T0244229

Revolusi

Revolusi

Indonesia and the Birth of the Modern World

DAVID VAN REYBROUCK

Translated from the Dutch by David Colmer and David McKay

W. W. NORTON & COMPANY
Independent Publishers Since 1923

for Wil

Contents

List of Maps

Prologue

No waves, no billows, no breakers. The calm Java Sea splits the moonlight into a thousand oyster-white shards that bob gently on the dark water. A mild northeast breeze brings some relief, but as always when the monsoon winds change direction, the heat lingers until after midnight, even at sea. Millions of stars sparkle in the firmament; the Milky Way is a swipe of chalk on a blackboard.

From the distance comes a faint thrumming, barely audible at first, but the sound intensifies, coming closer, now a distinct throbbing, an ever louder pounding – until it turns into a forceful, regular thumping. And in the moonlight, the unmistakable form of a steamship surges into view, a majestic white colossus parting the waters with her ramrod prow. Her masts, derricks and decks announce that this is a packet ship, carrying both passengers and freight. The broad funnel trails a horizontal wisp of smoke like a pennant. Now and then the stack disgorges a shower of red sparks; the stokers in the boiler room are raking the live coals. But the sparks soon fizzle in the open air, and the packet glides on through the lead-blue waters of the night.

The ship is listing to starboard a little, not much – she's just carrying a heavy load. But the angle of list is increasing, the vessel tilting further and further off centre. On the lower decks, the passengers look around in fright. Then the whistle sounds, six short blasts, one long: abandon ship. And again, and again.

Now everything happens fast. A few deck passengers rush out onto the promenade. Not everyone has a life jacket, and it's hard to assemble when the deck has become a slope. Stokers and trimmers are making their way up the steep ladders, but which way *is* up? The people on deck cling to pipes, cables, chains and ropes. Those who lose their grip slide down the deck, slam into the rail and fall, broken, into the sea. A shriek of terror, the crunch of impact, a cry of agony and then the splash.

A few minutes later, the ship keels over, her funnel smacking into the sea. She chokes, spurts water, takes in more and then suffocates in a death rattle of steam, soot, coal and salt. The big bronze propeller, half submerged, slows to an inglorious halt. The large flag that flew so proudly from the stern now floats on the dark water.

The once-mighty vessel lies on her side in the sea among the drowning people. Because the dynamo is on the port side, now facing up, many electric lights on deck keep blazing until the packet's final descent to the seabed. Glaring bulbs on a sinking ship. Brightly lit decks, wet coils of rope, a short circuit crackling. Then only bubbles rising to the surface.

Chapter 1

The VOC Mentality
Why Indonesia wrote world history

It was the loudest explosion I'd ever heard. I was at work in my hotel along Jalan Wahid Hasyim, a street in the centre of Jakarta, when from down the road came what sounded like a huge thunderclap. But the morning sky was a steely blue, as it had been the day before and the day before that. Had a lorry exploded? A gas tank? From my window, I couldn't see a plume of smoke anywhere, but my modest little hotel looked out over just one small corner of the city. Jakarta, with ten million inhabitants, is a sprawling megalopolis covering almost 700 square kilometres; if you count its satellite cities, the population is no less than thirty million.

Five minutes later Jeanne called, in a total panic. It seemed so unlike her. We'd met six months earlier at a language course in Yogyakarta. She was a young French freelance journalist and one of the most relaxed travellers I had encountered. Jeanne was based in Jakarta and, at that very moment, on her way to my hotel. We planned to spend the day visiting retirement homes in outlying districts, in search of eyewitnesses to history. She would interpret for me, as she had before. But now she was in tears. 'There's been an attack! I had to run from the shooting, and I'm hiding in the mall around the corner from you!'

Out into the street. The usual endless honking traffic had been replaced by a crowd of hundreds and hundreds. Multitudes of the city's poor were holding up their smartphones to film the scene. Four hundred metres further, at the crossroads of my street and Jalan Thamrin, Jakarta's central traffic artery, we saw a dead body on the ground – a man on his back, recently killed. His feet pointed into the air, an unnatural sight. Policemen and soldiers were holding back the crowd. The situation was not yet under control. On the pavement to my left, I saw Jeanne approaching. We stared at the scene in disbelief, hugged and rushed back to my hotel room. Today would not be about the 1930s and 40s.

The attacks of 14 January 2016 were the first in Jakarta in seven years. Members of an extremist Muslim group had driven up to a police post and opened fire. A bomb had gone off near a Burger King and a Starbucks – the bang I'd heard – and then two of the terrorists had blown themselves up in a car park. You can still find videos online. There were embassies, luxury hotels and a major United Nations office nearby, but we would later learn that those had not been direct targets. Eight people were killed, including four attackers, and twenty-four were injured.

Once Jeanne had recovered from the shock, she went straight to work. She wrote press releases for lots of French newspapers and websites, and she kept up with the latest news on my television so that she could send updates to Paris. We trawled the internet in every language we knew. By then I had made a few posts to social media, and the first newspapers and radio stations were calling for information and interviews. For the rest of the day, the hotel room became the nerve centre feeding information to the French, Belgian, Swiss and, to a lesser extent, Dutch media. (The Netherlands still has a few correspondents of its own in Jakarta.) I remember that at one stage Jeanne sat down on the carpet in the hotel corridor for a radio interview with France Inter, while I was talking live to a Flemish television channel on Skype. We went on without a break until late afternoon, by which time we both had splitting headaches and decided to stop for lunch.

The next day, it was all over.

As soon as it became clear that this was not an attack like the one in Bali in 2002 (which left 200 dead, mostly Westerners) or a tsunami like the one in Aceh in 2004 (which took 131,000 lives), international interest ran dry. Indonesia once again became the quiet giant you rarely if ever hear about outside Southeast Asia. It's a very peculiar thing, really – in population, it's the world's fourth-largest country after China, India and the United States, which are all in the news constantly. It has the largest Muslim community on earth. Its economy is Southeast Asia's biggest, and it supplies large parts of the world with palm oil, rubber and tin. But the international community just doesn't seem interested. It's been that way for years. In a quality bookshop in Paris, Beijing or New York, it's easier to find books about Myanmar, Afghanistan, Korea and even Armenia (countries with tens of millions of inhabitants or fewer) than Indonesia with its population of 268 million. One out of every twenty-seven humans is Indonesian, but the rest of the world would have a hard time naming even one of the country's inhabitants. Or, in the words of a classic expat joke, 'Any idea where Indonesia is?' 'Uh . . . not really. Somewhere near Bali?'

Let's start with a quick glance at the world map. Indonesia's place on the margins of that map reflects its marginal role in our image of the world: that mess on the lower right, that splatter of islands between the Pacific and Indian Oceans, apparently that's it. It's far away from compact Western Europe and massive North America, which are at the top – a historical convention, of course, since the surface of the earth has no centre and the cosmos no up or down. But if you shift the perspective and put Indonesia in the centre, you realise this is not some dusty corner of the world, but a strategically located archipelago in a vast maritime region between India and China. For seafarers in ages past, the islands made perfect stepping stones between East and West: a double row, mostly growing smaller further to the east. The Malay Peninsula practically rubs shoulders with colossal Sumatra in the southern row, and then there are Java, Bali, Lombok, Sumbawa, Flores and so on. The northern row consists of Borneo, Sulawesi and the Moluccas, which are massive, spindly and fragmented, respectively. The two strings of beads converge at New Guinea.

Indonesia is the world's largest island realm. Officially, it is made up of 13,466 islands, but it could also be 16,056. Or 18,023. No one knows exactly. Volcanoes, earthquakes and tides are constantly transforming the coastlines, and when the waters rise the number of islands increases. Once I witnessed it myself: the middle of a tropical

Map 1: Contemporary Indonesia (2020)

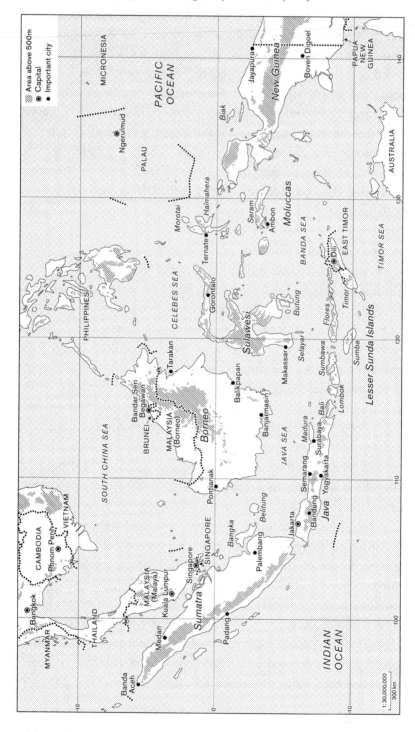

island disappeared for six hours at high tide. Were those two islands or one? Two, by the UN definition, but the locals had only one name for the place. Of those countless islands, only a few thousand are inhabited. Although most are tiny, Indonesia includes five of the world's thirteen largest islands: New Guinea, Borneo, Sumatra, Sulawesi and Java. The first two are shared with Papua New Guinea, Malaysia and Brunei; the last is the most populous island on earth. Java is about 1,000 kilometres long and 100 to 200 kilometres wide, only seven per cent of Indonesia's total land area, but its 141 million inhabitants make up more than half the population. No wonder so many historic changes began there. But Indonesia is more than Java. The whole tropical archipelago covers more than forty-five degrees of longitude, an eighth of the globe, spanning three time zones and more than 5,000 kilometres along the equator. If you could click on Indonesia and drag it over to Europe on the map, it would start in Ireland and end somewhere in Kazakhstan. Superimposed on a map of the United States, it extends almost a thousand kilometres out to sea on either side. That immense area is inhabited by nearly 300 distinct ethnic groups speaking 700 languages, but the official language is Indonesian, a young language derived from Malay with countless traces of Dutch, English, Portuguese and Arabic.

But these demographic and geographical superlatives are not the only things that merit our attention. Indonesian history includes an unprecedented event of global significance: it was the first country to declare independence after World War II. This milestone came less than two days after Japan capitulated. After almost 350 years of Dutch presence (1600–1942) and a three-and-a-half-year Japanese occupation (1942–5), a few local leaders announced that their archipelago would go forward as a sovereign state. It was the first domino to fall, at a time when much of Asia, Africa and the Arab world remained in the hands of a few Western European states such as Great Britain, France, the Netherlands, Belgium and Portugal.

The bold swiftness of this declaration, the Proklamasi, reflects its origins in the struggle of a very young generation. The Revolusi – the Indonesian war of independence that began in 1945 – was in every respect a youth revolution, supported and defended by a whole generation of fifteen- to twenty-five-year-olds who were willing to die for their freedom. Anyone who believes that young people cannot make a difference in the struggle against global warming and the loss of biodiversity needs to study Indonesian history *now*. The world's third-largest country would never have become independent without the work of people in their teens and early twenties – although I hope today's young climate activists will use less violent tactics.

But above all, what makes the Revolusi so fascinating is its enormous impact on the rest of humanity. It shaped expectations about the nature of decolonisation: not a gradual, decades-long process of increasing autonomy, but a swift transition to independence. Not limited to one small portion of the colony, but affecting the entire territory. And not restricted to a few specific powers or ministries, but constituting a complete transfer of political sovereignty. Fast, comprehensive, and complete: that was the model forged in Indonesia and actively pursued in many other parts of the world in the decades that followed.

In addition to shaping the decolonisation process, the Revolusi also encouraged all the newly formed nations to work together. In photographs of the bombing in Jakarta, you can see an extremely long billboard suspended above a footbridge over Jalan Thamrin. 'Asian African Conference Commemoration', it says, and below that are the words, 'Advancing South–South Cooperation'. The contrast with the smoke and panic below is striking. The billboard referred to a recent international commemorative conference; sixty years before 2015, Indonesia had extended its hand to other recently independent countries.

A few years after the final handover of power by the Netherlands, the fashionable Javanese resort town of Bandung hosted the legendary Asian–African Conference, the first summit of world leaders without the West. They represented a staggering billion and a half people, more than half the world population at the time. 'Bandung', as the conference became known, was described by the Black American author and participant Richard Wright as 'a decisive moment in the consciousness of sixty-five per cent of the human race'. What happened there would 'condition the totality of human life on this earth', he argued.[1] That claim may sound inflated, but it was not far from the truth. In the years that followed, every region of the globe was touched by the Revolusi – large parts of not only Asia, the Arab world, Africa and Latin America, but also the United States and Europe. The American civil rights movement and the unification of Europe were, for better or for worse, largely prompted by 'Bandung'. It was a milestone in the emergence of the modern world. A French study from 1965 did not mince words; evoking the storming of the Bastille on 14 July 1789, a key event of the French Revolution, it called Bandung no less than 'history's second *14 juillet*, a *14 juillet* on a planetary scale'.[2]

In the days that followed the bombing, Jeanne and I returned to driving from one retirement home to the next. The week before, we had written down some amazing stories, and it felt wonderful to return to finding and interviewing eyewitnesses. Although neither of us is Dutch or Indonesian, their life stories utterly fascinated us. They told a universal tale of hope, fear and longing, which spoke volumes about our own lives and today's world.

The Revolusi was once world history – the world got involved in it and was changed by it – but unfortunately, its global dimensions have been almost forgotten. In the Netherlands, the former colonial power, I had to justify myself a thousand times: Why write about Indonesia? And why me, 'a Belgian, of all people'? 'Because it doesn't belong to you any more!' I would say, laughing. Sometimes I added that Belgium had also suffered under Dutch oppression, that I was writing from my own experience, etc. But what I really believe is that the world's fourth-largest country should fascinate everyone. If we attach importance to the founding fathers of the United States, to Mao or to Gandhi, why shouldn't we also look to the pioneers of Indonesia's struggle for freedom? But not everyone saw it that way. After I had said a few things about my research in a weekly magazine, the far-right Dutch populist party PVV placed an indignant comment on Facebook: 'I think this moron should try writing a book about King Leopold and the Belgian Congo before he gets up on his high horse.'[3] But I had no intention of doing that again.

Processes of decolonisation are often reduced to national struggles between the colonial power and the colony: France vs. Algeria, Belgium vs. Congo, Germany vs. Namibia, Portugal vs. Angola, Britain vs. India and the Netherlands vs. Indonesia – like a series of vertical lines, side by side but never intersecting, a kind of barcode. But alongside that vertical component, there are also many horizontal processes. The participants include neighbouring countries, allies, local militias, regional actors and international organisations. Their influence must not be filtered out. If we do that, we are stuck in the nineteenth century, with the Western nation-state and its colonial borders as our frame of reference. If we look at the past only through the arrow slits, we won't see the whole landscape. The time is ripe to stop focusing on national narratives and recognise the global dimension of decolonisation. Yes, that takes some effort. A tangle of influences is harder to analyse than a two-sided schema, but such schemas do violence to historical reality – certainly when we turn to Indonesian history.

It's worth saying again: the world got involved in Indonesia's revolution and was changed by it. Yet today, the Revolusi is commemorated as a chapter in national history only in Indonesia and the Netherlands. In Indonesia, it has stood for decades as the unwavering foundational myth of the outstretched, ultra-diverse state. Whatever island I landed on, the local airport often turned out to have been named after a freedom fighter. Street names and statues form lasting tributes to the Revolusi. And in the cities, museums with dioramas, like the stained-glass windows of medieval cathedrals, offer graphic, canonical versions of a primal legend – in this case, the story of the nation. That story is essential for maintaining the archipelago's unity in the face of separatist tendencies, such as those of the strict Muslims of Aceh in the country's far northwest, or of the Papuans of New Guinea in the far southeast. Despite the contrasting ideologies of Indonesia's heads of state since independence, they have all drawn on the same historical narrative: the heroic *perang kemerdekaan*, the war of independence from colonial rule. The same pattern can be found in history textbooks for secondary schools. A new history text from 2014, *Sejarah Indonesia dari Proklamasi sampai Orde Reformasi*

(Indonesian History from the Proclamation of Independence to the Post-Suharto Era), devotes no less than the first half of its 230 pages to the brief *Revolusi* period, 1945–9, hurtling through the long span from 1950 to 2008 in its second half.[4] In recent years, a generation of young Indonesian historians have spoken out against an approach that is too Indonesia-centric and boldly turned against what they describe as the *tirani Sejarah Nasional*, the tyranny of national history. But the broader Indonesian public still sees the *Revolusi* as a chiefly national affair.[5]

Meanwhile Dutch perspectives on decolonisation are shifting. You can see that in the titles of influential publications. While an earlier generation of books emphasised what the Netherlands had lost – with titles that translate to *The Final Century of the Indies, Farewell to the Indies, Farewell to the Colonies* and *The Retreat* – more recent studies have instead focused on Dutch violence: *The Burden of War, Soldier in Indonesia, Robber State, Colonial Wars in Indonesia* and *The Burning Kampongs of General Spoor*.[6] In a parallel tendency, a new generation of journalists and activists are calling attention to the less flattering sides of Dutch history, which have often been covered up. Yet even after many years of richly nuanced and often superb historical writing, the impact on public awareness seems minimal. First-class diplomatic histories, meticulous political biographies, a few brilliant doctoral theses and some excellent books for the general public have done little to improve the very poor Dutch grasp of their own colonial and post-colonial history. In December 2019, when the British polling company YouGov investigated which European country was proudest of its colonial past, the Netherlands stood head and shoulders above the rest. A full fifty per cent of the Dutch respondents said they were proud of their former empire, in contrast to thirty-two per cent of the British, twenty-six per cent of the French and twenty-three per cent of the Belgians. What was still more striking was the exceptionally low number of Dutch respondents who were ashamed of colonialism: six per cent, in contrast to fourteen per cent of the French, nineteen per cent of the British and twenty-three per cent of the Belgians. More than a quarter of the Dutch people polled (twenty-six per cent) wished their country still had an overseas empire.[7]

What explains this peculiar attitude? Was Dutch colonialism really so much better than that of other European powers, giving the Dutch more objective reason for pride? Or has new information been so much slower to trickle in? Evidently the latter, because the historical literature does not make a strong case for national self-satisfaction. The insights of decades of thorough historical research inspire not pride but horror, yet this fact is still not widely understood in the Netherlands.

Maybe the striking ignorance about colonialism in the Netherlands is not surprising. In a country where it was possible as recently as 2006 for Prime Minister Jan Peter Balkenende, whose university degree was in history, in an address to the lower house of parliament during the annual debate on the government budget, the most important gathering of the political year, to call on the people's representatives to show more pride and vigour with a triumphant reference to 'the VOC mentality', can you really blame the public for having a generally positive image of this historical overseas venture? Spoiler alert: the VOC (Vereenigde Oostindische Compagnie), the Dutch East India Company, was responsible for at least one genocide. That was a well-established fact by 2006; in fact, it's been known since 1621. When a few members of parliament responded to Balkenende's rhetoric with indignant boos, the prime minister quickly hedged his statements, expressing a shred of doubt: 'Surely?'

This book is about that doubt. About pride and shame. About liberation and humiliation. About hope and violence. It aims to bring together the findings of numerous historians with a deep command of the subject, whose findings have not always become general knowledge. It builds on what other authors, journalists and artists in various countries have brought to light. But most of all, it draws on the memories of the people who experienced all this first-hand: the last remaining eyewitnesses to the Revolusi. I am a great believer in oral history. Despite many hours of being driven around on mopeds, the sometimes scorching heat and palpable air pollution in the cities, the hundreds of mosquito bites after a night on a ferry's afterdeck, and the stress of a terrorist attack around the corner, it was always worth it. Everyday people have so much to say. It was a privilege, in every respect, to hear their stories.

Between July 2015 and July 2019, I did about a year of fieldwork in total, including eight months in Asia. I visited countless islands and spoke to many hundreds of people. This led to formal interviews with 185 of them, at least half an hour long but typically lasting an hour and a half. Often our conversations went on much longer, or I returned later. I explained to all potential interviewees that I was working on a book about the history of Indonesian independence, and I asked their permission to interview them and share their testimonies. What I mean by a formal interview is that I asked for their name and age each time, went through their life story with them chronologically, took notes visibly and constantly, asked follow-up questions about particular topics and sometimes made recordings or photographs, always with permission. When people were unwilling to share certain memories, I abandoned that line of questioning. I prefer to work on a foundation of trust and respect. A few eyewitnesses asked for the opportunity to review any quotations that I used, and a handful preferred to remain anonymous. I always respected these wishes, of course. Although the general tone of these conversations was calm and quiet, they were usually far from emotionless. I saw anger, sorrow and vengefulness, but also wistfulness, remorse and regret, alongside humour, frustration and resignation. They laughed, they grieved and they fell silent. Most of my interviewees were very advanced in years, but the detail and specificity of their memories sometimes astounded me. If there's one thing I've learned from listening to elderly people, it's that the present fades faster than your youth, especially if your youth was eventful. Even after everything else is gone, sometimes the wasteland of memory still echoes with a children's song. Or a trauma. Some boulders refuse to budge.

The interviews took place in almost twenty different languages: Indonesian, Javanese, Sundanese, Batak, Balinese, Manado, Togian, Toraja, Buginese, Mandarese, Ambonese, Morotai, Japanese, Nepali, English, French and Dutch. Add a slew of dialects to this Tower of Babel and you can see the extent of the challenge. Although I could eventually manage a simple conversation in Indonesian, I always had interpreters to assist me during the interviews, if only because many older people don't even speak that newfangled national language. The interpreters translated into English, French, German and Dutch. Now and then, the translation had to take place in two steps, through Indonesian. Because translators and interpreters are the quiet heroes of globalisation, I give all their names in the back matter. Without them, I could never have succeeded.

I tracked down the eyewitnesses by asking everyone I met – an imam, the director of a retirement home, a young soldier – whether maybe they knew where I could find people. I told everyone around me that I was working on this project; that led to useful contacts. Social media provided me with a megaphone, and Couchsurfing

Map 2: Spread of *Homo erectus* (± one million years ago)

introduced me to amazing people. In Indonesia and Japan, I even found a few eyewitnesses on Tinder: man or woman, young or old, near or far, I always swiped right and accepted everyone. This enabled me to meet hundreds of strangers I would never have spoken to on the street. Sometimes I had to point out my profile, which explained who I was and that I was mainly interested in their grandmas and grandpas. It worked.

But the oldest Indonesian I met didn't come to my attention through a dating app. It was during a lunch break in Leiden, back when I was doing doctoral research. I cycled from the archaeology faculty to the natural history museum, where I admired his powerful jaw, robust constitution and handsome features. The palaeontology curator took the remains from a safe and laid them in front of me on a felt cloth. There they were, a molar, a femur and the top of the skull of Java Man, the first *Homo erectus* ever excavated. The Dutch physician and naturalist Eugène Dubois discovered him in Java in 1891. This was the find that confirmed Darwin's theory, the first true link between humans and other animals.[8] These days, he is thought to be one million years old. *Homo erectus* migrated from Africa to Java, which was not yet an island, but attached to Sumatra, Borneo, Bali and the Asian mainland. That's why elephants, tigers, orangutans and other mainland species can still be found there. The islands further east have a different, more 'Australian' fauna: echidnas, wallabies, quolls and other marsupials. A biological dividing line runs across the archipelago: the Wallace Line, named after Alfred Russel Wallace, the brilliant but often overshadowed co-creator of the theory of evolution. One million years – that's a long time ago. *Homo erectus* did not arrive in Europe until half a million years later, and it was not until about 12,000 years ago that both the Americas had human inhabitants. Unlike these far corners of the globe, Indonesia was part of the first wave of expansion by the world's first human inhabitants. Perhaps human evolution was also a kind of Asian–African Conference.

That is certainly true of the spread of *Homo sapiens*. If each millennium is a single swipe on Tinder, we have to swipe 925 times to see the successor to *Homo erectus* arrive in Indonesia from Africa. Around

Map 3: Spread of *Homo sapiens* (until ± 50,000 years ago)

75,000 years ago, the first small groups of modern humans went from the mainland to the archipelago; in those days, Europe was still home to Neanderthals.[9] The new arrivals in Indonesia were probably akin to Melanesians, with dark skin, curly hair and round eyes, the distant ancestors of the Papuans of New Guinea and the Aboriginal Australians. They crossed the Wallace Line – we don't know what sorts of vessels they used – and went as far as Tasmania. They were hunter-gatherers, of course, a lifestyle that prevailed for more than ninety-nine per cent of human history. But around 7000 BCE (another sixty-eight swipes later) they began to cultivate root vegetables such as taro and yams in inland New Guinea, along with sago palms and banana trees.[10] Around the same time, there were also experiments with food production in China. Instead of simply picking wild rice, some people started to grow it themselves. That went so well that it eventually led to population growth and migration, even overseas.[11] This development, known as the Austronesian expansion, brought people with typical Asiatic features – lighter skin, straight hair and almond eyes – to Taiwan, the Philippines, Borneo, Sulawesi and Java, where they arrived five swipes later, around 2000 BCE. Their vessels were double-outrigger canoes, stabilised by floats on both sides, like the *jukung* still commonly found in the archipelago. Wherever they went, they planted rice. They kept chickens and pigs and also grew millet, taro, sago, yam, coconut and bananas. They made earthenware and learned metalworking. Their lifestyle was sedentary; their wooden houses were elevated on poles and had attractive curved roofs. To commemorate their ancestors, they built monuments and menhirs, as the Toraja people of South Sulawesi still do.

In the millennia that followed (from 2000 BCE to 1200 CE) their way of life spread across a huge area, from Madagascar to Easter Island and Hawaii. The languages that emerged there were all part of the Austronesian family, which was the world's most geographically widespread group of languages prior to colonisation. Without a doubt, these peoples were 'the greatest sailors in history up to the fifteenth century'.[12] In Southeast Asian waters, they also benefited from a literal push. From November to March, the northeast trade winds are ideal for the voyage to China and India, and the southwest trade winds, which blow from May to September, speed the journey back. The average wind speed of 4 to 5 on the Beaufort scale made for comfortable sailing trips, usually undisturbed by high waves or heavy storms.[13] Only off the archipelago's south coast were the waves high – they rolled in from Antarctica. This is why, until the era of the steamship, contact between Java and Australia was rare.

Rice growing led to much more complex societies. Wet fields, or paddies, yielded more rice than dry fields, but required a much larger-scale approach. The earliest rice farms were tiny, but later entire plains were transformed into glittering paddies. Even slopes were turned into astonishing terraced fields. Anyone who has ever

Map 4: Austronesian expansion (± 3000 BCE – ± 1200 CE)

admired the ingenious irrigation systems that supply such fields understands that this is not the work of a single farmer, family or even generation. It takes far more consultation and co-ordination to maintain all those little dikes, canals and sluice gates. Chieftains became leaders, harvests increased and villages grew into cities. An agricultural society that produces surpluses can begin trading – in rice, vegetables, baskets, earthenware and also luxury goods. In the final centuries BCE, people were already trading bronze daggers, axes and drums, from Vietnam to southern China and Indonesia.[14] Local communities had become part of regional empires.

The archipelago was a crossroads of civilisations. Through its ports passed not only goods, but also gods. Itinerant priests from India brought Brahmanism, the precursor to Hinduism. As early as the fifth century CE, a ruler in Borneo offered Brahmans a gift of 'water, ghee, tawny cows and sesame seeds, as well as eleven bulls'.[15] Those words, etched into a stone pillar, are Indonesia's oldest surviving text. Two centuries later, a Buddhist from China wrote with enthusiasm about the archipelago: 'In the fortified city of Fo-Qi [now Palembang] Buddhist priests number more than one thousand, whose minds are bent on learning and good practices. They investigate and study all the subjects that exist just as in [India]; the rules and ceremonies are not at all different. If a Chinese priest wishes to go the West in order to listen [to] and read [Buddhist scriptures], he had better stay here one or two years and practice the proper rules and then proceed to central India.'[16]

The city now called Palembang in South Sumatra was the capital of a powerful Buddhist kingdom, Srivijaya. For six centuries, it controlled trade and maritime routes between China and India. Malay became the lingua franca of the seas. Religions from India also took root in Java, even reaching far inland. Forty kilometres to the northwest of present-day Yogyakarta, Borobudur, the world's largest Buddhist structure, was built around 800. Its astonishing terraced

Map 5: The spread of Hinduism and Buddhism

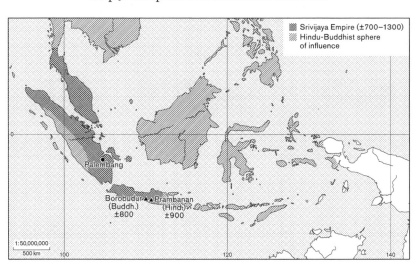

architecture was decorated with thousands of bas-reliefs and dozens of Buddha sculptures. Fifty kilometres away, the Hindu temple compound known as Prambanan was erected starting in 900. At least as impressive as Borobudur, it boasts the finest sculpture of a cow I have ever seen. Hinduism and Buddhism coexisted in peace.[17] In Java and Bali a unique blend formed, in which the historical Buddha was worshipped as the peer of the Hindu divinities Brahma, Vishnu and Shiva.

This cultural fusion reached its pinnacle in the fourteenth-century Majapahit empire, centred in Java, which spanned the archipelago from Malaysia to New Guinea. It was not as unified as the Roman empire; the ruler in the capital worked together with local vassals. But in the twentieth-century struggle for independence, Majapahit was the ultimate historical prototype, the proof that there had once been a great and glorious homegrown empire. Majapahit was the source of the red and white used in the revolutionary flag and retained as today's national colours. Architecture, wood carving, batik, dance and the Javanese language reached an unprecedented level of refinement. In the Majapahit courts, ancient Indian epic poems such as the *Mahabharata* and the *Ramayana* took on their characteristic Javanese form: a wondrous wayang play with

Map 6: Height of the Majapahit empire (1293–1401)

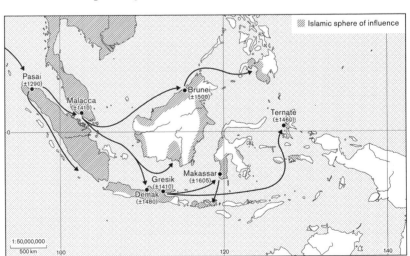

shadow puppets. The performances went on all night. The puppeteer sat cross-legged, telling and acting out the old stories, while an oil lamp projected the very evocative silhouettes of the buffalo-hide puppets onto a screen. They were magical performances: heroic, suspenseful, violent and occasionally funny. The play was accompanied by the soft, mesmerising sounds of a gamelan orchestra, the same elusive polyrhythmic music that would centuries later influence Western composers such as Claude Debussy, Erik Satie and John Cage.

The Chinese element also grew. From 1405 onwards, seven enormous expeditions were led by the eunuch admiral Zheng He. By way of the Indonesian archipelago, he travelled to Ceylon, India, Arabia and even the east coast of Africa. Some members of his expeditions stayed behind, forming the first seeds of the Chinese diaspora. Zheng He's fleet consisted at times of more than 300 vessels and 27,000 sailors. Some of his ships were 120 metres long. Consider the context: this was almost a century before Columbus set off with three caravels about twenty-five metres long and ninety men. Portugal, Europe's largest seafaring nation, had not yet dared to venture beyond Morocco.[18] Indonesia didn't need Europe to be connected to the world.

Map 7: The spread of Islam (until ± 1650)

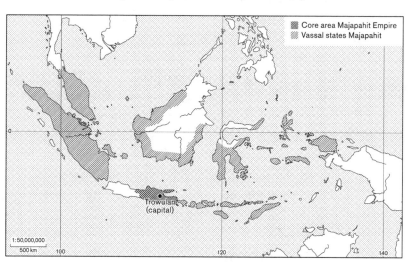

All those trade relations also permitted the spread of a new religion born somewhere far to the west. It especially appealed to merchants. Javanese feudalism was very hierarchical, but the new faith required everyone, from nobleman to nobody, to practise humility, kneel five times a day and donate to the poor. In the fifteenth and sixteenth centuries, Islam spread by way of Indonesia's port cities. This was not the result of large-scale immigration, conquest or force; it was the religion's egalitarian nature that made it so appealing. The earliest mosques were built in a Hindu-Buddhist style. Islam gradually spread throughout the archipelago, with the exception of Bali and Papua (which remained Hindu-Buddhist and animist respectively). Kings declared themselves sultans and kingdoms became sultanates, but the wayang plays were still performed and traditional beliefs in ancestors and spirits persisted – right up to the present. On a beach in southern Java, I was once advised not to wear a green swimsuit because Ratu Kidul, the goddess of the oceans, might swallow me up. After fourteen centuries of Hinduism and Buddhism and five centuries of Islam, such beliefs are still flourishing.[19]

'Java . . . what a mishmash that place is!' said 102-year-old Djajeng Pratomo, with a twinkle in his eye. Yes, that was one way of putting it. We sat in his room in a retirement home in Callantsoog, close to the tip of North Holland. It was four o'clock, an overcast summer afternoon. The dunes were dark with rain, the beach deserted and the sea pimpled. The room was swelteringly hot; Pratomo liked to keep warm. A nurse had just served us the most traditional of Dutch treats: the tiny pancakes called *poffertjes*, with powdered sugar. They brought a grin to the face of the short, thin man, whose chair was much too large for him. 'It's a very complicated affair, Indonesia,' he said, wiping a little powdered sugar from his trousers. 'Such a confusing mess!' To hear Pratomo's stories was to travel back in time. Apart from a couple of schoolboys, no one had interviewed him in the past thirty years.[20] I had first heard him mentioned in Jakarta; he was said to live 'somewhere in the Netherlands', but the spelling of his name was unclear. After a lot of online fuss, I found first his name, then a school assignment, then two boys, who put me in touch with their teacher.

That teacher referred me on to his daughter, who extended a friendly invitation to Callantsoog. And now here I was. Pratomo had just become the village's oldest resident and had his name in the local paper. He was amused by the thought that he, a Javanese man, was now the elder of a village in North Holland. 'Go on, have another poffertje.'[21]

As I chewed the lukewarm dough ball, it occurred to me that the Dutch colonial enterprise began not with a hunger for land, but with a hankering for flavour. The Netherlands did not invade an existing country to take it over. At first, it didn't invade any place at all and had no intention of taking over anything. All it wanted to do was take things *away*, in trade, particularly spices. For centuries, Asian spices had been treasured in Europe. In the only surviving cookbook from Roman times, *De re coquinaria* by Apicius, more than three-quarters of the recipes require large amounts of pepper.[22] In the mood for *pullus tractogalatus*, chicken with milk and honey? Then you needed an ingredient in your house from thousands of kilometres away. *Dulcia* with eggs and pine nuts? Without pepper from distant Asia, it lacked fire and flavour. Roman ships didn't balk at a few extra nautical miles. From the east coast of Egypt, they sailed to East Africa for ivory, to Arabia for incense and, furthest of all, to India for pepper.[23] 'India' stood for just about everything east of the Arabian Peninsula. That early trade also extended over land all the way to China. Precious goods travelled the Silk Road: lacquer, gold, silver, sugar, saffron, cinnamon.[24] In Syria, archaeologists have found skeletons from the Roman age wrapped in silk from Chinese imperial workshops.[25] Digs in India have unearthed Roman amphorae, oil lamps and statuettes. And Roman coins have been found as far away as Thailand.[26]

And the love of spices lingered. Medieval European cooking was much sweeter and more heavily seasoned than its modern counterpart. The habit of saving sweet flavours for dessert first formed in late-seventeenth-century French gastronomy.[27] Medieval cooks threw raisins, figs and cardamom into their sauces, combinations that to us are more redolent of Indian or Arabic cuisine. Compared to the herbs that could be picked in European fields, woods and monastery gardens – like chives, sage, sorrel, parsley and rosemary – the Asian spices were in a different league. Pepper, nutmeg, cardamom, cloves and cinnamon were hard and woody and had an extremely long shelf life. No one in Europe knew exactly what plants they came from. Only when crushed did they release their incredible aromas, which were so divine that various medieval authors situated paradise on earth somewhere in that mythical 'India'. And they were not only exceptionally tasty, but also extraordinarily healthy and medicinal. If your four humours (blood, yellow bile, black bile and phlegm) were out of balance, spices were the solution. Nutmeg was classified as hot and dry, ginger as hot and wet, and pepper as very hot and dry, while cloves helped to relieve toothache. Thanks to their magical perfumes, they fetched high prices. If a craftsman in London circa 1450 earned around eight pence a day, then a pound of pepper or ginger cost about two days' wages. A pound of cinnamon? Three days of work. A pound of cloves? Four and a half days. A pound of saffron? One month.[28]

For centuries, luxury items remained horrendously expensive, not only because they were produced far away (cloves and nutmeg came from the Moluccas, for instance), required a great deal of manual labour (as did saffron, picked from crocus flowers) or were extremely rare (like ambergris, which came from sperm whale innards), but also because so many intermediaries were involved. When the maid in an elite urban household in Bruges around 1500 grated a little nutmeg onto the cauliflower, it marked the last step in a journey around the world and through the hands of scores of merchants. A picker had harvested and dried the nut in Banda, the tiny group of islands in eastern Indonesia where the nutmeg was the only type of tree. His village chief then sold it to a Javanese or Malay trader, who resold it in a port in eastern Sumatra or the Malay Peninsula to Indian sailors who took it to Ceylon. There the nut was probably purchased by Gujaratis, Persians or Arabs, who sent it on to the south coast of the Arab Peninsula. If the cargo was shipped by way of the Persian Gulf, it ended up in the markets of Baghdad and the ports of Syria, which were linked to the Mediterranean trade network. But if it went by way of the Red Sea, then after stops in Cairo and Alexandria it came into the possession of Genoese or Venetian sailors, who took it to the

Map 8: Voyages of discovery and the spice trade

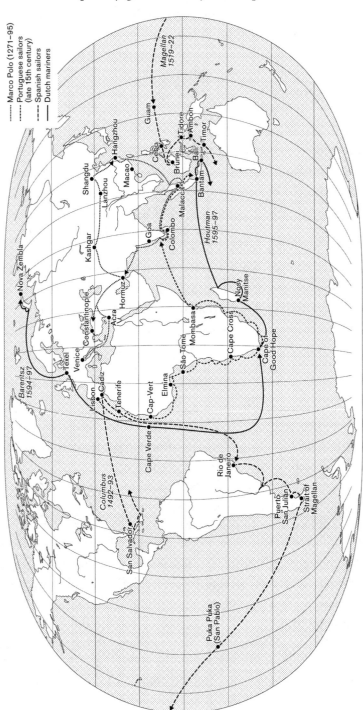

- .... Marco Polo (1271–95)
- ·-·-·-· Portuguese sailors (late 15th century)
- – – – Spanish sailors
- ——— Dutch mariners

Nova Zembla

Barentsz 1594–97

Texel

Venice

Lisbon

Cádiz

Tenerife

Cape Verde

Columbus 1492–93

San Salvador

Constantinople

Acra

Hormuz

Kashgar

Lanzhou

Shangdu

Hangzhou

Macao

Goa

Colombo

Malacca

Bantam

Houtman 1595–97

Cebu

Brunei

Guam

Tidore
Amboin
Bali
Timor

Magellan 1519–22

Cap-Vert

Elmina

São Tomé

Mombasa

Cape Cross

Nosy Manitse

Cape of Good Hope

Rio de Janeiro

Puerto San Julián

Strait of Magellan

Puka Puka (San Pablo)

Italian Peninsula. They were the first Christians to handle the nut after all the animists, Buddhists, Hindus, Muslims, Jains and Zoroastrians along the route. And then the little gem had to find its way over land, along the coast and up inland waterways to Bruges. And of course, every time it changed hands, the price increased, and each port had its own duties and transshipment costs. The consequences are easy to guess. Around 1500, once a handful of cloves had reached Venice, it might easily cost a hundred times as much as it had in the Moluccas (or 'Spice Islands').[29] Wasn't there a cheaper way?

Yes, there was, the Portuguese decided. Two hundred years earlier, Marco Polo had become the first European to land in Sumatra and to discover which islands produced what spices. Suppose we turn our backs on the Mediterranean and sail around Africa instead? How big could that 'country' be? Over decades, European seafarers learned just how big. From 1430 onwards, Portuguese expeditions began to sail south, planning to turn east as soon as they could, but the African continent proved far longer than they had imagined. Not until 1498, seventy years after their adventure had begun, did a Portuguese explorer, Vasco da Gama, first round the Cape. He sailed on to the west coast of India, where he learned that you had to go even further for the best spices: to Ceylon for cinnamon, to Sumatra and Java for pepper and much further still, to the Moluccas, for cloves, nutmeg and mace (the fragrant covering of the nutmeg seed). By 1525, the Portuguese had built up a modest commercial network throughout the region, with bases in Hormuz at the southern tip of the Arabian Peninsula, Goa in western India, Colombo in Ceylon, Malacca on the Malay Peninsula, Ambon in the Moluccas and later Macao on the south coast of China. In Ambon they erected a fort, the first Western settlement in what would later be known as Indonesia. They enriched the Malay language with words like *bendera* (from *bandeira*, flag), *gereja* (from *igreja*, church), *sekolah* (from *escola*, school) and *minggu* (week, from *domingo*, Sunday). The island of Ambon had a beautiful bay and was halfway from the volcanic islands of Ternate and Tidore, where they stocked up on cloves, to the tiny Banda Islands were nutmeg grew. From then on, Europe would have direct access to the source. Or at least, Portugal would, and it could sell its bounty – ten tons of nutmeg and thirty tons of cloves each year – in Europe at a large profit.[30]

Wasn't there a cheaper way? The same question occurred to the Spanish. But instead of struggling south, beating a course against the wind, they headed west. How big could the Atlantic Ocean be? If the world was round, then surely the Spice Islands were waiting for them on the other side? When Columbus arrived in Cuba in 1492, he thought he was in Japan. No, wait, he decided when he reached Haiti, *this* must be Japan.[31] So everything else in the area could only be India. All right, there were fewer spices than he'd expected, but wasn't that because it was winter? Be that as it may, he decided to call the locals Indians. A generation later, Magellan discovered that you could in fact sail westward to India, but you first had to make a large detour to the south, almost reaching Antarctica, and then pass below the South American mainland and sail on to the Pacific. The world was much larger than Europeans had thought. Magellan's voyage came to an end on a group of islands that he named after the Spanish king: the Philippines. He was killed by the locals, but afterwards his crew reached the destination they'd dreamed of, the Moluccas.

If the southerly and westerly routes are so difficult, the Dutch thought, then let's try going north. How big could Russia be? Willem Barentsz made three attempts from 1594 onward, but on his last voyage he became stranded in the pack ice of a sea that ever since then has been named after him. After his crew returned with tales of a fierce winter on the polar island of Nova Zembla (Novaya Zemlya), the northern route no longer seemed so attractive. Archaeologist friends who, in the 1990s, excavated the hut where Barentsz and his men spent the winter, said that to warn off polar bears they had to keep watch with flares every night. After dreaming of tropical spices, Barentsz must have been surprised to find himself repelling polar bears.

So the Portuguese route around Africa was the best one after all. Cornelis de Houtman from Gouda was the first Dutchman to accomplish the feat. With maps and information partly stolen from the port of Lisbon, he reached the west coast of Java in 1596, finding not only the Portuguese and the Chinese there but also pepper.[32] The Dutch were neither the first traders nor the wealthiest. De Houtman travelled on to Bali, picking up spices here and there, leaving a trail of destruction in his wake (just like the Portuguese) and returning to Amsterdam two years later. He earned just enough from this historic voyage to cover the costs, but the route to 'the Orient' was open for business.

The years that followed are referred to in Dutch as the era of the *wilde vaart*, 'wild seafaring', with scores of expeditions launched from Holland and Zeeland. They didn't set out in the name of their king and nation, as the Portuguese did, for the simple reason that they had no monarch and didn't exactly have a nation either. In 1588, the Netherlands had become the first country in northwestern Europe without a king, and the Republic was not a traditional state under centralised authority but an alliance of seven fairly autonomous provinces or states, which is why the name of the country still looks plural in so many European languages (the Netherlands, les Pays-Bas, die Niederlande, los Países Bajos, i Paesi Bassi and so forth). This confederate structure encouraged vigorous internal trade, to be sure, but it also led to intense competition. In 1602, the States General, the consultative body with representatives of all the Dutch provinces, decided it made more sense to join forces. All shipping companies in the Republic were merged into one, the Dutch East India Company (Vereenigde Oostindische Compagnie; VOC), which was granted a monopoly on trade with the East. This renowned corporation existed for two centuries and is unique for two reasons. For one thing, it was a private enterprise with far-reaching public powers. The VOC was authorised to conclude international treaties, administer justice, build forts and recruit soldiers. In other words, it had substantial diplomatic, legal and military responsibilities. Secondly, it was the first company in the world to issue shares of stock that could be traded; its co-owners could choose to sell at any time. They therefore did not have the same bonds of loyalty as the owners of a traditional family company. Shareholders wanted profit, and they wanted it fast. The combination of these two unique characteristics was every bit as explosive as you might guess. The VOC was hell-bent on turning a profit for its private investors and was equipped with the entire arsenal of public authority. There was no way this could go well.

The composition of the VOC crews didn't help. The sailors were anything but the flower of their nation. Although only four per cent of the nearly 5,000 voyages undertaken between 1595 and 1795 ended in shipwreck, the crews were buffeted by scurvy, dysentery, yellow fever, blackwater fever and brawls. A voyage took a year and a half, and two out of three sailors never returned home. No wonder the VOC recruiters resorted to desperate measures. Before a ship set sail, they would go to Amsterdam's shadiest taverns to round up 300 or so drunkards, rowdies and other lowlifes. In run-down boarding houses, they would sign up paupers, indigents, orphans and vagrants. Not all were Dutch; there were also many Germans and Scandinavians.[33] Having washed up like driftwood in Amsterdam's seedy harbourside district of De Wallen, they had nothing left to lose. Imagine dragging that crew to the Far East. The VOC did it.

The rough-hewn European mariners who stopped in the archipelago did not strike the locals as superior beings. They were physically depleted, their gums bleeding from scurvy after living on hardtack and beer. The senior VOC officials in their elegant trunk hose and wide collars were in better health, having dined on fresh vegetables and good wine during the voyage – there was a kitchen garden for them on the afterdeck and even a pen with pigs and chickens – but when they arrived, they raised eyebrows. Javanese and Malay chronicles describe them as loud, panting, sweaty fellows who kissed women openly in the streets.[34] Puppets and sculptures portray them as crude giants with bulging eyes, big noses, red cheeks, weird hair, large clumsy feet and – to the horror of the refined Javanese – visible teeth.[35] One captain was described as 'a raging demon with brusque gestures and a raspy voice', from whose 'open mouth saliva was dripping' and who gave off 'an unbearable odour of sweat'.[36]

Again, the VOC captains weren't there to conquer territory, at least not at first. They would ideally have liked to lay anchor in the bay or inlet of some tropical island and quietly bob there as sacks of spices were heaved on board, toasting the sale with brandy in their quarters – if their local trading partner drank alcohol, that is. But it was rarely so simple. The Portuguese got in the way, the Spaniards crossed their path and the locals proved to be canny negotiators. You could never be certain of your shipment of cloves, nor of the price. So they saw no alternative to establishing a presence on land. To ensure reliable access to the goods they craved, they had to leave men behind. In 1605 the VOC, with the aid of the local population, took over the Portuguese fort in Ambon. It was not large, several hectares at most, but it was the first patch of Dutch soil in Southeast Asia.

Looking out over the magnificent bay, I understood at once why the Portuguese and the Dutch had fought over the place. Nature could hardly have made it more strategic: a perfect inland harbour. On the far side of the bay I saw Kota Ambon, the city that had risen around the fort. A few rusty freighters were anchored there; smaller vessels arrived and departed. The fort itself was closed to visitors; it was still in use by the military. Even now, after 400 years.

Chapter 2

Assembling the Jigsaw Puzzle
Dutch expansion in Southeast Asia, 1605–1914

After my second poffertje I asked Pratomo about his year of birth.
'1914, in Sumatra.' I was glad to hear it. Not only was he the oldest
eyewitness to history that I could still talk to, but he'd been born in
the year the colonial empire became complete. You often hear
that the Dutch held sway over Indonesia for 350 years, from around
1600 to 1942, but that's a hoary myth kept alive by both nostalgic
colonialists ('We had such a long history there . . .') and furious anti-
colonialists ('That's how long the reign of terror lasted . . .'). Both
have the same oversimplified view of the colonial period: the Dutch
presence in the archipelago did begin around 1600, but for a long
time the Netherlands neither controlled the area nor had any ambition to do so. The idea that the Dutch captured and colonised the
archipelago from day one is simply wrong. Furthermore, in the year
1600 there was no unified area corresponding to present-day Indonesia, no cluster of islands acting as a political unit. The archipelago
was a geographical entity, not a national one. Even some individual
islands were home to a diverse range of kingdoms. The conquest of
all those islands and their incorporation into the colony of the Dutch
East Indies went very slowly.

It's helpful to think of the island empire as a jigsaw puzzle put
together over more than three centuries. The fort built previously by
the Portuguese in Ambon in 1605 was the first tiny piece of the puzzle to fall into Dutch hands, and the end of the Aceh War in 1914
completed the picture. The Indonesian historian Mochtar Lubis presents it very differently: 'In reality, however, the colony called the
Netherlands East Indies lasted no more than thirty to thirty-five
years.'[1] And it is true that the colony did not cover the entire territory

of present-day Indonesia for longer than that. Ambon belonged to the Dutch for 337 years, Aceh for only twenty-eight. Yet that does not make 1914 the starting point of colonial history, which began much earlier and can be divided into five stages.

The first stage in assembling the jigsaw lasted from about 1600 to 1700. For the VOC's first century, its motto was, 'The less land, the better.' Stations in the East were an expensive proposition, to be contemplated only when absolutely essential for trade. After the conquest of Fort Ambon in 1605, the Netherlands established settlements on Ternate and Banda Neira, two other Moluccan Islands, in 1607. These were obvious choices for commercial reasons; Ternate and nearby Tidore were the islands from which the trade in cloves was controlled, and Banda, a mini-archipelago 800 kilometres further south, was the only place where nutmeg grew. Cloves are the dried flower buds of the clove tree; when fresh, they are bright green, soft and fleshy. Nutmeg is the seed of a green fruit. The name comes from *nuces moschatae*, 'nuts that smell of musk'.

As you approach by air, you can see how small they are. Ternate and Tidore are two round, volcanic islands, no more than a few kilometres in diameter, glittering like two emerald-green cufflinks on the sleeve of the Pacific. Their fertile slopes are thick with mango, coconut and clove trees. Birds-of-paradise swoop from branch to branch.

'The Dutch went on land in Ternate. They didn't go by way of Jakarta, which didn't exist yet. They didn't conquer Java first. It was here that their encounter with Indonesia began. They turned up here after the Portuguese.' Husain Syah spoke the most beautiful Indonesian I had ever heard, as befits the Sultan of Tidore, one of the country's last traditional rulers. Although the political role of this ancient elite is mainly symbolic, the Republic recognises their status, and they are held in great esteem by the people. We spoke in his palace's impressive reception room. A servant crossed the white marble floor to bring us tea and cake. Sultan Husain showed himself to be an exceptionally charming and intelligent man with a passion for history. 'We sometimes forget that our own lives spring from the past and that history is the mother that gave us life. We must cherish it.' He described how the Portuguese, Spanish, British and Dutch tried to gain a foothold. For a time, the fort built by the Dutch on Ternate in 1607 even served as the headquarters of the entire VOC.[2] 'They established themselves here, and it was from here that they set up their administrative centre in Batavia, known to us today as Jakarta.'[3]

The sultan was right. The forts made it easier for the company to buy and store trade goods, but they were very far away from the primary trade routes. In 1619 Jan Pieterszoon Coen, the head of Dutch operations in Asia, decided to move the VOC headquarters more than 3,000 kilometres west, from the Moluccas all the way to western Java. The placid little port town of 'Jayakarta' on the north coast suited his purposes. It was at an intersection of maritime routes, had a good harbour and offered more than enough drinking water and wood for building. That made it ideal for repairing ships, storing goods, giving the men time to rest and organising new departures.[4] Coen drove out the British, who had a trading post there, and burned the local settlement to the ground. Batavia was born. The plan was not to conquer Java from there – quite the contrary. Coen looked out over the sea and lived with his back to the island. He wanted as little as possible to do with the two neighbouring sultanates – Banten in western Java and Mataram in central and eastern Java. The Javanese were not even allowed to live in Batavia, for fear of uprisings.

How did this desolate, charred, smouldering heap of rubble ever become a thriving hub of world trade? The answer was simple: by enslaving people, thousands of them. If you associate slavery only with the trade between Africa and America, it's time to widen your horizons. Slave markets were an age-old institution in Asia, of which the VOC made eager use.[5] In the late sixteenth century, an enslaved person cost about nine guilders there.[6] Between 1600 and 1900, an estimated 600,000 enslaved people were traded by the Dutch in Asia; that's not much less than the Dutch share in the transatlantic slave trade.[7] One-quarter came from Bali and the others from elsewhere in the archipelago, or from the Philippines, India, Madagascar or even mainland Africa. They were bought, plundered, stolen or taken as spoils after wars and natural disasters; the archipelago was, and is, frequently hit by volcanic eruptions, cyclones and tsunamis. Others couldn't pay their debts. Unlike in the Americas, they included many women, and enslaved people ended up mainly in cities and less often on plantations.[8] In the moist, blistering heat of Batavia, they dug canals, built warehouses, tarred ships or erected forts. Enslaved women did domestic work or served as concubines. Some VOC officers boasted of having as many as 300 slaves.

Towards the end of the so-called Dutch Golden Age, there were 27,000 people living in Batavia, and half were enslaved.[9] How many of them knew that their city was named after the Batavians, the forefathers of the Dutch from Roman days, celebrated for their love of freedom?

Batavia was dubbed the queen of the East and, with its canals, windmills and drawbridges, resembled a tropical version of Amsterdam. The city was never intended to become the capital of the Dutch East Indies – there was no such thing as yet – but it did develop into the nerve centre of an 'Eastern' trade imperium extending from Cape Town to Nagasaki. By the mid-seventeenth century, the VOC, the 'Praiseworthy Company', possessed Europe's largest commercial fleet. It had dozens of forts and 'factories' (or trading stations) in southern Africa, in the Indian Ocean, on the Arabian Peninsula, along the Persian Gulf and the coasts of India and Ceylon, throughout Southeast Asia, along the south coast of China, and in Taiwan and Japan. But it did not control a contiguous territory. At the Cape settlement in southern Africa, founded by Jan van Riebeeck in 1652, VOC ships could take on fresh vegetables and lemons to reduce the risk of scurvy. In Japan, the Netherlands was the only permitted foreign trading partner for two centuries. Between these two poles, the company traded in all directions: spices, tin, silver, sandalwood, camphor, cotton, silk, rice, shells, opium and enslaved people. In the archipelago, they used large numbers of Chinese traders. Batavia had the largest slave market in all of Southeast Asia.[10]

Long trade routes, small trading posts. But now and then, the VOC saw no option but to intervene in local affairs. That was because its success depended on the degree to which it could maintain a spice monopoly, by force if necessary. Growers in the Moluccas were not allowed to sell spices to anyone but the VOC, and a maximum price was set – not an attractive deal for them. From 1619 to 1629, Coen ruled from Batavia as governor-general. When it became clear in 1621 that Banda, in violation of its agreements, was still supplying nutmeg to other countries and companies, he sent a punitive exped-ition. The island's 10,000 to 15,000 inhabitants were massacred, and their land was assigned to VOC officials, who then imported thou-sands of enslaved workers to cultivate it. Today, we have a word for this: genocide. The genocide on Banda marked the transition from a purely mercantile project to a more territorial one. It was the first time that the VOC took over not a trading post but farmland.

Map 9: VOC factories and settlements in the seventeenth century

Coen was ruthless. In 1623, the VOC didn't hesitate to torture and kill some ten uncooperative Englishmen in Ambon. Two years later, when Coen learned that the neighbouring island of Seram had begun to grow cloves and sell them to other buyers, he had all the clove trees chopped down, 35,000 in total. It takes twelve years before a young tree bears fruit. He had urged his employers in Amsterdam to keep in mind 'that trade cannot be maintained without war, nor war without trade'.[11] His approach drew fierce criticism even in his own time. His predecessor Laurens Reael deplored 'all the unjust, yea barbaric, measures' that the VOC imagined necessary. 'On a desolate sea, in desolate lands and with dead people, no profit whatsoever can be made.'[12] Even the VOC directors in Amsterdam, seventeen pipe-puffing, white-collared worthies who expressed themselves in baroque sentences, would have preferred the monopolies to be acquired with a little less bloodshed, but they continued to give Coen their full support because he was so good for the bottom line.

The VOC quietly shifted its focus from the maritime to the military. After 1650, the company ordered the felling of no fewer than three-quarters of *all* the clove trees *throughout* the Moluccas, so that no rival could benefit from them. Islands and villages that dared to plant new ones were mercilessly torched and razed to the ground. In Java, the company managed to take the north coast, which had several excellent harbours, and also fought for the ports of Malacca and Sumatra. The hunger for land sometimes took strange forms. In 1667, after years of arduous struggle, the English were finally willing to concede Run – a tiny nutmeg island near Banda, less than four square kilometres in size – in return for another Dutch possession: New Amsterdam, later to become Manhattan. The Dutch seized the opportunity. What did they care that the island on the western edge of the Atlantic was sixteen times larger? It was a swampy tract where no spices grew. They had no way of knowing that they were swapping the future location of the world's most expensive square kilometres for a few nutmeg trees on a minuscule, deserted tropical island in the Banda Sea.

After 1700, a new stage began. In this period, the VOC was the most important European actor in the archipelago. It had sent the competition packing, secured its monopoly, expanded its network of ports, forged ties with Chinese intermediaries and earned very satisfactory profits. But then something happened that no one had anticipated: spices went out of fashion. The latest trend from Paris was *nouvelle cuisine*, an approach to cooking that swore by pure, natural flavours for a subtler experience and better digestion. Another game dish smothered in cloves, nutmeg and cinnamon? No, thank you. 'These days, spices, sugar and saffron are forbidden in France,' the *Nouveau dictionnaire* reported in 1776.[13] Truffles, oysters, lobsters, sweetbreads and *foie gras* were in, and champagne, a recent invention, was coming into its own; these sophisticated foodstuffs were not the kind of thing you drowned in a heavily spiced marinade. All over Europe, the aristocracy followed the new fashion. For a century, the VOC had fought for lucrative trade monopolies, but now that it had them, spices were not exquisite but common.

Weren't there other products they could sell? Yes, the good news was that Europe was developing a taste not only for a new cuisine but also for new colonial luxury goods: coffee, tea, sugar, tobacco and cocoa. At first it was only aristocrats in refined rococo salons who sampled the new hot drinks with their little fingers extended, and who took snuff, the sophisticated alternative to vulgar smoking. But the urban middle class soon followed suit.[14] Coffee houses popped up in every city in Europe, and soon became known simply as cafés. Their menus featured not only novel drinks such as coffee, tea and hot chocolate but also new treats made from sugar and cocoa; modern pastry was born. Cocoa came from Central America, but the other new commodities grew in Southeast Asia. The VOC began planting coffee and tea in western Java in 1707; twenty years later, it was the world's largest coffee producer, outranking the Arabian Peninsula. By 1725, it controlled half to three-quarters of the global coffee trade. Chinese immigrants in Batavia began growing sugar in the Ommelanden, the rural area surrounding the city. They too made huge profits. The wellspring of economic growth was no longer the Moluccas but Java and Sumatra.

But the new crops required land, a lot of land. What the VOC now wanted most was not harbours or orchards but vast agricultural areas. The whole region surrounding Batavia was cultivated; private plantations grew rice, cotton and sugarcane. In the interior, the VOC captured ever larger swathes of the countryside from local rulers. By around 1750, it possessed half of Java. The company also took parts of Sumatra, Borneo and Sulawesi, as well as smaller islands such as Madura, Sumbawa and Sumba. It obtained supreme authority over some areas, but most remained under the rule of local monarchs who acceded to the wishes of the Dutch officials in return for gifts. This marriage of convenience between the colonial overlords and local potentates would endure for centuries.

Batavia's population reached 120,000; only 7,000 were European. Along the way, it hit a few bumps. Starting in 1733, thousands of the city's inhabitants died of inexplicable fevers. More than half the VOC officials died within a year of arriving, some 85,000 in total by the end of the century. A constant supply of new men from Europe was required, at crippling costs. The lavish profits of old turned into debts. Batavia gained a reputation as the world's unhealthiest city, although the cause was not discovered until the twentieth century: the creation of fish ponds on the marshy land to the north of the city had provided ideal living conditions for the malaria mosquito.[15]

When, on top of all this, the international sugar market collapsed under the pressure of competition from Brazil and the Caribbean, unrest grew among the many Chinese sugarcane workers in the Ommelanden. The Europeans in Batavia lived in growing fear of a Chinese uprising, fear partly incited by the VOC. In 1740, after a few skirmishes, the Dutch killed almost all the Chinese residents of Batavia, regardless of whether they were menial labourers who had slipped in from the countryside or completely innocent merchants and craftspeople from the city centre. The victims included blacksmiths, furniture makers and proprietors of eateries and tea houses. Estimates range from 4,000 to 12,000 dead; it was the largest massacre since the Banda genocide of 1621 and, unfortunately, not the last time that the Chinese bore the brunt of the violence. As a typical intermediary class between the European regime and the native population, the Chinese community was consistently caught between suspicion from above and jealousy from below.

Map 10: VOC expansion in the eighteenth century

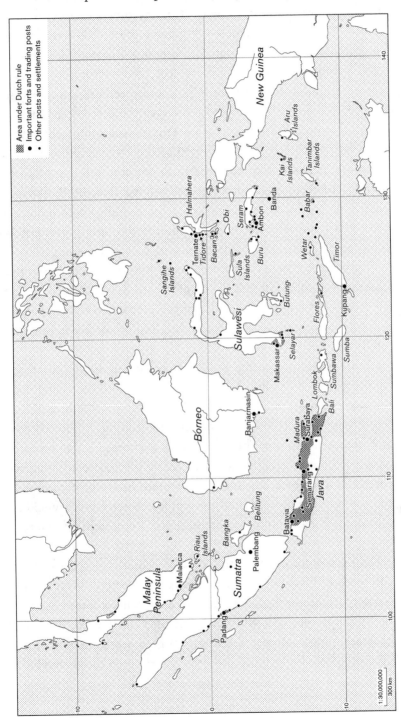

The burgeoning territory required a larger, more expensive governing apparatus, especially with so many officials succumbing to malaria. The VOC had to post a growing staff to stations throughout the archipelago, no fewer than 35,000 people in 1750.[16] As the company's spending soared, so did its debt, and corruption rose at a frightening rate year after year. Who could keep tabs on all the functionaries deep in the interior and at remote outposts? Adding insult to injury, the French botanist Pierre Poivre had smuggled nutmeg shoots to Mauritius in 1770, breaking the long-established VOC monopoly. And worst of all, the British declared war on the Dutch again in 1780 and blockaded the seas around Batavia. Bankruptcy became inevitable; on 31 December 1799 the company, once so profitable, was dissolved. The Dutch state took over the entire enterprise, including all its debts, which amounted to 134 million guilders, a quarter of the national debt. By this time 'the Dutch state' meant the Batavian Republic. The old Republic of the Seven United Netherlands, led by the quasi-monarchy of the House of Orange, had just metamorphosed into a unitary state inspired by the French Revolution. It was the end of an era.

It had seemed like such a good idea, equipping the VOC trading company with the political and military means to command lucrative monopolies. But in practice it became impossible to maintain. When every ship had to have soldiers and cannons on board, when every depot had to be a fort, when every anchorage had to be fought for, when monopolies obtained with great difficulty turned out to be worthless, when more and more trade goods had to be grown by the company itself, and when half the employees were quickly laid low and the other half couldn't be trusted, the 'Praiseworthy' enterprise became an expensive business.

The eighteenth century, the VOC's second century, had begun with renewed promise – coffee seemed to be the new cloves – but the company never matched its earlier successes. This led to a power vacuum in the archipelago, which other actors rushed to fill: the British, the Arabs, pirates, Buginese traders from Sulawesi, but above all the Chinese, whose importance had grown steadily in the second half of the eighteenth century.[17] Before the Netherlands had completed even a quarter of the jigsaw, the whole thing fell apart again.

The third stage of putting together the jigsaw was brief (1800 to 1816) but crucial. For the first time, the old commercial empire was transformed into something that began to resemble a traditional colony, at least on paper. But it began with disintegration. In 1804, the Batavian Republic became a vassal state of revolutionary France and therefore the enemy of Britain, which seized many of its overseas factories: the Cape, Ceylon, Malacca, the coasts of India and many islands in the archipelago. In Southeast Asia, the Dutch were left with nothing but Java and a few minor way stations.

Nonetheless, not much changed until 1806, when Napoleon himself took an interest in the Dutch question, transforming the Batavian Republic into the Kingdom of Holland and elevating his brother Louis Napoleon to its throne. To set Java straight and prepare for the possibility of a British attack, the new king sent Herman Willem Daendels to Batavia. An unsurprising choice: Daendels was quite possibly the greatest Francophile in the Netherlands, a doctor of laws, an admirer of the Enlightenment and an ardent patriot. After failing to overthrow the House of Orange, he had fled to Paris and been caught up in the French Revolution. He rose through the ranks of the French revolutionary army and returned to the Netherlands as a general in 1795 to establish the Batavian Republic. Louis Napoleon could hardly have found a more loyal subject.

On 1 January 1808, Daendels arrived in Batavia and did exactly what was expected of him: he expanded the remnants of the VOC administration (some 9,000 men) into a fearsome military force of 20,000, which included new indigenous troops from Java, Bali, Sulawesi and Ambon. He ordered the construction of barracks, powder magazines, arsenals and military hospitals, fortified the port of Surabaya and moved the centre of Batavia a few kilometres inland, where the climate was healthier. But that wasn't all. Just as Napoleon had ordered the construction of roads and waterways in Europe, Daendels had an east–west road built in Java, parallel to the coast, so that messages and troops could be dispatched more easily. This impressive thoroughfare, the Grote Postweg or Great Post Road, more than 1,000 kilometres long, was completed within a year. Some 12,000 forced labourers died while building it.[18] The travel time from Batavia to Semarang, for instance, was reduced from ten days to three or four. To this day, that road remains Java's main traffic artery.

Napoleon had carved France into departments and prefectures; Daendels introduced nine prefectures in Java. Napoleon saw himself as the defender of *liberté, égalité, fraternité*; Daendels improved the lives of the enslaved. Napoleon valued education; Daendels advocated schools for Javanese children. Napoleon despised the feudalism of the *ancien régime*; Daendels brought low the island's sultans and other aristocrats. Napoleon advocated the rational management of the national economy; Daendels reformed agriculture, forestry and water management, even introducing a general inspectorate for the coffee plantations. He was known as the Napoleon of Batavia, with all of his namesake's revolutionary and dictatorial tendencies.

What Daendels brought to Java was nothing less than the idea of the modern state. A crucial part of that was his conviction that all land was state property.[19] He regarded the remaining Javanese principalities as anachronisms, oppressing the populace and blocking the way to modernity. In Cirebon and Banten he smashed the power of

Map 11: The Great Post Road and the annexation of the
Javanese principalities (1800–1830)

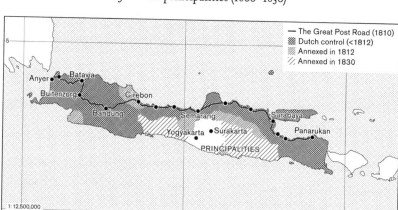

the nobility. He even went to Surakarta – also called Solo – and Yog-yakarta, the two central Javanese cities with their roots in the mighty sultanate of Mataram, where the local rulers still received generous grants from the Dutch. He wrote to Napoleon about the sultan of Yogyakarta: 'I have taken away his crown and placed one of his sons in charge. [. . .] I seized the opportunity to annexe a few of his districts, and I abolished a kind of annual tribute of 10,000 piasters that the administration had been paying him. A similar sum had been paid to the Emperor of Solo [the Susuhunan of Surakarta], and I abolished that too. Finally, I established commercial and political ties with the new sultan that should be very advantageous to us.'[20]

In short, Daendels was a man of action. But all his work couldn't prevent a British naval blockade of Java in 1809. A year later, Napoleon annexed all of the Netherlands, making it French territory. From that moment on, Java was officially a French colony. 'Inhabitants of Java, your interests have become those of the French empire,' Napoleon proclaimed. 'My priority, now that I may welcome you as subjects, is to make certain that this flourishing colony shall be protected from destruction by envious Britain, which has threatened it for so long. The French, who are now your brothers, unite with you to defend your possessions. From now on, your friends and allies will be your fellow citizens. [. . .] Princes and peoples of Java, your religion, your property, your laws and your moral codes will be respected. [. . .] We seek friends, not enemies. [. . .] I ratify all the treaties you made with Holland. Arm yourselves against your enemies; be brave and loyal. I will be a generous patron to you.'[21]

After these valorous words, Daendels raised the French tricolour; even though it was essentially the Dutch flag turned ninety degrees, many of the Dutch were unhappy with the change. To make matters worse, the British landed in Java in 1811 and took the island with a force of 12,000 men. The Gallicising of Java had long been a thorn in their side. Daendels' troops proved no match for them.

The new head of the administration was Thomas Stamford Raffles, and although he was British, he had absorbed Enlightenment ideals just as thoroughly as Daendels and was, if anything, yet more dauntless. He set out to territorialise the overseas area, to establish firm borders and, as far as possible, one contiguous territory, and to centralise the administration. He continued to chip away at the power of the native aristocracy, allowing only a few principalities in central Java to remain. And because the land that had belonged to the local rulers came into the hands of the state, every peasant now had to pay the colonial authorities at least one-quarter of their harvest in tax, sometimes as much as half. Although this new tax system was imposed only very gradually, it was a critical step in the development of the colony; the administration was expanding its influence over the lives of the inhabitants. Raffles made very specific, practical rules, even regulating how people moved. On the Great Post Road and other roads, he required horses and coaches to keep to the left, just as they did in Britain. That traffic rule is still respected, more or less, to this day; Indonesia is one of the very few former colonies where cars drive on the opposite side of the road to the mother country. The tireless Raffles also wrote the first, voluminous history of Java before moving on to a new project: founding the city-state of Singapore.[22] That's the kind of man he was.

Despite their brief terms of office, Daendels's three years and Raffles's five, their perseverance laid the groundwork for the entire colonial project. They reduced the influence of the aristocracy, established a central role for the state and set in motion the gradual process of transforming the old political order into a modern regime. Almost all their attention went to Java, but the transformation they effected there was the germ of all that followed. A bewildering patchwork of feudal principalities began its transformation into a single territory under a unified administration, with nationalised land that could be crossed on horseback, even if only on the left side of the road. The Netherlands, in power for 350 years? The true beginning was not a Dutch but a French and British initiative.

The fourth leader to work on the jigsaw puzzle was King William I. In 1813, the Netherlands had become independent again, and after Napoleon's defeat at Waterloo in 1815, it was expanded to include the territory of the later Belgium. For the new Kingdom of the Netherlands to function properly as a buffer state against France, it had to resume control of its overseas territories. So Britain had to loosen its grip on its recent conquests, but did so with great reluctance, keeping the Cape, Ceylon and the Indian trading stations for itself while returning Java to Dutch control. This is when it really began to make sense to speak of the Dutch East Indies (or Netherlands East Indies); the mercantilism of the VOC had been supplanted by Dutch colonialism. The new constitution gave the king absolute power in all colonial matters.[23] At first, William I continued along the same lines as Daendels and Raffles. Land remained the property of the state, and farmers could lease tracts in exchange for a portion of the crop. In the central Javanese principalities, the leases were awarded by the local aristocrats. When that led to wrongdoing and exploitation, the Dutch administration abolished the system. Prince Diponegoro, the eldest son of the Sultan of Yogyakarta, rebelled against the change, setting off the protracted Java War (1825–30). This was not a traditional battlefield encounter of the Napoleonic variety but an asymmetrical conflict in which Diponegoro used guerrilla tactics, like so many twentieth-century freedom fighters after him.

The Java War was the final attempt by the old Javanese aristocracy to contest foreign subjugation. It was unsuccessful: large areas of central Java were annexed by the colony, and only the south remained more or less autonomous, in the form of four principalities: Surakarta, Yogyakarta, Mangkunegaran and Pakualaman. The war cost the lives of 15,000 soldiers on the Dutch side, 8,000 of them European. On the Javanese side, the suspected death count is 200,000, one tenth in battle and the others due to hardship and famine.[24] It was an even deadlier conflict than the later war of independence from 1945 to 1949. When Diponegoro, after many years, agreed to negotiate with the Netherlands, the Dutch dishonourably clapped him in irons and banished him to Sulawesi. 'The Dutch are bad at heart,' he wrote during his lifelong exile.[25] Paying lip service to equality and then showing no respect for their opponent – this was a mistake Dutch authorities would often make during the Revolusi. No wonder Diponegoro grew into an icon of the anti-colonial resistance.

Pratomo was sitting up straight in his chair, telling me about his life. Then he interrupted himself: 'Does it seem at all plausible, what

I'm telling you? My memories are crumbling away.' I nodded. His stories fascinated me. Though he sometimes stopped and stared at the floor as if an unfinished sentence was a cup that had slipped from his hand, at other times his memory was crystal-clear. And what he had to say never failed to interest me. Take, for example, what he told me about his name, which in full was Raden Mas Djajeng Pratomo. 'Raden Mas is an aristocratic title. It means something like baron or viscount.' But in conversation with me, he didn't stand on ceremony; he invited me to call him 'Prat', like everyone else. 'I was born in Sumatra,' he said, 'but I really come from Java.'[26] I also learned that he came from one of the last four surviving principalities: Pakualaman, to the southwest of Yogyakarta. Maybe he was even a distant relative of Prince Diponegoro. His great-grandfather had been first in the order of succession, in any case, but he had left the palace behind him for good in dissatisfaction with the growing dominance of the Dutch and the loose morals that prevailed at court.[27] His decision had far-reaching consequences: Pratomo was the eldest son of the eldest son of the eldest son of the crown prince. He could have been a Javanese ruler, but instead here he was in a retirement home on the coast of Holland, munching on poffertjes.

As for that other monarch, William I, the Dutch king had great financial ambitions for his colony, but the Java War had cost a fortune, the tax system was not raising enough money and, to his great frustration, the year 1830 brought the secession of another Dutch territory he'd been exploiting for profit: Belgium. He had to say goodbye to the very substantial revenue from the Ghent textile industry and the coal mines in Wallonia. Until 1839, he continued to throw vast sums of money into the war against Belgium. It didn't help. Where could he compensate for the lost income? In the colonies, of course. 'If I cannot defend my kingdom,' he once grumbled, 'then I shall flood Holland and set sail for the Indies.'[28] What he could no longer squeeze out of Belgium would just have to come from the East. The ensuing exploitation of the Indonesian population was the indirect result of the Belgian struggle for freedom.

The king adopted an entirely new approach to colonial taxation: instead of claiming a fraction of each harvest, he forced the locals to dedicate some of their land to crops that could be exported at a profit. This was known as the Cultivation System (*cultuurstelsel*). Farmers had to devote twenty per cent of their land to crops that the colonial administration could auction off for a hefty profit on the Amsterdam exchanges, through the agency of a national trading society that William had founded: the Nederlandsche Handelsmaatschappij (NHM). Peasants with no arable land had to perform sixty-six days of *corvée*, a fancy word for unpaid work for the authorities – essentially, a form of forced labour. Countless Javanese peasants who grew sweet potatoes, coconuts, papayas and rice for their own use were also required to produce coffee, tea, tobacco, sugar, quinine or indigo, commodities that were of little or no use to them. They were paid wages for the crops they delivered, but because the cost of leasing land rose each year, their profit margins remained very small. In rural areas of the colony, the people who really profited from the system were the Chinese and European manufacturers who did the initial processing of the harvest (pressing sugarcane and drying tea and tobacco). But the greatest profits were made in Europe. The higher up the ladder, the richer the rewards.

A colonial administration was put in place to collect the crops. The governor-general, assisted by the Council of the Indies, appointed European officials in all parts of the colony. The highest in rank were known as residents and assistant residents. They were the equals, and later the superiors, of the local native leaders (the former aristocrats), who became known as regents. Java had sixty-eight regents,[29] who were still highly esteemed by the local population. Pratomo's grandfather, for instance, the son of the crown prince who had renounced his claim, became the regent of Wates, an area to the south of Yogyakarta. He must have been an impressive sight; he travelled on horseback, and young Pratomo and his other grandchildren had to kneel humbly before him with their hands on their chests and then leave the room by walking backwards. Their world was steeped in hierarchy and cultural heritage: Pratomo was initiated into the secrets of traditional Javanese dance. Although the regents tended to lead lives of great luxury, in terms of actual power they were subordinate to the colonial rulers. In short, local administration in the Dutch

colony was dual in nature, with a regent alongside a resident. In principle, the European resident (or assistant resident) oversaw the
activities of the Javanese regent, but in practice the relationship was
often reversed. The Dutch official was usually young and less experienced, had no local network and remained in that office for just a few
years, while the native regent was older and completely bound up
with his region, family and status. How could you persuade a person
like that to go along with a thoroughly European idea like the Cultivation System? The solution was simple: offer him a bonus. By basing
a portion of his wages on the size of the crop he delivered, the Dutch
hoped to increase productivity. No doubt this system did inspire
some native administrators to work harder, but of course it also left
the door wide open to exploitation. Many regents subjected their
people to decades of ruthless extortion, soon demanding that they
devote not twenty but forty per cent of their land to commercial
crops. The sixty-six days of unpaid labour for the colonial regime
soon became 200. King William I's Cultivation System was incredibly lucrative, even decades after the end of his reign in 1840. It
yielded 823 million guilders between 1831 and 1877 and often
accounted for more than half of annual tax revenue.[30] The Netherlands and Spain were the only two countries to exploit their colonies
in this direct fashion.[31] In the 1850s, the Cultivation System yielded
more than a third of Dutch public revenue, and this was no secret.[32]
In his annual Speech from the Throne in 1859, King William III discussed 'the highly satisfactory state of the national finances' and
acknowledged that this was 'largely the fruit of the benefits provided
to the Nation by possessions in the East Indies'.[33] But meanwhile, his
colonial subjects were being reduced to penury, as famine swept one
of the world's most fertile regions. In the years 1846 and 1847, tens of
thousands of people died in fever epidemics in central Java.[34] In 1851
and 1864, there were large-scale outbreaks of cholera.[35] Health care
was nearly non-existent.

It was against this harrowing backdrop that, in a garret in Brussels,
a former colonial official who had resigned in disgrace wrote the
scathing protest recognised today as the greatest Dutch-language
novel of the nineteenth century: Multatuli's *Max Havelaar* (1860).[36]

Under the new constitution of 1848, colonial policy was no longer the king's private playground but a public matter, the business of the Dutch government and parliament. Newspapers wrote about it, and members of the public weighed in.[37] Multatuli, the pen name of Eduard Douwes Dekker, did so with exceptional panache, or, as one contemporary put it, 'with a heat, a fire, a passion, an outrage – an all-consuming, unrelenting hatred of the system – that finally seems to have rudely awakened the Netherlands'.[38] His book was a motley collection of stories, letters, speeches, meditations, essays, poems and satire, but what undoubtedly touched the hearts of Dutch readers the most was the parable of Saijah and Adinda, the lovers whose lives were torn apart and destroyed by colonial politics. It was a tale of humiliation and impoverishment, of exploitation and embitterment and, ultimately, of radicalisation and resistance. This was the Dutch equivalent of *Uncle Tom's Cabin*, with all the magnificent formal chaos of *Moby-Dick* and the offhand but deadly wit of Guy de Maupassant or Turgenev.

Seldom has a single book so excited the masses.[39] The socialist leader Domela Nieuwenhuis called on the lower house of parliament to abolish the colonies, but that went too far for most, including Multatuli.[40] The majority agreed that the colonial regime should be made more humane and the Cultivation System should be abandoned. In 1860 the Netherlands abolished slavery, well after England (1833) and France (1848), although the practice persisted for many years in remote areas.[41] From that time onwards, the discredited Cultivation System was replaced, step by step, by the plantation system, in which agriculture was controlled not by the state but by private capital. Dutch companies were allowed to lease government land to set up plantations. The losses from the demise of the Cultivation System were more than made up for by new tax revenue.[42] Planters produced mainly coffee, tobacco and sugar in eastern Java, indigo and sugar in central Java and tea and quinine (from cinchona bark) in western Java. The state leased not only land but also licenses to provide services or other economic activities, which left the companies free to conduct those activities however they saw fit. For instance, there were licenses for selling salt and opium, running a pawnshop or a gambling house, collecting tolls or taxes, trading in trees, sponges, pearls or edible birds' nests and so forth. The Chinese middle class showed particular enthusiasm for this system, which became a major source of revenue.[43]

In this fourth stage of putting together the jigsaw puzzle, the emphasis was not solely on Java. After the death of William I, three large-scale military expeditions to Bali were mounted (in 1846, 1848 and 1849). That was possible because, after the Java War, William I had expanded his colonial forces into the Royal Netherlands Indies Army (Koninklijk Nederlands-Indisch Leger; KNIL), a full-scale colonial army that was separate from the Dutch military in Europe. Almost half the KNIL troops were European; the others came from Ambon, Sulawesi, Madura, Java and Sumatra and even from West Africa. From 1831 to 1872, some 3,000 soldiers went to the Indies from what are now Ghana and Burkina Faso. *Belanda hitam*, they were called: 'black Dutchmen'.[44] The plan was for this mixed-race professional army to put down local uprisings in Java and conquer the rest of the archipelago step by step. Bali was the first great test. In the expeditions of the 1840s, more than 12,000 people died. The KNIL had proved the superiority of its firepower. Yet it took the Dutch more than fifty years after that to subjugate the island completely. In the 1850s, the KNIL also fought for parts of Borneo, southern Sulawesi and the centre and east coast of Sumatra. Jigsaw puzzles could be a bloody business, but so be it; huge areas of land were added to the colony by military force. By the end of this period, in 1870, the Dutch had taken Java and were ready to rake in the rest.

In the fifth stage, from 1870 to 1914, the jigsaw was completed. This stage saw the greatest territorial expansion, with more than half of the colony's final territory first conquered – very late in the day. The KNIL conducted as many as thirty campaigns, ranging from minor incursions to long-drawn-out wars.[45] They attacked the Balinese in Lombok, the Batak and Minangkabau peoples in Sumatra, the Dayaks in Borneo, and the native inhabitants of Sulawesi, Flores, Sumbawa, Seram and the Riouw (now Riau) Islands. The whole archipelago reeked of gunpowder. These campaigns were euphemistically called

Map 12: Royal Netherlands Indies Army (KNIL) expeditions
between 1814 and 1870

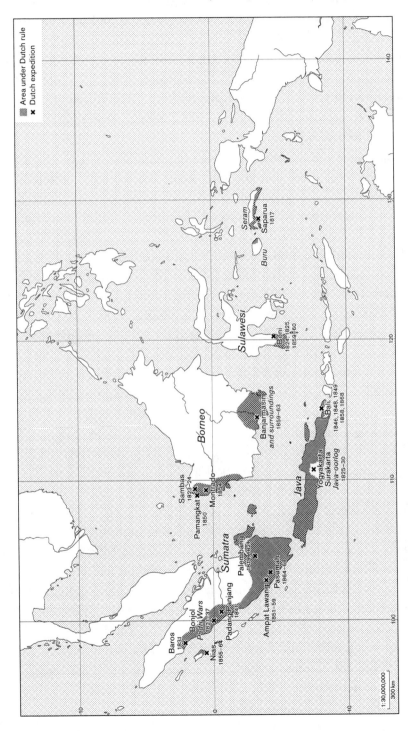

'pacifications', but in practice they were wars of conquest. The so-called Pax Neerlandica was the result of violent and often heartless military action. In this respect, Dutch colonialism was much like the way in which British, French, Belgian and German authorities pursued their imperial ambitions.[46] The human cost did not trouble them any more than the thought of the soldiers they sacrificed in Europe. Life was as cheap in the colonies as it had been in Napoleon's battles or would be in World War I.

But the largest conflict by far was the Aceh War. The northern tip of Sumatra, an area that had long adhered to a relatively traditional variety of Islam, was one of the last great blanks in this colonial jigsaw. (The other was New Guinea.) The opening of the Suez Canal in 1869 had increased its strategic importance; sailing ships and steamships no longer approached from South Africa in the southwest but from the northwest. No longer did they reach Batavia by way of the Sunda Strait between Java and Sumatra; instead, they used the Strait of Malacca, passing Aceh. That once-remote territory had become the gateway to the colony, so the Dutch felt it would be only prudent to grab it. But that was easier said than done; the Aceh War became the longest colonial war in history. It began in 1873 and went through several stages before ending forty years later in 1914, the year Pratomo was born. The intervening decades brought an endless series of sieges, campaigns and punitive expeditions that cost more than 100,000 lives. The Dutch fought Aceh longer than they ruled it: forty years of war for twenty-eight years of power. By the turn of the century, the KNIL had 1,500 commissioned officers and 42,000 soldiers and non-commissioned officers.[47] The many young European soldiers who enlisted in the course of the conflict included an unruly twenty-two-year-old Frenchman who, soon after arriving in Java, deserted. His name was Arthur Rimbaud. As a teenager, he had taken French poetry by storm, turned it upside down and then abandoned it. It wasn't that he had found a new calling as a soldier of fortune. He couldn't have cared less about the whole Aceh War; he just wanted to see the Orient. Soon after landing, he made a run for it, doubtless grateful to the Dutch for the free voyage and the enlistment bonus of 600 guilders.[48]

Steamboats and military campaigns may seem like relics of a bygone age, but this was not as long ago as it may seem. During my research in the 2010s, I did run across a few traces of that distant war. 'My grandfather fought in Aceh,' said a woman in Ede. 'He was shot at, but an Acehnese took care of him. Otherwise he would certainly have died.'[49] A very elderly Dutchman even told me that his father had fought in the war. 'He wrote a terribly dull book about it. You can buy it on Amazon if you're interested.'[50]

The methods by which the Dutch seized power were anything but subtle. The officer Hendrik Colijn wrote to his orthodox Calvinist farm family about the Battle of Lombok in 1894: 'I had to have 9 women and 3 children, who pleaded for mercy, heaped together and shot dead. A nasty business, but there was no other way. The soldiers enjoyed skewering them with their bayonets.'[51] In the 1920s and 30s, Colijn would serve for eight years as the Dutch prime minister; nineteenth-century brutality ran over into twentieth-century politics.

More horrifying still were the scenes in Bali, where in 1906 and 1908 the complete courts of a number of principalities chose to commit collective suicide (*puputan*). Hundreds of men, women and even children walked straight towards the Dutch rifles and artillery. They were dressed in traditional white garments and carried only staffs, spears and the finely wrought traditional daggers called krises. 'The rat-a-tat-tat of gunfire went on, the fighting grew fiercer, people fell on top of each other and more and more blood flowed.' A pregnant Balinese woman was one of the few who lived to tell the tale. 'Persisting in passionate fury, men and women advanced, standing up for the truth without fear, to protect their country of birth, willing to lay down their lives.' The KNIL soldiers couldn't believe their eyes: women hurled their jewellery at them mockingly, courtiers stabbed themselves with their daggers and died, men were mown down by cannons. The wounded were put out of their misery by their relatives, who were killed in turn by the Dutch bullets. Then the colonial army plundered the corpses. In the puputan of 1906, an estimated 3,000 people died. 'The battlefield was completely silent, aside from the rasp of dying breath and the cries for help heard from among the bodies.'[52]

And this event, too, has left traces. In December 2017 I travelled around a near-deserted Bali. Mount Agung's volcanic rumblings had put a stop to tourism for the time being, and in the ancient capital of Klungkung, I found the desolate ruin of the royal palace. It had been destroyed after the puputan of 1908. 'My grandpa, Dewa Agung Oka Geg, was there that day,' said Tjokorda Gde Agung Samara Wicaksana, the crown prince of Klungkung. We were sitting in the new palace, opposite the ruin, and drinking tea. It was Saturday and his servants had gone home; he had made the tea himself. 'The puputan of Klungkung was the very last one. After that, Bali was entirely subject to Dutch authority. My grandfather was only thirteen years old and nephew to the king.' Almost the entire royal family died; the king and the first prince in the line of succession were killed, the king's six wives stabbed themselves to death with krises, and 200 courtiers followed their example or were murdered. 'But my grandpa survived. To keep him from claiming the throne, the Dutch sent him to Lombok. They wouldn't let him return until 1929, when they made him the regent. In 1938, he was one of eight Balinese rulers to swear fealty to Queen Wilhelmina. He became the new king of Klungkung, but for the rest of his life he walked with a limp. He'd been shot in the leg during the puputan.'[53]

The Dutch gained control of the whole archipelago. Almost all the local leaders, around 300 in all, had to sign a 'Brief Declaration', a concise document by which they relinquished all their claims to power. 'I, the undersigned, X, administrator of territory Y, declare that territory Y forms part of the Dutch East Indies and hence falls under the authority of the Netherlands and that pursuantly I shall ever remain loyal to Her Majesty the Queen of the Netherlands and to His Excellency the Governor-General as the representative of Same, from whom I accept the task of administering the territory.'[54] *Hence . . . pursuantly . . . the representative of Same*; this was the type of prose in which they relinquished their freedom. The little kingdoms of old became colonial territories under Dutch sovereignty (*gouvernementslanden*); only the four principalities (*vorstenlanden*) of central Java, the crumbs of the once-great Mataram empire, near Yogyakarta and Surakarta, escaped complete control.

Map 13: Dutch military campaigns (1870–1914)

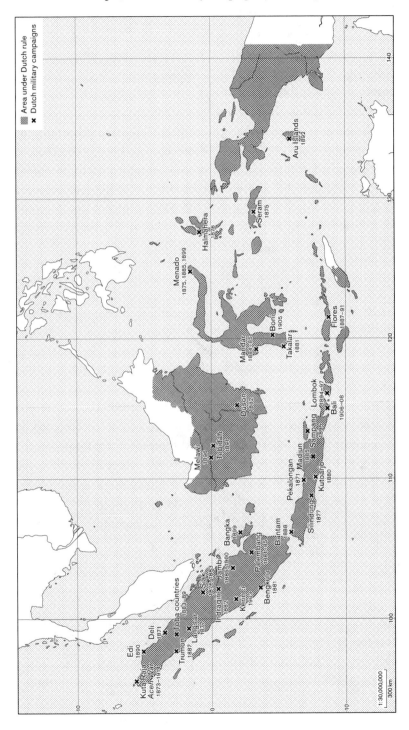

Area under Dutch rule
✗ Dutch military campaigns

Halmahera
1876
Aru Islands
1892
Seram
1875
Menado
1875, 1885, 1899
Bone
1905
Flores
1887–91
Mandar
1905, 1905
Takalar
1881
Lombok
1894
Duson
1905
Sampang
Bali
1906–08
Melawi
1906
Tebidah
1891
Madiun
1871
Pekalongan
Kutoarjo
1880
Slindung
1877
Bangka
1899
Bantam
1888
Palembang
1881–1907
Jambi
1885–1900
Siak
1875–1883
Indragiri
1882
Kerinci
1903
Bengkulu
1881
Toba countries
1883–89
Langkat
1873
Deli
1871
Trumon
1887
Edi
1890
Kuala Raja
Aceh War
1873–1913

1:30,000,000
300 km.

Meanwhile, the edges of the jigsaw were also nearing their final form, through a process of diplomatic negotiation and wrangling. As early as 1854, an agreement was reached with Portugal under which Flores became Dutch and Timor was split in two, with East Timor remaining Portuguese. In 1891, a convention with the British followed; Singapore and Malacca were already completely British, and Sumatra completely Dutch, but now Borneo was divided into two unequal parts. The smaller, northern part was brought into the British sphere and the south went to the Dutch. Finally, in 1895, the immense island of New Guinea was divided in three with a couple of neatly ruled lines: the western half was for the Netherlands, the eastern half for Germany (in the north) and Great Britain (in the south). The German border is gone now, but the other line remains. Again, this wasn't so very long ago.

By 1914 the job was done: the Dutch tricolour flew throughout the archipelago, from the northwest tip of Sumatra to the straight line that sliced New Guinea in two. The Netherlands possessed a colony nearly fifty times as large as the mother country. It belonged to a club of small European countries who were punching far above their weight as imperial powers; Belgium had the Congo, Portugal Brazil and Denmark Greenland. But while those territories were sparsely populated, Indonesia's demographics were impressive. Around 1900, there were barely five million people living in the Netherlands, but around forty million in the Dutch East Indies. Even great powers like Britain, France and Germany could not turn their noses up at that. The Netherlands, which also possessed Suriname and the Netherlands Antilles, had the world's third-largest empire, trailing only Britain and France. Obviously, this gave an incredible boost to the country's self-image. That little nation by the sea had recaptured some of its old glory; a new Golden Age seemed to have dawned. 'The East' became a source of great Dutch pride.

If we look at the whole region, we see that the British then ruled over what are now India, Pakistan, Bangladesh, Burma, Sri Lanka, Malaysia and Singapore. The French possessed Indochina: present-day Vietnam, Laos and Cambodia. Portugal was left with only East Timor; America had captured the Philippines from the Spanish in

1898; and Germany controlled the northeast of New Guinea (Kaiser-Wilhelmsland) and the adjacent maritime zone, which included the Bismarck Archipelago. Thailand, then called Siam, is the only kingdom that was never colonised. China remained independent, but the enfeebled empire had been forced to open up its seaports and lost Hong Kong to the British. The only Asian country with colonies of its own was Japan, which had taken Taiwan in 1895 and cherished far greater ambitions.

Light green fields of rice wherever I looked, and in the distance the massive silhouette of the active volcano Mount Merapi. A downpour had just ended, and as the sunlight returned, the rice fields gleamed. The scene was about as fresh, green and beautiful as Java gets. I was sitting with a farmer with silvery-white hair, a few hundred metres from Prambanan, the sacred Hindu site from the early tenth century. Harjo Utomo was barefoot and wore a dark green sarong. He sat in front of his house, staring out over the wet fields – a man of few words, ninety-eight years old and born in that very spot. Until several years ago he had fasted during Ramadan, but now he was getting a little too old for that.

My visit surprised him. He was an ordinary farmer – what had he ever experienced? The witnesses who think they have nothing to say are often the most interesting of all. Every life, however inconspicuous, reflects the light of history. 'No politics, no army, no stress.' That was his advice for a long life. 'Just eat and live, from day to day. And pray. And stay with your family, the children, the grandchildren. Even then, life is hard enough.' I asked him about his own childhood. His granddaughter translated into Javanese; he didn't speak Indonesian. To him, that was the language of the traders at sea, not the farmers in the interior.

'I'm the eldest of four and the only one still alive. The others are dead. I was born in 1918; I don't know the date. My father was a mason. He helped to build a Dutch factory nearby, a sugarcane plant. The buildings are still there.'

Aha, that didn't take long. A sugarcane plant. Around 1900, Java was one of the world's leading sugar producers. Its coffee, tea and tobacco also went around the world, along with cinchona (for quinine) and kapok (or Java cotton, for mattresses). But while most of these commodities could be shipped without a lot of additional steps, sugarcane was quick to rot and had to be processed where it was grown. Sugar refineries therefore became the first form of industrialisation in central Java. It was in agricultural areas such as this that a kind of industrial proletariat formed for the first time. According to oral history, the transition was far from gentle. 'My father had no choice,' Harjo Utomo said. 'He *had* to work for the Dutch. They didn't get breaks. It was just like the forced labour in the Japanese era.'

Around the turn of the century, the Dutch East Indies was the world's largest supplier of tropical products.[55] The plantation system proved a stunning success; the liberalisation of agriculture sent production soaring. The key to that success was the virtually unlimited supply of cheap labour. In many places, small farmers toiling away in their fields became employees and wage earners. They picked coffee beans in eastern Java and harvested sugarcane in central Java. In the gardens of western Java, women stooped to gather tea leaves. And at the end of each week, they received something very peculiar, something their fathers and grandfathers may never have heard of: money. That was what Harjo Utomo's father experienced. When I asked the nearly hundred-year-old man what his father had earned as a mason for building the sugar plant, he said, 'A little money and a little food.' A simple statement with a special significance. Along the coast, traders had been using coins for centuries, but in the interior, almost everyone still had to get used to the circles of metal, which were said to be worth as much as a chicken or a pineapple.

The monetisation of a thoroughly agrarian society brought ever larger groups of people into the fold of the colonial state. In 1855, there was only 45 million guilders of currency in circulation; by 1900, that figure had risen to 175 million.[56] Dutch authority no longer meant a monthly visit to your village by the assistant resident and the regent to see how the coffee bushes were coming along; instead it was inherent in the sticky handful of change you received weekly from your supervisor, which jingled in your pouch as you walked home. It had words printed on it: 'Dutch East Indies'.

Money opened the way to a new form of taxation. Rather than giving up part of your harvest, working for free or being compelled to plant commercial crops, you could simply hand over a portion of your income. But those who believed the worst suffering was behind them were wrong. In the fractious coastal region of Banten, recently hit by the eruption of Krakatoa, the new tax system provoked great unrest in 1888. Rains of ash, rivers of mud, tsunamis . . . and to top it all off, taxes? Many Dutch people were killed, but the colonial administration retaliated with a vengeance.[57]

In other regions, too, frustration was mounting. A European was someone 'with a forceful voice and a big stick in his hand, someone who never said anything to you but "Dammit" ', in the words of a Javanese colonial official.[58] From an early stage, attentive observers noted the widespread disaffection and even 'burning hatred' for the infidel rulers.[59] Harjo Utomo's father was no exception. Before I had even asked about it, his son told me: 'My father didn't like the Dutch. He hated them. Why? Because they colonised us.'[60]

Nowhere else were circumstances as wretched as in Sumatra's northeast coast. In 1863, the Dutch planter Jacob Nienhuys discovered that the banks of the Deli River were a good place to grow tobacco. In a time when Europe's bourgeoisie was taking to cigars, that was big news. And when Deli tobacco turned out to make the world's finest *capa* (cigar wrapper), this out-of-the-way area was overwhelmed by a gold rush. By 1881 there were 67 tobacco plantations in operation, and by 1891 no fewer than 169. Investors came from the Netherlands, England, Germany, Russia, America – across the Western world. In the middle of the ancient forest, they built the city of Medan from the ground up. This fast-growing commercial hub had banks, corporate headquarters and even electric streetlamps; today, it is Indonesia's third city. But where would the plantations find workers? The region was sparsely populated, and neither the Malays on the coast nor the Bataks in the interior were itching to fell gigantic trees or till the soil. Chinese indentured labourers were brought in, first from the Malay Peninsula (Singapore, Penang and Malacca) and later from China, in huge numbers: some 140,000 Chinese in total, plus around 35,000 Javanese from 1890 onwards.[61] These workers, referred to as coolies, weren't enslaved in the narrow sense of the word, since they received wages, but their five-year contracts allowed them so little freedom that the distinction was blurred. Deli became the Wild West of the Dutch East Indies. Large-scale gambling and opium use were encouraged among coolies, so that they would be so deep in debt by the time their contracts ended that they would have to renew. Opium also enabled them to keep working, oblivious to pain or exhaustion. The conditions under which they lived were deplorable. Whoever protested or walked away was punished severely: caned, whipped, placed in confinement or tortured. It was like working on a cotton plantation in the South of the United States. Raw capitalism wielded brutal, arbitrary, lawless power; public authority was all but absent.[62] A quarter to a third of the coolies died before completing their contracts.[63] And all this because gentlemen on the far side of the globe enjoyed puffing on cigars.

But not all the work was in plantation agriculture. The mining industry was also becoming active. In western Kalimantan, the gold mines began production in 1850; some 50,000 Chinese coolies laboured there. In Sumatra and southern Kalimantan, coal was found, a significant event with steam shipping on the rise. On Bangka and Billiton, two small islands near Sumatra, tin was mined on an industrial scale from 1900 onwards; the metal was essential for producing bronze. Around this time, the first rubber plantations were also established, in eastern Sumatra. The inflatable rubber tyre set off a revolution in motorised transport; planters and tappers couldn't keep up with the demand. But the most momentous finds were the first discoveries of petroleum, in northern Sumatra, later in eastern Java (near Surabaya) and most of all in eastern Borneo (near Balikpapan).[64] At first petroleum, literally 'rock oil', was merely fuel for oil lamps, but new uses were not long in coming. Small-scale mining operations made way for large companies. The year 1890 saw the founding of the Koninklijke Nederlandsche Maatschappij tot Exploitatie van Petroleumbronnen in Nederlandsch-Indië (Royal Dutch Company for the Exploitation of Petroleum Sources in the Dutch East Indies), known as 'de Koninklijke' (the Royal) for short. A year later, it was followed by the Shell Transport and Trading Company from the

United Kingdom. In 1907 they were amalgamated, becoming the Royal Dutch Shell Group, one subsidiary of which was the Bataafse Petroleum Maatschappij (Batavian Petroleum Company; BPM), which focused on oil production and refining. Just a few years later, BPM dominated the Dutch colony's entire oil sector, with forty-four concessions covering 32,000 square kilometres, an area larger than Belgium, Wales or Hawaii.[65] Oil became big business and would shape the archipelago's future.

The puzzle had been completed; now it was glued into place. The steamships of the Koninklijke Paketvaart-Maatschappij (Royal Packet Navigation Company; KPM) sailed back and forth, and telegraph lines reached the remotest corners of the colony.[66] Java even acquired its own railway. The export economy not only helped to unify the archipelago but also linked the colony to the rest of the world. The most powerful volcanic eruption in recorded history – Mount Tambora, 1815 – didn't make it into newspapers in the West, but the much smaller Krakatoa eruption of 1883 became one of the first news stories to circle the globe.[67] The world was growing smaller. Along with bags of coffee and telegrams, religions were also travelling further than ever. From the mid-nineteenth century, Protestant and Catholic missionaries arrived in the colony to spread their faith. The colonial authorities would not let them proselytise in the densely populated traditional Muslim areas, but on remote islands such as Flores, Timor, Ambon and Ternate and deep in the interior of Sumatra, Kalimantan, Sulawesi and New Guinea, they preached ideas and worldviews that were completely novel. By the end of the colonial period there were one and a half million Christians out of a total population of sixty million. Missions educated around 200,000 pupils.[68] Meanwhile, religion sent other people in the opposite direction, as steamships permitted more and more Muslims to go on pilgrimage to Mecca. In 1850, there were only 1,600 hajis (Mecca pilgrims) a year from Indonesia, but by 1900 there were already 7,000.[69] Their travels exposed them to new ideas, new developments and new insights. After returning home, they enjoyed the respect of their communities for the rest of their days.

★

There are fascinating images of the Dutch East Indies on the eve of Pratomo's birth. In 1912 and 1913, the Dutch soldier and amateur filmmaker Johann Lamster travelled across Java and Bali, shooting films for the Colonial Institute in Amsterdam.[70] These are the earliest moving pictures of Indonesia. They reveal two parallel societies, completely separate: Europeans in Victorian garb and plainly dressed Asians. The few Dutch women stroll the avenues of Batavia in their finest apparel: long dresses, and hats loaded with flowers and ostrich feathers.[71] Their husbands wear creamy white suits, leather shoes and pith helmets or straw hats. As they walk, they wave thin walking sticks, but they usually go by horse and carriage, and the very wealthiest already have 'automobiles'. A Javanese servant, barefoot, in a sarong and a tightly knotted headscarf, starts the engine with a crank. During the trip, he squats on the broad running board and clings to the handle of the door.

The shaky film shows Javanese girls spinning and weaving, mothers washing their children in a river, boys on the backs of water buffaloes and a few other exotic, idyllic scenes. But there are also shots of the railway workshops in Bandung and of an operation on a horse's trachea at a veterinary school in Buitenzorg (now Bogor). Two completely different worlds. In the most unforgettable sequence, dozens of shipyard workers in a dry dock in Tanjung Priok, the port of Batavia, are tarring the colossal hull of a steamship. Picture the scene: the gigantic screw propeller, the black steel hull and the otherworldly setting of the dry dock. And below, tiny and harmless, the milling crowd of anonymous workers.

Chapter 3

The Colonial Steamship
Social structures in a changing world, 1914–1942

On 25 October 1936, O. L. Fehrenbach, a harbour pilot from Surabaya, made a gruesome discovery. Standing on deck in his spotless
white uniform, he was looking out over the waves of the Java Sea,
where he normally kept an eye on the *prahus*, the region's traditional
sailing boats. One and a half nautical miles to the north of the western lightship, he saw four tattered, balloon-like forms bobbing in the
waves. Realising right away what this meant, he fired off a telegram
to Surabaya. It always takes a few days, he knew, before they float to
the surface. Those four – two Europeans and two Asians, by the look
of them – must have come from the *Van der Wijck*. All that week, the
steamship's sudden inexplicable disappearance had been front-page
news, even in the Netherlands. The hundred-metre-long steamer
provided an express service between Macassar (now Makassar) and
Batavia, with stops in Bali and Surabaya. Only fifteen years earlier,
she had made her maiden voyage from the Fijenoord shipyard in
Rotterdam, a fine, graceful ship known affectionately as 'the Gull'.
How could such a modern vessel have capsized in calm waters on the
familiar route between Surabaya and Batavia, straight along the
north coast of Java? Dozens of crew members and passengers were
still missing. Fehrenbach realised that the ship had sunk much further
to the west but the currents he knew so well had washed the bodies in
his direction. In the days following the tragedy, cabin trunks were
found as far away as the coasts of Madura.[1]

While a tug was on the way to pick up the bodies, the pilot took
another look at the grim sacks of flesh in the water. They lay with
their backs facing up, as usual, their hair drifting on the surface like
seaweed. Not only did he know which ship they came from, but he

could even say with some certainty on which decks they had stayed. The European corpses – not white or pink, but blue and greyish – must have come from the upper decks, where the lifeboats were. The two darker forms had to be passengers from the lower decks, or else stokers or trimmers from the hold.

Like all the KPM steamships, the *Van der Wijck* was divided into three classes. The luxurious first-class cabins on the uppermost deck accommodated sixty passengers and had sinks, water closets with running water and even electric fans. Ships like 'the Gull' were fitted out with every modern luxury: a dining room with attractive wooden wainscoting and marble on the walls, a smoking room with bronze reliefs, a promenade with wicker chairs and cushions and so on. Passengers could play bridge or chat there. The next deck down, second class, also offered comfortable cabins, but they were larger and had to be shared with strangers. Furthermore, they were closer to the engine and more affected when the ship rolled and pitched. There was room there for thirty-four passengers. First- and second-class passengers were collectively referred to as cabin passengers. The third class existed only on paper; in practice, there was a sharp transition to fourth class. Even this gap reflected the social system. On the *Van der Wijck*, as many as 1,000 passengers fitted into fourth class. Unlike the first- and second-class passengers, they did not have comfortable cabins but had to make do with one and a half square metres on deck for themselves, their luggage and a mat. In sunny weather, a canvas awning was raised. They often had to share the deck with horses and cows. At night, they pulled their sarongs over their heads to block out the electric light from the upper decks. They relieved themselves into the sea. The foreship had outboard toilet seats and footholds, the only sanitary facilities available during the many days of sailing. When the sea was rough, the splashing water rinsed both bow and bum.

These steamships were colonial society in microcosm. Nowhere else did you see the differences so clearly. People whose paths hardly crossed in everyday life coexisted on board for days. It had been like that since the nineteenth century. In *Aboe Bakar*, an excellent novel by P.A. Daum published in 1894, several young Dutch ladies in first class hear that one deck down, where passengers travel for half the price, there is a most peculiar man at the railing: 'Laughing and whispering at the prospect of seeing a handsome Arab who spoke Dutch, they went down the companionway and afore. And they elbowed each other, exchanging stealthy glances: "There he is!" ' They ask him in disbelief if he really speaks Dutch. When Aboe Bakar confirms that he does, 'with the elegant, polite gesture of a cultured Oriental', and even proves to speak a few words of French, they have no idea how to respond. 'They nodded and said, "Good day," without any honorific. How could a European lady call such a man "sir"?! They beat a hasty retreat up to the afterdeck, going over the peculiar incident, and accosted Mrs Slaters with a cry of, "Well, you've certainly missed something unusual!" '²

Encounters with working-class deck passengers, who paid one-eighth of the first-class price, were even stranger.³ When Aletta Jacobs, a champion of women's rights and the first Dutch woman to become a physician, toured the archipelago in 1912, she decided the deck passengers were much more interesting than her travelling companions. 'Over the railing around the bridge, I look down at them. They're all natives, the first mate tells me. [. . .] They make less trouble than the first-class lot. We complain about everything, say the mattresses are too hard, the cabin too small [. . .] the ice in our drinks not cold enough and the ten to twelve dishes on the menu three times a day not varied enough. The deck passengers all have just enough room to spread out their mats [. . .] They eat less than one-quarter of what we do, and they do it without fancy cutlery and crockery. No plates, no knives, spoons or forks, no napkins, no drinking glasses, none of the things we overcivilised people imagine we need [. . .] They sit packed together, without a hairsbreadth between them, and all seem content.'⁴

Even after the jigsaw puzzle was completed, the great class differences remained. From 1914 to 1942, the end of the Aceh War to the start of the Japanese occupation, the steamship was still a complete microcosm of colonial society. In this brief twenty-eight-year period when the Netherlands 'possessed' the colony as a whole, there was no better place to study its social structure than a steamer.

Let us take a look at the *Van der Wijck*'s passengers in 1936. The ship was not full: there were only 27 cabin passengers (first and second class combined) and 187 deck passengers. Who travelled first class? The answer is in the newspapers: Mr Schoevers, director of the Algemeene Volkscredietbank; Mr Mangelaar Meertens of the Handelsbank, Mr E. C. Hudson of the Union Insurance Company; Mr and Mrs Daniel Polsky, American tourists returning home from Bali; a certain Mrs Hartman with her daughter and baby . . .[5] They survived, but fourteen other cabin passengers died. Among the victims was the forty-four-year-old cipher clerk Mr Raaff from the headquarters of the Stoomvaartmaatschappij Nederland (Netherlands Steam Navigation Company) in Batavia. He and his wife were newly married and also returning home from a holiday in Bali. One of the unrecognisable bodies spotted by the harbour pilot was his; he was identified by his wedding ring. Mr Exley from Singapore, on the other hand, was identified by his teeth. He was a manager at the Ocean Steamship Company, which ran a shipping line between the United Kingdom and China. He had inspected one of their ships in Surabaya and was on his way back to Singapore. In a few months, he would have retired and returned to Europe. Another traveller, Dr Wisse from Mojokerto, survived the wreck but lost his wife and baby. Their funeral in Java was attended by 'many doctors, colonial officials, representatives of the sugar industry, Catholic clergymen, nurses and members of the Dutch East Indies Flying Club', to which Dr Wisse had belonged.[6]

But the luxury of a first-class cabin was not reserved exclusively for successful Westerners. Wealthy 'Indo-Europeans' could be found there too, such as Mr and Mrs Carli from Bandung, both in their early sixties. Ever since the days of the VOC, European men had had children with local women. Mixed marriages were very common until well into the twentieth century. Over the years, such children were referred to in countless ways: as mestizos, half-bloods, Indies Dutch, Indo-Europeans, Indos, Eurasians, Eurasiatics, biracials and so forth. Language seems to wear out fastest at the points of greatest friction. They formed a diverse group. During the Japanese occupation, the yardstick of how Asian you were was your great-grandparents; a Eurasian could be one-eighth European, for instance, or seven-eighths. If you looked back still further and distinguished other Asian backgrounds such as Chinese and Arab, the picture was even more complex. Although they were much greater in number than the 'European Dutch' in the colony (the figures in 1930 were 137,000 and 86,000), the Eurasians felt inferior to their lighter-skinned compatriots.[7] Novelist Marion Bloem, in her most recent book, wrote: 'My mother often said, "We're really just as good as the Dutch, even if we are Indos." '[8] That sums it up neatly. In the memorable words of Rob Nieuwenhuys, they were 'a fairly young group in historical terms, but with a long legacy of suffering'.[9] Although they were considered part of the European population, they always remained in a grey area between East and West, and between high and low, because 'class differences ran almost along racial lines'.[10] In short, they very often felt like the bottom layer of the upper crust.

And that spurred many of them to work their way up the social ladder. For some, travelling first class was a real statement. The Carlis had *earned* their fortune. Mr Carli had been an accountant at BPM, he taught bookkeeping at a secondary school, and he ran a well-known accountancy office in Bandung. A year earlier, they had lost their son, a physician in Buitenzorg. Mr Carli's outspoken belief in Western colonialist supremacy had led him to assume an active role in the Dutch Nazi party, the Nationaal-Socialistische Beweging (NSB), as a provincial inspector of finances. A quarter-century earlier, he had been involved in the Indische Partij (Indies Party), a progressive movement of Eurasians, but those days were long gone. In the 1930s, Nazi ideology was popular among Indos; it liberated them from humiliation from above and set them apart from the deck passengers below. After the couple died in the *Van der Wijck* disaster, the Bandung branch of the NSB flew the Dutch flag half-mast and organised a wake, which attracted plenty of visitors. 'Carli, a man you could depend on, a man with a heart of gold, an NSB man through and through, has left us!' Not long before his death he had asked, 'What would our lives be without the NSB?' The 'block leader' sounded the last call and the choir sang 'Ik had a wapenbroeder' (I had a brother-in-arms), a song 'to which all present listened in dead silence as they gave the fascist salute'.[11]

We will encounter these Eurasians many more times; they formed a diverse, complex group who could not be pigeonholed into one ideology or way of life. They had to redefine their position in Indonesia again and again – during the colonial era, the Japanese era and the Revolusi, and after the transfer of sovereignty – as they were sometimes deemed too Asiatic and sometimes too European. But they were in any event an essential, characteristic part of colonial society in the Dutch East Indies. I often refer to these part-Dutch Eurasians in the archipelago as 'Indos', a term which until recently was often considered offensive but is now being embraced in Dutch as a concise, attractive alternative to wordier terms.[12]

On to second class. Who were the passengers there? The victims included J. van Egmond, a shop assistant at Java Stores, where polo shirts and tweed jackets were sold. He was thirty-seven and unmarried. Then there was C. Brandes, a sixty-three-year-old lady who had worked at the Ondernemersbond (Business Owners' Association) for many years. She was travelling with her daughter. Both survived the wreck, but her daughter died of her injuries the next day. Other victims included J. A. D. Kesseler, a KPM second mate, and chief ship's engineer A. Kraanen, both travelling as passengers. The ship's only officer who died was the radio operator, twenty-eight-year-old M. J. Uytermark, who had stayed at his telegraph and worked until the end. His last message was 'S.O.S. listing severely'; he didn't have time to send the coordinates. We cannot know which of the Dutch victims were mixed-race and which were not; the family names tell us nothing. The proportion of Indos in second class was probably much greater than in first; 'the little Indo' was a well-known expression.[13] Though there was no strict colour bar, there was a continuum, sometimes referred to as a 'shade bar'; the darker your skin, the greater the invisible barriers and implicit restrictions.[14]

In second class we also find the Makatita family: a husband and wife, their two children and their nanny Saptenno. The Makatitas came from an elite Ambonese family, some members of which had been declared equal in status to Europeans in the late nineteenth century. This was very exceptional; in 1930, only 4,718 Ambonese, 2,051 Menadonese (inhabitants of Manado and the surrounding area) and 871 Javanese possessed this status, fewer than 8,000 people out of a population of 61 million.[15] Ambon and the Manado area of northern Sulawesi were the two parts of the archipelago with the most converts to Christianity; they served as soldiers in the army and officials in the civil service. The entire Makatita family drowned, and divers found the nanny in the wreck a month and a half later, caught in the ship's railing. She was identified by her gold earring.[16] Those same divers eventually discovered the cause of the accident: the ship's lowest portholes had been left open. During a long delay in the Surabaya harbour, the first mate had opened them to air out a shipment of fruit from Bali. It had been a stifling day, and the pineapples, mangos and mangosteens had started to stink as much as the durian, 'queen of fruits', which reeks like an open sewer. He had forgotten to shut the portholes when the heavily laden ship departed, listing slightly. During the trip, a little water had splashed inside now and then, bit by bit, until the ship had such a deep draught that the Java Sea came pouring in.[17]

We know very little about the 200 deck passengers and eighty native crew members. They included tally clerks and ship's store clerks with names like Latuperissa, Turang and Kaunang.[18] Fifteen crew members, nineteen deck passengers and three coolies were missing; none of their names are known to us.[19] Were the coolies Chinese or Javanese? Where were they going? In the newspapers, the deck passengers were always the last to be listed, a shadowy residual group without names or faces. When a few local fishermen out in their boats rescued some of the drowning people, Mr Schoevers the bank director, perhaps the wealthiest of the passengers, found himself lifted on board with paupers he would never have spoken to otherwise. He later told a journalist: 'There was also a terribly injured deck passenger in the prahu, with several wounds that were bleeding heavily and a missing finger. He had apparently become stuck somewhere.'[20] This is the only individual deck passenger I could find any information about, but the scene speaks volumes: hours after the disaster, passengers of all social ranks sat side by side in a rickety wooden boat with soaked garments, chattering teeth, wrinkled fingertips and fuel oil in their hair.[21]

The Act of 1925 regarding the colonial administration of the Dutch East Indies divided the population into three 'nationalities' (landaarden): Europeans, Foreign Orientals and natives.[22] This tripartite system was felt to be more satisfactory than the two-way distinction, dating from 1854, between Europeans and natives. Europeans included the European Dutch, the Eurasians and other Westerners, as well as the Japanese (recognised as 'European' from 1899 onwards) and the Turks (from 1926 onwards). Foreign Orientals (Vreemde Oosterlingen) were Asians who didn't come from the archipelago; most were Chinese, and others were Arabs and Indians. So while the Japanese were seen as Europeans, the Chinese were Foreign Orientals. Finally, the term 'native' (inlander) had long been used for the indigenous peoples of the islands; during the colonial period, it increasingly came to be seen as a term of abuse.

These ethnicities very roughly map onto the three groups on the steamship: there were many Europeans on Deck 1, many Foreign Orientals (such as Aboe Bakar in the Daum novel) on Deck 2 and many natives on Deck 3. The Indos complicate this picture. They could be found on both Deck 1 and Deck 2 (the 'big Indos' and the 'little Indos') but weren't allowed on Deck 3; as Europeans (of a kind), they could not be allowed to undermine the prestige of their race. In the economic crisis of the 1930s, unemployed Indos had to beg for permission to travel 'at the same rate as a native deck passenger'. KPM insisted that this would be wrong, 'especially in the case of European women'.[23] Tjalie Robinson, who wielded one of the sharpest pens in the Indo community, openly flouted this rule and sang the praises of his 'irregular, ever-changing, delightful voyages as a deck passenger on KPM ships'. When refused a ticket, he cried out, 'But I'm not a European!'[24]

The Chinese could be found on all three decks. A few of the colony's wealthiest inhabitants were Chinese. Take for instance Oei Tiong Ham, the greatest Chinese businessman of the colonial period; he began with an opium licence but invested in sugar, property, trade and moneylending. Tjong A Fie ran a commercial empire that stretched from Sumatra to Penang and Singapore; in Medan, he erected the city's most sumptuous residence. Kwee Zwan Liang came from a family of sugar producers, who in the 1920s were the only other owners of the make of luxury car driven by the emperor of Japan, the shah of Persia and US President Woodrow Wilson.[25] Elite Chinese families were wealthier than the Dutch and, of course, only travelled first class – if they didn't have their own shipping companies. But those were the exceptions. The Chinese passengers on Deck 2 typically ran small or medium-sized businesses: warehouses, restaurants, millinery workshops, match factories, rice mills or soft drink factories. Some had more financial roles, such as pawnbroker, moneylender or tax collector – work that could make them less than popular among the poor, who were often in their debt. The Chinese on Deck 3 were all paupers, coolies who travelled by ship only once in their lives, to the tobacco and rubber plantations on Deli, from which they never escaped. Arab and Indian merchants were much more of a rarity and usually travelled second class; only the wealthiest among them could afford first class.

And finally, the native population was not confined to Deck 3; a small fraction of them were permitted to travel second class. These were the members of the traditional ruling aristocracy, KNIL officers and the elites granted equal status with Europeans, such as the Makatita family. In each case, they came from groups that collaborated closely with the colonial administration.

In absolute terms, the groups were highly unequal. In 1930 the colony had only 240,000 European, 1.2 million Chinese and 60 million native inhabitants: 0.4 per cent, two per cent and 97.4 per cent of the total population, respectively. (The remaining 0.2 per cent were Arab, Indian and Malay.) More than 200,000 of the Europeans were Dutch, and only one-third of them had been born outside the colony. In other words, the vast archipelago with its thousands of islands was dominated by a group smaller than the 1950 population of Utrecht, Coventry, Perth or Oklahoma City.

The parallel between social and nautical classes was not mere coincidence. Among the colonial elite, there was a strong consensus that 'whether one travels on a vessel as a deck or cabin passenger is a reflection of one's social status in everyday life'.[26] 'Sophisticated people of a certain standing' simply could not be permitted to travel on an inferior deck; they were entitled to comforts 'commensurate with their class'.[27] The colonial administration also prohibited travel in a class 'higher than one's social position entails'.[28] And some Indo clerks complained when budget cuts forced them to travel on a deck to which 'their education and position did not suit them', namely 'alongside coolies and farm animals'.[29] In the 1930s, when class consciousness was at its height, there were lengthy debates about where different types of public employees should sit. Male civil servants with salaries of 250 guilders or more? First class. Women officials who earned less than 120 guilders a month? Second class. Non-commissioned officers in the army and navy? Also second class. Soldiers below the rank of sergeant? On the lowest deck. Even if they were Ambonese or Menadonese? Yes, but then they were entitled to European food. Great discernment was apparently required.[30]

This type of hair-splitting infuriated the famous essayist E. du Perron. When he returned to his place of birth, the Dutch East Indies, in 1936, on the run from European fascism, he couldn't believe his eyes. The KPM vessels struck him as 'pompous and expensive', and he described first class as 'a sun-drenched prison'; the conversations with other passengers were 'an ordeal': 'Seldom have I had such a strong impression of sharing cramped quarters with talking pigs.' But what disturbed him most was the racial divide. Du Perron was travelling with his wife, his young son and the boy's minder, a young Javanese man they had met in The Hague. On the voyage from Europe to Singapore, the young man had been given 'a decent cabin and the same food as everyone else', but as soon as they boarded the KPM vessel, they saw 'the dark side of the lavish first-class meals'; their minder was demoted to Deck 3 and prohibited ' "by regulations" from having tea or coffee – nothing but water, rice and a bit of fish'. Du Perron wrote: 'Since it's just for two days, he doesn't mind (besides, we bring him some fruit from the dining room), but [. . .] I am livid about the way of thinking here on board.'[31]

The racial divide was not merely a matter of some minor nautical arrangements; it was enshrined in law and influenced every aspect of society. According to the Act of 1925 on colonial administration, the Dutch elite (including the Indos, who were classified as Europeans) had the legal status of 'Dutch citizen'; all other inhabitants of the colony were merely 'Dutch subjects' without citizenship. One implication was that they fell under a separate court system. In civil cases, Europeans were tried according to Dutch law and the native population according to local customary law (which varied greatly from place to place), while Chinese merchants were included in the scope of European commercial law. In short, the administration of justice was to a large extent organised by race. 'Natives and Foreign Orientals could be held in preventive custody without any form of trial; Europeans and those of equal status could not.'[32]

Discrimination by law also affected many other domains. How much you earned, for instance, depended partly on your ethnicity. There was a well-known saying: 'The more pigment, the less payment.'[33] A European was paid more than a native for the same work, by both the colonial administration and private companies.[34] Not that many Indonesians received the kinds of jobs available to Europeans; a whopping ninety-two per cent of the top civil service jobs went to Europeans and a meagre 6.4 per cent to Indonesians. Native workers ended up as petty officials or in technical positions, where they made up ninety-nine per cent of the workforce.[35] This was all an obvious manifestation of structural inequality. In the late 1920s, an Indonesian's average annual income was sixty guilders, a Chinese worker's was 330 guilders, and a European's was 2,700 guilders. In other words, the average European earned as much in one day as a Chinese worker earned in eight days or an Indonesian in forty-five.[36] In 1939, the native population supplied more than ninety-seven per cent of the workforce but earned only sixty-nine per cent of the income, while Europeans contributed less than one-half per cent of the working population but took home thirteen per cent of the income. The Chinese, as usual, were in the middle: 2.4 per cent of the population and ten per cent of the income.[37] Tax revenue from this period shows the same pattern: the 240,000 Europeans paid more than 350 million guilders in taxes, while the great mass of

Indonesians, sixty million, paid only 446 million.[38] If you don't earn much, you can't pay much.

Your deck was your life. The person you married, the food you ate, the clothes you wore, the place you lived – all these depended in large part on your race and class. Occupation? Bankers, leading industrialists, planters, senior officials and officers on Deck 1, merchants, manufacturers and clerks on Deck 2, farmers, workers, soldiers and the unemployed on Deck 3. Religion? Protestants and Catholics on Deck 1, Taoists and Confucians on Deck 2, Muslims on Deck 3. Language? Dutch and English on Deck 1, Chinese, Javanese and Malay on Deck 2, all native languages on Deck 3. That's why it was so unusual to hear the Arab Aboe Bakar speak fluent Dutch on Deck 2. The figures reinforce this point: by the end of the colonial era, only 860,000 Indonesians used Dutch as their primary language, barely 1.2 per cent of the native population. The vast majority spoke one of the many regional languages. How could they speak Dutch, when they'd never learned it? They were too busy making ends meet. Twelve million people worked in traditional agriculture, a full seventy per cent of the native workforce.[39] Two million Indonesians worked in industry, one and a half million in plantation agriculture and one million in trade.[40] Their lives were very different from those of Dutch speakers. They wore simple loincloths, or sarongs, in contrast to the elaborate white tropical outfits and helmets on Deck 1. They ate bowls of plain rice with vegetables and sometimes a small piece of chicken or fish, or an egg, rather than the copious *rijsttafel* consumed on Deck 1, a gargantuan buffet of all the good things that Indonesian cuisine had to offer, twenty meals in one.

The Dutch East Indies was a fundamentally segmented society, and in the 1930s it even became a segregated society.[41] G. W. Overdijk-ink, a top official in Batavia and a canny observer, remarked just after World War II: 'A commercial orientation and a reserved attitude came to characterise the Dutch in Indonesia. [. . .] The result was indifference – yes, that's the word, an indifference to everything that concerned the other ethnic groups. What did the average Dutch colonial know about what was on the minds of the Indonesians or the Chinese? What did he know of native political movements, of their customs or moral codes? [. . .] The Dutch clustered together in exclusive residential districts, focusing on their business affairs or, if they were officials, on their salary scales, their new cars and the cottages up in the mountains where they spent the "weekend". They were completely out of touch with the Indonesian, the Chinese and even the Eurasian ethnic groups.[42]

The strict hierarchy of the colonial steamship was not entirely static. It permitted a small degree of social mobility: a certain number of people could change decks in the course of their lives. Downward movement was easiest. If you fell behind in social and economic terms, you had to descend to a more humble level. In his short story collection *Schuim en asch* (Froth and Ash), the Dutch ship's doctor and author J. Slauerhoff has a desperate European character say, 'Then I'll give up and become what I've never been in my life, a passenger, a deck passenger, what else can I do?' That wasn't a free choice: 'It smells terrible there, the food is disgusting, the crew look at me with contempt.[43] Very few of the people who descended to the level of the masses did so as deliberately and blithely as Tjalie Robinson, who shrugged off 'the cold stares of the class-conscious' and enjoyed the adventure.[44] After a long stay in the Netherlands, the poet Noto Soeroto had to raise money for his return trip, but the donations 'did not come in very swiftly', and he had no choice but to make the long voyage in fourth class.[45] Yet for others, travelling fourth class was a matter of principle, a moral decision, even a stubborn kind of freedom. The readers of the *Soerabaiasch Handelsblad*, an extremely right-wing Dutch-language commercial newspaper published in eastern Java, nearly choked on their coffee one morning in 1929 when they read that a native man in India had refused a free first- or second-class ticket for the long sea voyage from Rangoon to Calcutta. Who would do such a thing? 'But Ghandi [*sic*] will travel as a deck passenger and pay for his own ticket. He wants no favours from foreign capitalists and desires no luxury for himself.[46]

Rising in rank took a good deal more effort. The easiest method, if you were Indonesian, was to be a woman and at least somewhat attractive. Then you had a chance, however slight, of marrying a

Dutchman and automatically gaining the status of European. But this route was open to very few. A man could try to work his way up as a business proprietor or in the military, but the number of native officers was extremely small, and the middle class was largely Chinese, Arab and Indian. For most, the only way to a higher deck was a long and winding path through the educational system.

Since the turn of the century, the Netherlands had encouraged the people of the colony to earn a higher social status through schooling. In 1901, Queen Wilhelmina had said in her annual Speech from the Throne that the Netherlands, 'as a Christian Power', had a 'moral calling'.[47] She meant that colonialism should be more than the Western pursuit of profit; it should also benefit the local population. That was the start of the period of the 'Ethical Policy', twenty years in which the development of the colony and its people received greater attention. This policy called for more educational and economic opportunities, improved health care, more intensive missionary work and better infrastructure. Although the period from 1900 to 1920 was the most progressive in the colony's history, it was not free of internal contradictions. The Ethical Policy demanded a stronger emphasis on native culture but also made Westernisation a priority; it strove towards greater freedom from Western domination, but only under Dutch supervision; and it encouraged the struggle for autonomy, but not for independence. It gave to the natives with one hand and kept them in place with the other. But it did transform the educational system.

In the year 1900, fewer than 3,000 non-Europeans attended a Dutch-language primary school: 2,400 Indonesians and 400 Foreign Orientals. Education had been a very low priority, but the administration was determined to change that. From 1907 onwards, Deck 3 passengers had the option of attending the *sekolah desa*, or village school. This type of school offered a simple three-year programme of education for the rural population, provided in local languages by native teachers. In 1930, more than a million children benefited; in 1940, the number increased to 2.2 million.[48]

In the forests of western Sulawesi, I sat with bated breath as I listened to Hamad Puag Abi's stories. His wooden house was elevated on poles, and his memory was nothing short of phenomenal. He had outlived his four brothers and could put his own life in perspective. 'If I were a goat,' he said with a sigh, 'no one would buy me. All I'm good for is curry.' In his far-off childhood, he'd attended the sekolah desa. 'Next to the small bridge was the school, a wooden building that's not there any more,' his tale began. 'I used to walk there through the forest. Back then there was no road. The little school was just for boys; there were three classes. The headmaster's name was Ma'da, and my teachers were Sauda, Mahmud and Hadija.' Formal education, even of such a basic kind, was a break with tradition, reflected even in the clothes the pupils wore. 'My father was a farmer and grew coconuts. He was always bare-chested and never wore shoes. But I went to school in shorts and a shirt.' Village education was a revolution not only in apparel. Hamad was introduced to something his parents had never learned. 'My teachers taught me the Latin alphabet and Lontara, our own alphabet. In the first and second year we wrote on slates, in the third with pencil and paper.'[49]

But the large majority of children outside the cities remained uneducated, partly because of rapid population growth. In 1930, only ten per cent of men and 2.2 per cent of women could read and write.[50] Most Indonesian children had little or no contact with the colonisers. I discussed this with a few elders on Morotai, the northernmost of the Moluccan Islands. 'Dutch people? I never saw any. There were no Dutch people here,' Naji Baronga told me. He was born in the interior in 1932 and still lives there. 'All I did was climb high in the coconut trees and help my father with coconuts and cassava.' In Daruba, a larger village by the sea, I sat under a wooden lean-to, chatting with the sisters Yaya and Yomi Rauf. Our conversation attracted a growing audience, which eventually numbered in the dozens. 'We lived in the Dutch era,' the elder sister told me, 'but I never went to school. I did see Chinese people; they sold things.' The spectators listened, amused. 'We only saw the Dutch one time,' the younger sister added, 'when the whole family went to the doctor for *imunisasi*!' She pronounced the word very crisply, and then she and her sister began pulling at their clothing. To the hearty laughter of the crowd, they exposed their shoulders, revealing the characteristic scar of a smallpox vaccination, a souvenir of their one brief encounter with a Dutch person more than eighty years ago. The colony had literally got under their skin.

Not going to school did not necessarily mean remaining ignorant. I was impressed by the testimony of Timang, an elderly woman in a fishing village on poles on the Togian Islands, who was chopping wood for the fire at nightfall. As a traditional midwife, she had delivered more than a hundred children over a wide area. 'I speak eight languages,' she told me as darkness gathered over the sea. 'Indonesian, Buginese, Bajau, Bobongko, Saluan, Kaili, Togian and Baras.' Her dark blue silhouette calmly went on splitting wood for kindling. 'But not Dutch.'

Children on Deck 2 were given two options: the Hollandsch-Inlandsche School (Dutch-Indies School; HIS) and the Hollandsch-Chineesche School (Dutch-Chinese School; HCS), each of which offered seven years of primary education on the Western model, with a strong focus on the group's own culture. The curriculum was regarded as excellent but was not for everyone; in 1930, there were only 60,000 registrations for the HIS and 20,000 for the HCS. These low numbers were just as planned. The HIS was intended exclusively for pupils 'whose parents are at the forefront of native society owing to their occupation, origin, affluence or education'.[51] During my fieldwork in Java, I managed to track down a few alumni. Their fathers had been postal workers, stationmasters or teachers, loyal servants of the colonial state who looked up to the Netherlands. 'If I didn't speak Dutch at home, I didn't get my pocket money. Two and a half cents!' Chisma Widjajasoekma still laughed at the recollection – but her Dutch was flawless.[52] 'Our teachers were Indonesian, but they taught in Dutch,' Sri Lestari told me in the centre of Yogyakarta. She can still sing old Dutch children's songs in a high, clear voice, as well as an unforgettable version of the old southern German folk song 'Die Wacht am Rhein'. Her father was an architect in the sultan's palace, but she learned about a different dynasty: 'We sat at desks and learned the names of the Dutch kings,' she said.[53] For some, the love of the House of Orange would never fade: 'I still read books about the Dutch royals,' ninety-two-year-old Soeparti

Soetedjo ('call me Grandma Ted') told me in a Jakarta retirement home. 'I'm so fond of Juliana.'[54] But looking up to those they saw as 'above' them sometimes made them ashamed of being 'lower'. Social climbers often have strained relations with their communities of origin. Sukotjo Tjokroatmodjo's father had just been appointed as a stationmaster; he was issued a red kepi, and his family was allowed to live in a brick house belonging to the Staatsspoorwegen, the railway company owned by the colonial administration. But at school, his son made a social blunder: 'We were learning Dutch prepositions. "I wash my hands *before* or *after* a meal?" *After*, I said. I was the only one with that answer. At home, we were used to eating with our fingers. The others ate with a knife and fork. I was the laughing-stock of the whole class.'[55]

In homes for the elderly in Jakarta, I also spoke to a few Chinese Indonesians who had attended the HCS. 'We were taught in Dutch in the morning and Chinese in the afternoon. Our teachers were Catholic nuns from Holland and Chinese people from China. With my parents I only spoke Chinese.' Dorothea Tatiwibowo came from one of the many Chinese families that had taken on a local family name. Her father had been born in the southern Chinese province of Canton (Guangdong), but she grew up in Pontianak in Kalimantan. 'Indonesian is difficult for me,' she said. 'I never studied it. I just learned it by ear.' She spoke Chinese and Dutch.

Benny Bastian, an older man with a traditional Chinese goatee, told me his parents had spoken Dutch well. They had a hat factory where they made pith helmets. On the subject of the HCS, he told me: 'I learned to write Chinese at school. My teacher was a Chinese man from Indonesia.'[56] The HCS offered new educational opportunities. Dorothea even became a pharmacist's assistant. Nonetheless, she had something to get off her chest about the whole colonial system of 'emancipation': 'The Dutch didn't want to give us freedom at all. They never let people become truly independent. In fact, they wanted to keep everyone under their thumb. They didn't prepare us to stand on our own two feet. They left us in a state of confusion.'[57]

The Deck 1 passengers could send their children to the highest level of primary education: the Europeesche Lagere School (European

Primary School; ELS). This seven-year programme was entirely
based on Western models. The teachers were Dutch. In 1930, only
44,000 pupils received this type of education; most were European or
Eurasian (38,000), while only a few were natives (4,000) or Foreign
Orientals (2,000).[58] A few former pupils told me about their family
backgrounds. 'My father was a Dutchman and the captain of a KPM
vessel; my mother was Sundanese-Chinese,' said Anna Christina
Gunawan Bosschieter.[59] 'My father was a Swiss Catholic missionary,
my mother an Ambonese woman,' said Constance Amy Pattiradjawane.[60] 'My father was of Prussian descent and worked for the
Staatsspoorwegen, my mother was a *nyai*,' said Hans Dornseiffer. A
nyai was the Indonesian concubine of a European man.[61] 'My father
was an Indo and I'm complete chop suey,' said Nanny Kooymans with
a smile. 'He worked at the Department of Finance.'[62] 'My father was a
Chinese man granted equal status to Europeans. He exported pedicabs
to Kalimantan and was given a Dutch first name: Jan Max Ong,' said
Nora van Dorp, also known as Noortje. 'Shall I sing the Wilhelmus
[the Dutch national anthem]?'[63]

But the story of Joty ter Kulve illustrates how fluid some catego-
ries were. Who was really Dutch was never entirely set in stone. I
spoke to her in a service flat in Wassenaar. 'My first school had one
teacher, two classrooms and about twenty Dutch children of tobacco
planters and others in Cirebon. It was in Linggajati.' In that village
in the mountains, her father had designed a beautiful villa with
extensive gardens on the slopes of the Ciremai volcano. She had a
wonderful childhood there, surrounded by lush natural beauty. Her
father had been trained as an engineering officer in Breda, and in the
Indies he became a versatile businessman who laid water pipes, sewers and telephone cables. He married a beautiful Indo named Lizzy,
who had Javanese, Chinese, Portuguese and Flemish ancestry. 'When
I was born, the second of three girls, my father laughed and said,
"Now we have a blond child!" ' But he died in 1934, when she was
just six years old. 'He was only thirty-nine. Penicillin hadn't been
invented yet. That was when I learned what it's like to be discrimi-
nated against. At school, all of a sudden I was no longer Dutch but
an Indo. I didn't get a present for St Nicholas' Day any more, and my

sister was no longer invited to parties. Suddenly we were the children of an Indo mother.'[64]

Education for every deck; that was the idea behind the Ethical Policy. In a very limited number of cases, children could climb the social ladder, rising above not only their parents but also the people they'd grown up with. But only the most talented individuals, the fastest bloomers, could literally earn a place on a higher deck.

To go from Deck 3 to Deck 2, they had to complete what was called the Schakelschool (Linking School), a five-year curriculum taught in Dutch and introduced in 1919. This was a prerequisite for entering the European-style secondary schools known by acronyms such as MULO and HBS, and maybe, just maybe, going on from there to higher studies. The Schakelschool was the metal ladder between the lowest and middle decks, between the open air and the cabins, between native and European education. Children of parents with low-level bureaucratic jobs qualified for it, but not many were registered: fewer than 5,000 in 1930. This was because the Schakelschool charged for tuition. It was almost as if the colonial regime didn't really *want* progress.

In the city of Pare in eastern Java, nestled among volcanoes, I spoke to one of the last alumni of the system, Johannes Soewondo. 'The Schakelschool was a separate school for us. Dutch was spoken, but the teachers and the director were Javanese. I never saw a Dutch person at the school. They were in the sugar factories, and I never went there. We all came from the countryside near Klaten. My father was the village secretary. But the Schakelschool was very expensive and we had to pay for it all ourselves.' What was supposed to be a first step towards a Western education was, in practice, often an oppressive experience. The trouble began far outside the school gates. 'The walk to school was five kilometres. My father didn't have a car or a bicycle. I really wanted a bike, but only three people in our village had one, and they were all Javanese employees of the sugarcane plantations. Dutch and Indo children were brought to school on a factory lorry. We saw them drive past. That type of lorry was normally used for transporting sugar, but chicken wire and a zinc roof had been added for the schoolchildren. When we passed them on our way to school, we would shout, "Chicken coop! Chicken coop! Your lorry is a chicken coop!" If the lorry stopped, we scattered. Yes, I experienced colonialism in the streets. And when we wanted to play with Dutch children, their parents chased us away. They were very protective. But my parents didn't mind us playing with them.' He still felt some lingering animosity. 'Everyone, even my parents, hated the Dutch back then. For the simple reason that they snatched everything for themselves.'[65] Only after independence would Johannes Soewondo own his first bicycle.

Soewondo was not alone in his frustration. The very select group of Indonesian children who climbed from Deck 2 to Deck 1 also ran into all sorts of barriers. In 1930, at most 4,000 Indonesian pupils attended the ELS – a negligible fraction of the archipelago's twenty million children – but when I spoke to a few of them, I heard more resentment than pride.[66] 'You have no idea how hard it was to make progress!' Purbo S. Suwondo sat in a wheelchair in his well-appointed living room in Jakarta, and his voice was as clear as a bell. 'All the children at that primary school were Dutch or Indo or descended from the most aristocratic families, while I came from an ordinary native family in eastern Java. But my father had gone to the Hollandsch-Indische Kweekschool [a teacher training school for natives] and become a gym teacher at a teachers' college. They both spoke excellent Dutch and wanted me to have a European education. On my sixth birthday, I had to take an entrance exam. The head teacher wanted to know what language I spoke at home and especially what I spoke with my mother. I was accepted, and a totok, a "full-blooded" Dutch person, took charge of me. Seven years later, at the end of the ELS, twenty pupils took the entrance examination for the HBS [Hogere Burgerschool: a high-level secondary school in the European system, offering a grounding in science and technology]. Only four passed; I was one of them. The headmaster, Mr Spruyt, came to our house to congratulate my father on my results.' He shifted in his wheelchair to reach for a few photographs. 'At the HBS I studied with the sons of European officers, senior officials and owners of rubber plantations and sugar factories. My skin colour wasn't a problem, no, I had shown that I could earn better marks than the others. But however hard I tried, I never really belonged.'[67]

His experiences matched those of Cisca Pattipilohy, one of the very few girls to climb to Deck 1 of the educational system. In her apartment in Amsterdam-West she explained: 'My grandpa came from Ambon and was Christian. He was a KNIL clerk, and although he barely spoke Dutch, his only son, my father, went to the ELS. That was because our family was part of the feudal elite.' After secondary school, he studied architecture and became an architect. 'He designed a bank that was built in Makassar and houses in Borneo – the tigers still roamed all the way to the coast in those days! My father became terribly wealthy. He drove around in a dark red Buick, one of the most expensive cars on the market at the time. We spoke Dutch at home and even had a library.' When she took the HBS entrance exam, she was one of the few who passed. 'I had the highest mark for Dutch. There were only two Chinese and two Javanese people in my class. Everyone else was Indo or Dutch. The school fee was very steep: twenty-six guilders! I was by far the darkest-skinned girl in the class, but the dominance of the white race was unbelievable. Furthermore, the further you went in school, the fewer girls there were. The few who were left drew a lot of attention, of course, but not me, because I was so dark. I was small and skinny, but I was good at the long jump!' A lifetime later, she realised that her education had been a kind of 'long jump' up the social ladder. 'Yes, I was given many opportunities by the educational system, but millions of others were not. And for that, I feel the Dutch are very much to blame.'[68]

Ah, yes, those millions of others. What was their perspective? In the early days of independence, Indonesian poet J. E. Tatengkeng wrote a piece of satirical doggerel that opens with these lines:

> Until the age of thirty
> I was never more than a deck passenger
> Thanks to the struggle waged by my friends
> and the transfer of power
> I now travel first class.[69]

That was one way of looking at it. The rest of the poem ridicules the social climbers in the new government bureaucracy, but that's not relevant here. The point, once again, is that hierarchy was the engine of history. The Netherlands had organised colonial society on the model of a steamship, with hardly any opportunity to climb to a higher level, but that did not mean that everyone simply accepted the situation. From the very start, the whole system was challenged. What was striking was that the criticism began not among the impoverished masses on Deck 3, but at the top. There was certainly disaffection in the vast underclass, but it was not yet being channelled for political ends. It was on the upper decks that a few pointed questions were being asked, chiefly by the social climbers. That was no different in other colonial contexts; Gandhi didn't start out as an ascetic in a loincloth travelling in as little luxury as possible, but as a dandy in a three-piece suit who moved to London and played violin. The young Patrice Lumumba strove to appear as European as possible in language, culture, clothing and coiffure, until he was officially granted equal status to Europeans as a fully assimilated *évolué*. Decolonisation acquired a voice thanks to the frustration of a new domestic elite.

The traditional elite, in contrast, was often on quite friendly terms with the colonial regime. In the Dutch East Indies, the marriage of convenience with the European administration had been a profitable one for the governing native nobility. Over the preceding two centuries, the aristocrats had discovered not only new forms of prosperity but also a new culture, a new universe and even a new freedom. In the early nineteenth century, an Indonesian nobleman such as Raden Saleh could travel to Europe to become one of the great oil painters of his era. His romantic scenes are still greatly admired. A critic of colonialism he was not; he hobnobbed with the European jet set and regarded the Dutch kings William I, II and III as his benefactors; the third even made him court painter.[70] Raden Ajeng Kartini ('Raden Ajeng' is the aristocratic title for a girl or young unmarried woman) was also well disposed towards the colonisers. She believed it was the duty of the West to help emancipate the East. In her rhetorically charged letters, this accomplished daughter of a Javanese regent expressed her profound longing for freedom and educational opportunities for native girls. She devoured the writings of Tolstoy, Tennyson, Kipling and Maeterlinck and was more critical of Java than of Europe. 'It is so often said that we are more European than Javanese in our hearts. Sad thought! We know that we are impregnated with European ideas and feelings – but the blood, the Javanese blood that flows live and warm through our veins, can be denied but never destroyed.'[71] Kartini died at the age of twenty-five, too early to see her dream of a modernised Java become a reality. The poet Raden Mas Noto Soeroto, who was influenced by the Dutch poets known as the Tachtigers, made an explicit case in 1911 for the 'blessings Dutch rule has brought us: the railways, the waterworks, the postal and telegraphic systems, the legal order, public safety – in short, the introduction of material civilisation, the fruits of which we are now enjoying'.[72] No, the aristocratic elite couldn't be relied on to spark revolution. Not yet.

The atmosphere in Pratomo's room was stifling; he must have had the thermostat on a tropical setting. After telling me about his strict grandfather who was a regent, he abruptly changed the subject to his father, who had the opportunity for an adventure without precedent in his family: higher education.[73] 'My father became a doctor,' he said. 'He was one of the first to graduate from STOVIA.' Even privileged natives did not have a lot of educational options at the start of the twentieth century, and at the highest level there was really only one possibility: medicine. The colony had an acute shortage of medical professionals, as the cholera epidemics had made abundantly clear, and after successful experiments with natives administering vaccines, a true medical school was opened in Batavia in 1899. Its charming acronym was STOVIA (School tot Opleiding van Inlandsche Artsen; 'School for Education of Native Physicians').[74] There was a preparatory programme lasting three years, followed by a six-year curriculum. The students all boarded at the school, and all classes were taught in Dutch. Thanks to the heroic efforts of the first director, Dr H. F. Roll, the education rivalled that at Europe's finest medical schools. One of the earliest teachers, Dr Christiaan Eijkman, did groundbreaking research into the dreaded disease known as beriberi, laying the foundation for the theory of vitamins and receiving the Nobel Prize in 1929 for his insights. The few STOVIA students who earned a degree – only 551 by 1935 – were known as 'the flower and pride of the Indonesian people'.[75]

As a newly qualified physician, Pratomo's father worked in the Weltevreden military hospital in Batavia, for a gold mining corporation and for a rubber company, in that order. The Ethical Policy required private companies to provide medical care, of a minimal variety, to their workers. In the family archives, I found some noteworthy comments he had made: 'The company owner regarded the hospital, doctor etc. as a necessary evil, so to put it bluntly, it was not a pleasant place to work. And in the military hospital, which *was* a pleasant working environment, many of the patients were not ill but malingering.'[76] Finding a rewarding job was apparently not easy for a young native physician. But in 1911, Dr Pratomo saw an advertisement for a position as a medical doctor in Bagansiapiapi on the east coast of Sumatra. That was a town of around 9,000, where a large community of Chinese fishermen had formed. 'That's where I was born,' Pratomo told me. 'We lived near the coast, across the water from the Malay Peninsula, which is now Malaysia.' Bagansiapiapi expanded into a major centre of the fishing industry, supplying all of Singapore with the salted fish and shrimp pastes used in many recipes.[77] His father built a hospital near the Chinese school and learned to speak fluent Chinese. 'But I only ever spoke Dutch with him. I used Javanese with my mother, since she didn't know any other languages. We didn't have any religion. We were officially Muslims, but my father wanted nothing to do with all that, and I never set foot in a mosque. I did get to go with him on his rounds to see patients in nearby villages. Along the way, he taught me to hunt. We shot at crocodiles.'[78]

It was a new world, one in which stethoscopes were more important than the five daily prayers, Dutch felt more modern than Javanese and crocodiles had new enemies to watch out for. Only young natives of the highest social class could hope to earn a medical degree. They were among the most Westernised people in the entire Dutch colony. Over their traditional Javanese sarongs, they wore jackets with pocket watches and white-collared shirts.

At STOVIA, something like a national consciousness had its first stirrings. The students had seen the map of the Dutch East Indies on display in the classrooms of their secondary schools. Didactic prints for schools were a new phenomenon. They were the first to see how their own islands or regions of birth fitted into a larger whole. The colonial jigsaw became natural to them: this is who we are, this is our country. The map of which the Dutch were so proud made other people proud too. In history lessons, which dealt exclusively with the European past, they learned how the Batavians had fought back against the Romans and how the Netherlands had liberated itself from its Spanish overlords. It had all happened long ago and far away, but even so, it gave them food for thought, that dauntless struggle against foreign occupation.[79]

Young native men of high status from far-flung areas of the archipelago came together for the first time at STOVIA. Regional differences became secondary. In anatomy lessons, they stood around the operating table together in magnificent sarongs, with macassar oil in their dark hair. Their delicate aristocratic hands dissected human bodies, seeking out diseased tissue, fractures, bleeding and incurable conditions. They cut, watched and acquired keen powers of observation. Medical science at this level stimulated critical thinking and intellectual confidence.

And on 20 May 1908, they established Budi Utomo (Noble Endeavour), an association that was very sympathetic to the Ethical Policy. The founders included Soetomo and Tjipto Mangoenkoesoemo, two of the first Indonesian physicians. The association advocated Western education, trade, technology and industry, as well as the revival of ancient Javanese culture 'to ensure life with dignity for the masses'.[80] This was the earliest sign of political organisation among the colony's native people. Even now, 20 May is celebrated as National Awakening Day. That this political consciousness emerged at STOVIA is really no surprise. When a young doctor, after years of study, is forced to travel in third-class carriages while the lowliest Dutch functionary rides first class; when that doctor, who has memorised all the Latin names of muscles, tendons, membranes, bones and nerves, and learned to think critically, is expected to sit on the ground at a party where even the crudest European buffoon is offered a chair; when he has to endure humiliations like these day in and day out and is never treated with complete respect; then of course he is more apt to resent the colonial system than is a poor farmer working his meagre rice field just as all his poor forefathers worked theirs.[81]

Some STOVIA alumni believed that calls for a 'noble endeavour' and 'life with dignity for the masses' didn't go far enough. They wanted to bring injustice into the light of day. Tirto Adhisoerjo, a medical student who became engaged in journalism before the end of his studies, concluded that the outcries of the European minority 'receive more attention than those of a subjugated people' and longed for 'an organisation that will stand up for our interests as poor children of the Indies'.[82] Two other STOVIA students, Soewardi Soerjaningrat and Tjipto Mangoenkoesoemo, became acquainted with Ernest Douwes Dekker, an Indo and a distant cousin of Multatuli. The three of them, feeling Budi Utomo was too strait-laced and elitist, launched the colony's first political party, the Indische Partij (Indies Party), which promoted the interests of both natives and Indos. Strikingly, the party openly advocated independence from its year of foundation, 1912. That was a full thirty-three years before Sukarno's Proklamasi and more than forty years before similar positions were taken in Africa.

On the hundredth anniversary of the Kingdom of the Netherlands, in 1913, the Dutch authorities were counting on the financial support of all their people for the centenary celebration. That included the people of the colonies. Soewardi took up his pen and wrote a Dutch-language essay of mordant sarcasm: 'If I were Dutch'. It was published in Ernest Douwes Dekker's newspaper, *De Expres*. Soewardi asked what on earth the Dutch were thinking. 'We are about to celebrate the fact that one hundred years ago we were delivered from foreign dominion, and the whole event will take place before the eyes of the people who are still under our dominion. Wouldn't you think those poor oppressed people might likewise be yearning for the moment when they can celebrate such an event as we do now?' But wait, that wasn't all Soewardi had to say. 'Yet what truly offends me and my compatriots most is the fact that, once again, the natives must bear some of the costs of something that does not serve their interests in the least. What good will that celebration, which we are helping to bring about, do us? None at all, except perhaps to remind us that we are not a free people.'

Soewardi wrote of 'a sluggish period of awakening', a vivid description of those first years when the colonial steamship began to be called into question. Yes, the colonial jigsaw had been completed, the Pax Neerlandica had taken hold and the Ethical Policy prescribed a more humane brand of colonialism, but that did not mean everyone was happy with the deck assignments, or with a society that had such decks. Soewardi knew that this unrest would not remain confined to the elite; sooner or later Deck 3 would wake up. 'It is certainly a possibility worth considering that this nation, now still downtrodden, will one day outgrow its master. What then, when forty million fully awakened people come to demand an accounting from that gang of one hundred who form the Lower House of Parliament and are said to be the people's representatives? Would we rather surrender at the last minute, when the crisis has come to a head?'[83]

These words were prophetic, but the colonial administration was far from pleased. Soewardi and his comrades Tjipto and Douwes Dekker were banished without any form of trial, even though Tjipto had been knighted just a year earlier for his courageous work with bubonic plague sufferers as a young doctor. They had a choice: internment or 'externment', exile to some distant region of the archipelago or to the faraway Netherlands. All three chose the latter. The Indische Partij ceased to exist. In 1914, severe restrictions were imposed on freedom of expression; from then on, 'hatemongering articles' were prohibited. It didn't seem to occur to anyone in the administration that this crackdown might sow more hatred than any essay. They must have believed the colonial steamship offered plenty of scope for personal advancement.

Chapter 4

'Flies Spoiling the Chemist's Ointment'
Anti-colonial movements, 1914–1933

Search for this address in Google Maps: Surabaya, Jalan Peneleh, Gang VII, no. 29–31. Now take a close look at the satellite photo. You will see nothing – or at any rate, nothing that makes the traditional house with the tiled roof stand out in the endless sea of roofs in different shades of red, interrupted only by narrow alleyways and the sluggish meanders of the Kali Mas, the grey river along which Indonesia's second-largest city lies. Yet this is where it all started. This was the home of Raden Mas Haji Oemar Said Tjokroaminoto and his wife. Tjokroaminoto, Tjokro or Tjok for short, came from the traditional elite (hence his title, Raden Mas) and had done the pilgrimage to Mecca (hence the Haji). He was trained as a colonial official (hence the refined moustache in the earliest photographs) but ended up in the sugar industry, the trade union movement and journalism. In 1914, he became the president of Sarekat Islam (Islamic Union; SI), an organisation founded in Surakarta two years earlier. Under his leadership, SI grew into what Budi Utomo and the Indische Partij had never become: a mass movement. It advocated the general emancipation of the native population, and the roomy house in Surabaya and its courtyard was the place to find anyone who had anything to do with that cause.

At that same address, Tjokro's wife ran a boarding house for schoolchildren. For eleven guilders a month, about ten boys received food and lodging. She made sure that everyone rose at four, went to school, came home in time for dinner and went to bed at ten. Her boarders included Semaun, Alimin and Muso – teenagers whose names were then unknown, but who several years later would found the Partai Komunis Indonesia (PKI). This would become the third-largest communist party in the world, trailing only Russia's and China's. Kartosuwirjo, another nobody destined for greatness, was also a frequent guest there. Drawn to the religious component of Sarekat Islam, he became a journalist, as well as Tjokro's foster son and private secretary. A deeply religious Muslim, he felt a growing commitment to an Islamic state in Indonesia, a goal never shared by Tjokro, and in 1948 he became the leader of an army of fanatical rebels who fought the Republic of Indonesia for years. To this day, his legacy inspires Indonesia's radical Muslims.

And in 1916, a bashful fifteen-year-old boy arrived at the boarding house and was assigned a tiny room without a window or a mattress. He remained there for five years, sleeping on a mat of braided grass. He was the son of a Balinese mother and a Javanese teacher from the lesser nobility and had received a European primary education at the ELS. In Surabaya, where he was enrolled in the HBS, the most prestigious type of secondary school, he was terribly homesick at first, but fascinated by what he saw and heard at the boarding house. He looked up to Tjokroaminoto and, in his candle-lit room after dinner, would try to imitate his host's way of speaking. The unknown boy's name was Sukarno. Like many Indonesians, he had no first name – only the highest-ranking aristocrats wore strings of names. No one could have imagined that this shy, doe-eyed adolescent would lead the country to independence and even inspire the world with his struggle for freedom. Yet Tjokro's boarding house was the place where his story began. 'I loved mealtimes,' he said. 'Food was served family style so I could out-eat everyone and at the same time soak up the political conversation. [. . .] A person with creativity and high ideals, a fighter who loved his country, Tjok was my idol, I was his student. Consciously and unconsciously he moulded me.'[1]

Tjokroaminoto became so fond of Sukarno that he even asked the boy to marry his daughter – and Sukarno obliged him. Although the union did not last long, Sukarno went on regarding Tjokro as a father figure long after that. The boarding house was a place where politics, religion and society were debated openheartedly over plates of steaming fried rice and fragrant *gado-gado*, and a place where the great divides in Indonesian society first came to light.

In the colonial period, there were three great attempts to challenge colonialism: political Islam in the 1910s, communism in the 1920s and nationalism in the 1930s. None of these attempts succeeded. Political Islam fell prey to infighting and the other two to violent suppression by the colonial regime. Even so, their historical importance can hardly be overstated. The first attempt led to the establishment of the People's Council (Volksraad), a kind of proto-parliament; the second led to large-scale deportation; and the third to a police state. The discussions at Tjokro's house show that in the early days these three movements were not strictly separate. Networks overlapped, people knew each other, and activists evolved.[2] They were more like tendencies. The PKI grew out of the left flank of Sarekat Islam, and nationalism built on the legacy of communism. They were branches of the same tree. Most of the leaders were young men from Deck 2, whose education, origins or occupation raised them well above the masses. But to open the assault on Deck 1, they needed the support of Deck 3. How did they go about it?

Let us return for a moment to Harjo Utomo, the man who was looking out over the rice fields. He wanted nothing to do with politics, even though he disliked the Dutch just as much as had his father, who had helped to build the sugar factory. 'I had no plans to go to the factory, but I hated them too. After a few years at the village school, I went to work on a large tobacco plantation. I had to plant tobacco in the fields. Later I became a *sinder*, an overseer, and supervised a small group of workers.' The pay was not the problem. 'Every month we received our wages in cash. We earned enough to keep food on the table. I could even buy a bicycle. It was a long ride to the plantation. My wife still used a horse and cart, but we could afford a new house.' No, it was something else. He looked down at his weathered, wrinkled hands, searching for the right Javanese word. 'The boss was a brute. He didn't beat us, but he shouted a lot. He was living with a Javanese woman from Solo, who was not so friendly either. But she *was* beautiful. Her skin, her figure, yes, all that.' As his veiled granddaughter translated, her eyes widened and she spluttered with laughter. It was the first time she'd ever heard her ninety-eight-year-old grandpa sing the praises of feminine beauty. 'I never heard what they ate. No, I'm sure it wasn't tofu or *tempeh*!' His granddaughter was finding the conversation more and more hilarious. 'I do remember what they wore. The man always wore shorts, a hat and shoes. She always wore Dutch clothes, not a *kebaya* and sarong like everyone else, but a *skirt*!' He looked up in surprise when I told him that the Javanese word for 'skirt' was the same as the Dutch. But what did *he* wear? 'Me? Just shorts,' he said with a shrug. 'We didn't have sandals. We always went barefoot and bare-chested.'[3]

Harjo Utomo resigned himself to his situation, but his memories form a vivid illustration of the tensions on Deck 3. In other places, the response was organised protest. In 1912, a local batik salesman named Samanhudi – just thirty kilometres away, in Surakarta – became frustrated at the power of all those who outranked him: the Chinese middle class, the governing Javanese elite and the Dutch administration. He held a political meeting, which to his surprise attracted not dozens of Javanese, but several thousand. These weren't the cream of native society, graduates of the medical school in Batavia, but small shopkeepers, lower-middle-class people, artisans and humble clerks who were tired of being humiliated and craved respect. Sarekat Islam was born.

Under Tjokroaminoto's leadership, it grew into a huge movement. From the start, a few symbolic matters were crucial. In its Surabaya branch, members were forbidden to sit on the ground or squat; he'd had enough of that kind of feudal, colonial etiquette. Members had to wear long trousers and shoes.[4] Tjokro himself no longer wore the *blangkon*, the tightly knotted batik headwear of the Javanese nobility, but an Islamic *songkok*, a type of short black fez, which Sukarno too would sport throughout his life. Tjokro choosing to wear a songkok was like a Dutch baron exchanging his top hat for a French beret. Sarekat Islam was a modernising movement, influenced in part by the growing number of hajis who had encountered an austere new form of Islam in Mecca.[5] Utterly opposed to all forms of religious conservatism, they campaigned for better education, their own co-operative organisations and social assistance, a programme like that of the Christian workers' movement that was on the rise all over Europe at the time.

Sarekat Islam soon had branches in other parts of the archipelago – in time, more than 180.[6] Many were outside Java. Budi Utomo and the Indische Partij had been a purely Javanese phenomenon, but SI became the first truly national movement. In some parts of southern Sumatra, almost seventy per cent of adult men were members.[7] The organisation had 100,000 members by 1913, and as many as 700,000 by 1916; by 1920, it claimed the number had soared to two million.[8]

Tjokroaminoto's working-class supporters venerated him as a mythical saviour. That was thanks to his rhetorical gifts, an important asset in a country with a rich oral tradition. His booming baritone had a large range, and his utterances were clear. Crowds listened open-mouthed. It was better than wayang theatre. People saw him as the Ratu Adil, the righteous king who had been awaited for centuries. Many believed he'd been born on the day of the Krakatoa eruption – but he was really a year older.[9] Open-air meetings drew audiences of up to 20,000.[10] 'People were thronging around us,' one of his fellow activists observed after a speech. 'Tjokro was grabbed from all sides, and people kissed his hands, his shoulders, the hem of his jacket. Feeling stifled, he jumped up on a chair, but they crowded around his legs and kissed his feet. [. . .] It's hard, he said, being the leader of such a fanatical people. They adore me and would do anything I asked of them. And that's a big responsibility. I often think about stepping down, but I'm afraid to, because I don't know what the people would do.'[11]

He wasn't the only one to wonder what forces had been unleashed. The Dutch colonial press did not trust the situation. Incidents and disturbances had been reported in villages and cities.[12] Since the very start of the Ethical Policy, the *Soerabaiasch Handelsblad* had been grumbling: 'One might wish to give that rabble a good lashing with a long whip and teach them order and discipline. And one actually finds oneself longing for a modernised Cultivation System; at least there was something manly about that.'[13] Manliness played an ever larger role in colonial thinking, as the Ethical Policy drew growing criticism for being too soft, too 'weepy' and too feminine. *Het Nieuws van den Dag voor Nederlandsch-Indië*, an authoritative newspaper, described the native population on the front page of a Saturday edition in 1915 as 'a herd of indolent, stupid, uncivilised people, whose capacity for thought, if not entirely absent, is surely of the most primitive nature'. The newspaper went on: 'We believe the Javanese are children: naughty, impetuous, difficult and lazy, unreliable and cruel. Incapable of caring for themselves, incapable of performing any serious work unsupervised. [. . .] The native makes a poor and cruel coachman, a sloppy worker, a stubborn, backwards farmer, a lazy overseer, an indifferent subordinate, a harsh master. He is superstitious, unreliable, dishonest, dumb, negligent, childish, despotic and slavish. [. . .] Issuing reprimands is a task not for the subordinate, but for the Master. We are the masters.'[14]

But the supreme master, Governor-General Alexander Idenburg, the highest Dutch authority in the colony, refused to participate in this kind of primitive stereotyping. He believed wholeheartedly in the Ethical Policy and had taken careful note of a point made by Tjokroaminoto in his speeches: 'Sarekat Islam is not a political party, not a party that seeks a revolution, as many people believe [. . .] We are loyal to the colonial administration, and we are satisfied under the Dutch government. It is not true that we wish to fight. We do not, a thousand times no!'[15] In the early years, the leaders of the organisation were still very moderate and deferential to authority. But many of the Dutch were deeply sceptical and prepared for the worst. *De Java-Bode*, Batavia's oldest newspaper, warned that 'the mood among the natives, inflamed with religious mania' had reached such a fever pitch that they wanted to 'throw themselves into massacring Europeans'.[16] That butchery didn't take place, but this kind of overheated journalism did create such a demand for firearms that Java's weapons dealers couldn't keep up.[17] When the press gets emotional, reason often falls by the wayside. But Idenburg kept a cool head. To those who said he should violently crush the movement, he simply replied: 'I would do so if the movement were the root and not the fruit. If I suppress the movement now, the root will remain and give rise to covert action.'[18]

Idenburg did not ban Sarekat Islam but granted official status only

to its local branches. Furthermore, in 1916, the Politieke Inlichtingen-
dienst (Political Intelligence Service; PID) was set up to keep a close
eye on the restless movements of the native masses. From then on, it
sent agents to every public meeting, who were allowed to intervene
when they felt things were going too far.

But Tjokro did not give up. In the middle of World War I (in
which the Netherlands was neutral), he joined Budi Utomo in advocating greater political rights. They argued that if they might soon to
be required to join the military, then they also had the right to a representative assembly. This was a controversial proposal – the
Europeans were reluctant to make such a substantial concession, and
some in the Indonesian camp were unwilling to purchase their freedom with young men's lives – but it was taken seriously, with Japan
in the throes of militarisation. The Japanese had defeated Russia in
1905 and annexed Korea in 1910. A delegation from Sarekat Islam
travelled to the Netherlands and even had an audience with Queen
Wilhelmina. But the outcome was disappointing: the authorities
introduced neither conscription nor a parliament. Arming thousands
of young native men was felt to be too risky. In the archipelago, the
period of compulsory military service was only for Dutch citizens.
Beyond that, the administration decided to make do with the KNIL,
the colony's old regular army. Besides, Japan had sided with the
Allies, so maybe the situation was not so dire.

Still, the demand for representation was taken to heart. In 1916,
the governor-general announced the creation of the People's Council. This was far from being a true native parliament: the council
played a purely advisory role, was not directly elected and only fifteen of its thirty-nine members were native. That meant that
ninety-five per cent of the population had only thirty-eight per cent
of the power. Still, it was better than nothing; the People's Council
was the first place for official dialogue about numerous important
issues. Its members included Tjipto Mangoenkoesoemo and Tjokroaminoto, who were anything but yes men.

Only a few months after the People's Council began its work,
Tjokro said: 'We want the same set of rights as Dutch citizens – in
short, complete self-determination.'[19] Governor-General Johan Paul

van Limburg Stirum didn't even take this so badly; he was as committed to the Ethical Policy as his predecessor Idenburg. Just after World War I, he even spoke of the gradual emancipation of the Indonesian people – ringing words which, astonishingly, he had not run past the authorities in The Hague. They must have been livid when they heard the news. But the governor-general and Sarekat Islam were on the same wavelength. That movement had begun in the shabbier sections of Deck 2, won the enthusiasm of large portions of Deck 3 and achieved a rudimentary form of representation on Deck 1. Yet its hour on the political stage would soon be over, and that had much to do with a second, far more radical form of anti-colonial resistance.

Rukardi Achmadi parked his old wreck of a car. 'You have to see this!' he said, pointing to an old building with red roof tiles, shored up with wooden posts.[20] From the outside, it looked like plenty of other Indonesian structures. We went in. 'I helped to restore this,' the young journalist said, as he walked to the middle of the interior. In a shallow depression in the brickwork, he slid aside a small carpet. 'S.I.', read the letters on the old black tiles. He was beaming. 'Sarekat Islam. This is where they met! The building is from 1919. This is where the organisation was infiltrated by the communists!' Noticing my surprise, he added: 'Oh yes, in Indonesia the communists and Muslims worked together for a while.'

Semarang was the Reddest city in Indonesia. It had a long history as a port with a large Chinese community, but in the late nineteenth century the colony's railway company had established its headquarters there, taking advantage of the convenient location halfway between Batavia and Surabaya. The head office, from which railway traffic in all directions was managed, dates from 1902 and is still there today. Lawang Sewu, it's called, 'a thousand doors', a dazzling palace, cool and bright, with white walls, leaded glass and red roof tiles. Here, in this city of railway workers and engine drivers, the union of railway and tramway employees was founded in 1908. It became the colony's most ethnically diverse labour union.[21] And this is also where one of the most peculiar figures in colonial history unleashed his mayhem.

Henk Sneevliet came from a dirt-poor Rotterdam family and went to work for the railways at the age of seventeen. But in 1913, at the age of thirty, he arrived in the Indies, not as an official or a businessman, but as the secretary of the Semarang Trade Fair – and, secretly, as a socialist revolutionary. While leading the railway union in the Netherlands, he had clashed with socialists he felt were far too moderate, such as the well-known politician Pieter Jelles Troelstra. If Sneevliet couldn't unchain the proletariat in the Dutch polders, then he was determined to do so in the colonial paddies. In Semarang, he studied the railway union and founded the Indische Sociaal-Democratische Vereeniging (Indies Social Democratic Association; ISDV), the forerunner of the later Communist Party. Sneevliet understood what had gone wrong with Budi Utomo and the Indische Partij: despite their good intentions, they'd had no public support base. The elite couldn't save the proletariat on their own; what Sneevliet was after was a true native mass movement. One such organisation already existed, although it was heavily invested in the opium of the masses: Sarekat Islam.

Sneevliet became acquainted with Semaun, an ambitious young Javanese railway clerk who was a frequent guest of Tjokroaminoto's, having been a member of Sarekat Islam since the age of fourteen. When Semaun was sixteen, Sneevliet asked him to join the railway union and serve as the vice-president of the ISDV. Semaun moved to Semarang, became the chairman of the local Sarekat Islam branch at the age of eighteen and had joined the national committee by the age of nineteen. It was 1918, and the organisation had almost one million members. Sneevliet believed that Semaun was the ideal person to win over Indonesia to true socialism. 'This is where it all began,' Rukardi said. 'Through Semaun, Sneevliet infiltrated Sarekat Islam.'

It was a time of sweeping changes: the Russian tsars had been unseated, the German empire destroyed, and US President Woodrow Wilson was advocating the right of self-determination for all peoples. 'People of Java,' Sneevliet had written after the Bolshevik victory, 'the Russian Revolution has lessons for you to learn. [. . .] A people lives here, needy, ignorant. A people lives here, producing riches that for centuries have been diverted to the strongboxes of

Western Europe's rulers. [. . .] The only conceivable outcome is that the people of Java, of the Indies, will find what the Russian people have found: *Glorious triumph*.'[22]

The intelligence service concluded that Sneevliet was an agitator and a menace to the state and expelled him from the colony in 1918. Instead of retreating to the Netherlands, he travelled on to Moscow. At the request of the recently founded Communist International (Comintern), he returned to Asia, this time preaching revolution in China. Sneevliet debated with Lenin, befriended Trotsky, fell out with Stalin, inspired Mao, and had a hand in the foundation of the Chinese Communist Party. He was one of the most influential Dutch figures of the twentieth century. In World War II, he was executed on a heath near Amersfoort in the Netherlands, after his two sons had committed suicide. In China, millions of banknotes bore his likeness.

Rukardi puts back the carpet. 'Semaun was more than Sneevliet's puppet. He was really very intelligent. Come on, let's go see his near-namesake.'[23] Half an hour later, we were sitting in the living room in the home of Sumaun Utomo, ninety-three years old. I learned that he too had been the head of the national railway union, as well as the dean of social and political sciences at Indonesia's Open University. He had travelled to Russia, Romania, Czechoslovakia and East Germany for his studies and spent five years in China. The book he was reading lay on the sofa: *Selected Works of Deng Xiao Ping*.

'I was named by my father. When I was born, in August 1923, Semaun had just been exiled. My father had become a communist very early on. He couldn't read or write, but his Dutch was good, because he worked in the Hotel Sarkies.' That was the poshest hotel in Surabaya, officially named the Oranje Hotel. It would play a crucial role in the Revolusi. 'My father had to serve the guests there and was widely respected for his command of Dutch.'[24]

Henk Sneevliet's forced departure did not quell the unrest – quite the opposite. Semaun became a radical, partly under Comintern influence, and founded the Perserikatan Komunis di Hindia (Indies Communist Alliance), becoming its first president at the age of twenty-one. Shortly afterwards, he travelled by way of China to Russia and Europe and was succeeded by Tan Malaka, who was also young, only twenty-seven. The organisation, which soon became known as the Partai Komunis Indonesia (Indonesian Communist Party; PKI), was the first communist party in Asia to be recognised by the Comintern. Anti-colonial resistance always transcended the local. While Sarekat Islam had been inspired by new developments in the Arab world, the PKI had been influenced by what was happening in Russia. The dissidents had networks the colonisers did not.

At first, the communists were part of Sarekat Islam. As far away as Moscow, there were debates about whether the revolutionary prole-tariat and the Muslim liberation movement should make common cause. After all, weren't they both fighting for the freedom of the oppressed masses? In Java, Tjokroaminoto, who saw Islam as 'the religion of the poor and the oppressed', was trying to bring the two movements together despite their differences.[25] Yet those differences grew, and 1923 brought a final parting of the ways. The PKI went on independently and the lifeblood drained out of Sarekat Islam; by 1930, it had only 12,000 members.[26] Its leaders went on searching for a way to combine politics with Islam, but by this time the Muslim organisations with the most members were the apolitical ones, such as Muhammadiyah and Nahdlatul Ulama, which both did important social work.

The PKI grew fast. Its ideology was often a mishmash of Bolshev-ist slogans and messianic prophecies. In the faraway Moluccas, propagandists declared that all who refused to join the party ran the risk 'of having to return with the Dutch to their cold country'.[27] As dubious as such methods were, the desire for salvation was under-standable. During World War I, global trade had come to a near standstill; the submarine war kept export goods stockpiled in ware-houses, import goods had practically no way of reaching the Indonesian ports, and hardly any manufacturing took place in the colony.[28] The result was a tripling of prices between 1913 and 1920. In Europe, there were unions that could negotiate better wages, but most Indonesian workers remained poorly organised and therefore poorly paid. At the same time, their tax burden grew heavier. In less than fifteen years, the colony's public debt had swelled by one billion guilders, from 93 million in 1912 to 1,092 million in 1926.[29] The new governor-general, Dirk Fock, increased taxes and made drastic cuts in public spending, abandoning the commitments of the Ethical Policy in areas such as education and health care.[30] This was especially frustrating to employees: as prices rose, wages stagnated, public services deteriorated and they were expected to cough up more tax revenue. This destroyed any hope of a native middle class.[31] As conditions on Deck 3 grew worse than ever, the way to Deck 2 was barred.

All this could only lead to strikes.[32] In cement factories, tailors' workshops, furniture industries and newspaper companies, the first small-scale protests took place. In lending banks, a fifth of the employees refused to work. And the strike in the sugar industry involved no fewer than 20,000 workers. Governor-General Fock held the PKI responsible for all this unrest and could not tolerate the idea of an Indonesian Lenin, Atatürk or Gandhi. In May 1923, Semaun was arrested, half an hour after the birth of his son.[33] Fock banished him to the Netherlands without trial. This prompted a full 13,000 railway workers to go on strike, but their protest was broken up by force. Tan Malaka summed it up neatly: 'The saccharine tone of the Ethical Policy has now given way to the monotonous thud of rubber batons and the hiss of sabres.'[34]

Like Sneevliet, Semaun moved on to Russia, where he would remain for thirty years. He became an announcer at Radio Moscow and a member of the Comintern and was ultimately appointed head of the state design agency in Tashkent, Uzbekistan. He did not return to Indonesia until 1956.

Tan Malaka, his successor at the PKI, was also banished. He went to the Netherlands, where in 1922 he became the first Indonesian ever to stand for election to the lower house of parliament. He represented the Communist Party, the only political party that advocated Indonesian independence.[35] After that, he moved on to Berlin, Moscow, Canton (Guangzhou), Manila, Singapore, Bangkok and Hong Kong. As a Comintern representative in East Asia, he was constantly on the move. For more than twenty years, he lived in exile under more than twenty pseudonyms, often struggling with his health. In Canton, he wrote the visionary essay *Naar de Republiek Indonesia* (Towards the Republic of Indonesia), which made the case for an independent Indonesian state, possibly including the Philippines. It was the first explicit statement of the concept of the Republic of Indonesia. He saw that 'ninety-nine per cent of the population live in poverty and suffering' and contended that the 'skirmishes large and small now taking place in Java' were just the beginning. It was imperative to join forces, he wrote, and deliver 'the final blow [. . .] with such force, in the right place and at the right time, that Dutch imperialism will fall and its fall will be heard in all the other colonies in the East'. A quarter-century before it happened, he foresaw that 'Indonesia's freedom would lead to the freedom of the colonies in Asia, one after another'.[36] He also predicted that the United States and Japan would go to war over the Pacific, although he didn't know what consequences that might have for Indonesia. Not until after August 1945 did he dare to return to his homeland. He could have become president, but three years later he was assassinated.[37]

Sneevliet was gone, Semaun was gone, Tan Malaka was gone. The PKI was decapitated, but not defeated. Governor-General Fock thought he could put out a wildfire by blowing out a few candles, but his hard-line approach frustrated even the native elite. I. F. M. Salim, the son of a native public prosecutor in Sumatra, had received an entirely European upbringing. At school he belted out the Wilhelmus and other patriotic favourites. But as a young adult, he came to the painful conclusion that he and his friends 'were, after all, regarded by the Dutch colonisers as nothing more than natives'. Wherever he went, his high hopes of equal treatment were dashed, 'in their schools, in their clubs, in public buildings and above all in public transport'. You might think the European and Indonesian elites would have experienced a slow convergence of interests, but the opposite was true. Fock only increased their mutual estrangement. At the same time, the gap between colonial and native households grew, as more European women arrived in the colony – by 1920, there were around four for every five men.[38] Europeans took to spending the weekends with their families, playing tennis, riding or working on stamp collections. They trusted the nanny and the cook, but beyond that, less direct contact with Indonesians led to greater distrust. Systematic study of colonial newspapers has shown that public opinion in the Indies swung sharply to the right after 1920.[39] Support for the native cause dried up. Sympathy turned into loathing.

Salim thought he would always 'have to remain an underdog', but he felt 'an ever stronger desire' to make himself useful to his own people. He witnessed the poverty of coolies in Sumatra and thought it scandalous, considering the huge profits made by the plantations.[40] He found work as an editor for a few progressive periodicals that agitated for self-government.

Then came the moment when everything erupted. On Christmas Day in 1925, a few leading members of the PKI, meeting near Prambanan, cooked up plans for a communist revolution. Muso and Alimin set off for the Soviet Union to discuss the plans with Semaun at the Comintern. The three of them knew each other from their days at Tjokroaminoto's house. Now they found themselves in an office in the cold city of Moscow. During their discussions, it became apparent that the proposal was altogether premature. There was not enough support among the Indonesian masses for a workers' revolt. Many peasants felt what a colonial official had once described as 'the intense desire to be left in peace'.[41] The overconfidence of the would-be revolutionaries boggled even Stalin, who later remarked: 'The Javanese communists seemed to suffer from this deviation [of overestimating the possibility of revolution] when they, recently and quite wrongly, raised the slogan "All power to the soviets" in their country. This is a deviation to the left which threatens to sever the Party from the masses, and to transform it into a clique.'[42] When Stalin says you've moved too far to the left, you have a problem. The delegation returned to Asia, but the hotheads in Java would not be dissuaded. From Singapore, Tan Malaka tried with all his might to stop the madness, but the coup plotters forged ahead. The political intelligence service suspected that something was afoot. In early November 1926, messages were intercepted: 'All garments must be ground into *sambal*,' the generic term for the flavoured chili pastes essential to Indonesian cooking. 'Garments' sounded like a code name for the

European authorities.[43] The colonial administration responded, arresting a number of communist leaders. Other conspirators did not know that the plan had been foiled and went into action. In Batavia, they attacked the post office, the telephone exchange and the prison; in western Java, they destroyed bridges, railways and telegraph lines; in Surakarta, they set tobacco warehouses on fire. A few policemen, officials and other public employees were killed, including two Europeans. The plotters undoubtedly suffered much greater losses. In January, the fire spread to Sumatra, where mines, trains and railways were demolished. Although the revolution was exceptionally ill-prepared, the unrest continued for more than a month in some places. The colonial authorities restored order by brute force. A few of the people arrested were tied to trees covered with red ants; others were bound to metal plates and laid out in the sun. Some conspirators' corpses were hanged and mutilated.[44]

The communist revolt of 1926–7 had been an abject failure, but the European community was left in profound shock. 'Get out the hand grenades!' 'Why not line them up against the wall?' 'Fifty gallows in Koningsplein [Batavia's main square, now Medan Merdeka].[45] No fewer than 13,000 people were arrested. Some 4,500 of them received prison sentences, seven were condemned to death and three were in fact hanged – the death penalty, abolished in the Netherlands in 1870, remained in the colony's statute books until 1950. More than 800 people had been identified as instigators and troublemakers. Even if they hadn't been directly involved, they had to go. But where?

The twenty-five-year-old I. F. M. Salim was one of them. He had no personal connection to the revolt, but when the editor-in-chief of Sumatra's most influential colonial newspaper wrote that every rebel deserved a bullet through the head, he protested fiercely. For the colonial authorities, that was more than enough reason to shadow and arrest him. Just before he was taken away, he received a visit from his parents. 'My father was heartbroken but filled with confidence in God's justice and the infallibility of Dutch East Indies law; my mother was still sobbing, utterly bewildered. It made no sense to her straightforward mind. She'd never known me as anything but a son, incapable of any crime. It was the last time I would ever see them!'[46]

He and his fellow captives boarded a steamship. They'd been neither imprisoned nor convicted; no court had reviewed their cases. The governor-general had sent them packing with a stroke of the pen. His 'exorbitant rights' in this area stemmed from the days of the Dutch East India Company. His decision was not a criminal sentence, but an administrative measure to promote civil peace and public order. On board, there was very little of either. Salim and the others were bound together with iron chains in groups of five. 'Whenever one of us had to relieve himself, the other four had no choice but to attend the necessary event, while a soldier supervised us all.'[47] It must have been even more unpleasant for someone like Raden Sukaesih: 'There were 800 exiles on board, all men, I was the only woman.' This unmarried woman had been a member of the revolutionary committee. 'We were chained together, five to a group. During meals, they unchained one hand. We could not lie down until 9 p.m.'[48]

These sound like episodes from eighteenth-century slave ships, but they took place in the Dutch East Indies in 1927. The steamships headed east. The voyage took days, sometimes weeks, and ended in the most remote of all the islands: New Guinea. Deep in the ancient forest, a place had been made for them: Boven Digul, three days' journey up the Digul River. It was deathly silent and stiflingly hot, ridden with malarial mosquitoes, leeches and crocodiles. The captives on the boat sometimes saw naked, painted Papuans clamouring for tobacco.

Here, in this far corner of the world, 'unruly' individuals were sent to rot. Some entered the forest with dress shoes, Homburg hats and briefcases.[49] Almost half had worked as clerks for the colonial administration, the railways or the postal service. Others were peasants or craftspeople.[50] They could not believe the Netherlands would sink so low. More than half were under thirty; there were even a few teenagers among them. They lived in two camps: Tanah Merah, 450 kilometres from the coast, and Tanah Tinggi, forty kilometres further away, where conditions were even more spartan.

'My grandfather was sent to Boven Digul as a political offender,' said Dharyanto Tito Wardani over dinner in Tasikmalaya. I didn't understand. Tasikmalaya was more or less the hub of Javanese

Islamism. Had there been communists here too? 'Communism was just a social ideology. It wasn't about atheism. A lot of religious people participated.' And in fact, more than half the people interned in Boven Digul went on practising their religion there; they even built a house of worship.[51] Few of them had a thorough grounding in communist thought. 'My grandpa was a pious Muslim,' Dharyanto once told me. 'He'd stolen rice from the Dutch army to distribute among the poor. He was held there from 1927 to 1933.'[52] Most of the so-called communists did not advocate the abolition of private property or the bourgeois state, nor had they been striving for a Leninist dictatorship of the proletariat. What they wanted was a more equitable distribution of wealth. Salim wrote: 'It made a plausible story for the outside world to claim that all the internees were communists, and to hush up the fact that the event signalled the awakening of an oppressed people!'[53]

At Boven Digul's low point, it had 1,100 internees. They were accompanied by 1,000 family members, half of them children. Anyone who wished could have their family join them in the detention colony. And whoever chose to work was paid meagre wages and could spend them in the shop. The internees had a school, an infirmary, a church, a small library, two football fields and, of all things, a jail. Since they weren't technically prisoners, they could still be threatened with imprisonment.

But despite all these facilities, Boven Digul was a far from pleasant place. The fields proved unsuitable for growing rice. Fights broke out constantly. There were incidents of murder and suicide. And the medical conditions were horrifying. In the first two years, forty-seven people died of dysentery, malaria, beriberi or exhaustion. Even after health care improved, no one could escape lethargy and depression. Salim saw all the camp residents deteriorate into 'wrecks'.[54] Some tried to escape, but they were so far from the coast it was like trying to trek through impenetrable forest from Amsterdam to Paris. Internees went missing, succumbed to the brutal climate, or were found by Papuans, who sometimes chopped their heads off and sometimes returned them to their camps.[55] Those who were brought back after an escape attempt spent up to a year in jail. The Javanese captive

Sandjojo and a few accomplices made an especially spectacular attempt, fleeing on foot through the forest to the Australian part of New Guinea, rowing a prahu down the 400-kilometre Fly River to the south coast, renting a sailboat and crossing the Torres Strait to Australia without a compass. They spent a few months on Thursday Island, where one of them even gave haircuts to raise funds for the trip back to Java. But a letter home asking for money was intercepted by Dutch police detectives. They were all hauled in and sent back to Boven Digul.[56]

But it was Thomas Najoan from the Minahasa Peninsula in northern Sulawesi who had the most tragic story of all. He tried to escape not just once but three times. The first time, he reached Thursday Island, where he was arrested. The second time, he was caught by Papuans and returned. Back in the camp, he slit his wrists and wrote on the walls of his hut in blood.[57] The third time was in 1943, just before the camp was evacuated. If he had waited a little longer, he would have been liberated and taken to Australia. Instead, he was never heard from again. 'His skeleton is probably somewhere out there in the forest,' Salim mused, adding that maybe he had run into headhunters and 'his skull, dried or smoked, is part of the collection on display in a Papuan hut'.[58] Salim himself remained in the camp until its final day. He had lost fifteen years of his life, from the age of twenty-five to forty-one.[59] And all for writing a couple of editorials.

If Islamism came into its own in Surabaya and communism in Semarang, where was the cradle of nationalism? Leiden. There, in that university town in the Netherlands, a man named Soebardjo had hung a large red-and-white flag in his student room. The colours were inspired by those of the fourteenth-century empire of Majapahit. Soebardjo was a law student and the president of the Indische Vereeniging (Indies Association), a student club formed in 1908 for the few Indonesian students in the Netherlands. They all came from the native elite and studied law in Leiden, medicine in Amsterdam, veterinary medicine in Utrecht, economics in Rotterdam, engineering in Delft or agriculture in Wageningen. In the 1920s, the club never had more than a few dozen members. They often met at weekends in Soebardjo's large room. Before exams, some of them would spend a moment in contemplation in front of the flag.[60]

One of these regular visitors was nineteen-year-old Mohammad Hatta, who had been studying at a business school in Rotterdam since 1921. He came from the Minangkabau region of western Sumatra. Frivolous and sophomoric he was not. Under the influence of modern Islam, he stood out for his earnest dedication. He studied Marx's economic theories and acknowledged that colonialism was a manifestation of global capitalism but was unwilling to embrace the godlessness of communism.

In 1922 something seemingly trivial took place: the Indische Vereeniging changed its name to the *Indonesische* Vereeniging. Just two syllables, but a world of difference. It was the first organisation to use the word, two years before the Communist Party adopted the name of Partai Komunis Indonesia. The term 'Indonesia' had been invented by a British traveller in 1850: *nesos* was Greek for island, so names ending in '-nesia' were used for archipelagos, such as Polynesia, Melanesia and Micronesia.[61] This coinage, used by linguists and anthropologists, appealed to the small band of Indonesian students in the Netherlands. They began to use the geographical term more and more often as a political concept. It sounded good, because it didn't refer to the coloniser. 'Or did the Dutch speak of their own country as the "Spanish" Netherlands when it was still in the powerful grip of Philip II?' they wrote in their club newsletter.[62]

In 1923, Hatta became the treasurer of the Indonesische Vereeniging. In 1925, they changed their name again, now completely avoiding the coloniser's language and calling themselves the Perhimpunan Indonesia (PI), from the word *himpun*, 'gather'. In 1926, Hatta was elected president. By then the newsletter for members was called *Indonesia Merdeka*, 'Free Indonesia'. This slogan was another first. Twenty years later, it would became the foremost revolutionary battle cry, chanted by hundreds of thousands of young people. The first lead article in the renamed newsletter made the association's views abundantly clear: 'Sooner or later, every conquered nation will reclaim its freedom,' but it was up to the Dutch whether 'the birth of freedom will be accompanied by blood and tears or the process will unfold peacefully.'[63]

The PI was the cradle of nationalism, Indonesia's third great anti-colonial movement. The students in the Netherlands strove openly towards independence, calling themselves 'revolutionary nationalists'.[64] They believed their struggle transcended class and religion: 'Only an Indonesia that knows itself united, setting internecine differences aside, can overcome the power that dominates it,' they wrote in their statement of principles in 1925.[65] Hatta conferred with exiled communist leaders such as Semaun and Tan Malaka and found he could work with them. 'Anyone who wanted independence could become a member,' Pratomo said. 'That was the great cause that united us.' The 102-year-old from Callantsoog had joined the PI in the 1930s, after coming to the Netherlands to study – first, a year of medicine in Leiden, then economics in Rotterdam. Although Hatta had left by then, Pratomo knew all about his legacy: 'The Perhimpunan fought for independence all the way back in the 1920s!' His eyes were bright with enthusiasm. 'It was truly ahead of its time!'[66]

Compared to Sarekat Islam and the PKI, the Perhimpunan was still very small, but its impact was tremendous. Its members included some of Indonesia's most brilliant thinkers. They kept a close eye on the international scene – Japan, China and India, of course, but also Russia, Turkey and Egypt – and could write about it more freely in the Netherlands than in the Indies.[67] Inspired by Gandhi, they chose the path of non-cooperation, not wanting to place their talents and intellect in the service of the colonial administration. Their newsletter never had a huge circulation, but because copies were smuggled into the colony in suitcases, they infused the debate in the archipelago with an energy and audacity that were not possible there.[68] One of my eyewitnesses summed it up perfectly: 'Those highly educated Indonesians were few in number, but they were like the plutonium in an atom bomb.'[69]

In February 1927, Mohammad Hatta travelled from Rotterdam to Brussels for a historic but now nearly forgotten event: the founding of the League against Imperialism and Colonial Oppression. Stately Egmont Palace hosted this unprecedented gathering of intellectuals from Africa, Asia and Europe; for Hatta, it was a remarkable opportunity to meet people like Jawaharlal Nehru, who later became the first prime minister of India, Lamine Senghor, a communist from Senegal, and Mrs Sun Yat-sen, the widow of the man who had brought down the 2,200-year-old Chinese empire. The participants also included the Dutch poet Henriette Roland Holst, the British Labour leader George Lansbury, the French author and Nobel laureate Romain Rolland and even Albert Einstein, who by then had also won the Nobel Prize.[70] At the age of twenty-five, Hatta acquired an impressive international network and even joined the League's executive committee, serving alongside Nehru. He attended meetings in Paris, gave lectures in Switzerland, toured Germany, Denmark, Norway and Sweden, supported women's organisations and was respected wherever he went.[71]

Except in the Netherlands. There the authorities kept a suspicious eye on him. Could the League be a cover for the Comintern? (The answer later proved to be yes.) Was Hatta in communication with Semaun? (Yes, but he wasn't a communist himself.)[72] Did the PI support the use of violence? (No, this suspicion was completely groundless.) The communist revolt in Java and Sumatra had made the Dutch very distrustful, not just in the colony but also in their mother country. The homes of the leading PI members were searched by the police. Hatta was arrested, along with three others, and after a full six months of pre-trial detention, he said in the courtroom: 'Dutch rule is coming to an end, of that I have no doubt. It is merely a matter of time.'[73] The Dutch court acknowledged how flimsy the case against him was and set him free.

Hatta's extraordinary courage is clear from his rhetorical battle with Hendrik Colijn not long afterwards. Colijn was fifty-nine years old, an ex-prime minister and an ex-war minister, the former director of the Batavian Petroleum Company and even a former military officer who'd ordered the shooting of women and children in Lombok – the very incarnation of the colonialist-capitalist complex. Hatta was a twenty-six-year-old student who'd just spent half a year in prison. Colijn believed that the Ethical Policy 'had disturbed the deep rural peace of our East'. Western education had created a rebellious generation of 'the rootless'. Colijn argued that 'again today as in the past', education in the colony should focus on 'the needs of native society, which is still so simple'.[74] Hatta could not let this go unchallenged. He asked whether Colijn 'and all the other quacks of colonial policy' really wanted a return to 'the utilitarian education of the old days', which had served only to furnish the government bureaucracy and corporations with 'cheap low-level employees and "skilled" workers'? 'When the aim is to protect the value of colonial shares and guarantee the annual flow of millions from Indonesia to the Netherlands, no pangs of conscience protect the last little bit of high-quality education available to taxpaying Indonesians from degradation.'[75] But it was no use. For the entire period from 1933 to 1939, Colijn was the prime minister of the Netherlands, and from 1933 to 1937 he was also the minister of colonies.

I was sitting in a small, cluttered law office in Jakarta, peering at a black-and-white portrait: a three-piece dress suit, gleaming shoes and fashionable cufflinks.[76] 'My grandfather dressed entirely in the Dutch fashion,' Jefferson Dau told me. 'He was a district chief.' He descended from the Dayak people of Borneo, the ethnic group once portrayed as terrifying headhunters from the jungle, but he seemed to have embraced the colonial ideal of 'civilising the natives'. 'All the same, in the 1920s, he stopped working for the Dutch regime. He became a fervent nationalist, devoted exclusively to liberating Indonesia.' Was he one of the many native officials dismissed as a result of budget cuts? Did he deliberately choose the path of non-cooperation? The retrenchments forced many people with a European education to settle for jobs below their level, often as poorly paid teachers in small schools that did not receive public funds.[77] 'Since most children weren't allowed to attend Dutch schools, he opened a little school in our village of Kuala Kapuas. It was a Taman Siswa school. Have you heard of those?'

Yes, of course, I'd read about them. They were the brainchild of Soewardi, the man exiled to the Netherlands in 1913 because of his essay 'If I were Dutch'. On his return to Indonesia, he realised that political change would be a long-term struggle. If political parties weren't the solution, perhaps classrooms were. In 1922, he founded Taman Siswa, the 'Pupils' Garden', an educational system inspired by the philosophy of the Indian poet Rabindranath Tagore (the first non-Western Nobel laureate) and the educational principles of Maria Montessori. He also adopted a new name: Ki Hadjar Dewantara. The pupils were taught Western science, Javanese culture, traditional crafts and national history. This model caught on. A few years later, there were dozens of Taman Siswa schools teaching thousands of children. By the late 1930s, there were 15,000 pupils at more than 200 schools.[78] 'My grandfather knew Dewantara very well,' Jefferson Dau told me. 'They had a good rapport.'[79] And Dewantara was one of many. Governor-General Fock cut funding for education as the population grew apace. Many teachers were unemployed, and many pupils went uneducated. 'Wild schools' shot up like mushrooms. It was a movement of both men and women. 'My mother started a wild school with her women friends,' said Eli Kansil, who grew up in central Sulawesi. 'Only the wealthy could go to the Dutch school. She was a teacher, but being a native, she wasn't eligible for the highest qualification or the position of headmistress.'[80]

While in Leiden a generation of twenty-somethings was developing nationalism, tens of thousands of teenagers in Indonesia were also being raised with a very new frame of reference. I sat in the great mosque of Tasikmalaya in the interval between two prayers, listening to an elderly man. 'I attended a Taman Siswa school for three years,' Djadju said with pride. 'They really worked on your character there. It was not an Islamic school by any means; nationalism was far more important. The school strove for independence. We were taught science, Indonesian history and world history. We even learned about Diponegoro, who had fought against the Dutch!'[81] A refreshing change from the Dutch schools where Indonesian children learned to sing songs glorifying Dutch privateers and were taught that 'the Rhine enters our country at Lobith'.[82]

Change was slowly brewing. In October 1928, hundreds of young nationalists gathered in Batavia for a historic youth conference. On the final day, they made a declaration familiar to every Indonesian today as the Sumpah Pemuda (Youth Pledge): 'We sons and daughters of Indonesia acknowledge one birthplace, Indonesia. We sons and daughters of Indonesia acknowledge one people, the Indonesians. We sons and daughters of Indonesia uphold the language of unity, Indonesian.' The seeds sown by the PI came to fruition here for the first time. The word 'Indonesia', promoted some years earlier by the PI's leaders in Leiden as an alternative to 'the Dutch East Indies', became the national battle cry of an entire generation. No longer did they see their country as a section of the world map with fairly arbitrary borders, but as a natural, unified nation with its own name and its own people.[83] But what was 'the language of unity'? More than 700 indigenous languages were spoken. Dutch? Unthinkable. Javanese? Too feudal, too complex, with its own alphabet. Sundanese from western Java? Unacceptable to the rest of the archipelago. Malay, of course! The ancient language of trade was widespread, easy to learn and accessible to all. Even though it bore traces of Chinese, Hindi, Tamil, Persian, Arabic, Spanish, Portuguese and Dutch, it felt authentic. You could use it to negotiate, express yourself clearly and, not unimportantly, get a laugh. At the end of the conference, the young people sang the recent composition 'Indonesia Raya' for the first time. It would later become the national anthem. A Dutch observer at the event wrote to the governor-general: 'Its banal European melody and forced rhymes make it the epitome of degenerate taste, but it poses no political threat.'[84] Even so, it would soon be banned.

'My father was twenty and attended that conference,' said the constitutional law expert Ananda B. Kusuma. 'He was studying at the Hogere Kweekschool [European-style teacher training college] in Batavia to become a Dutch teacher, but after that conference he refused to teach Dutch any more. Seven years later, I was born. He no longer tolerated Dutch in our home after that. He raised me in Indonesian.'[85] That was how quickly things could go. Ananda's grandfather, a doctor from STOVIA, was one of the few people in the Indies to own the authoritative Dutch encyclopedia, the *Winkler Prins*, but his grandson never learned to read the expensive volumes. The decline of Dutch had begun.

Of course, these were merely the first small cracks. Most Indonesians still looked up to the Dutch language, but in the upper classes, some were making the switch. Herawati Diah was ninety-nine years old when I visited her in Jakarta. She was so distinguished that I felt

I was visiting royalty, a kind of Asian Jackie Onassis. Her spacious home was stylish, chic and – a rare luxury in the capital – quiet. Flawlessly coiffed, she sat in her wheelchair. 'My mother didn't want me to go to a Dutch school,' she told me in a voice like velvet. 'She was very progressive. She was one of the first women to drive a car, and she founded the women's magazine *Doenia kita* ["Our World"].'[86] Her father was another STOVIA graduate, but when Herawati was ready for higher education, she did not go to Leiden or Amsterdam. 'My mother said, "You must study in a country that does not have colonies."' The United States had just granted the Philippines far-reaching autonomy. 'In that era the decision to send me to America was revolutionary. No other Indonesian girl had studied there. Mother was ridiculed by her relatives, especially those who worked for the colonial government. But she was determined, and I left by ship.'[87] At Columbia University in New York, she studied sociology and became the first Indonesian woman with an American degree – and one of the first in her country to speak fluent English.

Not everyone had a mother like that. After his years with Tjokroaminoto, Sukarno went to Bandung to study architecture at the technical college there, in Dutch. In 1927 he organised a student club to debate political issues. Whether it was the PI in the Netherlands, the youth conference in Batavia, or the student club in Bandung, in every case young people took the lead. In 1926 Sukarno offered his analysis of the struggle in the article 'Nasionalisme, Islamisme dan Marxisme' (Nationalism, Islam, Marxism). The three major movements he had observed at Tjokro's house had descended into bickering between Muslims and communists, while nationalism remained the exclusive interest of well-educated, Westernised young urbanites. This was not the way forward. Sukarno wanted to combine these three currents into one great mass movement, with nationalism leading the way.

In July 1927 he established the Indonesian National Party (Partai Nasional Indonesia; PNI) and was constantly giving speeches. He had learned the art of oratory from Tjokro. At large outdoor meetings, the muscular pronouncements rolled smoothly off his tongue. He had the articulation of a machine gun, left dramatic pauses, repeated phrases, crescendoed, gestured dramatically and then fired off the key sentence. His audiences went wild. He was a highly educated man, but peppered his speeches with references everyone understood: characters from wayang theatre, archetypal figures from heroic poems and comparisons to buffaloes, tigers and snakes. Humour alternated with pathos. 'Engineer Sukarno' was a clear, straightforward speaker. He talked about *sini* and *sana*, here and there, us versus them. The Indonesians versus the Dutch.

When his political meetings took place in cinemas, the decor included red-and-white flags and portraits of nationalist heroes such as Diponegoro and Dewantara. The stage was decked out with red-and-white bouquets. A few supporting acts warmed up the audience. Then the man himself entered the theatre, and everyone leapt to their feet to sing 'Indonesia Raya'. He approached the stage with a manly stride, climbed the steps and treated the spectators to one of his bold and impassioned speeches.[88] Within a year, the PNI membership in Bandung had increased by a factor of *fourteen*. The party's supporters were teachers, clerks, officials, railway employees and a few workers. After Leiden, Bandung became the second cradle of nationalism.

In the Netherlands, the leaders of the PI followed the news of Sukarno's showmanship with a large dose of scepticism. To them he seemed vain, tiresome and unsophisticated, and a rabble-rouser to boot. What good would it do to whip up the masses if you didn't educate them? The executive committee had a new member, Sutan Sjahrir. He believed Sukarno and his allies were 'unsuitable to become leaders of a mass movement'.[89] Sjahrir was studying law in Leiden. Like Hatta, he came from the Minangkabau region of Sumatra, but the two could not have been more different. While Hatta was serious and studious, Sjahrir was jovial and nonchalant. He rarely attended lectures, devoured Marx, Engels and Rosa Luxemburg and frequented all kinds of socialist circles in Amsterdam, where he became involved with the Dutch feminist Maria Duchâteau, who was then married to Dutch socialist Sal Tas. He and Hatta were bona fide intellectuals, but it was the Javanese nationalist Sukarno who inflamed the masses as no other.

Although the PNI had at most 10,000 members, the colonial

authorities monitored its activities, just as they had monitored Douwes Dekker, Tjipto, Soewardi, Sneevliet, Semaun, Tan Malaka,
Hatta and all the others. In the Indies, political activism never went
unpunished. In December 1929, after more than one search of Sukarno's home, he was arrested. Governor-General Andries Cornelis
Dirk de Graeff refused to banish him, instead referring his case to the
court system. A year later, Sukarno was sentenced to four years'
imprisonment in Bandung, and the PNI was dissolved. The Dutch
overlords seemed to be stuck in a rut, with no other response to widespread disaffection but to treat the leaders like criminals – an
ill-advised strategy.

But Governor-General De Graeff did realise that these were not
just a few 'rotten apples'. He felt greater kinship with the early
twentieth-century promoters of the Ethical Policy than he did with
the reactionary brutes who came before and after him, Fock and De
Jonge respectively. He was aware of the social unrest, and to take the
wind out of Sukarno's sails, he wanted to give moderate nationalists
a greater say. To the severe displeasure of the European elite, he
arranged for greater representation of Indonesians on the People's
Council. From 1931 onwards, thirty of its sixty members were Indonesian, twenty-five were Dutch and five were Foreign Orientals
(mostly Chinese). It was a good-faith attempt to bridge the gap and
open the way to reasonable dialogue, but it went awry. The Dutch
thought the governor-general had lost his marbles. A right-wing
conservative association, the Vaderlandsche Club (Fatherland Club),
was set up to oppose 'the insane demands of the Oriental nationalists'.
With 9,000 members, it became the European community's largest
political grouping until the Japanese invasion.[90] Meanwhile, the
Indonesians remained committed to non-cooperation. After all, it
wasn't only the political system that was unjust; economic structures
were too. Yes, the Indonesian population had disproportionately
little political clout, but more importantly, they had disproportionately little income. That problem could not be solved by a few more
seats in the People's Council. And the Great Depression would only
make matters worse.

★

On a remote island off the coast of Sulawesi, I met Badora. How can I describe her? She had no family name. She didn't know her year of birth. She could no longer stand up straight and had to squat. Her skin was covered with a fine web of wrinkles. She must have been ancient; her first child had been born in colonial times. 'When I was a child myself, there were only three or four houses here. We hardly ever saw Dutch people. Now and then they made a quick stop here. Then they would go around looking inside all the buildings. We were scared of them.' Her father earned a little money selling copra, dried coconut flesh. 'We had a few coconut palms. We would cut the nuts in two and dry them over a fire. Then we would fill our bags, and my father would take them to Tongkabo on his small prahu and sell them to the only Chinese man who lived there. We used the money to buy sugar and cloth in his shop.' What seems like a very local trade was really part of the global economy. In the United States and Europe, the demand for margarine grew from 1910 onwards. Copra, a source of coconut oil, was much cheaper than animal fat.[91] It was also used in manufacturing soap. The United States looked to the Philippines and the Dutch East Indies for its supply. In 1917, there were some 24 million coconut palms growing in the Outer Islands of the Dutch colony.[92] They were mostly in the hands of locals like Badora and her family.

So in 1929, the Wall Street crash sent ripples all the way to those remote islands. In 1928, one hundred coconuts cost six and a half guilders; in 1935, less than one guilder.[93] Other export crops, such as pepper and rubber, dropped in value by half.[94] Between 1926 and 1932, per capita annual income in the Dutch East Indies plummeted from around fifty to twenty guilders.[95] But Badora and the people of her region were flexible; when the price of copra was low, they caught more fish, and when rice and cane sugar were expensive, they ate more maize and palm sugar. Money was nice to have, but not essential. 'Food was never a problem,' she said.[96]

But in Java and Sumatra, the shock waves were much greater. The colony had had an export economy for centuries, so it was at the mercy of the international market. Around 1830, eighty per cent of the sugar, eighty-eight per cent of the quinine, ninety per cent of the oil and ninety-six per cent of the tobacco were intended for export.[97] Furthermore, Great Britain abandoned the gold standard in 1931 as a stimulus to its economy, and Canada, South Africa, British India, Australia and Japan soon followed suit. Because the Netherlands clung to gold and its currency therefore retained its value, its colonial wares became unaffordable. Total exports from the Dutch East Indies shrank from 1.5 billion guilders in 1929 to less than half a billion in 1935. Sugar exports dropped from 307 million to 35 million guilders, rubber from 235 to 37 million and oil from 179 to 86 million.[98] From the largest coastal ports, the crisis spread to the smallest inland villages. In Java, numerous sugar plantations shut down; sugarcane remained in cultivation on only 28,000 of the former 200,000 hectares. In Sumatra, the rubber plantations and tin mines fell on hard times: 160,000 of the 336,000 coolies were sent away jobless.[99] Yet the native population was never radically impoverished.[100] Where sugar for export had once been grown, farmers could again grow rice for their own consumption. The colonial authorities eventually introduced a policy of small-scale industrialisation: sewing machines and looms led to a revival of cottage industries.[101] In 1930, there were only 500 modern looms in the archipelago; by 1940, there were 35,000.[102] These brought new economic opportunities, particularly for women.[103] And the weak yen led to an influx of affordable Japanese goods: light bulbs, bicycles, paper products, plates, preserves, textiles and soap, as well as cement, glass, steel, corrugated iron, tiles and electrical cables.[104] Badora touched the fabric at her hip and said, 'In the time of the Dutch, cloth was never expensive.'

On 31 December 1931, Sukarno was released early after two years in prison. Coincidentally, Sutan Sjahrir had also returned to Indonesia a few days earlier, after three years in Leiden. A few months later, Hatta would also return, with an economics degree. Both had been expelled from the PI, which had taken a sharply communist turn. The three greatest political minds of their generation were together in Java, but still in profound disagreement.[105] Could they overcome their differences? Hatta and Sjahrir still disapproved of what they saw as Sukarno's demagoguery. Education was more important to them than agitation. So they founded their own movement, the Pendidikan Nasional Indonesia (Indonesian National Education, also known as the 'new PNI'). Its mission was cadre training, an activity neglected by Sarekat Islam, the PKI and Sukarno's PNI. Only a well-organised movement would eventually be prepared for mass action. Sukarno, lacking the patience for this long game, became the chairman of the rival Partindo (Indonesian Party).

Hatta and Sjahrir had a more restrained style than Sukarno, but their ideas were more radical. Sukarno was primarily anti-colonial, whereas they were also anti-capitalist. For them, the fight against European rule also had to be a fight for social and economic liberation. Even so, Sjahrir acknowledged Sukarno's crucial role: 'At the moment, he remains a dominant political factor. He belongs to the revolutionary camp, despite his opportunism.'[106] But soon afterwards, something happened that would change their lives fundamentally.

On 2 January 1933, the armoured vessel *De Zeven Provinciën* left the port of Surabaya. At a length of one hundred metres, it was the navy's most heavily armed ship and one of the largest in the Dutch East Indies. The economic crisis had forced the Dutch military to cut spending drastically. The Dutch forces in the colony had been reduced from 37,000 to 31,000 men, and pay was about to be lowered for the third time, for a total cut of seventeen per cent.[107] When the sailors began to grumble, European men were granted a smaller reduction, but not the Indonesians. On 4 February, rioting broke out on the naval base in Surabaya, and nearly 500 people were arrested, one-fifth of the native naval personnel. *De Zeven Provinciën* was then anchored northwest of Sumatra, and the crew heard the news on the radio. In solidarity with their fellow sailors, they seized control of the ship when the commander was on shore. A few Europeans joined them – mostly seamen and engineers. The officers still on board were confined to the stern, the anchor was lifted, and the return voyage to Surabaya began. Not a drop of blood was shed.

'Mutiny!' exclaimed the headlines in the colonial press. To the Dutch colonials, it was the last straw. If you can't even trust the navy . . . Governor-General Bonifacius Cornelis de Jonge, a ruthless hard-liner who had taken office in September 1931, wanted to make short work of what he saw as his predecessor's craven half-measures. He received the full support of Prime Minister Colijn, who described the nationalist agitators as 'flies spoiling the chemist's ointment'.[108] A reprise of the communist revolt had to be averted at any price; Henk Sneevliet was already shouting, 'Long live the Dutch Potemkin!'[109]

De Jonge ordered the mutineers to surrender, but they telegraphed a response: '*De Zeven Provinciën* temporarily in the hands of the crew, everything proceeding as usual, on our way to Surabaya, no violent intentions, but protesting unfair pay cut and imprisonment of navy men in Surabaya.' For clarity's sake, they added: 'Absolutely no communist tendencies.'[110] It was obviously a labour action, as opposed to a political rebellion. Every morning, they raised the Dutch tricolour, all the officers on board were still served at the table and the portrait of Queen Wilhelmina remained undamaged. But none of that mattered. De Jonge brought out the big guns: one cruiser, two destroyers, two submarines, five seaplanes and three bombers. He ordered the aircraft to drop a warning bomb in front of the bow, but it hit the ship from a height of 1,200 metres, killing nineteen people, seriously injuring eleven and causing minor injuries to seven others.[111] Four more men later died of their injuries.

This fiasco did not inspire any trace of remorse. The newspapers outdid each other in indignation: 'unsavoury elements' had to be stopped from 'poisoning the souls of the masses'.[112] 'Keep your mouth shut, do your job and don't make trouble.'[113] The febrile tone in the press reached new heights of anxiety. The screeching no doubt helped to sell advertising, but reasonable social debate did not stand a chance. And the authorities did nothing about it. While native newspapers faced frequent restriction of their freedom, colonial newspapers could spew their gall with impunity.[114] One of them, *De Malanger*, wrote: 'If Italians need a Mussolini and Germans a Hitler, what our nation needs is a . . . Colijn!'[115]

Public opinion among the European population became even more uncompromising; no longer was there any hint of understanding of the Indonesians' grievances. One hundred and sixty-four mutineers received prison sentences of eighteen years, a total of 715 years.[116] The 500 navy men arrested from the Surabaya base were discharged, and their prison terms were increased.[117] Meanwhile, Governor-General De Jonge was on the hunt for all signs of unrest. In August 1933, he had Sukarno arrested and expelled to Flores without any form of trial. A year later, he sent Hatta and Sjahrir to Boven Digul; after a year there, they were transferred to Banda Neira, the little nutmeg island whose people had been wiped out by Coen's genocide in 1621. Their political organisations were completely forbidden to assemble.

Nationalism, Indonesia's third major movement, was dead and buried. And that wasn't all. In just a few years, De Jonge turned the Dutch East Indies into a police state, eliminating the final scraps of freedom.[118] Political parties were largely banned, associations that even began to dream of independence were shut down and teachers with nationalist sympathies were barred from the classroom. Newspapers, the post, telephone calls and telegraphy were all subject to sweeping censorship. Budgets were cut across the board, even for the army and navy, but the political intelligence services were given plenty of extra funding to shadow people and raid newsrooms. Indonesia went quiet.

Political Islam, communism and nationalism had all proved incapable of bringing down the colonial system. Sarekat Islam had the masses but lacked a clear plan. The PKI had a clear plan but hadn't yet reached critical mass. The nationalists could have had both but weren't given the chance. The troublemakers on Deck 2 had been exiled before they could mobilise Deck 3. The three movements seemed to have accomplished little. The People's Council had been established and now had an Indonesian majority, but the true centre of power was still Deck 1, where the colonial regime and the business sector were entwined in an intimate embrace.[119] And that's how it would stay, if it were up to Governor-General De Jonge. 'We Dutch have been here for 300 years,' he said. 'We will stay here for 300 more. After that, we can talk.'[120]

Travellers in the colony in those days saw taciturn peasants toiling away in the rice fields under the scorching sun. When the rice was high, you could see a homemade wicker hat sticking out here and there, like a circumflex in a French book from which all the letters have disappeared. A blank page, devoid of language. Silence may have been, in the words of the nationalist Singgih, 'the most dangerous form of anger in the East'.[121]

Chapter 5

Silence
The final years of the colonial regime, 1934–1941

'A day that will go down as one of the most glorious in Java's history.' The reporter at *De Indische Courant* piled on the superlatives: 'historic day', 'grand *selamatan* [festival]', 'lavish celebration'. But why such exuberance in an article about a deeply tragic event? A year after the loss of the *Van der Wijck*, a commemoration service took place in the northern Javanese fishing village of Brondong. Fifty-eight people had died in the accident, almost a quarter of those on board; it was the largest shipwreck in the history of the Dutch East Indies. But the death count would have been higher still if local fishermen had not gone out in the middle of the night. Kasilibin saved fifty-three people from drowning, Modwie thirty-two, Troenredjo twenty-two, Sratit twenty-one, Mardjiki seventeen and so on. They brought 140 people from the *Van der Wijck* ashore in their simple prahus, more than all the official lifeboats and seaplanes put together. Their selfless work was praised to the skies by the colony's Europeans: they were heroes, living proof that the bonds of friendship between the Dutch and the natives had been restored. Numerous Dutch papers and organisations collected money for the commemoration ceremony, raising thou-sands of guilders. It was to be a great tribute; a new lighthouse was even planned for the fishing village.

A procession of luxury cars wound its way to the humble village. Ceremonial gates had been erected over the road. The gamelan played and the fireworks banged. Six fishermen were to receive certificates of merit and new prahus from the governor of East Java; they 'were all squatting together, wearing fishing hats in red, white and blue'. I can picture no more depressing scene of colonial paternalism than these fishermen decked out in the colours of the Dutch flag. Or, come to think of it, I can. A few dozen other rescuers were given a little money 'as a reward for their altruistic and philanthropic labours'. When the governor asked one of them what he would use those few guilders for, an awkward silence fell. 'For food, sir,' the man said hesitantly.[1] In those days, people in rural areas spent no less than sixty per cent of their household budget on food.[2] The governor's wife hurried over to the building site for the lighthouse and laid the first stone. Afterwards, the fishermen had to give three cheers for their kind benefactors: 'Hurrah, hurrah, hurrah.' That lighthouse is still standing.[3]

And while Deck 3 was slaving away to make ends meet, Deck 1 was living it up on the archipelago's thirty-two golf courses. That was more than in the mother country; the game was extraordinarily popular among the colony's tiny European elite. New Guinea had what was probably the world's most remote course. If you accidentally sent your ball flying off into the primeval forest, you simply ordered your Papuan caddies to fetch it for you. At the golf club in Palembang, players had to shout *'Air!'*, the Indonesian word for water, if a ball landed in a pond. Local boys would dive naked into the water, and the lucky finder would receive a ha'penny.[4] Hurrah, hurrah, hurrah.

The final years of the Dutch regime were a peculiar time. In the nineteenth century, exploitation had been the norm; in the early twentieth, it had been diluted with a measure of emancipation. But after the crises of the 1920s, the promises of the Ethical Policy went unfulfilled. The ladders to higher decks became narrower and rustier and were sometimes removed altogether. The only recognised way of maintaining law and order was repression – the elite no longer extended a hand to the lower decks, but a clenched fist.[5] This seemed to work. Since 1933, there had been no more mass meetings, or strikes, or uprisings. The colonial steamship could puff onward in peace. But this silence was misleading, because it was in this period that the segregation of the Dutch from Indonesian life in the colony was completed. It was as if the entrance to the European deck from below had been closed off with a steel plate. At the same time, the native population began to form ties with a new group in the colony:

Japanese merchants. Officially, they belonged on Deck 1, but in practice they were much less haughty than the Europeans. To many children born after 1920 – the generation I was able to interview, the generation responsible for the Revolusi – these newcomers embodied an intriguing alternative form of superiority.

Meanwhile, people were having more and more children. In the 1930s, annual population growth was 1.5 per cent. That may not sound impressive, but it was dizzying; every year, at least 600,000 people were added to the lower decks. The child mortality rate was low. Of the sixty million people in the archipelago in 1930, some twenty-four million were under the age of seventeen. Where we have exact figures, we see that a full fifty-three per cent of the population was under twenty, and sixty-one per cent was under twenty-five.[6] Two-thirds of the population lived in Java and Madura – Java was in fact the world's second most densely populated region, trailing only the Nile delta – but less than ten per cent lived in cities.[7] Only six cities had more than 100,000 inhabitants: Batavia, Surabaya, Yogyakarta, Semarang, Bandung and Surakarta. Even Batavia had a population of around 500,000, smaller than Amsterdam's 750,000 and Tokyo's 5 million. In short, the silent 1930s witnessed the arrival of a new and different generation: young, rural, colossal and almost entirely cut off from the colony's Dutch elite – unless there was a golf ball to dive for.

'Oh, we often went swimming in Medan,' said Marianne Constance. 'A driver would always take us there.' 'Yes,' Brigitte Melissande confirmed, 'the swimming pool had a deep end and a shallow end. It wasn't mixed. All the children we spoke to were Dutch.' The three of us were sitting in a cafeteria at the Dutch beach resort of Kijkduin, part of The Hague. The two women had both been born in Sumatra around 1930. 'There were still tigers back then,' Marianne said. 'My father was a planter and a tobacco farmer; my mother played tennis and drank tea.' After the pancakes, out came the photo albums. A little dog named Flappie. A chair festooned with streamers for a birthday boy or girl. A doll's house with tiny furniture. The small black-and-white photos were captioned in an elegant hand: 'Behind the bungalow.' 'At the Grand Hotel.' 'Swimming pool.' I didn't see a single Indonesian in any of the photos. Yet Marianne said, 'We had a cook, a girl, a gardener and a water carrier.' And Brigitte added, 'In Sumatra, a servant was just called "boy". "Boy, *datang ke sini*." Come over here! You can't say that any more.'[8] I flipped the pages. Ah, there was one after all. In a photo taken at the magnificent Lake Toba, I saw an Indonesian holding the reins of a horse; on the animal's back, a Dutch toddler was gurgling. The man gazed into the camera with a solemn, impassive expression.

In the 1930s, the European upper crust had its own districts of large detached houses, swimming pools, tennis clubs and golf courses. The houses had verandas and gardens, electric fans, refrigerators and gramophones and were staffed with servants. In the cities, wealthy Europeans went out to the cinema or the club, fashionable forms of recreation from which ordinary Indonesians were excluded, except as waiters. The men wore white suits and smoked white cigarettes; the ladies were constantly paying visits to each other. They had affairs. They experienced moments of tedium, jealousy and lethargy, but also of pride, success and pleasure. On weekends, they left the stifling port cities for 'a breath of fresh air' at the cosmopolitan resorts in the hilly interior, such as Buitenzorg, Malang and Berastagi. But even there, the Europeans lived in a bubble, almost completely separated from the locals; after tucking into an extravagant rijsttafel on Sunday, they would play bridge or go to the horse races. It was a self-contained world, hemmed in by its own narrow-mindedness and wilfully blind to the native society all around it. They lived as if they were 'in Hilversum during a heat wave', as one of them put it.[9]

Leafing through *Populair Maleis* (Popular Malay), a language self-study book from that time, you get the impression that the most important verb form was the imperative. 'Boy, go to the shop.' 'Cook, fetch warm water.' 'Gardener, sweep the garden!' 'Girl, Madam is asking for tea.' 'Boy, please give me ice water.' 'Gardener, wash the car!' 'Driver, don't stop here!' 'Take away that dirty laundry.' 'Turn this flowerpot around for me.' 'Be careful with that silver.' But there were also indicative sentences: 'Master wants his dinner.' 'The dog and cat have not been fed yet.' 'You are a stupid creature.'[10]

Conversely, many Dutch words that found their way into Indonesian are domestic in nature, like *apel* (apple), *koki* (cook) and *sopir* (chauffeur or driver), or bureaucratic, like *pos* (post) and *amplop* (envelope). The Dutch administrative and educational system also influenced the form of Latinate terms in Indonesian. This explains the distinctive *si* ending of Indonesian terms like Proklamasi and Revolusi; the Dutch equivalents, *proclamatie* and *revolutie*, are pronounced virtually the same way.

The red carpet was rolled out for you even before you arrived in the colony. 'How astonishing it was, that first sea voyage to the Indies!' wrote Hetty Wertheim-Gijse Weenink, who departed in 1931. 'Suddenly we were uprooted from our ordinary Dutch lives and planted in a world of luxury. Excessive meals, extravagant parties and ever-present slaves, whose subservience was almost suffocating. Superiority was simply forced on you. If you tried to carry your own suitcase, everyone made it very clear that you must never do such a thing, that it would damage "our" prestige, that it would seem just as strange to the natives.' She observed that every colonial official, from the highest rank to the lowest, was permitted to travel first class. This form of equality pleased her at first, until she realised that it served only 'to accentuate the unity and loftiness of that community'. Her sardonic conclusion was that 'class barriers were dwarfed into insignificance by the sky-high walls between the races'.[11]

The author Bep Vuyk also vividly described her first voyage to the Indies: 'The modest man who boarded in Genoa is many degrees more important by the time he disembarks in Priok. It is an oxidation process that no one can escape. [. . .] For 300 years, each newcomer has, upon arrival in the Indies, automatically become a chieftain, a leader, a very important person. The moment he leaves Europe, he becomes a European.' And she added: 'The humbler his background, and the poorer his education, the quicker the process.'[12] Those who have never had power get used to it fast.

It was strange to Indonesians, that invisible but powerful layer above them. I saw Mulyono Darsono sitting cross-legged in front of his traditional dwelling in Kotagede, Yogyakarta's old town. Dozens of young cats were roaming his enclosed back garden. He had been a silversmith – what else? For centuries, Kotagede has been the centre of the silver industry; even now, you hear the soft tap of metal on metal from the traditional workshops. His business had an excellent reputation. 'We made silver for Queen Wilhelmina – a tea service and a coffee service, oh yes.' So if he had received such prestigious orders, he must have been in close contact with the colonisers, I said. He had just told me his wife was in charge of sales. He shook his head. 'No, I only *saw* the Dutch – at the police station, at the entrance to the market, or in their restaurants. I didn't speak to them.'[13] He casually stroked one of the kittens.

While in exile on Banda Neira, Sjahrir tried to keep up with political developments through the newspapers that reached him from time to time. He was less than enthusiastic about those 'rags' and their 'stupidities': 'I would rather read a month-old *NRC* [a leading Dutch newspaper from Rotterdam] than any newspaper from Java,' he wrote to Maria Duchâteau, who by this time was his wife.[14] 'The European press here is openly fascist. The average newspaper reader in Indonesia has an almost pathological hatred of anything "Red" and regards the fascists as the saviours of the world.'[15] This was no exaggeration. In 1933, the major Indies newspapers had reported on events in Germany with enthusiasm.[16] *De Java-Bode, Het Nieuws van den Dag voor Nederlandsch-Indië*, the *Algemeen Indisch Dagblad* and *De Locomotief* even fully supported the formation of a Nazi party in the archipelago. The colony's fascist movement was every bit as reactionary, nationalist, ultra-colonialist and openly fascist as in the Netherlands, but not as closely tied to German Nazism and antisemitism. It saw Japan not as an ally, but as an opponent. In just a few months, the organisation swelled to more than 20,000 members, both European and Eurasian.[17] Unlike in the Netherlands, public employees were allowed to join. Other reactionary organisations included the Vaderlandsche Club (Fatherland Club), the Nederlandsche Indische Fascisten Organisatie (Dutch East Indies Fascist Organisation), the smaller Nederlandsch-Indisch Volksfascisme Zwart Front (Dutch East Indies Popular Fascism Black Front) and the short-lived Ario-Indiërs Rassen Unie (Aryan-Indies Race Union).[18] 'Our new doctor's wife', Sjahrir wrote, 'greets her acquaintances with the fascist salute: "*Heil Hitler.*" She thinks it's fun and modern and understands no more about it.'[19]

In 1935, Anton Mussert, the leader of the Dutch Nazi party NSB, spent a month touring the Indies. This Mussolini of the Low Countries was the first and only Dutch party chairman ever to visit the colony. He gave speeches in packed theatres, oversaw parades of flag-waving members in black uniforms and saw many hundreds of colonists, both men and women, greet him with outstretched right arms. Not once but twice, he was the official guest of Governor-General De Jonge, a fact that caused greater commotion in the Netherlands than in the archipelago. The colonial Nazi party kept growing, and for years it sent tens of thousands of guilders to its Dutch mother party annually.[20] It had three times as many members as its counterpart in the Netherlands, drawn from the colonial population with Dutch nationality.[21] Sjahrir tried to understand. 'The appearance of success in Germany and Italy must encourage other territories ruled in a dictatorial manner, first among which are the colonial territories. It comes down to the belief that intimidation can create a positive, loyal mentality.'[22]

But was that true? It frustrated Sjahrir no end that the colonial administration wouldn't go to the trouble of looking beyond the nationalists' fury, which after all 'could be recognised as nothing more than a manifest sense of inferiority and [. . .] powerlessness'.[23] Didn't the authorities realise that they were achieving the exact opposite of what they intended? That after crushing the unrest, sealing off Deck 1 might not be the ideal long-term solution? 'To the administration, it looks like such an easy way of governing: sending all those difficult types to Digul and thus intimidating the population. But if they had a little more sense, they would understand that this is *too* simple and easy . . . Over time it will become ever clearer that the conditions for revolution here are being created by the regime itself, with its politically aggressive approach, which immerses deeper layers of the population in political consciousness.'[24]

He hoped the colonial regime would one day wake up to the fact 'that it has often been the one to destroy potential forces for true cooperation'.[25] In 1936 Soetardjo Kartohadikusumo, the very moderate president of the public employees' union, submitted a petition to the People's Council with a modest proposal for a conference that would, in a peaceful, reasonable fashion, contemplate gradual reform in the direction of greater autonomy, over the course of many years and always within the framework of the Dutch empire. There was no hurry, and radicalism was to be avoided. The idea was a kind of commonwealth like the one recently declared between the United States and the Philippines. The petition enjoyed very broad support among Indonesians, but the official response from The Hague took two years to arrive, and when it did, it could be summed up in a syllable: no.[26]

As the gap separating them from the Dutch became too wide to bridge, the Indonesians grew closer to another group, one that had never before had a substantial presence in the colony: the Japanese. In the 1930s, their numbers there had greatly increased. Since 1899, they had enjoyed the same legal status as the European population, but it was the weak yen that finally brought large groups of Japanese migrants to the archipelago. They ran shops with products that had until recently been unaffordable; there were even Japanese photographers. They were more welcoming to Indonesians than the Dutch, not like strict fathers but like big brothers to their customers.

'All of a sudden there were Japanese shops all over the place,' said Cisca Pattipilohy, the woman who was not entirely accepted even at the European-style secondary school, the HBS. Her apartment in Amsterdam was filled with books, which had dozens of bookmarks and sticky notes protruding from them. 'The Japanese sold pencils and office supplies. We preferred their shops. They were cheaper – friendlier, too.' She had grown up with Shakespeare and Beethoven and had a little library of her own by the age of sixteen. 'In Batavia, my cousin and I rode our bikes to Visser, a book shop, but they wouldn't serve dark-skinned natives. In the Japanese shops, on the other hand, they were very pleasant. That was quite exceptional.'[27]

Other witnesses also spoke with affection of those Japanese traders. Iskandar Hadisaputra even went to work for one of them. 'There were only three Japanese-run businesses in Salatiga at that time.' He leaned back sleepily in his armchair in a Jakarta retirement home. 'Puji had an ice cream factory. Heiso sold cars. And Ashimoto ran a shop, selling toys, school supplies and paper goods. I worked for him as an assistant. I was fifteen or sixteen years old. It was my first job.' Iskandar grew up with his uncle, a KNIL soldier who couldn't have children. His Japanese boss offered a warm domestic atmosphere that was new to him. 'Ashimoto spoke Indonesian and taught me some Japanese. He was around twenty-five, I guess. He and his Japanese wife rented a place not too far from where I lived. Since my uncle had to travel for the KNIL, Ashimoto let me stay in the back of his shop.'[28] To be so trusted by a foreigner was a new experience. In European households, children often emotionally bonded with the nursemaid, but young Indonesian men rarely received such affection.

Major-General Sukotjo Tjokroatmodjo, the man who was embarrassed at school because he still ate with his hands, discovered a more relaxed variety of intercultural encounter. 'We went to Banyuwangi on the Bali Strait to swim. There was a calm bay there. Sometimes on Sundays we saw a Japanese man who ran a grocery. We would go swimming with him. He even let me jump on his back in the water. He took a lot of pictures of the coast.'[29] Lying on the back of a lighter-skinned man, being allowed to put your arms around his shoulders, seeing his wet black hair glisten, getting dunked, coughing and laughing as you resurfaced – it all felt very new.

From exile on Banda Neira, Sjahrir saw more and more Japanese freighters, fishing boats and schooners passing by. He heard about the many new contacts. 'As far as I can tell, our country's entire Muslim population is now pro-Japanese,' he wrote to his wife. 'They admire Japan, they adore Japan.' The reason seemed clear to him. 'It's the very people who suffer most from a sense of inferiority who are so taken with the Japanese.' And he knew 'there was a purpose and a plan' in 'this winning of sympathy from Asian peoples'.[30]

It is certainly true that those friendly, informal contacts were accompanied by a major charm offensive co-ordinated from Tokyo. No other country in the region had undergone such a dramatic transformation as Japan. Its 'splendid isolation' had come to an end in 1853, when Matthew Perry, a commodore in the US Navy, muscled his way into the country's ports with the implied threat of warfare. Japan had no way of standing up to this gunboat diplomacy. Its feudal system had become an anachronism, colourful and folkloric but ill-suited to the nineteenth century. In 1868, Japan embarked on the Meiji Restoration, perhaps the most stunning leap of modernisation that any country has ever pulled off. Japan was ready to do whatever it took to become a modern nation-state. Archaic shoguns made way for a revitalised empire. The samurai were replaced with an army of 10,000 conscripts. The feudal domains became administrative prefectures, just as they had in Napoleonic France. The capital was moved from Kyoto, the imperial city of temples in the interior, to Tokyo, the commercial hub with a seaport. What had been a country of poor farmers soon became an industrial nation, with railways, factories, telegraph lines and steamboats. The cities were furnished with banks, cinemas and railway stations. Alongside kimonos, prints and lanterns, you could see more and more crinolines, photographs and gas lights.

Japan was bursting with self-confidence. It no longer shrank from foreign countries, but went out to meet them, full of ambition. In 1875, its forces captured several neighbouring islands. In 1895, it prevailed in a conflict with China over Korea. In 1905, it defeated Russia in the Battle of Sakhalin, winning the Russo-Japanese War; for the first time, a small, non-Western country had bested a great European army. In 1910, it annexed Korea. In 1914, it sided with the Allies. In 1918, it was a founding member of the League of Nations. And then the great moment arrived: at the Versailles peace conference, Japan advocated racial equality. More than any other nation in the world, it had proved that a non-Western country could become 'modern' on its own initiative, and in those days, 'modern' meant 'Western'. Its economy matched that of France; its navy was modelled after the British navy, its army after the Prussian army, and its banking system on the American banking system. But its request for racial equality to be enshrined in the Treaty of Versailles was laughed off by the Western powers. 'I would rather walk into the Seine,' said the Australian prime minister, William Hughes, 'or the Folies Bergères . . . with my clothes off.' The French prime minister, Georges Clemenceau, said with a sigh: 'To think that there are blonde women in the world; and we stay closed up here with these Japanese, who are so ugly.'[31] England and America were no more receptive to this demand; the League of Nations was about the equality of nations, not races, they insisted. When a general vote revealed a majority in favour of Japan's proposal, US President Woodrow Wilson overturned the newly adopted amendment single-handedly; too much opposition, he claimed.

It was a historic mistake. One of the Japanese negotiators, Prince Konoe, the scion of a long aristocratic line, harboured a serious grudge against the West for the rest of his life. In the 1930s he became prime minister. It is well known that Germany was humiliated at Versailles, but generally forgotten that even Japan, one of the Allies, was so crudely rebuffed. The country was apparently good enough to make the fifth-largest contribution to the League, but not to be treated as an equal. Humiliation is the quickest route to violence. That experience was one reason for Japan's rapid militarisation in the 1930s. Anti-Western, right-wing nationalist officers who sympathised with fascism acquired great power. In 1931, Japan occupied Manchuria; in 1933, it left the League of Nations; and in 1937, it invaded China again. As many as a quarter of a million people may have died in the Nanjing Massacre, and 20,000 to 80,000 women were raped.[32] Japan had transformed from a timid mouse to Asia's most aggressive political actor. There was no love lost between it and the Western powers in the region: the United States, Great Britain, France and the Netherlands. Its motto was 'Asia for the Asians'.

Understandable processes, appalling results. Sjahrir followed the news with a heavy heart. Japan, like Spain, Italy and Germany, had been taken over by people ruled by their hot tempers, he wrote, who would 'soon enough try to kill each other off again'.[33] It is almost unbelievable that a young man, still no more than twenty-five years old, who was suffering from severe attacks of malaria while in exile with no prospect of reprieve and limited means of communication, could analyse the period in which he lived with such insight, all the while keeping his moral compass intact. What he wrote in July 1936 is nothing short of astounding: 'The news of the civil war in Spain took me by complete surprise [. . .] I consider it by far the most important development in Europe, including all the questions of the League of Nations and German armament. In Spain, a new series of events has now begun, which already extends to France and Belgium and will spread throughout Europe. If the democratic forces in Spain can stand their ground, then the rest of Europe and the Netherlands will not remain immune to this wave of rejuvenated democracy; but if, on the contrary, the reactionaries win in Spain, then the triumph of fascism around the world will proceed more swiftly, and the democracies in France, Belgium and the Netherlands will stand on the brink of defeat. And then what awaits us, at first, will in fact be chaos, then barbarism will make the world an even greater hell, and then a greater destruction of human life than ever will take place. Then it will not be a Decline of the West, but of the whole world, because we here in the East have the huge reserves of cannon fodder, and because we too already have a supra-nationalism: fascism in Japan.'[34]

A visionary analysis, penned by a man whose favourite activities were enjoying his magnificent natural surroundings and playing in the sea with a few local children. 'We sailed, swam, rowed and spent four whole hours in the water,' he wrote a few months later. 'But I was a little stiff the next day, and dark red with sunburn.'[35]

Those sunny days were about to end. After Hitler annexed Austria in March 1938, Sjahrir wrote with clear-eyed pessimism: 'I stopped believing in separate resolutions of the Spanish or Pacific crisis long ago. Both will be resolved only as part of a general world crisis. When it will reach its low point and the global fire will break out is only a question of time. It depends on the fascists – whether Herr Hitler still needs a pause for breath after his latest success or not.' This unprecedented situation led him to make a crucial decision regarding Indonesia's struggle for independence. 'The old style of propaganda', he wrote, could 'no longer be our movement's primary mission, and non-cooperation can be shelved too, temporarily or permanently, there is no way of knowing that now.'[36] This was a historic turnaround. After fifteen years of non-cooperation, he committed himself to cooperation. Fascism was the greatest enemy, and only then colonialism. You have to know your priorities.

★

In Java, the same insight was dawning. After a slightly less despotic governor-general, Alidius Tjarda van Starkenborgh Stachouwer, took office in 1936, there was some opportunity for renewed Indonesian political activity. Political parties that were not too radical were allowed to meet again. And cooperative members of the People's Council were allowed to speak freely. Vigilant Indonesians kept an eye on events in Europe. Now that Germany was grabbing more and more adjoining regions – first the Saarland and the Rhineland and then Austria, the Sudetenland and the rest of Czechoslovakia – the question arose of whether the Netherlands too would fall prey to Hitler's thirst for power. And then what would become of the Dutch East Indies? Would the archipelago be swallowed up by Japan? Or divided between England and America? No one could say, but these disturbing questions did lead to greater solidarity than ever before.

May 1939 saw the birth of the Gabungan Politik Indonesia (Indonesian Political Federation; GAPI), a unified front of practically all the political movements that hadn't been banned or banished: cautious Muslim leaders, hesitant socialists and moderate nationalists. After the failure of Soetardjo's petition in 1938, Indonesians had recalibrated their political ambitions.[37] If a conference with the Netherlands to discuss partial autonomy was an unrealistic goal, might it not be better to strive for a more genuine popular assembly – not merely an advisory body, like the People's Council, but a legislative body with elected members? Wasn't that a feasible plan?

In September 1939, three weeks after the start of World War II, GAPI presented a manifesto calling for a new form of cooperation between the Indonesian and Dutch peoples. Cooperation was vital; the Netherlands had the power, but GAPI represented the masses. That was the only way the colony could respond effectively to whatever crises lay ahead. *Indonesia berparlemen*, the campaign was called: 'A parliament for Indonesia'. It became the greatest political initiative of those final years of colonialism. Student organisations, women's associations, youth movements and trade unions rallied behind the cause. In the autumn of 1939, many GAPI meetings took place, with more than 80,000 participants in total. Perfect silence? Just beneath the surface, Indonesia was very much alive. 'Never in the history of the Native political movement has there been as much unity as there is now,' one anxious Dutch observer noted.[38]

GAPI's standard-bearers – the cooperative nationalist Moham-mad Husni Thamrin, the cooperative socialist Amir Sjarifuddin and the moderate Muslim leader Abikusno Tjokrosujoso – drew inspir-ation from the relative autonomy that the United States had granted the Philippines not long before. But again, the Dutch government turned a deaf ear to their demands. Their own fully-fledged parlia-ment? Maybe, one day, later on, when the colony was ready . . . the usual waffle. The activists could hardly believe that their outstretched hand, their proposal to cooperate, was being waved away even now. What made the arrangement in the Philippines – constructive cooperation with the colonisers, as equals – so unthinkable in Indonesia?

Thamrin and Soetardjo, who both sat on the People's Council, went to the US consulate in Batavia in the utmost secrecy. Soetardjo was known for his earlier petition; Thamrin had become the most influential nationalist since the internment of Sukarno, Hatta and Sjahrir. The plea they made to the Americans was unorthodox, to put it mildly. If the Netherlands was occupied by Nazi Germany, would the United States be willing to take over the Dutch East Indies as a protectorate? Wouldn't that be better than a British or Japanese takeover? They obviously did not relish the prospect of British imperialism or Japanese fascism. The proposal was lunacy, and the American diplomats gave it no serious consideration, but it did show how fed up the Indonesians were with the Dutch attitude.[39] And in retrospect, this diplomatic initiative looks much less eccen-tric; after all, ten years later it was the United States that guided Indonesia to independence with a steady hand.

Sumaun, the man in Semarang who was reading the *Selected Works of Deng Xiao Ping*, had been personally involved in several key events of those pivotal years. In 1939, he was only sixteen years old. 'At my European-style secondary school, or actually from primary school onwards, we had active political lives. From a very early stage, I was part of the anti-fascist youth movement. We read about German and Italian fascism in the Dutch papers, and I knew Japan was fascist too.

Sukarno's book, *Indonesia Menggoegat* ("Indonesia Accuses"), had warned us about the threat from the north.' That book contained Sukarno's speech in his own defence from his trial in Bandung. 'Communists and nationalists were in close communication at the time,' Sumaun continued. 'Fundamentally, we were all anti-colonialists, and we all wanted a parliament. Our meetings took place in secret, of course; we still ran the risk of arrest. But we even spoke to young Dutch people who were anti-fascist. There weren't many of those.[40] Fascism changed everything: communists, socialists, nationalists, leaders of the Islamist movement and even some colonists were all in dialogue with one another. Adversity makes strange bedfellows. Even the Comintern had decided in 1935 that, in the struggle against deep black, dark red was allowed to mix with light red, pink and, yes, even pale off-white.[41]

The drizzle was still coming down as I sat talking to Djajeng Pratomo in Callantsoog. 'Well, we asked for a parliament, but the Netherlands rejected that,' the 102-year-old said with a sigh. In 1936, after he completed European-style secondary school (HBS) in the colony, his father sent him to the Netherlands, where his brother Gondho and his sister Soeprati already lived. After a year of medical studies in Leiden, he switched to economics in Rotterdam. Around Christmas, he saw a beautiful book about Javanese dance in a bookshop's display window. A pleasant coincidence, since he was a talented traditional dancer. What interested him even more was that a cute Dutch girl was examining the book. After they both walked on, he mustered the courage to strike up a conversation with her on a bridge. She told him her name was Stijntje Gret but everyone knew her as Stennie. She was seventeen, came from Schiedam and enjoyed ballet and modern dance. Twenty-three-year-old Pratomo stammered a few more questions. She wanted to study economics or journalism, he learned, but as a young woman, the most she could hope to become was a secretary or stenographer. Pratomo and I linger for a moment over that image: two young people on a bridge together. A few days later, they went dancing in a tent on Rotterdam's central boulevard of Coolsingel to the irresistible music of

Louis Armstrong and Josephine Baker. The war still seemed distant.

'Dear Prat, so awfully happy to hear from you,' Stennie wrote in her first letter. 'Your name isn't really all that difficult, and I think it's just lovely, nicer than all those Dutch names like Jansen, Pietersen, Gerritsen and so on and so forth. But tell me, what should I write on the envelope, Mr Pratomo, or just plain Pratomo?' They both had a lot to learn in their new cross-cultural relationship. Relationships between Dutch women and Indonesian men were still a rarity, although the converse had been happening in the colony for centuries. 'Would your mother and father ever approve of you stepping out with a Dutch girl?' At least she already knew that her own parents were 'not upset, and a good thing too, because I do as I please, no matter what!!'. It was the start of a great, irrepressible romance. 'It's so good to be with you, darling. I love you, your hair, your eyes, the way you dance!' Even the limits of language were put to the test. She was 'stormy with joy' when he managed to 'slap together' another 'divine letter', and she sent him 'a whole gang of kisses' for his unshaven cheeks. Her interest in Prat's country and people grew over time. She was awfully keen to see one of his dance performances but told him he would first have to 'explain a little bit about what the dancing means!'. She gave up hockey so that she could spend all her free time with him. 'I long for you terribly. [. . .] I think soon I'd better start learning a little Malay.' And through language and art, politics trickled into their relationship. 'Oh yes, when you're back you must tell me all about the PI's aims, so that I have a solid understanding of them.' True love, as Antoine de Saint-Exupéry knew, is not just gazing into each other's eyes, but looking outward together in the same direction. 'Have you read the government reports on the budget for the Indies?' she asked in one letter, a year into their relationship. 'Colijn seems intent on dismissing the Soetardjo petition. He says you're contradicting yourselves, although I don't really see what he means. I think he's just trying to wriggle out of it.' Then she closes with: 'I love you so very much and send you the warmest embraces.[42]

In the Netherlands, as in the colony, some people were wondering whether non-cooperation was still the best strategy, and whether fascism was not a greater evil than colonialism. The Communist Party changed its slogan from 'Indonesia independent from Holland now' to 'Indonesia independent from Holland'. And the PI newsletter was no longer called *Indonesia Merdeka* but *Indonesia*. 'Merdeka', freedom, would just have to wait. Pratomo's brother was one of the editors, and Pratomo himself became an active member. 'In Indonesia, we had to save a place at every meeting for the police, who could always drop by to listen in. Here in the Netherlands, we said, "Give us a genuine parliament after the war and we'll help you in your fight against the German Nazis." We weren't even asking for independence, no, just a genuine parliament.[43] But the leading issue at that time was the archipelago's relationship not to the Netherlands but to Japan. 'The Japanese question was a sore point for us. We argued about it at PI meetings. Some regarded Japan as an ally against colonialism, or even as our future liberator! That was a mistake, of course, but we had to watch what we said. Most of us, including me, were radically anti-Japanese. When Japan occupied Manchuria, we knew they were fascists. Setyadjit, from Java, was our leader in those days and set the course. We decided to fight fascism first and colonialism only afterwards.[44]

From his archive, he lent me the anniversary issue of *Indonesia*, published on the student association's thirtieth anniversary. The 'looming threat of fascist domination', I read, could be staved off only by 'a courageous turn in colonial policy', namely 'cooperation between the Indonesian People and its National Movement with the democratic Netherlands on the basis of equality and mutual respect'.[45]

In 1939, Pratomo and the PI went to London to raise funds for Japanese-occupied China. Their troupe performed Javanese dances, even making an appearance on the BBC. He was one of the soloists. 'Isn't it foggy in London? And are the ladies short there?' Stennie asked in a letter from Schiedam. 'Did you have to pay import duties for that spear?' Later in the year, he attended a peace conference in Brussels and went to Paris for the Rassemblement mondial des étudiants pour la paix, la liberté et la culture. At that stage, culture was still a weapon against barbarity. In one of the photographs in the family archive, I saw him as a dancer, in magnificent traditional attire. The same warm eyes, the same full lips. His expression, on the eve of the global conflagration, was dignified, modest and alert. No one had a crystal ball, but anyone could see that historic changes were coming.

Early in the morning of 10 May 1940, Germany invaded the Netherlands. Tanks and troops crossed the border, parachutists were dropped deep inside enemy territory, bridges were captured, aircraft destroyed and airports occupied. Just a few days later, the German columns were muscling their way west through the flat, wet landscape. When Rotterdam, the city where Pratomo was studying, was not surrendered promptly on 14 May, the old centre was bombed. Stennie was an eyewitness; in a quarter of an hour, 24,000 homes, thousands of shops, studios and factories, dozens of schools and hospitals and twenty-one churches were destroyed.[46] It was the first time a city in northwestern Europe had been reduced to rubble. That day, the Dutch government surrendered.

The German victory in the Netherlands surprised no one, but what were the implications for the Dutch East Indies? It was the first time since the British interlude from 1811 to 1816 that the Netherlands had not called the shots in the archipelago. The Dutch queen and government had fled to London a day before the capitulation and were trying to run the empire from there. Parliament had been dissolved, so the Indies budget for 1940, 1941 and 1942 was announced by royal decree in London. There was brief discussion of whether the queen should go to the Indies. This proposal had great advantages from a constitutional perspective: the monarch would be on her own territory. But Queen Wilhelmina remained immovable. In time, the government in London even included an Indonesian member: Soejono. This decision was made at the strong urging of H. J. van Mook, the progressive director of the economic affairs department in the Dutch East Indies administration and the minister of colonies in the wartime government. Soejono was the only colonial subject ever to hold the office of government minister. He was an aristocrat and a member of the People's Council and had worked at the ministry of colonies in The Hague. Wilhelmina appointed him to her team with great reluctance, and Prime Minister Pieter Sjoerds Gerbrandy is said to have mumbled that as far as he was concerned 'all Muslims were fuel for the fires of hell'.[47] In the war years, Soejono insisted again and again on the necessity of far-reaching autonomy for Indonesia, but to almost no avail. He died unexpectedly in 1943, when the Netherlands and Indonesia were still occupied.[48]

'Once the Netherlands was occupied by Germany, we could no longer communicate with the people back home,' Pratomo tells me. 'That led to considerable difficulties.' The 800 Indonesians in the Netherlands – students, nursemaids and sailors – were completely cut off from home.[49] Ships and letters could not cross the ocean. Because Stennie was working as a stenographer for the executive office at Wilton-Fijenoord, one of Rotterdam's largest shipyards, she knew what was going on in the port. 'There were a lot of Indonesian sailors in Rotterdam,' Pratomo said. 'They came from Java and Celebes and didn't speak a word of Dutch. Most of them were illiterate.' The PI decided to champion their cause and offer practical support. The students spoke impeccable Dutch and helped those hundreds of sailors and stokers find food, clothing and shelter in an empty port warehouse. Many of them had warm feelings towards Japan and saw it as a brave, dynamic nation. The PI was determined to keep them from falling for the charms of German fascism or going to Germany to work. 'We assigned people to propaganda duty,' Pratomo says. The war brought Indonesians closer together: the elite students from Deck 2 got to know the lowly nursemaids and rough-hewn stokers on Deck 3. What was frustrating was that students spoke Dutch and the sailors Malay. A participant at one cultural meeting said it was regrettable that 'most Indonesian students still haven't completely mastered our language of unity, Bahasa Indonesia'.[50]

In Pratomo's archive I found a pile of stencils and a typed Indonesian course, published in a low-budget edition in Leiden in 1941. It may seem bizarre that in the middle of the war, a manual for a language spoken tens of thousands of kilometres away had been published in a Dutch university town, but in fact the war was the reason it had happened. Now that fascism was on the advance, linguistic unity among Indonesians was more urgent than ever. Pratomo did not take a lot of notes, but the translation assignments are quite revealing. 'Every association has a board.' 'What was the state of the Indonesian people at the time?' 'The associations' collective campaign is also important.' A very different set of topics from that pre-war Malay phrasebook for colonists. The most striking sentence of all was: 'In time of crisis, their consciousness will mature more swiftly.'[51]

Another thing that made consciousness mature more swiftly was scholarship, and that was Pratomo's department. In September 1940, a few months after the German invasion, he published a brilliant essay in the student magazine *Soeara Roepi* under the title of 'Economic interests of the world powers in Indonesia'. His studies at his Dutch business school had turned him into an economist with a mind like a steel trap, who supported his arguments with the latest figures. He wrote the same way he danced, with grace, precision and apparent effortlessness. 'In no other colonial country except India is there so much foreign investment as in Indonesia. [. . .] Surplus foreign capital finds incredible opportunities for profit here.' Unsurprisingly, the Netherlands was the biggest investor, putting money into plantations, railways and tramways, ports, trading companies, oil and tin. All in all, this accounted for three-quarters of foreign capital. We now know that a full twenty per cent of all Dutch capital was invested in Indonesia.[52] Britain was in second place, owning large shares of petroleum companies such as Royal Dutch Shell and Standard Vacuum Oil Company. The United States also had investments in the oil sector and to a lesser degree in rubber. Although 'the Far East' produced only 3.4 per cent of the world's oil, eighty-two per cent of that came from Indonesia, Pratomo wrote. It was Asia's main oil producer, a fact that had not escaped notice in Tokyo. Japanese industry was running at full steam, but the country had only four per cent of the region's oil reserves. Eventually, the shortage was bound to become pressing. Japan already had a few modest oil concessions in Borneo, but those were not nearly enough. It had 'made many attempts to invest capital in Indonesia', so that it too could benefit from the archipelago's resources, 'as the Netherlands, Britain and

America do', but those attempts had been foiled by 'opposition from those three countries'.[53] In September 1940, in an amateurish student newsletter in Leiden with a small circulation, Pratomo thoroughly explained and predicted the conflict that would be played out with devastating consequences in the years that followed. In that same month, Germany, Italy and Japan concluded the Tripartite Pact.

In the Indies, the news of the German invasion came as a bombshell. Deck 1 was thrown into disarray. Planters, officials, business owners and missionaries were left without news of their friends and family. The mother country had fallen, and no one knew what to do next. Deck 2 responded in a surprising way: not only the traditional ruling aristocracy but even the nationalist leaders joined the colonial regime in ruing the loss of the Netherlands. Consider the case of Tjipto, Dr Tjipto Mangoenkoesoemo, a STOVIA graduate and one of the earliest anti-colonial activists, the co-founder of Budi Utomo and the Indies Party, banished to Europe in 1913 and sent to Banda Neira permanently in 1928 for his supposed involvement in the communist revolt. What did he do, after twelve years in captivity? He openly declared his support for the Dutch government and called on other activists to follow suit – which they did, en masse. How could that be? Yes, they had been muzzled, exiled and put in chains. Yes, they had cursed and deplored the colony. But they didn't wish an invasion like that on their worst enemy.

In spite of everything, many Indonesians had an emotional attachment to the Netherlands, the country that had shaped and influenced them. But Governor-General Tjarda van Starkenborgh Stachouwer ignored their declarations of support completely. It was as if he saw himself as a man in mourning at his beloved mother's deathbed, with no desire to be disturbed by some exotic houseboy's eager condolences.

The mood on Deck 3 was very different. Ordinary rice growers, satay sellers and young people on the streets just shrugged their shoulders at the news from Europe. The weaker their ties to the colonisers, the less they cared. 'I was in my first year at primary school when the Netherlands was occupied by Germany,' Soerachman recalled. He was living in Yogyakarta at the time. 'The teacher told us about it in class. We had to sing songs and pray to God for the Netherlands to rise to its feet again. I didn't know that Wilhelmina had fled to London. No, everything stayed just the same. We still used guilders.'[54]

Nothing stayed the same, of course, but the colonial administration did all it could to keep up the appearance of normality. Behind the calm facade, drastic measures were taken: an immediate state of emergency was declared, public gatherings were banned and individuals who formed a potential threat to the state were arrested. The government interned all 2,800 German residents of Indonesia, as well as 500 prominent members of the NSB, the Dutch Nazi party. The Germans included innocent missionaries, public officials, physicians, scholars, scientists, engineers, planters, merchants, sailors and even a few Jews who had fled Nazi Germany. The German artist Walter Spies, who was in Bali to follow the example of Paul Gauguin in Tahiti and wanted absolutely nothing to do with fascism, also lost his liberty, and later his life.

Nor did the colonial administration intend to let nationalism spread unchecked. Boven Digul remained in operation, Sukarno, Hatta and Sjahrir remained in confinement, and questions in the People's Council about a conference with the Dutch government or a parliament remained unanswered. The usual business of politics was put on hold. The governor-general in Batavia and the government-in-exile in London had a point when they argued that such momentous decisions would have to be debated in the Dutch parliament, which would not be convened until after the war. The nationalists in the People's Council responded with more questions: No conference about the future? No parliament of our own? Then can we at least talk about equality under the law? Indonesians still had a different legal status from Europeans. Couldn't that legally sanctioned racial discrimination be brought to an end? Wasn't it about time for some form of 'Indies citizenship' for all? No, that wouldn't be possible either. Then can't we at least do away with terms like 'Dutch East Indies' and 'native' and replace them with 'Indonesia' and 'Indonesian'? Even that was tricky, apparently. No, there could be no question of changing the name of the colony, but if absolutely necessary, 'native' (*inlands*) could be replaced with 'indigenous' (*inheems*) in official documents, and now and then even with 'Indonesian'. And in truth, that was more or less the biggest concession made by the colonial administration after thirty years of struggle: two adjectives.[55]

On 11 January 1941, Thamrin, the businessman and founder of GAPI, died a few days after being placed under house arrest. In the People's Council, he had become the leading critic of colonialism, and in the US consulate he had called for an American takeover, but in the end he was falsely accused of pro-Japanese activity.[56] His funeral in Batavia drew many tens of thousands of people; it was the first important mass event in years and also the last of the colonial era. Despite the silence imposed on the Indonesian people, the independence movement was alive and kicking. Thousands upon thousands followed Thamrin's bier through the streets and alleyways of Batavia. They grieved, they hoped, they despaired. The powder keg was in place. Now for the match.

Ichizo Kobayashi strode resolutely along the Tanjung Priok waterfront. As the Japanese minister of commerce and industry, he had come to lend weight to his country's demands. Mere days after the German invasion of the Netherlands, Tokyo had placed its order with the authorities in the Dutch East Indies: Would the colony be so good as to supply Japan with one million metric tons of petroleum annually (almost twice as much as the archipelago's total exports at the time) and to grant several very large petroleum concessions? Its shopping list also included 200,000 tons of bauxite, 150,000 tons of nickel ore, 100,000 tons of scrap metal, 100,000 tons of salt, 50,000 tons of manganese ore, 20,000 tons of rubber, 5,000 tons of chrome ore, 4,000 tons of castor seeds, 3,000 tons of tin, 100 tons of molybdenum and 600 tons of cinchona bark.[57] Now the time had come for direct negotiations. In September 1940, Japan raised its opening bid a little, no longer demanding one million but three million tons of oil a year, for a period of five years. Kobayashi's interlocutor was H. J. van Mook, the director of the colony's economic affairs department, who had been promoted to envoy extraordinary and minister plenipotentiary. Van Mook had been born into a family of Freemasons in Java. In the 1930s, he had opposed the unhealthy rigidity of colonial society, partly in concert with the 'Stuw group', progressive activists associated with the journal *De Stuw*. No one else in the European community took the grievances of the Indonesian population as seriously as he did. Van Mook combined a humanistic outlook with an enormous appetite for work and an extremely obstinate nature. He was not easily impressed, not even by a Japanese minister in wartime who had come to pick up mountains of raw materials. He heard Kobayashi out and then sent him on to Royal Dutch Shell and Standard Vacuum, the two main oil-producing companies.

In December 1940, a new Japanese delegation arrived, this one led by Kenkichi Yoshizawa, the former foreign minister. He presented demands that were still more extreme, namely for the Dutch East Indies not only to supply oil, but also to become an integral part of the Greater East Asia Co-Prosperity Sphere, in which Japanese goods and people would circulate freely. Van Mook realised this was tantamount to a takeover, but he managed to draw out the negotiations for more than five months. It was June 1941 by the time he gave his answer: unfortunately, the Netherlands could not grant Japan's requests, but of course Tokyo was free to talk to the private oil companies and other concession holders again. Talk about nerve! Tjarda van Starkenborgh feared that Japan would declare war on the Netherlands, but that didn't happen. Van Mook had brushed off the Japanese demands poker-faced, and then he had done it again. He was the first Dutch national to make the cover of *Time* magazine: 'Thanks to him, the Dutch have had time to get ready,' read the caption.[58]

Although the leading actors from those days are all dead and gone now, I did catch one final glimpse of that great diplomatic achievement. Fred Lanzing was not involved in the oil negotiations with Japan; he was only eight years old. 'But my father was an aide to the governor-general, and he was there.' I spoke to him in his book-crammed apartment in Hobbemakade in Amsterdam. 'My father started out as a KNIL artillery officer, following in his own father's footsteps. After that he was responsible for the commissariat: buying rice, meat, coats et cetera. Our household didn't have a typical military atmosphere. My father was a very cultured man and was offered a position as Van Starkenborgh's aide. That was a great honour. The governor-general had two aides, one officer from the KNIL and one from the navy. My father was in charge of protocol, receptions and dinners. We lived in a wing of the palace. The governor spent a lot of time in Bogor, which had a cooler climate than Batavia. His predecessor De Jonge was a cur of a man; Van Starkenborgh was nicknamed Si Pepsodent, because of his flawless teeth. He often invited members of the Indonesian nobility to his home, so my mother met many high-status Indonesian women. The threat of war led Van Starkenborgh to move to Batavia to be closer to the colonial departments. That's why my father was present at the negotiations.' Fred showed me a photo from 1941. His father, in a spotless white uniform, was escorting two Japanese negotiators up the palace steps. He also showed me a beautiful silver box that the chief negotiator, Yoshizawa, had presented to his mother shortly before the talks broke down. The lid was decorated with some melancholy bamboo stalks. 'My mother gave that box to a highly placed Indonesian woman for safekeeping when she was interned.'[59]

The people of the occupied Netherlands could hardly believe their eyes when, in the course of 1941, thousands of soft little packets whirled down from the sky. As the roar of the aircraft died away in the distance, they landed in fields, pastures and city squares: round, fragrant little packets with fluttering notes attached. Farmers stared in surprise, children snatched them up with a laugh and mothers closed their eyes and inhaled the fragrance. A blissful smile appeared on their faces: finally, the familiar scent of dark, robust, autumnal tea from Java. Everyone looked up with pride. The many thousands of teabags dropped by the British bombers had tags with the Dutch tricolour and the words, 'The Netherlands will rise again. Greetings from the free Dutch East Indies. Take heart!'[60]

    This heartwarming event fitted perfectly into Deck 1's new, self-imposed mission: helping the mother country. The power relations had suddenly been inverted. The colony was no longer dependent on the Netherlands, but the Netherlands on the colony. Throughout the archipelago, funds were raised for the Red Cross, aluminium was saved for British Spitfires, and socks were knitted for the boys back home. There was a cheerful atmosphere of determination and esprit de corps, with Spitfire parties, Spitfire auctions and even Spitfire board games. One such aeroplane cost £5,000; the campaigns in the Indies raised enough to pay for one hundred. There was even enough left over for a few dozen bombers. The RAF aircraft were all named after places in Indonesia: 'Bandoeng', 'Ceram', 'Batavia', 'Merapi', 'Soebang', etc. Strange to think that the British air force was flying over continental Europe in those aeroplanes with names evoking the Indies.[61]

The discussion of how to defend the Indies unleashed even more patriotic zeal. By this time, it was clear that Japan had its eye on the archipelago. During the global economic crisis, the KNIL had been reduced to a military police force of 31,000. The first step was to get that number back up to 40,000. The navy began to operate jointly with the British – which was permissible now that Dutch neutrality had been violated. And necessary too, because with only three cruisers, seven torpedo-boat destroyers, fifteen submarines, a few seaplanes, supply ships and a few minelayers, they could never defend such a vast maritime realm on their own.[62]

The colonial administration promptly placed large orders with British and, above all, American companies: a few hundred fighter and transport aircraft, more than 1,000 tanks and light armoured vehicles, 100,000 rifles and 3 million cartridges.[63] The whole Dutch community felt the same devotion to the cause. A full 32,000 men signed up for the Volunteer Drill Corps (Vrijwillige Oefencorpsen; VOC); most were former army personnel. Women joined the Commission for the Organisation of Women's Labour in Time of Mobilisation (Commissie tot Organisatie van Vrouwenarbeid in Mobilisatietijd; COVIM) and the Women's Automotive Corps (Vrouwen Automobiel Corps; VAC) and prepared to provide transport in evacuations and care for the wounded. Other new services included the City Guard (Stadswachten) and the Home Guard (Landwachten), the Air Raid Civil Defence Service (Luchtbeschermingsdienst; LBD) and the Disposal and Destruction Corps (Afvoer- en Vernielingscorpsen; AVC). In the case of withdrawal from the colony, these last corps were responsible for blowing up bridges, making roads unusable and, most importantly, setting the crucial petroleum installations in Borneo and Sumatra on fire. A modest local arms industry even popped up, with workshops in Java producing naval mines and ammunition.[64] Off the coasts, the navy laid minefields.

During my fieldwork, I had the chance to speak to three veterans who witnessed this lightning militarisation from close by. All three were Indos born in the colony. As a child, Hans Dornseiffer liked to be alone. He climbed trees to play with frogs and chameleons. 'One day everyone started collecting pots, pans and kettles,' he told me one afternoon in The Hague. 'All that aluminium was for the Spitfires.' At the age of eighteen, he received the letter summoning him for compulsory military service. 'I had to report to Bandung right away for the medical exam. I hadn't graduated from secondary school (HBS) yet; I'd had to repeat the third year. I'd failed my language subjects because I was dyslexic. But German had been cancelled because of the war. Boy, was I happy about that!' No more German case endings, but he did have to join the military. In Bandung, he was surprised by the nonchalance he encountered. It was early December 1941, one week before Pearl Harbor. 'The doctor looked at our group. "Am I supposed to examine you all? Right, then, you're all approved. If there are any special issues, I'm sure I'll notice." '[65]

Dick Buchel van Steenbergen had completed his compulsory military service in 1939. 'When the war began in the Netherlands, my father said, "You may as well make that your career now. There are no jobs to be had anyway. War is coming." ' That's how it was; the approach of war was less a threat to life and limb than an employment opportunity. Dick was ninety-seven years old when I met him in Waalre, near Eindhoven, and still living independently. 'It was an expression of my father's desperation. He worked at a rice mill. That's how I became a career soldier, like both my grandfathers.' He was rejected for pilot training, but because his hobby was photography, he was assigned to the aerial photography service. When I spoke to him, he still had a collection of antique cameras on display in his living room. 'I was sent to Yogyakarta. People used to belittle the Japanese soldiers: "With those slit-eyes, they can't see a thing. They have inferior weapons. They're weaklings."'[66]

Another young man called up for duty was Felix Jans, the son of a Belgian father and a Javanese mother. I spoke to him in a care facility in Loosduinen, near The Hague. 'I had no plans to join the military, but I received a summons, and so did my brother. If I had to go, I wanted to join the navy, I said. They had a nice uniform! White with a blue collar. Real seamen!' Like Hans and Dick, he could not begin to imagine what horrors awaited him. 'We received six months of training in Surabaya. Lots of sports, lots of marching, lots of hand-to-hand combat.' It wasn't a bad time. 'They kept telling us, "We'll get those Japs!"'[67]

To the natives of the archipelago, this sudden wave of militarisation was bewildering. It was insane enough that they were massacring each other in Europe, but to bring the war to the peaceful rice fields was utterly absurd. Sukotjo, the boy who had gone swimming with a Japanese grocer, was mystified. 'Everything changed at school. Our whole life changed! All of a sudden, I saw my Dutch teachers turn into soldiers. There was a barracks across the street from our house. One day I saw my teacher, Mr De Wit, there in uniform!'[68]

Some young people were swept up in the militaristic fervour. In the Moluccas, for example, where the KNIL had recruited many soldiers since the late nineteenth century, there was a strong sense of affinity for the colonisers.[69] 'I am a child of the KNIL,' Julius Nunumete said with a smile on the island of Ambon. 'My father was in the KNIL, my uncle was in the KNIL, my brother was in the KNIL. I knew that I too would fight for the Netherlands.' The Moluccas were one of the most Christianised parts of the archipelago, strongly influenced by Dutch culture. 'Like many Dutch people, we celebrated St Nicholas's Day on 5 December with St Nicholas and Black Pete. The only difference is that in our case [instead of Pete wearing blackface] it was St Nicholas who wore white face paint.' When the City Guard and Home Guard were formed, he did not hesitate. Half the auxiliary forces were European and half were Indonesian and Chinese, 28,000 troops in all. 'I was eager to answer the call! I wanted to fight for the Netherlands and joined the Home Guard in Ambon. We were issued ordinary rifles, not automatics or semi-automatics.'[70] Many of those rifles were cast-offs from the Italian army, taken by the British in Ethiopia as spoils of war – not the best firearms.[71]

Others were less enthusiastic. The communist Sumaun refused to participate, of course. 'The City Guard had been founded out of fear of Japan. We were anti-fascist, to be sure, but we weren't about to get involved in that.'[72] Cooperation ended where cannon fodder began. The nationalists, likewise, were unwilling to take up arms. Having been ignored for decades, they were expected to spring into action now? When the colonial administration contemplated introducing compulsory military service for native people in 1941, the nationalists demanded political concessions. They felt morally supported by a speech made by Queen Wilhelmina in May on the radio from London, which had held out the prospect of 'the adaptation of the structure of the overseas territories'. And they pointed to the Atlantic Charter issued in August, in which US President Franklin D. Roosevelt and UK Prime Minister Winston Churchill emphasised 'self-government' and 'the right of all peoples to choose the form of government under which they will live'.

It was all to no avail. Compulsory military service for Indonesians was introduced anyway, without the slightest concession. Ever since World War I, the colonial administrators had been loath to arm the masses, and now that they had changed their minds, it was far too late. In the second half of 1941, some 6,000 young men were called up for duty, the first and only group of native recruits in the history of the Dutch East Indies. They would not make much difference. But for the young Sumarsono, there was no way out; despite his communist convictions, he would have to take up arms for the Dutch. He was wearing braces and a cap when I talked to him in his daughter's home in Jakarta. 'We were forced into that army! They called us *milisi*, the people's force. Unpaid troops, that's what we were. I was working for Borsumij, the Borneo-Sumatra trading company, but every Monday and Friday they gave us time off for military training.

We were issued military uniforms. My commander was a Dutch officer, Bakker. The City Guard was supposed to defend cities, but we
were rushed through training to fight Japan as part of the Dutch
military.'[73]

By late 1941, the Dutch East Indies had a total of around 76,000
troops. Not an insignificant number, but were the Dutch really
ready, as *Time* had claimed? Most colonists thought so. Purbo
Suwondo was in an HBS secondary school with children of European and Indo officers. 'They said, "Those Japanese are bowlegged
soldiers with thick glasses. We have nothing to be afraid of. Their
legs are too short to fly a plane." '[74] But even those who did not
indulge in such unadulterated racist fantasies doubted that Japan
could fight on so many fronts, so far from home, with such long
supply lines.[75] Surely it was a logistical impossibility? On the other
hand, many of the colony's own orders of weaponry had not been
delivered on time. Of the seventy tanks ordered in Britain, only
twenty had arrived. Of the 600 tanks expected from the United
States, only seven had been delivered, and those had no guns. Of
the 400 American light armoured vehicles, only twenty-five were
ready in time. The US war economy could not serve all comers.
One hundred thousand rifles? Order cancelled. One hundred and
sixty-two Brewster dive bombers? Never delivered. The same
number of B-25 bombers? Never delivered. Twenty Lockheed
transport aircraft for paratrooper units? Delivered, but . . . without
parachutes. There were also severe shortages of machine guns, field
artillery, mortars, anti-tank guns, anti-aircraft guns and, above all,
experience.[76]

And there was something else too, something hard to capture in
figures. On 29 November 2017, I walked into the room of an old man
in a Catholic retirement home in the Sumatran city of Medan. He
was seated in a wheelchair, having dinner. It was the shortest of all
my interviews. As usual, I started by asking for basic biographical
information. When were you born? '1941.' Where? 'In a Batak village
an hour from Medan.' What is your family name? 'Sembiring.' And
your first name? 'Nippon.' I beg your pardon? The Japanese word for

Japan? 'Yes, my father liked the sound of it.'[77] All right, Nippon. 'And I know someone else from my generation with that name. He lives not far away.'

I was struck dumb for a moment. Nippon. Maybe it just sounded modern, that new name, but what does it say about the mood in a country when humble village farmers name their sons after the supposed enemy? What would it have said about the Dutch attitude to the war if, just a few months before the invasion, farmers in Zeeland or Drenthe had been naming their sons 'Deutschland'?

Chapter 6

The Pincer and the Oil Fields
The Japanese invasion of Southeast Asia,
December 1941–March 1942

Everyone knows the attack on Pearl Harbor was a turning point in the history of World War II, but few realise how much that attack had to do with the Dutch East Indies oil reserves. When Japanese forces set out to destroy a military base in the middle of the Pacific, six time zones to the east, in the early morning on 7 December 1941, they had a powerful motivation: to make sure the Americans would not stand in their way in the south.

For more than fifty years, Japan's economy had relied on imported oil. Since 1937, the country's war with China had only increased this dependence. The endless convoys of military trucks, the huge fleet of battleships and submarines, the hundreds of combat and reconnaissance aircraft, the tanks, machine guns and mortars required diesel, petrol, aviation fuel and lubricant, and that is not to mention the many factories where all those instruments of war were produced. Automobiles weren't the biggest guzzlers; at the time of Pearl Harbor, there were only 210,000 cars in all of Japan, as compared to 32 million in the US.[1] In 1940, Japan needed 48 million barrels of crude oil a year, and more than three-quarters of that came from abroad, half from the United States and one-quarter from the Dutch East Indies.[2] When the oil negotiations with the Dutch colony fell through on 17 June 1941, it was a serious economic setback, especially because Japan hoped to push on from China to Russia. On 2 July, scarcely two weeks later, high-level consultation took place in Tokyo; even Emperor Hirohito was present. The conclusion was that Japan must continue its war on China but, in order to do so, would need to tap into the Dutch East Indies oil reserves. That meant expanding the war, if necessary, even to include the United States and the United Kingdom.[3] Another two weeks later, a peculiar meeting took place in France. Marshal Pétain, the leader of the collaborationist Vichy regime, granted an audience to the Japanese ambassador. The stakes were high. Japan urgently requested to station troops – lots of troops – in the south of the French colony of Indochina, with the kind permission of Pétain's government. A year earlier, Japan had invaded the north of Indochina, the better to attack China from the south. But in 1941, its interest in the south of the French colony signified something quite different: Japan planned to open a new front, and this time its target was the Malay Archipelago.[4]

Although anyone could see that this amounted to a military occupation of Indochina, Pétain didn't dare to protest. After all, Japan was an ally of Nazi Germany. Besides, in return for this concession, Japan pledged that France could keep its colony. Strange . . . wasn't the Japanese war cry 'Asia for the Asians'? But in this case, there was a higher priority: oil for the Japanese. If the French could supply it, their colonialism was not a problem. That also explains why Japan did not hesitate to bring Thailand, the only country in Southeast Asia that had never been colonised, into its sphere of influence. Independence was a beautiful thing, but a clear path for the Japanese advance was essential. In short, Tokyo established a presence on the land mass that jutted out towards the Dutch colony. To conquer an archipelago, you need a shore from which to launch your ships.

On 26 July 1941, the first Japanese soldiers arrived in the south of Indochina. At Cam Ranh Bay, they built their largest naval base in the region. The US was infuriated. The invasion of northern Indochina had led to an American trade embargo on scrap metal and aviation fuel, but this southern initiative was a much greater threat, with the potential to destabilise the entire region. President Franklin D. Roosevelt immediately froze all Japanese assets. A few days later, he announced a new embargo, this time on oil. To avoid war, he had hoped at first to keep a trickle of exports going: 'There was a method in letting oil go to Japan with the hope – and it has worked for two years – of keeping war out of the Southern Pacific for our own good.'[5] But while he was away for consultations with Churchill, assistant

Map 14: The Japanese invasion of Southeast Asia (December 1941–April 1942)

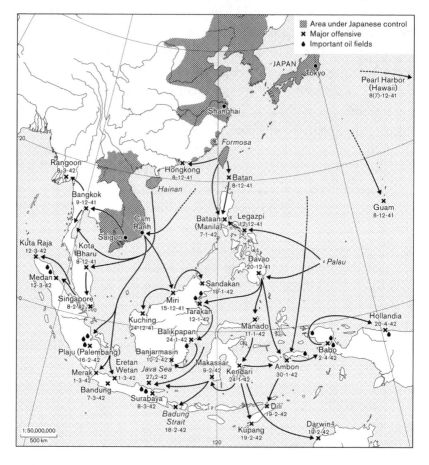

secretary of state Dean Acheson brought all trade with Japan to a halt. When the United Kingdom and the Netherlands followed suit, Roosevelt had no more room to manoeuvre and could not reverse the decision. Japan was cut off not only from its US assets, but also from its US oil supply. Its reserves would last twenty-four months, or eighteen in wartime.[6]

The Netherlands' decision to join the American embargo – and go even further – was understandable but unwise. It not only departed from prior trade agreements with Japan but also left Japan completely deprived of oil. The Dutch government in London apparently felt it was more important to display its resolve to the United States and

Great Britain than to make a realistic appraisal of the threat of war. In essence, the Dutch leaders were modelling their foreign policy after their approach within the colony, strictly punishing any undesired behaviour in the assumption that this would solve the problem. But compared to a few young Javanese and Sumatrans who had become politically conscious, the Japanese empire was a threat of a different order. If the Netherlands had continued to honour its commitments, Japan would certainly not have resorted to war so quickly, and history could have gone very differently.[7]

On 3 December 1941, Roosevelt spoke to the Japanese government about the Indochina question. It was too late. Two days earlier, at an imperial conference in Tokyo, the top secret decision had been made to go to war. On the morning of Sunday 7 December, nearly 400 Japanese aircraft attacked the naval base at Pearl Harbor in Hawaii. The surprise strike went on for two hours. Four US battleships were sunk, and three destroyers and three cruisers were obliterated, along with almost 200 aircraft. More than 2,400 people were killed. The Pacific fleet, the air force and the port infrastructure weren't completely demolished, but the damage was so severe that it would take the US months to recover its strength in the Pacific. And that was exactly as Japan had intended.

What few people know is that one hour before the attack on Pearl Harbor Japanese troops landed on the east coast of the Malay Peninsula, and Japanese planes bombarded Singapore. For Japan to gain access to Dutch East Indies oil, it had to neutralise not only the US but also Britain, the other great power in the region. Singapore was the base of the Royal Navy's fleet in the Far East and just as important to the British as Pearl Harbor was to the Americans. Only by removing both threats could Japan take the Dutch East Indies in a pincer movement. The meticulous plans for the Japanese attack – the result of many hours of war games with scale models – called for a two-part manoeuvre: the conquest of the Philippines to the northeast of Java and the Malay Peninsula to the northwest. These American and British colonies were crucial stepping stones to the Dutch East Indies. The pincer movement looked straightforward on the map but would require complex co-ordination of air, sea and land forces; after

Japanese aircraft attacked strategic targets, the navy would deliver ground troops to take airfields from which fighter planes could venture further south.

And so it began. On 10 December, after three days of combat, Japan invaded the Philippines and sank the British navy's two largest battleships near Singapore. A few days later, it captured Hong Kong and British Borneo, gaining its first, small oil field. Meanwhile, the United States lost Guam and Wake, two bases in the Pacific.

Immediately after Pearl Harbor, the Netherlands declared war on Japan. Again, it showed exceptional belligerence; the US and Great Britain did not follow suit until a few hours later. Governor-General Van Starkenborgh felt that this early declaration of war was good 'for outward prestige', and the government and queen agreed.[8] But how much was that 'prestige' worth, when the Netherlands had no more than a hastily patched-together army? Even Japan was taken aback. The Dutch diplomat who presented the declaration of war in Tokyo had the document returned to him – surely an event without precedent in diplomatic history. Did the Netherlands know what it was saying? Japanese officials asked. And did it understand the consequences? Japan did not regard itself as being at war with the Netherlands and merely wished to make the same type of arrangement in the Dutch colony that it had in Indochina. But if the Dutch insisted on a contest of strength . . .

The Netherlands, with its weak military forces, was counting on the power of its allies in the region. In late December, this military cooperation was formalised in the American–British–Dutch–Australian Command (ABDACOM). Although these forces had never drilled or conducted exercises together, and the American and British navies had sustained serious losses, the four countries' military leaders joined together to try to repel the Japanese advance across a territory extending from Burma to Australia. The British general Sir Archibald Wavell became ABDACOM's commander.

The colony's leaders were also concerned about domestic security. What was to become of the Japanese who had settled in the Dutch East Indies? Most Japanese shopkeepers, fishermen and merchants had returned in the preceding months, but was there a danger that those who remained (about 2,000 in number) would form a fifth column for the advancing Japanese troops? The colonial authorities rounded them all up and deported them to a camp in Australia.

And what was to be done with the last few hundred detainees in Boven Digul? For the time being, nothing changed for them. They were eventually sent to Australia, but not until 1943. The most prominent political prisoners were kept in the colony, but their living conditions were improved. The fact that all three were very critical of Japanese fascism undoubtedly worked in their favour. Sukarno was moved from Flores to a more comfortable location in Sumatra; Hatta and Sjahrir were transferred from Banda Neira to West Java.

And then there were the Dutch Nazi party members and the Germans, who had been in detention since May 1940. What if the Japanese liberated them? For safety's sake, the worst Dutch Nazis were sent across two oceans to Suriname, the largest Dutch colony in Latin America. The ship transporting them there had dynamite on board so that the captain could scupper it in an emergency, killing all prisoners.[9] The captive Germans, in contrast, were sent to British India to be interned. The first two shipments of prisoners conveyed the most dangerous individuals to Bombay, but the third went terribly wrong. The *Van Imhoff* was transporting the last 473 Germans, all less serious cases: retired officials from the colonial administration, ex-KNIL fighters of German origin, elderly missionaries, a few anti-fascists and Jews who had fled Europe, a number of stranded German sailors, a few mentally ill people and the artist Walter Spies. They were kept in cages between-decks and on the aft deck, surrounded with barbed wire and guarded by sixty-two soldiers. The *Van Imhoff* also had a civilian crew of eighty-four. At departure, there were plenty of life jackets but not enough lifeboats. The captain reported the problem, but the commander of the navy, Conrad Helfrich, ordered him to sail anyway. There was no red cross or other warning sign on deck to show that the ship was transporting prisoners. The Japanese bomber that spotted it off the west coast of Sumatra saw it as a warship like any other and attacked. The damage to the ship seemed limited at first, and panic did not break out, but after a few hours, from inside the barbed wire, the prisoners saw the Dutch lowering the boats and moving away. The only possible conclusion was that the *Van Imhoff* was doomed. To their astonishment, they saw that the lifeboats were nowhere near full. The steamship slowly started to list. A group of prisoners managed to free themselves and jumped into the water, making it onto a few rafts and a forgotten lifeboat. But 200 others drowned. A day later, two Dutch ships passed by. The first did not rescue anyone; the second asked the survivors if any of them were Dutch. Helfrich – him again – had sent secret instructions to allow only 'trustworthy elements' on board and 'prevent other Germans from reaching land'.[10] A Jewish jeweller who had fled the Nazis in his own country made a desperate attempt to climb on board but was swallowed by the waves.[11] Sixty-six of the 473 prisoners reached the island of Nias on a small lifeboat; they were the only survivors. After they arrived, one of them committed suicide: a former KNIL soldier, who could not believe that the Dutch East Indies, which he had served for years, would do such a thing to him.

The *Van Imhoff* disaster had a lasting impact. Even before the war ended, the Netherlands was ordered to pay the German occupiers four million guilders in compensation, but in 1956, the appeals court in Amsterdam decided that it was unnecessary to prosecute the captain. And the source of the orders, Helfrich, never faced court proceedings of any kind; his secret letter didn't surface until later. The Dutch broadcasting company VARA made a television documentary about the affair in 1965 but was prevented from airing it. The Netherlands insisted that it had been a victim in the war and suppressed any claims that it had committed war crimes.

In January 2016 I flew to Manado, a city near the tip of Sulawesi's northern peninsula, which points towards the Philippines like a finger. This was where, on 11 January 1942, the first Japanese troops landed on Dutch soil. Manado itself did not have any oil wells, but it did have a large enough airport to serve as a starting point for the advance south. I wondered if I could find living witnesses, but it seemed unlikely. Still, the first place I went after landing was the veterans' home, to try to rustle up a few addresses. To my surprise, I stumbled onto a reunion in progress. The home was full of former soldiers in uniform, who had just begun their lunch. After a morning packed with speeches, they were restoring their strength with fragrant *nasi kuning* in banana leaves, chicken legs, sweet tea and plenty of tales from the old days. Sometimes luck is on your side.

Hendrik Pauned Muntuuntu's memory was as clear as ever. He had been almost fifteen years old: 'The Japanese warships arrived in Kema, thirty-five kilometres away. I come from a nearby village. I saw those boats on the beach at Kema.' This is consistent with Japanese military reports, which say that 1,400 soldiers coming from the Philippines landed on Kema Beach. Another 1,800 came ashore on the west coast of the peninsula.[12] Hendrik made a sketch in my notebook: 'Here. First they went to the place where the Dutch army was. Then they took Langowan Airfield.' That too chimed with the official Japanese reports. Throughout this operation, there were no ABDACOM ships to be seen. The Allies flew a few defensive sorties, but without doing much damage. The airfield was captured in part by Japanese parachutists – Japan's first ever combat airdrop. Hendrik Muntuuntu said: 'I saw the first Japanese soldiers. Of course we were scared! We fled to our fields to hide and didn't return home until a week later. Then they moved on to central Sulawesi. Japanese civilians stayed behind as civil administrators.' They felt more familiar. 'There had been lots of Japanese fishermen here before the war, in the 1930s, living near Bitung. They cleaned and cut fish, sending tons of it to Japan. Their leader was called Ike-san. Then they were all called back to Japan for military service.' There had been some 4,000 fishermen in total.[13] 'They returned on the naval vessels. My parents took me to Bitung harbour to see. We listened to speeches by the Japanese. It took a couple of hours. The Dutch had left, they told us; now Japan was in charge of everything, and the Japanese administration would work with Indonesian officials.'[14]

Hendrik was an eyewitness to a historic beginning. After the centuries-long Dutch presence in the archipelago, it was the dawn of the Japanese period. Ventje Memah, another veteran, added: 'We fled to our fields, but later the Japanese gave us sugar and broken watches.'[15] He was only eight years old at the time and didn't know what to do with those strange gifts. Another veteran, from a village a hundred kilometres away, said: 'There wasn't much fighting in our area. There were no Dutch troops left. When the Japanese arrived, the villagers fled into the forest. I was twelve. We children had to catch chickens for them to eat.'[16] For those Indonesian children, the new era began with broken wristwatches and squawking chickens.

That same day, Japan attacked Tarakan, a major oil field off the east coast of Borneo. The oil produced there was so pure that it could be used almost untreated as marine diesel.[17] But the Dutch East Indies administration had given orders to destroy everything of value in the event of an invasion. This destruction had been planned in exhaustive detail by engineers in the military and oil industry. A Dutch employee of BPM described the procedure: 'After a few orders, we heard the dull booms of the explosions, and the first heavy columns of smoke began to block out the sun. Magnificent installations that had cost hundreds of thousands were transformed into burning ruins in mere seconds. After the explosion, the oil wells spouted their final jets into the air. It was especially painful for us BPM employees, who had put so much work into the company. Then it was time for the tank farms, both the one on the Pamusian drilling site and the one in Lingkas. Two times eighty million litres of oil went up in a tremendous sea of flame. The river of burning oil in Lingkas destroyed everything it touched on its way to the sea: roads, warehouses, homes and jetties. Columns of white and black smoke blotted out the sky. The white was evaporating seawater that had come into contact with the burning oil.'[18]

The Japanese landing troops were enraged by this sabotage and threatened to wipe out all the Europeans if the scenario repeated itself 600 kilometres to the south in Balikpapan. This had been the world's largest oil refinery in the nineteenth century, and it formed a much richer source of oil.[19] Japanese aircraft dropped leaflets announcing in flawless Dutch that 'those who destroyed oil wells, oil company facilities, oil tanks etc. [. . .] would be shot dead at once, along with their immediate and extended families.'[20] This didn't stop the colonial authorities. Balikpapan produced 1.2 million metric tons of petroleum and derivatives annually. The fire there burned for four days, covering a seven-kilometre strip. The smoke was visible more than one hundred kilometres away. 'Destroyed: all tanks, engines, pumps, generators, turbines, distillation units, boiler rooms, steam boilers, water pipe steam boilers, pipelines and hoses, the drum factory, the can factory, the paraffin factory and the petroleum factory, batteries of twelve combustion chamber boilers, transformer stations and the complete power plant.'[21] Lubricant, aviation fuel, asphalt, sulphur and paraffin were also burned, 25,000 barrels in all.

Japan was furious. The soldiers got their hands on seventy-eight Europeans and herded them onto the beach a few weeks after the landing: two colonial bureaucrats, a police inspector, a health officer, a few engineers, several clergymen and even some hospital patients. The locals were forced to watch. The two officials had to kneel and were beheaded with a slash of the samurai sword; the others were marched into the sea up to chest level, where they were shot dead – regardless of whether they had played any role in the sabotage.

But the colonial administration carried on with its plans for destruction. In Borneo, Sumatra and Java, which had the largest oil fields, as well as on a few smaller islands, more than 3.3 million cubic metres of petroleum went up in flames, the equivalent of the annual amount that Japan had demanded from Indonesia.[22] Only in the southern Sumatran town of Plaju were the destroyers too late. Plaju was then home to the largest oil refinery in all of Southeast Asia and of vital strategic importance as the only place in the Dutch East Indies that produced the low-aromatic fuel needed for modern warplanes.[23] The systematic demolition was supposed to continue for four days, but Japan was hell-bent on capturing the oil field; otherwise, the entire operation would have been pointless. In haste, about one hundred Japanese paratroopers were dropped near Plaju and neighbouring Palembang on 14 February 1942, another pioneering parachute drop of troops in Japan's military history. In response to this sudden move, the KNIL took over the work of the specialists in the destruction corps. This involved a good deal of improvisation. In a small flat in Leiden, I discussed it with one-hundred-year-old Ton Berlee: 'I was a sergeant, sent to Sumatra to retake the oil fields. A small body of Japanese troops had seized the Plaju field. Twenty-seven of us were there to drive them back.' Berlee was born in Cimahi; his parents came from Beverwijk and Enkhuizen in the Netherlands. Following in his father's footsteps, he joined the KNIL as a professional soldier. Now he and his men were making their cautious way through an eerie industrial landscape of forbidding distillation columns, baffling pipelines and dozens of warehouses. The official Japanese reports describe 'an Allied unit of around thirty troops, armed with two light machine guns', which 'launched a fierce counterattack and came within forty to fifty metres'. It is exceptional to be able to hear both sides of the story: 'As the bullets flew back and forth, the oil began to gush from the tanks and pipelines,' the Japanese sources tell us, 'and the Allied unit opened fire with mortars. The lines that took direct hits burst into flames, and black smoke filled the air.'[24] Sergeant Berlee described the scene in earthier language: 'We torched the place with mortars. One lad had an anti-tank rifle and used it to shoot through the pipelines. The flames stretched as far as the eye could see! We had to destroy whatever we could, since we had no chance of recapturing anything. They shot at us from behind, where they had cover. We took our mortars and fled. It was over fast. We started in the morning, and by evening we were already on our way back to Java.'[25]

A number of storage tanks were also set on fire, for a total of 850,000 cubic metres of oil that went up in smoke in Plaju.[26] Even so, the Japanese paratroopers managed to take control of a relatively undamaged refinery that still had very large reserves. This was such a crucial gain that it inspired a marching song which became popular in Tokyo: 'Sora no Shinpei' (Divine Soldiers in the Sky). It began with a quintessentially Japanese image:

> In the sky, bluer than indigo blue,
> In an instant bloom thousands of
> White roses, what a sight!
> Behold, parachutes descending in the sky!
> Behold, parachutes conquering the sky!
> Oh, the greatest flower, parachute![27]

The song did not mention that black oil had more to do with it than white roses.

Although the advance of the Japanese troops was unstoppable, ABDACOM inflicted a few serious losses on them. It was not the American or British vessels but the Dutch submarines that achieved the most spectacular results, heavily damaging or sinking at least six Japanese warships and transport ships. Even Winston Churchill had to acknowledge that the Dutch submarines, intrepidly deployed, had been responsible for sinking various Japanese ships.[28] In the late 1930s, there had been endless back-and-forth in the Netherlands about the construction of a few battlecruisers that were prestigious but fantastically expensive. The money would have been better spent on modern submarines. After all, the Dutch navy had pioneered the development of the wolfpack tactic in the 1920s: a co-ordinated attack on an enemy vessel by several submarines. This method, in combination with seaplanes, could assuredly have slowed the Japanese invasion. But the Netherlands had compounded its two diplomatic blunders – reneging on its commitments to deliver oil, and declaring war despite not having been attacked – with a military miscalculation: preferring battlecruisers to submarines, prestige to precision.[29] The 1930s were sometimes an era of foolish pride.

In the east of the archipelago, Australian forces put up brave resistance. Australia feared a Japanese attack on its territory – a possibility that was in fact under discussion in Tokyo. In February 1942, Darwin was bombed in a series of air raids, and Japan was even said to have its eye on India. The island of Ambon became the site of a blood-curdling clash between just under 6,000 Japanese soldiers and 3,000 Allied troops – 400 from the Netherlands, 1,400 native fighters and 1,200 Australians. Julius Nunumete, the Ambonese man who loved the Netherlands and St Nicholas, was serving in the Home Guard: 'I was assigned to the airport, alongside Australian soldiers. We had ordinary rifles, and the Australians had machine guns, but even with those, they were almost as helpless as we were. The Japanese force was overwhelming. They had many more fighter planes; we had two. And their ground troops surprised us from behind. There was a lot of shooting at the airport that day. Everyone fled back home to the mountains. Some of us even wanted to hop on the boat to Australia.'[30] He remained in hiding for a month, so he didn't see what the Japanese soldiers did to their Allied POWs. Sixty Dutch and 260 Australian soldiers were beheaded. The killings took place at night, by the light of an electric torch, and each one was greeted with loud cheers.[31]

By mid-February 1942, this was the situation for Japan: the American and British navies were still severely battered, Indochina and Thailand had been conquered, most of the Philippines and the Malay Peninsula had been taken and the attack on the Dutch East Indies was in full swing. In Sulawesi, Borneo, southern Sumatra and Ambon, the main airfields and oil wells were controlled by the Japanese, who immediately started rebuilding the demolished refineries. But the struggle was not over yet.

The main centres, Singapore and Java, still remained untouched. Singapore was said to be an impregnable fortress, and some later analysts believed that Java could have become 'a second North Africa', a place where the enemy were brought to their knees and the tide of war was turned.[32]

But 15 February brought what no one had considered possible: Singapore, the city with a million inhabitants, the hub of the British navy in Asia, the 'Gibraltar of the East', where no fewer than 120,000 British, Australian, Indian and New Zealand troops were stationed, suffered an ignominious defeat. It was the biggest surrender in British military history, after less than a week of fighting. 'We were very disappointed,' said a Nepalese man who had served in the British army and been sent to Singapore. 'A few days after we arrived Japan took over, without any kind of fight, without any confrontation with the enemy. We had to turn over all our weapons, except our cutlery.'[33] It was a blow from which the world's greatest colonial empire would never recover – and for Japan, it left the door wide open to the conquest of Java. The fall of Singapore sealed the fate of two great colonial powers: Britain and the Netherlands.

'So you'll stay and you'll fight it out,' said Helfrich, the naval commander, on the telephone in late February, speaking to his immediate subordinate, the Dutch rear admiral Karel Doorman.[34] After the fall of Singapore, ABDACOM had broken up into three regions: Burma, Java and northern Australia. Helfrich was in charge of the Allied naval forces in the Java region. Although East Java did not have the archipelago's richest oil fields, Java was critical to the Japanese; most of the native population lived there, the most fertile agricultural land in Southeast Asia could be found there, and it was the heart of colonial and military power.

The decisive engagement before the invasion of Java was the Battle of the Java Sea on 27 and 28 February 1942. It was one of the first major naval battles since World War I.[35] A convoy of dozens of large Japanese troop transports was carrying the invasion force to East Java, escorted by two heavy cruisers, two light cruisers and fourteen destroyers. The Allies tried with all their might to prevent this troop movement, a feat that did not look impossible on paper; their Combined Striking Force consisted of two heavy cruisers, three light cruisers and nine destroyers. But events unfolded very differently. The Japanese vessels were better armed and armoured and, most importantly, had a new type of fast torpedo that could hit targets from up to forty kilometres away. That was twice the range of the Allied torpedoes. The Allied ships – four Dutch, four British, five American and one Australian – had never conducted exercises together, and after weeks of patrolling under life-threatening circumstances, their crews were exhausted. Furthermore, they had hardly any reconnaissance aircraft at their disposal for this final operation, while the Japanese convoy had ample air support.[36] The Allied forces were led by Rear Admiral Karel Doorman, a conscientious officer who realised beforehand that there was no hope. 'We're fighting with our backs to the wall, especially after the fall of Singapore,' he wrote to his parents-in-law, 'so the chance that I will next see you in the hereafter is greater, on the face of it, than my chance of seeing you again in this world.' His words to a fellow military man were more prosaic: 'In a few days, I'll be fish food.'[37]

This was the situation as the two forces approached each other. At quarter past five in the afternoon on 27 February, the *Kortenaer*, a

Dutch destroyer, was hit by a Japanese torpedo – the first major loss. Over the next two days, another seven of the fourteen Allied ships were sunk, including the *De Ruyter*, Karel Doorman's flagship. His gloomy prediction – or rather, his realistic assessment – had proved accurate. A total of 2,300 Allied troops died.

Felix Jans, the man who had joined the navy because sailors had 'a nice uniform', recalled being in the middle of this debacle. 'The fear we felt as we put out to sea' – he was on watch on the *Kortenaer* – 'I honestly wouldn't wish that on anyone.' When we spoke, he was the last survivor of the Battle of the Java Sea. 'We didn't have a chance.' I remember his measured words, his silent anger. 'I lost all my friends. All drowned.' He glanced outside. Said nothing. Then more words came. 'In the afternoon, we put out to sea. From Surabaya.' Silence. 'I was standing on deck. I saw the Jap ship in the distance.' A deep breath. Then he said, 'When a torpedo is coming at you, you can see it from the foam, the white trail through the water.' A sigh. 'And then, boom! The whole ship shook. We had been hit.' The *Kortenaer* had been struck amidships and broke in two. The two halves stood up straight for a moment 'like the towers of a cathedral', in the words of another eyewitness.[38] Felix remembered it. 'Down went the front end, up went the rear end. It was sinking fast. The commander said, "Jump into the water." Whenever there was action, we wore life jackets.' He looked at his fingernails and said he didn't like to talk about it. I didn't push him. He went on with his story, even though I hadn't asked – or maybe because I hadn't. 'I wouldn't want anyone to go through something like that. The fear. The fear when you're in the water. The waves all around you. Dark, dark, dark. You can't see a thing, you don't know where you are. The sea wasn't rough, but the wind was cold. It was a clear night. I was a good swimmer, but I thought I'd never make it. I thought I would die. There were more than a hundred of us in the water. We clustered together. Everyone was screaming. Wounded. Broken arms, legs. Shots were still being fired.'

And it was true: the battle was still in progress. The explosions sent columns of water rising many metres into the air like geysers of froth, a forest of liquid pillars surging up and crashing down, filling the darkness with thunder and clamour. But the most terrible thing of all happened several hours later. At ten o'clock at night, Dutch ships sailed at high speed past the place where Felix and the other survivors of the shipwreck were bobbing among the wreckage and the fuel oil on their little balsa wood rafts. Tossed by the waves from the bow, they shouted and bellowed to the people on board. But there was no time to help; at most, an emergency beacon light was thrown into the ship's churning wake. Combat came first, and then rescue. 'I was in the water with Hakkenberg, my pal from basic training in Surabaya.' Hakkenberg was the youngest sailor in the battle, barely eighteen years old. They could not do much but pray. 'At daybreak, the British came to pull us out of the water.' This was HMS *Encounter*, a British destroyer. 'They threw down a ladder and brought us back to Surabaya, back to the barracks.' There they swapped their dripping wet, oil-stained uniforms for khaki army uniforms. They were done with that nice navy blue. 'We had drifted in the water for half a day.' When the casualties were counted, he learned that he had lost fifty-seven of his comrades. A day later, HMS *Encounter* would follow them to a watery grave.

He said nothing. He hesitated, and then asked if he could tell me something else.

'We were no match for the Japs. They had the most advanced destroyers. We had always underestimated them. "We'll fix 'em!" No, they fixed us. It was Dutch arrogance that did us in. We always know best, we can always do it best, but really the others are just as good, if not better! Our problem is our supremacy.'[39]

The Battle of the Java Sea couldn't stop the advance; the Japanese invasion force reached Java just one day later than planned. This pitiful result raises the question of whether Helfrich should have sent the available ships to safe waters – for instance, to Australia or Ceylon – to wait until the time was ripe for an Allied counteroffensive many times more serious than that senseless suicide mission, which was more a product of late-colonial arrogance than military realism. Give up Java without a fight? Well, there comes a point where a healthy sense of honour turns into a form of destructive madness. Calling a delusional operation a 'battle' will not bring a country's glorious maritime history back to life.

★

Mrs Natsui served extraordinary green tea and unusual sponge cake – I couldn't guess a single ingredient. Not that I was concentrating on that. After combing the capital unsuccessfully for almost two weeks, visiting museums, archives and embassies but all to no avail, I found myself in a quiet house in the Japanese countryside, seated opposite the friendly Mr Natsui. That morning, the bullet train had brought me and an interpreter through the snow-covered mountains to the west of the country. Spring had just begun on the coast; the birds sounded timid, but the sun was bright and its warmth was very welcome. Funny, box-like little cars from an agricultural co-operative were driving around. A few days earlier, the interpreter and I had found Mr Natsui's testimony on a CD-ROM at a documentation centre for disabled veterans in Tokyo, and when we searched the internet for a death notice, nothing came up. Could he still be alive?

I had come to Japan to get to know their side of the historical narrative. As I've said, the decolonisation of the Dutch East Indies was not simply a struggle between the Dutch and the Indonesians. The three-and-a-half-year Japanese occupation played a decisive role in setting off the Indonesian revolution and deserves as much attention as the other chapters of the story.

Seiji Natsui was sitting up straight with both feet on the floor. He wore a checked shirt and a cardigan. The frame of his glasses had a thick upper edge. I could see that his left eye was not almond-shaped, but wide open and wet. Who were the real people behind the image of the fearsome Japanese soldiers? Were they all confirmed fascists? Were they ultranationalists, ready to die for their emperor? 'I was the fifth child in my family and had twelve siblings. As the third son, I had no opportunities. My father was a rice farmer, so only the eldest son could follow in his footsteps. I was nineteen, I hadn't had a good education and the economy was poor. So I volunteered for the army. Ten yen every ten days! The army paid much more than a rice farmer could earn.' Food on the table – sometimes it was that simple. 'I was examined and admitted to military school for a year. I still know all the military ranks by heart. I became a *socho*, sergeant major, the seventh rank.'

He spoke in a calm, clear voice, with his left hand resting on his knee and his right hand beating time. Step by step, he told his story. In 1939, he had been sent to Manchuria – or more precisely, Manchukuo, as it had been called since the Japanese occupation. On the border with Russia and Mongolia, a series of insignificant skirmishes had grown into a serious border conflict, a dramatic prelude to World War II. In what became known as the Nomonhan Incident, Russia deployed 57,000 troops to Japan's 38,000; both lost more than 8,000. 'I was there. Nomonhan was a ghost town. I wasn't involved in the fighting myself. All I had to do was guard the food. A thousand mounted Japanese soldiers couldn't flee and were killed by the Russians. I was also in the cavalry, I rode a horse too. Many, many Japanese soldiers were mowed down.' In the late 1930s, Japan still had four cavalry brigades. In the border conflict, it also used mounted Mongol auxiliary troops. But the Russians had many more tanks at their disposal than the Japanese: hundreds and hundreds of tanks, facing men on horseback. 'The Japanese government learned its lesson,' Natsui continued. 'The age of the horse had ended. They motorised the cavalry. Tanks were the solution, so I was sent back to Japan in 1940 and retrained as a tank driver. This was at the training centre in Sendai. We were supposed to be sent back to China, but then World War II began and I had to wait.' For quite a while after that, Japan still hoped to conquer Russia from Manchuria, but the American oil embargo led to a change of plans. 'Suddenly we had to go to Java. We had no idea why. We weren't given any explanation. We sailed from the port of Hiroshima on a very modern ship, with ten tanks on board and many types of soldiers. That was a deliberate choice: if we were hit, it would not mean the loss of any complete unit. But we had no worries. There were a hundred or more Japanese ships on their way to Java. Navy ships and aircraft accompanied us. There weren't any Japanese soldiers in Java yet. We stopped in Taiwan, we stopped in Cam Ranh Bay, and had to wait there for two or three days. Singapore was still British. It was February and very warm. After being so cold in China, we went swimming in the ocean! That's how relaxed the mood was. And the people there welcomed us!'

As the interpreter translated his words with care, it dawned on me that many Japanese soldiers must have seen the trip as a kind of holiday. Southeast Asia was a different, warmer and sunnier region of their continent. Maybe they were like the many northern Europeans who feel at home right away in southern France or Italy. But this was no pleasure cruise. Seiji Natsui was one of around 55,000 soldiers in the 16th Army who were preparing to invade Java.[40] Meanwhile, the 25th Army was headed for Sumatra, and the navy was responsible for the Outer Islands. The invasion force for Java was the largest one. Led by General Hitoshi Imamura, it was to be Japan's greatest joint operation ever. There were eastern and western convoys; the eastern convoy went through the Battle of the Java Sea, and the western, with Natsui, went south from Cam Ranh. This pincer movement had begun with the attacks on Pearl Harbor and Singapore, and now the two sides were closing in. The eastern troops aimed to land in East Java and the western force in the west of the island. Four places along the north coast had been chosen for this delicate operation. Once they were on land, the pincer would shut, and – after the defeat of some 60,000 troops – the conquest of the Dutch East Indies would be complete.

With a friendly bow, Mrs Natsui set down another tray, laden with crackers, biscuits and apples. 'After the fall of Singapore, we were able to sail on towards West Java,' her husband continued. 'We

Map 15: The Japanese invasion of Java (March 1942)

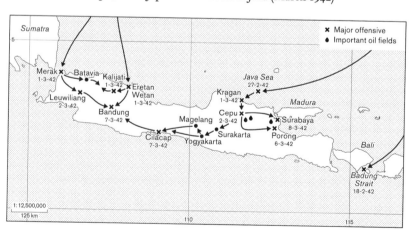

landed in Merak before dawn on 1 March 1942.' We looked at the map. That was the westernmost corner of northern Java. 'Our landing ship was the *Akitsu Maru*. Before we landed, we could see shooting to our left, between the ships and the land.' His right hand traced the arc of the projectiles. 'All sorts of colours. It was pretty, really, kind of like fireworks.' Banten Bay saw heavy combat. The KNIL infantry was guarding the beach with machine guns. Two cruisers, one Australian and one American, joined the fray, while American B-17s bombed the approaching fleet.[41] Three of the fifty-five transports were damaged and two were sunk, perhaps by friendly fire. This included the ship transporting Commander Imamura, who was able to swim to safety. Meanwhile, Seiji Natsui reached the coast. 'Our ship had a loading hatch; from there, I had to drive onto the beach. I was driving the first of our ten tanks. I wasn't scared, no. We knew we were very strong. We weren't impressed by the Dutch; we knew where they were. We had to get them, those were our orders. If they got us first, we had to kill ourselves. Being taken prisoner was extremely shameful.' He waved his right hand again. 'Our senior commander was Nasu. My commanding officer was Lieutenant Colonel Noguchi Kinichi, originally a teacher. The tank commander was Hiroshi Nakamura; he was also the gunner. It's cramped inside one of those tanks. There's just enough room for two, him and me. I was seated very low, on a little futon.'

It was March 2017, and I realised that in this beige living room in the Japanese countryside, I was listening to a veteran who had been one of the very first soldiers in the imperial army to set foot on land in Java. His division was even a little ahead of schedule. 'With those caterpillar tracks, you have a maximum speed of fifty kilometres an hour, but it feels very fast. The road was excellent, paved with asphalt. The landscape was flat. We had maps and aerial photos. It was like I already knew the way! "Faster, faster," I heard my commanding officer say.' The unit had to capture and guard a few strategic locations as soon as possible. 'Since I only had a narrow slit to look through, I opened the hatch so that I could see more clearly. The plan was to advance towards Bandung and guard a bridge along the route. After an hour's driving, we had travelled thirty-five to forty kilometres.

The next tank was well behind us. Then, fifty to one hundred metres ahead of us, I spotted a Dutch truck. Our gunner took aim. A big explosion. He had blown up the truck. All the soldiers were dead, seven or eight Dutch soldiers, I think. Right after that came an enormous flash of light, followed by complete darkness. I tried to keep driving the tank but couldn't any more. The caterpillar tread was broken. There must have been a landmine next to the truck. I felt something warm on my forehead, but it didn't hurt. I touched my face and felt blood all over it. Metal had flown in through the open hatch. I bandaged my head. I was carried off and was soon in terrible pain. They took me to a hospital boat. After a few days, they sent me to a hospital in Thailand for treatment. For ten days, I was completely blind. I remained there for a month. The hospital ship that had brought me was sunk soon afterwards. My left eye is false, and there are still bits of metal in the right one, so I can't have an MRI scan.'

Mr Natsui's hands were on his knees again. He did what Japanese men his age often do: gave a quick bow and a nervous, apologetic laugh. 'I'm sorry I couldn't tell you more. I was only in Java for an hour. I didn't see any Indonesians or Dutch people. You came all this way for nothing. Please excuse us.'[42] He nodded and smiled awkwardly, his wet glass eye still staring at me.

The Dutch ground troops and the Allied aircraft tried to stop the Japanese advance, but the landing troops were far too much for them. To the east of Batavia, a smaller detachment had landed near Eretan Wetan. Ton Berlee, the KNIL sergeant who had helped to destroy the Plaju oil field, had been sent to the area. He lived through the first day of the war: 'Java was protected with pillboxes, except in the marshy area near Indramayu. That was where I was sent. I was still the commander of my twenty-seven-man unit. The Japs moved through the marsh fast, they had done good espionage. All those shopkeepers had passed on information; some even spoke fluent Dutch. We were trapped in that marsh. I stayed calm and quiet. If the commander gets scared, the native soldiers beat a hasty retreat and disappear into the crowd in civvies. We were searching for a house to give us cover.' An intense firefight followed. 'Only three of the twenty-seven survived the shooting: two Menadonese soldiers and me. We were no match for them. They had been capturing territory in China while we were still waiting for our plans from the USA. Then they went on to Kalijati Airfield.[43]

Kalijati was a crucial base for attacks on the rest of West Java and had good roads to Batavia, Buitenzorg and Bandung. By the afternoon of 1 March, the airfield was in Japanese hands. For the Dutch soldiers, it was a moment of 'dismay, deep humiliation and shame', in the words of a later report.[44] The next day, the air force and the KNIL made furious but haphazard attempts to recapture it. More than ever, the greater experience and motivation of the Japanese troops became apparent. Not everyone on the Dutch side was a trained professional soldier willing to make the ultimate sacrifice. Hans Dornseiffer, the man who had been mobilised a week before Pearl Harbor and approved for service without an examination, saw things differently. 'The Japs had taken over the landing strip. That night, we set off with a large convoy of trucks and artillery. I was part of the mountain artillery, a mobile artillery force that normally transported howitzers on horseback.' I had seen photographs of the mountain artillery: horses wading across a mountain river, laden with light cannons. They'd looked more like images from the late-nineteenth-century Aceh War than preparations for a world war in the industrial age. Hans worked in the 'farrier school', but there was no longer any time for such rustic modes of warfare. 'We weren't allowed to make any light. The *kampongs* [native villages or compounds] we passed were very quiet and completely dark. I was in a truck transporting oil for the cannons and got oil all over me. By morning, we were nearing the airport. We saw small Jap reconnaissance planes. We shot at them with our little rifles, but of course that didn't work. Then Japanese dive bombers came swooping towards us. Explosions. Trucks burst into flames. Dead bodies. We hid in the craters left by the bombs. The explosions had wiped away all the bamboo. The Japanese bombers had two gunners, one at the nose and one at the tail. When another plane came our way, we would hide on one side of the crater; when it flew back over us again, we would search for cover on the other side. It was raining. Everything was soaked, everything turned to muck.'

Farrier school seemed like a distant memory. 'We were only a couple of kilometres from the airfield, but we never saw Kalijati. We withdrew.'

This mortifying retreat had a deadly effect on troop morale. 'There was a rumour that the Japs were shooting mainly at officers,' Hans Dornseiffer continued. 'I was a private second class – there was nothing lower. Well, third class, but that was for the natives. Anyway, all those big-mouthed officers took off their epaulettes fast! The retreat led us from Bandung back to Cimahi. We slept in the officer training school, where the barracks had real beds with white sheets. The officers were dancing! I thought to myself, well, they know how bad things are, this is the Last Supper. The next day, the leader of the training programme gathered everyone together. There were trumpets playing fanfares and everything. We were ordered to fight. The KNIL was going to 'wage a final battle', the Dutch government in London had decided. Not capitulate, but fight a guerrilla war. Oh, right, great idea, I said to myself. We had little rifles with bayonets, while the Japanese had much longer rifles with gleaming bayonets. How were we supposed to fight them man to man? It was madness. I didn't go! I went outside instead and sat in the sun. The next day, the Japs reached the barracks.[45]

Sumarsono had a similar experience. He was one of the few Indonesian conscripts. 'But when the war began, we did nothing. I slept in the barracks, ready to fight, but when the Japanese approached, Commander Bakker was nowhere to be found. All our officers had run off! We woke to find Japanese guns aimed at us. "Atsumero," they shouted: assemble.[46]

Most Indonesian soldiers were not especially willing to die in combat. Iskandar Hadisaputra, who had worked in the Japanese shop, was used to seeing his uncle in uniform as a KNIL corporal. 'He wore long, dark green trousers with tapered legs with pockets on them. But when the Japanese arrived, he didn't feel like fighting and getting killed. The KNIL hardly put up a fight anyway. They gave everything away, including their vehicles! The Europeans were being taken prisoner, but he was afraid he would be killed. He took off his uniform and went home – in his underwear! I was playing football outside and couldn't believe my eyes. He came walking up in his underpants and singlet and shouted, "Quick, lock the door." For the next two or three days, he didn't come outside.[47]

Despite blown-up bridges, felled trees and a few heroic attempts by the Allies to resist, the Japanese invasion force made remarkably fast progress. In just a few days, the imperial army spread to every corner of Java. Almost half the Dutch troops did not engage in combat.[48] On 1 March, the Japanese took Kalijati Airfield; on 2 March, the Cepu oil field; on 3 March, the city of Bojonegoro in East Java; and on 4 March, Batavia was declared an open city to avoid a bloodbath. Nor was there any battle of Buitenzorg. The colonial forces entrenched themselves in Bandung, the city in the mountains. Governor-General Van Starkenborgh ceded supreme command to Lieutenant General Hein ter Poorten, the commander of the army. Helfrich had left for Ceylon; the navy no longer had any role to play. On 5 March, Japan took Batavia without significant fighting. Along the city's leafy avenues, the locals gawked at the columns of grimy soldiers marching by in their beige uniforms. They wore caps with neck flaps and had strikingly long rifles. On 6 March, Buitenzorg fell, and the port of Surabaya was attacked from the air, after the Netherlands had sunk more than fifty of its own ships and submarines there. One of the last departing aircraft took Van Mook, who had hastily been appointed lieutenant governor-general, to Australia, while Van Starkenborgh remained in place. On 7 March, Japanese troops headed for Cilacap, the port on the south coast where the Allies were trying to escape. That evening, they took the mountain village of Lembang, eight kilometres from Bandung. In barely a week, the pincers had closed almost completely.

'Great confusion. Chaos. No leadership any more.' And on top of all that, Dick Buchel, who came from the Dutch town of Steenbergen and worked for the aerial photography service, had just had malaria. 'I was back on my feet and had been discharged from the military hospital in Yogyakarta. In the middle of the night, we drove to Bandung. All the troops were ordered to go there. There were already Japanese aircraft overhead. Bandung was supposed to be a bulwark, but that plan failed. It was in a river basin, and Japan had the mountains. The mountain ridge was the only place where any fighting happened.' He received permission from the medical service to go home to recover. Soon afterwards, he saw the first Japanese residents move into the elementary school behind his parents' home. 'The speed of their advance was unbelievable. Their aircraft were superior. I even saw their ground troops on bicycles. Wherever they went, they stole bikes. Their legs were too short to reach the pedals. They were little men, but they achieved great things.' Some even spoke of a 'bicycle *Blitzkrieg*'.[49] 'Their self-sufficiency was remarkable too. They cooked for themselves; there was no central kitchen.'[50] Many Dutch people felt so humiliated by the military superiority of the Japanese that they declared them inferior in every other respect. A civilian official in South Sumatra described them as 'ugly little men, unbelievably dirty' who let out 'raucous cries' and 'stank of the war'.[51] 'How is it possible,' one soldier lamented at the time of the surrender. 'Those little Japs! You could piss straight down on their heads . . .'[52]

Better weapons, better training, more experience, more discipline, more fanaticism – many factors contributed to Japan's lightning advance. Cruelty also played a role. Although General Imamura had expressly ordered his troops not to misbehave, they sometimes massacred civilians, including many colonial officials. Indonesian and European women were the victims of gang rape, and some who complained to the local commander were raped again, this time in the commander's presence.[53] Many prisoners of war were beheaded, killed with bayonets or mowed down with machine guns. Japan had signed the Geneva Conventions but never ratified them, and according to its own imperial doctrine, to be a prisoner of war was a shameful thing. 'As long as you live, you will never undergo the disgrace of captivity,' their disciplinary regulations said. Either you won with honour, or you died with honour – there was nothing in between.[54] 'Assume that death is lighter than goose down' was the kind of thing that soldiers were told.[55] Historian Fred Lanzing sums it up: 'While German soldiers learned to kill, Japanese soldiers were taught to die.'[56] Men subjected to this kind of brainwashing could not be expected to show much compassion to enemy POWs. 'A Japanese soldier confiscated all our belongings,' said one Dutch soldier who had surrendered on the mountain ridge north of Bandung. 'Fountain pens, watches, money, even our dog tags and our military passbooks [. . .] When that was done, we had to cross our hands behind our back. Our wrists were bound with puttees, and we were tied together in groups of three. The groups were lined up, and I heard the commander shout another order. Then I saw and heard that we were being shot at with a machine gun set up about ten metres away. I felt the bullets hitting me in the belly and fell over. The two men attached to me fell on top of me. I think they died instantly. [. . .] When the firing stopped, twenty-five to thirty Japanese soldiers charged at us with levelled bayonets. I played dead, but for an instant I saw the Japanese walking up to soldiers who were still groaning and writhing on the ground. It gradually grew quieter, and after a while I couldn't hear the victims any more. I lost consciousness again. I don't know how long I was out, but I guess about three hours. It was deathly quiet around me.'[57]

Just on this one occasion, approximately eighty POWs were killed. Some corpses were headless or had their eyes gouged out.

There was yet another reason the advance was so rapid. In Tokyo, I had a very hard time getting in touch with Ryuichi Shiono, but once I had found him, the words kept rolling out of him. It began as the interpreter and I were removing our shoes in the corridor of his traditional Japanese home. '*One hundred and one years! Too old!*' He even spoke a little English.

Shiono was energetic, cheerful and untiring. 'I have to keep trying new things,' he continued in Japanese. 'If I do nothing, I'll end up senile. I learned sign language at the age of eighty-eight and watercolour painting at ninety-three. *I am something trying new always!*' Without pause, he went on to the Japanese word for Holland: '*Oranda, Oranda!*' Then something about a ship breaking in two, swimming, swimming, swimming, for eight hours without stopping. Meanwhile, he was rummaging through a pile of papers and magazines. The interpreter was having trouble keeping up with him. Wait, what was all this about? He paused for a second. 'I have to tell you everything in the right order, or it will all be a mess. People like me don't have much longer to live, and when we're not around, everything will be forgotten.'

Shiono took a seat and made himself comfortable. His birth date was 15 January 1916. His father had been in charge of the carriages for the imperial household. But Shiono had wanted to work on a more modern form of transport: aeroplanes. He found a job at the Nakajima Aircraft Company but was called up to serve in the war against China.

'There was a special draft at the time. We had to go to the front.' His sentences grew shorter. 'In China, in the mud. We marched through the mud every day. Then fought again, then marched again. That was how we advanced. It was brutal, but our army was tough as nails. The bullets flew in all directions. *Pisha, pisha, pisha.* It was like a hailstorm in a rice field. We had to make it through them. I did that many times. There was no time to be afraid, you just wanted to get through them as fast as possible. That was your mission. I carried my rifle and was covered with mud from head to toe. I was capable of extraordinary efforts, thanks to my pride in my country, my loyalty to the emperor. I'd been taught those qualities since early childhood. In the battlefield, you're on the threshold between life and death. Then you need a powerful symbol: the nation, the emperor. That's the way to make even a weakling strong. Many of my comrades fell in battle, so when I go to Yasukuni Shrine [the monument to the war dead in Tokyo], I can't help crying. We all fought for the emperor. Many died for him. Many went down with their ships. Many shouted "banzai" for the emperor when they died. They were proud of our country and emperor. But your own mother is also very important. They called out for their mothers until the very end. "Mama, mama . . ." they shouted. And that was how they died.'

He no longer looked nearly as cheerful as he had just a few minutes earlier. For the moment, he was the young man in the mud again. 'In China, one of my comrades went to fetch water and didn't come back. He had walked down from our camp in the mountains. I went to look for him. His throat had been cut. We were dealing with a terribly barbaric, cruel people. Your life hung by a thread. Compared to that, the war in the south, in the Philippines and Indonesia, was a normal fight between two armies. After China, I was posted to the island of Hainan to be trained as a radio operator. Communication by telegraph and telephone. I still know Japanese Morse code by heart: *i, ro, ha, ni* . . . That was not a gentle process. They kicked and whipped it into me. That's how we learned so fast. The only way to memorise things that fast is if they're pounded into your body. Our training was brutal. We were covered with welts.'

Unconditional love for an emperor worshipped as divine, remorseless training and harrowing experiences in China. Shiono embodied the type of soldier later sent to Indonesia: a fighting machine, pounded flat, hollowed out and pumped full of nationalism. 'You can put a lot of things in an empty vessel,' a Belgian paratrooper once told me. That was certainly true of the Japanese soldier. Shiono stopped leafing through his documents, having finally found what he'd been looking for.

'I first fought in the Philippines. On 17 February, we embarked in Lingayen and sailed south through the Macassar Strait to Java. On 21 February, we crossed the equator. On 23 February, we ran into an enemy fleet and turned around. On 26 February, we were attacked and had to search for cover. On 27 February, we were attacked by a high-altitude bomber.'

That was all he saw of the Battle of the Java Sea in his troopship. That confrontation was a ripple in the water on the way to Java. 'We landed near the village of Kragan. Not in a port, but in little boats with sturdy bottoms that we beached. From there, we moved on to Surabaya, which was still some distance away. I was part of the motorised infantry and rode in a truck. I worked for the liaison office, a small unit separate from the main force. Whenever a plane flew low overhead, a Spitfire or a Hawker Hurricane, I reported it by telephone.'

The troops ahead of him were capturing Cepu, Java's largest oil field. 'The battle had reached its climax, the oil fields were going up in flames. Our trucks had to stop because of all the smoke.' And then something happened that he would never have believed possible, an experience unlike any his fellow soldier Natsui had had during his brief nocturnal tank drive, a far-fetched incident that still surprised him and made him laugh many decades later. 'The locals came up to us, smiling, and gave us food! Bananas, coconuts, papayas. Such friendly people. They seemed grateful we had come. People in China had been genuinely hostile, but here they felt sympathy for us. The women were very friendly too.' It seemed more like the end of a war than the beginning. 'Their faces resembled Japanese faces, but they wore headgear that looked like a flowerpot and also a kind of turban.' He was talking about the *songkok*, a kind of black fez, and the *blangkon*, a knotted batik cloth. 'And they wore sarongs, a kind of skirt, and short jackets. There was a local legend that they would be freed from colonialism by people from the east, and they projected that onto the Japanese. They saw us as their liberators, that's why they were so good to us.'

He was referring to the legend of Jayabaya, who prophesied that, after centuries of hardship, a saviour would come. Without the enthusiastic reception, the Japanese troops would have had a much harder time invading the country. There was no Indonesian resistance, no sabotage, no underground.

'It didn't feel as if we were waging a war, but as if we were at home in Japan on a military exercise. We won all the battles in no time. Outside Surabaya, there was heavy combat at a place called Porong, which had a fort and a river with crocodiles, but other than that, fighting the Netherlands seemed more like a field day than a real war. The Japanese army was so strong back then.' He had time to enjoy the landscape. 'Java was a place with a lot of vegetation, light and beauty. It was mountainous, but the roads were good. It was warm, but the shade of the many trees and the trade winds made it pleasant. The climate was not too damp, the food was good and the people were welcoming. A delightful place, I would have liked to spend my whole life there. I understand the Dutch people who crossed the seas long ago to travel to Indonesia. Everything is there in abundance, there's plenty of delicious food. Meat, fish, rice. The rice farmers have more than one harvest a year. What I remember best are the wonderful prawns. During battle, infantrymen had miso powder and rice with them, but once we were quartered and eating outside the barracks, we found out how good the prawn dishes were. When we went to an Indonesian restaurant, we said "terima kasih," thank you. Compared to China, the war in Indonesia was a lot of fun. People were very friendly to us right from the start. We spent whole evenings listening to their gamelan music.'

Even though there was a war on, ordinary Japanese soldiers were also starting to forge real ties with ordinary Javanese civilians. The fact that a soldier like Shiono found himself attending long gamelan performances after dark and still had fond memories of the experience some seventy-five years later speaks volumes about the pleasantness of those initial encounters. But what was confusing for the Japanese was that some Indonesians served in the colonial army. 'Along the road, I saw a young Indonesian who had been wounded. He was dying by the roadside. I couldn't help him, he was one of the enemy, but his eyes, that look in his eyes – I can't forget it, even now.' By this time, Dutch soldiers were drowning their troubles in drink and belting out songs like 'Surabaya, Singapore, *alles is nu naar zijn moer* [everything has turned to shit]'.[58] Was this the superior European race? 'When we attacked Surabaya, we took a lot of Dutch prisoners. They had surrendered, and their hands were tied behind their backs. Our front soldiers had to keep them in their sights until the auxiliaries could take charge of them. I never faced them eye to eye. I didn't have to kill.'

Still, Shiono was able to distinguish between economic necessity and ideological propaganda. 'Above all, the Japanese military invaded Indonesia for the oil. Because of the boycott, Japan could no longer import any oil or scrap metal. In the process, we happened to liberate Indonesia. I don't know how the higher-ups saw it. I do think that liberating the Indonesians was part of the plan, but natural resources came first.'

The Netherlands had completely miscalculated the response by the local population. Before long, countless Indonesians were going around with Japanese flags on their bicycles or their sleeves.[59] Children and young people had their heads shaved bald so that they looked like Japanese soldiers.[60] Japanese flags were flying everywhere.

In the countryside, many colonial houses were plundered. Even a poorhouse in Central Java was targeted. Everything had been taken, the director said, 'even my dentures, which I'd been about to put in'.[61] This was more than theft and vengeance; it revealed just how tooth- less the Netherlands was.

'When the Japanese arrived, I saw all those soldiers taking off their uniforms,' Purbo Suwondo told me. He was still indignant about it. 'Forget about "We would rather stand and die than kneel and live," as the head of the KNIL had said. The KNIL proved to be all talk and no trousers. Were we still expected to look up to those people? When we saw the Japanese, we said, "Hey, here are Asians who never stud- ied at a European university, and they can defeat a world power just like that." '[62]

Iskandar saw more of the invasion than just his uncle returning home in his underwear. To his astonishment, he ran into Ashimoto, the Japanese shopkeeper he'd stayed with. 'I didn't recognise him at first! When he'd left for Japan, the Dutch had closed his shop. But now he was back, in the uniform of the Kempeitai, the military police, with a samurai sword! We hugged. He still treated me like a son.'[63]

Sukotjo Tjokroatmodjo, who'd been laughed at by his classmates, was also reunited with an earlier acquaintance. 'The Dutch barracks across the road from our house were occupied by the Japanese. One day a car with a blue pennant stopped there. The generals had yellow pennants, red was for majors and colonels and blue for lieutenants and captains. A Japanese man with a sword a full metre long called my name. I was frightened, of course! But then I laughed. It was the Japa- nese grocer who had let me swim on his back!' And that was not the end of the story. 'He opened his bag. Inside were hundreds of photos of the coast of Java. Then I understood why he had always been tak- ing pictures on the beach. Every time we went swimming, he was helping to prepare for the landing.'[64]

Iskandar and Sukotjo didn't feel betrayed by their Japanese acquaintances. These were tales of happy reunions, not of disillusion or resentment. They even seemed proud to have known Japanese offi- cers personally.

★

It was a subdued gathering, the evening of 8 March 1942 at the air-field in Kalijati. Governor-General Van Starkenborgh and Lieutenant General Ter Poorten had been summoned there to negotiate with General Imamura, the commander of the Japanese invasion force for Java. The aircraft were ready and waiting to reduce Bandung to rubble.

'Do you represent all the military forces, public officials and inhab-itants of the Dutch East Indies in your capacity as governor-general?' Imamura asked.

'I do,' Van Starkenborgh replied.

'In that case, can you, here and now, declare either your surrender or the continuation of the war?'

'No, I cannot.'

'Why not?'

'As governor-general of the Dutch East Indies, I was until recently the supreme commander of the armed forces, but when General Wavell became the commander-in-chief of the Allied troops, I was divested of that power by order of the queen.'

Imamura turned to Ter Poorten: 'And what about you?'

'I do not have that authority either.'

'In that case, what is your role as the head of the Dutch East Indies military?'

'I command the troops.'

Imamura stared at the two men. 'If this is how things stand, gen-tlemen, then why on earth did you come here?'

'It wasn't our idea to come,' the governor-general reminded him. 'You invited us.'

'But why did you send a messenger with a flag yesterday to offer a ceasefire?'

'We offered a truce so that we could yield Bandung as a bulwark,' the governor-general said. 'It would be unbearable to go on exposing Bandung to the depredations of war.'

'And what would you say to surrendering the whole Dutch East Indies?' the aggravated Imamura responded.

'That is impossible, because I lack the authority.'

'Are you telling me you can wage war but cannot surrender?'

'Only the queen can decide to surrender. As we lack any means of communicating with her and requesting her permission to surrender, we can do nothing.'

Commander Imamura drew a sharp breath. 'We are at war with each other. This is no time for diplomatic negotiations. We are here to discuss capitulation or the continuation of the conflict. That discussion leaves no room for dickering with you.'

Then he had all the civilians leave the room, including the governor-general. He asked Ter Poorten: 'Will you surrender, even if the governor-general does not support your decision?'

'Conditions in and around Bandung are abominable. Bandung has become completely indefensible, and the army is as good as disbanded. It is totally unthinkable to subject civilians to the horrors of war any longer. I will surrender a large area around Bandung. Can you accept that?'

'The surrender of Bandung is not of the least importance to the Japanese army. Capturing Bandung alone would be child's play for our elite military corps. If surrender is so impossible for you, then there is no point in continuing this conversation. The Japanese forces demand your complete and unconditional surrender. If you cannot oblige, leave now, and we will resume hostilities without delay and maintain the use of force until the Dutch East Indies has been destroyed.'

It was 8 p.m. The next afternoon, Ter Poorten spoke on NIROM, the Dutch East Indies radio broadcasting service, as required by his agreement with the Japanese military leaders. 'After thorough reflection, I had no other option but to meet the Japanese demands. I order you to cease the hostilities in progress.'[65] Ter Poorten's decision reflected neither weakness nor cowardice but realism. Unlike the governor-general, the commander of the navy or the head of the Dutch government in London, he was one of the few who realised that continuing to fight was senseless in the face of such overwhelming force.[66] The closing of the pincers could not be reversed. That evening, NIROM aired its final broadcast. The announcer ended with these words: 'We will close our doors now. Farewell, until better times. Long live the queen.'[67]

★

Three months to the day after Pearl Harbor, Japan had achieved its goal, one month earlier than anticipated.[68] In a single season, it had taken over all of Southeast Asia and deprived no fewer than five colonial Western powers of their influence over the region: Britain, the United States, France, Portugal and the Netherlands. To its list of conquests, which began with eastern China, it could add the Philippines, Indochina, Thailand, Malacca, Burma and the Dutch East Indies. It had captured the oil fields, and the repairs to the refineries were going so swiftly that it expected to be able to export at least 1.75 million tons of oil by the end of the year.[69] The other spoils of war in the Dutch East Indies included 152 aircraft, 367 tanks, 1,567 machine guns, 97,000 firearms and one million cartridges, grenades and explosive devices.[70] The entire operation had cost Japan just over 2,000 lives, 845 of which had been lost in the Dutch East Indies and only 255 in Java – a very small number, in view of the scope and significance of the mission.[71] The Netherlands lost 2,549 troops, and its allies in Java mourned around 1,000 other fatalities, mostly American.[72] Though fairly large, the poorly trained and equipped army that had been scraped together was no match for the Japanese invasion force. In just three months, the Netherlands lost the entire jigsaw puzzle it had pieced together over three and a half centuries. All the islands were taken, aside from part of Timor and inhospitable New Guinea, where Japan would never capture more than the northern coast. That left Boven Digul, the internment camp for unwanted individuals of all stripes, as one of the last areas in Dutch hands. In an irony of history, it was those who loved the Dutch administration least who had to go on living under its authority longest.

For a brief while, sporadic fighting continued. Some Dutch commanders refused to accept the surrender and instead resorted to guerrilla tactics, but this method relied on the support of the local population, support that was practically non-existent. Japan relentlessly defeated these rogue units one by one. Only on the Bird's Head Peninsula, the northwestern peninsula in New Guinea, did one small commando still hold out against the invaders, with the aid of the local Papuans, until they were liberated by the Americans in 1944. By then their unit of sixty, including one Ambonese woman, had only fourteen survivors.[73] Their struggle is the stuff of feature films but made no difference to the larger history.

When Japan conquered the Dutch East Indies, it took approximately 110,000 POWs. The Indonesians among them, some 50,000 in number, were soon released, as a brother race to the Japanese. This included Sumarsono. 'We all had to line up. "Are you Indonesian?" they asked. If you were, you had to step forward. There weren't many of us, there were a lot more Indos. They sent the Indonesians home and held the Indos captive.'[74] Yes, the colony's Europeans and Eurasians faced an uncertain future. Ton Berlee, the Dutchman who had set the Plaju oil refinery on fire and fought in the marshes of northern Java, was captured when he tried to take a bus from Bandung to Cimahi. 'They saw my rucksack and threw me in a camp surrounded by barbed wire, the KKK, the Kale Koppen Kamp [Bald Head Camp]. They shaved all of us bald.'[75] The three Indo recruits I spoke to were also interned. Felix Jans, who had barely survived the Battle of the Java Sea, was arrested in Surabaya. 'And that was how I became a POW. While other guys were chasing girls, I was swinging a pickaxe.'[76] Hans Dornseiffer, who had decided to go sit in the sun after Kalijati, was told to stay in his barracks. 'The Japs didn't bring us any food or water that day. I still had a couple of cans of condensed milk from Friesland. I used my bayonet to punch holes in them.'[77]

But the most remarkable story was told by Dick van Steenbergen, the man who was lying at home in Bandung, recovering from malaria.

'I wasn't wearing a uniform any more, but my mother said, "Go and register!" Everyone in the military had to sign up for internment, or else they'd kill your family. I went to the old fairgrounds. There were Japs at the gate, but the KNIL soldiers who were already inside said to me, "Go home, there's nothing going on here." The Japanese were still preoccupied with finding housing for themselves. A week later, I reported to the fairgrounds again. Two of my brothers had been interned by then. They were soldiers too. I did it to save my skin and for my family. I just walked in. There was no registration. It was a partly covered site where the annual trade fair had been held. In a fairly large building, I found a spot on the bare earth. There were about 200 people there. No one knew how long we'd be held. A few months, everyone said, if that! I told myself I could be there till 1945. I don't know what made me come up with that date, but I clung to it. It helped to have such a long, practically endless, period in mind. Then you have no expectations. Because if you have hope, you lose heart completely.'[78]

Chapter 7

The Land of the Rising Pressure
The first year of the occupation, March 1942–December 1942

'The Japanese occupied all of Indonesia,' said Djajeng Pratomo in his retirement home in Callantsoog. 'They went all over . . . for the spices!' He meant petroleum, of course, but even if 'spices' was merely a slip of the tongue, the metaphor is apt. Oil was the nutmeg of the twentieth century, and Japan's brutality was certainly reminiscent of the Dutch East India Company's. When Pratomo heard the news of the Japanese invasion, he had just turned twenty-eight. After the bombing of Rotterdam, he had moved to Leiden, home to the central board of the Perhimpunan Indonesia (PI). In that historic university town, with its small alleyways and calm water, he lived with several other Indonesian students on a branch of the Rhine, a fifteen-minute walk away from their clubhouse in Hugo de Grootstraat. They were dismayed by what had happened. 'Indonesia had supposedly been liberated by the Japanese,' he scoffed. 'But really they were conquerors. Japan used pro-Japanese students who believed they shouldn't work with the Dutch but with the Japanese.' This is true: immediately after the invasion, the Japanese set up a propaganda machine. Young members of the Indonesian intelligentsia, such as the influential poet and journalist Sanusi Pane, were permitted to write friendly pieces in the newly established journal *Asia Raya* (Great Asia) about the fall of the Occident and the rise of the Land of the Rising Sun.[1] Pratomo and his comrades were thunderstruck. If students in their homeland were so quick to support fascism, then they would have to resist all the more fiercely in the Netherlands. By then, the PI had been outspokenly anti-fascist for some time. When the German occupiers had dismissed Jewish professors and instructors in November 1940, they had boldly cast their lot with the resistance. It is worth emphasising how remarkable this was; the Indonesian students, who were mostly Muslims, chose to risk their lives at the moment when Dutch Jews came under threat. On 26 November 1940, when Rudolph Cleveringa, the dean of Leiden's law faculty, delivered a now-famous speech protesting at the dismissal of some of his colleagues, the PI encouraged students in Leiden and Delft to go on strike. Its president, Setyadjit Soegondo, even joined the editorial staff of *De Vrije Kath-eder*, an underground magazine that grew out of that protest. The Germans responded with round-ups and by closing the universities in Leiden and Delft.

'Oh, yes, the Perhimpunan remained in operation and formed the basis of the Indonesian resistance. We worked together with Dutch resistance members,' Pratomo recalled. And that too was out of the ordinary; the colonised came to the aid of the coloniser, despite their opposition to colonialism. Why? Because they saw fascism as a far greater evil. And because they had always been more anti-colonial than anti-Dutch. As far back as the 1930s, the PI had declared that they were not 'fundamentally hostile to the Dutch people, but that they did reject reactionary colonial policies'.[2] During a talk in Paris in 1939, Setyadjit had said: 'There is a different Holland from the Government's, which practises oppression and injustice, a different Holland from that of the rich bankers, who have exploited the colonies for profit; it is the part of the Dutch population with democratic feelings.'[3] Statements like this had always been dismissed by the leading colonial institutions as 'demagoguery'.[4] Yet the students' democratic idealism was perfectly sincere. During the war years, they would offer an impressive demonstration of how far they were willing to go for their democratic ideals, hand in hand with Dutch anti-fascists. Pratomo told me: 'I worked together with Wim Jorritsma, who had studied with me at the business school in Rotterdam.' After our conversation, I looked up the name: Jorritsma was a young communist from Rotterdam, who was executed in Scheveningen at the end of the war. That Rotterdam business school, the Handelshoge-school, was the precursor of the Erasmus University. 'And that's where I'd met Jusuf Muda Dalam too. He came from Aceh and was a member of the Perhimpunan.' I scribbled down the names and let him go on talking, hoping that more memories would surface. 'Jusuf helped to write pamphlets. That was how we could express ourselves.' His voice faltered. 'Hmm . . .' he sighed. 'It's a long story.'⁵

I managed to reconstruct this story, with some difficulty, from his exceptionally interesting personal archive. It was an essential and fascinating puzzle to solve, because the role of Indonesians in the anti-German resistance is practically unknown.⁶ Because the Dutch reverted to seeing them as adversaries after World War II, their heroic acts were deleted from the national memory. Not until 2019 was a book released in which their role was discussed in detail, and even that was self-published.⁷ I see this selective memory as an injustice. The Dutch have forgotten the risks taken by Indonesian resistance fighters and the dangers they confronted in a country that was not their own, and which had in fact been occupying their homeland for centuries. The Dutch have forgotten that the well-known resistance member H. M. van Randwijk – founder of *Vrij Nederland*, the underground wartime newspaper that grew into a major national magazine after the war and is still published today – wrote about 'our Indonesian friends' after the liberation of the Netherlands: 'We were all volunteers in the same underground army. [. . .] We fought for the same ideals of freedom, humanity, justice and truth.'⁸ The Netherlands has forgotten Professor Cleveringa's words of May 1945: 'When there was resistance here in the Netherlands, we didn't have to ask, Where are the Indonesians? They were here and they stayed at their posts. They made the sacrifices. They were in the concentration camps, they were in the prisons, they were everywhere.'⁹ The Netherlands has forgotten how the PI was cheered at the huge celebration of freedom on the Dam in Amsterdam in May 1945; its members marched in the procession with a red-and-white flag and a banner reading 'Indonesia'.¹⁰ The Netherlands has forgotten that the PI had an audience with Prince Bernhard, the supreme commander of the unified Dutch resistance forces (the Binnenlandse Strijdkrachten), and that after the war a number of Indonesian resistance fighters joined national advisory committees and even the Dutch emergency parliament.¹¹ The Netherlands has forgotten that, after the war in Europe, some PI members planned to organise the resistance against

Japan in Indonesia, and that the PI's president, Setyadjit, even became the deputy prime minister of the Indonesian government during what the Dutch euphemistically called their First Police Action. The Indonesian resistance in the Netherlands fuelled the Indonesian independence movement that erupted after the war, and Pratomo played his part in this development.

Of the approximately 800 Indonesians in the Netherlands at the time of the German invasion, sixty to one hundred were involved in the resistance: 7.5 to 12.5 per cent.[12] In other words, they made a much larger contribution, relative to their numbers, than the Dutch community; even when the resistance reached its height in the final year of the war, it involved only 0.25 to 0.5 per cent of the Dutch population, 25,000 to 45,000 people out of a population of nine million.[13] To put it yet another way, one out of thirteen Indonesians joined the resistance even by the most conservative estimates, as opposed to one out of every 360 Dutch people. The myth of the Netherlands as a 'country of resistance' has been deflated even by comparison to France and Belgium, where twice as many citizens took part in the resistance, but the contrast with the Indonesian figures is astounding. Even if we keep in mind that the Indonesians in the Netherlands were mostly young people – students, sailors and maids – and therefore more willing to become involved in clandestine work, their participation rate was still exceptionally high. They joined the resistance not only in large numbers, but also early in the war, when only a few hundred Dutch people had dared to do the same. They included both men and a number of women, and a few of them were Chinese Indonesians.[14] The Indonesians printed and distributed illegal anti-fascist newspapers, they aided Jews and other people in hiding, and they forged identity papers. After a while, they also began to attack rationing offices and police stations and to train a militia of their own. Eight of them paid with their lives, seven of those in concentration camps, while another seventy-eight Indonesians died during the war of disease, deprivation or violence. This death rate is twice that of the Dutch population in the war years.[15] But they are not commemorated anywhere in the Netherlands. Dutch citizens from the Indies were also over-represented in the resistance and the struggle against the

Nazis. They participated by the hundreds. For example, eleven per cent of the Engelandvaarders, resistance members who fled to Britain, had been born in the Indies.[16] That included the most famous Engelandvaarder of all: Erik Hazelhoff Roelfzema from Surabaya, the 'Soldier of Orange'.[17]

'Resistance and more resistance, that was our battle cry,' Pratomo told me.[18] When I interviewed him, I knew he was the last surviving member of the Indonesian underground in the Netherlands. How can we explain their willingness to fight? Most of the Dutch population had been raised to respect authority, but the board of the PI had grown used to operating in the shadows, even before the war. Its members knew what it was like to be spied on and persecuted through the justice system. Two of them had spent months in Dutch prisons with Hatta before the war. Furthermore, they were far from their parents and therefore freer to make their own decisions.[19] In their clubhouse in Leiden, Pratomo helped to organise secret discussion groups. His housemates Suripno and Sunito gave him copies of the underground newspapers *Vrij Nederland* (Free Netherlands), *Het Parool* (The Watchword) and *De Vrije Katheder* (The Free Lectern) to distribute. In Rotterdam, where his brother Gondho was working for the resistance, he and Wim Jorritsma organised meetings at the business school. Pratomo put Jorritsma in touch with Stennie, who was still working for the port, to arrange for the printing of illegal newspapers, and she provided him with copies of the communist newspaper *De Waarheid* (The Truth) to distribute among his fellow students. He was a link between the docks and the lecture halls.

In June 1941, the Sicherheitsdienst (SD), the Nazi intelligence agency, raided a number of student residences in Leiden. Two PI board members managed to escape and were added to the Gestapo's blacklist; two others were arrested. Pratomo's brother was sent into the lion's den: the Sicherheitsdienst headquarters in The Hague, which happened to be in the old ministry of colonies building – same building, different enemy. He gave away nothing. Soon afterwards, publication of the newsletter *Indonesia* was suspended, and the PI was split up into autonomous divisions. Setyadjit and the other fugitive board member went into hiding where Gondho was staying in Rotterdam. Pratomo, too, moved in with his brother in early 1942. But all these comings and goings made the building's owner suspicious, so about six months later Pratomo had to move again, to The Hague this time. There he shared living quarters with Moen Soendaroe, who like him was a member of the Insulinde dance troupe. They made a little extra money by performing weekly at the Colonial Institute in Amsterdam.[20]

In Rotterdam, Pratomo's brother Gondho had found a building on Aelbrechtskade that was more suitable for their clandestine activities. By day, the area was a hub of inland shipping; by night, it was quiet. Above a grocer's storeroom was a room that was thoroughly closed off from its surroundings. There they could print underground newspapers, with a hand-operated roller at first and later with a Gestetner stencil machine. The fact that a few dark-skinned young men managed to smuggle in that cumbersome machine in the middle of the war shows how discreetly they operated. Gondho's girlfriend, a Dutch fashion designer, travelled to Leiden twice a week to pick up the lead articles for *De Vrije Katheder*. The authors included a Jewish chemist in hiding who listened to the radio illegally. The only time they could print was at night, when the stencil ink was sometimes so cold it remained solid. The young men of the Indonesian resistance were hungry and chilled to the bone, but they printed *De Vrije Katheder*, *De Waarheid* and *De Vrije Pers* (The Free Press) and helped to distribute *Vrij Nederland*, *Trouw* (Loyalty) and *Het Parool*. Pratomo didn't like to brag about it. 'It was a strange time,' he said. 'I wrote and distributed pamphlets.'

The printing press, the paper, the ink – it was a lot of evidence against them in one small space. Prat's friend Jusuf Muda Dalam believed they should arm themselves. 'What if they catch you at it? You're bound to die anyway, so you may as well sell your life for the highest possible price.'[21] He began to amass a cache of weapons: four pistols stolen from a police station in The Hague, two carbines passed on through the resistance network, nine jute sacks of hand grenades, some disassembled Sten guns and bullets from an RAF supply drop. Gondho took the weapons to their hiding place in a bread delivery cart, an operation fraught with danger, during which the cart nearly collapsed. Later they had to go to Leiden, where the PI was training a squad of Indonesian students. You couldn't take the train any more. So you cycled there – on a bicycle without tyres. Or you went on foot with a baby carriage and your weapons hidden under the baby. Or you went alone, from Rotterdam to Leiden, a thirty-kilometre trek, in the middle of the winter famine, with a few hand grenades hidden under a pile of swedes or carrots and the Feldgendarmerie, the German military police, thinking you were Chinese and asking you something about *Kartoffeln*. And you crossed the bare fields with your dark skin, your rumbling stomach, your emaciated body. 'First your legs start to hurt and seem to drag along behind you like lead, and then the pain spreads everywhere. You press on, and eventually you feel nothing. You see the road ahead of you, straight ahead, and you think to yourself, that road leads to my goal. But after a while you don't think any more either. You start counting in your head, one-two, one-two, and walking, walking, walking on and on.'[22]

Survival was often a matter of luck. In Leiden, Irawan Soejono tried to transport a stencil machine on the back of his bicycle. He had carefully wrapped it in jute, but he ran into a Gestapo patrol. When he tried to flee, he was shot dead. He was the son of Minister Soejono, the only Indonesian ever to have served as a Dutch government minister. Stennie helped Jews go into hiding, but on 16 January 1943 she learned that she had been betrayed; she and Jorritsma were arrested for distributing communist literature. At the home of Stennie's landlady, the Sicherheitsdienst found the address of Stennie's sweetheart in The Hague. Soon afterwards, inspectors came to Pratomo's door in Regentesselaan. 'I was arrested because the woman I loved had been betrayed,' he told me. 'My brother witnessed my arrest.' Gondho's eyewitness account was like a scene from a film: 'As I approached his address, I saw an unfamiliar car parked in front of the door with a few men standing around it, enveloped in the infamous SD overcoats and wearing their broad-rimmed felt hats. It was too late to turn back, so I slowly walked on and was nearing the place at the exact moment when Mr R. M. Djajeng Pratomo was being led out of the door into the van.'[23]

To Gondho, his brother's arrest came as 'a complete shock'. He went into hiding at a flower bulb nursery in the countryside near Sassenheim. But he wasn't safe there either. The farmer had a German non-commissioned officer billeted with him in a room across the corridor from Gondho's. It was a nerve-wracking ordeal. 'Sometimes I didn't even dare to sleep, for fear of snoring.'[24] Pratomo, his housemate Moen Soendaroe, and two Indonesian workers were taken to the Rotterdam police headquarters in Haagscheveer and subjected to probing interrogations. After a month of confinement, he and Moen were sent on to Kamp Vught in the Dutch province of North Brabant, the only SS concentration camp outside Germany. It was in the forest to the south of the city of 's-Hertogenbosch and had only been in operation for a few weeks, but it would soon become a fully-fledged *Konzentrationslager* with 32,000 prisoners: Jews, resistance members, political prisoners, Roma, Sinti, Jehovah's Witnesses, homosexuals, homeless people, criminals, etc. Between the tall barbed-wire fences was a wide canal. The guards in the watchtowers always fired live ammunition. Pratomo was shaved bald and given a blue-and-white striped uniform. He slept in a barracks with 240 other prisoners. The sacks of straw on the bunk beds formed a stark contrast with his daytime duties. 'I worked on the Philips assembly line,' he says. Radio valves, dyno torches and electric razors – the prisoners assembled the devices in return for better food and better treatment. Furthermore, they were not as heavily guarded there. Pratomo got a message to Gondho that he had been interrogated only about the Jorritsma group and not about the PI. His brother could come out of hiding.

There were also women prisoners at the camp, in separate barracks. One day, Pratomo saw a familiar face through the barbed wire: Stennie, in the same striped uniform. They had a moment to talk. She shouted that she was healthy and also working for Philips. During their year and a half at the camp, they had a few opportunities to speak to each other. The days of 'divine letters', 'gangs of kisses' and dancing to Josephine Baker seemed long gone. War makes love tougher, darker, leathery. Did she hear about the tragedy in the bunker: seventy-four women crammed into a single prison cell for the night – ten of them suffocated? Did he know their dark-skinned fellow prisoner who had opposed colonialism in Suriname, Anton de Kom? Had they seen those 1,800 Jewish children leave?

And the birches around the camp in Vught sprouted new pointed leaves that turned dark green and then yellow and red and brown, until only black branches protruded from the thin white trunks in the white snow. And very occasionally the living quarters of the sparsely furnished barracks were the site of a minor miracle. There was one small stove to provide heat for 240 men, and now and then Pratomo's former housemate Moen Soendaroe would bring a little sunshine into his fellow prisoners' day by dancing for them. In the oppressive atmosphere of the concentration camp, in the middle of the war, an audience of listless, hollow-eyed Dutch prisoners were treated to some of the most graceful bodily movements that human beings have ever devised: traditional Javanese choreography, with refined gestures and evocative facial expressions, performed in a prison uniform.[25] Moen Soendaroe was twenty-four years old. A few months later, he died in Neuengamme concentration camp.[26]

Roller skating. Yes, even that was forbidden in Jakarta (as Batavia was now called) 'in the vicinity of buildings where the Nipponese live'.[27] Dutch women were no longer allowed to wear trousers. Smoking was prohibited under the age of twenty. The cigarette brands Mascot and Double Ace were renamed Kooa and Sekidou, 'Asia Awakens' and 'Equator'. If you ran into a Japanese soldier in the street, you had to make a deep bow; even cyclists had to dismount or risk a beating. Java fell under the military authority of the 16th Army, Sumatra under the 25th Army and the Outer Islands under the navy. But the pattern was the same everywhere: respect for Japan was beaten into you, and everything Western was beaten out.

Dutch banks and the editorial boards of newspapers were shut down. Political activities were banned.[28] In the cities, wooden structures were erected with loudspeakers that played Japanese music and propaganda all day long. Wherever you went, you heard 'Kimigayo', the Japanese national anthem. News broadcasts were in Indonesian, Javanese and Sundanese, but never in Dutch, and there were daily

Japanese and gymnastics lessons.[29] Owners of radios had to have them locked so that they could be used only for official Japanese broadcasts. Listening to foreign stations in secret could be punished by death – and was.

Cinemas were given Japanese names and showed only films such as *Bouquet in the Southern Ocean*, *Sacred Snow* and *Flower of Patriotism*. These never included café scenes or smoking women; instead, they glorified self-sacrifice, patriotism, respect for the elderly and bashful femininity. Ticket prices dropped, half the seats were available at the lowest rate and there were hundreds of open-air screenings in the countryside. Some films attracted more than a million viewers.[30]

The propaganda machine swung into action with surprising speed. Japan had sent a team of 200 journalists, novelists, poets, cartoonists and interpreters to Indonesia.[31] They immediately launched a campaign known as AAA: Japan was 'Asia's light, Asia's protector, Asia's leader'. So many things changed: the language, the objects, the times. Don't say Japan, but Nippon. Don't call the central square Koningsplein, but Lapangan Ikada. Don't say Dutch East Indies, but Southern Territories. Don't celebrate Queen's Day any more, but the Emperor's Birthday. Don't depict chrysanthemums any more; choose a flower that doesn't symbolise the divine head of state. Don't print books in Dutch any more, except for the Bible. Don't treasure your old teaspoon with a W for Wilhelmina. Don't put 'Orange Nassau soup' on your menu. Forget all the Dutch, Christian and Chinese holidays; celebrate only the Japanese, Shinto and three approved Muslim holidays. Don't say 1942, but 2602; the imperial calendar went back further. Don't say six in the morning, but half past seven – the clocks were set to Tokyo time. Don't use stamps with Wilhelmina's face; instead, adorn your envelopes with Mount Fuji, the Buddha or a young pilot.[32] Pay in guilders, but use the ones minted in Japan, with an inscription in Dutch: 'The Japanese Government Will Pay One Guilder to Bearer'.[33] Later the Dutch inscription became Japanese and Malay and the guilders rupiahs.

It worked. Many Indonesians adjusted to the new normal. 'Speak Indonesian, why don't you!' a man hissed at Chisma Widjajasoekma and her friends as they strolled through Pasar Baru, a popular marketplace, chatting in Dutch. It came as a shock. She *had* to speak Dutch at home, or she wouldn't get her pocket money. Her father was a professor at a Dutch-Native School (HIS). 'From that time on, we didn't dare to speak Dutch above a whisper. My first job was in the office of a court. My boss was Japanese, so I had to learn to speak Japanese. The only place we still spoke Dutch was at home.'[34] Japanese at work, Indonesian in the streets, Dutch at home. That was how fast things could change; Dutch transformed from a respected, admired language of government into an idiom whispered at the kitchen table.

The entire colonial steamship was turned upside down. Everything Dutch disappeared into the hold. Deck 1 was exclusively for the Japanese. The masses on Deck 3 had to be re-educated. But how did the Japanese relate to the passengers on Deck 2? Pragmatically. Yes, the native aristocracy had collaborated with the Dutch, but their authority and governing experience could still be useful. Yes, the Chinese were the enemy elsewhere in Asia, but here their factories and businesses were indispensable. And yes, the 'little Indos' seemed very European, but why not take advantage of their skills? And what were the Japanese to do with the highly educated, politically active elite?

Deck 2 was a grey area for the Japanese. The masses on Deck 3 could be massaged in the right direction with suitable propaganda, but the Deck 2 passengers weren't as easily influenced. The fundamental goal was to turn them into the link between the military administration and the lower echelons. The old aristocratic regents were permitted to remain in their positions, but their allowances were halved. No more expensive ceremonial positions; from now on their job was to put Japanese policies into practice and set a good example. They were even encouraged to grow their own fruit and vegetables.[35] The Chinese middle class was also allowed to go on with business as usual. 'Japan needed us,' Go Gien Tjwan told me. 'My parents were resellers in the import-export trade. They continued to buy rice, soap and fabric from Javanese farmers and resell it.' His family felt a much greater affinity for China than for Japan – his brother, a physician, had gone to Manchuria to help – but that was no problem.[36] Benny Bastian's parents were also allowed to continue making headwear at their factory in Jakarta, but the demand for pith helmets was decreasing. 'After a while, we had to close the business anyway and start searching for food.'[37] These were hard times for the Chinese on Deck 3. Tjong King Poek sold coffee in a Japanese military canteen in Aceh. 'I was scared of them! If you forgot to bow, they hit you. If that knocked you over, they kicked you while you were down. Our Asian brothers? They were *kejam*, cruel and implacable!'[38] And the small Chinese community on Deck 1 had to work hard to get along with the new regime. Noortje van Dorp's Chinese father had gained equal status with Europeans. 'We Chinese had been here for centuries, and that made the Japanese very suspicious! Silence is golden – that was my mother's attitude. She called herself Li Bik, two short names. That looked more Japanese than Li Bik Nyo, her real name. She even wore a kimono in those days. The Japanese went to her for intelligence about who was wealthy in our area and who had received higher education, what nationalities people had and what their religions were. She gave them names. My father was never arrested, but our neighbours were.'[39]

The Indos had to find a place for themselves too. They had always been a little too Asian for the Dutch, and now they proved to be too European for the Japanese. Japan hoped to knead them into loyal subjects of the new empire, but they didn't seem overjoyed at the prospect. 'Japan wanted us on their side,' Bol Kerrebijn said. 'On the outside, I do look like an Indonesian, I'm a half-blood, but on the inside I was staunchly in the Dutch camp. Every Jap is one too many, that's what I thought.'[40] Nanny Kooymans's experiences were mixed. She had seen her father set off with the KNIL as a militiaman. Now he was a prisoner of war. 'We visited him in prison. He was in a little room. I said, "Will we all go home together now?"' She was eleven years old at the time. 'I bawled my eyes out.' But she also saw a different side of the occupation. 'The Japanese were very sweet to children and the elderly. As a child, I had a fringe. A Japanese officer with a magnificent sabre told me I looked like a Japanese child and invited me to come to the city with him. All the other Japanese people bowed to him. And to me! That bowing was their way of greeting. We went to a Chinese restaurant to order food, and the Chinese people bowed to me too! We ordered enough for the whole family, all eleven of us. Afterwards, I took a rickshaw home with all that food. I won't speak evil of the Japs, because what came afterwards was *much* worse.[41]

And then there were the leaders of the national movement on Deck 2: Asian by birth, European in education and anti-colonial in ideology. The day after their victory, the Japanese authorities contacted a few of them.[42] In March, Hatta and Sjahrir were released after eight years of confinement. Despite his lacerating criticism of Japanese fascism, Hatta was put up at the fashionable Hotel des Indes in Batavia at the expense of the occupying regime and assigned an impressive DeSoto to ride around in.[43] In July, Sukarno was even permitted to return to Jakarta from his place of internment in Sumatra. He had asked the Dutch to take him to Australia with them, but the colonial authorities had rejected this proposal, in effect handing him over gift-wrapped to Japan. They would have plenty of opportunity to rue that decision.[44] As soon as Sukarno arrived, he conferred with Hatta and Sjahrir, his former rivals. He and Hatta decided to become advisers to the Japanese military regime; Sjahrir chose not to join them and instead kept a very low profile. Would Japan elevate these Indonesian leaders into the elite? Would it be open to the nationalists' dreams of independence? The first step, in any case, was the abolition of the much-despised racially segregated court system.[45] In addition, the use of Indonesian was strongly encouraged, and people were allowed to call themselves 'Indonesians' for the first time. But the red-and-white flag remained banned, and none of the nationalist leaders were promoted to high positions; the Japanese leaders did not yet feel entirely sure of them. How reliable were people who advocated radical independence? For smooth cooperation with the native population, Japan preferred to work with a movement that seemed less dangerous: organised Islam. The nationalists were too headstrong for the Japanese, and the communists were intolerable, but the Muslim organisations could be put to good use. The traditional Nahdlatul Ulama and the reformist Muhammadiyah were apolitical and had hundreds of thousands of members, many in rural areas. They were people of faith, like the Japanese; they were not insistent about independence or democracy; and they turned out to be extremely well organised.[46] Nationalists like Sukarno – engineers, artists and economists who dreamed of independence – were dismayed to see devout Muslims without any political vision given greater power than them.

But the most important method of cultivating a new spirit was education. To make Indonesia an integral part of its empire – Japan believed this was just the beginning of a very long presence in Southeast Asia – it immediately began moulding the children on Decks 2 and 3. Less than two months after the conquest of the archipelago, Japan reopened elementary schools for Indonesian children to mark the birthday of Emperor Hirohito on 29 April 1942. The Dutch, Chinese and Arabic schools remained closed.

The publisher and sociologist Toenggoel Siagian had just turned seven and was enrolled in the first year of the HIS, the Western-style primary school for natives. 'It was the same school, but the Dutch headmaster had disappeared. We kept using our old textbook. There was a story in it about a tiger who ate the villagers' goats, until a man with a rifle, a Dutchman, of course, solved the problem for them. After the Japanese invasion the word "Dutchman" was replaced with "a man with a gun". Yes, Japanese indoctrination was very subtle.' New customs and rituals came into being. 'Each morning, we had to bow towards Tokyo. We had to sing "Kimigayo" and take the pupils' oath. I remember all sorts of new songs and fairy tales: one about a child who fell off a melon and one about a young fisherman who saved a turtle, that kind of thing. There were no more Dutch classes. The lessons were in Indonesian, and we were also taught a lot of Japanese.' The earlier years received three hours of Japanese a week and the later years up to ten hours.[47] 'We hardly ever saw the Japanese, but after three and a half years I could write Japanese well,' Toenggoel said. '*Katakana* and *hirakana*, of course, those are the easy syllabic writing systems, but also *kanji*, the Chinese characters used in Japanese. I knew a few hundred characters by then.'[48]

Primary school was made free, and growing numbers of children attended, some 2.6 million at the peak in 1944 (as compared to 2.2 million in 1940).[49] It was almost unbelievable: 50,000 Japanese colonisers reached more students in two years than 300,000 Dutch ones had in several decades. Teachers were better paid, schoolmistresses were brought in from Japan, and Indonesian spread like wildfire through the schools. Young Soerachman was fourteen by then. 'It was completely new to me! I spoke Dutch with my father at home and Javanese with my mother. At our HIS, our Dutch teachers were gone. Instead of *maandag*, the Dutch word for 'Monday', I was suddenly supposed to say *Senen*, with the stress on the final syllable. I mispronounced it, stressing the first syllable, but no one laughed at me. It was new to everyone.' The curriculum was thoroughly reorganised. Pupils everywhere spent a lot of time on Japanese history, morals and gymnastics; they had to make handicrafts and do volunteer work and military exercises. Soerachman said: 'Every school had daily training. We learned to march, move stealthily, shoot wooden dummy rifles and charge with a bamboo spear. Every day. They played on our feelings, saying, "We will give you independence."'[30]

Girls were also spoon-fed the new culture. Liza Yusuf summed it up for me: 'More singing, more parades, more gardening.' I was visiting her at a retirement home in Jakarta. She had just had an eye operation but was still as mischievous as she had been in those days. 'We learned to plant *singkong*, cassava, for baking bread. We also learned to bow. For an ordinary soldier? Deep. For the emperor? Very deep. During roll call, they pulled your hair until you bowed deeply enough. Then in your heart you start cursing the emperor and calling him names, of course. Drop dead, I thought.' That wasn't all that bothered her. 'The Japanese burned all the books. My father hid *Les Misérables* and *The Hunchback of Notre Dame*, which we had in Dutch. If we weren't allowed to speak Dutch at home any more, I decided I would just have to read those.' Resistance began not with big words but with little actions. Her father, a customs officer, was arrested for giving cigarettes to a few Australian POWs. 'The Japanese kept him in custody for three or four days. They put out their cigarette butts on his forearms.' She looked at my notebook with her one working eye and turned it towards her. Then she wrote a column of five exquisite Japanese characters. 'A, i, u, e, o', she read aloud. 'My Japanese teacher was a lady from Japan, Yoshino-sensei, Miss Yoshino. We loved her very much.' All of a sudden, she was singing 'Aikoku no Hana', the title song from the film *Flower of Patriotism*. She still thought it was just beautiful. She'd had such mixed feelings: detesting Hirohito, cherishing Victor Hugo, seeing her father's forearms . . . and at the same time, hearing poignant songs, learning to write elegant characters and adoring her new schoolteacher. 'When the Allies returned, I heard Miss Yoshino had performed hara-kiri. Didn't she want to go back? Was she ashamed? Had the man she loved abandoned her? Did she have an Indonesian lover? Who knows.' She stared into the distance with one eye, as if the answer lay there.[51]

Cisca Pattipilohy, one of the few girls at the HBS Western-style secondary school, loved Japanese education. 'Until 1942 I was a nobody. I'd done well in school in the Dutch period, but I didn't count. Then, for the first time, I was treated as an equal, and for the first time I felt like a normal human being.'[52]

Education offered girls new opportunities, but as much as Japan proclaimed its objective of Asian brotherhood, and as much as its films celebrated the ideal of the chaste, refined woman, Indonesian girls and young women were, from the beginning, at serious risk of sexual violence. The topic arose with disturbing frequency during my conversations in Indonesia. I heard stories of young women who, during the occupation, 'tied pillows to their bellies every day so that they would look pregnant'.[53] Stories of grandparents who kept their granddaughters hidden in the rice fields.[54] Stories of girls who married young for safety.[55] Or who quickly found a boyfriend, saying, 'I need to borrow you.'[56] Stories of Japanese occupiers who burst into people's homes and shouted, 'Onna! Onna!' (Women! Women!).[57] But what made the deepest impression was a story told by 'Grandma Ted', not because it was so dramatic, but because it was so characteristic. Her full name was Soeparti Soetedjo; she cut a graceful figure and spoke polished Dutch, with an impressive vocabulary. 'I was eighteen when the Japanese arrived here. An officer on horseback came into the garden. "Are there girls here?" he asked. "No," my mother lied, "they're all gone." She had hidden me. I was peeking out from a corner, very frightened. The Japanese soldiers were twenty to thirty years old. Their shock troops were Koreans: short, crude, shabbily dressed people with helmets. Their officers were taller and Japanese; they wore caps, sabres and insignia. They were well dressed. They enjoyed Jakarta night life and hungered for women, but fortunately I was spared.' To escape being abducted, women took extreme steps. 'Although at one point I was suffering from bacillary dysentery, my mother refused to take me to the doctor. She didn't want anyone to see me, because she was afraid they'd take me to work in a brothel. Instead, she treated me at home with traditional Javanese medicine, boiling papaya bark and giving me the liquid to drink. It was so bitter!' The fact that a worried mother in Batavia decided to treat her daughter's serious illness with home remedies rather than seek medical help speaks volumes about the risks women faced in the streets.

Still, they couldn't stay in hiding forever. Soeparti searched for a better solution and found one. 'I took a Japanese course, purely in self-defence. After all, if you spoke Japanese, they didn't take liberties. A girlfriend and I received private lessons from a Japanese officer, Mr Mimura, who was around the age of forty. He was like a father to us. He had daughters of his own back at home and would never have dreamed of brutalising us.' That was her euphemism for rape. 'Twice a week, we would go to his apartment in Cikini, where he would give us lessons from three to five in the afternoon. In the end, I was never brutalised.' And befriending a Japanese officer had other advantages. One day they saw an advertisement in the newspaper; the Japanese were in search of an Indonesian beauty to turn into 'a superstar'. Soeparti was eager to audition. 'Don't do it,' Mimura said, 'it's a trap.' Advertisements for actresses, hostesses and students were pretexts 'for abducting you'. Instead she should stay safe and continue her language lessons, he advised her. Japan couldn't import enough teachers from the mother country and was looking for native instructors. 'I spoke the language well and started to teach Japanese at an elementary school: katakana, hirakana and kanji, all three. Now I've forgotten everything.' Her language skills also proved useful in other situations – and even in the lion's den. 'After a year I went to Semarang. There I found a job at the Lawang Sewu building.' That was the imposing former headquarters of the Dutch East Indies railway company. 'The Kempeitai, the Japanese military police, had moved into it. It had the reputation of being haunted.' The Kempeitai were as feared as the Gestapo in Europe. Its members committed countless war crimes. 'Down in the cellar was a dungeon where people were tortured. I never went there to look. I worked on the second floor as a typist for the personnel department. I spoke Japanese, Javanese and Indonesian, so the Japanese respected me.'

Soeparti discovered that other women had developed their own strategies for coping with sexual violence. 'In Jakarta, I visited an old school friend, a sweet young woman with a Dutch father and an Indo mother. She called to me to come inside. On a chair, I saw a Japanese officer's sabre and cap.' Soeparti stared at her friend in disbelief. 'She had become his "wife", she said. She was shacked up with him. He was taking a shower. She couldn't let me stay for long. "I had to do it," she whispered. "Otherwise I would have been sent to the internment camp." I never saw her again.'[58]

And sometimes words fall short. Lia was mopping the corridor in the soldiers' barracks. She was thirteen years old, an Indo girl who'd had a carefree childhood, born in Batavia, raised Catholic and sent to board at a convent school. That school was closed now. Instead, she had to do the laundry, the ironing and the cleaning in a Japanese air force barracks. A group of soldiers noticed her there: her slight figure, the way she moved, the light in that long, quiet corridor. Suddenly she felt hands tugging, clothes ripping. Suddenly there were arms grabbing her arms. Suddenly there were torsos, leering faces, dripping sweat. She didn't know what was happening. She didn't want it to happen. But it happened, that day, the next day and every day afterwards. And suddenly there were no days left, only minutes, minutes that lasted weeks, and always the same leering faces, the same dripping sweat, from different torsos every time. She was raped several times a day. She was thirteen and pregnant for the first time. The military doctor forced her to have an abortion, even though it was against her religion. Afterwards, it started all over again. Hands, skin, hot breath, saliva. She turned fourteen and became pregnant again. This time she was allowed to have the child, but as soon as it was born it was killed before her eyes by two Japanese men. Suddenly there was nothing left in her life: no one, no soul, no light. A Japanese air force officer took charge of the bundle of skin and bones called Lia. He gave her food and then a bed, he showed her attention and then his fists. She turned fifteen and became a mother. She turned sixteen and became a mother again. 'A child with two children.'[59] After the Japanese capitulation, the officer took both children from her and spirited them off to Japan. Lia was a sobbing bundle of skin and bones again. It was the start of a desperate search that lasted a lifetime. When she died in the Netherlands in August 2007, she still hadn't found her children.[60] How thoroughly can a life be destroyed?

The problem of Japanese troops' sexual behaviour had been evident in the Russo-Japanese War of 1922, when a third of them returned from Siberia with syphilis and gonorrhea.[61] After the Nanjing Massacre of 1937, in which tens of thousands of Chinese women were raped by Japanese soldiers, the decision was made to set up army brothels with sex workers. There had to be at least one prostitute for every seventy soldiers; the women received medical care, partly to protect the health of the troops.[62] Japanese soldiers were exposed to a great deal of stress, but instead of sports, films or leave, they were offered brothels. The Japanese army took this philosophy to the newly conquered areas in the south.

It is remarkable how quickly it began, and how systematically they went to work. As early as July 1941, months before the start of the Pacific war, a senior official in the Japanese medical service took a clandestine trip to the Dutch East Indies to compile a secret report. 'We must take careful steps to prevent any rapes from occurring,' he reported to Tokyo, 'because that would undermine the confidence of the locals in Japanese military discipline.' But the established brothel system was an unsatisfactory solution, because venereal disease was present 'on a large scale'. So it was important 'to make the village chiefs responsible for comfort girls, so that they can guarantee to us that the women are rigorously examined for venereal disease'. There it was, in black and white, in an official document written even before the war began.[63]

For the officers, light-skinned women were brought in from

Taiwan and Japan; for the soldiers, native women were 'recruited'. The 'comfort girls' signed a document declaring that they were performing sex work voluntarily, but many signed under duress. The usual method was to snatch them off the streets or out of their homes. Here is the experience of Johana and her elder sister Rika, two girls who worked in a wire factory. 'Our father tried to hide us, but that was hopeless. The soldiers searched room after room and found us. My parents were forced to turn us over and told that they would be paid for us. If they hadn't agreed, they would have been killed instantly. With tears in their eyes, they gave us away.'[64] The two sisters were grouped together with dozens of other girls from Java, Sulawesi and the Moluccas. Throughout the country, young, attractive women were sent to hotels and restaurants that had military licences to run brothels – that was how official the system was.

Others ended up in the institutionalised military brothels in the barracks. They received salaries, medical check-ups and a portion of the income, but they weren't permitted to leave. Some were only twelve years old.[65] After a month in Jakarta, Johana and Rika had to go to Borneo, where they were sent to a fortified camp named Sakura, 'cherry blossom'. 'We were each assigned a room. Rika and I were in different rooms in the same camp. We were also given Japanese names, which were on the doors of our rooms. I was called Yoko-chan. We were provided with some clothes and make-up and told to dress up nicely and do our faces. One evening around seven, a soldier came to my room. I was forced to entertain him. At first I didn't want to. He shouted at me. Then I squatted down to defend myself. He hit me and pulled off my clothes. It wasn't long before I'd been robbed of every scrap of pride and dignity. The same thing happened to Rika and the other girls . . . We couldn't defend ourselves and we couldn't walk away, because the camp was so heavily guarded. In the end, we had no choice but to accept our fate . . . They should be ashamed of taking our childhood away from us like that. We had to service five to ten soldiers a day, and if we refused we were beaten or tortured.'[66]

The number of women and girls who worked as comfort girls is difficult to calculate. A Japanese study arrived at a figure of more than 22,000, but that included both the many 'mistresses' of Japanese officers (such as Soeparti's friend) and the women who were raped (like Lia).[67] The number of women actually forced into prostitution was much lower.[68] The life that awaited them was generally full of shame, trauma and cigarettes, lots of cigarettes.[69] The number of children born of such unions is unknown – probably several thousand.[70] The number of women of European origin used as military prostitutes, generally against their will is estimated at 200 to 300.[71] Professional sex workers were also employed. Sukarno, by his own account, 'gathered 120 [prostitutes] into a segregated district' of Sumatra at the request of the occupying regime 'and penned them in a camp surrounded by high fences'.[72]

What is not nearly as well known is the sexual violence endured by some boys. Two Dutchmen have anonymously testified that, as boys with blond hair, they were sexually abused by Japanese servicemen. This was systematic abuse by multiple men, who threatened to kill the boys' whole families if they refused to cooperate. They say they were twelve and eight years old at the time.[73]

What did it mean, in reality, that everything Dutch was sent to the hold of the colonial steamship? The Dutch forces had become prisoners of war; that was standard military practice. But no one had expected European civilians to be interned as well. Immediately after the March 1942 invasion, a few thousand prominent Dutch people were placed in confinement: judges, police officers, bankers, merchants and professors. This was a reprisal for the 2,000 Japanese civilians deported to Australia. A month later, all European public employees were dismissed and replaced with Indonesians; all Dutch people older than seventeen were required to register with the occupying regime.

May 1942: the first round-ups of Europeans. Jobless Dutch people were interned in hotels, schools and factories. In most colonial households, there was little change; they still had their domestic employees, and their suppliers still delivered door to door. October 1942: the first transports of European women and children to 'protected neighbourhoods' where they could retain the services of their native nursery maids and laundresses.[74] But the supreme commander, Hitoshi

Imamura, did not think it necessary to intern all 90,000 Europeans and 190,000 Indos. How could these relatively small communities stand in his way if '50 million natives are working with us'? If you have Deck 3 on your side, you don't have to worry about the upper decks, he reasoned. 'Out of considerations of humanity, I did not intend to intern all those people for no special reason.'[75] But his considerations of humanity irked the senior military commanders in Tokyo, who felt that this was no time for old-fashioned samurai ideals or Zen Buddhist compassion. In November 1942, he was replaced by a hard-liner who swiftly transformed the protected neighbourhoods into joyless mass internment camps. It should be added that Imamura's chivalry was not merely a posture. When, after the war, he was condemned by an Allied tribunal to ten years' imprisonment for war crimes committed by his subordinates, he decided the sentence was not severe enough. After his release in 1954, he had a copy of his three-*tatami* prison cell built in his garden. He remained there until his death in 1968. His cell can still be visited in Nirasaki today.

Of all the countries occupied by Japan, the Dutch East Indies had the largest European population. Almost 100,000 European Dutch nationals were confined to Japanese civilian internment camps: men, women and children. No exception was made for the elderly. Nowhere else in Southeast Asia were there more internees than POWs. Nowhere else were so many camps required: hundreds of centres in urban districts, warehouses, mental asylums, monasteries and convents, sanatoriums and boarding schools. Nowhere else were women and children separated from men as systematically.[76] 'Our neighbours were Dutch,' Kartika Affandi, an Indonesian, told me in an interview. 'I could hear the screaming when the husband and wife were separated by force.'[77] About one out of six internees did not survive, 13,000 Dutch people in total. The survivors went to live in the Netherlands after the war, as did a large group of Indos. No other Western European nation suffered such a profound collective trauma of long-term mass internment in civilian camps where conditions were usually wretched.

In a quiet retirement village beside the dunes in Wassenaar, near The Hague, I discuss all this with Joty ter Kulve. She was the girl who grew up in the villa in Linggajati but stopped celebrating St Nicholas' Day after the death of her European father. 'My mother had to go to Kempeitai headquarters in Cirebon. I was fourteen, my elder sister seventeen. The commander said to my mother, "You can go home now, madam, but we'd like to hold on to the two girls for the brothel here." "Over my dead body," my mother said. "You can't have them." "Think carefully," said the commander. "We'll shoot you dead otherwise." I was fourteen and had never heard of sex. At most I'd had a crush on a boy at school. The way the Japanese rounded up women! A week later, he asked my mother if she had changed her mind. "No, you won't get your hands on my daughters as long as they live." "Then get out of my sight!" the commander shouted. My sister and I had to go to the internment camp. Without the business about the brothel, we would have been spared that.'

Her mother, grandmother, grandfather and youngest sister were with her. They were sent to Kareës, a former residential area of Bandung fenced in with bamboo and barbed wire. There were already quite a few Dutch girls there when they arrived. 'All of a sudden, I was considered a full-blooded Dutch girl again. "We'll fetch your suitcases for you," they said. "Oh, great." But when the suitcases were brought to us, they were empty. These people were hungry, I realised. We shared a small room with nine other people in a house where no fewer than ninety people lived. But at least it was a house! The food came from the camp kitchen: in the morning two slices of bread without butter or anything else, at lunch time a handful of rice and some leaves and in the evening a piece of tapioca-flour bread. It was not nearly enough and anything but nourishing. After three months, my grandpa died.'[78]

The beginning of internment was a radical departure from the past for everyone, but few had already been through so much as the several hundred Jewish Dutch nationals who had fled Europe.[79] Their dramatic story has fallen through the cracks of history. Take Lydia Chagoll. After the war, she became an influential choreographer, filmmaker and writer, but when it began, she was a refugee, fleeing Europe with her parents.[80] 'My grandparents were typical "orange

Jews", selling fruit from a pushcart in Amsterdam,' she told me one winter day in her wooden cottage full of books in the woods near the Belgian town of Overijse. Classical music was playing; we drank tea with whisky. 'A few months after I was born, my parents moved to Brussels,' she said assertively. There her father founded *Het Hollandse Weekblad*, the city's leading newspaper for Dutch expats in the city.[81] They lived in a wonderful house in Lambermontlaan, a stately avenue along beautiful Josaphatpark. One day she noticed that her mother was packing and her father was withdrawing their money from the bank. She was nine years old. Germany had invaded that day; they had to go to the station as fast as they could.

That was the beginning of her wanderings. She hardly knew what it meant to be Jewish – the family was not very devout – but that didn't make any difference. From Brussels they went to De Panne, on the border, and continued on foot to France. Minibuses, vans, lorries. Saint-Omer, Abbeville, Rouen, Dunkirk. 'I remember Dunkirk,' she tells me. 'We stayed near the station. A day after we left, it was bombed.' Paris, Bayonne, Biarritz. Couldn't they get a boat to England from there? No. Then on to Pau, and after that, Toulouse. Sleeping in stations, parks and schools, sleeping on farms. Along the way they saw wrecked military vehicles, houses shot to pieces, smouldering remains. After a year in a refugee camp, they had the chance to travel on to Spain and Portugal. How about South Africa? they thought. They took a ship to the Portuguese colony of Mozambique and continued by train to South Africa: Pretoria, Johannesburg, Durban. 'Unwelcome everywhere we went. They all told us we were stealing their jobs.'

So they went on to the Dutch East Indies. Not of their own free will – soldiers put them on a ship. 'Surely they knew there had been a US embargo against Japan for months! Surely they knew the Dutch East Indies had oil reserves! Surely they knew that something was bound to happen there!' But whatever they knew, it made no difference. 'That ship was packed with people with Dutch passports.' After a year and a half of wandering the globe, they reached Batavia in November 1941 and found host families. They didn't want to seem ungrateful, but still, 'the way those people treated their servants! A bunch of rotten colonials is what they were. We were genuinely anti-colonial.' A month later: Pearl Harbor. They were devastated. Imagine crossing three continents to escape one war only to end up in the middle of another. When the Japanese army invaded, they were so scared of being killed that they fled to the interior in their car with the headlights off. The family of four spent days in hiding on a tea plantation – only to be captured and interned in the end, not because they were Jewish, but because they were Dutch. 'Eleven hundred and thirteen days behind barbed wire. Three years and eighteen days. Five different camps,' she fumed. In one camp, Tangerang, there were other Jews, including the world-famous violinist Simon Goldberg and the brilliant pianist Lili Kraus, who had been on tour together when Japan invaded. There was also a Hungarian variety artist. Lili Kraus did yoga. 'We all thought that was bonkers, but Frau Müller, a German Jew, told us it was "gymnastics, Indian-style".' In any case, it seems it did no harm to her resilience. 'Lili had to perform for the Japanese officers. She wove strains from the Wilhelmus and Jewish songs into her melodies. They were unrecognisable to the Japanese, but clear as a bell to us.' She fell silent. I said nothing. On a shelf of her bookcase, I saw a menorah alongside a beautiful wayang puppet and a portrait of Che Guevara. 'You longed for freedom like, like . . .' – for the first time in our conversation, she was at a loss for words – '. . . like a fish with its mouth open.'[82]

Life in the camps became more spartan as time dragged on. They were no longer allowed any contact with the outside world. When the Japanese suffered their first military defeats in the Pacific Ocean, they feared some Dutch internees in the camps might escape to assist the British and Americans. If you tried to flee the camp, you put your life at risk. Any suspicion of espionage or sabotage was ruthlessly punished.[83] In the autumn of 1942, Soerachman was a fifteen-year-old in Yogyakarta. 'I was on my way to see a friend. The path passed the sports field at the technical school, which had barbed wire around it. I knew our Dutch teacher and his family had been sent to a camp. "Stop!" a Japanese soldier shouted. He forced me to watch. A few Dutch people were being forced to dig two holes, side by side, on the football field. There was a pole at one end of each grave. A large, blond Dutchman was tied to one pole. He had run away, but the Japanese had caught him.' To make his story clearer, he sketched a map in my notebook, drawing the classrooms and the toilets. 'This is where the sports field was. These were the holes, and these were the poles.' He drew an X on the spot where the blond man and another man had stood, followed by an arrow pointing straight at them. '10–15 metres', he wrote next to it. At the other end of the arrow he drew an angular figure carrying something that looked like a stick. 'This here is a Japanese man with his bayonet. He got off to a running start. "Ooooowaaa!" Right in the belly. His guts came bulging out. The first Dutchman died instantly, but not the second one. "Uuuuurrgh," he groaned. They untied the rope and kicked and stomped them into the holes. Their friends had to fill the graves.'

This made a deep impression on Soerachman. Only later in life did he find the words to express it. 'Treating us gently is a good way of maintaining law and order,' he said. That was how the Dutch system worked in its best years, in his opinion. 'Treating us harshly, on the other hand, makes us angry.' That sounded like the 1920s and 30s. 'But if you treat us very harshly, we get scared. That was the Japanese system.'[84]

While the civilian camps were places of great misery, the prisoners of war were even worse off. For months already, they had been interned in a few large barracks in Java. They slept on the ground, were hungry all the time and hunted for 'roof rabbit' – if you called it that, it didn't taste as much like cat. Every day they had to form a line and hit each other if the line wasn't straight enough. They saw an interpreter who had made a translation error confined to a barbed-wire cage in the burning sun for twenty-four hours. They saw other people shot dead. 'But one day 600 of us were sent to Batavia to board the *Takuma Maru*,' said Ton Berlee, the KNIL sergeant who had started the fire at the oil refinery. 'We were sent to Rangoon in Burma. There we had to sleep on concrete in the British prison. Not much fun. We were black and blue from lying on our bones. A few of the boys had died on board, the biggest and strongest first.' Felix Jans, who had survived the Battle of the Java Sea, was put on a transport to

Singapore. He and thousands of others bobbed in the hold of a Japanese freighter for four days, surrounded by the unbearable stench of sweat, urine, faeces and vomit.[85] 'From there, up to Bangkok by rail, and then we continued on foot.' Both Ton and Felix became forced labourers on the Burma Railway, known around the world because of the film *The Bridge on the River Kwai*.

The Burma Railway was meant to help Japan supply its troops in Burma without having to sail around the Malay Peninsula, a long and dangerous maritime route patrolled by British submarines. Burma was of crucial importance to the Japanese; it cut the interior of central China off from the coast, had fertile rice fields and a few oil wells, and it opened the way to attacking British India. The railway was intended to link the Gulf of Thailand to the Bay of Bengal; from Bangkok, it went northwest, first passing through the green, flat lowlands and then climbing through the jungle until it reached the Burmese border at Three Pagodas Pass before descending to the Burmese coast south of Moulmein (now Mawlamyine), a journey of more than 400 kilometres through inhospitable, overgrown terrain with cool nights and day after day of oppressive heat. There were no fewer than 600 bridges to be built. Ton and Felix worked their way towards each other, Ton from the Burmese and Felix from the Thai side.

Ton Berlee: 'There was a crew that cut down trees. There was a crew that made holes in the rocks for dynamite. And I was on the crew that had to build the embankment. Behind us came the team that laid the sleepers and the rails. We had to add one cubic metre per man per day. That's a lot! And it wasn't exactly sand!'

The construction of the Burma Railway was the largest building project of the entire war in Southeast Asia to use forced labour. Japan sent 62,000 POWs there: 30,000 were British, 18,000 Dutch, 13,000 Australian and a few hundred American.[86] The KNIL prisoners of war included Moluccan soldiers. There were also tens of thousands of Asian forced labourers, known as *romusha*. Estimates vary from 70,000 to 190,000.[87] At first, the work was supposed to be completed in five years or less, but as the war situation changed, with Japan suffering ever-greater losses, new demands were made: it had to be finished in a year and a half – no, in a single year. At one point, the exhausted,

Map 16: Japanese POWs and forced labour in World War II

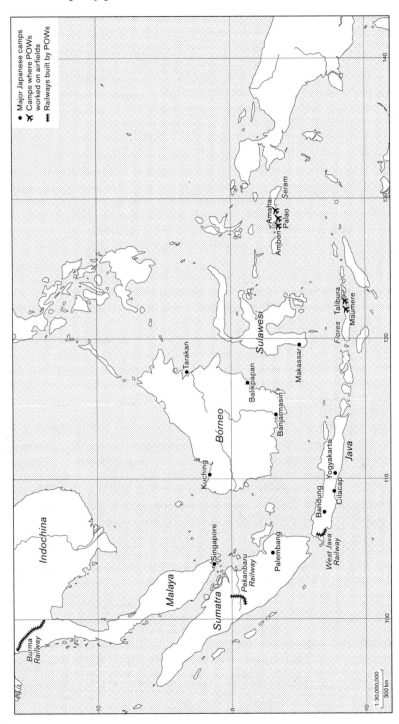

- Major Japanese camps
- ✈ Camps where POWs worked on airfields
- ⊞ Railways built by POWs

Amahai
Ambon
Palao
Seram
Flores
Talibura
Maumere
Tarakan
Balikpapan
Banjarmasin
Makassar
Sulawesi
Bórneo
Kuching
Yogyakarta
Bandung
Cilacap
Java
West Java Railway
Palembang
Pekanbaru Railway
Singapore
Malaya
Sumatra
Indochina
Burma Railway

1:30,000,000
300 km

starving, emaciated forced labourers were expected to move as much as three and a half cubic metres per person per day.[88] They walked barefoot in the rain over the rocks and along the muddy paths; they wore threadbare garments, and if anything, conditions were worse on the Thai side than on the Burmese.[89] Felix Jans told me about that: 'We had to move earth, we had to carry bags of sand and stone. And we were as skinny as this little finger of mine! You weren't allowed to rest, you had to keep working, otherwise you'd get a beating from the Japs.' The camp was guarded by Japanese soldiers and Korean auxiliary troops. To them, POWs were men without honour, cowards who had failed to defend their countries until their dying breath.[90] It still made Felix angry. 'They were always beating someone. They liked to give beatings, they did it out of habit. They were very cruel, even to each other. Their own soldiers took regular beatings too. The Japanese are intelligent, hard-working people, but also sadistic. I was beaten too, but not much. Some of the Japanese stayed calm, but others would strike out for no reason. And they enjoyed it. They would look on and laugh. Some of them were super-sadists who loved to knock the living daylights out of us. Fucking Japs! I've always said they're a shitty race, and I stand by that. No, that was not a great time. When I see a Jap, I turn away.'

Along the route was a shabby, improvised camp, eight kilometres long. The workers slept there under canvas or in bamboo huts with leaky palm roofs. The nights were cold and wet. Hygiene was non-existent, food extremely scarce. It was very difficult to bring supplies along the slippery paths trod into the mud. 'All we got was a little watery rice,' Ton recalls. 'No vegetables, and hardly any meat. Cows weren't cows any more, but coat racks. The Japanese ate the good bits first and then left the rest of the carcass for 500 men. If you found one drop of fat floating in your soup, you were lucky. A lot of fellows from the Indies knew about plants and would go searching for edible and medicinal plants in the forest. We ate cockroaches, giant earthworms, beetles, iguanas and snakes. Snake has the best flavour, just like eel. A cat made the mistake of coming into our camp. We were on it in a flash! And a dog – we fried it in a little oil. We'd kill for a treat like that!' But these additional sources of food didn't help much.

'Boy, were we skinny! We would wash ourselves naked, and all you saw was skin and bones. We were skeletons under a thin layer of hide. One of our pals said, "I haven't done my business for twenty-eight days." A doctor said, "That's possible. When you eat so little, your body stops producing waste." Twenty-eight days!'

Dysentery, cholera, malaria, kwashiorkor, scabies, gangrene, boils, beriberi, pellagra, dengue, diphtheria . . . the list of illnesses was endless.[91] So was the list of the ill. And that of the dead kept growing. 'I was never ill,' Felix told me, 'but I threw them into graves by the dozen. One, two, three, alley-oop! Chuck some sand over him, on to the next one. They died like rats. We dug the graves ourselves. I kept losing friends – to diseases, or they were beaten to death by the Japs, that kind of shit.'

The death figures were very high. Of all the Western prisoners of war, an average of twenty-one per cent died. The figure for the British and the Australians was a little higher, and for the Dutch it was seventeen per cent. 'We were still protected by our KNIL injections,' Ton said. By comparison, the death rate for POWs in Germany was only four per cent. Out of 62,000 Allied prisoners, probably about 13,000 did not survive the hell of the Burma Railway, despite being hardy young men.[92] Among the romusha, the Asian forced labourers, the death rate was about fifty per cent, and the total number of people who died may have been around 100,000.[93]

One cause of death is rarely mentioned: suicide. Surviving family members didn't generally want to hear that their father, son or brother had taken his own life. Some family members were told that their loved one had 'fallen, hit his head on a rock and died in the sun', as Brigitte Melissande Sparwer-Abrams put it.[94] What that meant was not always clear. Ton Berlee wanted to shatter the taboo. 'There were lots and lots of suicides, especially among young people. They would spend the whole day worrying. You shouldn't do that, you have to stay positive. I always found something to do – making a cup out of a condensed milk tin, or whatever. But a lot of Dutchmen sat around fretting and committed suicide.' But how did they do it, without pills, bullets or trains? 'If you wanted to die, all you had to do was taunt a Japanese soldier armed with a bayonet. In a camp in Thailand, there was a Japanese brute who loved to stick his bayonet into people. One young fellow asked an interpreter, "Teach me the worst curse words in Japanese." We were building a bridge across a river at the time – twenty, twenty-five metres high. Below it was granite. He climbed a rope ladder and started to swear a blue streak at that Jap brute. The Jap was furious and threw the boy off the ladder. Twenty metres down, the impact flattened him.'

On 17 October 1943, the railway was finally completed. The first train to use the line brought not only ammunition and provisions to the stations along the route, but also a group of six or seven older Korean prostitutes.[95] That was part of what those thousands of men had died for. On the way back, the train took wounded Japanese soldiers out of Burma, broken young men without arms or legs. Ton was transported to the starting point in Thailand. 'The railway was finished. We were all gathered together in Kanchanaburi. There was a Japanese examination system. We were all examined and had to eat lots of vegetables. I was told I had to go to Japan, but I managed to swap with another fellow in secret. Luckiest thing I ever did. The boat that was taking him to Japan was torpedoed.'[96] That was yet another possibility: you could go through hell in Burma and come out alive, only to drown because of an Allied torpedo. Approximately 11,000 prisoners on Japanese transports died that way.[97]

Felix remained in Thailand until the end of the war. 'The greatest moment of my life was when the British forces arrived! The world was turned upside down. They put the Japs behind barbed wire and told us to guard them. In war, anything is possible.' Felix, the man who had drifted in the Java Sea fearing for his life for hours after a Japanese torpedo sank his ship, the man who had hurled bodies into graves along the Burma Railway, now had an unexpected taste of power. 'It was our turn to do the beating. He hit me yesterday, so I hit him today. I didn't abuse my position, though I'm sure I kicked a Jap or two. If they were disobedient, we laid one on them. It's always easy to judge another person. I saw fellows on our side do things that made me think, No, I sure wouldn't do it that way. They were just like beasts. I could write a book, but I won't. No one needs to know. It would only be a story, anyway. You'll never go through what I experienced – good thing, too. War is always cruel and unjust. There are no good wars.'[98]

In Tsuga, on the furthest outskirts of greater Tokyo, I visited the Kawais. Kazuko Kawai still had clear memories of her father, who had been the chief engineer for the construction of a railway in West Java. 'He sent me lots of letters and even presents, like a pair of leather shoes. He was living in a big house with a swimming pool and a maid. In his letters, he always said how friendly the Indonesians were. He went mountain-climbing there and was very happy.' She showed me photos of him in a rattan chair, his white shirt unbuttoned. 'He worked at Lawang Sewu in Semarang but travelled a lot. He was a civilian in a military uniform.'[99] The railway in West Java was needed to transport coal from the interior to the south coast. How many died there? Fifteen thousand? Twenty thousand? Sixty thousand?[100] We will never know. The labourers ate leaves from the trees and drank water from rice fields and sewers. And how many people worked on the Pekanbaru Railway in Sumatra? Seven thousand POWs and perhaps 120,000 Javanese romusha. Some 80,000 of them are said to have died – all for nothing. The railway for transporting coal was not completed until the last day of the war.[101] And the airfields in Flores and the Moluccas, how many people died building those? About 24,000.[102] The Burma Railway was certainly not the only major infrastructure project.[103]

But as horrifying as these statistics are, some personal stories leave a far stronger impression. Take Nanny Kooymans, who had howled as an eleven-year-old girl because her father was a prisoner of war and couldn't come home with them. She had seen him for the last time as he was taken away to the harbour in a truck to do forced labour in the Moluccas. He was probably involved in building an airfield there. 'About six months later, my mother received a telegram informing us that he had died of bacillary dysentery. We heard they got one portion of rice a day.'[104]

Dick and Hans, two other Indo KNIL soldiers, were also put on a transport. They had to go to Surabaya. 'There was no logic to it,' said Dick, who had turned himself in as a POW. 'You were supposed to go to the harbour, but you didn't get any news about where you were headed. You never knew what to expect.' In Surabaya, Hans came down with amoebic dysentery. 'When I heard we were about to embark, I went to the latrine. That was a little ditch with running water. You rinsed yourself off with an empty tin. I heard someone groaning. "Are you in pain?" I asked. "Yes," he said. "Bleeding?" I asked. "Yes." "Here, put some in this tin for me." And I took that tin of mucus, blood and crap and showed it to a Japanese soldier. They were terrified of disease! They told me I didn't have to leave yet.' But his brother Erich did have to go and was sent to Flores to build an airfield, from which Japan hoped to attack Australia. Later, he was transferred to Sumatra to work on the Pekanbaru Railway. 'But the ship that was supposed to take him to Sumatra, the *Junyo Maru*, was torpedoed by a British submarine.' The sinking of the *Junyo Maru* is still remembered as one of the biggest maritime disasters in history. Of the 6,500 people crammed into the vessel, 5,620 drowned, all POWs and forced labourers.[105] By comparison, some 1,500 people died in the sinking of the *Titanic*. 'I never saw Erich again.'

Shortly after his brother's departure, Hans was forced to board a ship too. The voyage took a month: Batavia, Singapore, Taiwan . . . 'We followed a zigzag course for fear of torpedoes. I was wearing a blue band, which was for people who often had to go to the toilet. I slept on the edge of the beds, so I could get to the handrail faster to relieve myself. But whenever you saw a Jap, you had to make a deep bow, even if you urgently needed to go.'

Hans and Dick eventually arrived in Japan, where only a few thousand prisoners of war from the Dutch East Indies ended up.[106] Because many Japanese labourers had left for the front, they were forced to work in heavy industry. Dick was assigned to the shipyards of Nagasaki, where he had to help build supply vessels, welding plates onto the hull. In those days, they still used rivets. 'I was lucky. Our Japanese supervisor was not too strict. If there was an incident, he would inform the navy about it at break time, in the shack where we ate. Only then did the military get involved and possibly punish you.' There were only about 200 Dutch POWs there. The living conditions were basic: 'We slept in barracks divided into sections for twenty men each. We had bunk beds with tatamis, four wide and four high. In the beginning, we worked five days a week, but later in the war we sometimes worked non-stop for three weeks. There were also POWs working in the kitchen, and they would smuggle in Japanese newspapers with maps in them. We would try to follow the progress of the war that way.'[107]

Hans was less fortunate. He was sent to the Ashio copper mine north of Tokyo, where he started out working near the rim of a huge vat of molten metal. 'It was one of those pear-shaped Bessemer converters. You blow oxygen into it to keep the metal fluid. Never heard of it? I had to melt down whole rooms full of coins! And beautiful bronze bells from China, which were brought to us in rattan baskets. They needed the copper for cartridges.' The war industry was running full tilt, and everyone had to pitch in. 'I saw Japanese women doing heavy labour there.' Then, in the middle of the winter, he had to roast ore on a red-hot sheet of metal. While the ice-cold wind whipped across his back, the heat seared his abdomen as he stirred the glowing ore. Meanwhile, the snow drifted down through the holes in the broken roof, and the crows cawed. 'Kaa, kaa, kaa . . . In the middle of the snow.' The prisoners were wearing only the sackcloth garments they'd received on the ship. Many died of pneumonia. One day, when Hans tried to wash his itchy clothing, it froze into a rough sheet of ice. 'It was always January in Japan,' the Dutch poet Leo Vroman wrote in a poem about his experiences as a prisoner of war there. 'We became thin, crooked objects.'[108]

On the Emperor's Birthday, the factory was closed, and they had to remove the scraps of tin from the chimneys – dirty, demanding and dangerous work. The scraps fell down the shafts. 'People were sitting under the tin and were terribly burned.' They bathed in open water tanks full of murky water and discarded metal. The food was poor: a little rice and sometimes a fish head. 'When packages arrived from the Swedish Red Cross, we had to pose behind a large table with cans of Spam and mandarins. Smile! Photos! Smile! And then it was gone. The Japs took everything useful from the packages, and we went hungry. In our camps, there were maggots crawling over the ground. We had open latrines and saw that they lived on our faeces. We started to collect those maggots and lay them in saw-dust. That way they got clean. As long as they had a black stripe, they still had poo inside them. We kept an eye on their droppings until they were clean. Then we fried them.' The whole time, he was still suffering from severe amoebic dysentery. He was sent to the hospital for POWs in Yokohama. But even there the food was no good, des-pite the fresh vegetables. 'They grew lettuce on the beach but fertilised it with our own latrines. Eventually everyone caught amoebic dysen-tery.' But the worst part of all was the work in the depths of the mine, more than one hundred metres underground. Before taking the lift down, he was given a carbide lamp. There were no matches. They had to use tinderboxes, dried moss and flint to get it working. 'Blow-ing and blowing until you had a flame.' The work was organised hierarchically. At the top were the Japanese, responsible for the dyna-mite. Next came the Koreans, who tended to be cruel supervisors. Then the POWs, who had to fill carts with stone and push them down long, low tunnels. Old rooms were filled with debris to keep them from caving in. One man lost two fingers, another shattered his leg, two Australians were crushed and a lift came plummeting down and killed a couple of the Japanese.[109] It's a miracle that Hans, with his fragile health, survived. 'I was growing weak, I knew I wouldn't make it. But there were empty shafts, and I saw how to get there. I went there and blew out my carbide lamp.'[110] And there, in utter dark-ness, he would remain for hours, waiting in deathly silence until mealtime. He heard scuttling in the dark and knew it was the sound of blind white rats that could no longer tolerate the daylight. He heard dripping and knew there was an underground reservoir, home to blind white fish. Creatures from a different, quieter world. And maybe that is the ultimate image of the Japanese period: waiting in fear, in profound darkness, for it to end, as despair drips from the ceiling and you don't know if you'll make it.

Chapter 8

'Colonialism is Colonialism'
Mobilisation, famine and growing resistance,
January 1943–late 1944

On 5 December 1942, Sukarno did something unprecedented: he gave a speech on the radio. Ever since his release several months earlier, his life had been one unbroken string of surprises. No longer was he a political pariah under Dutch rule; all of a sudden, he had the ear of the highest authorities. Hitoshi Imamura, the commander of the Japanese army that controlled Java, had called him a 'true samurai' and made him an adviser with a monthly salary of 750 guilders.[1] As the charismatic leader of the Indonesian anti-colonial movement, he had a luxurious villa at his disposal in the most fashionable part of Jakarta and a sleek black Buick – both confiscated from Dutch colonists sent to the camps. Sukarno had transformed into an impeccably dressed gentleman, even eating fruit with a knife and fork. He had criss-crossed Java in his new car to give lectures and meet with leaders. In Jakarta, he had spoken to Hatta and Sjahrir. In Yogyakarta, he had been to see Ki Hadjar Dewantara, the founder of the Taman Siswa educational system. In Surabaya, he had visited Mas Mansur, the leader of the country's largest Islamic organisation, Muhammadiyah. He was free to travel, hold meetings and make speeches without disruption. And on the first anniversary of Pearl Harbor, he was permitted to address the nation on the radio, a privilege never accorded to him in the colonial era.

The importance of this speech is almost impossible to overstate. Under Dutch rule, Sukarno had sometimes spoken to a crowd of thousands, but his audience now was on an entirely different scale. Not that so many Indonesians owned radios, but the Japanese system of public loudspeakers brought his voice to hundreds of thousands of listeners. In parks and squares, along avenues and in railway stations, ordinary people heard him speak for the first time: a crackling voice, punctuated with static. Sukarno said: 'If this war does not end in victory, all of our aspirations, all of our hopes, all of our efforts will be shattered, and we shall once again suffer and be oppressed and exploited by Allied imperialism. Only a Japanese victory can save us, can save all of Asia.' He knew, of course, that he had made himself the willing mouthpiece of Japanese propaganda – the conflict in the Pacific was still in progress – but his attitude was highly pragmatic: 'The Japanese needed me and I was aware of that. But I also needed them to make my country ready for revolution.'[2]

His Indonesian was as bombastic as ever. He stressed every syllable of the word 'Indonesia', and his rhetorical pauses were perfectly timed to allow for applause from the unseen crowds. In Jakarta's central square, the former Koningsplein, people were seated on risers, listening breathlessly. His young audience was especially entranced.[3] Leo Jansen – as an interpreter for the Japanese radio, one of the few Dutch people who could still move freely – wrote in his diary: 'Every Indonesian boy looks up in admiration at the heroism of the Japanese forces and at the hero of his people, Sukarno. It's a kind of romanticism we'll never share. We offer them good salaries and Frigidaires and radios if they will come and work for us. [. . .] We're always at a disadvantage, because we're more aloof, less interested, more level-headed, less family-minded.' That day, he saw thousands of bare-chested children with wooden rods march through the streets. These *bantengs*, 'wild bulls', as they called themselves, had been brought to the city on hundreds of military trucks, and they 'greeted each other with outstretched arms and *hidup Sukarno*', 'long live Sukarno'.[4]

In his speech, Sukarno stressed the need to 'build a new society in Indonesia' and announced the establishment of the Pusat Tenaga Rakyat (Centre of the People's Power). This organisation, Putera for short, was to be run by Sukarno in cooperation with the economist Mohammad Hatta, the education expert Ki Hadjar Dewantara and the Islamic leader Kyai Haji Mas Mansur, under Japanese supervision. *Putera* means 'son', an appropriate name in view of the youthful virility that the movement sought to project, and Japan's self-appointed role as an elder brother. 'Son', 'wild bulls', bare chests . . . there was plenty of carefully staged masculinity around this time. Putera was meant to replace the old, top-down AAA propaganda initiative. From Japan's perspective, Putera was a way of winning hearts and minds to the war effort, with the help of influential Indonesians. To Sukarno, however, it was nothing less than a new popular movement dedicated to the glorious prospect of Indonesian independence. 'Come, come, Indonesians,' he said, 'let us roll up our sleeves, let us get to work. Let us bravely work alongside the Japanese, combining all our powers, so that we may move mountains. [. . .] Art thou a *putera*? Answer only: Yes, I am a *putera*, a son of the new era, a son of the new struggle, a son of the new society, a son of Indonesia!'[5]

In the past, great emphasis was placed on Queen Wilhelmina's famous '7 December speech'. This English-language radio address, which despite the popular name was actually held on 6 December 1942, the eve of the Pearl Harbor anniversary, was of special importance because it was the first time the Dutch head of state in exile said that 'after the war it will be possible to reconstruct the Kingdom on the solid foundation of complete partnership'. That went far beyond any pre-war pledge. What she had in mind was 'a commonwealth in which the Netherlands, Indonesia, Surinam, and Curaçao will participate, with complete self-reliance and freedom of conduct for each part regarding its internal affairs, but with the readiness to render mutual assistance [. . .] This would leave no room for discrimination according to race or nationality.'[6] In short, the colonies were to be granted a high degree of sovereignty within the Dutch empire. But in Indonesia, Sukarno's radio speech was many times more influential than Wilhelmina's, which couldn't even be heard legally there. Not the queen, but Sukarno was the voice of the nation, especially in the minds of the youth. One young Eurasian who had not been sent to the camps had her misgivings about Sukarno's growing popularity: 'Nippon has now put some rotten native we banished in charge of the government.'[7] When Putera finally became active – in March 1943, on the first anniversary of the capture of Java – Sukarno spoke in the centre of the capital to a crowd of around 200,000.[8] Batavia had been officially renamed Jakarta in December 1942, Koningsplein had become Ikada Square, and that very morning, the statue of Dutch East India Company pioneer Jan Pieterszoon Coen in Waterlooplein had been pulled down.[9] The tide had turned.

'Oh, yes, I still remember Sukarno's house very well,' Kartika Affandi said with a laugh in her lush garden outside Yogyakarta. 'We had breakfast there every Sunday. I was eight or nine at the time.' It was the first half of 1943; Sukarno had just been appointed head of Putera. Kartika is the daughter of Affandi, the greatest and most original Indonesian painter of the twentieth century. 'Every Sunday, there was a big meeting with lots of artists,' she said. 'It was a modern colonial house with a terrace and a big, big garden. It must have been fifty metres back from the street. Sukarno was an architect by training, but he also painted and sketched.' That's true: Sukarno was a more than proficient artist, especially in watercolours. You might have expected him to be an expressive oil or acrylic painter, but he preferred dreamy, harmonious landscapes in watery pastel tints.[10] It was around this time that he began his private collection of modern paintings, which would grow to several thousand works and is still the finest in the country. As the chairman of Putera, he had an unparalleled network, which included all the big names in the visual arts. 'Sudjojono, Agus Djaya, Emiria Sunassa . . . They were all having breakfast at one big table. I couldn't follow the conversation. They were speaking Dutch! We only spoke Sundanese at home. Fatmawati was there too. She was so young and so beautiful.' This was Sukarno's third wife, just twenty years old to his forty-one. After his marriage to Tjokroaminoto's daughter he had wed Inggit, a woman from Bandung. A generous mood prevailed at those Sunday brunches: 'The atmosphere was anything but stiff. They were light-hearted events. "Affandi," Sukarno once said to my father, "what is your favourite food?" "Fried tempeh in newspaper," my father said, "with sambal and soy sauce!" The most ordinary food you could imagine. "Done!" said Sukarno. A week later, there was tempeh in newspaper waiting for him.'[11]

Those were golden years for Indonesian artists. In the early days of Putera, Sukarno invited Affandi to come to Jakarta.[12] Before then, Affandi had made his living by painting film posters in Bandung. 'All of a sudden, my father had a place to work and a salary. For the first time, we could have three meals a day!' And before that, they had lived in Bali for a few years, 'half-naked', Kartika says, close to nature in what was then still an island paradise. Affandi was a bohemian who hated conformism. 'He didn't think school was so important. It was better to learn from life, he said. He taught me to play marbles, make kites and ride a boy's bicycle.' But Putera offered him new opportunities. 'He no longer had to exchange his paintings for clothes. Sukarno bought several from him, saying, "Affandi, I love your work because you're honest. You show a person as he is."' That was undeniable. Affandi painted the poor, workers and prostitutes; he depicted wilted sunflowers and messy cockfights. His bright colours and popular themes were reminiscent of Van Gogh. He developed a technique all his own: painting directly on canvas with the tube and then using his bare hand to spread the oil paint. If he had been a European or American artist, he would undoubtedly have developed into a leading light of figurative expressionism.

During the Japanese era, Affandi also became friends with Chairil Anwar, another phenomenon. 'Yes, that famous poet was a friend of Papa's,' Kartika said. Anwar was a young man in his twenties, fifteen years younger than Affandi, who just a few years later would be hailed as Indonesia's greatest poet. He had studied the work of the greats, such as Auden and Rilke, and leading Dutch writers like Marsman and Slauerhoff, and his work demonstrated that Indonesian – that young, utilitarian language – lent itself to surprisingly fluid verse. Chairil Anwar was also the prototype of the *poète maudit*, a 'doomed poet' who led such a turbulent life that it destroyed him, indulging not only in poetry but also in opium and prostitutes. In his work, he aimed to take 'no ordinary photos, but X-rays to the white of the bones'.[13] He was skinny, pale and scruffy and died of typhoid in 1949 at the age of twenty-six. About Affandi, he wrote: 'Let me be there on the high tower/ Where you alone surmount the others.'[14]

Chairil Anwar wrote half of his small body of work (about seventy-five poems) in the war year of 1943, when Sukarno's Putera was formed. Many of his poems did not get past the censors – too individualistic, too tormented, too Western – but the important poem 'Dipo Negoro' did make it into print.[15] It is clear even on a quick reading that the poem is about more than just its title character, a rebellious nineteenth-century Javanese prince. It opens with the lines: 'In this time of building, forging/ You live again/ And astonished embers burn'. A few lines later, it seems to herald an imminent war:

Forward

These soldiers beat no drums
They show their faith by attacking

To mean something, once
Then death

Forward

For your country
You lit a fire

Better destruction than slavery
Better extermination than oppression
It may come after our death
But life has to be life

Forward.
Attack.
Charge.
Strike.

The poem reads like a kind of military exercise, and that's probably how it was intended. That same spring, in 1943, the Japanese began drilling young Indonesians. Guadalcanal, the largest of the Solomon Islands, northeast of Australia, had been lost to the Americans in

February. Even more than the Battle of the Coral Sea (May 1942) and the Battle of Midway (June 1942), both won by the Allies, the capture of Guadalcanal after eight months of heavy fighting was a turning point in the Pacific theatre: the island was the southernmost Japanese territory and the first of a long chain of islands extending northwest towards the Philippines, Taiwan and Japan. What's more, it had an airport. From there, American and Australian troops could begin their long advance. The supreme command of the Japanese military realised that, in the event of an Allied landing, capturing Java would be like taking sweets from a baby; after the invasion, Japanese force levels had been reduced from 55,000 to 11,000–13,000 at most, and many of those troops had relatively little training.[16] That made it essential to mobilise the young generation of Indonesians, not just politically but also as a military force. Sukarno was more than happy to contribute to the campaign. At meeting after meeting, he raised his fist and inflamed the masses: 'Amerika kita setrika, Inggris kita linggis' (We'll squash the Americans, we'll bash the British). The masses chanted the slogan along with him. Rice farmers and schoolchildren learned to hate distant countries their parents might never have heard of.

In the course of 1943, Japan set up four major youth organisations. Seinendan and Keibodan became active in April. Seinendan's members, aged fourteen to twenty-five, learned to patrol and keep watch. Keibodan, for young men aged twenty to thirty-five, served as an auxiliary police corps and maintained order, tracked down criminals, kept an eye on suspicious characters and so on. According to Japanese figures, Seinendan had half a million members and Keibodan one million. 'Everyone automatically became a member,' Soemardi tells me. 'It was compulsory. We had to march, we were drilled and we were given all sorts of little jobs to do. We didn't have any weapons yet, only bamboo spears, but it was real military training, no doubt about that.'[17] This type of training, alongside all the physical exercises at school, prepared a whole generation for military duty. For many young people, it was the main source of pride, social status and self-confidence.

In the second half of the year, the heiho and PETA also became

active. The heiho were auxiliary troops in the Japanese army. Immediately after capitulation, Indonesian KNIL soldiers had been
incorporated into the Japanese army, and now that corps was
expanded to a total of more than 60,000 young soldiers.[18] The enthusiasm of the young volunteers was striking. 'We were drawn to it by
the way the Japanese dressed, their smart uniforms and long trousers
that went down past the knee,' said Johannes Soewondo. 'I stood and
watched them in shorts and bare feet.'[19] Some people went to great
lengths to become members. 'I dreamed of becoming a heiho in the
Japanese army,' said Soenyaro Goenwiradi from Yogyakarta. His
father, a teacher of Islam, had already joined and was training young
soldiers. 'Japan was very clever! My father was a Muslim, but anyone
could join. They were very tolerant. Every day, my father was training young people. That appealed to me! I was in good shape, but I
was still too young. One day there was a big recruitment drive across
from the Sonobudoyo Museum. I think the Japanese needed a lot of
soldiers. I registered and was accepted. I was very happy. I was only
fourteen! Japan told us, "The Netherlands is colonial and will take
away your things. We're your elder brother. We'll protect you from
other countries." That was why we loved Japan. It was going to liberate us.'[20]

Becoming a heiho meant subjecting yourself to the rigours of
Japanese military discipline. 'Ouch! They were so strict!' Soejono
exclaimed when I spoke to him in Malang. 'Couldn't speak proper
Japanese? They beat you. Didn't stand up straight for roll call? They
beat you. And if you keeled over during a march, no one looked back.
But I was put in charge of a forty-man section. I was the only one
with a gun.'[21] Sumaun Utomo, the communist from Semarang, and
his small group of anti-fascist friends saw a strategic opportunity:
'We joined as volunteers, not to aid Japan, but to learn to use weapons. There weren't many who saw it that way, only the leftists. Japan
arrested and executed lots of communists, so I had to be very discreet.' Sumaun received six months of basic training. He learned to
shoot an old Dutch gun and was assigned to the air defence division.
'There I learned to calculate an aircraft's distance from its speed and
direction. There were twelve of us measuring, loading, aiming and

firing. The gunner sat on a little metal chair. The Japanese soldiers just looked on.' Later, when Allied aircraft really did appear in the skies over Surabaya, Sumaun knew what he had to do. 'We didn't want to fight that enemy at all! When we calculated the distance, we made deliberate mistakes and missed on purpose. We never downed a single aircraft! All we had wanted was the training. They didn't know we were their opponents; our resistance was underground. We said, "If Japan stays for a long time, we'll fight fascism. If Japan stays for a short time, we'll fight for freedom." '[22]

Finally, on 3 October 1943, PETA was founded. The abbreviation stood for Pembela Tanah Air, the defenders of the motherland. PETA was not a militarised youth movement or an auxiliary military or police corps, but a real native fighting force with Indonesian officers under Japanese command. The battalions of around 500 men were headed by teachers, public officials or other local leaders. Ever since World War I, Indonesian activists had been talking about troops of their own, but now, for the first time, the occupying regime was permitting large-scale mobilisation. No fewer than sixty-five PETA battalions were eventually formed, in total 37,000 soldiers. They had at their disposal 17,000 rifles, 900 machine guns and ninety light mortars. For the first time, Indonesia was armed.

'The Japanese were masters of social mobilisation,' says Purbo S. Suwondo, the man who had felt so ostracised in his European-style secondary school. When I interviewed him in July 2016, he was one of the last living former PETA officers. 'The gymnastic exercises at school, Seinendan for young people, the heiho auxiliary troops, the PETA battalions – all forms of collective life were designed to ignite nationalism and patriotism. These methods spread the fighting spirit to the most remote villages. By 1945 we, the world's gentlest people, had all become tigers!'

Purbo's encounter with the Japanese army was a breath of fresh air. In PETA, he was valued as never before. After basic training in Bogor, he reached the status of *shodan-cho*, platoon commander, and after further specialisation he was given responsibility for training recruits at military school.[23] At the ceremony in Jakarta where he was promoted to officer, he received a uniform, a rank and a samurai sword. Now he really belonged. The Japanese model was far more democratic than the Dutch one: what you were capable of mattered much more than who you were. Social class, economic status and religious preference became less important. For the first time in centuries, a generation rose up that did not look to people's ancestry but to the future. The distinction between Decks 2 and 3 grew vague. Young people no longer cared who was rich, who descended from the aristocracy or who practised traditional Islam; instead, they saw themselves as a unified whole with a single mission: to defend the fatherland.[24]

'Sukarno and Hatta are often said to have "collaborated" with the Japanese,' Purbo added. 'A parallel is drawn to collaboration with the fascists in Western Europe. But that's unfair.' It certainly did make quite a difference whether your country was free or colonised; in the latter case, you might join forces with the occupiers simply because you were anti-colonial. Furthermore, the Japanese had a policy of 'anti-colonial fascism', an ideological combination unheard-of in Europe. Totalitarian regimes such as Mussolini's in Italy, Salazar's in Portugal and Pétain's in France had colonies of their own; not one autocratic regime in Europe was anti-colonial. In contrast, as we have seen, Indonesians had various reasons to side with the occupiers. To add still more weight to this point, Purbo added: 'Don't forget that Sukarno and Hatta had been freed from prison by the Japanese!' That's true too. They'd been incarcerated for eight years. And on top of that, 'Sukarno believed that, if we wanted freedom, we had to form our own army with our own officers. He said it was pointless to generate ideas without generating power. In short, PETA was the embryo of the later national army.'[25]

In other words, strategic cooperation with the occupiers was a necessary part of moving forward with the national struggle, a form of opportunistic cooperation rather than ideological collaboration. Sukarno himself called PETA 'the vital tool in our forthcoming Revolution'.[26]

Yet the road to independence had its potholes. Putera was meant to become a large mass movement but lost much of its prestige when the Japanese set up a range of parallel organisations that escaped its control. Young people had Seinendan, women were given their own umbrella organisation and Muslims were brought together in a new Islamic federation, Masyumi.[27] There were also separate organisations for sport, culture and education, and Putera never had any economic powers. 'Within Putera, the question often arises of what is left for Putera to do,' Hatta grumbled in August 1943.[28]

What was even more frustrating was that Burma and the Philippines had been declared 'independent' by Japanese Prime Minister Tojo as early as January 1943. Although they were still part of the Japanese empire, their new status corresponded exactly to what the Indonesian nationalists had requested from the Netherlands before the war: independence within the empire. The Indonesian nationalists would still have jumped at the chance for such a status, but that great leap forward remained very distant. The reason was simple: Indonesia had too many strategic resources for Japan to loosen its grip so quickly.[29] In November 1943, when the Greater East Asia Conference was held in Tokyo, with delegations from occupied territories, Indonesia was not even represented – to Sukarno's fury. Why should he go on spreading Japanese propaganda and lending legitimacy to the occupying regime without even a symbolic quid pro quo? A month later, he and Hatta were appeased with a junket to Japan and an audience with Emperor Hirohito. It was Sukarno's first trip abroad. PETA officer Purbo S. Suwondo still recalled those days clearly. 'Sukarno and Hatta received an invitation from the Japanese emperor, but nothing changed. Our red-and-white flag and our national anthem remained banned.'

If 1942 was the year of politicisation and 1943 the year of militarisation, 1944 proved to be the year of total mobilisation. The international situation looked unpromising for Japan. Germany had been halted at Stalingrad, North Africa had been lost and Mussolini had surrendered. Meanwhile, the Americans were advancing in the Pacific. In November 1943, Admiral Chester W. Nimitz and his fleet, based in Hawaii, conquered the small but strategically important Gilbert Islands. From there, he began to use his tactic of island hopping, crossing the sea by way of the Marshall, Caroline and Mariana Islands to the islands off the

Japanese coast. The army, in contrast, advanced by what was called leapfrogging: from Guadalcanal, one of the Solomon Islands, General Douglas MacArthur chose to leap ahead to larger islands such as New Britain and New Guinea in order to retake the Philippines and Borneo and bombard Japan from there. Even though these plans literally left Java and Sumatra to one side, the repercussions of this double advance were felt throughout the archipelago. Japan, fearing invasion, demanded total mobilisation of the Indonesians working in agriculture, mining and infrastructure. Invincible Japan had become a very nervous occupying power.

To plan and execute the mobilisation, the occupying regime founded two new organisations: the Central Advisory Council and Jawa Hokokai (the Java Service Association); Sukarno had a seat on both. He was the director of the central office of Jawa Hokokai, established in January 1944 as a successor to the collapsed Putera organisation; Hatta became the vice-chairman of the advisory council. Anyone over the age of fourteen could be mobilised for the war effort. That included sixteen-year-old Johannes Soewondo. I had a long conversation with him in the East Java town of Pare; we sat in his living room, and his grandson Anton, a sociologist at the State University of Malang, was our interpreter. 'The Japanese said, "We need young people. We're going to bring you up properly. We are all Asians."' After basic military training and a crash course in Japanese, both of which involved frequent corporal punishment, he was sent to Sekiyu Kogyo Gakko, a training centre for petroleum extraction connected to the Cepu refinery near Bojonegoro. At first, he loved it there. 'It was fun in the beginning, that Japanese uniform. Discipline was strict, but we learned useful skills. Me and 700 other students slept in a huge warehouse under a sugarcane roof.' Then he was transferred to an oil refinery in Surabaya. 'My job wasn't in prospecting, but in refining. The crude was piped in and we had to determine the levels of fuel oil, asphalt and paraffin and filter it. We stored the paraffin and asphalt in separate containers and refined the crude oil into kerosene.' Of course, this fuel was not intended for flickering oil lamps in the utter darkness of night in rural Java, but for Japanese warplanes. Now that the Allies were sinking more and more oil tankers at sea, oil production had to be increased. But it wasn't a safe activity on land either. Surabaya was Japan's main southern port; the oil installations had great strategic value. 'When the air-raid siren sounded, we all had to go to the underground shelter. To reduce the probability of bombing, the Japanese even built a decoy of our factory! One night I saw an enemy American aircraft being "caught" by three large searchlights and shot at from the ground.' But as he filtered all that crude oil, the product of his homeland, something was slowly but surely happening to him. His enthusiasm transformed into its opposite. 'I loved the Japanese, but later, not any more. They were cheating us! They were taking away all our resources!' He said it with great intensity. Every day he had seen the proof on his plate. 'The Japanese were bad at feeding people. Our usual staple food is rice, but rice became expensive, so we were given rice mixed with maize. Eventually it was only twenty per cent rice and eighty per cent maize. But meanwhile, we could see trucks driving past loaded with rice.' Japan or the Netherlands? His conclusion was rock-solid: 'Colonialism is colonialism!'[30]

In 1944, rice became extremely expensive in Java. Early in the year, twenty-nine-year-old Hertha Anna Hampel, a Eurasian woman in Jakarta, wrote in her diary, 'The rice ration [given out by the Japanese] is not enough to sustain anyone,' so she had to buy rice on the black market, 'and that already costs 1.60 guilders a litre'.[31] In just a few weeks, the price had risen from thirty-five to eighty cents and then to 1.40 guilders, and in June 1945 it would soar to 2.10 and then peak, not long afterwards, at 7.50 guilders.[32] 'Rice?!?' she scrawled in outrage in her diary. 'Nippon buys up everything, and if they find out that you're buying rice outside [i.e. on the black market], you're in for a beating. At the pasar [marketplace] they beat someone half to death as a warning.'[33] There was scarcity outside the capital too. In the city of Semarang, the price of a kilogram of husked rice rose from forty-five cents to 2.10 guilders in less than a year, even though the official price of a kilogram of rationed rice was pegged at twelve cents.[34]

Where did this huge price increase come from? Wasn't Java one of the most fertile rice-growing areas in the tropics? Its stunning terraced green rice fields, the *sawahs*, stretched to the horizon. Furthermore, Jawa Hokokai had introduced the *tonarigumi* system, neighbourhood associations that allocated rations and basic health care among ten to twenty households. Its power thus extended to the smallest dusty alleyways of remote rural villages. But in spite of all this, after two tough years of occupation the economy was in a shambles; the export of agricultural produce had come to a halt, irrigation systems were suffering from neglect and livestock numbers were shrinking. Consequently, erosion was increasing, the rice fields were crumbling and the roads were going to pot. There were fewer cows and buffaloes to work the land, fewer lorries and trains to transport rice to the cities and also, very simply, fewer people who could farm the land full-time without being forced to work for the occupying regime. Besides, 1944 was a very dry year, one of the twenty driest since measurements had begun in 1787. Fortunately, the years just before and after were especially rainy.[35] Under normal circumstances, this temporary downturn could have been easily covered by the available reserves, but these were not normal circumstances, and that had less to do with the rain than with the Japanese forces.

The high cost of rice was mainly due to bad policy.[36] The military administration in Java had come up with the unfortunate idea of organising rice distribution itself. It imposed a quota for each residency (administrative division below the provincial level), offered farmers everywhere the same low price, banned rice hoarding and clandestine sales, and forced the farmers to bring the harvest (an amount stipulated in advance) to one of the large rice mills that worked exclusively for the government. From there, the gleaming white grains were distributed to the army, the civilian administration, the markets and the shops, where the maximum sale price was twelve cents a kilogram. This centralised approach sounds appealing: efficient distribution, an adequate supply and low prices. But it was based on the assumption that the roads and railways would remain available. This was not the case. Before the war, there were 1,200 locomotives in Java; after the war, fewer than 300. The number of lorries dropped from 11,000 to only 1,400 — for the whole of

Indonesia.[37] Without adequate transport, 'informal distribution', a euphemism for smuggling, became a very attractive alternative.

The large rice farmers had already been grumbling for some time about being forced to supply their product at such ridiculously low prices, but now they began to hide a large portion of their harvest, waiting until prices rose or they had an opportunity to sell the rice under the table. For example, a poor farmer in Indramayu could buy hand-husked rice from a rich farmer for twenty-five cents a kilogram and resell it to Chinese shopkeepers in Jakarta for 2.50 guilders.[38] Everyone benefited: the grower, the intermediary and the shop-keeper. But consumers paid ever-higher prices. The rice that was sold through official channels had the strange property of shrinking in volume at every step; each buyer, husker, transporter and govern-ment official took a cut and sold it on the black market. Chinese distributors often paid native inspectors a fat 'tip' to turn a blind eye while a few sacks of rice were snatched.[39] An oxcart here, a delivery van there, what difference did it make? A little extra was always wel-come in hard times, wasn't it? Since the system was as leaky as a sieve, the volumes delivered remained well below the volumes demanded, so the demands increased, and with them the motivation to hoard, smuggle and defraud, in a vicious cycle. As a business model, it was far from flawless.

The consequences were dire. While tons of rice lay in storage in the interior, waiting for a serious buyer or simply for a working train, the prices in the cities, home to ten per cent of the population, sky-rocketed. And while in fertile areas much of the harvest was left to rot, elsewhere more and more people were driven to begging. Ultim-ately, the farmers didn't even go to the trouble of producing large surpluses, since they had nothing to gain by it. A smaller harvest was much less work, easier to hide and just as profitable on the black mar-ket. No, it wasn't so much the drought as the Japanese occupiers' misguided measures that made the lean year of 1944 such a brutal blow. In the late 1930s, Java had had no trouble meeting all of its own demand for rice – it produced as much as 8.5 million tons of paddy rice in 1939 – but the occupiers' clumsy, inefficient approach reduced the harvest to 5.6 million tons in 1945.[40]

The average number of calories available per capita dropped from 2,070 a day before the war to 1,320 in 1944 and 1945; an adult Indonesian's minimum daily requirement was around 1,900. Furthermore, the regional differences were very large; in the leanest years, the average Jakartan had access to less than 900 calories a day, while in Bojonegoro, the region where Johannes Soewondo was complaining about the food at the oil industry training centre, this figure was less than 700. The available protein per capita also plummeted during the occupation, from 47 to 30 grams a day. The consequences were inevitable: in the final years of the war, children under the age of fifteen were five centimetres shorter than children of the same age had been just before the war.[41] The experience of famine, scarcity and need, of sheer physical degradation, contributed to the radicalisation of young Indonesians.

In the internment camps, which held some 100,000 Dutch inmates, food shortages became extreme, especially when, from 1944 onwards, the hundreds of small camps were regrouped into larger ones, many of which had several thousand internees under the direct authority of the military administrators. The very large camps in West Java, such as Cideng, Cimahi and Cikudapateuh, had approximately 10,000 inmates each; Cihapit had 14,000.[42] Malnourishment was especially severe there. Internees in the women's camps often received no more than 1,100 calories per person per day, sometimes as little as 800.[43]

'We were skinny and dressed in rags,' said Joty ter Kulve, the girl from Linggajati. 'When we were sent from Bandung to Buitenzorg, we hadn't been outdoors in a year. After a night on the train with no food or water, we disembarked and were jeered at by the Indonesians. Something has changed here, I realised. There was no more respect. Suddenly the Dutch were nothing to them.' In the new camp in the mountains, they lived in open barracks. 'There was one tap, maybe, for 1,500 women. When we bathed in the nude, I could see how emaciated we'd all become. Skin and bones. The number of deaths there was shocking. We, the women aged fourteen to twenty, had to bury them. We wrapped them in banana leaves, dug the graves and heaved them in. There are memories you'd really rather not have.' After

Map 17: Japanese civilian internment camps in Southeast Asia (1942–1945)

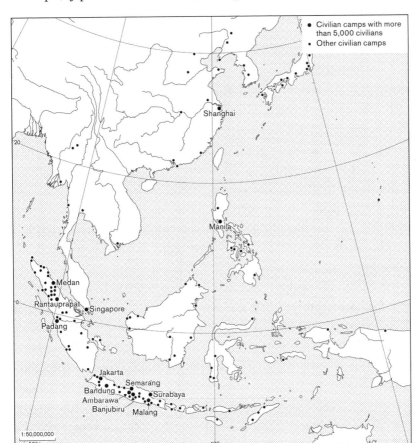

these words, she paused for a moment. 'And when trucks brought maize and musty rice, I had to carry the sacks on my back. The camp commander sometimes shouted at me to squat. Then he would toss me some meat as if I were a dog.'[44]

An estimated 13,000 people died in the civilian camps, most of hunger and hardship. In 1944 the sisters Tineke and Berthe Korvinus, daughters of an orthodox Calvinist missionary, were seven and six years old respectively. 'No milk, no fish, no meat. Starchy gruel, yes, that was what we ate: a mix of old hard maize and a few grains of rice. It gave you a bellyache.' They were held in camps in Central Java. Berthe came down with amoebic dysentery and nearly died, but pulled through. 'In the rainy season we had to gather snakes and frogs for people who were ill, for the protein.'[45] Marianne Pulle told me: 'In the end my mother, who had given birth to three children, only weighed thirty-two kilograms.'[46]

Everyone scraped together what food they could. Lydia Chagoll, the Jewish girl who had fled Europe with her parents, had a couple of solutions: grass and wax. 'We filled jars with grass and salt water and left them out in the sun: pickled grass! And melted candle wax was a rare treat. To the adults, it must have tasted like caviar. We children thought it was heavenly, just like butter.'[47] Brigitte Sparwer-Abrams sampled the fiddleheads of young ferns. 'They were disgusting but nutritious.' And with a survivor's bitter sarcasm, she added: 'I was assigned to carrying duty and was always pleased when we had another corpse to take outside. "Is someone dying? Wonderful! We can go pick ferns again soon."'[48]

And from the ranks of all those starving women, Japanese soldiers sometimes picked out girls and women for sex work. Eight young Dutch women were taken away without warning from an Ambarawa camp to a private brothel.[49] In Solo, girls disguised and mutilated themselves to escape forced prostitution, tearing their dresses, cutting off their hair and making themselves stink.[50] In Semarang, thirty-five young women were dragged from the camps to the brothel.[51] In Banjubiru, near Ambarawa, the Korvinus sisters saw an unforgettable scene: 'Fifteen women were rounded up for service there, including four girls aged fourteen and fifteen. The camp rose up in outrage, but the Japanese crushed the protest. Then a few Dutch women offered themselves in the place of those young girls. They were ex-prostitutes from the port city of Surabaya. They sacrificed themselves and were taken away. We never saw them again.' Tineke and Berthe's mother, who was continuing her husband's missionary work in the camp, preaching, baptising and leading 'pastoral group discussions', had to acknowledge after that incident that prostitutes could be 'good people after all'.[52]

Joty ter Kulve acknowledged that there was moral ambiguity. 'Some women would spend the night with a Jap in return for food. They weren't whores, but respectable ladies. The Japanese officers could now and then be very civilised. In the camp in the Kramat district of Jakarta, I had to serve them dinner one evening. There was one girl sitting there, with long, blond hair; she had such sad eyes. I don't know what happened to her, but I still have nightmares about her.'[53]

In the Netherlands, there has been a decades-long controversy about how bad the Japanese internment camps really were. *Sunken Red*, Jeroen Brouwers's famous novella from 1981 about his time in Cideng from age two to five, depicted them more or less as Asian concentration camps with watchtowers, floodlights and machine guns, where rape and torture were an everyday occurrence. The essayist Rudy Kousbroek, another former internee, was critical of this 'inauthentic representation of matters', describing the story as 'big words' with lots of 'tomato ketchup'.[54] Fred Lanzing was another author who drew a good deal of hostility in the Netherlands; he published his camp memoirs under the provocative title of *Voor Fredje is het kamp een paradijs* (To Freddie, the Camp is a Paradise), a sentence from his mother's camp diaries.[55] When I spoke to him about it, he said: 'I'm sick of seeing the Dutch and the Indos play the role of victim. It's not based on any real knowledge of what happened. East Indies Camp Syndrome is the unwillingness to face up to a colonial history full of racism, hypocrisy, violence and lies. People would rather nurture their own victimhood.' Lanzing was in the same camp as Jeroen Brouwers. 'Cideng was terrible, no question about it. Ten thousand women and children in a camp with room for only two thousand. There were fleas, cockroaches and mountain rats. The sewers were overflowing, and camp commander Kenichi Sonei was a notorious, volatile war criminal who terrorised the camp with his fits of temper about the most trivial things.' But, he adds, 'apart from that life was not so bad, at least when I was there'. Until mid-1944, children could play outside all day there. They played hopscotch, roller-skated, built treehouses and played with praying mantises. 'It was a carefree time for us. Always on holiday, never at school.'[56] But as the son of the last governor-general's staff officer, he enjoyed a special status. 'Sonei took me home with him, gave me tea and bananas, and even took care of the sores on my feet!'[57] After the war, Sonei was sentenced by a Dutch military tribunal to death by firing squad.[58]

Lydia Chagoll offered some wise reflections on the debate. 'There were huge differences between camps and even between barracks, especially when it came to punishment. You can't generalise. We were all confined to our own barracks; you had no idea what was going on a kilometre and a half away. Besides, everyone deals with the psychological impact in their own way. Don't attack one another. Respect each other.'[59] One of the reasons so many people had such difficulty coming to grips with the past is that, when they arrived in the Netherlands, the survivors found that their trials and tribulations were rarely acknowledged. Most of them, and certainly the children, had never lived in that cold country on the North Sea. 'The mother country?!' said Brigitte Sparwer-Abrams, who came to the Netherlands for the first time at the age of fifteen. 'The stepmother country, more like! We were never granted a voice. They told us, "We had the winter famine; you were nice and warm." Pff! We had lost everything! Our houses, our fathers, our future . . . "We had to eat tulip bulbs," they told us. Well, I would have been happy to eat a tulip bulb in the camp! But now I understand that the Netherlands was just coming out of the war too and had its own suffering to work through.'[60]

But there was also an outside world. There were around 100,000 Dutch internees in the camps, but twice as many Indos and seventy million Indonesians in the rest of the country. What was that time like for them? The writer Beb Vuyk was part of a group allowed to leave the camp now and then as part of a transport squad. She could see that ordinary Javanese were even worse off than the Dutch: 'the same kind of wasted emaciation, they were starving like us, but two stages further along.'[61] And that was really the greatest tragedy, a tragedy that has received much less attention than the infamous *jappenkampen* ('Jap camps'). When the dry season of 1944 began, food shortages in Java led to outright famine, with increasing shortages not only of rice but also of maize and cassava. In 1942, 8.7 million tons of cassava were harvested, and in 1945 only 3.5 million tons. In the same period, maize production shrank from 2.2 to 0.9 million tons.[62] And prices rose accordingly; in 1945, a chicken cost thirty guilders in Jakarta, a month's salary.[63]

The memory of this time of exceptional scarcity resurfaced in numerous conversations with Indonesian, Eurasian and Chinese witnesses. 'We no longer had any rice and ate papaya leaves with soy sauce; even boiled, they were bitter.'[64] 'All we had to eat was old, dry cassava, indigestible. Those were the worst days of my life.'[65] 'We were so hungry.'[66] 'We ate only twice a day.'[67] 'We ate only *once* a day.'[68] 'We even ate banana peels.'[69] 'We lived on cassava and maize.'[70] 'We lived on sago we extracted from palm stems.'[71] 'We lived on coconuts and drank water from puddles.'[72] 'We took our dogs out hunting for wild pigs; when a dog was slashed open by a pig's tusk, we had to finish it off with a machete.'[73] 'We had a little plot where we grew sweet potatoes, cassava and nuts.'[74] 'Our cow still provided a little milk.'[75] 'We still had two fishponds outside the city.'[76] 'Since we were Chinese traders, we still had a little rice.'[77] 'We had a shop selling rice, oil and wood, until we had to close it.'[78]

Poverty took increasingly serious forms. 'We had to stand in line for rice every Sunday: 400 grams per adult, 200 per child.'[79] 'We were allotted one kilogram of rice a week for the whole family.'[80] Some Indos saw beggars jumping onto a rubbish truck; they ate everything. Some had no clothes left and simply went naked.[81] They saw people paying for food with a piece of cloth; money no longer had any value.[82] They saw them in rags or with bits of mat tied to their feet.[83] Indonesians told me: 'We traded in our dresses and trousers for a little rice.'[84] 'We wore clothes made from rice sacks, which were ridden with fleas; we had sores all over our bodies and had to bathe in foul-smelling sulphur.'[85] 'We wore burlap bags.'[86] 'We had shorts made of burlap.'[87] 'We were covered with lice, and the itching was terrible. Even washing ourselves didn't help.'[88] 'We didn't have any more cotton, so we beat the bark of a tree until it was soft and dressed in that.'[89] 'We wore loincloths made of bark.'[90] 'We no longer had any medicine and used banana bark for bandages.'[91] 'We queued up along the riverbank for a small spoonful of boiled cinchona bark to fight malaria.'[92]

Hunger led to hatred. Japan had been feared and admired at first, but over time it was hated more and more. I learned that too from the chorus of voices. 'We worked in the rice fields, but when we harvested we couldn't take any for ourselves; the Japanese took it all from us.'[93] 'We saw them make off with whole warehouses of rice; it was like they were kicking sand in your eyes.'[94] 'We saw them take away cars.'[95] 'We even saw them demand scrap metal and send it to the port.'[96] 'They took buffalo, they took girls, they behaved like wild animals.'[97] But an Indonesian who stole could expect no mercy; that much soon became clear. 'We saw the welts on a friend's back. He'd been tortured for stealing a little maize; we saw the madness in his eyes.'[98] 'We saw a thief who had been arrested and was tied to a pole; whoever passed by had to cut him with a razor blade and squeeze lime juice on the wound.'[99] 'We saw a flag being raised, no, not a flag, but a man. He was raised like a flag, his face black and blue, blood running from his ear.'[100]

The most striking remarks were about the banality of death. 'The sight of walking skeletons no longer surprised us.'[101] 'We saw two shrivelled corpses on the sidewalk.'[102] 'We saw many dead bodies in the streets.'[103] 'We saw the dead lined up in rows at the pasar.'[104] 'We saw them dying by the roadside.'[105] 'We saw the sick and the dead lying all over the place, out in the street, under the trees, at the edge of the forest. Corpses were just like litter.'[106] 'We lost so many people who were close to us.'[107] 'We lost the prettiest girl in our class – was it dysentery? Typhoid? The bubonic plague? The city was filthy.'[108] 'We saw a child, a skeleton, a bag of bones with a mother, clawing at the empty skins of her breasts like an animal', as Beb Vuyk put it.[109]

In one of the world's most fertile agricultural regions, an estimated five per cent of the Javanese population died of hunger, one in twenty people.[110] In absolute figures, 2.4 million died. By comparison, 22,000 people died in the Dutch winter famine of 1944–5, 0.24 per cent of the population.[111] Many dozens of books are devoted to the internment camps, but the huge famine in Java, one of history's most severe, has received much less attention. The only scholarly study of the subject is no longer in print.[112]

Meanwhile, in that famished country, Japan demanded a mass mobilisation of the available workers.[113] In Java alone, at least two and a half million people became romusha, forced labourers; some estimates are around four million.[114] Most were put to work fairly close to home, but some 300,000 had to toil overseas, especially in Sumatra and Borneo.[115] I learned how brutal that was from Eman Sulaiman, a rather timid man I met in the lobby of a home for the elderly in Jakarta. 'My parents were rice farmers near Bogor. My father hoed the fields. One day the Japanese army just took him away. I was playing and saw it happen. They trained their guns on him. I wanted to go with him, but they pushed me away. He was sent overseas. It was the last time I saw him. I was nine years old.'[116]

Elsewhere in the archipelago, too, people were forced to work. In Ambon, the former reservist Julius Nunumete had to report to his village early in the morning. 'The Japanese would pick out some of us to put to work. They made all the men work for them. We were under their command.'[117] On the Togian Islands, normally so tranquil, young people were forced by the Japanese army to 'dig pits four metres deep and four metres wide to use as shelters from enemy aircraft'.[118] At the northernmost tip of Sulawesi, even 'older people were forced to dig caves for use as bunkers'.[119]

These were sometimes short-term assignments, but many people were forced to labour over a long period in the most wretched of circumstances, mining coal, building railways or digging tunnels. Many tried to get out of it, bandaging their heads or claiming serious illness, but in the face of this reluctance, Sukarno did exactly what was expected of him: he urged his people to put all their energy into this work.[120] To make his words more compelling, he even had his photograph taken as a kind of elite romusha. He, a man who earned 750 guilders a month, stood leaning on a spade in a smart pair of shorts and a jaunty sun hat, peering resolutely into the distance. Meanwhile, in the background, a little railway was swiftly being laid. This idealised picture stood in stark contrast to the harsh reality. 'I had to work as a coolie in Merak, in the South Banten district of West Java,' Siswodwidjo said. 'I had to dig for coal. It was very demanding work. Many people died of hunger and diseases like malaria, dysentery and skin conditions.'[121]

In a cobbled-together food stall at the foot of a few skyscrapers in the centre of Jakarta, the owner, Corrie, told me her story. Her father had been snatched away to work on a railway somewhere. She didn't know what had become of him. 'When he finally returned, I was very happy.' But she noticed that something had changed. 'Every time he ate soup, he would make a terrible mess. The Japanese had made a hole in his upper lip. It was horrifying. The soup would leak out of the hole.'[122] Other romusha are known to have had their eardrums pierced with a hammer and pencil for trivial offences.[123] And those were the lucky ones. All in all, approximately 400,000 Indonesian forced labourers died.[124] Of the 300,000 Javanese sent overseas, only 77,000 returned.[125]

Sukarno's role in the deaths of romusha has been very controversial in both Indonesia and the Netherlands. Young nationalists considered his willing participation in such a murderous system unforgivable; the Netherlands saw it as the ultimate proof of his traitorous collaboration with Japanese fascism. Sukarno himself looked at it in purely mathematical terms: 'If I have to sacrifice thousands to save millions, then I will.'[126] Was his choice to work with the enemy really an act of pure pragmatism? I asked the person who knew him best, Naoko Nemoto. She first met Sukarno in 1958 at a tea party in the Imperial Hotel in Tokyo. A beautiful nineteen-year-old Japanese woman, she worked as a hostess in an expensive nightclub.[127] A few years later they were married – Sukarno had several wives at the time – and she was henceforth known as Dewi Sukarno.[128] 'Sukarno knew a great deal about Japan and had great respect for the country and the Japanese people. He told me he'd studied Russian, French and Japanese while in exile. He had also looked into Japanese history.' We were conversing in her sitting room in Tokyo, surrounded by a forest of orchids; it was not long after her birthday. Dewi Sukarno was an upper-crust socialite with a murky past in the business world. 'Why do older Dutch people accuse him of collaboration? I don't understand. I mean, Sukarno was freed from prison by the Japanese. He loved Japan like an elder brother. During the war, he must have met all the great Japanese generals, the army and navy officers. To run Indonesia, they needed his help. I think that was when he saw the discipline, strong moral sense and pride of the Japanese people. Without Japan, independence would never have come. Japan even wanted to help with independence.'[129]

However you look at it, it is difficult to make a case that Sukarno had fascist sympathies. Japanese imperialism never excited him, and he was never tempted by militarism or totalitarianism. All his political engagement was directed towards a single objective: Indonesian independence. To achieve that ideal, he was prepared to make extremely far-reaching concessions to the occupiers, all the more so because they came from a country he admired for never having been colonised and yet having become modern and prosperous on its own.

One of the few to document the great famine was the painter Affandi. He drew emaciated bodies, rail-thin dogs and staggering skeletons. 'When he ran out of canvas, he would buy a pedicab canopy if he had to,' his daughter Kartika says. He drew in ink and watercolour on tissue-thin rice paper, scraps of cardboard and pieces of plywood. In 1944 he created *Dia datang, dia menunggu, dia pergi* (He Comes, He Waits, He Goes), a triple portrait of a haggard old beggar who asks for food but receives nothing, an emotionally powerful work reminiscent of Oskar Kokoschka or Käthe Kollwitz.[130] 'A Japanese officer who painted saw it at the art association,' Kartika says. 'He said, "As an artist I agree with you, but as a Japanese officer I cannot accept this." It was too critical.'[131]

In general, the Japanese regime was very sensitive to criticism. When you're occupying a country and draining its resources, you have to expect the locals to run out of sympathy at some stage. 'At first Japan was good to us, but step by step it became very bad indeed,' as one witness concisely put it.[132] No matter how hard the Japanese tried to suppress criticism and rebellion, things were bound to fall apart eventually. And 1944 was the turning point. In February of that year, a religious leader in the strict Islamic city of Tasikmalaya preached against the requisitioning of rice, the romusha system, the appalling Japanese treatment of women, the abuse of the Koran and the ban on political assembly. During one of his sermons, the Kempeitai burst in, but this provoked such a forceful response from the congregation that two Japanese soldiers were killed in the scuffle. The next day brought severe reprisals: eighty-six people died in the fighting, 800 were arrested and twenty-three were executed.[133]

Map 18: Uprisings against Japanese rule

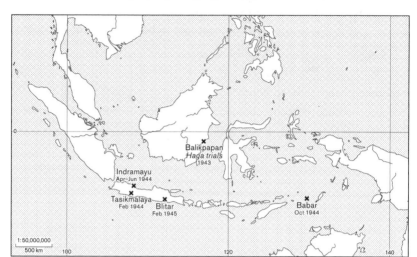

The situation also got out of hand elsewhere in West Java. In April, May and June, villages in the Indramayu area rose up against the draconian rice requisitioning. Hundreds of people were killed or taken captive.[134] These spontaneous riots were always local and short-lived, never forming a threat to the regime as a whole.

The violence was probably most brutal on the remote island of Babar in the southern Moluccas. Babar was known for its excellent tobacco, but even that export trade had imploded. The islanders were getting by on coconuts, papayas and bananas and wearing bark. In late October 1944, a Japanese trader in the coastal village of Emplawas, known among locals for his quick temper, bought a large shipment of tobacco for the navy. When it was delivered, there was a heated dispute about what price had been negotiated. The conflict descended into violence when other villagers came to vent years of pent-up frustration with the trader. They chopped off his fingers and toes, cut out his tongue, stuck a spear in his anus and hung him upside down from a tree. Fearing vengeance, the villagers hid the women and children in the forest. They requested assistance from other villages and killed two Japanese soldiers. The navy brought in reinforcements and struck back ruthlessly. After torturing and murdering one hundred men, they said the women and children could return. Among the locals who did show themselves, they picked out the twenty most attractive young women and took them away; the others were massacred. The stench of corpses was still in the air months later. Of the island's 700 inhabitants, 500 had been killed.[135] One of the survivors was Donisius Unawekla: 'It happened eight kilometres away from my village. Emplawas was wiped out completely. They cut off young women's breasts, threw babies into the sea. Almost my whole family was killed. I lost ten people.'[136]

But the anti-Japanese violence was not confined to spontaneous outbursts in desperate rural communities. Some actions were more premeditated. Sumaun and his comrades became heiho auxiliary soldiers in order to learn to use weapons in the struggle against fascism. Others listened in secret to broadcasts from Australia, New Delhi and Ceylon on the radios of interned Dutch families.[137] The idea that all resistance in Indonesia ended after the defeat of the last Dutch units is incorrect. Nor did the locals merely wait in resignation to be liberated, trembling in fear of their Japanese overlords. There was an organised resistance. Information about the Allied advance was gathered and disseminated. Underground newspapers circulated. Communists formed armed cells that prepared for battle. Obviously, all this was done in the utmost secrecy. Even so, we possess an extraordinary document of this activity: a near-forgotten account by Sintha Melati, a young woman from Semarang. She took the train to Lasem, another town along the north coast of Central Java, for a clandestine training programme with 'many female teachers among them'. From there, she went to Surabaya with underground printed material in her luggage, hidden under pineapples. The magazine *Menara Merah* (the Red Minaret) had a hammer and sickle on the cover, referred to a religious building and advocated democracy 'of the people, by the people and for the people'. It was communism, Islam and Abraham Lincoln all rolled into one. In Surabaya, one of her contacts whispered, 'These are what Japan has given us: gunny sack sarongs, a diet of snails and romusha forced labour.' 'And geishas,' she added.[138]

The underground resistance was financed by discreet donations from sympathisers, but in the port of Surabaya, Sintha was astonished to see another source of income: a forge where a few resistance members had figured out how to make false twenty-five and fifty-cent pieces. A clandestine organisation that could forge currency in the middle of a crisis despite its primitive equipment was more than a bunch of amateurs. Sintha Melati was not filled in on the big picture, but she knew that many other cells were active. She and two comrades travelled back to Lasem. This time, her luggage was heavy baskets full of household items, meant to give the impression that she was moving house. She suspected that a typewriter or rolls of ink were hidden somewhere inside, but when she arrived, she learned she'd been transporting firearms. 'They said there were plenty more.'[139] Then she went on to Bandung and Jakarta; her work took her all over Java. The resistance had branches in many places, was well organised and possessed some weapons; its members included a striking number of women. In the capital, she was told that 'Oom Kecil' ('Little Uncle') was also involved in it; that was a name used for Sutan Sjahrir, who listened to the BBC in secret and had become the mentor of a small group of radical young people. In a shop selling traditional herbal preparations, she heard that Sukarno, behind the facade of all his pro-Japanese speeches, was a regular donor to the resistance. 'Could this really have happened? Behind all his impassioned speeches and his camaraderie with the high officials of the Japanese it seemed he was also in close contact with underground movements.'[140] It was very possible. Sukarno realised that his popularity as a folk hero was eroding because of all the horrors he had to endorse. He needed to stay friendly with the occupiers, but without losing the trust of the native leaders, the young intelligentsia and the masses. In other words, he needed to win over Decks 1, 2 and 3, all at once. He had to furnish the resistance with discreet support to maintain his credibility there. 'Risky or not,' he wrote in his autobiography, 'I kept in secret communication with the underground.'[141] Above all, he wanted to make certain that the most radical groups would not turn against Japan prematurely, but would instead save their blood and energy for the possible future arrival of the Allies, because once they landed, the prospect of an independent Indonesia would be further away than ever.[142]

As for Sintha Melati, she belonged to the generation less amenable to compromise than the older nationalists. She wanted action, speed, change. She smuggled stencils and printing plates to Semarang. While travelling to Surakarta she saw starving romusha, poor people dying of disease and abandoned corpses. She opened a snack bar in Blitar that was intended as a front for everyone working in the resistance there. But in February 1945 she and twelve others were arrested, interrogated and tortured. Someone must have betrayed her. 'If you jump in the water, you must expect to get wet,' she wrote laconically.[143]

Japanese fears of the resistance could trigger complete paranoia, as shown by events in South and West Kalimantan. The occupying regime suspected a conspiracy among the former Decks 1 and 2: Dutch internees, rebellious Eurasians, Chinese merchants, native teachers, journalists and anyone else who still spoke Dutch. Over a period of several months, more than 1,500 civilians were beheaded for no clear reason; in numerical terms, this was the greatest war crime of the occupation.[144] 'They arrested my grandpa,' says Jefferson Dau. That was the man in the three-piece suit in the black-and-white photo, who had opened a nationalist Taman Siswa school. He had become an educator, a pioneering journalist, a newspaper publisher and one of the leading critics of colonialism in the region, but none of that saved him. 'He'd cut his ties with the Dutch back in 1922, but the Japanese thought he was spying for them! One late afternoon my grandma was coming back from the rice field and people said, "Don't go home, the Japanese are there." Her husband and three of their sons had just been taken away to prison in Banjarmasin.'[145] In prison, his grandfather shared a cell with Dr Bauke Jan Haga, the former governor of Kalimantan. They would not survive their detention. Hundreds of others were tortured – by waterboarding, beating, electrocution and every other available method – until they 'confessed' or signed a blank form later filled in with a declaration that they'd sought to overthrow Japan.[146] And not one act of resistance had been committed, not one shot fired. Not a single radio had been confiscated.

This stands in stark contrast to the PETA revolt in Blitar, the occupation period's largest uprising, which did involve armed resistance. Four hundred PETA soldiers, led by the junior officer Supriyadi, took up their rifles in February 1945 to liberate 250 prisoners. Sintha Melati was still a free woman then and lived through the events: 'Between midnight and dawn, while the whole city was sleeping, I heard a burst of rifle fire from the eastern barracks. It was hard to tell what was going on. More explosions soon followed. When the clock struck five, we mustered the courage to go and look. There was no laughter to be heard, no voices, a very strange atmosphere. A neighbour said that a Japanese man had been assassinated in the Sakura Hotel. From that hotel, the PETA brigades took the main road to the prison. The troops shouted, "Merdeka! Freedom! Whose path to freedom will you follow, the Japanese path or the PETA path?"' The insurgents occupied the police station, the Kempeitai headquarters and the telephone exchange.

Not only the scale of the revolt but also its origin caught the Japanese by surprise. These were not starving farmers, not fanatical communists or wealthy late colonials; these were PETA troops, the group most closely tied to the Japanese occupiers – essentially, their own soldiers. This was mutiny pure and simple, worse than the betrayal of the Dutch on the *Zeven Provinciën*. But the motives were not just military. 'The Blitar incident was not caused solely by the frustration of a few battalion officers,' Sintha Melati wrote. 'Within PETA, the treatment of native people had created bad blood. The senior positions were always reserved for the Japanese. But what really infuriated them was the plundering of food, which left people to starve to death like animals, as well as the oppression of the romusha labourers and the cruelty towards anyone who dared to protest.'[147]

For the first time, Japan did not come down hard on the rebels – only six were sentenced to death, a very small number by Japanese standards. But if even their most loyal subjects were rising up against them, they had a problem. Two weeks later, a political working group, formed by the occupying regime, began paving the way to a degree of autonomy within the Japanese empire.

Chapter 9

'Our Blood is Forever Warm'
The tumultuous road to the Proklamasi, March 1944–August 1945

Sometimes one look at the map tells you enough. When you see what a vast territory the Japanese empire controlled from 1942 onwards – from Timor in the southern tropics to the Aleutians, an island chain stretching towards Alaska, in the north (a distance of more than sixty degrees of latitude), and from Burma in the west to the International Date Line in the middle of the Pacific Ocean in the east (a distance of ninety degrees of longitude, a quarter of the earth's circumference) – you naturally begin to wonder how the whole thing could be defended. If this was not imperial overstretch, what is?

In the 1930s, Japan had fought China and Russia on the mainland; those fronts seemed to have stabilised. To access the oil in the Dutch East Indies, it had then had to expel Great Britain and the United States from the region. That plan had been a spectacular success. But since then, those two great powers had re-armed and co-ordinated their efforts. In the west, British forces based in India, commanded by Vice Admiral Louis Mountbatten, were in the process of reconquering Burma in the hope of pressing on to Singapore. In the east, the Americans were still trying to take the Pacific by leapfrogging and island hopping, the two lines of attack developed by MacArthur and Nimitz for large and small islands. Once-invincible Japan was now under threat from two sides. Furthermore, America had support from Australia, and the British were fighting side by side with Chinese units. The Dutch East Indies lay in the South West Pacific Area (SWPA), the American area of operations in the Pacific, with the exception of Sumatra, which was in the British theatre, the South East Asia Command (SEAC). The Netherlands played no significant military role; the mother country on the North Sea was still occupied by Nazi Germany and no longer had its own army, while its colonial troops were still in Japanese POW camps. At most, it contributed a couple of freighters for use in the Allied offensives.

But what the Dutch government-in-exile in London did manage to do, in 1944, was set up the Netherlands Indies Civil Administration (NICA), based in Brisbane in Australia. The indefatigable Acting Governor-General Hubertus van Mook had begun organising a Dutch East Indies government-in-exile in Australia, and NICA was its vanguard: a corps of a few hundred officials, police officers, interpreters and nurses tasked with restoring Dutch authority as soon as the occupied territories were liberated. The plan was for them to provide emergency aid (food, clothes, housing and medical assistance), form the beginnings of a new colonial administration and even circulate new paper money, denominated in what was referred to as NICA guilders, to replace Japanese currency. Even though these were all civilian tasks, NICA was organised in a military fashion, with ranks and grades. Formally, NICA fell under American command, but in practice, the corps acted on behalf of the Dutch queen. Its fundamental mission was to start governing as soon as MacArthur had liberated a Dutch colonial territory.[1]

In late March 1944, MacArthur opened the attack on Hollandia, an administrative centre on the north coast of New Guinea and a strategic stepping stone in his advance towards Japan. With a huge force of more than 200 ships and eight aircraft carriers, he began by bombing the airfield, destroying hundreds of Japanese aircraft. Most of the Japanese troops stationed there, about ninety per cent, were reserve units, often poorly trained, made up of older conscripts.[2]

One such conscript was Nobuteru Iwabuchi's father. When sent to New Guinea in 1943, he was thirty-three years old and married with children. 'Japan was recruiting ever-older men. In Hollandia, he worked for a logistical unit that unloaded cargo.' Nobuteru was showing me around the museum he had founded in the northern Japanese prefecture of Iwate. His father had died in the American bombardment, when Nobuteru was just three years old. 'Nothing at all was left of my father. We have no remains. Japan left more than a million bodies behind in the Pacific. Family members often received

Map 19: Allied conquests (1944–1945)

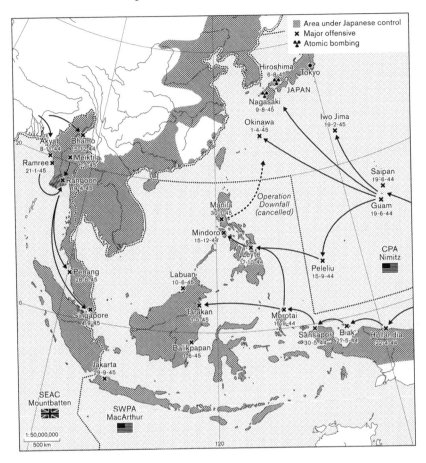

no more than a so-called fragment of bone that was actually crumbling coral.' For years, Nobuteru did research in the former war zone, visiting more than 200 times and repatriating more than 1,500 skeletal fragments. In his museum, he displays the canteens, ballpoint pens and belt buckles unearthed in archaeological digs. Sometimes he could offer surviving family members the consolation of an object engraved with a name or serial number: a rusty mess tin or a helmet with a bullet hole. 'I have to continue my work,' said Nobuteru, now in his seventies. 'The least we can do is never forget the war.'[3]

On 22 April 1944, 50,000 American troops landed in Humboldt Bay (now Yos Sudarso Bay), where Hollandia was located, in one of the largest amphibious operations of World War II. The Japanese soldiers there, approximately 11,000 in number, put up less resistance than expected and fled into the ancient forests; even reserve troops refused on principle to surrender. The Allied invasion transformed the sleepy government town, where a mail boat arrived once a month, into a gigantic military base. Hundreds of ships sailed in and out of the bay, 250 Dakotas landed at the airfield daily, bringing materiel, and hangars, barracks and camps popped up all over. The number of American troops rose to 150,000. On the edge of the forest, where Papuans continued the Neolithic way of life that they had preserved for millennia, a massive military complex rose in the blink of an eye, with seventy cinemas showing the latest Hollywood films.[4]

The first part of the Dutch East Indies had been liberated, and already it was clear how crucial the role of the United States had become. Two days later, the first NICA detachment arrived. These were the first Dutch East Indies officials since Japan had occupied the colony. Most of the Japanese soldiers who had fled inland trekked west through the mountainous forests in the hope of reinforcing the troops further along the north coast. But as they fled, they were pursued by small groups of Papuans egged on by NICA, which promised a reward of twenty-five cents for every Japanese soldier they killed. Apparently, slaughtering the enemy was part and parcel of 'civil administration'. As proof of their killings, the Papuans had to hand over their victims' severed ears. A number of American soldiers sent Japanese ears home from Hollandia as souvenirs.[5]

The retreat through the forest turned into a full-scale massacre of Japanese troops. They had to contend not only with the Papuan attacks but also with a terrible shortage of food; they'd had no choice but to leave most of their rations behind, few of them were familiar with the tropical rainforest, and many tried to eat grass, roots of trees, insects and worms. Out of 11,000 soldiers, 10,000 died.[6] This same pattern was played out throughout the war zone. Accounts of cannibalism are amply documented. The unforgettable film *The Emperor's Naked Army Marches On*, one of the greatest documentaries of all time, broke the supreme Japanese taboo by showing that Japanese soldiers had fed on the flesh of Asian auxiliary troops, Allied prisoners of war and indigenous people, and even each other's. Nob-uteru Iwabuchi, after all his research into the war in New Guinea, was quick to confirm: 'The Japanese ate each other up.'[7] Chandgi Ram, an Indian soldier in the service of the British colonial army, described what had happened when a single-engine American air-craft had to make an emergency landing. 'The Japanese ran over and grabbed the pilot, who can't have been more than twenty years old. About half an hour after his emergency landing, the Kempeitai beheaded him. I watched from behind a tree and saw some Japanese soldiers cut the flesh off his arms, legs, hips and buttocks and carry it back to their quarters. I was so shocked by the sight that I followed the Japanese to find out what they planned to do with that flesh. They cut it into pieces and fried it.'[8]

In Tokyo, I had the chance to speak to one of the very last survi-vors of the Japanese retreat through the forests of New Guinea: Nobuyoshi Fukatsu. In April 2017, I visited him twice. He and his wife have a humble dwelling to the north of Ueno Park, famous for its annual wealth of cherry blossoms, but he remembers other vegeta-tion. 'New Guinea? Jungle!' Those were the first words out of his mouth. He was twenty years old at the time and an X-ray technician. In January 1944 he was stationed in Hollandia as part of a local intel-ligence team named Agent God. 'Agent God's mission', his commander Niiho told him, 'differs from that of ordinary units. You must never die in combat.' For Japanese soldiers, this was a novel idea. 'Make sure to come back alive. Only if you come back alive can we gather information. That is our mission, never forget.' Niiho was an exceptional intelligence officer; before the war, he had posed as a journalist and done important espionage work in and around the Sumatran oil refineries. After Pearl Harbor, the Dutch East Indies authorities had arrested him and shipped him to Australia. He had been released as part of a prisoner exchange when he was still thought to be merely a reporter. Now he was back, this time in New Guinea, with the task of winning over the local Papuans to the Japanese side. Niiho ordered Fukatsu to do something very un-Japanese: remove his uniform, put on a loincloth and grow out his hair. He spent weeks with the Papuans, observing their dances, photographing their villages and sleeping in their huts. For the whole duration of the war, he never fired a single bullet. When the United States bombed Hollandia, he had just left on a march along the coast. 'When the enemy landed, we went deeper into the jungle,' he said. He and dozens of others began a trek through the forest that would go on for five months. '*Jalan, jalan*,' he said in Indonesian, 'walking and walking.' The intention was to move their base to the west, but the coastal route was no longer safe. They suffered great hunger, but Papuans taught them to extract sago from the wood of the sago palm, a laborious procedure. 'Sago saved my life,' he said. He showed me a sketch of the preparation process. 'We made it into a kind of porridge, which we fried. It contains a lot of water, so your hunger soon returns, but it was very important.' By the journey's end he was as skinny as a rake, but now and then they could catch a catfish, snake or bat. About cannibalism, he said: 'I never saw it myself, but I heard about it. Even among the Japanese, there are roughnecks.' In a hut along the route, they ran into an American pilot whose Lockheed had crashed. They took him into custody, and Fukatsu shared a mosquito net with him. 'Whenever he got up at night to relieve himself, I had to stay awake and make sure he didn't flee.' They communicated without language and gradually developed a rapport. The pilot showed Fukatsu pictures of his friends and family. When they decided to move deeper into the forest, Lieutenant Watanabe decided enough was enough. Fukatsu can still hardly believe it. 'It was cruel. On that day . . . deep in the mountains . . . he was killed.' The pilot was beheaded and thrown into the river, to the outrage of Commander Niiho, who was informed too late. After the war, Niiho was brought before a Dutch military tribunal for war crimes committed under his authority. Of the 1,000 Japanese officers on trial, 240 were condemned to death.[9] Niiho was one of them. Fukatsu still can't understand it. 'There was no reason to kill him. He was a reasonable man.'[10]

Meanwhile, the American advance continued. In June 1944, a few weeks after the Allied landing in Normandy, General MacArthur captured the island of Biak and had airfields constructed there. In July and August, Admiral Nimitz took the Mariana Islands of Saipan and Guam, from which American B-29 bombers could reach Japan without stopping to refuel. The loss of the Marianas was such a crushing blow that the Japanese prime minister, Hideki Tojo, had to resign. In September, the American forces pushed all the way to Morotai, the northernmost of the Moluccas and the perfect springboard to the Philippines. From September 1944 onward, Morotai was to the United States what Manado had been to Japan in January 1942: the ideal stepping stone between north and south.

When the Battle of Morotai began, the sisters Hatijah and Yomi Rauf fled with their whole family, their nine children and their two parents, taking a wooden prahu to a neighbouring island. From there they could see the battle in progress: 'The Americans first dropped bombs and then arrived by ship. Not by parachute, just by ship. We saw a lot of military ships and a lot of planes.' Alligator amphibious tanks, Kitty Hawks, Douglas Havocs, Catalinas, B-17s – they didn't know what they were seeing. Once America got things under control, the families that had fled decided it was safe enough to return. The sisters were young teenagers at the time and, like everyone else, wore sacks. 'America was good to us!' they said, laughing, when we talked beneath a lean-to in their village. 'They gave us biscuits, beef and clothes! They were nice. Not the Japanese! They took women away and murdered them. They made our people dig pits and then killed them with knives. We were terrified of them! And we were so hungry!' The end of the Japanese occupation meant the end of the worst period they'd ever experienced. Would the time of rice, plantains and fresh fish now return? It appeared so. 'Our eldest brother was fifteen. He helped unload the American ships in the Wawama harbour. He carried their provisions. He wasn't paid in money, but in food. We were happy then.'[11]

For the locals, it was the dawn of a new era. Naji Baronga was used to climbing high in the coconut palms with a machete, just as his father, grandfather and ancestors had done before him. But now he saw something new: 'There were lots of soldiers then. They had cars, boats and aeroplanes. They came from all over. There were even black soldiers! The American army was integrated.' More than 50,000 soldiers landed on Morotai, many times the number of inhabitants.

'They had plenty of food and clothing. We felt safe again.' He knew exactly what they were there to do: 'The Americans were building landing strips in the south.'[12] They lengthened the strip that was already there, and parallel to it, they added new parking places for aircraft. Morotai became the main air force base for retaking Borneo and the Philippines. Nowadays the old landing strips and the place where the aircraft stood are largely overgrown, except for one runway that is still in use. But they're easy to spot on Google Earth. When I walked around there in July 2016, I could still see the old markings for arriving pilots on the cracked asphalt. Hatijah Kira also remembered the many aircraft, but what struck her most was something else. Her teeth blood red and crumbling from chewing betel, she said: 'In the interior, the Americans even built a soft drink factory!'[13]

Despite how elated the locals were by the American invasion, there is a statue on Morotai of a soldier from the Japanese army: Teruo Nakamura. What did he do to deserve that? Well, when the Allies landed on Morotai, Nakamura did not surrender but retreated. He was a man from Taiwan enlisted into Japanese military service, and the accepted options – a fight to the bitter end or else suicide with honour – did not appeal to him. He and a few others fled into the primeval forest. One by one, his comrades-in-arms died or disappeared, but Nakamura bravely held out, living in a hut on bananas and root vegetables that he grew himself. He was not found until December 1974, naked and as thin as a stick. Indonesian social workers had approached his hiding place while singing the Japanese national anthem and waving a Japanese flag. He had been in hiding for more than thirty years, in the firm belief that the war was still on. He was the last World War II soldier to surrender. Word had never reached him of the American victory in the battle on the large Philippine island of Leyte from October to December 1944, nor of the landing in January 1945 on the island of Luzon, where the Philippine capital of Manila is located. He didn't know that the Allies had captured the Japanese islands of Iwo Jima and Okinawa in February and April 1945, in unbelievably violent battles in which some 30,000 American and more than 120,000 Japanese combatants lost their lives. The firebombing of Japan from January to March 1945, the use in August, not once but twice, of a new type of bomb that wiped away a whole city at once and maimed an entire generation of survivors, and the emperor's surrender shortly afterwards – Teruo Nakamura heard about all this only thirty years after the fact.

Meanwhile Shiono, the 101-year-old telegraph operator who had received such a warm welcome from the Indonesians, was back in Japan. 'After I had been a soldier for three years, they sent me back to Nakajima Aircraft. There was a shortage of technicians.' The string of defeats had made it very difficult for Japan to supply its forces. The country needed to build new aircraft and vessels, fast. Furthermore, in the autumn of 1944, military leaders had decided to use kamikaze tactics, so there was a demand for manned torpedoes, one-man submarines and, above all, suicide aircraft. Shiono tinkered with the vehicles that some of the 4,000 kamikaze pilots would bring crashing down onto American boats and bases. 'At Nakajima, I worked on the engine for the Zero, the kamikaze warplane.'[14]

Japan also wanted to build V2 bombs and Messerschmitts, but how could they get their hands on the blueprints? Not by land or by air, and at sea the Japanese ships were being systematically sunk. Were there no other channels? Yes, in fact: submarines. It was vital to Germany that its ally in the Far East win the war. In May 1943, it had set up the Gruppe Monsun (Monsoon Group), a naval unit operating in the Atlantic, Indian and Pacific Oceans. At first, the unit's mission was just to torpedo enemy ships, but from 1944 onward it also provided transport. The Gruppe Monsun was the only form of cooperation at the practical level between Germany and Japan at any time in World War II, and Indonesia was the main site of that cooperation.

It was not until he reached the west coast of Spain that Martin Müller was told his destination: Indonesia, the essential link between East and West. 'None of us had ever been there, though there was a marching song we had sung during training: *Auf Java, sind die Mädchen braun, haben Augen wie ein Reh.*' (In Java the girls are brown, have eyes like does.) A few days earlier, he had joined the crew of the

U-195 in the port of Bordeaux as a volunteer fighter. It was late August 1944; he was twenty. As soon as they reached Atlantic waters, all hell broke loose: they and another submarine came under fire. 'A mission was always carried out by two boats. It was taken for granted that at least one would be lost.' The other U-boat was hit by a depth charge and went down with its entire crew. His own submarine was also damaged; at a depth of 150 metres, the water spurted inside 'in deadly jets' through a few air valves. He would remember those minutes of terror all his life: plugging the leaks, diving deeper and planting the vessel in the ocean floor, 225 metres deep. Hearing more explosions in the distance, using as little oxygen as possible, lying perfectly still on your back. Leaving the work to the few people who manned the instruments. 'If you have to die, you might as well die that way. Uninjured, in the comfort of your steel coffin.' The U-boats were the most dangerous units in any branch of the German armed forces; the average life expectancy of their crew members was around sixty days.[15] And the Gruppe Monsun was the riskiest assignment of all; of the forty-one submarines that Germany sent to Southeast Asia, only six returned in good condition and only two delivered their cargo. 'But it was an elite unit. In the mindset of those days, who wouldn't have wanted to be part of it?' And then the U-195 wrenched itself loose and travelled on in silence.

'Japan was in a bind,' Martin remembers. 'They didn't have the weapons they needed. We had V-2s on board and blueprints for the new Messerschmitt, so that the Japanese could make their own.' The torpedoes had been removed to make room for 250 tons of mercury and optical instruments. In the ports of Indonesia – Tanjung Priok in Jakarta and Tanjung Perak in Surabaya – they would hand those goods over to their Japanese allies. 'And then we would return with rubber and other commodities.' The plan was to bring back a freight of raw materials for the German war economy: rubber, tin, tungsten, molybdenum and manganese for steel plating, but also quinine, iodine and opium for medicines.[16] That last product was especially important. After the loss of North Africa and the defeat at Stalingrad, the Third Reich had lost its access to the Moroccan, Persian and Afghan poppy fields. In a country with many tens of thousands of heavily injured people, opium derivatives were indispensable as painkillers and anaesthetics. Furthermore, many leading members of Hitler's regime used opium as a mind-expanding drug. Hitler is known to have received regular injections of Eukodal, which contained opium, from 1943 onwards, so that he could maintain his former energy level.[17]

The voyage to Java took at least ninety days, but the U-195 was in trouble. 'We had been damaged by those depth charges in the Bay of Biscay and were leaking oil. Would we even make it to our destination? Only the port diesel and the electric motor were still running and that made our progress much slower. To go faster and take in oxygen, we surfaced, but then we were harassed by Allied planes. The British and Americans had bases and defences everywhere. We had to repel several air attacks.' As an artillery mechanic it was his job to maintain the anti-aircraft guns on deck. 'After each dive I had to prepare the guns.' Instead of taking just over three months, the voyage took five, all that time in an incredibly confined, dark and filthy environment, with the engines roaring constantly and temperatures rising to over forty degrees. But it looked like they were going to make it. 'We sailed around Africa.' Approaching Java, it became highly dangerous again, but on Christmas Eve 1944 they arrived in Jakarta in one piece. There was no welcoming committee from the Japanese navy, not even someone to help them dock. While his mates went ashore, Martin capped five claustrophobic months at sea with sentry duty. Fortunately a few Javanese arrived with a basket of tropical fruit for him. The spiky fruit, the exotic colours, the heavenly flavours: what a luxury after those long grey months.

After earlier trips to Penang and Singapore, the German U-boats were now only docking at the large ports in Java.[18] Just as the archipelago had linked India and China in the distant past, Indonesia was now a stepping stone between Germany and Japan. How was the local cooperation? Between the officers, correct; between ordinary soldiers, much surlier. 'The Japanese were as suspicious as hell,' Martin Müller said. 'We couldn't exchange a single word with them.' In Jakarta he took a pedicab to a Japanese officers' mess. 'Their attitude was, "We're the occupiers. We decide what happens." We were not allowed to carry weapons or wear our uniforms. We were in civvies, in white, with a small swastika as our only emblem. We even got into street fights with our Japanese allies!' Java was a stepping stone, but not a springboard. Looking back, he was under no illusions: 'The coming together of two completely different cultures, with different attitudes and mentalities, both entirely unprepared, did not provide any basis for normal interactions.'

Martin Müller was still able to enjoy a relaxed, carefree stay. There were billiard tables, dances and, above all, potatoes. Nature was overwhelming. You walked around in short trousers and saw monkeys playing in the trees. The war seemed very distant. Only once did the crew have to put out to sea for a tricky supply mission off Madagascar, but that turned out well. He was incredibly lucky. During his leave in the interior while their boat was in dry dock in Surabaya, a fourteen-year-old girl caught his eye. He realised she was far too young, but waited and would marry her after the war all the same. They lived in the Netherlands in Overveen, near Haarlem, until his death in 2014.[19]

While a young German ended up unexpectedly in Indonesia, a young Indonesian found himself equally unexpectedly in Germany. After D-Day the SS began evacuating the concentration camp in Vught in the south of the Netherlands. Djajeng Pratomo, the economics student who had carried out resistance work with his brother, was put on the large transport to Dachau, near Munich, while his fiancée Stennie Gret was sent to the women's concentration camp Ravensbrück, north of Berlin. 'Dachau was a terribly large camp with thousands of people locked up in it. On arrival we were examined to see who was still able to work. You had to take off all your clothes and go and stand naked in front of a doctor. He saw that I wasn't Dutch. I was dark all over. "Aus Indonesien? Hier?" he said. "Das haben wir noch niemals gehabt!"' We've never had that here before!

In 1944 Djajeng Pratomo, the young man who had once walked through the forests of eastern Sumatra with his father, was the sole Indonesian among 32,000 European prisoners in Dachau. Number 69053. And just as in Vught, they put him to work. 'I had to do soldering and assemble machine guns for the German army at the Messerschmitt factory. You had to attract as little attention as possible, that was the tactic.' From Dachau he was allowed to write letters to his love in Ravensbrück – in German, so they could be censored. They were like holiday postcards. 'Sunrise and sunset are sometimes very beautiful here, very colourful. It would be wonderful if we could take photos of it, like we used to. We have had some snow too, but not very much as yet. On clear days we can see the Alps in the far distance,' he wrote in November 1944.

The war seemed hopeless, but the influx of prisoners from other camps raised suspicions of new developments. The newcomers also brought a dangerous disease with them, typhus fever. 'The German who had been appointed leader of the camp picked me out to work together with a Russian doctor. As a student, I'd done one year of medicine at Leiden. That medical knowledge saved me. Dachau was a transit camp but there were also gas chambers and ovens. I was lucky, I ended up at the sickbay.' 'Lucky' was a highly relative term. He first worked on the ward for skin and venereal diseases, but was later sent to Block 7, the *Infektionsbaracke* for contagious diseases, including typhus. Pratomo worked under Dr Kowalenko, a Soviet POW. Barbaric work, no hygiene, no hope, lice everywhere. Many of the doctors and nurses died from the disease themselves. 'I could never have imagined that, so close to liberation, my most terrible period was about to begin.'

At the age of 102 he could no longer talk about it. Now that his life was coming to an end, the nightmares had returned, as harrowing as ever. 'I wake up and don't know where I am. Images of the camp. Totally confused. Then I look at the photos on my wall. My wife and child. Tulips.' When he told me that, I couldn't help but think of the austere poetry of Ed Hoornik, who had been imprisoned in the same camp as Pratomo. 'Dachau shut my soul off with a grid./ That's why I flinch when I am reading in my chair;/ that's why it's a night shelter where I make my bed.' The unforgettable lines: 'And every day I have to force myself again/ to the duel with all the ordinary things: I do it, but sometimes feel like I can't breathe.'[20]

Once, long ago, Pratomo tried to describe the indescribable, once only, never again. 'Every morning when I got up I found dozens of dead in the beds, succumbed to typhus. [. . .] With an assistant, a Russian boy of fifteen, I took the dead to the *"Totenkammer"*. So many prisoners died that in the end there was no more room in that Totenkammer. We had to lay the dead on the street next to it. Every morning there were dozens more. In the end we had to pile them up on top of each other. The pile got higher and higher. We had to use a ladder to put the dead on top of it.'[21]

But even in the camp he persevered with subtle acts of resistance. With the Americans advancing, the SS began executing prisoners. He and Kowalenko admitted resistance men who were in danger of being killed and categorised them as 'highly contagious' without even examining them – even if nothing was wrong with them. A fake but highly alarming fever chart at the foot of their beds served to keep the Nazis at bay. They also attached the names and numbers of living anti-fascists to the big toes of fresh corpses and told the Germans who came to look for them that patient X or Y had unfortunately just died.

A survivor from Azerbaijan remembered 'the impressive concern Pratomo had for the patients and his irrepressible, selfless efforts to do good and alleviate their suffering, regardless of their nationality. He was small in stature, with dark skin and expressive eyes. He was terribly thin and often spoke to Russian, Yugoslavian, Czechoslovakian and other prisoners to see how he could help them.'[22]

On 29 April 1945 Dachau concentration camp was liberated by American troops. Pratomo rejoiced and wept. He walked back to Block 7, sank down on a chair and sat there staring into space for a long time.[23] Then he sprang into action again. 'The Americans had liberated us with a very small unit. They asked who could handle a gun. Well, I'd hunted crocodiles with my father. They were glad to hear it and gave me a gun: a small rifle with twelve bullets. I ended up in a special command guarding the camp.' Among his papers I found a pass signed by US Lieutenant Colonel Martin W. Joyce, commandant of liberated Dachau, stating that Pratomo was a member of 'the permanent staff of the International Prisoners' Committee' and that he had a 'free pass' to move 'in and out of the compound'.[24]

Crocodile hunter, scion of an aristocratic family, medical student, economics student, courier for underground newspapers, concentration camp prisoner, nurse of typhus patients and now, camp guard at Dachau. Some people live at least ten lives in one. But real life, the thing that would give his life meaning, was yet to begin. He sat up straighter. 'Dachau had been liberated, but Indonesia was still under the Japanese. We wanted an independent Indonesia. The war wasn't over yet. It was only just beginning!'[25]

In early May German forces surrendered all over Europe. The Netherlands was liberated, Wilhelmina returned, only the Dutch East Indies still needed to be quickly sorted out. The resistance publisher the Bezige Bij released a peculiar anonymous picture book entitled *Jappenspiegel*, the Jap Mirror. It consisted of a series of political cartoons in which Japan was depicted as a fat, ugly, grimacing little fellow with a simian face and yellow skin. 'Holland was there at Tarakan . . .' went the caption of one of the last drawings: a blushing sailor holding down an enormous sumo wrestler. 'At the final victory too!' said the penultimate cartoon: a slim, blond youth kicking a fat Japanese officer to the ground. 'And now . . . rebuild,' the last picture concluded: an enormous Dutch tricolour planted in a Japanese soldier's ribcage, flying triumphantly over his twisted artillery piece and green body.[26]

These caricatures encapsulate the conflict that would break out in the coming years: the liberated Dutch assumed unquestioningly that the Indies would soon be theirs again. The war had been an unpleasant interlude, but now their overseas venture could be resumed. Perhaps there would need to be a little more independence and equality, maybe old-style colonialism had had its day, but that didn't alter the centuries-old link between the Netherlands and the archipelago. Nonetheless, the combined resistance movements had warned a week before the liberation of the Netherlands that the struggle for Indonesia 'will be a liberation and not a reconquest'.[27] And immediately after liberation the Perhimpunan Indonesia had got down to brass tacks in a pamphlet: 'The Dutch nation has now experienced what it means to suffer and be deprived of one's freedom. As a result it understands our situation.'[28] Whether that was really the case remained to be seen.

On 8 May a peculiar scene took place in the port of Surabaya. Two large trucks full of Japanese soldiers drove up and the troops climbed out with fixed bayonets to assume positions around the friendly U-195. 'We didn't know what was happening,' said artillery mechanic Martin Müller. He saw two Japanese officers go on board and exchange a few words with his commander, after which they walked across the deck of the submarine. 'After several commands that were incomprehensible to us, the flag was lowered and the Japanese rising sun was raised. The German flag was handed to our captain, who buried his face in it in sorrow.'[29]

Italy had been defeated. Germany had been defeated. Of the Axis powers only Japan was still on its feet. Given their great military shortages, they immediately confiscated the submarine – leaving Martin Müller and his mates nothing to do but polish off the supply of drink. Although they were now officially prisoners of war of the Japanese, who ordered them to prepare their ship, none of them felt like risking their lives in a war that was no longer theirs. They came up with a delaying tactic. 'In the daytime we were allowed into town, so we'd take small objects from on board – tools, spare parts, engine components – and sell them to the Chinese! We could even have sold torpedoes but they were too big! We had plenty of money. We were able to go out on the town and our boat couldn't dive. The Japanese were furious!'[30]

One thing he noticed on shore was the declining popularity of the Japanese occupiers. 'Most people hated the Japanese, who had bled them dry.' At the port he had seen several times how the Japanese would chain petty thieves together in a circle and then beat them mercilessly with sticks. He was not the only one to realise that the honeymoon was long over. There were rumblings everywhere. In 1942 only the people on Deck 1 had had a hard time of it – losing their authority and jobs, being made prisoners of war, internment – whereas Indonesians on Decks 2 and 3 had been presented with new educational opportunities, new ideas and racial equality. In 1943, in addition to schools and picture shows, youth movements and militias had been introduced for the young – greatly increasing their self-esteem. What's more, the barrier between Decks 2 and 3 had blurred, especially within the Asian community. But by 1944 conditions had grown difficult for everyone. The Europeans and Indos in the camps, the impoverished Chinese and Indos in the cities, the famished Indonesians in the cities and the countryside, the exhausted and emaciated romusha everywhere . . . Aside from the nationalistic, well-educated upper layer of Deck 2 that included Sukarno, Japan had very few supporters left. Repression on that scale was unsustainable.

To counter the growing mass discontent, Japan was prepared to make far-reaching concessions, motivated not by humanitarianism but by opportunism. Hunger and poverty had stirred resistance within the archipelago, just when Japan needed to concentrate on external defence. It could not afford to wage two wars at once. On 7 September 1944, at the height of the drought, Prime Minister Kuniaki Koiso tried to reduce the pressure by announcing a vague but radical decision in the Japanese parliament: Indonesia would become independent 'in the future', possibly gaining the same status as Burma and the Philippines, autonomy within the Japanese empire. On top of this a new army corps was formed a week later, Barisan Pelopor (the vanguard corps), led by Sukarno. Barisan Pelopor was intended to channel the young nationalists' rampant frustration about the rice shortages, the romusha, the coarse clothing – an estimated 80,000 joined. No firearms were provided; they drilled with bamboo spears. The members were trained to fight and die, not for Japan but for Indonesia.

In December Barisan Hizbullah was also founded, a militia for young Muslims with 50,000 members. And lastly there was the Angkatan Muda, a movement for better educated, generally left-wing youths, intended to redirect their sympathies for the underground in a Greater East Asian direction.[31] Three organisations with three Indonesian names to appease the three movements in the Indonesian struggle: the nationalists, the Muslims and the 'communists', or those who went by that name.

Appeasement was also the purpose of Koiso's promise of independence 'in the future'. It wasn't until eight months later, in April

1945, after the worrying PETA revolt in Blitar, that a first working group was assembled to consider possible independence. It was all very conditional. Even the name made that clear: the Investigating Committee for Preparatory Work for Independence. The word 'Indonesia' wasn't even included. For the time being it was only about the composition of the working group, not the actual meetings. The Japanese were trying to combat unrest with political symbolism. When it came to delaying tactics they were as expert as the Dutch.

Speaking of delays, a month after liberation Pratomo was still at Dachau waiting for transport home. When none came, he and his mates repaired a broken German bus and drove back to the Netherlands themselves in their striped concentration camp uniforms.[32] Stennie's trip back was very different. She was freed from Ravensbrück by the Red Cross and driven in a convoy of trucks through shelling and bombing raids to Denmark and Sweden, where she would stay for several months. The lovers' prolonged separation was extremely frustrating, but their correspondence was extraordinary. In the months between the German and Japanese capitulations, they had plenty to say about the future of Indonesia. 'Darling,' Stennie wrote from Stockholm on 9 July, 'the idea of you being there when I arrive in Holland, the idea of us being there together after these miserable two years is the most terrific thing that could ever exist!' Her youthful effervescence was back. Her political engagement too. 'Say, Prat, the Indonesians are awfully active, aren't they? At least, I've heard on the radio what the PI is up to now and I found an article about you all in *Vrij Nederland*! It's such fun to hear and read all these things, especially knowing you all so well!'

Prat wrote back that it was true that the PI was operating openly again. There was a new committee and a new clubhouse, and they could publish the magazine *Indonesia* again, monthly at first, later even as a weekly. He himself had joined the executive committee! Djajeng Pratomo had been appointed undersecretary and treasurer of the illustrious association that, with figures like Hatta and Sjahrir, had already argued for independence in the 1920s. He'd moved to Amsterdam for that purpose and was living in Van Breestraat. The organisation was nearby on Jan Willem Brouwersplein. 'Dearest Stennie! We're leading a busy life in Amsterdam and need all the help we can get. We have a wonderful clubhouse now, close to the Concertgebouw. When you're back we should throw a big party there for the Indonesians who have come back from the concentration camps and for you. The building is magnificent, parquet floors everywhere. There's a piano! The second floor is entirely occupied by the PI. That's where we have our offices. As I'm on the executive, Adjit and Ripno and I have set up one of the front rooms as an office. Awfully posh, you know!' And he added: 'We have to work hard, but we love this work deeply, as you know, so we never tire of it.'

Stennie suspected that, thanks to its resistance work, the PI would 'have now acquired a very different position in Holland'. After returning to the Netherlands she no longer wanted to work as a secretary, but become a journalist instead. Pratomo heartily approved. It is moving to read these political love letters between two young, inspired people who saw each other as equals and could finally talk, think and dream freely again. 'Your not being here in Stockholm is such a pity,' Stennie wrote. 'Especially now it's summer and the nature all around is so terribly beautiful! When the sun shines like this on the silvery water and the rocks around the harbour, and you feel the wind in your hair, you suddenly feel so homesick for the people you love.'

But the letters are about Southeast Asia more than Scandinavia. 'Now Japan,' Stennie wrote on 20 July, 'but that might take a while yet!' Nobody could have suspected that the war would be over three weeks later. The general assumption among the Allies was that Japan wouldn't surrender until 1946 at the earliest. 'Indonesia must surely be longing for liberation too,' she wrote, 'and hopefully it will be a real liberation!' She wanted to know if the Netherlands was already preparing. 'What's the situation with enlistment for Indonesia?' Would military service be introduced or would it just be volunteers? Had the resistance resumed organising yet? 'I hope you're not in Indonesia when I arrive in Holland! That's selfish of me, of course, I realise that, but it would be a pity, don't you think? Anyway, what must be must be!'

★

Just before liberation the underground papers had, at the request of the government-in-exile in London, issued a collective call for voluntary enlistment to continue the struggle in the Netherlands and the Dutch East Indies. The response was massive. In May and June 1945 170,000 residents of the liberated Netherlands signed up, among them 60,000 women.[33] A new edition of the textbook *Populair Maleis*, Popular Malay, was even published for those who were about to leave for Indonesia, 'expanded with Malay for the military'. Printed on the last page was the reading assignment: 'Tida lama lagi Tanah Hindia merdéka djoega.' It won't be long before the Indies too are free.[34] Jan Langenberg was eighteen. His father had been in the resistance near Haarlem, they'd survived the famine in the last winter of the war by eating bulbs and sugar beet, and as soon as they were liberated he signed up 'to kick out the Japs!' When he was rejected because of poor eyesight, he begged to be allowed to go. He became a quartermaster.[35]

Goderd van Heek was twenty-two and came from a prosperous family of textile manufacturers in the east of the Netherlands: in the late nineteenth century his grandfather had set off 'to sell some cotton' in India and the Dutch East Indies; his father now ran the textile factory; he himself was a student at the textile school in Enschede. At Huis Bergh, the family castle in 's-Heerenberg, the famine hadn't been too bad. 'We had a cow in the garden. We called her Irene.' Van Heek turned out to be a witness with an impeccable memory. He was ninety-three when I first spoke to him and he was still overflowing with energy. He'd done Nijmegen's annual four-day walking event three times, skated the almost 200-kilometre Elfstedentocht four times and cycled the route eleven times. Yes, endurance was his forte. He'd avoided forced labour in Germany by working as a deckhand on a barge, but after being liberated by the Canadians, higher duties called. 'Now we're going to go tackle those Japs! They're still occupying Insulindia.' The only witness who still used Multatuli's poetic name for the archipelago, he enlisted out of pure idealism. 'We knew about the camps and wanted to free the Dutch prisoners.' Just as the Canadians had liberated the Netherlands, the Dutch would now liberate the Indies. It would be heroic and noble. 'After Japan had ransacked the country, we would help with the reconstruction. The Netherlands would return it to prosperity. We remembered Wilhelmina's speech from 1942: the Indies would be free, we were not going back to a colonial regime. My father's reaction was positive. He told my uncles, who were also board members, "Let him go. It's a noble goal."' Goderd went to the recruiting office two days after liberation, signed up for an indefinite period and left for training at Warley Barracks, near Brentwood in the English county of Essex. 'After five years of occupation we wanted to see something of the world too,' he said with an affable smile. 'We were keen as mustard!'[36]

Besides volunteers there was another, very different reservoir that could also be drawn on. The Roman Catholic Church in the Netherlands proposed that young collaborators who had been in the SS could be sent to the Indies 'and rehabilitate themselves that way'. Because no matter how you looked at it, a Catholic memorandum stated in June 1945, ultimately these boys 'had at least had the selflessness to risk their lives for their ideals'. It was possible to put a spin on anything. 'These SS soldiers, who took up arms to sin against their own nation, could now be given the opportunity to serve that nation under arms.' There were some 4,000 troops involved. Prince Bernhard formulated proposals of a similar tenor. From a purely military perspective the SS men were, without a doubt, the best trained and most experienced soldiers in the Netherlands, but ideologically their participation was hard to endorse. The Dutch government didn't take up these insane suggestions, but there were some former SS troops among the conscripts who were later dispatched.[37]

Even as many prepared for departure, what had been happening in Indonesia all this time was a mystery to everyone. The PI had not had any contact with the home front for the last few years, the Dutch government in London was in the dark, and the British, Australian and American intelligence services were complaining about the very patchy information they were getting. In short, nobody outside the country knew the situation on the spot. Famine, revolts, militias, indoctrination, the new generation . . . it was

all very vague. To placate its nervous allies, the Dutch government
had set up the Netherlands Forces Intelligence Service (NEFIS).
With the greatest possible caution, Indonesian infiltrators were
transported to the archipelago from Australia and Ceylon – by
parachute, by submarine – but although several attempts were
made, none of these clandestine operations lasted long enough for
relevant information to be transmitted: most of the spies were murdered fairly soon after landing. The population's hatred for the
occupier had reached the outside world, but the conclusion that was
automatically drawn was that they must be longing for the old days.
This was the limit of the knowledge that got through. From January 1944 NEFIS was led by Simon Spoor, the future commander of
the Dutch troops in Indonesia. He was convinced that the so-called
struggle could be put down entirely to Japanese 'rabble-rousing'.[38]
But the fact that very few Indonesians seemed prepared to help his
secret agents should have given him pause for thought.[39]

What was the situation on the ground? After the fall of Germany,
the loss of Iwo Jima and yet another change of command in Tokyo,
Japan allowed a new political step for Indonesia. On 28 May 1945 the
Investigating Committee for Preparatory Work for Independence
met for the first time in Jakarta, while in Surabaya the Allies began to
bomb the port. The committee had sixty-six members: sixty Indonesians, four Chinese, one Arab and one Eurasian, assisted by eight
Japanese advisors. They met in June and July to consider what this
new Indonesia should comprise. Shouldn't the Malay Peninsula be
included, so close to Sumatra? And wasn't all of Borneo more logical
than just Kalimantan? Should East Timor remain Portuguese? And
wouldn't it be better to shuck off West New Guinea? The time for
jigsaw puzzles seemed to have come around again, but in the end they
opted for simply maintaining the existing borders of the Dutch East
Indies. More important was the issue of the archipelago's political
foundation. On 1 June Sukarno put forward a proposition for a
national ideology. Didactic as ever, he proposed five fundamental
principles: belonging to one state (nationalism), solidarity with all of
humanity (internationalism), striving for deliberative consensus
(democracy), equitable distribution of wealth (social justice) and belief

in God (monotheism). Together he called this the Pancasila, literally 'the five columns or pillars' in Pali. The term was derived from Buddhism and referred to the believers' five precepts, but also recalled the Five Pillars of Islam. To this day, all Indonesians can reel off these principles. More than just a piece of wartime political propaganda, the Pancasila contained the ideological blueprint for an independent Indonesia and a political programme that could unite the three different factions. Nationalists attached importance to the unified state and democratic decision-making, the left approved of the international and social aspects and Islamic leaders appreciated the explicit religious reference and enquired whether that fifth principle could not be made the first. Sukarno had no objection, as long as the other religions were still recognised. Indonesia was a monotheistic country, but not exclusively Islamic. Pluralist monotheism you might call it. Anyone who takes a domestic flight in modern Indonesia can find a card in the seat pocket in front of them with a prayer for a safe flight in five variants: Islamic, Hindu, Buddhist, Protestant and Catholic. For Sukarno the Pancasila was the synthesis of everything he had struggled his whole life to achieve: a reconciliation of his country's three great political movements, reuniting what had grown apart since Tjokroaminoto's boarding house in the 1910s. The goals that had been formulated there over dinner could finally be realised on a national level.

But while Sukarno was carefully smoothing out the ruptures between the political factions, a new breach was opening between the young and the old, one that would become enormous. The most important political change of that moment was taking place outside the walls of the grand conference room where the archipelago's leaders were smoking and orating about borders and constitutional principles. It was taking place in the heads – and bodies – of many thousands of people in their teens and early twenties who saw the older generation as passé. The young felt betrayed by their leaders' endless kowtowing and postponing. Teachers, low-level clergy and the administrative elite had all participated in Japanese rule – as educators, militia leaders, rice collectors, romusha recruiters or whatever. What use were people like that? Even the national bigwigs were a disappointment. To a fifteen-year-old from Java, Sukarno was an old man of forty-five who had been on the scene forever and collaborated with the occupier. Only Sjahrir, almost the only one who had not gone along with the occupier, could still count on the sympathy of the young progressives, but compared to Sukarno and Hatta he had very little real power. Without access to the national media, he was also much less known. Still, in Jakarta various student unions held meetings where they candidly debated the country's future with him.

Sintha Melati, the young woman from Semarang who was in the resistance, wrote: 'Our attitude towards the older, more experienced people was still a source of tension. The problem was how to establish contact with them without having to accept a subordinate role. It was difficult for us to win their trust.' She asked herself, 'Did there have to be a rift between the older and younger generations? Did there have to be discontinuity in the evolution of the struggle??' At that moment it seemed inevitable. 'The youth regarded the debate of the Committee for the Preparation of Independence as too compromising. [. . .] The youth wanted a firm demand for immediate independence.'[40]

From 16 to 18 May 1945 young nationalists from all over Java gathered in Bandung for an important youth congress, which became the setting for outspoken calls for independence. 'Anyone who stands in our way is an obstructionist and a traitor!' exclaimed Chaerul Saleh, a young leader from Jakarta.[41] The participants' motto left nothing to the imagination: 'Merdeka atau mati!' Independence or death.[42] Their tone was vastly more radical than the strategic approach deployed by Sukarno, who needed to stay friends with everyone, carefully inching towards a little more autonomy under Japanese tutelage.

The young were the *pemuda*, the youthful spirits who had been politicised since 1942 by Japanese propaganda, militarised since 1943 in all kinds of military and paramilitary organisations, enduring a terrible famine since 1944 and completely sick of it all by 1945. The pemuda had seen their mothers starve to death, their fathers dragged off as forced labourers, their sisters abducted as comfort women. The pemuda were the wiry scrags who had been drilled endlessly to rush the enemy with nothing more than bamboo spears, sticks and fake wooden guns, screaming loudly. The enemy – the Enemy – who would soon arrive: 'Amerika kita setrika, Inggris kita linggis.' We'll squash the Americans, we'll bash the British. Wide-open eyes, wild gaze, sacred fury. The pemuda were all those young intellectuals secretly listening to the radio and enthusiastically discussing imperialism, fascism and capitalism. And there were plenty of them. A tally of the number of members of PETA, Seinendan, Keibodan, heiho, Barisan Pelopor, Barisan Hizbullah and several other youth organisations came to more than two million . . .[43]

An infiltrator dispatched by the Netherlands wouldn't have noticed it right away, but a volcano was rumbling in Java and that volcano was youthful enthusiasm. It was contagious, it was fiery, it was seething everywhere. Despite their social divisions – rich or poor, urban or rural, educated or illiterate – the young increasingly saw themselves as a separate, unique generation that would make a historic difference. Even a hyper-individualistic poet like Chairil Anwar was sensitive to this stirring vitality. He was twenty-two when he wrote the poem 'We're Ready' in late 1944, with the telling subtitle 'To my generation'.[44]

> By then your hands will be stiff,
> By then your heart will have stopped beating,
> By then your body will have turned to stone,
> But we'll quickly find others,
> We'll go on carving this Monument.
>
> By then your eyes will be only glass,
> By then your mouth will have forgotten speech,
> By then your blood will have stopped pounding,
> But we'll quickly find others,
> We'll push on to a World of Triumph.
>
> By then your voice will be stifled,
> By then your name will have vanished,
> By then you won't want to march forward,
> But we'll quickly find others,
> Advancing together, to Victory.

Our blood is forever warm,
Our bodies are forged of steel,
Our spirit is strong, is brave,
We'll repaint the skies,
We're the bearers of real happiness.

[. . .]

Everything's burning!
Everything's burning!

Friends, oh friends,
Let's rise up knowingly
Stabbing the new light deep under the skin.
Friends, friends,
Let's swing our swords toward the Bright World.

The question was who were they going to rise up against? This generation had been whipped up into a frenzy to fight the Allies, but . . . the Allies hadn't arrived. After reaching Morotai, General MacArthur had decided against liberating Java first, pushing on to the Philippines instead. He needed all available ships for his offensive against Japan; the rest of Asia could wait. The bamboo spears had been sharpened, but nobody showed up.

A smoking volcano, a rumbling volcano, a seething volcano – but no eruption came. The Allied army passed Java by on its way north. Where was all that irrepressible, youthful energy going to go?

Deep under the surface in the pitch-black coalmine of Ashio, Hans Dornseiffer was still waiting for events to unfold. How long had he been a POW in Japan? He didn't know any more, time had turned to dust, endless debris. He wouldn't make it, he knew that, he had no strength left. What's more, there were American bombing raids now too. He even noticed them underground. 'At a depth of 110 metres, the deepest level of the mine, the lights suddenly went off. The Americans had hit the power stations on the coast. The ventilation cut out too. You heard the pumps go silent, the ground water started rising.' In the end he was rescued, but he was so exhausted physically that the camp doctor decided to send him to the POW hospital in Yokohama. He was dispatched on a boarded-off prisoner transport. The mine was north of Tokyo, the hospital south. Through the chinks between the boards he could see the capital city spreading out in all directions: a vast tangle of wooden homes with paper walls and straw mats, home to millions of people. Travelling back three months later, he couldn't believe his eyes: the whole city was gone. 'The American bombers had dropped enormous numbers of incendiaries. They burst open and sprayed napalm. Tokyo was on the coast. The wind fanned the flames. The roofs were on the ground, the people were living under corrugated iron. When you saw those Japanese mothers fleeing with their children you couldn't help but feel for them.' The devastating fire in Tokyo on the night of 9–10 March killed 100,000 people, wounded a million, and made as many again homeless. 'So much suffering,' Hans sighed. 'If you've seen that, you can't hate the Japanese.'[45]

Dick Buchel van Steenbergen was still working at the Nagasaki shipyards. The drone of the American bombers kept getting worse. He had to help build a bomb shelter. 'A concrete box with a concrete lid on it. It wasn't very safe. Once it shook so much the lid fell on someone's head. Dead.' On 9 August 1945 he was back at work again. When an Allied plane flew over late in the morning, he fled into the bomb shelter with ten others. False alarm, it seemed. It was only a reconnaissance mission. In the factory yard he went back to clearing away rubble from a previous bombing raid. When a second plane approached everyone raced off again. 'I went into the factory. That was stupid. I didn't hear the bomb itself falling, it exploded in mid-air. I did see the flash, like a camera's. I was blown over. The roof of the factory collapsed. By chance I was lying in a good position, in the middle of an open square in the construction of the roof, between the rafters. I only had a few grazes. But another Dutchman was just under one of the rafters. I couldn't get him out from under it. Eight of us tried, but we couldn't free him. He wasn't hurt, that lad, he was just stuck.' It was an exhausting, infuriating job. 'Then the factory caught fire.' Even more tugging, more lifting. It was no use. 'In the end we had to leave him behind because of the smoke.'

What he and his mates saw when they went outside was shocking. 'The dust was still hanging in the air. Chaos everywhere. So much destruction. Our Japanese guards had run for the woods. They just left us to our fate. They weren't heroes any more.' And the indescribable view. 'Suddenly you could see really far. Of the metal buildings, only the skeletons were left. Everything wooden had been flattened.' He had a clear view across a zone of several square kilometres. But the strangest of all was what was close by. 'Our barracks was lying at an angle towards the bomb. It hadn't been blown over, but sucked towards it. "What is this?" we said. It was unlike anything we'd ever seen before. What could cause so much destruction? "A blockbuster?" In the days before there'd been whispering about some kind of bomb. We'd heard vague stories about Hiroshima.'

From the ravaged shipyard, Dick looked out over what had been the large city of Nagasaki. The atomic bomb had exploded a few kilometres away from him. In normal conditions, he wouldn't have survived, but because of poor visibility the bomb, on parachutes, had been dropped a couple of kilometres north of the planned site. What's more, it had exploded at a lower altitude than in Hiroshima, so the impact area was smaller than intended. Although 'Fat Man' was a good bit heavier than 'Little Boy' three days earlier, it 'only' caused 40,000 deaths in the first minutes after the explosion, as opposed to 70,000 in Hiroshima. The total death toll would end up being more than a quarter of a million. It was America's recently inaugurated President Harry S. Truman who had made the decision to use atomic weapons. It was later claimed that a conventional marine landing would have cost the lives of a million American soldiers and at least that many again on the side of the Japanese. 'There was no wind that day,' Dick said. 'I was put to work in the city for four days: collecting bodies, collecting wood, wood to burn the bodies. I slept outside for five days, in that fall-out the whole time. Lying in that stuff for weeks. The Netherlands never showed any concern for me at all. I was never examined.' Dick Buchel van Steenbergen was ninety-seven when I interviewed him in North Brabant. He still lived independently.[46]

And then it all happened very quickly. The day the bomb was released over Nagasaki, the Russians invaded Manchuria. That morning Sukarno and Hatta had flown to Saigon in occupied Indochina for consultations with Field Marshal Hisaichi Terauchi, supreme commander of the Japanese troops in all of Southeast Asia. This time it wasn't a casual junket at the occupier's expense. Terauchi gave them formal notification that Japan had decided to grant Indonesia independence. On 14 August they landed back in Jakarta, and that same evening a new, smaller committee was assembled, the Preparatory Committee for Indonesian Independence, with Sukarno and Hatta as chairman and vice-chairman respectively. This committee was made up of twelve Javanese, three Sumatrans, five members from the rest of the archipelago and one representative of the Chinese community. The first meeting was scheduled for 18 August. The plan was for the transfer of power to take place soon after, perhaps as early as 24 August.[47]

But world history changed on 15 August. Against the advice of the army generals, who thought that Japan should fight to the bitter end (anything was more honourable than surrender), Emperor Hirohito decided to throw in the towel. Never before had a Japanese emperor addressed his subjects directly. In factories all over the country workers laid down their tools, took off their caps and bowed their heads humbly. In schools, in hospitals and on the streets, life came to a standstill. All of Japan stood motionless with their chins against their chests listening to their divine head of state. In extremely sophisticated Japanese that very few understood, but with a voice of liquid crystal, the emperor announced in guarded terms that the war was over. Although he scrupulously avoided the word 'surrender', the tenor was clear: he accepted all the conditions that Truman, Stalin and Churchill had set at the Potsdam Conference a few weeks earlier.

Ryuichi Shiono was still working on the engines of kamikaze planes at the Nakajima Aircraft Company. 'Our factory was attacked by an American B-29 bomber. While the factory was being rebuilt, the news about the end came. We heard the emperor's announcement on the radio.[48] Hans Dornseiffer saw American planes dropping leaflets over the coalmine. 'They told us how to get to the closest garage, where trucks would pick us up.[49] And at the devastated shipyards of Nagasaki, Dick Buchel van Steenbergen heard his camp commandant say that peace had come. 'We were standing in an open area listening to him. I couldn't make out a word of it. Then it was finished. No Wilhelmus or anything like that.[50]

On the other side of the world, in a small room in Amsterdam, Pratomo wrote a letter to Stockholm: 'Dearest Sten! Japan's capitulated! Now definitive!' For once he used just as many exclamation marks as she did. But his exuberance didn't last long. Several days later he reported on the national celebration in Amsterdam to mark the liberation of the Indies. 'I've never seen a celebration as listless as yesterday's. There was absolutely no enthusiasm.' No joy, no parades, no streamers. He could understand 'why the people here were less enthusiastic than they had been about the liberation of the Netherlands – Indonesia is so far away', but he saw that even the Indonesians 'weren't so very passionate . . . That's because they have to continue the struggle, of course.' Which they promptly did. 'Many of us will be leaving soon. Goenara from The Hague already left today. He's going to Australia first, then to Indonesia. Tomorrow Dick, Tamzil, Uncle Nazir and three others will be leaving from The Hague. Indonesians will be leaving from Amsterdam soon too, Soeripno among them. I don't think they will still be here when you get back.' This sudden exodus was stunning: they had only just stopped fighting fascism, and now they were off to resume the struggle against colonialism. But what about those who had found a Dutch partner in the meantime? 'You must be wondering about my intentions,' he continued. 'I will be staying here for now. I'll wait till you're home first and then we'll see. I don't want to decide anything without you. I love you much too much to suddenly head off to Indonesia without you. So if it's at all possible come back as fast as you can, then we can discuss whether we should stay here for the time being or go to Indonesia.[51]

Meanwhile Pratomo continued his tireless work for the Perhimpunan Indonesia, working day and night with the three editors of the association magazine *Indonesia* on a special two-colour edition. The result was a historic document. Pratomo and his friends asked themselves if the people of Asia had suffered so much 'only to return to the former, outdated conditions of colonial relations in Asia?' Again the PI leadership's analysis was strikingly consistent. 'The barrier of fascism has fallen, but we are faced with new obstacles that are rooted in the same soil that nourished fascism: the self-interest of groups that profit from disenfranchisement and the curtailment of the rights of the masses. These are the grandees of the Indonesian plantations, of the tin and the oil, who fear the prospect of Indonesians having a greater say and whose influence extends into the ministries, the press and through the whole fabric of government in Indonesia . . . As long as there are colonies, there will be a source of conflict.'

The news of the Japanese capitulation surprised friend and foe alike. The war had been long, definitely, but the final chord had come sooner than expected. The evening before, Hatta and Sjahrir had visited Sukarno at home. It was clear that Japan was losing. Sjahrir thought they should proclaim their independence without Japanese permission. That would keep their freedom from being tainted and help gain recognition from the Allies later.[52] Sukarno and Hatta disagreed: the process had already advanced significantly with Japanese support; crossing them now seemed unwise. After all, Japan was their only definite ally.[53] On 15 August Sukarno and Hatta visited Rear Admiral Tadashi Maeda, the liaison between the Japanese army and navy and a great sympathiser with the Indonesian struggle. It was from him that they heard the news that Japan really had surrendered. They didn't know what to make of it: just now when they were so close to realising their dream! Rumours of capitulation were already spreading among the capital's politicised youth. A number of them, like the radical nationalist Chaerul Saleh and the young journalist B. M. Diah, had already been involved in consultations with nationalist leaders in the previous weeks. Now that the news of Hirohito's speech had reached them, they were not bothered about an orderly transfer of power or possible recognition by the Allies. They had to strike while the iron was hot. And that moment had come. The city was extremely restless. Youngsters were gathering knives, spears and cleavers to press their demands. A delegation visited Sukarno at home but he wasn't impressed by their willingness to die. Yes, maybe they could liberate Jakarta, but outside the city they wouldn't stand a chance. He had no desire to see a repeat of the cack-handed communist uprising of 1926. Militancy without strategy was folly. But strategy without militancy was cowardice, his young critics countered. They refused to be persuaded and demanded that he proclaim independence that very day. A knife was even drawn. 'Don't you threaten me. Don't you dare command me. You will do what I want. I will never be forced into YOUR will!' Sukarno leapt up and offered them his throat. 'Here, here is my neck. Chop it off . . . go on, cut my head off . . . you can kill me . . . but I will never risk unnecessary bloodshed because you want me to do things your way.'[54] He knew they wouldn't do anything to him. They still needed him.

At four o'clock the next morning, 16 August, Sukarno and Hatta were visited by several pemuda, among them Chaerul Saleh. The revolution was about to break out, they said. The young members of the heiho and PETA were going to take up arms. A bloodbath threatened in Jakarta. It was better if they, the pemuda, took their leaders to safety. Sukarno and Hatta let themselves be persuaded and got into a waiting car that drove them away from the city. Hours later they arrived in the small town of Rengasdengklok, where an Indonesian PETA officer had already raised the Indonesian flag. What was the intention of this peculiar kidnapping of the country's two most senior leaders by a group of hot-headed youngsters? Was a violent uprising really planned for the capital? Or was this another attempt to force an immediate proclamation? Neither happened, in any case. Jakarta remained quiet and Sukarno and Hatta stuck to their position: no proclamation without Japanese support. 'I met that group of young guys,' said the Dutch veteran Piet van Staveren, who had sympathised with the liberation struggle, 'I happened to get to know them. They had mostly leftist tendencies, "communist", but that's a term I have difficulties with. Sukarno wasn't so very left-wing. He fought

for the Republic, he was a real nationalist.'⁵⁵ Sukarno suspected that
Sjahrir had incited the youngsters to carry out their action. He hadn't,
but he did agree that independence should be unilaterally declared
without delay. He and Sukarno had never got along very well and
now not at all.⁵⁶ In Sjahrir's eyes Sukarno was overly pragmatic and
had let Japan lead him by the nose. Sukarno considered Sjahrir an
excessively principled intellectual who had stayed on the sidelines.
Towards the end of the afternoon Rear Admiral Maeda managed to
convince the young radicals to release their leaders.⁵⁷ He guaranteed
Sukarno and Hatta's safety and, more than that, invited them to his
home to discuss how a possible declaration should be drafted.

That evening, 16 August 1945, Sukarno and Hatta went to see
Maeda and spoke to several sympathetic Japanese officers. The situation was complex: the capitulation meant that Japan was obliged to
maintain the status quo in the territories it occupied. Formally it was
impossible for it to quickly grant an enormous country like Indonesia
independence at the last moment. The Preparatory Committee for
Indonesian Independence could not do anything either. As an official
Japanese organisation it had lost all authority. A spontaneous action,
then? A purely Indonesian initiative? No, that wasn't possible either,
said Major General Otoshi Nishimura, chief of the General Affairs
Department, at least 'not as long as he knew about it'. But, he admitted, that implied that it could be done 'without his knowledge'.⁵⁸ The
defeated military administration would neither grant nor encourage
independence, but simply turn a blind eye. This strange compromise
allowed the senior Japanese officers to respect the orders from Tokyo
to maintain the status quo, yet also accommodate the wishes of the
older Indonesian nationalists, while reducing the risk of mass bloodshed by the younger nationalists. Maeda succeeded in convincing the
senior command of this position and went to bed. The Indonesians
were left to carry on working undisturbed. It was their independence, after all.

They spent until five in the morning polishing the text of a
speech – nobody got much sleep during that feverish week – while
Fatmawati, Sukarno's wife, quickly stitched together two pieces of
fabric to make the first official national flag. The final text was short,

smart and simple. 'We the people of Indonesia do hereby declare the independence of Indonesia. Matters concerning the transfer of power and other matters will be executed in an orderly manner and in the shortest possible time.' Signed, 'Djakarta, 17-8-05. In the name of the people of Indonesia, Soekarno/Hatta'. The document used the name the Japanese had given the city and the Japanese calendar – '05' referred to the imperial year 2605 – but nowhere did it state that Japan had transferred power. After all, the Indonesians had declared themselves sovereign. There was no call for violence either – the document spoke of an orderly transition. And there was no more dawdling: 'in the shortest possible time' meant *before* the Allied invasion. The Japanese officers, the older nationalists and the young pemuda could all be satisfied.

And so it happened. Several hours later, on Friday 17 August 1945, Sukarno stood in front of his home in Jakarta, flanked by Hatta, and read the Proklamasi. Both men were dressed in smart white suits, and both were pale with exhaustion. To avoid disturbances they had not made a mass demonstration of it, despite how much Sukarno would have loved to address the crowd. The handful of photos that have survived show a few hundred people. A PETA officer raised the flag on a bamboo pole. Those present sang 'Indonesia Raya'. With this short, restrained ceremony, the history of the fourth largest country in the world began – on a sunny Friday morning in August at ten o'clock with a small number of tired people raising a homemade cotton flag. In the Netherlands no one had a clue.

Chapter 10

'Free! Of! Everything!'
Republican violence and the British nightmare,
August 1945–December 1945

Out of a population of sixty-eight million, a United Nations study put the number of deaths in Indonesia at no less than four million, almost six per cent.[1] It hardly registered internationally, but Indonesia emerged from World War II as one of the worst-hit countries. The Indonesian death toll was the fifth highest globally (after the Soviet Union, China, Germany and Poland, and before Japan); for civilian deaths it was the highest. In Japan and Germany, civilians made up 23.3 and 28.4 per cent of the victims respectively, in the Soviet Union 57.8 per cent, in China eighty-one per cent, in Poland – partly because of the Holocaust – around ninety-six per cent, but Indonesia was worst of all: 99.7 per cent.[2] What's more, these innocent victims fell in a war that was never theirs, dying of starvation and deprivation in a military and economic clash between Japan and the Netherlands for the mineral wealth of their country.[3] Once you understand that, you understand much better why the people of Indonesia were so opposed to the return of either one. 'Free! Of! Everything!' shouted ninety-five-year-old Toernowo Hadiwidjojo in Dutch when I asked him about his motivation for taking up arms.[4] He was hard of hearing and articulated it extremely clearly. 'Vrij! Van! Alles!' Yes, that more or less summed it up.

Still, it would take another four and a half years before Indonesia was really free of everything, a liberation process that would drag on for a year longer than the entire Japanese occupation. The transfer of sovereignty would not be signed until December 1949. Until then the country would battle the Netherlands for control of the archipelago. But it wasn't just coloniser and colonised. British troops and diplomats would also be involved, along with Indian and Nepali soldiers, Australian troops and dockworkers, American officials and advisers, Ukrainian diplomats and a Belgian politician. Colonial histories are never binary processes, and that applies a fortiori to the first major post-World War II decolonisation war. Again, the world got involved and it changed the world.

To make sense of the tangle of events and players, it's useful to divide the period between August 1945 and December 1949 into four phases and name each one after the party that had the upper hand politically: the 'British year' lasted from August 1945 to November 1946, and was followed by a short 'Dutch year', until August 1947. This gave way to a longer 'American year': September 1947–December 1948. Finally there was a 'UN year' that lasted until December 1949. This breakdown is somewhat artificial, especially given the partial overlap of the US and UN efforts in the later phases, but it has the advantage of highlighting the complex international dynamics of the conflict. And, of course, all these years were also 'Indonesian years' – that was what it was all about.

In the Netherlands, the phase between 1945 and 1949 is still often referred to as 'the time of the Police Actions'. There is a gradually growing awareness that the term 'police actions' was a euphemism for conflicts that were part of an unmistakable decolonisation war, but not enough people realise that the 'actions' – there were two – lasted less than a month altogether (two weeks in July 1947 and two weeks in December 1948), while the whole war lasted fifty-two months. It's not very useful to reduce a period of almost four and a half years to two brief Dutch offensives, just as we don't call World War II 'the time of the Battle of the Bulge' or 'the time of Operation Market Garden'. It was a much wider conflict. This doesn't mean there were pitched battles between regular armies every day as in World War I. This war went through phases of great intensity, followed by periods of relative 'calm', but it also simmered with what we now call 'low-intensity conflict': scattered but regular violent incidents without an ongoing co-ordinated offensive.

We mustn't let the considerable attention paid to the violent side of the conflict in recent years – were the Dutch 'excesses' incidental or structural? – obscure the fact that the period 1945–9 was distinguished most of all by the alternation of military and diplomatic initiatives. Although the diplomatic side is increasingly at risk of being forgotten, it is completely impossible to understand the story behind the battles and other eruptions of violence without knowing about the peace treaties and ceasefires that were negotiated and agreed in the intervening periods. Put simply, the revolutionary violence of what the Dutch call the Bersiap (late 1945) was followed by the Linggajati Agreement (November 1946). This agreement led in turn to the first of the so-called Police Actions, the first Dutch offensive of July 1947, after which the Renville Agreement was signed (January 1948). Breaches of Renville were the prelude to the second Dutch offensive (December 1948), which led to a guerrilla war against the Netherlands (first half of 1949). The Roem–Van Roijen Agreement (May 1949) sought to end this conflict and resulted in the ceasefire of August 1949, the Round Table Conference of November 1949 and ultimately the transfer of sovereignty in December 1949. In short: war – negotiation, war – negotiation, war – negotiation, with the negotiations resulting successively in the Linggajati, Renville and Roem–Van Roijen Agreements. Overlooking the diplomatic side would mean missing half of the history. Von Clausewitz's classic axiom that war is 'the continuation of politics by other means' is more applicable than ever to the drama that unfolded in Indonesia between 1945 and 1949.

The British year, then. Volunteer Goderd van Heek, the son of a Twente textile baron, began his military training at Warley Barracks, near Brentwood in Essex, in June 1945. Great Britain and the Netherlands were allies, so there was nothing out of the ordinary in young Dutchies, while awaiting an army of their own, receiving military training from experienced Tommies before fighting Japan together. Bayonet training made the intentions clear. 'There were sackcloth dummies filled with straw. In a bush, behind a tree, in a trench. They were the Japs. They all had slanty eyes!' Goderd learned the commands in English. 'Fix bayonets! In-out! They taught us that wounded Japanese soldiers keep fighting. We had to give them a jab too: In-out! A friend of mine said, "Stuff that! It's against the

Geneva Convention!" We were idealists.' The months in England felt like a new beginning after four long years of war. 'It was a marvellous, carefree time.' Dancing with English girls, going on leave with mates in Scotland, a warm welcome everywhere from people who wanted to hear your stories about the German occupation . . . 'Primary Training was followed by Infantry Corps Training with Dutch and Brits together. This brought us into contact with real London cockneys, a strange hotchpotch who were almost as dirty as they were funny.' A new world and a new vocabulary opened up for the respectably raised Goderd. And the chance to send a first batch of troops to England for training was a godsend for the Netherlands. 'A whole army needed to be built up,' Goderd explained, 'and we were going to be the officers and NCOs for the first divisions of conscripts.'[5]

The British had been helping the Dutch against the Japanese for some time. They had committed to assisting attempts to liberate Sumatra and had launched a dozen small-scale commando raids on the island since April 1944. Militarily these hadn't achieved much, but once Burma, the Malay Peninsula and Singapore were retaken, the British forces would move south into Sumatra while the Americans liberated the rest of the Indies. Dutch NICA units would go ashore with each landing to re-establish the civil administration. 'You're in the Indies to fight until the last Jap is driven out,' according to a book of instructions distributed widely among American soldiers from 1944.[6]

But in April 1945, after the Battle of Manila, something crucial happened. While MacArthur was given the task of pushing on to Japan, Washington asked London if Mountbatten could finish the job in the territories that would be left behind. This would hasten the end of the war *and* – though this wasn't said in so many words – absolve the US of the difficult task of reconquering the Dutch, French and Portuguese colonies. The British had little choice: the forces at their disposal were not up to such an enormous responsibility, but was that grounds for prolonging the war? During the Potsdam Conference of July 1945 the decision was made to enlarge the British operational area: in addition to Burma, the Malay Peninsula and

Sumatra, their South East Asia Command (SEAC) would now also cover French Indochina, Thailand, the Dutch East Indies and Portuguese East Timor. It was a massive expansion. Mountbatten had already had power over the fate of forty-five million people; this was now increased to 125 million.[7] Command was scheduled to be passed to the British on 15 August, coincidentally the day Japan surrendered.

The Dutch were not sure what to make of this transfer of military authority. On the one hand, it was a tremendous setback given that America was much more powerful both politically and militarily. What's more, Dutch–US collaboration had always gone smoothly. In Australia Van Mook had got along excellently with MacArthur; his NICA units had accompanied US troops, and tons of emergency aid for the Indies were awaiting shipment from Australian harbours. This seemed certain to generate a lot of goodwill among the impoverished inhabitants. 'Ten shiploads of food and textiles from Australia,' said Van Mook, 'and the whole Javanese population will flock to the docks to unload the ships.'[8] This well-oiled collaboration now came to an end. The British operated from Ceylon, not Australia. They had less of everything: ships, soldiers and experience. Their knowledge of Indonesia was minimal. They had not received any intelligence reports from the Americans, for the simple reason that none existed. There still wasn't anyone who knew exactly what was happening in Java. That wasn't encouraging.

On the other hand, relations between the Dutch and the British were unmistakably warm. The government-in-exile in London, the mutual admiration between Churchill and Queen Wilhelmina, the shared struggle against fascism, the connections between the Dutch resistance and the United Kingdom (the escape route from the occupied Netherlands was across the North Sea; the RAF had airdropped supplies) – all these things had reinforced the countries' trust in each other. In Asia, Dutch and British troops had operated together under ABDACOM, suffered together in the Battle of the Java Sea and shared the same fate as prisoners of war on the Burma and Sumatra Railways. And now the two countries were training together. What's more, the British had colonies in the region themselves:

India, Burma, Ceylon, the Malay States. Wouldn't that make them more sympathetic to Dutch concerns than the Americans, who could not wait to make the Philippines independent? Weren't they a more suitable liberator?

Not that the Netherlands had any say in the matter. The country wasn't a participant at Potsdam – only Truman, Churchill and Stalin had seats at the table – and without a military of its own there wasn't much it could do. The Netherlands was working diligently to rectify that last failing: besides the troops in England that included Goderd van Heek, a thousand Dutch soldiers were being trained in Australia and 4,500 marines in the US. But what use was learning how to bay-onet straw dummies now Japan had surrendered? 'That was a complete unknown,' said Goderd. 'We were in the middle of train-ing, but we heard that Japan had been defeated. It seemed it would no longer be necessary to fight to liberate the Indies. Minister of War Meynen came specially to Essex to speak to us. There was a chance we were going to be sent to Germany as occupation troops. Disap-pointment all round. We wanted to go to the Indies!'

The end of the war in Indonesia was most peculiar of all, 'a liber-ation without liberators' in Henk Hovinga's pithy description.[9] There were no tanks rolling through the streets with laughing soldiers on them, no cigarettes or chocolate bars being strewn around. Nobody was dancing. Nobody jumped into bed with the likeable liberators, simply because there weren't any. And at the same time, it wasn't clear what exactly it meant for a colony to be liberated.

On Friday 17 August 1945 Herawati Diah saw her husband arrive home in the afternoon. 'Apparently, he hadn't slept a wink all night.' Herawati was the woman who had studied at Columbia. During the occupation she had worked for Japanese radio and that was where she had met her husband, now a deputy editor of *Asia Raya* and a prominent nationalist youth leader. That morning he had been one of the very few present at the ceremony in front of Sukarno's house. 'He was there at the house as a journalist,' she said.[10] On arriving home he told her: 'I have just distributed the text of the Proclama-tion of Independence. I am satisfied that some of the population of

Jakarta already know that we are free.' Herawati gave him a questioning look. 'He showed me a crumpled piece of paper from his shirt pocket and I saw the handwriting of [Sukarno] which began with the word "Proclamation".'[11]

The Japanese military administration did nothing to prevent this historic event. On the contrary, Rear Admiral Maeda let Sukarno use his printing press to make copies to distribute. The Japanese telephone and telegram services were also made available. The news reached Bandung around midday. That evening it could be heard here and there on the radio. At the end of the war Japan had almost 300,000 troops in the archipelago, including some 60,000 in Java.[12] According to the conditions of the capitulation they were only permitted to maintain the status quo. Not that they still cherished many ambitions: they had been shamefully defeated and most of them just wanted to go home. Still, they did take one more important measure one week after the Proklamasi. To avoid disorder, they disarmed PETA and the heiho, the two most important of the native militias they had founded.

A power vacuum is less a place without political players than one where too many players are biding their time. Who would be the first to reach Deck 1 now that Japan had vacated it? The British? The Dutch? The nationalists? Theoretically it was, from 15 August, the UK's turn to make a move, but the area of British authority covered all of Southeast Asia. Mountbatten proceeded one step at a time: first liberate the Malay States and Singapore, then Thailand and French Indochina – freeing the POWs there from their terrible camps – and only then, right at the end, sail to Indonesia to demobilise the Japanese there too, evacuate the camps and re-establish civilian rule.[13] There was no hurry; it was peacetime. Starting in September he would send a few small units to assist the people in the camps, but the main force wouldn't land until 4 October, more than six weeks after the Proklamasi.

Van Mook repeatedly urged Mountbatten to bring the deployment forward, but the logistics ruled out arriving any more than five or six days earlier. Militarily, the Dutch were completely dependent on him. In the Netherlands the war had ended later than expected (spring '45 instead of autumn '44), in Indonesia sooner (August '45 instead of '46). Although it was naturally impossible for the Dutch authorities to raise an army of their own in the three and a half months between May and August 1945, everyone in the Netherlands besides the communists still assumed that they would once again take the lead role in the Dutch East Indies, at least for some time to come. Opinions differed about how long that period would last (five years? twenty-five years? a few more centuries?) – the left thought short, the right thought long. And how close the ties should be was also unclear – the left thought loose, the right thought close – but for virtually everyone, the Indies simply belonged with the Netherlands. The economic importance of the colony was indisputable. In 1945 statistician J. B. D. Derksen and economist Jan Tinbergen (later winner of the Nobel Prize for Economics) calculated that before the war the Dutch East Indies was responsible for fifteen per cent of the Netherlands' annual national income, more than five billion guilders. In addition, approximately one sixth of Dutch national capital was invested in the Dutch East Indies.[14] The raw materials, the cheap workforce, the markets . . . It was obvious that all these economic advantages were of great importance to Dutch reconstruction, but there was also a psychological attachment. For decades many Dutch citizens had felt that the East gave them international stature. Even farming families in the polder who didn't own shares in any kind of colonial enterprise still felt a sense of national pride. And it really was an achievement for such a small country to be at the helm of an enormous empire. But this pride could easily lead to a blinkered perspective. Officially the Indies was dependent on the Netherlands, but economically and emotionally the Netherlands was just as dependent on the Indies.

Pratomo and the PI tried in vain to change Dutch attitudes. After the war he and Stennie stayed in Amsterdam, where they were very active: Stennie in the women's movement, Pratomo as a zealous advocate of Indonesian independence. 'We organised a large meeting at the Concertgebouw,' said Pratomo. 'It was packed. Indonesian seamen working for the shipping companies Rotterdamsche Lloyd and the Nederlandsche Scheepvaartmaatschappij came. There were a lot of women there too.' Clandestine resistance work was no longer necessary. 'We applied for and received permission for our demonstration. I was involved in the organisation and marched with the red-and-white flag. I gave a speech about the liberation of Indonesia.'[15] Some 2,000 sympathisers showed up, a significant number, but nothing compared to the bulk of the Dutch population who simply wanted to reclaim the Indies.[16]

In Australia that seemed strange. Why couldn't their large neighbour be free? During the war Australia had been a refuge for the Dutch East Indies and Van Mook's base of operations, like England for the Dutch government. But after the war, protest increased, chiefly among Australian dockworkers. During the occupation they had met the Indonesian sailors and stokers of the exiled KPM, as well as Indonesian KNIL soldiers and even the left-wing detainees from Boven Digul. A high level of solidarity developed between the Australian trade unions and the Indonesians struggling for independence, as shown by the 1946 Joris Ivens film *Indonesia Calling*. The dockworkers arranged a very well-publicised boycott of the planned shipments and none of the tons of relief supplies waiting in the warehouses was shipped to Indonesia. Already lacking an army, the Dutch didn't have any goods now either. With neither a stick nor a carrot, they were in no position to make demands. With Japan inactive, the British absent and the Australians striking, it was all very difficult.

Meanwhile the Indonesian nationalists were wasting no time in establishing their own power. Immediately after the Proklamasi of 17 August they made a series of important decisions. On 18 August the Preparatory Committee for Indonesian Independence accepted the constitution they had already prepared under Japanese rule: the Republik Indonesia would be a unitary republic, not a federation of independently governed islands, but a strongly presidential country with a central government in Jakarta – not so very different from the colonial model. They also adopted the colonial borders: what had once been an arbitrary jigsaw puzzle was now seen as a self-evident territory. Sukarno and Hatta were immediately appointed president and vice-president. On 19 August eight provinces were created. On 21 August Sukarno called for the establishment everywhere of 'national committees', new revolutionary bodies to assist the existing organisations in their administrative tasks. On 22 August the BKR was founded (Badan Keamanan Rakyat, the People's Security Corps) as a replacement for the now defunct heiho and PETA – still not a real army, but a self-defence force and the start of national defence. On 27 August a first national advisory council was convened, the KNIP (Komité National Indonesia Pusat, the Central Indonesian National Committee), a kind of unelected proto-parliament. On 30 August a large conference for civil servants was held and on 31 August a first government was established. To sum up, a constitution, a head of state, a parliament, a government, something resembling an army and the start of a new administrative apparatus were all realised in less than two weeks. Soldiers and civil servants were immediately assigned places in the new state, which had already reached out to thousands of villages and islands. Decks 2 and 3 were ascending to Deck 1 together.

But people started jostling on the stairs. The unruliest element in Indonesian society was undoubtedly the pemuda, the politicised and militarised youths who were ablaze with militancy and impatience. How did they see the future? They sympathised with independence, of course, but could they also accept Sukarno's bureaucratic approach? Daily meetings, setting up all kinds of bodies, publishing decisions in a new bulletin of acts, orders and decrees – was that how they saw the struggle for freedom? Their poverty continued unrelieved, they were still starving.[17] They were a powder-keg waiting to go off.

While Goderd van Heek was in his barracks in Essex wondering if he would ever be sent to 'Insulindia', Sukotjo Tjokroatmodjo was having the time of his life. The son of a native stationmaster was now seventeen. At school he had been embarrassed about still eating with his hands. He had swum on a Japanese grocer's back when he was a child and seen him return during the war as a friendly officer. He'd experienced the occupation at school in Malang: bowing for the emperor, learning Japanese, drilling with a fake wooden gun. He hadn't heard anything about Hiroshima and Nagasaki from the public radio masts: they were still blaring daily gymnastic exercises through the streets at six every morning. Not a word about the capitulation. About the Proklamasi, even less. Until the big news reached him on 23 August. 'Sukarno called for the foundation of national committees. They had to assist the district heads. The Japanese were still in Malang. Most people didn't dare to do anything, but we stole a pickup from them! There were eight or nine of us youths. One of us could drive. We drove to Blitar to meet the *bupati*, the regent. We wanted to set up national committees, but the Japanese chased us away. We had hundreds of red-and-white paper flags with us; they'd been printed in Malang. From Blitar we drove to Tulungagung and Kediri. Everywhere we went, we'd ask for the local administrators. We also spoke to the PETA soldiers, they'd just been demobilised by the Japanese. We said, "You have to protect the older generation so they can set up a national committee." We were on the road in our pickup for days. We slept at our friends' parents'. The people in the villages didn't feel safe. They were still scared of the Japanese, but we weren't scared any more! The Japanese sat in their offices and didn't come outside any more. We didn't have weapons yet. All I had was my pocketknife, ha-ha! But national committees were gradually formed in the villages and the Japanese left them in peace.'

Sukarno had every reason to be satisfied: young Indonesians were spontaneously helping to build up his Republic. It was late August and his incredible gamble of 17 August seemed to be coming off. Japan was leaving him to it, there were no signs anywhere of the British, the Netherlands seemed a distant memory, and the Indonesian youth, that unpredictable factor, were making sure that the few hundred people present at the Proklamasi was growing into a national movement that reached the smallest hamlets. Symbols mattered, nobody realised that more than Sukarno. A country does not live by bureaucracy alone. On 1 September he decreed that the red-and-white should fly everywhere. Around the same time *'Bung'* – brother, mate – came into fashion, by analogy with the 'citizen' and 'comrade' of the French and Russian Revolutions. More and more often he himself was being referred to with the amicable 'Bung Karno' – the prefix 'soe' or 'su' in many Javanese names comes from Sanskrit and means 'good'. And thanks to this national revolution, Indonesians no longer greeted each other with *Selamat pagi*, blessed morning, but with *Merdeka!* Freedom!

In September 1945 the British appeared on the scene. After the formal signing of the Japanese surrender on 2 September, a first team of four paratroopers landed at Kemayoran, the airport of Jakarta, on 8 September. Their goal was the co-ordination of medical care for POWs and interned civilians. A week later a first British boat moored at the port of Tanjung Priok, followed by a Dutch ship with several administrators. Van Mook had visited Mountbatten in Ceylon shortly before. The British were to disarm and repatriate the Japanese, evacuate the camps and prepare the area for the return of civilian rule; the Australians would perform the same tasks in the sparsely populated east of the archipelago, where the Japanese navy had been in charge. Van Mook assured Mountbatten that none of this would present any kind of 'operational problem' – he had no knowledge of the pemuda movement in Java and Sumatra and thought that everything would go as smoothly as it had in western New Guinea, Morotai and Borneo.[18] In the remote provinces that had been liberated since 1944, the Dutch tricolour was flying again and the grateful people had gathered to sing the Wilhelmus.[19] But there was something else. He had heard on the radio that Sukarno and Hatta had declared independence. These figures were, however, extremely 'compromised with the Japanese', he told Mountbatten. 'It is obvious that the Sukarno "government" has been formed by the Japanese and is completely under Japanese control.' It could become 'a centre of Japanese Pan-Asian propaganda' if Mountbatten didn't declare it void.[20]

Mountbatten didn't consent to that last request. If the government really were a Japanese creation, it would be up to Japan to dissolve it – but it wasn't. There were decolonisation movements in other colonies too: Gandhi in India, Aung San in Burma, Ho Chi Minh in Indochina. In Burma he, Mountbatten, had entered into direct talks with Aung San, the later Nobel Prize-winner Aung San Suu Kyi's father, who had also collaborated with the Japanese. What would justify him taking action against the nationalists in Indonesia? And now

Map 20: Proklamasi and Revolusi (August–December 1945)

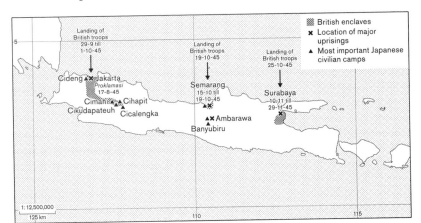

of all times. After all, the socialist Clement Attlee had just been elected in the UK. Mountbatten apparently added that things might have been different if they had still had Churchill. Then something might have been possible.[21] For a senior military officer, his own views were quite progressive. His wife, Lady Mountbatten, England's wealthiest heiress, was even distinctly socialist. Socialite and socialist in one, a fairly unique combination. No, his troops would readily smooth the way for a Dutch return, but one could not expect him to pass judgement on an internal matter.

And maybe it wouldn't come to so very much anyway. A British intelligence report anticipated that the Indonesians 'will welcome the return of the Dutch by whom they were well treated, except for a small minority who will have profited materially under the Japanese'.[22] Van Mook's closest colleague, head of intelligence Simon Spoor, had also, with an abundance of confidence, written: 'The radio reports definitely do not give the impression that the population is inspired by a fanatical willingness to back these collaborationist leaders in a struggle for a completely independent Indonesia. On the contrary, going by the official reports it is even difficult to take the independence movement seriously.'[23]

It turned out very differently.

★

The months September, October and November became a real nightmare for Mountbatten. Every time he landed troops, the pemuda
reacted with even more youths, even more fury and, above all, even
more violence. It began reasonably innocently. When the first British
soldiers drove through the streets of Jakarta, they were surprised to
see freshly painted slogans on the trams and trains – which were even
in English. 'We want to be free and we shall be free.' 'We need just
now independence.' 'We don't like the DUTCH!' It was unclear
who had painted them. The English was almost perfect; sometimes
they were even professionally designed billboards. This had clearly
been ordered from above. They also referred to the Atlantic Charter
('For the right of self-determination') and American history, a favourite parallel of Sukarno's (US President Monroe's famous 'America for
the Americans' became 'Indonesia for the Indonesians').[24] In one case
we know for certain that Sukarno was behind it: he personally asked
Affandi to design a poster calling on the young. The result was the
legendary 'Boeng, ajo boeng', an incredibly powerful graphic design
showing an angry young man breaking his chains while holding a
red-and-white flag high on a bamboo. The catchphrase – 'Come on,
man!' – was from the poet Chairil Anwar, who knew it from his
brothel-going in Jakarta: it was how prostitutes tried to attract potential customers' attention. That poster too appeared on streets all over
the seething city.[25]

On 18 and 19 September, small-scale Allied parachute drops in
Bandung, Magelang and Surabaya followed. These enraged the
pemuda. In their eyes these interventions were intended not just to
intern and evacuate the Japanese, but also to bring the Dutch back
into the country. They were absolutely right: along with the British,
the NICA landed, together with several high-ranking administrators, including Charles van der Plas, Lieutenant Governor-General
Van Mook's right-hand man. Didn't NICA stand for Netherlands
Indies Civil Administration? Not Indonesia, but a shameless 'Netherlands Indies'? And in what sense was it a 'civil administration'? The
NICA workers wore army uniforms. And their banknotes were in
Dutch again. Free of everything? It didn't look like it.

On 19 September the pemuda organised a gigantic demonstration

in Jakarta. The initiators were figures like Chaerul Saleh and Adam
Malik, the same radical elements involved in kidnapping Sukarno
and Hatta a month earlier. Young people from working-class districts, perhaps more than 200,000, answered their call to come to the
centre of town to show how dissatisfied they were with the British
landings. Young Indonesians really were capable of mobilising on a
massive scale, something that had previously only succeeded under
the authority of the Japanese state. Sukarno responded to the initiative with irritation and caution. At first he had forbidden it, but when
the masses flooded in anyway, he let himself be persuaded into giving
a short, conciliatory speech. Japanese troops were standing by with
machine guns and tanks. Once again his oratorical brilliance was
revealed. He began with a classic *captatio benevolentiae*: 'Brothers and
sisters, we are not retracting a single word of our Proclamation of
Independence and will defend the Republic until our last breath!'
Frenzied cheers rose from thousands of throats. This was just what
they wanted to hear. 'I know that you have come here to see your
president and hear his orders.' No, actually, they had come to kick
out the Brits. Inggris kita linggis. Sukarno had said it so often, we'll
bash the British! But this time he expressly avoided the slogan. He
asked a question: 'Do you trust your president?' Thousands of throats
roared yes. 'Well, all go home then, calmly and serenely, and await
our orders.' One man facing almost a quarter of a million screaming
adolescents. There are not many politicians from the twentieth century who managed to keep a cool head in such a tense situation and
bend an irate mass to their will. Sukarno did it masterfully. The
youngsters slinked off meekly. Bu Law Ennie was there that day. She
was sixteen. 'I don't remember exactly what he said,' she related, 'but
Sukarno was extraordinary. He spoke without looking at his notes,
addressing the crowd directly. His charisma was unbelievable.'[26]

In Surabaya too there was a great gathering of young people, but
no Sukarno in attendance. The day before, a team of four British and
four Dutch paratroopers had been dropped to prepare the evacuation
of the camps. Afterwards a Dutchman had the stupid idea of running
up the Dutch tricolour again for the first time over the Oranje Hotel,
the city's modernist luxury hotel. Talk about unsubtle. 'It was a large

flag,' recalled Sumarsono, who lived in Surabaya, 'one metre by more than two metres! Clearly visible from every corner of the city!' Pemuda like him could hardly believe their eyes. This was the ultimate proof that the British were smoothing the path for the Dutch.

Sumarsono was one of the instigators of the riot that followed. He had been one of the rare conscripts in the colonial army, but after three years of Japanese occupation, he was now giving his all for the young Republic. 'Five people came to my house to tell me that a red-white-and-blue flag was flying. I was furious. I told them we had to take it down. Putting up that flag returned power to the Dutch. We went there on foot. It was a long way. We were impatient. The whole way I shouted, "A red-white-and-blue flag is flying! Come on, come on! We're taking down that flag! *Belanda mau kembali*! The Hollanders want to come back! Just look at that flag!"' His group soon swelled. 'A lot of young people who heard me went to the hotel with us! Hundreds! When we got there, we shouted, "*Turunkan bendera*! Take down that flag!" Five hundred turned into a thousand, a thousand became ten thousand. Even more people arrived. Ten thousand of us were standing in front of that hotel. Then a big strong Dutchman came out, Ploegman, a professional boxer with a wooden club, just like Samson! He waved it around to break us up, hitting us. Some people got injured. I took a blow too and screamed in pain. The pemuda chased him, a hundred metres at least. He went back inside like a dog. I shouted that he had to come back so we could fight. I went forward with a lot of people following me. We shouted that the flag had to come down. Twenty or thirty people climbed up onto the roof, nine up onto the mast. One of them was Ana, someone from our organisation, alongside two Ambonese. I didn't climb up myself but gave the order. The blue strip was torn off the flag and the red-and-white was raised.' How significant a role he really played is difficult to reconstruct; tumult has many leaders, especially in retrospect. 'Meanwhile Ploegman came back out with his club, three times even. The third time I saw that he was bleeding. Someone must have stabbed him, not a pemuda, but a Madurese, I suspect, maybe a pedicab rider with a sickle? I didn't know him. The blood flowed. Ploegman fell to the ground and died.'[27] Victor Ploegman, a middle-aged Eurasian, was possibly the first fatality of the decolonisation war.

Sumaun was there too; his father had once worked in that fancy hotel. His matter-of-fact account confirms the broad details. 'There was a great rush of people. Some youths were carrying bamboo spears. One of us climbed up and tore the blue off the flag. A Dutch captain came out seething and drew his sword, but we pelted him with stones. There was nothing he could do. There were hundreds with *bambu runcing*, bamboo spears. That's how he was killed.'[28] There are different versions of Ploegman's death; the story made a great impression on people.[29] In Surabaya, the city where Tjokroaminoto's boarding house had been located, you could, after this incident, hear a twelve-year-old boy shouting, 'I want to see Dutch blood!'[30]

The struggle for Deck 1 had begun. In the cities the young took over the most important public buildings, things like railway stations, post offices, food storehouses and radio stations. They also managed to gain control of the trains and trams. The red-and-white flag was flying everywhere. In Ceylon, Mountbatten realised that relieving Indonesia would not be an easy task. His wife, the colourful Lady Edwina – beautiful and polyamorous – had, as head of a medical aid organisation, visited several civilian camps in Java, where the European population was still interned. During her trip, she too saw the political slogans and countless flags and, after returning home, she was able to tell her husband how deeply the Republic had already taken root. At the end of September, Mountbatten informed Van Mook and Van der Plas of an irrevocable government decision: the British would disarm the Japanese and liberate the camps, but liberating all of Indonesia in anticipation of the reinstatement of Dutch rule was, in these circumstances, no longer possible. They would concentrate solely on several port cities that were needed for the evacuation of the camp residents and the Japanese: Jakarta and Surabaya in Java, Medan and Padang in Sumatra. NICA could operate freely in those key areas; beyond them, it was at their own risk. For the Netherlands this was an enormous disappointment. The country had hoped to regain the vast jigsaw puzzle it had gone to such lengths to assemble during the colonial era, but now had to make do with four miserable little pieces on the edge. Important harbours, it was true, but what good are harbours without hinterland? Or even worse, with hostile hinterland? It was like being flung back to the seventeenth century. To make matters worse, Mountbatten insisted on Dutch talks with Sukarno. That was how he had done it in Burma too, and that had prevented a civil war. Even progressive figures like Van Mook and Van der Plas found this utterly unimaginable. They wanted Sukarno and Hatta arrested immediately.

Mountbatten appointed General Philip Christison commander in the Netherlands East Indies and, in Singapore on his way to his posting, Christison gave a press conference at which he stated that the British did not want to meddle in internal affairs. 'The Indonesian government' would remain responsible outside the four key areas he would occupy, but he was always ready to bring 'representatives of the Netherlands and Indonesian leaders' together.[31] The Netherlands exploded. Although he later qualified his remarks, they amounted to de facto recognition of the Sukarno government, legitimisation of the Republican project and the reduction of the Netherlands to just one of the parties involved. The Netherlands had hoped for an ally, but had gained a go-between at most. 'You have let us down,' said an embittered Van Mook.[32]

Was perfidious Albion up to its old tricks? Were the British taking over again in a moment of Dutch weakness, like they had with Raffles in 1811? No, anything but. Very few British interests were at stake. They too had limited means and the war was over. 'We don't want the Dutch East Indies. We don't want anything at all. All we want is to go home,' said a British commander.[33] To complicate things, their task was not at all clear-cut. Whatever they did, it would always be too little for the Dutch and too much for the Indonesians. Once a puzzle has been put together, it can only have one owner, unless you take it apart again and start sharing out the pieces. But both players wanted the whole thing. The British were caught between two hostile camps. And that in peacetime.

In October 1945 things went horribly wrong. The immediate cause was the arrival of the 1st Indian Infantry Brigade in Jakarta on 29

September. Within three days 4,000 soldiers went ashore in Tanjung Priok. Most were from the Indian army: Sikhs from Punjab, Rajputs from Rajasthan, Gurkhas from Nepal. Many had fought in Burma or been imprisoned in Singapore; their officers were British. Although the soldiers were Asians too, the pemuda were anything but glad to see them.

Those who *were* glad about their arrival were the Europeans in the civilian camps. Rescued at last after three years of misery! 'And then one day the door of the camp was thrown wide open. The Gurkhas had come to protect us! We were allowed out!' Joty ter Kulve remembered. 'The last days there was no roll call in the mornings any more. We no longer needed to bow in the direction of the emperor. Sometimes the Japanese were even blind drunk.' In order to evacuate the inland camps the British had extended their area of activity to Bogor and Bandung. The pemuda looked askance at that too: were they about to lose another piece of the jigsaw? 'In Bandung I went out with English officers every evening,' Joty recalled. 'I was seventeen. We hadn't seen any men for three years! My mother said, "I promised your father. You're not doing anything, no matter who the chap is! You can kiss, but that's it!" Well, I stuck to that,' she said with a smile. In any case the greatest danger came from a completely different direction. 'During an Officers' Ball in the middle of the jungle I was

Map 21: Republican civilian internment camps in Java (1945–1947)

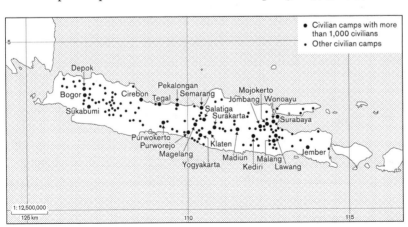

dancing with an English officer. Suddenly bullets were whizzing past our ears. The Indonesians' fury had turned against us.'[34]

The Korvinus sisters were still stuck in the Ambarawa camp in Central Java. 'The Gurkhas took us to Semarang in trucks. There we spent three nights in the warehouse of a cigarette factory. The bullets were whistling over us. We had to hold our mattresses over our heads.'[35] In Sumatra friends Brigitte Sparwer-Abrams and Marianne Constance Pulle were liberated by soldiers of the Indian army. 'They were big, dark-skinned men with turbans and beards. We were scared of them!' Violence broke out there too. 'It was bizarre,' said Brigitte Sparwer-Abrams. 'First we were interned by Japan, then we were liberated by Englishmen and Gurkhas [presumably Sikhs] and in the end we were protected by the Japs!' The world really had turned upside down. The Japanese, who had barked orders at the Europeans for years, now had to guarantee their safety and prevent the pemuda they had radicalised from entering the camps and killing or injuring them.

Again, the British arrival turned out to be a Trojan horse. At the start of October more Dutch officials returned to Jakarta in their wake, and hardly the least prominent: Admiral Helfrich, head of the navy; Lieutenant General Van Oyen, commander of the KNIL; and even Lieutenant Governor-General Van Mook, the Dutch administration's number one man. In the weeks that followed, seven KNIL companies of a hundred men each landed from Australia, plus an approximately 600-strong battalion of former POWs from Singapore. These were no longer NICA officials in uniform, but real soldiers. Ton Berlee was one of them. He came back from Saigon, where he had ended up after the forced labour on the Burma Railway. 'The KNIL was ready for action right away.' He went to work with the KNIL military police. In 1942 he had helped set fire to the Plaju oil refinery, now he would help put out this grassfire. 'In some kampongs we were given a grand welcome, even honoured! The people said, "You've come to drive out the bandits!" But the youths were hostile and all worked up. Sukarno had stirred them up.' He sighed. 'They should have shot him dead! And we should have had the Americans, not the British!'[36] Former KNIL native troops – Ambonese, Menadonese and Javanese – also reported back for duty with the Dutch. On top of the 4,000 British troops there were now a few thousand Dutch soldiers available. This stirred up so much ill feeling among the young revolutionaries that they cooled their fury on everything that seemed European: the Dutch, the Eurasians, the British and all the soldiers fighting on their side. Even Chinese traders, who had always benefited from the Pax Hollandica, were now sharing the suffering.

Jakarta was completely on edge. 'After the British landing, fire-fights broke out regularly in the streets,' remembered Toenggoel Siagian. 'Those were turbulent times. My uncle joined the pemuda and disappeared. My aunt was raped and murdered. Friends died. Two streets from here, a twelve-year-old boy was gunned down by a Dutch soldier because he had a copy of the newspaper *Merdeka* on him. Our street was closed off when there was fighting around the Kramat II camp. The British took away the red-and-white flag and we children were furious! You saw naked, emaciated people on the street. Japanese dead. A headless Dutch body . . .'[37]

For fourteen-year-old Nanny Kooymans the first months after the war were 'much worse than the Japanese period'. As a Eurasian she had belonged to the well-off upper class, but the days of comfort and domestic staff were over. There was robbing, looting and murder. 'Nobody was in power. The pemuda were wandering around with red headbands. They carried bamboo spears and screamed, "*Bersiap!*"' That battle cry – Indonesian for 'Attention!' – is still used in the Netherlands to indicate this period of disorder, the so-called Bersiap. In Indonesia, the term is not applied and people speak simply of the Revolusi instead. Not a unique historic event that requires a distinctive name, but a classic process of great social and political upheaval comparable to the French Revolution. In a short period, the Revolusi violently settled its score with the *ancien régime*, without being centrally led by any one party.[38] Nanny Kooymans: 'I lost two cousins. One was very blond and was taken from his house in Surabaya. The other one was fourteen and went to the market in Jakarta. He was chopped to pieces.' With most of the Europeans still in the camps, the Indos were the group that suffered the most attacks.

'Indonesians came into our house too with a *klewang*, a sword. "Is there a man here? If we find him, we'll cut off his head!" My younger brother was blond and they swore at him; he was six. It was only when Ambonese with red berets came that they fled.' Gunshots in front of the house. Blood on the pavement. Yelling. Nanny Kooymans still trembles when she hears people shouting. 'I saw an Indo who was on guard duty shot dead. A pregnant Chinese woman was murdered with a bambu runcing. They cut out the baby. My uncle was missing for a couple of days. A few days later there were bodies in Ciliwung Canal. We were looking down from the bridge. "Look, there's Uncle Jan!" His chest was cut open. I also saw an Indies Dutch girl's body floating in the water: naked and nailed to a raft.'[39]

The Indies Dutch were again the target of violence. Too dark in the colonial era to pass as 'real' Dutch men and women, too light-skinned in the Japanese period to count as 'real' Asians, and too European to be spared during the Revolusi. 'We always got it from both sides,' Bol Kerrebijn agreed at Bronbeek, the Dutch veterans' retirement home in Arnhem. 'During the Bersiap everything turned against us. The Dutch were still protected in the camps. I was one of the "stray Indos". There was no authority. The neighbours had been murdered by marauders. I told my mother, "Ma, now it's our turn. The moment one comes over that fence, I'll stick my knife into him."' Nobody was going to mess with Kerrebijn. He was eighteen and had fourteen dogs. During the Japanese period he'd used them to hunt wild pigs. He let his fists do the talking. '"No, don't," my mother said. I cried, "Then I'm leaving now and you're coming with me."' He set off through the interior of West Java, but was picked up after just a few kilometres. 'We've got an Indo!' the pemuda screamed. It was another twenty-five kilometres' walk to Bogor. The crowd following them grew to several hundred. 'Finish him off! Finish him off!' It still made Bol furious. 'Those pemuda were my own age! God-damned jerks. Cowards. And they're the heroes of Indonesia! It still winds me up. I spoke their nasty little language, Sundanese. I spoke the broadest Sundanese they'd ever heard. "You can all bloody well go . . ." That's what saved me.'

Bol Kerrebijn was taken to the prison at Bogor, where other

Eurasians were also being held. 'Gurkha shock troops came and freed us. They had a Scottish commander and they were tremendous! Those Gurkhas were used to the mountains. They were very calm and humble. They washed and shaved. All very respectable. They didn't visit prostitutes, they preferred playing volleyball.' Bol's experience of the blind violence of the pemuda would determine his choice of profession forever. 'I joined the army out of revenge! I wasn't going to let them kill me! All I thought about was surviving and killing.' In the process he developed his own military code. 'Take the Gurkhas as an example. Be one hundred per cent loyal to the system. And make sure you're as vicious as your adversaries.[40]

The pemuda's cruelty knew no bounds. In deliberate sadism they often surpassed their Japanese teachers. They tortured and murdered entire families. They bashed children's heads on drain covers to crush their skulls. They raped girls, then killed them by ramming bamboo spears up their vaginas. It is difficult to say just how many people were murdered – the latest, authoritative estimate puts the figure at 6,000.[41] What explained this insane orgy of violence? This was more than a sudden, intoxicated rush brought on by gangs of youths stirring each other up in late 1945. This was not just the fault of British troops arriving too late and in insufficient numbers (September 1945). It was not just a consequence of the famine and terrible suffering of the preceding years (1944–5). It could not be blamed entirely on the Japanese occupiers, who had turned the heads of the young and hardened their bodies (March 1942–August 1945). This was also caused by events of the Dutch era.

The pemuda who went so wild in the last months of 1945 had been children and young teenagers in the twenties and thirties, the period when the emancipatory ideals of the Ethical Policy gave way to the much more repressive attitudes of late colonial society, which reached a low point in the early thirties. Boven Digul, the mutiny on the *Zeven Provinciën*, the totalitarian police state, the Soetardjo petition . . . They may not have known about any of these things, any more than they knew about the three failed attempts at political mobilisation (Islamist, communist and nationalist). But over and over again they had directly experienced the systematic mistrust, the far-reaching segregation and the everyday humiliation. Their education had been an attempt to train them in docility. Toenggoel Siagian summed it up as 'You participated, but you were still shut out.'[42] No matter what they did, they were stuck on Deck 3, third-class citizens in their own country. There were many of them, but they didn't count. They had dreams, but found only frustration. The Japanese occupier had given them the fleeting illusion that this situation did not need to last forever, but after that promise too had led to starvation and death, the last thing they wanted was to return to the demeaning world of their childhood.

Volcanoes don't explode just like that. Slow, subterranean processes come first, seismic tensions that build up so subtly that they remain invisible for a long time. In 1956 a Dutch parliamentary fact-finding commission put together a list of ten causes for the Bersiap, but not one went further back than the Japanese period, as if the problem had only started then. A 2005 study did admit that pre-war policies regarding the nationalists had been too 'rigid', but didn't seem to realise that this was only the tip of the iceberg.[43] All of colonial law was fundamentally based on racial discrimination; colonial society of the twenties and thirties was completely permeated with an assumption of superiority; the relentless prosecution of communists and nationalists betrayed fear more than wisdom; and the obstinate rejection of virtually every proposal for political reform showed the myopia of the colonial government – that miserable colonial steamship just kept bobbing along calmly as if the internal tensions were not reaching breaking point and a world war had not appeared on the horizon, and all this contributed to the explosion of violence. 'The natives make you just want to hit them,' noted a young Eurasian in her diary at the start of the war. 'Today they refused to get out of my way.'[44] The young Indonesians of 1945 had grown up in an atmosphere of mild but constant humiliation. This is why the Revolusi's burst of flame was also a reply to the smouldering fire of the late colonial period. The Netherlands cast a shadow over their lives, Japan made death easy – their own death and the deaths of others.

For Indos it was a bitter pill twice over: they were the most disadvantaged of the most privileged. What you might call the rejects of Decks 1 and 2. Despite their Dutch citizenship, they had suffered discrimination from the European Dutch for years, and now they were the first to be attacked by Deck 3. They felt like they were being victimised twice: first from above, now from below. The history of real injustice they had experienced often blinded them to the much greater injustice taking place below them. The terrible slaughters the furious masses now carried out in their ranks caused years of embitterment and misunderstanding.

I spent an evening in Jakarta at the home of a former pemuda. Leaning over a plate of brown rice and vegetables under a bluish low-energy light bulb, Soerachman told me about his youth. 'I didn't like the Indos,' he soon admitted, 'they always felt superior, even though they had Indonesian mothers too.' At the start of the Japanese occupation he'd had to watch while two Dutchmen were killed with a bayonet. The brute violence shocked him, but a few years later he would turn violent himself. How did that happen? 'The Dutch were using the British troops to come back! When I saw that, I resolved to fight for my country to my last drop of blood! It was an inner compulsion, a passion, a feeling. I had to do it.' And he added something crucial. 'Under the Dutch, life had been good. They knew how to run a country, but they worked with the elite and kept us in our place. We were like children, hushed to sleep by their lullaby. They were very clever, the way they did it. Japan, on the other hand, taught us how to fight, supposedly for our independence, but that was camouflage for their own war against the British and Americans.' When Japan was defeated, Soerachman said, 'Now I'm going to build up my country!' But his father said, 'You're still a child! Don't take up arms!' Later he could understand that reaction. 'My father worked at the post office for the Dutch and that had influenced him. Respect your superiors, that was his attitude. Always be obliging – the Dutch fostered that mentality. I shouted, "My friends are going too!" ' He was seventeen. Every day he tuned in on the radio to listen to Bung Tomo, a radical militant from Surabaya who gave blistering speeches calling for battle. Anyone who loved their country had to let it grow! And not have sex until Indonesia was free! 'He influenced me. It was magic! We were free! Suddenly everyone wanted to join the fight! Against the Dutch, against the Japanese! We were all volunteers, we didn't have any weapons. Only the police had guns.' As he talked about it, Soerachman's voice was still full of fire; he forgot to eat. 'I took the iron rail from the garden fence and sharpened one end. I bought the leaf spring from a car and said in the garage, "Turn it into a samurai sword!"' At this point in the conversation I put down my fork and gave him a quizzical look. It seemed like a fairly unusual request for a mechanic, to turn part of a broken suspension into a feudal blade. But while enthusiastically continuing his account, Soerachman walked over to a corner of the room and picked up a long wooden scabbard from which he drew an impressive sword. The garage keepers of Java were apparently highly versatile. 'I walked around Yogyakarta with this! I was proud! I started a *laskar*, a people's militia, in our neighbourhood. I climbed up onto the roof and, using my hands as a megaphone, shouted, *"Kumpul! Kumpul!* Gather!" I gathered some thirty youths together and lined them up. They were young men of seventeen, eighteen. I trained them for a month. Nobody got paid. You did it automatically. Yes, sometimes I got cigarettes, but I didn't smoke.'[45]

This sense of sacred duty came up often in my conversations with the last living Indonesian veterans. Take someone like Ahmad Muhadi, a ninety-four-year-old farmer in rural Central Java. His perspective – and that of many thousands of his contemporaries – seldom makes it into books, although it's essential to understanding the events of the time. 'It was my own choice. We did it of our own accord. The mosque didn't call on us, the school didn't call on us, we didn't have a radio and my father didn't encourage me either. He was just a farmer, here in this same house.' While children and chickens walked in and out of his simple home, he told me about life before the revolution. 'My mother sold *jamu* in the village, traditional herbal tonics. I sold *getuk*, sweet cassava cakes. I didn't like the Dutch and I didn't like the Japanese. The Japanese were different, but they were still foreigners. So I felt responsible and reported to fight. Young people joined up everywhere. In the south the ones from the south fought, in the west the ones from the west, but we all fought for Indonesia. We fought day and night. We didn't get any training or uniforms, there wasn't time for that, but we felt responsible. The young had the responsibility to fight for Indonesia.[46]

Johannes Soewondo came from Klaten and had been forced to refine oil for the Japanese. He was seventeen. 'There were numerous militias, some based on religion, others just local. I joined a *laskar pelajar*, a student militia. We weren't paid and we didn't have any uniforms.[47] Sriyono from Surakarta was only fourteen. 'There were lots of us and we helped each other: the militias, the PETA soldiers, the Christian pemuda, the Muslim pemuda.[48] Toto, a farmer's son from Tawang, was twenty-one. 'I joined Barisan Hizbullah. There were thousands of us in each village. All we had to fight the Dutch with was bamboo spears.[49] Soemardi, a country boy from Temanggung, was eighteen. 'The Netherlands wanted to keep Indonesia, but no longer had that right.[50] Suradi Surokusumo from Yogyakarta was twenty-two. 'I would have been ashamed not to fight the Dutch. I was proud of being a nationalist, proud of being Indonesian, proud of our national anthem "Indonesia Raya".[51] Toernowo Hadiwidjojo from Semarang was twenty-four and worked as a telegraph operator for the railways. 'I already had a two-year-old son but took part without a second thought. The reason? There was no reason! Merdeka was a must! I had no fear. I preferred war to colonialism!'[52]

For this generation the old three-way split between Islamists, nationalists and communists was of lesser importance; the Revolusi had brought them all together. Some recited verses of the Koran during their improvised training exercises, others sang 'Indonesia Raya', yet others whistled 'The Internationale'. And sometimes the commands were even given in Japanese. 'We didn't want to fight separately. All the young people fought together. We didn't care if someone was a communist or not. As long as there was an enemy, we fought together,' according to Sumaun.[53]

But with so much unanimity, the social pressure was enormous. Iskandar Hadisaputra from Salatiga was twenty-two. 'I didn't hate the Dutch, but I had to fight. Everyone took part. If you didn't join in, you were considered a Dutch spy. I had no choice.'[54] That applied all the more for young Chinese who still had no idea what place they would have in this new Indonesia. Benny Bastian from Jakarta, son of a Chinese hat manufacturer, was eleven. 'If I hadn't taken up a bamboo spear, all the other boys would have hated me. We had a large garden about eighty metres deep. The youths gathered there with their bamboo spears with small red-and-white flags fluttering on the ends. They asked my father's permission to train there. It was allowed. They marched and shouted, "Siap!" Attention! The troops were mainly Indonesian but Chinese joined in too. Other Chinese said, "That's their problem, not ours." '⁵⁵ But some Chinese youths made a radical choice to be part of the Revolusi. Go Gien Tjwan was one of them. I spoke to him in Amstelveen shortly before his death. 'The Bersiap difficult? Not at all, it was fabulous! I was in Malang and I spoke on the radio just before Bung Tomo. "I'm speaking on behalf of 20,000 young Chinese . . ." – that was how I started.' He spread the ideals of the uprising with great enthusiasm.⁵⁶

The great majority of the pemuda did not hesitate. Only the Japanese could have restrained them – they were still there in large numbers and armed – but they felt little inclination to do so. They were anti-Western themselves and had stoked the young Indonesians' hatred. And since September they had been engaged in a peculiar process of self-internment. The Kempeitai and several residual infantry units remained in the cities, but large parts of the occupying army withdrew into sparsely populated mountainous regions to avoid falling prey to possible disturbances.⁵⁷ While awaiting their definitive repatriation the troops stayed in very large secured camps – 20,000 near Malang, 30,000 on Seram, 40,000 on Halmahera.⁵⁸ They mainly left their weapons under guard in depots, but the soldiers charged with guarding these depots were only given five bullets each. This was the state of affairs in Java at the start of October: approximately 4,000 British and approximately 2,000 Dutch soldiers, fewer and fewer Japanese with less and less ammunition, and several hundred thousand rampant youths.

During my many long trips in Indonesia I often stared out at the countryside. Few things in the archipelago are as moving as tall, rustling clumps of bamboo: the thin leaves lisping in the wind, the swaying of the smooth, dark-green trunks, the light filtering down to the ground. I saw them everywhere on the roadside. The wood combines an incredible range of qualities: it is light as a feather and as strong as iron, watertight and amazingly fast-growing. You can use it to build houses and you can make furniture from it. You can transport water and cook food in it. You can use it to make musical instruments and clothes. It's even edible. But you can also use it to commit murder. Without bamboo there wouldn't have been an Indonesian revolution. The Japanese had taught hundreds of thousands of young men how to quickly turn a charming plant into a fearsome weapon. Hack off a stem that's not too thick, sharpen it – and if you like, harden it in the fire. Anyone who has ever threaded a piece of beef onto a bamboo skewer knows that if you apply enough pressure, you'll overcome the meat's resistance. The human body was no different. The cruel *bambu runcing* would become the mythic weapon of the Revolusi, the emblem of a collective struggle, the ultimate proof that the new state was not an elitist project, but the expression of a broad national craving for independence.

But what good would it do you if you were facing the Lee-Enfield repeating rifles and Madsen and Bren light machine guns that the Dutch and British had just brought ashore? The pemuda changed up a gear. In August they had driven around with little flags, in September they'd daubed slogans on walls, but in October they started stockpiling arms. For someone like Iskandar Hadisaputra it was very simple. He saw the Japanese shopkeeper he had lived with, who was now with the Kempeitai, just before he left for Japan. 'Ashimoto gave me his gun and his address in Tokyo.' That was kind of him. 'But I never visited. I had no more sympathy for him. All I wanted was independence.' Iskandar also saw Ashimoto's commander 'handing out weapons too'. It was like that in many places. When it came to defending the Japanese arsenals, it wasn't just ammunition that was lacking. Soemardi from Surakarta said: 'Some Japanese soldiers agreed with us and gave us all their weapons, uniforms and gear.'[39]

Another option was to steal weapons. Soenaryo and his mates went to Wates, outside Yogyakarta, where a battalion had been bivouacked. The main building had been a colonial villa, but not much of that was left. 'Wates Camp was complete chaos. Everybody was going there to loot it.' His father, the Islamic teacher who had trained a heiho unit, shouted: 'Don't steal!' But Soenaryo couldn't remember anyone listening to him. 'Everyone was carrying beds, chairs and tables outside. They even tore out the ceilings and doors for the metal. In the end only the walls were left.' He too preferred the call of the motherland to his father's admonitions. 'I took a desk and a samurai sword. And a pistol! Later I sold that sword to my cousin. For too little. We were still paying with Japanese money.' But he kept the pistol. He also went to the city with scores of other youths. 'We asked the Japanese to give us their weapons. They'd lost, after all. Normally they would hand their weapons over to the British, but we said, "No! No, don't do that!" Their commander refused. He wanted to obey the rule that the loser surrenders his weapons to the victor, but we took them first. My first rifle was one of those long Japanese carbines with very little recoil.'[60]

What could a detachment that had been left behind on guard duty with very few bullets do against a large group of highly motivated youths with very sharp bamboo spears? It all went very quickly for then fourteen-year-old Sriyono. 'East of Solo there was a Japanese arms depot. We went there to get weapons. That's how I got my first rifle.'[61] Ahmad Muhadi had to make more of an effort. 'My first weapon was a bambu runcing. I used it to kill an enemy and took his gun.' He pointed his walking stick at me to demonstrate, poking me in the stomach. 'You have to stab here: very painful, very bloody.'[62] Johannes Soewondo knew that the Japanese were very scared of that 'biological' weapon. 'With a gun you're dead right away, but with a bambu runcing it can take a long time. I saw them writhing on the ground.'[63] Iskandar remembered that it was 'easy' to kill someone that way, but recalled an incident where the spear broke before a fighter had finished the job. 'The victim lived for a whole day before we shot him.'[64] The witness accounts were unemotional, dry even. With their years of militarisation, the Japanese had created a monster that had now turned against them. They were, in the words of Sudarpo's astute summary, 'destroyed by the ideals of their own propaganda'.[65]

And Surabaya was once again the centre of the Revolusi. On 1 October hundreds of young people stormed the offices of the once feared Kempeitai. 'It was a marvellous fight!' said Sumaun. The pemuda had no fear and that was terrifying. 'We went to the head-quarters of the Kempeitai. The Japanese opened fire on us from upstairs, but we went inside. We were like a firehose: the water gushed out so terribly hard that they didn't know which way to turn.' The dozens of dead were the price of freedom. Hario Kecik also compared it to water. 'As soon as we went at our goal in large num-bers we were like a human tidal wave filling the street, like a flood dragging everything along with it.'[66] The Kempeitai suffered heavy losses and even ran out of ammunition. 'In the end Japan surrendered with a white flag,' Sumaun said. 'We demanded all of their weapons and put them in prison. We seized an enormous number of weapons that day.' The haul really was incredible: '19,000 rifles, 800 subma-chine guns, 700 light and 500 heavy machine guns, 148 grenade launchers, seventeen infantry support guns, twenty field and moun-tain guns, sixty-three heavy mortars, 400 light mortars, twenty anti-tank guns, 140 anti-aircraft guns, four howitzers, sixteen tanks, sixty-two armoured cars and 1,900 other vehicles.'[67] Enough to arm half an army. With this, the Revolusi took a decisive turn. Barefoot youths got Japanese rifles that were taller than they were. Mines and mortars went from hand to hand. Hundreds of grenades were passed out to children 'as if they were fried bananas'.[68] The impoverished people from Deck 3 suddenly had power. 'In contrast to the rags they were dressed in, their weapons were shining.'[69]

Sukotjo Tjokroatmodjo, the man who had gone everywhere with his little flags to announce independence, got his hands on his first rifle. 'All the weapons had been brought together, at least 17,000 rifles, in the old Surabaya Club, now called the Building of Youth. "Do you want a weapon?" "Yes." "Then you have to go and fight straight away." I tried to go to school with my gun, but the headmas-ter said, "What do you want? To go to war or to go to school?" "I want to go and fight," I said.'[70] Soon after he enrolled at the military academy in Malang, one of the country's first training institutions. On 5 October, shortly after the British landing in Jakarta and the

Japanese transfer of arms in Surabaya, Sukarno reformed the BKR (the People's Security Corps) as the TKR (the People's Security Army), a first formal army. This shouldn't be envisioned as a tightly organised military apparatus. It was no more than a kind of extensive pemuda militia, but one that was led by former PETA officers and with the beginnings of centralisation and a military hierarchy. Soemardi was one of the very first sergeants. 'I was in the 3rd Company, 54th Battalion, 18th Regiment of the 3rd Division.'[71] But Sriyono, who was also there from the beginning, added some context. 'It wasn't until 1946 that I got my first uniform. Well, it wasn't yet entirely standardised. We all wore different uniforms.'[72]

Sukarno's creation of an army did not mean he was choosing armed struggle. On the contrary, with an eye to international recognition of his Republik Indonesia he continued to advocate a peaceful transition. Misconduct by the pemuda would reflect badly on the new state he had just founded. It was his task to convince the world, and especially America, that his actions were defensible. He called for calm on the radio and travelled hither and thither to clear up conflicts and let the British carry out their humanitarian work. His most remarkable decision was to move all of the Indos into camps. He realised that they needed to be protected from the pemuda. Even if life in the camps was far from comfortable, it was an essential security measure to prevent unnecessary bloodshed. Some 46,000 people were interned, with the last unable to return home until May 1947. Sukarno did not use them as hostages.[73]

The tension between the Republic and the Revolusi, between the older and younger generations of nationalists, did not disappear overnight. It was clear that Sukarno needed the pemuda, but their delirium could also ruin things. The formation of the TKR was an important first attempt to channel their energy into a constructive project that would serve the new state. This did not always succeed. Young radicals also attacked Japanese garrisons to obtain arms in the Central Javanese cities of Magelang and Ambarawa. In Semarang their actions were especially rash. After the Japanese Major Shinichiro Kido refused to disarm, the pemuda resorted on 14 October to taking 200 Japanese civilians hostage – most of them railway employees – transferring them to the women's prison in Bulu. Iskandar was there. 'We didn't want to kill them, we only wanted their weapons, but they refused to give them to us. Our enemies were the Dutch, the British, the Gurkhas, the Indians, the Australians, not the Japanese, but we had to attack them to get rifles, and again the next day for the heavier guns.'[74] The confusing, extremely tense situation culminated in a massacre at Bulu Prison. 'It was complete chaos. No command. No idea who was giving the orders. Everyone died. They were unarmed and couldn't escape.'[75] Rumours about what happened in Semarang were sometimes difficult to verify. Toernowo was able to tell me more. 'We wanted to take the Japanese hostage, but we killed them. The hostages chose bullets rather than bamboo spears. Our plan was to kill the Indos after that, but that evening Governor Wongsonegoro gave a speech under pressure from the Japanese in which he called on us to stop.'[76] The final result was clear: the pemuda had murdered 200 Japanese, whereupon Japan killed hundreds and possibly even several thousand pemuda in house-to-house fighting that lasted for five days.[77] In the end British troops arrived to reinforce their positions. Strange, given that they had been each other's enemies just two months earlier.

Kazuko Kawai was eagerly anticipating the return of her father, who had been working as a railway engineer in West Java. 'After three years my father was finally going to come home! I wanted to see him again so much. I was just fourteen. When our emperor surrendered, I was so happy! Father wasn't a soldier, so he could come home straight away. He was already preparing for the trip back.' But he was based in Semarang and was taken hostage and sent to Bulu Prison. The precise events remained unclear for a long time, but later she received more details from the Japanese negotiator Aoki. 'He told me that my father was standing at the front and tried to talk to the Indonesians. At two in the afternoon he was wounded and three hours later he was still alive. He was bleeding from his belly. There were many wounded. He told Mr Aoki, "Help the others first." He lived for a few more hours after that.'[78] There is now a Japanese monument in Semarang.

In Indonesia many more Japanese died after the war than during it: 255 during the 1942 invasion, 717 in the last months of 1945, plus another 205 missing and 387 wounded.[79] Nowhere did this become clearer to me than in the hospital ward of the brand-new Agano Hospital near Niigata, which I visited late one afternoon in March 2017. Tomio Yoshida was seriously ill, as were the three other patients in the ward. I found my presence inappropriate and wanted to leave immediately, but the interpreter tried to start up a friendly conversation with Yoshida anyway. Always follow a country's etiquette, I told myself, no matter how strange it seems. Yoshida had been recommended to us by Seiji, the man who was in Java with his tank for just one hour. Yoshida, on the other hand, was there much longer. He went ashore in a tank as well and was in Bandung at the end of the war. He could have been an exceptional witness, but we were too late. Still, his short testimony encapsulated the entire Japanese period. 'At first the Indonesians were so friendly to us. So friendly. But after the war not any more.' He said it again. And then again. More than twenty times he repeated the same sentence. Then he sat up in his hospital bed. 'They were so angry at us. I was in Bandung. I knew Japan had lost the war. They took us prisoner. They took away our rifles and our swords.' He was silent for a moment. 'Such a shame. Such a shame. Such a shame. We lost. We lost. We lost. At first we were so good and then not any more.'[80] A whole life summarised in a few stammered sentences.

In total the pemuda captured approximately 50,000 rifles, 3,000 machine guns and a hundred million bullets and shells in a few weeks.[81] Mountbatten exhorted Van Mook repeatedly to go and talk to Sukarno and Hatta, but the directives from The Hague were clear: at the start of October the Dutch government had formally declared that it did not under any circumstances want to negotiate with Sukarno, a position that won the support of the parliament. Collectively, the Dutch continued to see the Republic as a product of Japanese fascism. Shortly after the war the Netherlands still thought in terms of 'good' and 'bad' and for the Dutch Sukarno counted as terribly bad. He was the Anton Mussert of the Indies, the Asian equivalent of the leader of the Dutch Nazi party. It was a convenient caricature. Once the other has been demonised, there is no longer any need to take them into account. Even so there was something strange about it. During the colonial era, Sukarno and Hatta had been too left-wing, now they were suddenly too right-wing. Van Mook, headstrong as ever, gritted his teeth and went to Lieutenant General Christison's house to speak to Sukarno and Hatta. The next day the Netherlands was in a tumult and the cabinet demanded Van Mook's dismissal – only Queen Wilhelmina's objections saved him. What seemed inevitable in Jakarta remained incomprehensible in The Hague. Mountbatten had two more points to make to Van Mook: NICA should be relabelled with a less colonial name and, for the time being, the Netherlands were not to send any more troops as that would be like throwing oil on the flames. He took the first to heart and had to accept the second.

Yes, leave the occupation of the key areas to the British troops, then it will be clear that the intentions are purely humanitarian. So they thought. On 25 October 1945 the British finally went ashore in Surabaya, a month after Jakarta. But instead of a port city full of bamboo spears, the almost 4,000 soldiers of the 49th Indian Infantry Brigade entered one full of firearms. From the deck of one of their ships, a British intelligence officer saw 'a lot of agitated natives dashing about. They were armed to the teeth with bandoliers of ammo, tommy guns, rifles, grenades, swords and anything else portable you care to think of.'[82] The British commander, Brigadier Aubertin Mallaby, resorted to unarmed consultation with the Republican authorities, assuring them that he had only come to evacuate the Japanese soldiers and the interned Europeans. He was given reluctant permission. 'I can now take this place without a shot being fired on either side,' concluded an overconfident Mallaby.[83] But the next day leaflets calling on the population to lay down their arms and deliver them to the British floated down over the city. 'The leaflets were a disaster, but for the British, not for us,' according to pemuda leader Hario Kecik.[84] Radio host Bung Tomo incited his many thousands of young listeners 'to drive the British into the sea'. After Jakarta and Semarang, Surabaya was the only large port in Java that had not yet fallen and it had to stay that way. On 28 October thousands of young fighters attacked all of the British posts in the city simultaneously. Mallaby's few thousand men were faced with 20,000 soldiers from the regular TKR and 140,000 youths. Within the first ten minutes eleven British officers and forty-four British Indian soldiers had lost their lives.[85] A British convoy accompanying hundreds of internees, all Dutch women and children, from the camp at Gubeng to the port of Surabaya was attacked on the way; a hundred civilians and sixty British Indian troops were killed. Sumaun, who had already experienced the flag incident in September and the storming of the Kempeitai barracks in October, now helped to overwhelm a column of trucks. 'It was a night patrol. We took up positions on both sides of a wide road, Jalan Pasar Cilik. I had a revolver. The convoy was made up of eight trucks. As camouflage the British soldiers had blackened their faces.' Then they opened fire. 'The convoy stopped. There were about a hundred dead, I think. Some of them were able to get away. There were a lot of dead on our side too. In the morning the Red Cross came to pick up the bodies.'[86]

The situation continued to escalate. On 29 October Sukarno flew into Surabaya. On 30 October he managed to calm his regular and irregular forces and impose a ceasefire. But five hours after signing the agreement, Brigadier Mallaby had to make his way through a crowd in his car. Jostling, shouting, furious people. Who was provoking who? A shot. A hand grenade. Another shot. A throng of fleeing people. A dark patch growing on a brigadier's uniform. Forty-five-year-old Mallaby, one of the highest-ranking officers in the British forces in Indonesia, died on the back seat of a private car. During a peace operation, just after concluding a ceasefire.

Then it all blew up. Mountbatten immediately sent the 5th Indian Division to Surabaya. No longer a brigade, but an entire division: four brigades, altogether 12,000 men, reinforced a few days later with another 9,000 and twenty-four Sherman tanks. It was more than a revenge action, it was a large-scale demonstration of military power after a month of faffing about. On 9 November the British military authorities issued an ultimatum, demanding the Indonesians lay down arms. As expected, it was ignored. Surabaya was then bombed from the air and shelled from the sea. The ground troops moved through it from north to south. Pitting their military experience against well-concealed snipers and gangs of fanatical youths house by house, street by street and neighbourhood by neighbourhood, the British conquered the city. The Battle of Surabaya lasted from 10–29 November, almost three weeks of outright warfare in Indonesia's second-largest city, exactly what Mountbatten had wanted to avoid. Several hundred British troops died, compared to an estimated 15,000 people on the Indonesian side. Some 200,000 residents fled. The Battle of Surabaya was the biggest and most deadly conflict in the four and a half years between the Proklamasi in August 1945 and the transfer of sovereignty in December 1949. There were also serious disturbances in Central Java, Aceh and East and West Sumatra. On 1 December the Republic had over 125,000 weapons at its disposal in Java and 65,000 in Sumatra.[87]

The British had set out to carry out a few humanitarian tasks, but now found themselves in an impossible urban guerrilla conflict that was part of the first big post-war decolonisation war.

Meanwhile England was in the grip of a cold, snowy winter. Goderd van Heek was getting ready to start officer training at Wrotham and Sandhurst. It was a tough course: running up hills in full kit, throwing live hand grenades, learning how to operate machine guns, things like that. His fear of being sent to Germany suddenly turned out to be unfounded. 'During the Bersiap extremely large disturbances occurred. The disorder became clearer and clearer. A British big shot was assassinated in Surabaya and a fierce uprising broke out. The situation was very insecure. A lot of Brits were killed. It was clear then that we would be going to the Indies.'[88] He was right – Mallaby's murder and the Battle of Surabaya had changed everything. Indonesia had turned out to be a nest of vipers and the British wanted to get out as fast as they could. The Netherlands decided to send its own large-scale military force, but before it could come to that, there needed to be an agreement with the Republic, according to Mountbatten. Whether that would be possible was very much the question. The situation was infinitely more difficult than it had been in August.

Chapter 11

'An Errand of Mercy'
The British year, January–November 1946

Kartika Affandi had gone inside for a moment. I was still on the patio in front of her house with a few members of her family. Only now did I see that she had even painted the back of her wheelchair – with a portrait of her father. She always decorated everything everywhere. The garden where she exhibited her canvases and sculptures was bursting with light and flowers and full of traditional wooden architecture. Her dress was a self-portrait she had had printed on the fabric. She even wore her hair up as a baroque artwork in its own right. This ebullient artist was like the Frida Kahlo of Southeast Asia but without the anxieties and depressions. Under a roof was an enormous canvas she was working on, an evocation of Borobudur, the temple she, as a Buddhist, held so dear. Walking with difficulty, she came back out. 'Sorry again about having to go to the dentist this afternoon,' she said with a toothless smile. 'Last night the dog slurped up my glass of water and took off with my false teeth! We can't find them anywhere!' She shrieked with laughter while telling me, and the others kept cracking up about it. Grandma seemed to have a patent on these kinds of antics. I realised that seeing yourself in perspective lies at the base of all Buddhism.

She flopped into the wheelchair. The garden sloped down, behind us rose the majestic flanks of the volcano Merapi. 'Behind that shed is where I want to be buried,' she said roguishly. 'The pit's already dug, but the tomb isn't finished yet. I want to put mosaics on it with animals. I want it to be a playground for the children, not a cemetery. Do you understand?' I said I did. What I didn't understand was how she, after Bali, Bandung and Jakarta, had ended up in Yogyakarta. Toothless or not, she was happy to tell me. 'In 1946 Sukarno moved to Yogyakarta. Papa and all the other artists went with him. The Sunday morning breakfasts simply carried on. Every Sunday we now went to the *istana*, the presidential palace.' She was twelve. 'The sultan of Yogyakarta offered to house all those who had fled Jakarta. Most of them were highly educated. We lived here free of charge for three years in a house with thirty-three others!'[1]

On 4 January 1946 Sukarno and his government exchanged Jakarta for Yogyakarta. If the British left, the Dutch would be the only power in the capital and that could not bode well for him – after all, they had already imprisoned him twice before. To make matters worse, their primarily Ambonese KNIL troops were extremely trigger-happy. Shortly before, in late December, the freshly appointed Prime Minister Sutan Sjahrir had evaded an attack.[2] Minister of Defence Amir Sjarifuddin had escaped death too.[3] Yogyakarta was safer, especially now that the Gurkhas had been driven out of Central Java, with the exception of Semarang. The young Sultan Hamengkubuwono IX, who had attended university in Leiden as 'Henkie' – Pratomo had seen him there – was very sympathetic to the new republic and extended an invitation to the revolution's leaders. He was joined by the heads of the other three monarchies in Central Java, Kasunanan, Pakualaman and Mangkunegaran. It seemed like a return to the days of the Dutch East India Company when Batavia was exclusively Dutch and a native kingdom ruled over the interior from Yogyakarta. Until the end of the war in 1949, Yogya would remain the capital of the Republic and the anti-colonial resistance. Sukarno moved into the white, neo-classical governor's residence, a stone's throw from the *kraton*, the sultan's extensive complex of historic palaces.

Many freedom fighters moved with them. People streamed into Yogya from the British enclaves of Jakarta, Bandung, Semarang and Surabaya. Toernowo, the man who wanted to be 'Free! Of! Everything!', fled south after the bloody conflict in Semarang. 'With my wife, my son, my mother and one bicycle, we went on foot from Semarang to Temanggung. From there, we took the train to Magelang and Yogyakarta. Yogyakarta and Surakarta belonged to the Republic. It was safer there.'[4] Herawati Diah ended up there too with

her husband, the journalist who had spread the news of the Proklamasi and now headed the newspaper *Merdeka*. 'Yogyakarta! It was a
city of dreams for republicans who were staying in regions under
NICA control,' she rejoiced. 'There were no white-skinned soldiers
patrolling in jeeps. There were no armed Gurkhas hunting for "terrorists". Here, even the Japanese army had turned in its weapons.'
The hotels and boarding houses were packed. 'Yogyakarta became
the official capital of the Republic of Indonesia on January 4, 1946.'[5]

Meanwhile much had changed in Sukarno's government. While
Sukarno was enjoying a few days' leave in October 1945, Vice-
President Hatta had made several drastic decisions to democratise the
country. The KNIP, the president's central advisory council, was
expanded into a fully-fledged legislative parliament with 137 members. These were still unelected – the first free elections would not
take place until ten years later, in 1955 – but the first political parties
were already forming. This made the strongly presidential regime
more parliamentary.[6] And Hatta went further: he charged Sutan
Sjahrir, his former colleague from the PI committee in Leiden, with
forming a new government. Sjahrir, who had been playing a waiting
game all this time, chose democratic people who had not sullied
themselves by collaborating with the Japanese. He claimed the three
most consequential posts himself, becoming not only prime minister,
but also interior minister and foreign minister. At thirty-six he was
the world's youngest PM. Amir Sjarifuddin became defence and
information minister. Amir was a left-wing politician with communist sympathies who had pushed for a full parliament before the
war and had, at the request of the Netherlands, led the underground
resistance to Japan at the start of the occupation. He had been sentenced to death for these activities, but was released after Sukarno
interceded on his behalf. Amir too was distinctly anti-Japanese.

The formation of Sjahrir's government was not ideal for Sukarno –
he lost power to the prime minister – but he recognised its advantages:
it could only advance the international recognition of Indonesia.
Sjahrir's principled anti-Japanese and anti-fascist positions made him
a much more acceptable negotiator. He had also studied in Leiden, he

was married to a Dutchwoman, and he loved European culture – all these helped too. But his pamphlet *Perjuangan Kita* ('Our Struggle', in Dutch, *Onze strijd*), published by way of a government policy statement, was a frontal assault on Sukarno and his associates. 'Those who have sold their honour to Japanese fascism deserve to be expelled from the leadership of our revolution.' It can't have been an enjoyable read for Sukarno. Sjahrir spoke of 'collaborators' who should be considered as 'our own fascists' who 'have betrayed our struggle and our people's revolution'.[7] He also condemned the violence of the pemuda. 'Starting as drills with spears, this has now blossomed into looting and slaughter.' Japan had indoctrinated the young so much that 'the only skill they have is to become soldiers, that is to march and obey orders – to charge, to attack – and sacrifice themselves in the most literal sense'. The youths used the same agitation and propaganda 'they had seen and learned from the Japanese . . . therefore fascist'.[8] These observations didn't make him many friends either.

Thanks to his age and outlook, Sjahrir had always been an intermediary between the older nationalists and the young revolutionaries, but now he was caustic about both parties, adamant that their past misbehaviour and present misdeeds were damaging the young republic. His criticisms were not only principled but also pragmatic: those dark memories were not helping the cause, definitely not now that 'the fate of Indonesia, more than that of any other country, depended on the international situation and developments'.[9] He was completely right about that – an internal revolution without foreign recognition was worthless – but reconciling the international players, national politics and the pemuda was a mighty challenge. What's more, Sjahrir's task had been made even more difficult because the TKR, the national army, had chosen its own supreme commander two days before his appointment: General Sudirman, a former teacher who had become a PETA officer under the Japanese. That's right, the chief of staff of the armed forces had not been appointed by the government, as he should be in a parliamentary republic, but by the soldiers. For Sjahrir this meant another potential adversary. The army's evolution from a spontaneous grassroots movement to an instrument of the authorities was far from complete.

While the Republic moved to Yogyakarta, Sjahrir stayed behind in Jakarta to negotiate with the British and Dutch. Talking might have been more tedious than fighting, but it could often be more efficient. Even during his exile on Banda Neira he had kept a close watch on foreign politics and its significance for the colony. The post-war world was going to become more international no matter what. At the start of February 1946, during one of the very first meetings of the UN Security Council – only two weeks old and still seated in London – the subject of Indonesia was immediately put on the agenda. The Ukrainian representative, an extension of the Soviet delegation, agitated against the fact that Japanese fascist troops had fought alongside the British in Semarang and asked whether the United Kingdom's violent suppression of Indonesian independence did not contravene Article 1, Paragraph 2 of the United Nations Charter concerning the right to 'self-determination of peoples'. No, the British and Dutch answered in chorus, the Netherlands was still the sovereign power, world peace was not threatened and Article 2, Paragraph 7 forbade the Security Council from intervening 'in matters which are essentially within the domestic jurisdiction of any state'.[10] The British envoy Ernest Bevin was more than annoyed by the Ukrainian insinuations. His country had performed 'an errand of mercy', and now, in his own capital of all places, he was being 'accused of attacking the Indonesian Nationalist Movement!'[11] He made a point of clarifying a few things. The British were operating solely under Allied supreme command and aimed to carry out their task as quickly as possible. The Netherlands was open to the idea of an international commission to investigate British actions. Mexico, Poland, China, France, Brazil, Egypt and the Soviet Union became involved in the discussion. But the vote did not lead to a majority for the Ukrainian proposal. Despite this, the meeting was highly important: for the first time it became clear what kind of role the new international body, the UN Security Council, would play in decolonisation. Countries you had once had little or nothing to do with were now suddenly able to formally meddle in what had always been an internal question, the colonial policies of a sovereign country. The times were changing and Sjahrir knew it.

A crackling fire, mince pies and tawny port. During the 1945

Christmas holiday at Chequers, the country house of the UK prime
minister, Clement Attlee had given his word to Dutch Prime Minister Schermerhorn, who had taken office in June 1945, and Lieutenant
Governor-General Van Mook, who had flown over from Batavia:
the British would stay in Indonesia until a political agreement had
been achieved. He was hoping for late March but in the event it
would be the end of November. All that time his country wanted to
mediate between the two parties, as it had been proposing since September. Meanwhile, the mood in the Netherlands was also ripe for
change. The very serious disturbances in Java and, to a lesser degree,
Sumatra had opened people's eyes: the Republic was more than just
Japanese origami. Sjahrir's taking office also created a first opening
for negotiations, especially after the favourable reception in the
Netherlands of his pamphlet. Like Schermerhorn and Attlee, Sjahrir
was part of the anti-fascist, social democratic family. In October the
Dutch coalition of socialist, Catholic and Protestant parties had
refused talks with the Republican leaders. In November it suggested
the possibility that Indonesia might become autonomous for internal
affairs. In December, after the Battle of Surabaya, the coalition first
considered independence for Java, which it envisioned as continuing
to belong to the Kingdom of the Netherlands as part of an Indonesian
federation. But it would still take most of a year to reach agreement
on this. The British year was far from over.

What did this year mean in practice for all those Asian troops in the
service of the British empire? Of the thirty battalions that left for
Indonesia, only four were all British; the rest were Asian.[12] They liberated the camps, disarmed the Japanese, fought in Java and Sumatra.
They gave their lives, but their story is never heard. Their names are
completely unknown. Maybe it's time to shine a light on their side of
events.

In the spring of 2017 I travelled to Nepal, without knowing if I
would still find any witnesses. Although not all of the 'Gurkhas' in
the story were really Gurkhas – in Indonesia the name was commonly used to refer to all British Indian troops – the soldiers from
Nepal were undoubtedly the most remarkable of all. In contrast to

India, Nepal had never been a British colony. Although the British had fought a fierce war against the kingdom between 1814 and 1816, they had never managed to conquer it, only establishing the border between British India and Nepal where it remains to this day. The British officers were, however, most impressed by the courage and application of the Nepali troops. 'Under our government they would make excellent soldiers.'[13] And so it came to pass: Gurkha volunteers and prisoners of war ended up in British regiments, just as later Sherpas would accompany British mountain-climbing expeditions. Gurkhas still make up the British army's most seasoned combat units. During the annual recruitment in Nepal some 11,000 applicants undergo highly arduous selection tests for just 170 available positions. In World War II they were sent to the Middle East and Italy. But over the last half a century they have also fought in the Falklands, Iraq, Yugoslavia and Afghanistan.[14] In both Nepal and Britain, the Gurkhas have attained a mythical status: they are said to be extraordinarily brave, loyal and fearless. Thirteen of them have been awarded the Victoria Cross, the highest British military decoration.[15] One could also say that, as foot-soldiers from poor, isolated, traditional villages, the Gurkhas took on (and take on) the dirty work Western soldiers were no longer willing to do.

'You've come here to catch the last flicker of the British candle!' laughed John P. Cross in his study in Pokhara, Nepal's second city. He was wearing a traditional Nepali hat and was bronzed by the sun. Although he seldom used his English any more, it was still a delight. If something seemed nonsensical to him, he politely called it 'taurine dung'.[16] Born in London in 1925, he turned out to be the second Brit ever to have been naturalised as Nepali. He lived with the family of his Nepali adoptive son and spoke fluent Nepali as well as half a dozen other Asian languages. This proficiency had often proved useful to him as an officer. 'Oh yes, the tongue is more potent than any sword. It is better to win a battle without fighting.' Sometimes he had achieved more by patrolling in civvies with an umbrella than in uniform with a gun.[17] During the war he had joined the army with his brother. His brother was killed in the Netherlands liberating Venlo; he was sent to Burma to fight Japan with the Gurkhas. After the capitulation they had to disarm Japanese soldiers in French Indochina. 'So ignorant were we, none of us knew where it was. We had to go to a local schoolmaster to get an atlas.'[18] He had not been sent to Indonesia himself, but as a lieutenant colonel with years of being partly responsible for recruitment in West Nepal, he was sure to be able to tell me something about how the Gurkhas were recruited. 'They came from the foothills of the Himalaya. There are four castes in Nepal. We take them from the third layer, the traditional martial classes. People who enlist are the ones who are unhappy. They feel dominated by the higher castes.' So they were low on the social ladder, but lived high in the mountains. Cross nodded. 'People from the same village were brought together in a battalion, just as in the county regiments in England. If you have people from the same region they would stick together far more.' Something else that encouraged them to stick together was the language. 'Gurkhas weren't allowed to speak English. They've already left their village, why make them leave yet another thing? They might turn politically and appreciate the Indians.' Ah, that was the real reason. 'The Indians were not happy with their army's serving the Dutch colonialists when they were fighting for their own independence.' Cross took off his thick, horn-rimmed glasses and rubbed his eyes. He still considered the end of British India 'one of the blackest days I have ever experienced'.[19] Whether there were any Indonesia veterans who were still alive was something he couldn't tell me with any certainty.[20]

I had arranged to meet several military men in the garden of the Gurkha museum in Pokhara. The oldest was a hundred. Bhagta Sing Pun was born in 1974 on the Nepali calendar, 1917 CE. What did he remember about his recruitment? He didn't need to stop to cast back his mind. 'Someone who was already with the Gurkhas came to our village to recruit young people. I was twenty but lied that I was seventeen because I was keen to join. My father was an ordinary farmer. He grew wheat and millet.' Bhagta was in a wheelchair, his eyes almost closed, but very expressive with his hands. 'The recruiter quickly measured me up – height, chest size – and they were fine. I was glad and proud. As my parents didn't know about it, we left that same night. They never would have let me go. It took me eight days to walk to Pokhara with the other recruits from the same valley. Barefoot, of course, we never wore shoes. I only had the loincloth I was wearing and a piece of fabric that served as a shoulder bag. From there we went by rail to the training centre at Dehra Dun in India. It was three years before I saw my parents again.'[21] A dog barked in the distance, someone swept some leaves together, a chicken cackled under a bush: each interview had its own soundtrack. He told me much more. How his British officers had trained him in Nepali. That the only English words he learned were right and left. That the punishment for using English was seven days. During the war he was taken prisoner in Singapore and was put to work loading and unloading Japanese ships. But he wasn't sent across the strait to Indonesia.

I spent the weeks that followed travelling through the valleys where soldiers who had been sent to Indonesia could have been recruited. Travelling times were long, contacts hard to make. Several of the larger villages still had a small British army office that paid out veterans' pensions, but their lists were confidential. It also turned out that many Gurkha units had become part of the Indian army after Indian independence, an administrative tangle that made them even more difficult to track down. And most of the veterans had already died of course. Of the more or less 50,000 Gurkhas who served in Indonesia, only a few dozen were still alive. I tried to track them down. Long dusty days following long dirt roads through the mountains. Once, after five hours' jolting, we arrived in one of those quiet, misty mountain villages. Yes, the old Gurkha was still alive. Yes, he served in the right battalion. 'Come with us, he's out in his field.' And, after a couple of minutes, I heard: 'But I didn't go to Java. I stayed behind in India as a trainer at the training centre.' Oh, well. The evening conversations with the interpreter and the driver over a plate of *dal bhat* were instructive. The national dish of lentil curry was a feast. And the view of the Himalayas in the morning – massive, white, mythical – made up for everything.

Still, I was able to speak to ten or so of them, all born between 1916 and 1928. For virtually all of them it was the first and last time they told their story outside of the circle of family and fellow villagers. One of them, Purna Bahadur Chhetri, was bedridden and, according to his children, hadn't spoken for two and a half months, but the conversation perked him up miraculously. He sat up, told us that his rifle was 'a .303', showed us how you had to hold it and where you wore the ammunition. The body is slow to forget. Many of them still remembered that it was 'nine days and nine nights sailing'. On arrival, Indonesia turned out to be a pleasant land. 'Java was a bit hotter than Nepal, but they get a good sea breeze.'[22] They had 'very good fruit' there, said another, 'watermelon, coconut, peanuts, cucumber'.[23] 'They get so much rain. Their country was so wet: rice, rice, rice. A good three harvests a year. And we only get one!'[24] On the other hand, after the war the people there were 'poorer than in Nepal', one of them remarked, 'very poor. They lived in houses made of bamboo.'[25] I enjoyed hearing their first impressions of the archipelago, but what about their war experiences?

Ninety-four-year-old Sop Bahadur Rana was sitting outside his mud hut surrounded by goats and weaving a basket. Smiling, he put down his work to draw on his excellent memory. He had fought in Burma and been decorated for it. Afterwards he was sent to Indonesia. 'It wasn't a big war there. There weren't many killed. We had to protect a few Dutch buildings.' He chased away a few flies with a languid wave of his hand. He was put on sentry duty in Jakarta, a piece of cake for someone who had been through the hell of Burma. 'It was a big city with cars. They even had running water. There were no burnt-out houses.' The European residents were terrified of the pemuda, but for him it didn't amount to much. 'I didn't need to fight or shoot much. Now and then they shot at us and we shot back.' Did he know anything about the political context? The Gurkhas didn't get in-depth briefings about the country, people, culture and political situation before they were deployed somewhere. 'The Japanese had already left,' Sop said, 'they had lost.' Their self-internment had begun in September 1945. 'We had to protect the Dutch government. For three months we guarded the palace in the city.' On 2 October, Van Mook had moved into the old palace on the Koningsplein.[26] Was it there? 'A white building with five or six floors. It was an hour's march from the harbour. It was in a garden with tall trees that was overgrown at the back.' That seems like too many storeys for the governor-general's residence. It might have been a military headquarters. 'The commanding officers met in that building: generals, majors, captains . . . British and Gurkha commanders. We patrolled around the building.' That really wasn't the most dangerous place to be stationed. Compared to Surabaya, very few Japanese weapons had been captured in Jakarta. What was the local population like? He remembered that too. 'They look like Nepalis. They have the same colour skin. The women wear similar kinds of clothes, but they speak a different language. They are beautiful women, but they are Muslims, like in Burma.' He found it odd that 'nobody carries baskets like they do in Nepal', on their back with a headband, when that's so practical. He laughed and returned to his basket weaving.[27]

'It was a minor war. The people were not armed. We were.' Tul Bahadur Thapa was also sent to Jakarta. The ninety-five-year-old was in the same battalion as Sop. He has forgotten how many Japanese he killed in Burma, but remembers that the mission in Java and Sumatra was 'just sentry duty'. 'The war was already under control. We didn't need to fight.' He was staggered by what Japan had done. 'They had stolen all the food and couldn't take it home with them. It was rotting on the ground and no longer edible.' Many houses had also been destroyed. They were bulldozed. But it wasn't really a miserable period. 'Some Gurkhas went out with the women there. Some started a family. Nice women, definitely, but I wasn't interested. We didn't go out. If you drink, you can't aim straight any more.'[28]

Others had to disarm the Japanese. Certainly not a difficult job, related the imperturbable ninety-six-year-old Hari Bahadur Chhetri, sitting cross-legged in front of the colourful mud hut he shared with his family and two buffaloes high on a lush slope of the charming Marsyangdi Valley. Hari had fought in Italy during World War II, and disarming the Japanese in Indonesia was nothing compared to that. 'Several of the Japanese killed themselves with a pistol or rifle, but the rest surrendered immediately. We didn't need to fight. They put up their hands and we took them prisoner. We had about 200 of them. One of them said, "I'm not fighting with you. I've already lost anyway." Because I liked him, I shared my rice with him. He ate with chopsticks! As thanks he gave me a mirror you could use to start a fire. His name was engraved on it.'[29]

Yet others were charged with liberating the internment camps. The diffident ninety-four-year-old Lal Bahadur Khatri lived with his son in a very remote location and in extremely modest circumstances. The track to get there through the mountains was so bad and so dangerous that the sweating driver didn't dare continue and parked his four-wheel-drive until a lorry driver came by to take us the last ninety rattling minutes. But Lal's testimony was worth the effort. 'Europeans were imprisoned at Ambarawa,' he told me shyly while handing me a cup of warm buffalo milk. More than 8,000 Dutch women, children and elderly men were liberated there, but we never hear the Gurkhas' side of the story. 'They were very happy when we arrived, but they looked so skinny! They didn't get any food in the camp. And their clothes were very old too. The cotton was worn. The colours were grey. But they were very happy. I was grateful to be able to help those people. I don't know what happened to them afterwards. Did they go back home?'[30] Purna Bahadur Chhetri, ninety-two, remembered that 'everyone we got out of the prisons went on ships'.[31] The liberation of the large women's camp of Ambarawa involved a lot of violence. Pemuda had killed some forty people with hand grenades.[32] 'We had to shoot our way into those camps,' related ninety-five-year-old Khamba Sing Bura in his sleepy mountain village, where two girls were using a flail to thresh grain. 'The Javanese fled. We let them go. We had to liberate the camps. There were so many women locked up in those prisons. They were skin and bones and begged us for food.'[33] Lal, Purna and Khamba risked their lives to free the Dutch internees – but are there any memorials to them anywhere in the Netherlands? Has the government ever expressed its gratitude? On the contrary, not so long ago an authoritative Dutch study still labelled the British actions 'catastrophic'.[34]

The penniless Lal was even there during the struggle for the ports. 'The fighting began even before we landed. We were on our boats, but were not allowed to shoot back. The RAF helped us by bombing. The fire from land kept coming. I never thought I'd survive but

I was wearing a helmet and God helped me. They'd planted sharpened bamboos and I cut my right leg open on one of them. It bled terribly. The wound was large and painful.' After the Battle of Surabaya he was sent to the chaotic interior of Central Java, where the British Indian forces were so inadequate that they had to call in the help of residual Japanese units. Three months earlier, the British and Japanese had been enemies, now they were fighting side by side against the uncontrollable violence of the pemuda. 'There weren't many Japanese left in the jungle. They had beautiful rifles, but no longer wanted to die. They stayed in the rear and shot from a distance. We were in the front line. The Javanese facing us had bamboos, sticks and rifles, but they didn't want to fight man to man, because then we drew our kukris.' The kukri was the Gurkha soldier's most feared weapon, a thick, curved machete almost half a metre long, much heavier than the Japanese samurai sword or the Javanese klewang. Once I saw a billy goat being slaughtered with one in a Nepali mountain village: not a pretty sight. 'We always wore the kukri on the left,' Lal explained. 'If someone came too close, you drew your knife. That was why a lot of Javanese didn't dare approach us.' A rifle could always miss its target, but there was no escaping a hack or a thrust from a kukri. The wound in the neck or belly or on the arm was always grave. Lal didn't like to talk about it. 'I killed more than ten with it.'[35] The liberation of the civilian camps of Ambarawa and Banjubiru involved man-to-man combat that claimed the lives of at least fifty pemuda.[36]

Most Gurkhas were Hindu or Buddhist – the two religions blend together in Nepal – but that didn't mean they were non-violent. One of the veterans gave a pithy summary: 'We went to war to kill or die. Then you don't think about God.'[37] What's more, the British gave them extremely little information about the enemy. 'During our briefing in India and Java our officer said, "They are our enemy. Don't be sentimental. Don't kill any women, but don't fall in love with them either. Don't respond to their advances. They are enemies too."' That was enough. In a military ceremony at the end of their training, each Gurkha had taken an oath in which he solemnly swore on the ornately decorated Queen's Truncheon to blindly obey all orders. Purna Bahadur Gurung summed it up well: 'We follow every order, even if we have to kill a family member. If the officer says kill, we kill.'[38]

Many remember the conflict in Central Java as a hellish ordeal. They went through the interior on foot, past the flanks of Merapi and Merbabu. 'It was so hard to walk there. Your feet were constantly sinking into the ground. We had to lay down mats to make progress!' 'Six months we were in the jungle. Moving from place to place with our patrol. We carried a small tent and a thin blanket in our backpack. We used the backpack as a pillow.'[39] 'We didn't see any rice fields, just jungle with sometimes a little bit of maize. In a village I only saw old, emaciated people. No young people! How do they survive? I wondered.'[40] 'The enemy knew the volcanoes better than we did.'[41] 'The jungle was thick. The trees were so tall you couldn't see the tops. There were monkeys in them that were bigger than in Nepal. My friends ate monkey. Not me, I didn't eat meat. Our food was airdropped but often we couldn't find it. We suffered terrible hunger.'[42]

At times the rationing was very precarious. The British had no cross-country supply lines. 'The rations came by air: they dropped biscuits. We ate very little. Two or three of those biscuits with water.'[43] 'And it was very difficult to find water. We used our hands to scoop up water to drink out of filthy puddles.'[44] 'A plane dropped us food, American army biscuits, but the Javanese chased us off. They were well armed and we had to leave the food behind. The forest was enormous. Many died.'[45] The young revolutionaries became increasingly formidable adversaries. 'The Indonesians didn't have bamboo spears, but professional rifles and bombs.'[46] 'We had to bury our dead in the ground, there was no time for cremations. I helped dig the pits.'[47] 'One of us was killed by the enemy. We put him on a stretcher but the fire was so intense that for three days we couldn't move him. We were ordered to dig a grave, but the ground was so hard we only got one and a half feet deep, just enough to cover the body. We took his boots off first.'[48]

Some testimonies gave a glimpse of what the war was really like. 'There were a lot of roadblocks with tree trunks. Three Javanese threw themselves on our column. One had a sword and two guns. Another came at me with his rifle pointed at me. While my friend shot down the other two, I grabbed the rifle out of his hands and split his head open with it. I killed him and broke the rifle.[49] In the middle of the Revolusi the Gurkhas did the real dirty work. Birbahadur Pun recalled: 'They opened fire with heavy guns and our men returned fire. I fired all six of my bullets but didn't know if I'd hit anyone. An Indonesian looking for cover jumped into our trench. He wasn't armed and I didn't have any bullets. We started fighting with our bare hands. He punched me on my eyes and I saw stars. I knocked him down and while falling he kicked me in the chest, making me fall too. I went wild. I must have grabbed some earth that contained a rock from the wall of the trench with my outstretched arm. I still had no idea what I was doing but I must have hit him with that rock. He yelled and tried to get away. Then I realised what I was doing again. I grabbed him by the foot and dragged him back. I took my rifle with the grenade launcher on it and used it to beat him to death.'[50]

A humanitarian mission in peacetime? An 'errand of mercy'? In the absence of the Dutch army, the British were helping to wind down the war, but in practice it came down to poor Nepalis punching poor Javanese, or vice versa. It was like a Balinese cockfight, a fierce life-and-death struggle in which two combatants give their utmost while the watching crowd whoops and hollers.

Of all the Gurkhas I spoke to, Purna Bahadur Gurung had the most historical knowledge. This ninety-three-year-old former butcher poured a glass of homemade *raksi* for me, a distilled alcoholic drink that smells like dark, wet soil and is made from steamed barley. He said: 'We went there to help the Dutch people who were still stuck there. Japan had occupied Indonesia and at the end they said, "We've taken your country but now we want to give you your freedom." But the Dutch said, "No, no, this is ours!" The Indonesians knew that we had come to help the Dutch. That was why they were so angry at us.' The whole conflict in a nutshell. In the course of a long conversation with Purna, I realised how much he had come to mistrust Indonesians. He kept returning to that point. 'I was in a village with a lot of coconut trees. We were on patrol with four men. The local population was being very friendly towards us. They smiled and said, "Salaam! Salaam!", but as soon as your back was turned they killed you.' He shook his head. 'We didn't understand their language. It was so difficult to trust them. They were very smart. They dressed like traditional peasants: short trousers, bare chests, baskets with tools. And suddenly someone whistled and they attacked us. Their weapons were lying on the ground under the bushes. It wasn't fair.'

Even after the big battles in Surabaya the conflict continued. There were skirmishes throughout 1946. 'Early one morning, women, children and men came towards us,' Purna remembered. 'They looked innocent, but started shooting. Then we killed their captain. They left his body behind. He had a rifle, a pistol, a compass and a map on him. He was tall and terribly thin. His rifle was very strange: as long and thin as my walking stick here. Had he made that himself or bought it off a Japanese?' These kinds of contained surprise attacks would become a trusted tactic in the coming years. PETA soldiers had already been taught guerrilla tactics during the Japanese period. 'They even used women because they knew we wouldn't attack them.' He took another sip of his raksi. 'Aside from the time we accidentally killed a native woman with a mortar. That was a big mistake! When you're firing you often can't see whether or not you've hit anyone.'

This ongoing conflict caused moments of great frustration. One Saturday morning Purna was asleep when the camp was suddenly shelled. The attack made the men furious. The previous night they had stayed up late playing cards and that day they were intending to cook a little and relax. Now one of their officers had almost been hit. 'We took vengeance. A British officer ordered us to destroy their rice. He said, "Leave the women in peace, but burn their rice and houses." We set fire to their harvest. The fire burned for a week. It was good rice. They kept it in huts. There was fire everywhere. "*Hati-hati*!" cried an old blind man who was inside a hut and couldn't walk. He begged us to spare him with his hands pressed together. "Please! Don't murder us!" But we'd already set fire to his hut. Some got out, but he couldn't escape.' Those images would never let Purna go. 'I still regret it. We had fathers and grandfathers ourselves. Only once did we burn down a village like that. I wasn't happy about murdering those people, but we never attacked first. We only reacted. It was a pity, but that was our task. We did our duty.'[51]

The atrocities committed by the Japanese during the war are familiar. The horrific violence of the pemuda during the Revolusi likewise. An awareness of the many war crimes committed by Dutch troops is, after seventy years, finally sinking in. But that British troops also carried out excesses that seriously contravened the Geneva Conventions is much less well known. Purna twice stated that his British officer had given the order to burn down the village. For the British, the war was over; none of them had any desire to die in a conflict they didn't actually have anything to do with.

Even army commander Mountbatten showed sympathy for the reprisals.[52] After the murder of the entire crew of a crashed British Dakota, the nearby town of Bekasi was mercilessly reduced to ashes. After an attack on a food convoy, adjacent Cibadak was bombed. After a British major who had gone for a naked swim with a Red Cross nurse one night in Padang was murdered with bamboo spears, a kampong in the neighbourhood was razed and local youths were summarily executed. These kinds of reprisals and punitive expeditions were regular events. 'We were repeatedly shot at with automatic weapons. We saw that all of the local inhabitants participated, so we went there and burnt down as many villages as we could,' said Buddhiraj Limbu.[53] Lal Bahadur Khatri, the man with the buffalo milk, also testified that the orders came from above. 'We didn't take any prisoners. They either got away or we killed them. Our British commander told us, "Even if they're wounded, finish them off!"' Killing the wounded is prohibited by the Geneva Conventions. For once Lal breached the old ban on English to pass on his officer's orders verbatim. 'He said, "Bloody bastards! Kill them!" That was normal.'[54]

With the passing of time, several veterans suffered remorse. I spoke to ninety-seven-year-old Champa Singh Thapa above a grocer's in a roadside village. 'I'm sickly because I have killed so many people,' he said while rubbing his temples. 'Because I have sinned so much, I can't hear, understand or remember properly any more. I'm like a child again. I don't have any energy left, no more ideas.' And then, while looking down at his old, weather-beaten hands, he added: 'They looked like us, those enemies, they were just like us.'[55]

The last place I visited was also the most remote: the mountain village of Gumchal, some 200 kilometres southwest of Dhalaugiri, a summit of over 8,000 metres. It was a place where time seemed to have stood still. The grain was still threshed by hand, they fired their own clay pots, lentils simmered in earthenware on wood fires. Khamba Sing Bura was snoozing peacefully with a woolly hat on and leaning back against a basket. As a Gurkha he had always been a Bren-gunner and he still matched the stereotype of a machine-gunner: burly, big-boned, good-humoured. 'The Bren, that's tadadadada! You need two people, a gunner and a loader.' He joked and was quick to respond. 'Why is this Westerner asking so many questions?' But in the course of the conversation he had to admit that he did have some strange memories of his mission in Indonesia. 'Do you know what they said when they surrendered? "Sama, sama!" That's to say, together, we are the same. "I am a soldier, you are a soldier, we are fighting for our country, just like you." Our British officer didn't say anything.' It was unbelievable to hear a few words of Indonesian coming from the mouth of an almost hundred-year-old man leaning on a cane basket in an extremely remote mountain village at the foot of the Himalayas. '"Terima kasih!", they said that too. "Terima kasih banyak!"' That means 'thank you, thank you very much', but literally 'accept my love'. He straightened his thick woolly hat. 'They had the same kinds of faces as us. They had the same colour skin as us. They even gave us little cakes.'[56]

The British could not stay forever. From a total deployment of approximately 36,000 troops they suffered 627 dead (of whom 550 were Asian), 330 missing (of whom 300 were Asian) and more than 1,300 wounded.[57] After the Battle of Surabaya, the Dutch government decided to mobilise a large-scale military force of its own, something that wouldn't be possible with the available KNIL troops and volunteers alone. In addition to the professionals, large cohorts of conscripts were needed. In late 1945 the Netherlands had around 10,000 troops at its disposal in Indonesia. In March 1946 these were strengthened with 15,000 volunteers.[58] Simon Spoor, head of NEFIS, the Netherlands East Indies Forces Intelligence Service, was appointed army commander in the Indies and found these numbers insufficient. In the course of 1946, no fewer than 95,000 young men were called up in the Netherlands, of whom more than three-quarters were found 'fit for the tropics'.[59] There was, however, one formidable problem: Article 192 of the Dutch constitution stated that Dutch soldiers could not be dispatched to the colonies without their consent. The law was hastily amended – invoking emergency powers as if the country were still at war with Japan – but formally this only took effect in August 1947. This meant that the first troop ships had a very tenuous legal basis, or were in fact unconstitutional.[60]

On a warm day in July, I spoke to ninety-year-old Piet van Staveren in a garden in Assen. 'We were the first conscripts after the war.' We were sitting in the shade of a tree and drinking tea. Piet came from a working-class family and had been in the resistance. He read Marx and Engels, but still found it strange to call himself a communist. 'Were all those ideological divisions necessary?' Cooperation was what interested him. 'When we emerged from the underground, I met the Indonesian students from the Perhimpunan Indonesia who had also been in the resistance. As a result I already knew a lot about Indonesia, more than most young people in the Netherlands.' In the summer of 1946 Piet was twenty-one. The small, battered Netherlands was trying to quickly set up an army in the middle of reconstruction, but not every young man felt called to do his bit. There was an exemption for conscientious objectors, but Piet did not apply for it. After all, he had been in the resistance. 'I wasn't a conscientious objector on principle, but after a couple of months we were told that we had to go to the Indies to establish "peace and order".' That changed everything. Now the struggle was no longer against Japanese fascism, but against nationalist freedom fighters. 'We started campaigning against it in the army. We held a meeting in Amersfoort and wanted to found soldiers' councils like in the Soviet Union. Our draft was named the 1st 7 December Division. We were going to be added to the large group of volunteers who had intended to fight the Japs.'

The Netherlands was determined not to repeat its NICA mistake: rather than referring to the colonial past, the new division's name invoked a new future like the one Queen Wilhelmina had sketched in her speech on 7 December 1942. This new designation could not prevent some from pulling out. Besides the small group of principled conscientious objectors – fewer than 200 were recognised annually – there was a large number of 'Indonesia objectors', people who were willing to do military service but did not want to be sent to Indonesia.[61] Some couldn't leave the farm for an extended period, others were the breadwinner for a whole family, yet others had suffered war trauma. The news reports about the Battle of Surabaya had not done anything to engender a fighting spirit. What's more, many had political objections. During training they were told that peaceful Indonesia was being ravaged by 'thieves, murderers and radicals who had been stirred up by the Japanese', but Piet van Staveren knew better. 'We had just been liberated from German oppression and now we were going to Indonesia to do what the Germans had done to us: occupy the country. It was too idiotic for words.'[62]

Public opinion in the Netherlands was extremely divided. A poll in July 1946 revealed that only fifty per cent of men and thirty-six per cent of women supported sending troops.[63] Professor Wim Wertheim of Amsterdam, a sociologist and a member of the Netherlands-Indonesia Association, presented the government and parliament with a petition with no fewer than 230,000 signatures calling for a peaceful solution.[64] Not only communists, but also various social democratic and Protestant organisations joined the protests.

A first contingent of 2,500 men was due to leave by ship for Indonesia on 24 September 1946. The soldiers had been given ten days of embarkation leave to say goodbye to family and friends and had orders to be back at the barracks a week before sailing, but thirty-eight per cent of them didn't report back. This was desertion on an unprecedented scale. Piet van Staveren remembers it well. 'The minister and the commander of the Dutch army said on the radio, "All those soldiers have let themselves be misled. Return to barracks!" They were promised a general pardon.'[65] This appeal reduced the number of deserters to fifteen per cent, but the next ship had to leave with twenty-two per cent fewer troops than intended. 'Some 3,200 men didn't show up. That was an enormous number.' The 7 December Division was intended as a unit of 20,000 men, but ended up being 16,000.

Two days before the first departure, protests in Amsterdam turned violent, even leading to one death.[66] Pratomo, who had become editor-in-chief of the PI magazine *Indonesia* in the meantime, dedicated an editorial to it. 'With the true zeal that characterises the people of Amsterdam, the nation's capital showed clearly and unambiguously that it will not support the army command's military obstinacy.' The article attracted the attention of the Dutch security service, so much so that 'editor-in-chief Djajang [*sic*] Pratomo' was named in a secret report; there was concern that the PI belonged to the camp in which 'no stone is left unturned in a continual and highly irresponsible attempt to criticise government policy in this area'.[67]

All kinds of measures were taken to make the first sailing a festive, patriotic event. Military bands played on the platform at railway stations where troops were leaving. And on the trains, Marvas – volunteers from the Marine Vrouwenafdeling, the women's naval service – gave the soldiers a chocolate bar and ten cigarettes each. On the dock another brass band was playing the Wilhelmus to further encourage the troops and console those they were leaving behind.[68] But the carriages of the trains still had 'Meat transport Amsterdam–Batavia' daubed on them.[69] And as a precaution at the new Prime Minister Louis Beel's request, the queen had signed a royal decree allowing the declaration of martial law or even a state of war in case of serious riots.

Just as in Indonesia, a generation gap was developing in the Netherlands, with the difference that a growing number of young Dutch men did not want to go and fight whereas the Indonesians did. Of course the government and military headquarters didn't have a good word to say about the Indonesia objectors. Unlike the first wave of volunteers, these were no 'men of action', but 'inferior' youths, too lazy and cowardly to serve their country and rescue the poor people of Java and Sumatra from extremist gangs.[70]

Until 1949 tens of thousands of recruits were drummed up annually. There were various ways of avoiding conscription. Many crossed the border. Jos van het Groenewoud left with his girlfriend for Brussels, where their son Raymond would be born and later develop into the godfather of Flemish rock.[71] Poncke Princen, who would become known as a Dutch deserter and Indonesian human rights activist, initially hitchhiked to France.[72] The poet Remco Campert, called up when he was just eighteen, found a less laborious method. 'I ate less around that time and kept my hair dishevelled. A psychiatrist friend who had also been in the resistance declared me S5.' I had to look that up. In the Dutch army, S5 meant 'completely unfit' in terms of emotional stability. A missive to psychiatrists described the conscientious objectors as 'psychologically disturbed people [. . .] slightly neurotic, soft youths [. . .] morons, psychopaths, eccentric sectarians and incipient schizophrenics'.[73] All these things undoubtedly apply to many poets, but in the case of Remco Campert something else also played a role: his great-grandmother was Sumatran. His great-grandfather had met her as an officer in the KNIL. 'I really like having something of the Indies in me. My great-grandmother lived to a very advanced age. I always had to play cards with her in The Hague and was given thousand-layer cake afterwards. She was always cooking. There were always pots on the stove.' Should he go and fight against her country now? Out of the question. 'We artists were in favour of the liberation struggle and strongly opposed to Beel. In retrospect we were right, but you know how difficult it is to change the course of history.'[74] The poets Armando and Hans Andreus were also rejected, one feigning madness, the other homosexuality. Fellow poet Lucebert was going to be sent to the Indies as a conscript, but was passed over by clerical error and received an honourable discharge.[75]

In total no fewer than 120,000 Dutch conscripts would depart between 1946 and 1949, an enormous number that approached the general mobilisation before World War II (150,000). Six thousand recruits who were examined and judged 'fit for the tropics' refused to embark. Many of these were tracked down and hauled out of their beds by the military police. This hunt for deserters went on until

1958!⁷⁶ Strict sentences were passed on 2,565 war resisters. Almost three-quarters received custodial sentences of up to two years, the rest remained in jail even longer.⁷⁷ Altogether a total of fifteen centuries of prison sentences were pronounced, a remarkably large amount compared to the complete immunity granted to later war criminals.⁷⁸ The conclusion was clear: those who refused to kill were locked up, those who murdered without reason went free.

Didn't the colossal military build-up form an obstacle to the political negotiations the British were advocating? How could they discuss things calmly in Yogyakarta while jeeps and tanks were rumbling off the ships in Jakarta? They had to. And more to the point, the pressure was deliberate. 'Negotiating without any force backing you up' was, in the eyes of former prime minister and by then chief negotiator Willem Schermerhorn, 'a thankless pursuit'.⁷⁹

The talks had been initiated by Lieutenant Governor-General Van Mook. In November 1945 the Dutch government had wanted to remove him for having spoken to the devil incarnate Sukarno, but after the intense fighting in East and Central Java, the realisation grew that the right of self-determination, a basic principle of the Atlantic Charter, needed to be recognised in Indonesia as well. This important change satisfied Mountbatten and in March 1946 he decided to admit the Dutch volunteer battalions to Indonesia (for safety's sake he had been making them stay in Malaya and Thailand). The danger of escalation was now many times smaller. In April the British began transferring posts to the Dutch, just as the first major talks with the Republic were taking place. Dutch and Indonesian delegations carried out high-level formal talks for ten days in the sedate St Hubertus Hunting Lodge in the Hoge Veluwe National Park in the Netherlands.⁸⁰ Van Mook launched his master plan flanked by Prime Minister Schermerhorn, Minister of Foreign Affairs Van Roijen, Deputy Prime Minister Willem Drees, and Minister for Overseas Territories Johann Logemann. It was a compromise in which he tried to run with the hare and hunt with the hounds: the Republic of Indonesia would be recognised only in Java, where its authority was actually established, but beyond that the Netherlands would remain in charge and the Republic would not have a say in anything. In those other places, colonialism would simply continue, even if the term was to be avoided. The Dutch East Indies would become a so-called federation of states, of which Java would be just one, albeit with more autonomy than the rest. On top of this, the federation would still remain part of a Dutch commonwealth. Java was the Republic, the Republic was part of a federation, and that federation was part of a Dutch commonwealth. The French had already come up with something similar for Indochina.

The Indonesian delegation could like it or lump it. Formally they had been hoping for a real *treaty*, not the half-hearted *protocol* the Dutch government was putting forward. And they had hoped to take over the jigsaw puzzle of the Dutch East Indies in its entirety. It was true that they were being offered the puzzle's crucial middle piece, but only within a complicated construction in which the Netherlands retained power, with 'free' Java wedged into a federation and that federation tied to the former coloniser. All of the other states would remain under Dutch rule, including Sumatra, the island where Sjahrir and Hatta were born. This was something Sjahrir could not possibly justify back home, where his position was already greatly weakened. Proponents of diplomacy like Sjahrir, Hatta, Sukarno and Amir were faced with ever louder calls for conflict. The pemuda bellowed 'one hundred per cent Merdeka' and would accept no less. Sudirman's army wanted to fight, not talk. And Tan Malaka, the legendary leader of the communist party, had returned after twenty years of anonymous wandering in Asia and was pressing Sjahrir hard. The government had very little leeway.

The conference at the Hoge Veluwe failed, even after Schermerhorn insinuated that war could be the alternative. What became obvious in 1946 was that the Indonesian camp was nowhere near as monolithic as often assumed. Just as the Netherlands was deeply divided regarding the Beel government's dispatching of troops, Indonesia was deeply divided about which course to take with regard to the Netherlands. Decolonisation was not a struggle between two clearly defined camps – Indonesia versus the Netherlands, perpetrator versus victim – but one with constant internal tensions. On 3 July in

Indonesia there was even an attempted coup against Sjahrir, just after
he had sent Van Mook a proposal for a new compromise. The coup
failed but showed what a perilous course he was steering between
diplomatic negotiations and fanatical advocates of independence.

After the Dutch elections of May 1946 brought Louis Beel to
power at the head of a coalition of Catholic and socialist parties, former prime minister Schermerhorn was made chief negotiator for
Indonesia. In the week that the first ship with conscripts sailed, he
landed in Jakarta for talks with the Republic as head of a three-man
General Commission. The detailed diary he recorded with a Dicta-
phone during his stay proves that diplomatic history – with its endless
working lunches and tiring cocktail parties – can be at least as fascinating as military history.

After just two days he remarked that the Dutch and Indonesian
ways of thinking were 'hopelessly different' and saw 'for the ump-
teenth time' proof that 'in reality the Dutch are actually hopeless and
possibly helpless sticklers for convention'. Surprising words from
someone who until recently had been prime minister himself, but
research on the spot always leads to better insights. 'Confronted with
the violence of the facts', his General Commission had to make its
own 'very radical decisions'. That too was strong language.[81]

Schermerhorn spoke approvingly of Lord Killearn and the other
British diplomats operating as mediators. The British year was
drawing to a close, but had not yet been crowned with a political
agreement. Lord Killearn, who as British ambassador to Egypt had
been involved in lightening the colonial yoke, was now Special Commissioner in Southeast Asia. It was at a luncheon at his residence in
Jakarta on 30 September that Schermerhorn first met Sjahrir, an
encounter that he looked forward to 'with more than ordinary curi-
osity'. Later he observed: 'Sjahrir is quick to laugh and likes a good
glass of wine.' After lunch Lord Killearn left the two of them on the
patio and they continued the conversation in Dutch, a language they
both spoke better than English. Schermerhorn said that if they, as
kindred socialist spirits, could not succeed in finding an honourable
solution for both parties, it might never succeed. His diary is moving
proof that world history is always partly a question of personal

relations, of people who start out as strangers but then learn or do not learn to trust each other. The first long discussion was instructive, but Schermerhorn found it 'extremely difficult' to judge whether Sjahrir was being 'fully honest' with him and whether he was seeing what was really 'in his heart'.[82] But over the days and weeks that followed, their mutual understanding and appreciation grew. Even if, during some meetings, the Indonesian prime minister was 'incredibly dogged in his demands' – his job, after all; he represented seventy million people – Schermerhorn appreciated his 'common sense'. On 14 October, after less than two weeks of negotiations, an important first breakthrough was achieved: a provisional truce. 'I am happy,' Schermerhorn told Lord Killearn. It gave him 'confidence in the authority of the opposite party and above all in Sjahrir's personal reliability'.[83]

The ceasefire was badly needed. No sooner had Dutch troops taken over British posts than they had begun seizing Republican territory. General Spoor dreamed of re-occupation and had already widened the Jakarta–Bogor–Bandung axis and extended it to Tangerang. By August 1946 he already had more land under Dutch control than the British had ever occupied. To establish benchmarks for the mutual stabilisation of military forces, Sjahrir had requested troop numbers. The moment in peace talks when the strength of the forces is discussed is always a delicate one. Both sides need to have enough faith in each other to show their hands, but they also need to retain their effectiveness as a military deterrent. Schermerhorn provided the figures the next day. According to army command, the Netherlands would have 93,000 men at their disposal by the end of November: 52,000 KNIL soldiers and 41,000 members of the Dutch army, including the 7 December Division. 'I had the impression', he remarked, 'that Sjahrir was genuinely shocked by our military strength in numbers.' The figures were padded: many of the conscripts were far from combat-ready. 'I have to honestly say that I too had never imagined we currently had 56,000 men here in West Java. I could quite imagine his shock.'[84] Besides strategy, diplomacy always comes down to empathy. Sjahrir in turn stated that the Republic had 140,000 regular troops in Java and Madura and 60,000 in Sumatra. He didn't specify what he understood as 'regular'.

Schermerhorn and Sjahrir gradually grew closer. 'This feeling each other out is the only fruitful method we can apply at this stage.' The former Dutch prime minister's descriptions of Sjahrir went from 'a sly little fellow' to a chairman 'who is extremely calm and an exceptionally good listener' and a leader who analyses problems with 'extraordinary subtlety'.[85] They realised that their fates were intertwined: as their viewpoints came closer, the potential distance from their own governments increased. During a dinner at Lord Killearn's residence, 'an extraordinarily sociable evening with relatively little engagement with politics', they even said so in as many words. Sjahrir 'stated frankly that a rejection of these proposals would mean his resignation. For myself I then declared forthrightly that I was of the same opinion.' Schermerhorn remembered all too well one of his fellow diplomats' remarks on the trip out: 'Friends, from now on we have to count on everyone in Holland thinking we're mad.'[86]

The negotiators were now meeting in the pleasant setting of Sjahrir's home, with the Indonesian prime minister providing the meals. Schermerhorn described another dinner as 'extremely enjoyable, awash with a copious amount of champagne, of which the old gentleman [Killearn] turns out to be a great enthusiast'.[87] Lord Killearn and his team helped where possible, but acted with discretion: as long as the talks made progress. And they did. At the start of November the time was ripe for formal, diplomatic negotiations. But where? There was no question of the Dutch delegation making their way to the lion's den in Yogyakarta: that would be too great a symbolic concession. On the other hand Sukarno and army commander Sudirman did not trust the Dutch enough to travel to Jakarta. They could always be taken prisoner, like the Javanese Prince Diponegoro in 1830, a story of Dutch betrayal that was familiar to every Javanese. Sjahrir knew an ideal spot halfway: south of the coastal city of Cirebon, on the flank of the volcano Ciremai, was the charming town of Linggajati. It was in Republican territory, but far enough away from the hotbed of Yogya to be safe and acceptable. There was an old colonial villa there with a large garden that could certainly serve as a meeting place.

This now historic villa was where Joty ter Kulve, who spoke to me in a service flat in Wassenaar, grew up. Her father, who died young, built the cool, spacious house in the 1930s and she spent what were possibly the most beautiful years of her life there. 'As a toddler I was once in the bathroom when the volcano began to rumble. Everything was shaking. I ran out into the garden without any clothes on!'[88] In this house, another seismic event was about to take place: the final talks between Indonesia and the Netherlands from 11 to 13 November 1946. It is now a magnificent museum that stylishly evokes the historic negotiations, a rare rapprochement between colony and coloniser.

The extreme tension of the military situation was apparent from the moment they arrived. As soon as the Dutch negotiators' Catalina flying boat landed on the water a row broke out over who would take them ashore, a Dutch or a Republican naval vessel. It almost came to a firefight. Fortunately the fuses in the villa itself were not as short. Lord Killearn took on the role of chairman, with the four-man Indonesian delegation led by Sjahrir on his left and the matching Dutch delegation led by Schermerhorn on his right. Also present was Van Mook, an indefatigable but now quite frustrated advocate of greater freedom for Indonesia, who had pressed for more autonomy before the war and had convinced the queen to deliver her 7 December speech in 1942. Waiting in the garden for the outcome of the talks were journalists and photographers. Sukarno and Hatta themselves were deliberately not taking part – for the outside world they were still too controversial – but staying nearby, ten kilometres to the south in the town of Kuningan. Schermerhorn was sensible enough to go to pay his respects immediately. 'Both gentlemen were friendly and courteous' towards him and he observed: 'They are two completely different people: Sukarno, a Javanese, and Hatta, a Sumatran. Sukarno more or less a charmer, setting great store on the phrasing and during the conversation seeing in his mind's eye the necessity of making the result acceptable to his people. Hatta, a man who is much more Western and pragmatically rational in his reasoning. This man makes a first-rate impression on me.'[89] When the formal talks began, the main points were quickly agreed: the Netherlands would in fact recognise the Republic's authority not just in Java but also in

Sumatra. This was an important concession considering that vast island's highly important tobacco plantations and oil reserves. It was the world's fifth largest island and would give the Republic control over eighty-five per cent of the Indonesian population. In exchange it would accept becoming part of the 'United States of Indonesia', a federal construction that, in addition to the Republic, would contain two more states: Borneo (the world's third largest island) and the Great East (the rest of the Outer Islands). This federal construction would in turn be part of the Netherlands–Indonesia Union under the Dutch Crown. Besides the United States of Indonesia, the Union would contain the Kingdom of the Netherlands, made up of the Netherlands, Suriname and the Netherlands Antilles. It was a complex compromise, certainly, but Schermerhorn thought it defensible for all. 'In our opinion this preserves the bond between the states [important to the Netherlands] while giving the republic the recognition it demands. I am hopeful that it will be successful.'[90]

Sjahrir and his team still saw several difficulties: large parts of Indonesia were calling for 'one hundred per cent Merdeka' but this construction left a lot of power and a lot of land in Dutch hands. What's more, the new state would become 'free' but not yet

Map 22: Linggajati Agreement: the United States of Indonesia
(15 November 1946)

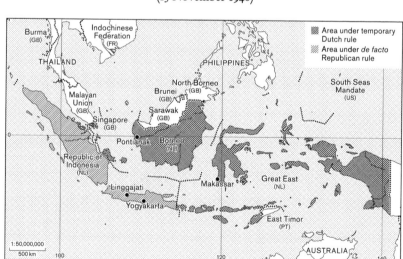

'sovereign'. In its foreign affairs, for instance, as it would not have the right to build up its own diplomatic service, whereas Sjahrir already had extensive contact with Nehru in India. Was a country really a country if it wasn't recognised as such abroad? And when would all this take effect? How long would the people have to wait for their freedom? It was agreed that everything would be arranged on 1 January 1949.

At the end of the first day, Schermerhorn decided against returning to the Dutch navy ship in Cirebon with the rest of the Dutch delegation, spending the night in Linggajati instead. He claimed to be suffering heart problems, but did it mainly 'out of political motives'. Together with Sjahrir, Hatta and Sukarno he went to a gamelan concert that made a great impression on him. Afterwards they enjoyed 'a delicious Chinese meal with bird's nest soup, shark fins and all the ingredients of a good Chinese dinner'. The dinner went on until eleven-thirty. You can still visit the negotiators' bedrooms today. They shared the bathroom where little Joty had once heard the rumbling of the volcano. Schermerhorn got a good night's rest 'in Linggajati's delightful climate'. The next day they again went to visit Sukarno and Hatta, without Sjahrir, who had a headache. One of the Indonesian negotiators suggested that, in the agreement they were writing, the adjective 'free' should be replaced with 'sovereign', as this would considerably raise the Republic's standing and make it easier for it to sell the compromise to its supporters. Schermerhorn described the minutes that followed in detail. 'Van Mook then asked Sukarno and Hatta, if, in the event of our getting this alteration through and accepting it, we could then say that we were finished. Sukarno confirmed this without hesitation and even said that, in that case, he would be prepared to deploy the whole weight of his person and position to make it acceptable to the population of the Republic.' Schermerhorn added: 'As anyone can imagine, a small shock passed through the Dutch delegation at that moment, because we now had the consent of the highest authority.'[91]

The only one who was less than happy with the result was Sjahrir. Once again Sukarno had beaten him to it, just as with the Proklamasi. But his greatest concern was that he now had to defend what

Sukarno had just decided. Work on the agreement resumed until Sjahrir too found the result sufficiently robust. The final document comprised seventeen articles and was six pages long.[92] For Schermerhorn 'the text was now definitive', a text his General Commission considered 'no longer actually open to any further alterations'.[93]

On Wednesday 13 November the delegations returned to Yogyakarta and Batavia, as the Dutch still called Jakarta. On 15 November 1946 the document was initialled in Sjahrir's living room in Jakarta prior to the official signing. The photographs suggest a relaxed atmosphere. Van Mook even signed with his shirt unbuttoned and a cigarette dangling from his lips. In the evening Schermerhorn and Sjahrir ate their last meal at Lord Killearn's residence. The British had been pulling strings from the beginning to the end. 'Killearn was in the best of moods and that was completely understandable,' Schermerhorn dictated afterwards. 'In these circumstances the departure of the English on 30 November will cause quite a bit less tension than it would have without an agreement.' And, he added, 'the four of us drinking four bottles of champagne in the course of the evening was not so terribly surprising, particularly since we'd seen earlier that the old gentleman is extremely fond of it himself.'[94] Four men seated around a table just after agreeing measures for the rearrangement of the world's third largest colonial empire. With midnight approaching, Sjahrir wanted to go home before the curfew as he would otherwise have to deal with the police. In Jakarta the authority of the prime minister of the Republic was very limited. Schermerhorn noted in his secret diary: 'He gave me a lift home in his car and remarked on the way that he'd probably never drunk as much champagne in his life as he had that evening. I must say, however, that he seemed no more bothered by it than either of the other gentlemen.'[95]

Keep this picture in mind for a moment: two tipsy gentlemen on a drive through night-time Jakarta. The tall, highly contented Schermerhorn next to the small, invariably cheerful Sjahrir. Willem was 52, Sutan 37. Years later, in 1966, when Sjahrir died in a Swiss hospital at the age of 57 after years of imprisonment – Sukarno had cast him aside – his body was flown back to Indonesia via Schiphol. At the airport Schermerhorn gave an improvised speech during which he, the serious statesman, had difficulty 'controlling his nerves'. 'It was not only that we were here commemorating an extraordinarily gifted man, but you will understand that, with those words, our shared struggle rose in my mind along with the defeat we suffered at the hands of the forces of extremism. That whole image moved me more than I could bear at that moment.' But we're getting ahead of ourselves. It is still 1946. Watch them riding through the night, the prime minister of the new country and the former prime minister of the old country, see their car driving down the city's avenues, see them growing smaller. It was the first time that a Dutchman and an Indonesian at this level had interacted with each other with such warmth, almost as friends. It was also the last time. The car disappeared into the distance.

Chapter 12

The Trap
The Dutch year, November 1946–July 1947

The history could have ended here. The Japanese were evacuating, the British were sending their troops home. The Republic and the Netherlands had entered into an agreement that ended hostilities and laid the groundwork for a new future as equals. The superpowers' reactions were extremely positive. British Prime Minister Attlee congratulated the Dutch ambassador in London on the result they had achieved.[1] The US government praised both delegations' 'high statesmanship'.[2]

Even Piet van Staveren, with his strong left-wing views, decided he could no longer remain in hiding in the Netherlands. 'After Linggajati I had no reason not to go,' he told me in his sunny garden in Assen. 'I went to the barracks and said, "Here I am again, reporting for duty!" There was a pardon, inasmuch as I wasn't punished but was sent immediately to the Forwarding Depot in Schoonhoven. I had to go under escort. They sent a sergeant with me.' What happened next took him by surprise. 'I arrived and it was a complete mess. I immediately got a Sten gun shoved into my hands. I said, "What's this?" The lads in the barrack room said, "Ah, just put it in the back of your locker." Jan Princen was in the same room. He'd also reported back and we immediately struck up a conversation.' Jan Princen, better known as 'Poncke' Princen, the man who went over to the other side, is a name Dutch baby boomers remember vividly: loathed by many, admired by some. Piet and Poncke left for Indonesia on the same transport ship. 'We had bunks in the hold,' Piet recalled, 'four or five tiers. Princen slept in the bunk over mine. I had a lot of long discussions with him.'[3] The ship carried 800 Indonesia objectors who had surfaced after Linggajati. Poncke Princen wondered how well-considered it was 'to put poorly motivated soldiers together on a ship for three weeks'. He was, in any case, impressed by one of his fellow passengers. 'I ended up in a bunk near Piet van Staveren. [. . .] Piet had written *"Kita datang sebagai teman, tidak sebagai moesoeh"* on his helmet – we come as friends, not enemies. Compared to him I was just an unthinking adventurer.[4]

Not everyone wrote messages of peace on their military equipment, but Linggajati did signal the dawn of a new era. At least, in theory. 1947 was to be the year the Netherlands finally retook control, no longer as a coloniser, it told itself, but as a partner joining Indonesia in striving for a new legal system. It turned out completely differently. The 'Dutch year' – my term of convenience for the period between November 1946 and August 1947 – was the first year since the Japanese advance of 1942 in which the Netherlands again had a free hand at administering the archipelago, but it ended as a grand fiasco. The arduously achieved Linggajati Agreement was systematically undermined by the imposition of new Dutch conditions, which soon eroded the fragile trust between the Dutch and Indonesian delegations. At the same time extremely cruel methods were used to suppress the liberation movement in South Sulawesi and, to cap it all, the Netherlands launched a large-scale military offensive, the so-called First Police Action, which did the opposite of what Linggajati had promised: conquering instead of relinquishing. All this took place in just over six months. How was it possible that a rare chance of peace could be so thoroughly squandered?

Initially everything went well. In Indonesia the first response to the draft agreement was cautiously positive: even the reactions of business people, officers and officials of European and Eurasian origin were 'not at all hostile', as Schermerhorn observed at public talks he gave.[5] It is possible that these people knew the situation in the country well enough to realise that 'a political solution was inevitable and the military path impossible'.[6] On the Republican side, too, Sukarno, Hatta and Sjahrir – still president, vice-president and prime minister respectively – set to work faithfully to convince their supporters that the agreement was sound. They gave radio speeches in which they brought their full political weight to bear. Hatta tried to sell it as a 'springboard' to more and Sjahrir described it as 'merely a phase' in the struggle for independence.[7] Even journalists who were confirmed Republicans were 'definitely not unsympathetic' to the proposed new collaboration.[8] Meanwhile senior functionaries of the Dutch East Indies government were making the first agreements on recognition of each other's currencies, the NICA guilder and the Republican rupiah.[9] People carrying Republican money in a Dutch enclave were no longer committing an offence. Someone who pulled out NICAs at a market in Republican territory would no longer be berated. It was a start.

But the sparks began to fly in late November when Schermerhorn landed back at Schiphol. While the Republican leaders were consistently promoting the agreed compromise, the Dutch government was far from convinced. Unlike Sjahrir and the other Republican leaders, the Dutch ministers had only been able to follow the process from a great distance. It was still five days of flying from the Netherlands to Java, with stops in Rome, Basra, Karachi, Calcutta and Singapore. All official communication had been by telegram. These terse messages between government and commission were sometimes a source of confusion, annoyance and incomprehension. Schermerhorn landed at Schiphol for what he called 'the great battle' with the Dutch authorities.[10] Besides an official welcoming committee, he was also met by an elated delegation from the Perhimpunan Indonesia, but thanks to 'all kinds of unpleasant stories' he had picked up en route, his spirits were 'really below zero'.[11] The country's highest military authorities, head of the navy Helfrich (from the Battle of the Java Sea) and chief of staff Hendrik Kruls, had openly warned the queen of what they saw as the disastrous consequences of the agreement Schermerhorn had just reached. Several lawyers even considered it a contravention of the constitution and international law. Other experts condemned the absence of financial and economic guarantees. In the days that followed, the rumblings in the polder continued. While the Dutch-Indonesia Association amassed 230,000 signatures in favour of a peaceful and amicable solution to the dispute, conservative lobby groups such as 'the Indies in distress' and the 'National

Committee for Maintaining the Unity of the Kingdom' managed to collect a total of 300,000 signatures against Linggajati. The latter committee was led by heavyweights such as former prime minister Pieter Gerbrandy, former minister of colonies Charles Welter and former commander-in-chief of the army Henri Winkelman. The most important right-wing party leaders joined them. The Netherlands was revealed as deeply divided. A Dutch opinion poll in December 1946 showed that thirty-six per cent of those questioned were opposed to Linggajati, thirty-eight per cent in favour and twenty-six per cent had no opinion.[12] In these extremely tense circumstances, Schermerhorn had to enter discussions with Prime Minister Beel's coalition of Catholic and socialist parties.

It went better than expected. Communication is easier around a conference table with coffee and ashtrays on it than through a series of telegrams. Misunderstandings can be corrected, experiences shared and doubts expressed. Schermerhorn considered the mood 'excellent' and there was even 'a degree of mild humour'.[13] Finally he could provide background information about the emergence of the agreement, the reasons behind certain articles and why the result was definitely not at odds with the Dutch constitution: rather than establishing a new legal structure, it only provided the parameters for it. Correctly, he stated that there were no longer 'twelve solutions' but only two: either 'the acceptance of the formal and even factual equality' of the opposing party or 'the method of striking a blow, which of course means striking hard'. Linggajati represented the first path, military intervention the second. 'We are convinced that there is no middle course.'[14]

It was normal that questions should arise, but he considered the imposition of new conditions problematic — not just internationally, where the Netherlands was in danger of being considered unreliable, but also with regard to the Republic. 'Gains on one side, for instance, for the Netherlands' meant 'the Indonesian delegation losing face before their people.' Fiddling around with the terms could undoubtedly lead to 'a certain distrust of Dutch intentions'.[15]

And that was exactly what happened. The Dutch government suddenly attached great significance to New Guinea, a jungle territory that had swallowed up the occasional missionary in the colonial era and otherwise been used for little more than dumping dissidents at Boven Digul. All at once the Dutch were arguing that West New Guinea needed to be kept separate from Linggajati and outside the planned state of the Great East, so that the Indies Dutch could be resettled there, on the world's second largest island. The sparsely populated territory would thus be retained as a colonial possession. The coasts of New Guinea, modernised since the American invasion, would offer a new luxury deck, now that the passengers from Decks 2 and 3 had climbed to the top in the rest of the archipelago. None of this had been discussed a month earlier in the villa at Linggajati.

It wasn't the only new condition. Shouldn't the importance of the Crown be increased somewhat? Weren't financial and economic agreements needed alongside the political one? Couldn't the preamble be rewritten a little? 'If we start tinkering with this agreement,' Schermerhorn realised, 'we can rest assured that the other side will also come up with counter proposals.'[16] Unfortunately, after his General Commission's technical explanation, the cabinet wrote its own interpretation to present to the Lower House. Here several epic debates that attracted great attention were held between 10 and 19 December 1946.

At that time the political landscape in the Netherlands was made up as follows: on the far left were the communists (with ten of the 100 seats in the parliament), beside them the social democrats (twenty-nine seats), the Catholics (thirty-two seats), three smaller Protestant parties (together twenty-three seats) and, lastly, the liberals (six seats). The social democratic and Catholic coalition held a wide majority of sixty-one seats, but when it came to decolonisation the opinions in the government were divided. Before the war, only the communists had been principled advocates of independence. After the war – once Koos Vorrink had restructured the old SDAP (Social Democratic Workers' Party) as the PvdA (Dutch Labour Party) – the socialists had come around as well. The breach now ran through the Catholic People's Party: General Commission member Max van Poll defended Linggajati, whereas former minister of colonies Welter was distinctly opposed. On the right, the Protestant and business parties were also against Linggajati, appealing to church, queen and capital.

The minister of overseas territories, Jan Jonkman, an independent and a magistrate who had been the chairman of the People's Council of the Dutch East Indies, realised that he could not convince the parties on the right. When they asked if it would not be better to re-establish 'peace and order' first by military means and then negotiate, he retorted: 'because of our refusal to negotiate when we were still in power, we are now obliged to negotiate when we are no longer in power.'[17] These apt words summarised colonial politics from 1920 to 1940 and linked the repression of those years to the current revolution. The Netherlands was reaping the whirlwind.

To win over the hesitant Catholics, Jonkman explained the specifics of the Linggajati Agreement. First, the deadline of 1 January 1949 was not absolute. At most it was the date by which the new legal structure 'could possibly prove' to be ready – until then the Netherlands would formally retain power. Second, it was necessary to retain the possibility of 'mass resettlement' in West New Guinea of the Dutch and Indies Dutch who wished to continue living 'under their own system' – not everything needed to be lost. Third, the rights and obligations of both countries meant that all the debts of the Dutch East Indies would 'have to be assumed by federal Indonesia'. Fourth, the agreement's 'immediate' reduction 'in troop strength on both sides' did not need to be taken literally, and would not be carried out 'without the strictest guarantees'. And fifth, the international arbitration clause at the end – a far-reaching measure Sjahrir had insisted on – was merely a 'psychological concession' which naturally required 'further elaboration'. In short, things were nowhere near as black as they seemed.[18]

Jonkman realised that Linggajati was lost without the Catholic vote. The government would fall, the Netherlands would lose a great deal of international credit and the future in Indonesia would look very sombre. There was nothing unusual about such an important question being debated at length – after all, it was the post-war Netherlands' largest political issue. Besides all the commercial aspects, it remained a dossier that aroused 'a certain national pathos', and even

what Schermerhorn called a 'possessive passion'.[19] In a democracy it
was completely normal and healthy for there to be disagreements, for
the parliament to press the minister, request explanations, formulate
objections and require guarantees, especially when the country had
just been through five years of fascist occupation. But what followed
was less edifying. In order to pass the agreement, the Catholic and
socialist chairmen together submitted a motion to agree to Linggajati
only if the General Commission's explanation and the government
declaration were included as an integral part. In short, the primary
text would be not just the agreement reached at Linggajati, but also
the spin The Hague had put on it. The motion was passed and the
six-page negotiated agreement was unilaterally expanded to a working document that was several dozen pages long.[20] Hmm. That might
have resolved the problem for the time being – sixty-five members
of parliament did vote for it – but in the long run it placed a heavy
burden on the fragile agreement that had been reached with such
difficulty. Linggajati should have been accepted or rejected in its
entirety – with all the consequences. But this chicanery was along
the lines of *ni pour, ni contre, au contraire*: we're neither for nor against,
on the contrary! Only the communists still backed the original
agreement.

Schermerhorn had emphatically hoped that the parliament would
not 'stand on all of the Republic's corns at once', but was obliged to
conclude that it had 'puffed up its breast and probably wasn't strong
enough to back it up'.[21] After the vote he left for Indonesia in a less
than cheerful mood. His General Commission was given less freedom in continuing the discussions and would henceforth be directed
by politicians in a bubble in The Hague, many of whom had never
even been to Indonesia. It was a debacle for Schermerhorn, whose
personality and vision had been deciding factors, and it considerably
weakened his negotiating position. Shortly before leaving, he was
asked by several journalists whether the Indonesians 'could be
trusted'. He answered sharply 'that the Indonesians ask themselves
exactly the same question with regard to the Dutch'.[22] Schermerhorn
was a pragmatist who wanted to make progress. As on many other
occasions, he showed considerable insight when he wrote: 'I know

that in all kinds of areas equality does not exist, but precisely where personal reliability is concerned, I take the liberty of denying that. There is nothing worse than impugning an adversary's humanity and many Dutch colonialists are still prepared to do just that to the Indonesians.'[23]

Linggajati should have been a treaty between two equal partners, but its 'presentation' by the Dutch politicians had seriously skewed it. Sukarno stated shortly afterwards that he considered the result 'a violation of the original agreement', and he was right.[24] Was it then strange that the more fanatical side of the Republic – the armed youths, army command, the communists, the older nationalists – felt little inclination to respect a treaty the Netherlands itself did not respect? They hadn't been convinced of the value of the compromise in the first place. Nowhere did the mistrust grow faster than on the borders between Dutch and Republican territory. 'At first I was in favour of Linggajati,' said a former pemuda, 'but unfortunately enough, the Dutch didn't respect it. They moved back into our territory.'[25] Pemuda militias also regularly breached the demarcation line with the Dutch enclaves, while Dutch fighter planes flew over Republican territory. 'The demarcation line wasn't visible,' Sriyono said, 'but there was gunfire almost every day.'[26] Bol Kerrebijn, the young Indo who had joined the KNIL, snorted, 'The demarcation line? In Batavia the tram drove through it!' The many border disputes took a toll. 'We saw dead people on the side of the road every day,' he said.[27]

The Netherlands decided to impose a naval blockade to cut off Republican export and supply routes by preventing Republican ships from putting out to sea. The Republic responded with a food blockade and refused to continue supplying the Dutch enclaves: rice and vegetables no longer arrived from the interior. The Dutch troops had to survive on instant mashed potato from leftover American supplies on New Guinea. The troops called it 'reinforced concrete'.[28] A peace process is a succession of cautious steps forward and swift strides back. As the Dutch saying goes, trust arrives on foot but leaves on horseback.

★

Much more disastrous for mutual trust were events in the Outer Islands. The fundamental assumption of Linggajati was that Java and Sumatra were already as good as 'lost' to the Netherlands, but that the rest of the archipelago remained calm and docile. The goal was to bind those territories to the Netherlands by quickly founding loyal, non-Republican states. If Java and Sumatra left two large holes in the great puzzle of the old colonial empire, the rest had to be glued in place as soon as possible. And that was exactly what Van Mook had been doing for months. In July 1946 he had organised the Malino Conference in a holiday resort on the southern tip of Sulawesi, close to Makassar. Here, for the first time, he had presented his federal plans to scores of regional leaders: the territories outside of Java and Sumatra, the so-called 'Malino territories', would be given their own administrative bodies. In December 1946, immediately after Linggajati, he had convened the Denpasar Conference, where the first non-Republican state was founded, called the Great East or East Indonesia. The territory covered the entire eastern half of the archipelago. The capital was Makassar, the country's largest city outside the Republic. The inhabitants were given their own government, parliament and authorities. Many local administrators saw this as massive recognition. There had long been a simmering annoyance at Java's political dominance, and Van Mook skilfully capitalised on this by offering the peripheral regions a tremendous boost in prestige. Borneo too was to be given such a status.

Not everyone in the Outer Islands was pleased with this arrangement, but I only realised how true this was on the evening I spoke to the Balinese Murtini Pendit. 'My father had held a good position in the Dutch era: he had been the district head and even had a car. In the 1930s! But he was opposed to the whole idea of "East Indonesia". He wanted a single country, not a colonial concept like that.' The border between pro- and anti-Republican did not coincide with the straits. 'He was thrown into jail because he wanted the country to be free.' In the Japanese period her father had been the commander of a Japanese PETA battalion; after the Proklamasi he was put in charge of a Republican PKR unit (the People's Security Corps, established by Sukarno). During a flag incident similar to the one in Surabaya, her father had been the one to tear off the blue strip. Here, too, youths had daubed 'Go to hell, Holland!' on the fences. Bali was receptive to the Republican ideology. Leader of the local troops was Ngurah Rai. 'He was murdered during the fighting against the Dutch,' Murtini related. 'My husband joined the pemuda too. He was eighteen at the time. He too was imprisoned for a while by the Dutch.' Her husband, Nyoman S. Pendit, would later become a versatile intellectual who translated the three greatest works of Hinduism – the *Ramayana*, the *Mahabharata* and the *Bhagavad Gita* – into Indonesian. He met Gandhi and Nehru and was photographed with Sukarno.

The Revolusi was not an exclusively male concern. Young women like Murtini were involved too. On the day of the Proklamasi she turned fourteen. 'My father said, "No! You're too young!" But I joined the Red Cross anyway.' This wasn't the international, neutral aid organisation, but the revolution's volunteer medical corps. 'All the older boys said, "You have to support the struggle too! We'll take care of the guerrilla warfare, the girls join the Red Cross." And so I learned how to bandage.' Murtini summed up the situation in a few words. 'There were two groups in Bali, pro- and anti-Dutch. As in Java, the old elite was pro-Dutch, but the new elite, for instance those who had trained as soldiers, were not. All my family and friends supported the Revolusi.'[29] Dissent like this seriously frustrated Van Mook's plans. No wonder Murtini's father and brother were thrown into jail. Linggajati could only succeed if the Outer Islands were content to toe the line.

It became even more difficult when Javanese pemuda went to reinforce the troops in the Outer Islands. Despite the naval blockade, a number of them succeeded in reaching the other territories, including some women. Lying on a hospital bed in a depressing retirement home in Jakarta was Siti Aishah. Her testimony was incredible. 'Siti Aishah was not my real name. I was actually called Yeti Rosa, but during the struggle my friends gave me this name so I could stay anonymous.' She still remembered the year. 'In 1947 I went to Kalimantan.' By no coincidence, that was just after Linggajati, when Borneo was slated to become a separate state. 'I was fourteen. I left with friends. That way I was able to get away from my mean stepmother too! It was four days by ship. We went to Balikpapan. There were still Japanese there! I joined the Red Cross and learned how to provide first aid. In the jungle I had to nurse and cook. I didn't wear a uniform, just ordinary trousers and an armband. Sometimes I took part in the fighting. I wasn't paid. We were in the forest as volunteers. We moved every two days. There were twenty of us, eighteen boys and two girls. We drank from coconuts, we drank from the river. We washed in the river, quick, quick, because there was fighting. Clothes back on, shoes back on. Friends were shot dead. We buried them immediately. They're sad stories. I got grazed on the leg.' To prove it she pulled up her sarong to show me a patchy bit of skin, scar tissue that had lost its pigment. 'We took the victims' weapons. I got a gun that way too. The enemy had planes. They dropped bombs. Ah, I don't want to think about it.' Her voice breaking, she sang a marching song from those days: '*Berjalan terus tak mengenal haus/ Menjaga perjalanan musuh/ Otak meletus musuh menjadi kalang kabut/ Demikianlah gerangan gerilya Indonesia.*' Loosely translated: 'Always walking, even thirst won't stop us./ Always looking to see where the enemy has gone./ Silently we strike: chaos among the enemy./ This is who we are, the Indonesian guerrillas.' She fell silent. She groaned, coughed. Then continued. 'Our group was mixed. I was the youngest. There were Dayaks among us, but also Ambonese and Javanese. Our leader was Javanese.' The Revolusi exported its youth. 'Hassan Basry was the big leader of Kalimantan back then. He was famous.' After Linggajati he chose to continue the struggle until all of Indonesia was liberated. Later his militia would be integrated into the government army and he would be made a lieutenant colonel. But at this stage his movement was still part of the resistance. 'We didn't have any tents. We slept under the trees. We were not allowed to light fires, otherwise the enemy would see us. We saw them. Sometimes from far away, sometimes close by. They wore uniforms, some of them had cars. We did everything on foot. The whole day long. Everyone carried something. I had the medicine, the others the ammunition. We went very hungry. Once I fell asleep while marching. There were snakes and wild pigs. And lots of orangutans! We kept our distance from them! They're dangerous if you go too close!' And then she said something that Van Mook would have found alarming. 'Now and then we went to the villages. Not to sleep, no, we never stayed long. But the people gave us food and drink. They supported us.'[30]

In the Outer Islands there was no demarcation line between Republican and Dutch territory – according to Linggajati they all belonged entirely to the Netherlands – and countrymen came up against each other. 'I fought against Hassan Basry!' said Donisius Unawekla, a KNIL veteran from the Moluccas. 'He had a big army in the jungle near Banjarmasin.'[31] Julius Nunumete, the Home Guard soldier who had been charged with defending the airport of Ambon against the Japanese, was sent to Borneo. 'From 1947 on, I was in Balikpapan. It wasn't a real war. We had to patrol in cars and protect the oil refineries.' Kalimantan was important to the Netherlands not just politically but also economically: the oil companies were gradually starting up again.[32] Like many KNIL soldiers, Julius remained extremely loyal to the Dutch queen. The Ambonese troops were actually the Gurkhas of the Dutch East Indies. 'Orders are orders! I was opposed to the Proklamasi. As a KNIL soldier I felt protected by the Dutch government.' His patrols sometimes led him into the jungle. 'There were wild animals there. I saw orangutans!'[33] Siti and Julius, children of the same country, separated by Linggajati – but united in their fear of the most magnificent of the anthropoid apes.

In an outer suburb of Makassar, the former capital of the state of East Indonesia, I was able to talk to Puling Daeng Rannu. She was sitting on the side of her bed in a very modest home, but spoke with undiminished passion. 'I became a pemuda! The Red Cross taught me how to dress wounds. Lots of fighting, lots of wounds! Bullets in hands and legs! My husband was a policeman. I stole his gun and left a note: "If I get arrested, make sure you look after yourself." '[34]

She was far from the only one. In the so-called 'Malino territories', Makassar became *the* place where resistance to Linggajati took on dramatic proportions. The freshly inaugurated capital of the new state was meant to become a peaceful administrative centre, but the situation remained restless far into the countryside – partly because of the brutality of the KNIL. Other than in Bali, even the traditional nobility was on the side of the Republic. The most inspirational figure was Sam Ratulangi, a Zurich-educated mathematician from North Sulawesi who had been on the Preparatory Committee for Indonesian Independence. Following the Japanese capitulation he had installed a Republican administration, but shortly afterwards Sulawesi had been taken over by the Australians, with NICA and the KNIL in their wake. In April 1946 Ratulangi was dragged out of his bed; the Netherlands banished him to an island off the coast of New Guinea as if it was still 1926 instead of 1946. As an attempt to extinguish the Republican fire, this failed completely.

'After that happened, Makassar really wanted to fight.' General Bachtiar was one of the last who could tell us about it. 'I was sixteen at the time. The Netherlands was trying to colonise and exploit us again. They opened a school, but we refused to go to it. We pemuda preferred to go to the schools run by Dr Ratulangi, who had been appointed governor of Sulawesi by Sukarno.' They did more than just study. 'When Dutch convoys passed we shot at them. We had Japanese and Dutch carbines. I was living at Dr Ratulangi's when he was arrested and banished. Then I went by boat to Java to fetch weapons and military equipment.' He tagged along with important freedom fighters like Andi Mattalatta and Saleh Lahade, who went to see Sukarno.[35] He said, 'Are the people of Sulawesi really prepared to join Indonesia?' 'If we weren't ready, we wouldn't be here, *bung*,' they answered. 'Splendid,' Sukarno said, 'I don't need a million pemuda. A thousand is enough, no, a hundred is enough, as long as they are as brave as you.'[36] Armed with a mandate and means, the delegation returned to South Sulawesi in late December 1946. 'We weren't satisfied with the Linggajati Conference. A federation made up of separate states? They were *negara boneka*! Puppet states! We had to eliminate them.' They didn't go back to Makassar itself, but sailed to a safer coast in three prahus. Attacks were coming thick and fast at the time. A year after Semarang and Surabaya, Makassar seemed to be becoming the main hotbed of resistance. Besides rebels, it was also overrun with marauders and common bandits. Was a large-scale military operation like the one on Surabaya imminent? No. Bachtiar remembered well that the Netherlands opted for a different tactic. 'They set Captain Westerling's special forces on us.'[37]

In the mid-sixties, if you went to the outdoor swimming pool of Doorwerth, a peaceful village in the Dutch province of Gelderland, you could easily strike up a conversation with a charismatic lifeguard.[38] Raymond Westerling was the name, nicknamed 'the Turk'. Born to a Dutch-Greek couple in Istanbul in 1919, he had undergone commando training during World War II. After his period in the Indies he had run a second-hand bookshop in Amsterdam and taken opera lessons in Brussels.[39] Now he sat in his lifeguard's chair and languidly watched over the swimmers in the pool with the wave generator, a curiously calm existence given his history. In Indonesia he had led the Special Troops Depot, an elite unit whose training had been modelled on the British commandos' so that they could be deployed in demanding conditions. When the violence in South Sulawesi became uncontrollable, army commander Spoor sent Westerling there – without precise instructions. How could a unit of some 120 men, consisting of thirty Dutchmen and just over ninety troops from Ambon and Manado, restore peace and order in a coastal area more than 300 kilometres long, when the British had needed more than 20,000 soldiers to pacify a single city? The answer was simple: the Westerling method.

Immediately after arriving in Makassar, Westerling gathered as much intelligence as possible about rebel movements. He then had his men surround a suspicious kampong in the early morning and wake all the residents. Anyone who tried to escape had something to hide and was gunned down mercilessly. The remaining villagers were herded together on a central square while the soldiers searched their houses for weapons and documents. Sometimes owning a torch or a green shirt was enough to make a person a suspect. After searching the houses, Westerling addressed the silent crowd and went through his list of suspects. Those who heard their name had to stand. Among the crowd he had informants who discreetly signalled whether or not someone was a pemuda. Village elders were also compelled to point out rebels. One after the other, the suspects were forced to squat. In front of everyone, Westerling then personally shot them in the head. If the villagers refused to name names, they would be murdered themselves, after which Westerling would randomly pick out another ten victims. In some villages he had his men form a firing squad. After the 'clean-up' he invariably appointed a new village council that had to swear there would be no more terror or support for the Republic. And finally, to drive it home, he burnt the houses in most of the villages down to the ground.

The 'Westerling method' was not an impulsive act of retribution, but a strategy deliberately designed by the captain.[40] Despite the agreements of Linggajati and Malino, what he called 'terror, chaos and danger' reigned in South Sulawesi, both politically and economically. A state of war had been declared, but no conventional forms of warfare were acceptable. 'A purely military answer to the situation would have meant making no distinction between the one per cent that needed to be eliminated and the vast majority of the population who, in fact as a result of our shortcomings, had fallen into the embrace of our real adversaries.' It came down to identifying the often young 'fanatical nationalists' who did not shrink from violence and the 'pseudo-nationalists' who only sowed terror and destruction. They alone deserved 'the death sentence and that in a spectacular fashion'. In Westerling's view, summary executions in public were 'the only possible way to pacify southern Celebes in an efficient, lasting and, above all, morally responsible manner'.[41] It was conditional on 'self-control and, above all, fire discipline on our side'. The introduction of 'summary justice' was 'essential' to regaining the trust of the people and something 'the Oriental mentality' would certainly appreciate. He considered his method 'a combination of being hard but fair, alongside humane and flexible actions'.[42]

This simple logic was totally unsound. Where to begin? With the number of active pemuda possibly being higher than one per cent? With the flimsy evidence of their 'guilt' or the extreme vagueness of the notion of 'summary' justice? His lack of a mandate to that end? His having crowned himself as a military magistrate or, more than that, acting as judge and executioner in one? With the possibility that the 'Oriental mentality' might be more complex than he could fathom after one and a half years in Indonesia? Or that pacifying a territory is not the same as traumatising the population? All these aspects simply escaped Captain Westerling. And that's before we begin to discuss his much vaunted 'self-control' and 'fire discipline'. Westerling thought he was operating in the style of a modern commando – he had done his training in Scotland – but his methods were no different from the way Governor-General J. B. van Heutsz had pacified Aceh around 1900: with brute theatrical violence that was not just imposed, but was meant to be seen and talked about. Also no different was the reaction of those responsible at the highest level: Lieutenant Governor-General Van Mook, Commander-in-Chief Spoor and Attorney General Felderhof knew very well that Westerling and his troops were acting illegally, but they let him carry on because he achieved such tremendous results, just like J. P. Coen around 1620. The attorney general, the highest legal authority, glossed over Westerling's behaviour as 'military action based on emergency powers'.[43] Worse still, in late January 1947, other officers were given permission to resort to this 'emergency summary justice'.[44]

During the first action on 11 December 1946, forty-four people were killed in a village east of Makassar. Two days later: eighty-one dead in a village further south. Another two days later, Westerling and his gang moved on the village of Kalukuang, home to Puling Daeng Rannu, the woman who had stolen her husband's pistol. She remembered it as if it were yesterday. 'It was five in the morning. "Get up! Get up!" I was married, but hadn't had any children yet. I worked as a nurse in a hospital, but was already a pemuda. There were a lot of thieves and marauders then too, but they were not real pemuda. We were all very scared. All those soldiers and their guns! And their camouflaged faces! We all had to go to a field. They shot over our heads to force us to sit down. We sat in the sun; we had to pull up our knees. There were a lot of people! From all kinds of neighbourhoods! Our house was searched. Afterwards it turned out that the Ambonese had stolen all my jewels. Westerling was a hand-some man of about thirty. He had a high nose and wavy hair. He didn't know I was a pemuda, otherwise I would have definitely been killed, even though I hadn't done anything wrong. I hadn't murdered anyone. They asked where this or that person was. If you didn't know, they shot you dead. If you said, "I know the person you're looking for," they stopped shooting. The bodies were carried off on two bamboos with a sarong stretched between them.' More than eighty people were killed that day according to official reports. 'The first one shot was Regge, a cousin of mine. I was sitting three metres away from him. They shot him six times. In his right foot, his left foot, his right knee, his left knee, the right side of his chest, the left side of his chest.' Fire discipline in practice. 'It was Westerling himself who shot him. He didn't say anything. He drank a soft drink, threw the bottle in the air and shot it.'[45] So this was the new equality promised by Linggajati? A young Dutch captain who riddles your cousin with bullets, then plays the cowboy. For almost three months, Westerling and his troops sowed terror in all of South Sulawesi. Sometimes he made two suspects wrestle with each other: the loser was shot. 'My father was a victim,' related Sitti Saerah of Bajeng, south of Makassar. She was eleven and stayed home that day to look after her sick grandmother. The rest of the family was forced to go and watch. 'Relatives carried his body home in a sarong. They shot him twice, once in the forehead and once in the left of his chest. My mother saw it happen at the market. The KNIL left his body lying there. The other victims were all related to me too, eight in total. After my father's death we only just scraped by. We moved to my grandfather's house. My mother had five children and made clothes so she could send us to school.'[46]

But things could always get worse. Westerling's right-hand man, Sublieutenant Jan Vermeulen, and two KNIL officers, Major Jan Stufkens and Captain Berthold Rijborz, headed north where they intensified the 'Westerling method' to a grim new level. Lists of suspects were abandoned, interrogations superfluous. If no rebels could be caught – many had long since fled to the interior – they simply emptied the local prison. Pick them up, shoot them and, above all, make sure it was seen. Abubakar Lambogo, a rebel leader who was returning from a military conference, was not only killed but also beheaded, after which his head was put on public display. 'Every week we went to Enrekang on market day. When we were there we saw Abubakar Lambogo's head impaled on a post at the entrance to the market. I only looked for a second, but recognised him immediately. He used to visit us at home sometimes. There were a lot of people standing around the head, which was guarded by KNIL soldiers.[47] Another eyewitness knew exactly what the intention was. 'The Dutch did this deliberately to scare the people of Enrekang and surroundings, who no longer dared leave home. There were some dark-skinned KNIL soldiers there. Ambonese, I suspect. Their captain was called Blume, but I didn't see him. One of them said, "Here is your hero!" I swear on my faith that the Dutch army did this.[48] In September 2020 the Dutch state awarded the son of the beheaded Lambogo damages of 874.80 euros. The son refused to accept this absurdly low amount.[49]

The Westerling method had an enormous impact. Young Sergeant-Major Bachtiar experienced it first-hand. 'In the beginning it was easy to get food and logistical support. Everyone cooperated! But because of Westerling's massacres and fire-raising, many people had to move. They were asked to leave the forest and live close to the road. The villages were empty. We lived in the forest under the trees and ate leaves.' Reinforcements from Java? Requesting them wasn't easy either. 'I had to find a prahu, but nobody wanted to help us any more. The people were scared to death.'[50]

Westerling's troops acted like death squads that had to answer terror with terror – conveniently forgetting that the earlier unrest had been stoked just as much by the KNIL as the pemuda.[51] Sixteen-year-old Arifin was not a pemuda but fled anyway. 'I walked almost 300 kilometres to a friend's in Palopo, where there was no fighting. Many people fled. If the Dutch had caught me they would have said that I was a fighter and killed me. Some of my friends were murdered like that.'[52] Between 3,500 and 6,500 people were killed in the operations in South Sulawesi, with Westerling stating that he accounted for 563 of those personally.[53] Despite several highly incriminating reports, neither he nor the officers Vermeulen, Stufkens and Rijborz were brought to trial – if they had, the entire colonial leadership in Jakarta would have been implicated. The enthralled swimmers of

Doorwerth could carry on listening to his dramatic stories. It was
not until March 2015 that the court in The Hague held the Netherlands responsible for the bloodbaths in South Sulawesi and ordered
the payment of damages to the victims' widows and children.

It was four in the morning when the car dropped me off in front of
the bamboo house. Hours earlier we had left Makassar after a long
delay, and now I was finally alone, in a deathly silent coastal village
called Pambusuang. The sea wasn't even murmuring, it was whispering. I glanced at the parts of a traditional sailing boat lying in front of
the house – a boom, a mast, a hull – which matched the description
I'd been given. A sleepy Iwan opened the door barefoot and in a sarong. He had a goatee and wore his hair in a bun. He led me past piles
of books and magazines, pointed to a mat on the floor and climbed
back into his hammock. We'd talk tomorrow.

Iwan – real name Muhammad Ridwan Alimuddin – was a young
sailor, boat-builder and local historian. He turned out to have the
best book collection for miles around, and liked to share his library
with others. High-school and university students came by to read
and learn. In his traditional sailing boat he sailed to remote regions
with crates full of books, an initiative he jokingly called the book
armada. This was Mandar Regency in the southwest of Sulawesi. In
February 1947 a small force led by Vermeulen, Stufkens and Rijborz
reached this place, 300 kilometres north of Makassar. What ensued
was more than an offshoot of the bloody spectacles in the south. This
was where the greatest slaughter of all took place.

Iwan started his motorbike and we rode to Galung Lombok, the
scene of the massacre. *Galung* means rice field in the local language.
Lombok is the name of the nearby village. The site was slightly
inland, not far from the first mountains. 'This used to be all rice
fields,' he said after turning off the engine. 'There were no trees. It
happened on 1 February, just after the harvest. The Dutch picked up
prisoners from the jail in Majene, a town four kilometres away, and
brought them here. The residents of ten villages in the surroundings
had to come and watch.' He sketched a map in my notebook: Lawarang, Tinambung, Lekopadis, Kandeapi, Baruga, Tadolo, Tande . . .

These people too needed a lesson in loyalty. The villagers were forced to squat and watch as several dozen prisoners and suspects were executed one after the other. Afterwards Vermeulen asked who the other troublemakers were. When the villagers said they didn't know anyone who was guilty, he picked a few men out of the crowd at random and had them executed. 'But then the news came that three soldiers had been killed in their vehicle in a nearby village,' Iwan said. 'In response the Dutch shot the residents of that village who were present here.' What the Dutch history books call a '*vuurpaniek*' broke out, a 'firing panic'. This is a euphemism: the unarmed villagers were mowed down. At least 364 were killed, among them Iwan's grandfather's brother. Iwan had heard an interesting hypothesis about the direct cause of the massacre. 'The story goes that the Dutch had harassed some local girls. In Mandar culture, if you have sex with a girl without the family's permission, the family gets furious, even if the girl wanted it herself. Even now people still get stabbed to death for that.'[54] Recent research indicates that the Dutch really did commit sexual assault during their operations in South Sulawesi.[55]

We walked through the grass to a monument with the names of the victims. A peculiar silence hung over the site; no sound but the rustling of grass. 'That's where Kama Patta is buried. That's my great-uncle.' Further back are the semi-decayed remnants of the cemetery. I counted 153 nameless wooden planks and crooked, subsiding tombstones. Iwan and I decided to comb the area on his motorbike to gather the last testimonies. 'I wasn't there myself,' said Yusuf Rambe, who lived close by, 'but my cousin and uncle were murdered here.'[56] 'Yes, and my mother's first husband too,' added his wife Isa.[57] We rode criss-cross through the silent landscape, past extensive rice fields and through cool riverside forests. In the shade of an enormous mango tree we saw a very old woman lying on a bamboo chair. Her name was Hafsah. 'My uncle and brother were murdered that day. They were ordinary citizens. I didn't see it. I had fled into the mountains and forest. That was rebel territory.' That confirmed the proposition that the resistance had not been defeated, but at most driven off.[58] 'I slept there in a cave for a week. My other uncle helped bury the bodies. He told us what had happened.'[59] 'My father came home at midnight,' said Abdul Samad Bonang. 'He had helped to bury the bodies. They didn't have any tools and couldn't dig deep graves. The bodies were half buried and half covered. Three months later the dogs were still coming to feed off them.'[60]

Maemunah was the first eyewitness we found. She lived close by and had experienced the events from early in the morning. 'It took a long time before all those people were gathered. The men were separated from the women and children. Eight houses were set on fire. In the morning there were executions with a pistol. I saw a Dutchman with a sharp nose. The prisoners were sitting in a row. In the afternoon they opened fire at random with the Bren gun. I didn't see who was shooting, I only heard the screams. Some of the soldiers shouted, "Lie down! Lie down!" I lay down on the ground and survived.'[61] In the village of Lekopadis we found someone else who had been there herself. Like many of the men and women in that rural region, Umi didn't know the year of her birth and didn't have a family name, but her memory was intact. 'My mother carried me to Galung Lombok on her arm. I could already walk. My father was killed there. I didn't see how. Women and children were standing apart. My mother protected me by throwing herself on top of me. I was an only child. You are the first European I have seen since.'[62]

Iwan and I went to see Haji Harun Masa, the son of a carpenter. He was ten that day. 'It was seven o'clock in the morning and I was with three friends catching crickets at the river. We'd put them in a box to make them fight each other. "*Ayo, kumpul!*" we heard. Gather! We all had to fall in line and walk to Lombok together. I walked with my parents for more than an hour. We passed a house where you could get your hair cut. Some of the people there didn't want to come with us. A soldier, I think he was Ambonese, immediately shot them dead. I cried, "They're going to shoot us all."' When he arrived, he saw the horror. 'We children had to sit apart. The prisoners from Majene were brought by truck and then executed one by one. There were no interrogations or anything. They were "fighters". They were shot from one metre away. They weren't blindfolded. Their bodies were stacked like pillows.' Now Vermeulen went in search of other rebels. 'Where are the rebels here? Who is "red-and-white" here?' But the worst was yet to come. 'At three o'clock in the afternoon a jeep full of angry Dutch soldiers drove up. The jeep stopped in front of the mosque. "Where are the people from Baruga?" The soldiers surrounded them. They were wearing red scarves. *"Bunuh semua orang Baruga!"* Kill all the inhabitants of Baruga. But we were all mixed up together. The shooting started immediately from the jeep the three Dutchmen were sitting in, but all of the soldiers were firing. The bullets were like a chain. A lot of people ran for it. I threw myself down and lay in the dirt. A lot of houses were on fire. The rice fields were burning too after the harvest. If you had a lot of wounds afterwards, they finished you off. Some of the wounded were carried home. It grew very quiet. I couldn't hear any voices any more and thought I was the only survivor. "Are you still alive? Go and start burying them then." But there were no tools. "If it's not done, I'll come back and murder you." My father said, "Go home. I have to dig." The bodies were thrown in a drinking pool for water buffalo.'[63]

The days I spent with Iwan gleaning the testimonies under a leaden sun almost seventy years after the fact were peculiarly intense. In the evening I strolled around his village: children playing in dusty alleys, fishermen keen to start up a conversation, looking out over the calm sea together.

The testimony I found most moving was that of Hamad Puag Abi, the man who had such precise memories of his village school. He was seventeen when the massacre in Galung Lombok took place. 'At eight o'clock in the morning my brother and I were making a traditional leaf roof from planks and sago palm leaves. Heavy work. I was sitting on the roof; others below were passing things up. Suddenly some Ambonese in Dutch army uniforms appeared. They had red flags around their necks and gathered everyone together. We had to go by foot from Lawarang to Galung Lombok. When we arrived there at ten, there were already quite a lot of people dead. That was the prisoners from Majene, their bodies were piled up. The Dutch said they were bandits. Anyone who was a rebel was killed. Then came the news that three Dutchmen had been killed and they started mowing us down with the machine gun.' At this point in his testimony Hamad became very emotional. He shivered and sobbed. 'I hope that my grandchildren never have to experience anything like that.' A long silence. Twisted shoulders. 'All those people from our village. Tomati, Ka Camba, Kacaputi, Pusi, Kamacamba, Kapa, Pa' Su, Naku, Nuhun, Gasa, Tepu . . . Some died less than five metres away from me.' His veins were visible on the back of his thin hands. 'Nuhun tried to run away, but a Dutchman shot him dead. I don't know who was shooting: Ambonese, Timorese, Menadonese. The Javanese said, "Lie down!" They still had hearts, the others were *mabuk*, drunk.' Alcohol, that's also possible. The KNIL soldiers were rarely Muslim. 'Even the imam of Baruga was killed. He was wearing the pilgrim's white cap and didn't want to sit down. "I am a haji," he said. Among us, someone like that is highly respected. "Liar," the soldier said, "you're not a real haji." He took his cap and put it on himself. "Now I'm a haji." He kicked the imam in the back of the knee to force him to kneel down, then shot him.'

We sipped our tea. Hamad, too, had been forced to bury the bodies. That night he didn't take the normal route home. 'We didn't dare use the bridge, we waded through the river. Afterwards I couldn't eat for three days. Even now I still remember the sound of the rifles. And the blood. Blood everywhere.' He was now almost blind, but the old images did not fade. 'I still have nightmares. I still see those pictures before me. That Saturday was the worst day of my life. You're the first European to come and interview me. I expect nothing from the Netherlands. Absolutely nothing. Only peace.'[64]

It seemed like it would never happen, but on 25 March 1947 the Linggajati Agreement was finally officially signed, four months after it was initialled. Following the lead of the Dutch parliament, the Indonesian parliament had now come round as well. Sukarno had pushed it through by expanding the parliament from 200 to 514 members, without changing the constitution to that end. First-rate political manoeuvring. The two largest parties, the Islamic Masyumi Party and the nationalist PNI resigned in fury, but farmers, workers, rebels and minorities were now represented.[65] The mood at the signing in Jakarta was different from how it had been in November, if only because both parties were approving a different text: Indonesia, the original agreement; the Netherlands, the expanded variant. The euphoria was gone. Rumours about the massacres in South Sulawesi had also reached Java.[66]

The Netherlands had in fact betrayed Linggajati from the very beginning. The new states were to be founded in consultation with the Republic, but the Netherlands did it all itself. The states were to be large and extensive, but the Netherlands suddenly came up with 'West Borneo' (because it couldn't get the rest of Kalimantan under control) and even 'West Java' (which officially belonged to the Republic). The Netherlands was supposed to reduce its military presence, but was actually increasing it. The Netherlands was to surrender its enclaves in Java, but was actually consolidating its positions. The Netherlands was to give the Republic de facto recognition, but its naval blockade was preventing trade. To his frustration, Schermerhorn saw among his compatriots no 'real willingness to find a peaceful, albeit difficult, means of resolving this matter'.[67]

The Republic too repeatedly violated the agreements: it sent military support to Borneo and Sulawesi, whereas it had no business intervening in these Malino territories. It appointed governors, raised its flag and seated numerous MPs from those territories in the Republican parliament in Yogyakarta. According to Linggajati, the Republic had to limit itself to Java and Sumatra, but it did not give up the Outer Islands. Officially it was not allowed to maintain its own foreign relations, but the contacts with India, the Philippines, Australia and Egypt were frequent and excellent. The Republic sent representatives to those countries and traded with them; and with a few planes it started a national airline company, Indonesian Airways.[68] Egypt offered Indonesia a pact of friendship and was the first country to not only recognise the Republic de facto, but also de jure: in practice and on paper.[69]

In the confusion of events, it is difficult to work out who caused exactly what, but mutual irritation was growing by the day and the fragile trust was clearly evaporating. Schermerhorn considered it 'an appalling state of affairs'. 'There is no longer any question of productive work, only waiting and standing idly by, while on both sides everything is slipping away.'[70]

In the Netherlands, mistrust of the agreement took insane forms. Former prime minister Gerbrandy, a man who had never been to the Indies, was not content with giving fiery tirades on the radio, writing letters to the queen and government and consulting with conservative Professor Carel Gerritson of Utrecht to organise mass petitions for maintaining the unity of the kingdom, but also conceived a serious plan for a coup d'état. In the Netherlands. In peacetime. In a parliamentary democracy. That seems rather revolutionary for somebody who for years had been the standard-bearer of the Anti-Revolutionary Party but, in the eyes of Gerbrandy and his cronies, it was the violation of the unity of the kingdom and the mutilation of the realm that were truly revolutionary. In such circumstances they considered violence more than justified. They gained the backing of Admiral Helfrich and General Kruls, the heads of the navy and army respectively, and in Indonesia of Major General Simon de Waal, territorial commander of the KNIL in Central Java. No less a person than resistance hero Erik Hazelhoff Roelfzema, World War II's universally acclaimed 'Soldier of Orange', played the main role in the conspiracy. The man who had helped liberate the Netherlands from fascism would now save it from parliamentary democracy. It beggared belief. After escaping to England during the war, Hazelhoff Roelfzema had built up excellent relations with Queen Wilhelmina and he sought contact with the palace now too. 'On Monday, 14 April 1947, I received a call from Hazelhoff Roelfzema in London,' wrote François van 't Sant, the queen's private secretary, to Wilhelmina. With Gerbrandy's express support, Hazelhoff Roelfzema would be arriving 'for a very important discussion'. The secretary's letter to the queen, written 'immediately after Hazelhoff's departure', was only recently discovered by historian Sytze van der Zee in one of the most spectacular finds of post-war Dutch political history.[71] A longer quote: 'He told me that the resistance groups have decided to put an end to the current government; that resistance troops drawn chiefly from the Westland will arrest all ministers and that they will be directed to a certain location; that this will take place on Thursday, 24 April 1947; that this deed, after having taken place, will be announced through bill posting, on the radio and in the newspapers; that Helfrich and Kruls have declared that they are willing, with army and navy staff, to take action for the country's peace and security; that at the same time the army in the Indies will take action under General De Waal – not under General Spoor; that De Waal is aware of everything and has already been involved in the aforementioned plan; that senior police officials are informed and will take part; that the assumption is that martial law will be declared immediately after the completion of the plan; that the protection of non-strikers has been arranged [the conspirators were counting on a general strike by the left but wanted to avoid the economy coming to a standstill]; that they hoped that the order would soon be given [by the queen] for a national coalition government with the exclusion of the communists; that Gerbrandy and Hazelhoff would play a major role in the initiative; that [former minister of the navy] Fuerstner was behind Helfrich; and that, according to Hazelhoff, the success of this plan was completely assured.'

In short, the Dutch right wing was planning a coup and requested the support of the queen. Hazelhoff Roelfzema went so far as to request an immediate answer, but of course Van 't Sant could not possibly respond to 'a communication of such boundless scope'. He forwarded the information to the queen with the words: 'Should I receive no further instructions from you, then I have *not* informed you.' The following day he sent her a second letter. He had asked Hazelhoff Roelfzema what would happen if he took action against the instigators. 'Hereupon Hazelhoff stated with great conviction and determination, "Then disaster would strike the Netherlands. The matter has already gone too far. That would mean bloodshed. If anything were to happen to the leaders of this movement, it would mean civil war."' He did not just ask for Wilhelmina's support, he *demanded* it. The Soldier of Orange's having been born to a Dutch family in Surabaya undoubtedly played a role. Towards the end of his life he acknowledged his attachment to the colonial cause and seemed to admit, in more or less veiled language, that 'many of us, blinded by sadness, lost sight of the majestic flow of events'.[72]

Wilhelmina's reaction is unknown. What is certain is that the queen found the Linggajati compromise 'very complicated' and hoped that it would not damage the national interest.[73] And she was highly sympathetic towards Gerbrandy. Several months later she even suggested to sitting prime minister Beel that it might be best if Gerbrandy formed a new government.[74] But that does not necessarily mean that she would have supported a coup. Perhaps she preferred to return him to power herself rather than see him deploy violence to take charge. In any case, on 24 April 1947, the day of the planned coup, two armed men spent hours driving up and down the Benoordenhoutseweg in The Hague waiting for Koos Vorrink, founder and chairman of the PvdA, to come home. The organisers of the coup were insistent that the exceptionally gifted orator from the hated government party, responsible for forcing Linggajati through parliament, would be the first to be killed. That would be the signal to arrest all ministers and install a new regime. The plans had been devised together with Gerbrandy. Arrests would also take place in Jakarta and Surabaya. News that the day's plans had been cancelled because the military intelligence services had been informed (by the palace) had not reached the two assassins. Vorrink stayed in Amsterdam that night. Unable to accomplish their mission, the two men proceeded to Gerbrandy's office in The Hague to tell him that they had failed in their attempt to murder the socialist Vorrink. Gerbrandy informed them in turn that the whole thing had been called off, but concluded nonetheless with the words, 'The Fatherland will be grateful to you.'[75]

Linggajati had been signed but the negotiations about what would come next could not drag on forever. For the Netherlands, a large overseas military force was essential to maintaining pressure, but also tremendously expensive. In 1947 the Netherlands was impoverished. The country was in ruins, the economy disrupted, Marshall aid not yet a topic of discussion (it only began in 1948). What's more, it was the coldest winter since 1789. Inland shipping was impossible for weeks; hundreds of coal barges were stuck in the ice. Villages were cut off from the outside world by snowstorms. On the coast, the

North Sea froze and in the Wadden Sea, the ice piled up six metres high. Finance Minister Piet Lieftinck, a thoroughly earnest man who as the conscientious bookkeeper of the post-war Netherlands had already been nicknamed 'Pete Panic', wrote a long, 'highly serious' letter with a simple message to Prime Minister Beel: the money has run out. 'The foreign currency position of the Netherlands and the Netherlands Indies' was in such an alarming state that 'the Dutch economy was facing a highly serious reversal'. In his view, the border 'had not only been reached but already crossed'. The military and civilian requirements in Indonesia were costing the Netherlands more than three million guilders a day. The available foreign currency and gold supplies would be exhausted by the end of June and not in autumn, as had been previously calculated. Not only was the Netherlands Indies as good as bankrupt, the Netherlands itself was 'on the edge of the abyss'. He considered further military spending 'completely irresponsible'. 'We are facing a hard fact here, and our desires and emotions are colliding with it.' The government could consider applying for a substantial dollar loan in the US, but then the Netherlands Indies would need to be more or less stable – otherwise America would consider repayment impossible. It was striking that Lieftinck – who had studied in the US – looked to the Americans for a solution rather than the British.[76]

Several days later, his alarming letter was discussed at length by the Council for Military Affairs. A general gnashing of teeth. The Netherlands was finally able to take some initiative in the Indies, it had finally managed to mobilise an army – at great effort – and now the coffers turned out to be empty. Minister of War Alexander Fiévez observed drily that there were three options for lowering military expenditure: unilaterally reducing their military forces, agreeing to a mutual reduction in military forces *or* delivering a powerful military blow to reconquer the old plantation areas and recommence exporting. The first was the fastest and cheapest, but meant 'abandoning our interests and that is something I would never countenance'. The second was also cheap, but required immediate collaboration with the Republicans – which was 'far from preferable'. That left one thing, the military option. More expensive and riskier, but it could raise a large amount. Estimates assumed a cost of 200 million guilders compared to an expected return on the investment of 300 million.[77] This appealed to Minister of the Navy Jules Schagen van Leeuwen's sense of the situation. 'I do not trust the natives at all. [. . .] The natives keep us talking, realising that we are running out of time.' He condemned 'the Republic's treacherous attitude', was making plans for 'the elimination of warlords and their gangs' and believed that there was no room for any further procrastination. Prime Minister Beel concluded that from now on they needed to follow 'a rigid political course based on our interpretation' of the Linggajati Agreement, and do so 'without delay'.[78] Beel became a hard-liner.

Lieftinck's letter changed everything. The amicable rapprochement between Kingdom and Republic – something Dutch historian Loe de Jong described superbly as 'an attempt to win trust by giving it' – was supplanted by a much harsher attitude.[79] The financial weakness of the Netherlands led it to act tough politically. It was a questionable decision. Like all previous Dutch governments, this one too was composed solely of men, but it seems as if the war had created an ideal of heightened virility and indomitability. As if the key to participating in international politics was imitating Churchill's inflexibility. As if every opponent was automatically an enemy. The money was exhausted and so was their patience. This firmed their resolve. But their great economic vulnerability could also have led them to policies of humility, consultation and generosity. That course was rejected.

At the start of May, Prime Minister Beel and Minister of Overseas Territories Jonkman went to Indonesia themselves to demonstrate how serious they were. It was the very first time that the leader of a Dutch government had visited the colony while in office. Schermerhorn's reflections on what he heard from the two ministers were scornful. 'When they say the Netherlands wants to implement Linggajati faithfully and generously, I take the liberty of denying it. The entire Dutch community here, with only a few exceptions, is simply incapable of doing so. Events in Makassar have demonstrated that.'[80] After the ministerial visit, an ultimatum was delivered to the

Republic on 27 May 1947 summing up the Dutch conditions for the transitional period that would end at the earliest on 1 January 1949: officially the Netherlands remained the sovereign power; the Republic would rule over Java and Sumatra in practice, but had to open its borders (allowing Dutch proprietors safe access to their plantations); the administration would be placed in the hands of an interim government led by a representative of the Crown (which sounded like a new governor-general). The Dutch and Republican armies had to pursue 'police collaboration' and merge into a single gendarmerie (which sounded like the Republic disbanding its forces and relinquishing its territory). The Republic also had to withdraw from the Outer Islands and give up foreign relations (which sounded like going back to zero). Historian Herman Burgers described the proposals aptly. 'They seemed more like a form of "limited recolonisation" than "limited decolonisation".'[81]

The Republic was given two weeks to respond. Meanwhile the Dutch cabinet agreed that military action should not be excluded in case of an 'unsatisfactory reply'. Minister for Social Services Drees, who would become prime minister a year later, stated: 'After all, the Dutch troops have been sent to the Indies for a reason.'[82] On 7 June the Republic, still represented by Prime Minister Sjahrir, proved willing to go along with quite a few of the proposals, but the tone of his reply was reproachful and discontented. How could it be otherwise? Specifically he agreed to the planned transitional government and to open up economically, but not to the merged gendarmerie or the suspension of the Republic's diplomatic activities. On 19 June, under threat of war, he even agreed to Dutch sovereignty during the transitional period and the return of a representative of the Crown. These radical concessions caused such dismay in the Republican camp – among the military command, the nationalist and Islamic parties, and even within his own party – that his government fell and his prime ministership ended. Sjahrir's political career was as good as dead. By constantly increasing its demands, the Netherlands had lost the most important bridge-builder on the Republican side.

The Netherlands' extreme demands had not been met. For large segments of the home front, the Beel government had been shown up. 'Option three', military force, was gradually growing inevitable. If you flex your muscles, you have to be willing to use them too. Even moderate figures such as Schermerhorn and Van Mook were increasingly trapped in the logic of violence. Was there any point to further negotiations? Lieutenant Governor-General Van Mook became so disgruntled that, at the request of the Beel government, he prepared a modest military attack for 30 June – not to destroy the Republic but to give it a hard rap on the knuckles. A few days before-hand a *deus ex machina* in the form of US Consul General Walter A. Foote intervened: if the Dutch and Republican governments cooperated, the State Department was willing to make a large sum of money available to assist in Indonesia's reconstruction. But even that didn't help. In July things derailed completely. Van Mook wrote dir-ectly to Sukarno with five minimum demands: concede to Dutch sovereignty during the transitional period; allow the businesses to return; participate in the federal administrative body; end your own diplomatic activities; and accept the mixed gendarmerie. Sukarno agreed to everything except that last point: the Republic had been able to establish itself thanks to its shock troops, its bamboo spears and its Japanese weapons. What makes a state a state is its monopoly on violence; dismantling that capability meant dismantling all polit-ical claims. The Republic would just become another province. More sighs from Van Mook. The alternative was the cessation of all hostili-ties, and the withdrawal of Republican troops within five days to ten kilometres behind the demarcation lines. Abandon the military pos-itions and expose the troops in the open field? Out of the question, said Sukarno, that was tantamount to a unilateral abandonment of all military positions. Westerling could murder to his heart's content, but the Republic wasn't even allowed to man its borders. Sjahrir had wanted to avoid war at all cost, but Sukarno gambled that a Dutch offensive would be frowned upon internationally and could give the Republic an advantage. Cynical, but it was what it was. Van Mook had little choice but to declare the Linggajati Agreement invalid on 17 July 1947: the Netherlands was no longer bound by its stipulations. Three days later the Dutch launched the offensive they called the First Police Action.

The 'Dutch year' had begun hopefully in November 1946 but the position taken by parliament, Westerling's misconduct, the administration's acceptance of it, Van Mook's one-sided approach and the cabinet's aggressive tone reduced the scope for calm and respectful talks until violence seemed the only solution. Even the queen agreed. On the eve of the offensive she wrote to her daughter Juliana: 'Things have gone wrong in the Indies. Even I have no objection to a police action (use of troops to establish *peace* and *order*; this, of course, is still *secret*). Instead of accepting our further details, namely the elaboration of the reached agreement in principle, they advanced a new proposal which really was unacceptable.' The ongoing Dutch violence, both military and mental, that had begun six months earlier, seemed to have eluded her.

And the fact that Dutch actions had forced the exit of the most reasonable Republican negotiator was accepted as part of the bargain. 'My father was actually more an educator than a politician. Perhaps he wasn't cut out for politics. Writing suited him more,' said Upik Sjahrir, Sutan Sjahrir's youngest daughter, in her light, spacious living room in Jakarta. 'He was a humanist who devoted himself to justice and equality. Papa always told us, "Live without mistrust or hate." He could roar with laughter, but also get angry. He was very expressive. I am still very grateful to him, but why was my time with him so short? He died when I was six . . .' Tears welled up in her eyes. 'He believed in duty and responsibility. He could get on well with the Dutch, but he didn't like colonialism. His ideas, his values, his struggle, his way of living are rarely included in the history books. But his political diplomacy was crucial to ensuring international recognition of Indonesia as a free and sovereign country.'

In later years his prominent role was suppressed by Sukarno and Suharto. Nowadays there are millions of banknotes in circulation in Indonesia with portraits of Sukarno and Hatta, but Sjahrir doesn't adorn anything. Jakarta's international airport is called 'Soekarno-Hatta', regional airports were given the names of regional freedom fighters, but only half an avenue and a chocolate shop in Jakarta have been named after Sjahrir. Upik had to laugh. 'Even if he is hardly known, we don't want a Sjahrir cult. It's not about a statue or a monument, it's about his values: cooperation, honesty, freedom, equality – between men and women too.' She herself did not go into politics. She became the director of a nursery school. 'I help my country by making better children! Children who can appreciate diversity. At our school we celebrate Chinese New Year, Christmas and Eid.'

Upik looked at a black-and-white photo of her father and gave a melancholy smile. She went upstairs and returned soon after with a small box. Silently she put it on a chair and carefully raised the lid. Suddenly it was lying there – serene, tranquil and awkwardly intimate – Sutan Sjahrir's death mask. He died at fifty-seven. 'After his second stroke, he couldn't talk any more. He was still a political prisoner and Sukarno wouldn't let him go to the Netherlands for treatment.' Neutral Switzerland was chosen instead. Sjahrir was treated in a hospital in Zurich. Upik visited him there. 'There was classical music playing in his room and he was crying. "Why is he crying?" I asked my mother.' We looked at the death mask. 'My mother answered, "They are tears of joy." '[83]

Chapter 13

'Unacceptable, Unpalatable and Unfair'
The American year, August 1947–December 1948

'The First Police Action? That was more *funfair* than *warfare*!' It still brings a grin to Goderd van Heek's face. At first he was going to be dispatched to turbulent Sulawesi, but in the end he was sent to the relative calm of Jakarta. 'And I wasn't much of a city boy . . .' Fortunately he came into contact with a few Marvas, the 'motivated, pleasant young ladies' of the Dutch navy. Nothing wild, he said, but in general he had a very relaxed time during the offensive. 'We could do all kinds of entertaining things.'[1]

He was no exception. Dick Buchel van Steenbergen, the man who had survived the atomic bomb on Nagasaki, saw action in Sumatra in the area around Medan. 'I volunteered so that I could experience something exciting. Just to be part of it. Not that I saw much combat. I became a driver for the radio service that maintained contact with the planes. We returned to base every night.'[2]

'I never knew I took part in it,' said Bol Kerrebijn, who was a KNIL military policeman. 'I had to cut the lines to explosives under the road to Tangerang. Afterwards the troops used the road. That was my First Police Action; I'd never heard of it.'[3]

The First Police Action, really the First Dutch Offensive, was the tragic low of the short Dutch year that began with the British departure in late November 1946. After months of fruitless negotiations, the Dutch felt they had no other option than to take a hard line. From an armyless country that could only look on impotently as the Japanese, British and Indonesians manhandled its former colony, the Netherlands had grown once again into the region's most powerful player. The military offensive was meant to prove this to all concerned, and commander-in-chief Spoor considered American involvement 'particularly undesirable'.[4]

The amassed forces were definitely impressive. In July 1947 the Netherlands had some 100,000 troops at its disposal: 52,000 men of the KNIL, 41,000 of the Dutch Royal Army, 5,000 with the navy and 3,500 in the KNIL air force. 75,000 of these were stationed in Java and 21,000 in Sumatra. The Republican numbers were also formidable: approximately 195,000 soldiers in Java and Sumatra, alongside 168,000 irregular troops, supplemented by a few hundred Japanese and British Indian deserters.[5] 'Men with turbans,' Dick said, 'they were the snipers!' The regular army was now called TNI (Tentara Nasional Indonesia, the Indonesian National Army). Dutch intelligence knew better than to fixate on these astronomic numbers. The TNI hardly had any tanks, jeeps or trucks. The navy? A few small freighters. Air force? Ten or so Japanese hand-me-downs. Firepower? Approximately one firearm for every three soldiers.[6]

On 20 July 1947, at 11 p.m., Lieutenant Governor-General Huib van Mook, acting on the instructions of the Beel government in the Netherlands, gave the starting shot. General Simon Spoor, the commander-in-chief, who had been fine-tuning his plans of attack for months, immediately rounded up the Republican leaders who were still in Jakarta. Sukarno's famous house – where the Proklamasi had been made, where Linggajati had been officially initialled and where the Republican headquarters were located – was occupied. Public services that had been in Republican hands for almost two years – the post office, radio, telephone and telegraph – were also taken over with little difficulty. 'I had to go and occupy Radio Republik near Koningsplein,' Van Heek related. 'Well, I managed without firing a single shot.'[7] Had he gone through that difficult officer training in England for this? But, of course, it wasn't only about Jakarta. General Spoor had settled on a spearhead strategy: motorised columns set out for the interior from all of the Dutch enclaves in Java and Sumatra simultaneously, with the goal of penetrating deep into hostile territory. The tens of thousands of troops that had been stuck for one and a half years in Indonesia's hot and humid port cities were finally allowed to enter the cooler interiors of Java and Sumatra. Each column was made up of tanks and armoured cars, followed by the artillery's gun carriages and the infantry's trucks and jeeps, with the supply trucks bringing up the rear. Some columns encountered quite a lot of resistance from Republican positions while leaving the enclaves, but once the demarcation line had been passed, the roads wound through the landscape, the morning sun shone, and everything remained conspicuously quiet. Rural women appeared here and there with baskets of fruit, a gesture that was immediately taken as proof of their unwavering loyalty to Dutch rule, forgetting that Japanese soldiers, the crews of German U-boats and even Westerling's death squads had also been treated to kilos of mangos and papayas. A submissive smile could mask fear just as easily as indicate gratitude.

'Comrades-in-arms!' said the marching orders General Spoor had given his men, 'you are advancing not to bring war to this country, but to return it to peace. You will be coming not as conquerors, but as liberators.' In villages and homes the troops had to behave correctly. 'Ordinary politeness towards even the simplest of Javanese peasants, will achieve targets that bullets cannot.'[8] The silent, bitter and hostile glances the columns attracted further inland were attributed to the pernicious influence of a handful of hotheads in Yogyakarta. Everyone supports us, too bad about the few rotten apples; in 1947 the Dutch saw things just as they had in 1927. They simply refused to grasp the collective nature of the Revolusi. What's more, resistance was rare and easily overcome. Taken by surprise, the Republican soldiers had no time to apply scorched-earth tactics. Yes, some bridges were mined and roads blocked, but the Dutch troops advanced too quickly to allow thorough sabotage. The engineering corps quickly repaired any damage. The Dutch army rolled over the Republic of Indonesia just as the Japanese army had rolled over the Dutch East Indies: with astonishing ease. Its tactical, technological and ballistic advantages were patently obvious, its co-ordination of air, sea and land forces superior. And the logistic achievement of continuing to supply all those rapidly advancing columns with fuel, ammunition, medical assistance and food was considerable. Entire bakeries and slaughterhouses advanced with the troops.[9] Supplies

Map 23: First Dutch offensive in Java (20 July–4 August 1947)

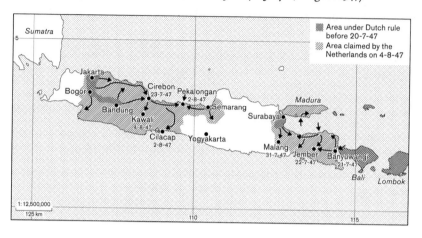

Map 24: First Dutch offensive in Sumatra (20 July–4 August 1947)

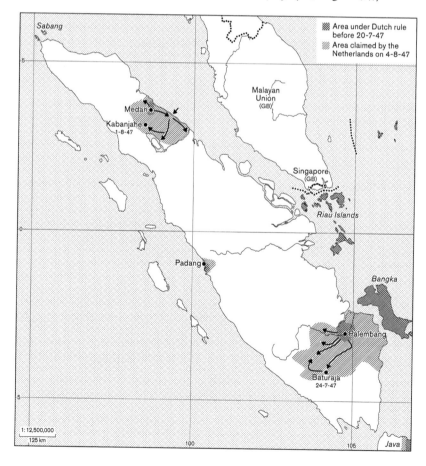

were airdropped to units that were hard to reach. To treat 'the boys' to fresh chops, live pigs were even parachuted in.[10]

Within a few days the Dutch troops had seized a very extensive territory. From the city of Medan in Sumatra, they had occupied the entire surrounding area of Deli, the region of tobacco and rubber plantations. From Palembang they seized the nearby oil wells, coal mines and production areas. But the greatest territorial expansion took place in Java: starting from the axis Jakarta–Bogor–Bandung virtually all of West Java and a substantial part of Central Java was seized. In one blow, the ports of Cirebon in the north and Cilacap in the south were Dutch again and the isolated enclave of Semarang had been linked to the Jakarta zone. In East Java they proceeded south from Surabaya to Malang, and from there to the eastern salient, the so-called Oosthoek, an area they were able to conquer rapidly thanks to attacks by the navy. On the eve of the campaign, the Dutch controlled a territory of more than 9,000 square kilometres split up over six urban enclaves (Medan, Padang, Palembang, Jakarta, Semarang and Surabaya). They had now increased this by a factor of fifteen and ruled over 143,000 square kilometres: three and a half times the size of the Netherlands.

But it was not just about land area, more important was *what* they had captured. In this regard the codename for the First Police Action was very much to the point: 'Operation Product'. Seldom has an offensive been given a more honest name. Three-quarters of colonial production had been brought back under Dutch control:[11] in Sumatra, for instance, fifty-six per cent of the palm oil, sixty-one per cent of the rubber acreage, sixty-seven per cent of the tea-growing area and eighty-four per cent of the fibre production. In Java these figures were even more substantial: fifty-nine per cent of the coffee, seventy per cent of the rubber, eighty-six per cent of the cacao, ninety-one per cent of the cinchona and ninety-two per cent of the tea.[12] The entrepreneurs could get back to work. Minister of Finance Lieftinck could relax: this war would raise more than it cost. For the time being the bankruptcy of the Netherlands and its overseas territories had been averted.

★

It was an enormous blow to the Republic. Not only had it lost the most important economic zones, its population had also been reduced to thirty of its original sixty million.[13] Did this mean that everyone in the occupied territories immediately surrendered? Far from it. The Dutch army had been able to penetrate deep into Republican territory, but only by sticking to the main roads. The TNI troops withdrew into the mountains, the sawah, the forests. 'For three days we marched south through the mountains,' related Sukotjo Tjokroatmodjo. As a platoon commander, he had tried to stop the Dutch advance at the strategic bridge over the Porong River, but failed. 'The Dutch troops had automatic and semi-automatic weapons, Brownings and Bren guns, while we still had rifles from World War I. And their planes strafed us from the air.' He lost one cadet, a boy who had borrowed his binoculars for a moment. Then he withdrew south with his men, 'parallel to the main road the Dutch tanks were driving on'. When the Dutch reached the city of Malang at the end of July, he stayed in the mountains with his platoon searching for the best way of making life difficult for the Dutch in Malang. His experience was symptomatic of a greater process: regular warfare gave way to guerrilla tactics. If the TNI was incapable of launching a major counteroffensive, it could still harass the enemy.

Maps that represent the First Police Action as an immediate expansion of the area under Dutch control are misleading: drawing a new line was not the same as colouring in a new area. At the very least that area should be hatched to show that Republican elements were far from eliminated. More than that, the Dutch army gave fragmented units like Sukotjo's ample opportunity to regroup and reorganise. Spoor did not distribute his troops evenly across the newly acquired territory, but concentrated them strategically on the new border in the hope of soon being able to push on to Yogyakarta. Platoon commander Sukotjo took advantage of the situation. 'I moved my troops to a rubber plantation southeast of Malang. From there I could see Malang.'[14]

Pushing on to Yogya was the dream of many in Jakarta. For the military command it was a foregone conclusion. '*Ceterum censeo Djocjakartum esse delendam*,' Spoor wrote to army's supreme commander in the Netherlands: 'Furthermore, I consider that Yogyakarta must be destroyed.'[15] Accordingly he called his second plan of attack 'Cato', after the Roman orator who wanted to raze Carthage – another highly revealing code name. As long as Yogyakarta stood, Sukarno and his ilk would continue to spout propaganda, Sudirman and Bung Tomo would continue to encourage the troops in the occupied territories and Central Java would remain a base of operations for Republican attacks in East and West Java. But the civilian leaders – Van Mook, Van Poll and even Schermerhorn – had also come to the conclusion that the military campaign could not be stopped here, but had to be allowed to culminate in smoking out Yogyakarta, which the otherwise so tactful Schermerhorn called the 'nest of intellectual infestation'.[16] Everyone in Jakarta agreed, but Jakarta still had to obey The Hague.

The First Police Action was a political compromise on the part of the Beel government: the Catholics got the forceful action they had been demanding for so long and the socialists were willing to go along with it as long as the Republic itself wasn't overthrown, something their supporters would never endorse. Even this limited campaign had attracted heavy criticism: 7,000 members of the PvdA left the party. For the socialists, pushing on to force Yogyakarta to its knees would have been nothing less than political suicide. But in Jakarta, Van Mook was so tired of the political tussling in The Hague that he threatened that, if forced, he would personally give the order to march on the heart of the Republic himself. Didn't anyone in the Netherlands understand that this half-hearted dawdling was severely damaging the country's reputation? Yes, someone understood: Queen Wilhelmina. At the start of August she made it clear to Prime Minister Beel that as far as she was concerned they could clear the 'Yogya hotbed'. In the months that followed she again indicated that she 'could not accept a solution that failed to do away with the extremists'. She was annoyed by the 'slow pace of our national character' and the 'courtship of Yogya'.[17]

The First Dutch Offensive was a massive economic success, but it failed to yield the desired political and military results: the disturbances continued and a solution was further away than ever. The hope that a hard blow would make the Republic see reason had been proven terribly naive. The Republic did not need to be compelled to see reason; it had always been fairly reasonable – Sjahrir, Hatta, Sukarno and the new prime minister Amir had bent over backwards to accommodate the Dutch, invariably in opposition to their own roaring mobs. It was the Dutch who had let themselves be whipped up to more and more unreasonable demands and increasingly hysterical ultimatums, despite the equality they had avowed so solemnly at Linggajati.

Piet van Staveren, the man who had sailed for Indonesia after Linggajati with a message of peace written on his helmet, came to the same conclusion. 'A friend of mine told me, "Yesterday they handed out maps of Indonesian territory." All of the column commanders had been given topographical maps with the route from Bandung to Cirebon marked. I knew right away: this means we're going to march in.' When he met up with Poncke Princen a little later, he said, 'I don't know how you feel about it, but military operations are coming . . .' Piet didn't say any more, not to anyone for that matter, but when he returned to his unit, his mind was made up. It was the night of 13 July, one week before the big offensive. 'We were encamped next to the demarcation line. We had positions with sandbags where we often slept. A few days earlier there had been an incident with gunfire. That night I walked to the barracks, grabbed my stuff and crossed the demarcation line. The border was a wide strip. I walked, but I couldn't see anything at all. Until I encountered a group of Indonesian soldiers on patrol. "Merdeka!" I said. That was the magic word.' It must have been a bizarre sight for those soldiers, one of those lanky Dutchmen, well over six feet tall, in uniform and greeting them with the Republican call for freedom. 'They took me to their military commander. I had a letter of introduction with me that I'd received from the Indonesia Committee in the Netherlands. That letter was invaluable! I told him, "A military campaign is coming. The Netherlands is going to attack." And they were. Just a few days later it happened. I stayed at his house for a week.'

Piet van Staveren was one of the very few Dutch soldiers who found the conflict so unjust that he went over to the other side, well aware of the risk he was running. He was sent to Yogyakarta. 'Trains were still running in the Republic at that stage. They were firing the steam engines with wood for lack of coal, so big sparks were coming out of the chimney! So big that the roof of one of the carriages caught fire! It had to be extinguished! When we finally arrived in Yogyakarta, I was immediately taken to the presidential palace. Douwes Dekker was sitting there, Multatuli's great-nephew!' Almost seventy by then, he had been a champion of independence since 1912. 'I had a conversation with him. We were going to talk again the next day, but that night the Dutch troops attacked and I was taken to a sugar plantation south of Yogyakarta.' He didn't want to take up arms again, but accepted a civilian role within the TNI. 'I became the political spokesman on Radio Gelora Pemuda, literally, "youth fervour radio". The Indonesians appreciated my participation on their side. Doesn't every nation have a right to freedom?'[18]

Piet van Staveren may have been an exception, but on the world stage he was not alone. For all that the Dutch presented their actions as maintaining internal order, the battlecruisers, combat aircraft and columns with tens of thousands of khaki-clad soldiers didn't seem very much like 'policing' in any usual sense of the word. The world looked on in astonishment at this *agresi militer Belanda*, as the Indonesians describe it, 'Dutch military aggression'. At the outbreak of the offensive, both Great Britain and the US promptly offered their 'good offices', a diplomatic way of saying they wanted to help negotiate. The Republic did not take them up on it – the disastrous results of British mediation were still too fresh in their memories – but it was striking that the US would make such a generous diplomatic offer on top of the financial support they had offered to provide at the end of June. This much more active positioning contrasted sharply with America's 'neglect' of Indonesia during the last year of the war, when the US had passed the archipelago by. What was the reasoning? Had the region suddenly become so much more important to US foreign policy? No. The Netherlands had become much more important.

In 1947 large sections of Europe had become entirely or partly communist: the communists had gained power in six Central and

Eastern European countries; in Italy and France they were on the verge of taking over the state; in Denmark, Norway, Finland, Austria and Belgium they were already represented in the government. There was a very real chance of the impoverished Netherlands also falling victim to the 'Red Menace': the communists had already gained ten per cent of the seats in parliament. Spring 1947 was the moment when the Cold War became undeniable and America really began to panic about the supposed Sovietisation of Western Europe. From a more level-headed perspective this reaction seemed exaggerated: the Soviet economy was a third the size of America's, Russia was in ruins and had lost twenty million people – compared to fewer than 300,000 in an unscathed America. What's more, it didn't have any nuclear weapons.[19] But that made no difference. According to Truman the world was divided into the camps of the free and the unfree, and 'the moment has come to place the United States at the head of the Free World'.[20] The Truman doctrine of March 1947 was expressed in the Marshall Plan of June 1947: America would pump almost $13 billion into the European economy to create what Secretary of State George Marshall called 'the political and social conditions in which free institutions can exist'.[21] Keeping the Netherlands within the US sphere of influence was very much in America's interest. Sukarno could plead on the radio during the Dutch offensive that 'just as your American ancestors fought 170 years ago for your liberty and independence, so are we Indonesians fighting for ours', and Indonesian diplomats could be as emphatic as they liked about it being '1776 in Indonesia', but when it came down to it, America pursued an unmistakably pro-Dutch course in this first phase.[22] Its having made the Philippines independent a half-year earlier was not a factor. Greater interests were now in play: preventing communism in Europe.

During the long American year, the period from August 1947 to December 1948, we see Washington feverishly tacking between its geopolitical interests in Northwest Europe and Southeast Asia. Remaining on good terms with the Netherlands without frustrating Indonesia was the task at hand. The US carried out this delicate balancing act primarily through the United Nations' involvement with the issue. As a permanent member of the Security Council, America manipulated multilateral diplomacy masterfully to protect its own, often conflicting, interests. For a long time the US saw the Netherlands as a favoured partner, but a combination of factors – above all the rapid rise of communism in Asia – brought an abrupt change. In 1947 the US was distinctly pro-Dutch, in 1948 pro-Indonesian. This dramatic about-face would prove extremely important.

Immediately after the start of hostilities, Australia and India had put the Indonesian question on the agenda of the UN Security Council. The British had given India the prospect of independence just two weeks earlier. The Council met on 31 July 1947, no longer in London, but on Long Island near New York City. According to India, the Dutch offensive in Indonesia could 'endanger' international peace (Article 34 of the UN Charter); according to Australia it was a 'breach of the peace' (Article 39). It was still unclear to what degree the Security Council's authority extended to these kinds of colonial conflicts, given that they were not really international (in the sense of involving more than one distinct state), but also not purely domestic (the Republic already had the de facto recognition of quite a few countries, including the Netherlands). Australia proposed a forceful resolution, but America watered it down and suggested that all references to the charter be scrapped.[23] It was a way of remaining noncommittal: recognising the seriousness of the situation in Indonesia while not offending the Dutch. On 1 August 1947, ten days after the start of the Dutch offensive, Resolution 27 was adopted. The text was short and decisive: both parties were called upon '(a) to cease hostilities forthwith, and (b) to settle their dispute by arbitration or by other peaceful means and keep the Security Council informed about the progress of the settlement'. This short text was a milestone in the history of post-war diplomacy: for the first time the UN called for a ceasefire and gained jurisdiction over an ongoing conflict.[24] In the coming years the Indonesian question would remain at the top of the UN agenda. No fewer than seventy-two Security Council meetings were dedicated to it between 1947 and 1949, resulting in fourteen resolutions. The UN played a decisive role in the Indonesian question, just as the question was decisive in shaping the still young UN.

Always having to defer to The Hague was extremely aggravating for Jakarta, but in the new world order The Hague could not ignore New York either. And when New York spoke, Washington could be heard in the background. The devil-may-care days were over. Even guzzling champagne with a British lord would no longer help. Colonial issues had become world politics. Having an international resolution against you passed by the world's newest and most-elevated security organ? The first-ever UN call for a cease-fire? The Netherlands was not pleased. If it had been up to Queen Wilhelmina, the country would have withdrawn from the UN.[25] But the government realised its international credibility was on the line. On 4 August, with its tail between its legs, it announced a ceasefire.

In late August, the Security Council voted on two new resolutions. Resolution 30 stipulated that the fragile ceasefire would be monitored by the consuls of the countries seated on the Security Council. Resolution 31 stated that the Security Council offered its 'good offices' – that term again – to settle the dispute peacefully. This proposal came from the Americans. Instead of having the question decided by international arbitration (which could have been very disadvantageous for the Netherlands), the US proposed settling the dispute amicably like adults. No strict verdict by an independent court, but restrained mediation in-country. To this end, a three-member 'Committee of Good Offices' was to be formed: both the Netherlands and Indonesia were allowed to allocate a country that was a Security Council member, and those two countries would ask a third. Alongside the five fixed members (the USA, the USSR, China, France and the UK) the Security Council of summer 1947 was made up of Australia, Belgium, Brazil, Colombia, Poland and Syria. The Netherlands could have asked the mighty UK, but as the British year had been far from a display of unconditional loyalty, the Dutch opted for their neighbour, Belgium – puny, but very understanding when it came to colonial affairs. The Belgians had just helped to found the Benelux; they voted consistently for the Netherlands on the Security Council; and they had Congo. They knew what it was like for a small country to have a large colony in a world with new, major players that didn't.

Indonesia, in turn, had been charmed by the way Poland had defended its interests in the Security Council, but understood that, in 1947, that choice could be problematic for the US. Instead it chose Australia, a country that had supported the Netherlands during the war, but had since become pro-Republican under a Labor government. And who did Belgium and Australia choose as the third country on the Committee of Good Offices? The US, of course, which thus gained the central role in negotiating the Indonesian question. What couldn't be arranged bilaterally had been achieved multilaterally. Truman could be content.

At the same time the Committee of Good Offices was a first in the history of the UN Security Council. The high standing of its members increased its prestige. The Belgian representative was former prime minister Paul Van Zeeland, a Catholic politician who had led two governments in the 1930s. Australia nominated Judge Richard C. Kirby of the Commonwealth Court of Conciliation and Arbitration, an expert on social issues with a decidedly progressive profile. America appointed the historian Frank P. Graham, president of the University of North Carolina and a champion of disarmament, economic justice and civil rights. In Belgium, Van Zeeland had opposed the fascism of the Walloon agitator Léon Degrelle; in their respective countries his colleagues had defended the interests of Aboriginals and African-Americans. Their committee replaced Schermerhorn's all-Dutch General Commission.

The 'internationalisation' of the Indonesian question was immediately felt in Jakarta. The Committee of Good Offices arrived on 27 October 1947 with a consular commission that included dozens of consuls and military attachés. It required some adjustment from the Dutch. Mans Spoor-Dijkema, wife of commander-in-chief Simon Spoor, wrote: 'With the presence of so many foreigners, the party circuit expanded tremendously. Ambassadors, international businesses and of course the Lieutenant Governor-General gave receptions and dinners. [. . .] We couldn't avoid it either. In November we gave a cocktail party for, among others, the military observers and Dutch officers, approximately one hundred guests.' It didn't enthuse her. 'We had simply been inundated with all those foreigners and then in your own interest you have to make the best of it.' She noticed that many of her compatriots also 'loathed all those foreigners'.[26]

Had the era of cocktail parties also dawned in the occupied territories? Not at all. Officially a ceasefire had been in place since 4 August, but on announcing it, General Spoor had explicitly stated that it only applied to 'new – repeat, new – territory'. The borders had been expanded, but within those new borders there was still work to be done: 'To safeguard population, our troops and objects within – repeat, within – now occupied territory.'[27] It was enough to make you despair – repeat, despair. This was more a cease-drive than a ceasefire. The Netherlands presented the First Police Action to the outside world as a two-week pinprick, but in fact the fighting lasted 'six months, until the signing of the Renville Agreement', as brigade commander Kawilarang experienced first-hand.[28] Less than a month after the resolution of 1 August, the UN was obliged once again to call for the ceasefire to be respected.

Initially Sukarno behaved more correctly than Spoor: after the truce he called on his troops to lay down arms wherever they were and not fire unless the enemy opened fire first.[29] 'In our thousands we withdrew into the forests,' related Iskandar, the man who had been given his carbine by his Japanese shopkeeper boss and was now fighting in a people's militia. 'In the forest we slept on the ground with our rifles in our arms. "My gun is my wife," we said. We were starving a lot of the time. When we came to a village we'd ask for food. If there were no villages, we'd look at what the monkeys were eating. If there were no monkeys, we'd fast. We couldn't quench our thirst with coconuts, because if we'd climbed up into the trees, the Dutch would have seen us and shot us. We just drank water from the river. We washed in the river. Or we didn't wash at all! For days on end we wore the same clothes. I didn't have a uniform. Just a red-and-white headband.' A lot of pemuda had resolved not to cut their hair until the country had been freed. 'Despite the hunger we could still move quickly when the Dutch came. They patrolled on foot and were better armed than we were – automatic rifles, whereas we could only fire one shot at a time! – but we had scouts everywhere. A chain of messages ran through the forest!' In those first weeks it stayed fairly calm, said Iskandar. 'The Dutch searched the villages. They left the women and children in peace. There was no violence.' But one day he had to go to the provincial town of Salatiga for medicine for his friends. 'Before I left, I hid my carbine in the ceiling of a house, but I was surprised by Dutch soldiers. "Hey, stop! Hands up!" They arrested me and took me to Salatiga, and after a couple of days they sent me to Semarang prison. You had A, B, C and D prisoners there. A were the political prisoners, I was B: POWs. The cell was packed with sixteen, sometimes as many as thirty-two people. There was a tiny ten-centimetre window. We didn't have any mattresses or pillows. You had to go to the toilet in front of everyone. We all came from different rebel groups, but you couldn't say anything confidential. The Dutch listened in. At first I was scared I was going to be executed. We were given bread to eat. I used it as a pillow and broke a piece off now and then because I thought I was going to die the next day.' Iskandar was in the cell for a year. 'Nobody was executed. I wasn't beaten. The Dutch treated us well. I was even given five cigarettes a week. It wasn't real tobacco, but at least it was something.' And then something miraculous happened: the Committee of Good Offices visited. They were looking into the fate of prisoners of war. 'The Komisi Tiga Negara [literally, the Three-Country Committee] interviewed me. About the conditions, the food, the sleeping arrangements. I said we only got *bubur*, porridge, but no rice. In the days after that, the food got better.'[30]

In their newly acquired territories, the Dutch tried to round up their adversaries. Goderd van Heek was made military commander of the small prison of Tangerang and was later allowed to go out on patrols as well. 'They were so-called peace patrols. There wasn't much action then, the guerrilla warfare hadn't started yet. The planters returned, the rubber companies were operating again, and the doctors had resumed providing medical care to the population. We were still motivated by reconstruction!' He had to qualify that: 'Yes, of course there were soldiers with venereal disease but my unit was disciplined. It was made up mainly of Protestant lads from Friesland and Catholic lads from Limburg. In the evening I would hear my

soldiers ending the day by singing psalms in the kampong.' Still, it
didn't take much to disturb the apparent calm. 'Sometimes it happened that we were shot at from a kampong and then we opened fire
on the kampong. Then you might hit innocent civilians.'

It was not always clear who was provoking who, but you couldn't
consolidate conquered territory with tea parties. In West Java, Van
Heek was facing troops from the Siliwangi Division, one of the
Republican army's best units. 'Yes, the TNI was quite well trained.
And the student army too, they weren't just tearaways! They really
thought things through. Afterwards, too, their guerrilla warfare was
well structured. You can respect that too.'[31] The Republican forces
were not the disorganised rabble they were often made out to be.
Sukotjo, who like Van Heek had trained as an officer, provided proof
of this. After retreating from Porong, he had regrouped in October
1947 near Malang, which was in Dutch hands. 'In the morning they
attacked us near Ngadipura with 400 men, then they were moving in
a long line along a ridge. I only had forty men: twenty cadets on my
left and twenty Madurese on my right. Our position was lower and
we were up to our calves in mud; the rice had been cut. We only had
two machine guns as well. But we advanced anyway. When the right
flank moved, the left flank provided cover; when the left flank pushed
forward, the right flank did the shooting. We were all under fire,
but nobody was hit. The bullets were making the plants move, but
nobody was hit! At fifty metres I saw the Dutch commander standing
there in his khaki uniform, took aim and missed. I was so angry with
myself! Then I drew my klewang. My forty men stormed forward
with their bayonets. The marines fled and we occupied the ridge. It
was the only time we were able to dislodge the marines.'[32]

Direct confrontations like this were rare. Much more often the
Republican resistance consisted of isolated incidents from the bush.
Since a swarm of mosquitoes can sometimes bother an elephant more
than a single buffalo would, the Republican forces settled on guerrilla tactics, and the word itself, derived from the Spanish diminutive
for war, was soon written in Indonesian as *gerilya*. Guerrilla warfare
wouldn't bring victory, but it held off defeat, while exhausting your
adversary. The tactic could hardly have come as a surprise. Frans

Goedhart, a former resistance hero and a leading light of the PvdA, who'd been in Jakarta during the First Police Action, had predicted it perfectly: 'This is an insane and completely hopeless undertaking. The "limited use of military force" now in progress will only make the Indonesians dislike and mistrust us even more, and increase their hatred for us. One can subject them to military defeats, but the Republic's willingness to voluntarily cooperate with the Netherlands will evaporate entirely. We can expect furious guerrilla warfare.'[33] And that is exactly what they got.

The Netherlands had the main roads, the Republic the hinterland. The connecting roads were long and the convoys a cherished target. 'It still gives me goose bumps,' related Soerachman. 'The Dutch used tanks, armoured cars, jeeps, trucks . . . If you shot at them, they got out and you could shoot at the driver.'[34] Soewondo was in position for an ambush when a KNIL truck stopped. 'They got out to drink and smoke. I chose a target and aimed. A Dutchman. He was wearing a helmet, boots, a uniform. I was bareheaded and barefoot. I kept my gun trained on him, but didn't get the order to shoot.' He let him go. But on other occasions, he added, he had downed 'a few people'.[35]

During the First Police Action the Dutch army lost just 76 soldiers; the guerrilla war that followed killed many more. And that led to constant anxiety among the troops: the enemy was invisible and poorly armed, but could strike at any moment. A comrade you'd enjoyed playing cards with the previous evening could be inside a body bag with a label on his big toe the next afternoon. It was enough to drive you crazy. 'Your first funeral for a Dutch soldier made an impression,' related Jan Langenberg, who was stationed in a barracks in Medan. 'I didn't know the man; he was shot during an ambush on the road from Medan to Berastagi. Life goes fast there. Afterwards we all grabbed a beer.'[36]

'I had to take photos of the dead and wounded,' said Ton Berlee, the man from the Burma Railway and the fire at the refinery. After the Proklamasi he'd set up a photographic service with the KNIL military police. 'I sometimes rode a hundred kilometres into no-man's land on an old Harley. Nobody dared to do that work. "Berlee, go there!" they said. And then I set off again.' He had a Leica 35mm camera and saw the most magnificent dawns and sunsets. Shame there wasn't any colour film back then, he thought. 'The first body was the most horrific. A young Indo had been hacked to pieces, just because he was Dutch and had fallen into the hands of a bunch of those idiots.' During the advance of the Dutch army the pemuda had once again vented their anger on the defenceless, slaughtering a hundred Indos and 1,500 Chinese. 'I got him on a bier, cleaned up and respectable. He was all in pieces, in a bag. That was a blow!' But that wasn't the end of it. 'After that it was non-stop. In hospitals, in a pit, after operations. I must have taken photos of at least a hundred dead like that. If you see a pile of bodies, you don't feel very well. Doctors cut them open to determine the cause of death. I kept a hankie with eau de cologne on me. A doctor said, "There's nothing unusual about bodies. Stench is part of it." Yes, it was a strange job. It was about tormenting them as much as possible. Tongue out, eyes out, scalped, privates off. I had to photograph it. If you'd seen your mates so terribly mutilated, tortured and killed, you shot at everything that moved. And then we're the war criminals! Agreed, our side did things that weren't right either, but you just went mad.'

Berlee was a seasoned soldier: he'd survived the Japanese invasion, survived the Burma Railway, survived the Revolusi. His eyes were wide open. 'At first there wasn't any hostility and I did everything normally. But I became determined and brazen. When I went into a village, I gave a demonstration first. I could shoot just as easily and accurately from the hip. Someone held a bottle over his head and I shot it to pieces. They were on their guard after that! Most of the enemy were bad shots, but sometimes they had a sniper at the top of a coconut tree. You always had to watch out for that. I shot two or three boys right out of a tree. First the rifle fell, and only then the body.'

Berlee gave a terse summary of his attitude. 'I became icy, calm and steady.' You couldn't say that of all the newcomers from the Netherlands, the conscripts and volunteers who had hardly outgrown their village churches. 'The *barus*, the greenhorns, were so naive. They arrived by ship and thought people here still used bows and arrows. Us KNIL troops felt sorry for them. We understood the language and the mentality, but they were sent into the jungle completely unprepared. I heard about a commander who dived behind a sawah bank at the slightest sign of anything, scared to death, in all the mud! I heard about a captain who sat there crying like a baby when his troop got surrounded! An ordinary sergeant had to save his company . . .'[37]

One of those newcomers was Goos Blok. In late 1947 he arrived in Bali as a conscript without, in his own words, 'any knowledge of the tropics'. 'The first night they gave us fried rice. One of our boys said, "I want rice with raisins. With sugar and cinnamon and a little pool of melted butter in the middle." Ha!' At school Goos had only learned to rattle off the names of the volcanoes of Java, that was all. And during training it had not been much better. 'We had to sing like the German soldiers in the streets of Rotterdam. "Where the pale tops of sand dunes/ Gleam in the sunny glow/ And the gently frothing North Sea/ Greets the Lowlands' narrow coast . . ." On Bali!' Those manly choruses couldn't hide a certain degree of panic, as soon became evident. 'During a march our lieutenant screamed, "Take cover, damn it!" We dived into the ditch. There was a puddle of blood on the road! The KNIL was brought in. Well, it turned out it wasn't blood, but red spit from chewing betel. Three centuries of experience in the tropics, but that was something our lieutenant had never heard of . . .'

Goos Blok spoke with remarkable candour about the effect this culture of fear had on him. During the voyage out he had learned a little Malay and that was sufficient to immediately be assigned to the intelligence service. That sounded like a soft job, but in a guerrilla war the intelligence service is the place where all of the anger, frustration and fear converge. Interrogations have to provide information fast. 'We had captured a kid of fifteen and had to question him. "Where are they?" "*Tidak tahu.* I don't know." "Really?" We hit him. "Where are they?" "*Tidak tahu.*" We fetched the field telephone. "Where are they?" "*Tidak tahu.*" We used the dynamo, jammed the poles into his hands, and shocked him.' *Where our forebears' shining virtue/ Has never yet been shunned/ And peace in hearts and houses/ Make folk and monarch one . . .* 'Another shock.' *Rejoice, on all your streets and strands :/ I love you so, my Netherlands!*

Goos Blok again: 'Yes, that's what I did. For three whole months. Not every day, but often. A total disgrace.' And then to realise that Bali wasn't even officially Republican, but 'friendly' territory. He didn't want to stay quiet any longer. 'At an outpost the KNIL was in charge of an interrogation. They put a funnel with a tube in the prisoner's mouth. Water in! He was writhing on the ground . . .' *Blessed by God, my dearest Fatherland/ Your strength is unity!* 'One morning we went out on patrol at five-thirty with five of us, led by a Balinese KNIL soldier. We went to a ravine. We saw footprints in the sand. The lieutenant opened fire with his Sten gun and a little further along we found a man with a wound in his buttock. He was still alive, it was a clean wound. He wasn't armed and turned out to be in hiding because he hadn't paid his taxes. The lieutenant told me, "Finish him off. This gorge is too difficult for the Red Cross." I said, "You can't do that!" I should have protested. The Law of War? Rules of Engagement? The Geneva Conventions? If you brought things like that up, it was all, what *are* you talking about?' *Unto death may you stay loyal/ To the Law and Monarchy!* 'Someone else shot him in the ear.' In 1986 Goos Blok went back to Bali for the first time to show his wife the narrow sawah embankments he'd walked along back then. In a church building he addressed the local community: 'I said I was sorry for having stood in the way of Indonesian independence.' All present applauded him. It was one of the most striking moments of his life.[38]

Stef Horvath couldn't work because of the yelling. He had to man the radio post twelve hours a day. It was located on a plantation in East Java. 'But the prisoners were questioned in the workers' houses. You heard constant screaming and cries of people being tortured. Military intelligence was mainly made up of people from the KNIL. An Ambonese was making whips and called them "fat dicks". For fourteen days I heard that screeching every evening and every night. None of us in the signals unit could work. Besides the whip they also used the generator, which they connected to the prisoners' balls.'[39]

On the ship to Indonesia an inconspicuous conscript from The Hague celebrated his twentieth birthday. His name: Joop Hueting. Nobody could suspect that he would become the most important whistle-blower in Dutch post-war history. In 1969 he was the first person to speak on Dutch television about what he and his men had done during the war in Indonesia. During the last years of his life, I was able to talk to him at length several times in Amsterdam, sometimes in an old people's apartment, sometimes at a rehabilitation centre. Once we went to eat oysters at an outdoor café with his daughter. His testimony is as disconcerting as ever. 'I first saw torture in Jember. A member of the TNI had been hung up by his feet with his head down. An Indo lad from the KNIL tortured him by gently pulling on the rope, multiple times, so that his head hit the floor. They kept going until his skull broke. I walked away. I couldn't bear it.[40] He didn't know then that he himself would be involved in atrocities several months later. War is not a precipice, but a gradual slope.

The 'police actions' drew international attention, but the worst phases were the months that followed. 'Then all hell broke loose!' Joop Hueting exclaimed during one of our conversations. The periods in which the most war crimes were committed were the second half of 1947 and, above all, the first half of 1949, each time in the wake of an offensive.[41] Not all violence is a war crime. War crimes are forms of violence that are inadmissible even in the context of war, as they are contrary to the prevailing laws and customs of warfare.[42] Second Lieutenant Sukotjo made that distinction very clearly. 'Firing at us? No problem. It was war and then killing each other is normal. But I hadn't expected atrocities. On the side of the road to Ngadipura we found a man with a baby. The man had been killed with a bayonet, the baby's skull was split open. They had been killed the night before when the Dutch army passed by. They killed everything that moved. The man was only carrying a bundle of clothes. They must have been going somewhere.[43]

Legally, it is possible to question whether one can really speak of war crimes in a colonial war. Is the international law of war applicable to a conflict that is not really international, in the sense of involving two states? Do the Hague and Geneva Conventions apply if one of the two parties is not yet really a country? In the case of Indonesia, definitely. Linggajati was de facto recognition of the Republic by the Netherlands and, by consenting to United Nations mediation in 1947, the Netherlands acceded to the principles of the UN Manifesto and hence to international law. In 1948 it signed the Renville Agreement, reached under UN supervision. From that moment at the latest, international law and the laws of war applied. In the meantime Dutch courts have acknowledged in so many words that these were extremely serious irregularities and misconduct that also contravened military and ordinary criminal law.

And then there were the atrocities of gross negligence. Radio operator Stef Horvath witnessed a horrific catastrophe. After having to listen to torture for days on end at a plantation, he was assigned to a mobile radio station that had been set up in a modified goods carriage. Every day he criss-crossed occupied East Java by rail to maintain contact with the radio posts. It was 23 November 1947, and in the afternoon he was going from Malang to Surabaya. At the station in Bangil three large wagons were coupled to the train. 'They were hermetically-sealed cold storage wagons.' They contained hundreds of POWs who had to be transported from Bondowoso to Surabaya. Most of them were farmers, with a few teachers, traders and soldiers among them. Many of them had been previously tortured with generators: electric shocks to their hands, electric shocks to their genitals, convulsions, pain. Personnel officer Post described the transport as a 'filthy mess'.⁴⁴ The prisoners had been in transit since the morning. At various stations along the way the train stood for hours in the sun. It was a scorching day. When they banged on the doors of the dark vans, they heard, 'Shut the fuck up!' When they begged for water, the answer was, 'All we've got for you is bullets.'⁴⁵ When they groaned, it stayed quiet. In one van they prised open a small hole in the floor. With a rolled-up banana leaf they sucked a little air into the van. In the other vans, they grew dizzy, drank their urine, fainted . . . After an eleven-hour train journey, the doors finally opened. In a living room in North Amsterdam, Stef Horvath still found it difficult to tell the story. 'One station before Surabaya [Wonokromo] the doors opened. *"Keluar! Keluar!"* they shouted. Out! Out! But nobody came out!' In the third van nobody had survived, in the second there were a number of dead. Of the hundred prisoners, forty-six died. The survivors had to carry out the bodies themselves. Afterwards a few of those responsible received mild punishments – the most severe being eight months' imprisonment. 'There must have been more senior people who were responsible,' Horvath said. 'I'm the only witness. That death train was so stupid. I'm getting emotional about it again.' Stef sobbed for the forgotten dead of days gone by.[46]

Two weeks later the criminality that followed the first Dutch offensive reached an absolute low point. Early in the morning of 9 December 1947 some eighty soldiers of the Dutch Royal Army – ordinary conscripts, not Captain Westerling's special forces, not KNIL diehards, not Ambonese whose extreme loyalty made them brutal, but 'decent' newcomers from the Netherlands – entered the kampong of Rawagede. The small village was in the marshy lowlands east of Jakarta, an inaccessible and rebellious area. The Dutch troops were looking for a local guerrilla leader, but when it turned out that he was long gone, they massacred the village's entire male population. At least 300 and possibly more than 400 civilians died. Women and children were intentionally separated, not a single firearm was found on the victims' bodies and there were no Dutch casualties. Even after the village had been conquered, men were still summarily executed. The Committee of Good Offices established an independent observation team that interviewed witnesses on location. Its findings were implacable: 'the action undertaken by the Netherlands army was deliberate and ruthless.' Although the Dutch authorities also lied to the investigators, there was no doubt at all about the 'most brutal use of force'.[47] Those responsible were never prosecuted, but in 2011 a Dutch court held the state responsible for the damages suffered. Nine widows received compensation of 20,000 euros each.[48]

And then something very peculiar happened. The Bondowoso death train was raised at the UN Security Council in New York at the end of December 1947, but . . . it had no consequences.[49] The massacre at Rawagede astonished the Committee of Good Offices, but . . . it was kept out of the UN Security Council's first interim report.[50] Why? Because America was protecting the Netherlands.[51] Turning a blind eye to keep out communism. The Netherlands needed to recover economically and its colony could help. What's

more, Indonesia was rich in raw materials – tin, oil, rubber – and that
was good for global trade. With the Dutch still at the helm, US access
to these resources seemed more secured. America was much less anti-
colonial in practice than on paper. That also emerged from the
numbers: in Indonesia the Netherlands received '$70 million for
Marshall Plan aid and $60 million in grants. The Dutch also received
$75 million in surplus arms and another $100 million in arms made
available if the Netherlands so desired. In 1947 Secretary of State
George Marshall formally confirmed that the United States had
equipped a Dutch Marine Brigade fighting against the Indonesian
Republic, and that the United States had provided the Dutch with 54
bombers, 64 fighters, 266 mortars, 170 pieces of artillery and 159
machine guns.'[52] No death train or ghost village could outweigh that.

For Indonesia the situation seemed completely hopeless. In December 1947, Herawati Diah, the woman who had studied at Columbia
University and moved to Yogya with Sukarno, set off for the All-
India Women's Congress. India had gained its independence in
August and had passionately defended Indonesia in the UN Security
Council. In a break from the congress proper, Herawati and several
colleagues visited an old man in a garden. It was bitterly cold but the
man with the friendly smile received them outdoors, bare-chested
and wearing a loincloth he had woven himself: Mahatma Gandhi.
This encounter with the father of the world's largest democracy made
a lifelong impression on her. 'He was very progressive,' she said when
I interviewed her. That I, deep into the twenty-first century, might
be able to speak to someone who, as an adult, had conversed with
Gandhi, was something I hadn't dared hope for. Like so many Indonesian freedom fighters, Herawati had been at her wits' end. 'Will the
Indonesian struggle succeed?' she asked him with bated breath. His
answer was more moral than political. 'When you truly believe that
it will succeed, then it will surely succeed,' he said encouragingly.
Gandhi himself would not live to see it. A month after Herawati's
brief visit, he was murdered in that same garden by a radical Hindu.[53]

It was back to square one. The years 1948–9 seemed like a repetition
of the years 1946–7. A phase of extreme violence was followed by

arduous political negotiations, in which the Netherlands constantly imposed new conditions on the Republic, while itself again violating the fresh agreements. These breaches generated new reactions, setting off another spiral of violence and escalating the situation further: the Netherlands made non-negotiable demands, the Republic sought guarantees, the Netherlands delivered an ultimatum, the Republic gave in and the Netherlands unleashed a military offensive anyway, with renewed guerrilla warfare as a result. There are few historical periods to which Karl Marx's famous adage that history always occurs twice, first as tragedy and then as farce, can be applied as literally as to the decolonisation of Indonesia – with the proviso that here the farce was worse than the tragedy. Nonetheless, there were important differences. When the USS *Renville* put down anchor in Jakarta Bay at the start of December 1947 to provide a location for the peace talks, the situation was very different from the negotiations in Linggajati a year earlier. Then it had been a British initiative, now it was American. Then the UN hadn't played a role, now it was happening under the auspices of the United Nations. Then the British had been quite pro-Republican, now the Americans were pro-Dutch. Then there had been trust, now only mistrust. The negotiations at Linggajati took four days, those on the *Renville* almost six weeks. Even the fact that they had to resort to a ship outside the three-mile limit showed that the delegations refused to enter the other's territory. A residence in the mountains versus a warship at sea: didn't that sum it up?

Could the Linggajati Agreement be revived? That was the question. The Indonesian negotiators were led by Prime Minister Amir Sjarifuddin. The delegation for the Netherlands was made up of Dutch experts and the pro-Dutch leaders of the Indonesian states,[54] and headed by Abdulkadir Widjojoatmodjo, Secretary of State for General Affairs and for years a faithful adviser to Van Mook. His appointment was meant to show that this was not Europeans against Asians, but a conflict between federalists and the advocates of a unitary state. The Republicans saw this as a cheap trick to present the conflict as a purely internal affair. Giving a significant number of dark-skinned people a seat at the table didn't make the issue any less colonial.

For weeks both camps met on the *Renville*'s shaded afterdeck: from 8 December 1947 to 17 January 1948. The discussions did not go smoothly. The Netherlands wanted a military agreement before talking politics, the Republic wanted to discuss both simultaneously. After a lot of back and forth, three documents were on the table by mid-January. In a nutshell: the weapons had to be silenced, the civilians had to speak and the politicians had to cooperate.

The military proposal was a triumph for the Netherlands: it stipulated that a ceasefire had to be implemented, that for the time being the territorial expansion of the First Police Action was to be accepted, and that the Republic had to withdraw its troops behind the new demarcation lines. What's more, a demilitarised zone had to be established: fifteen kilometres on either side of this 'Van Mook Line'. Score so far: 1–0 for the Netherlands.

The political proposal for the transitional stage was a win for both parties: the Netherlands retained sovereignty over all of Indonesia and was free to establish a provisional federal government (2–0), but referendums were required within six to twelve months to determine which occupied territories would become part of the Republic. From bullets to ballots, in the words of the American mediator Frank Graham. The Republic was confident that the areas it was now

Map 25: Renville Agreement: the United States of Indonesia (17 January 1948)

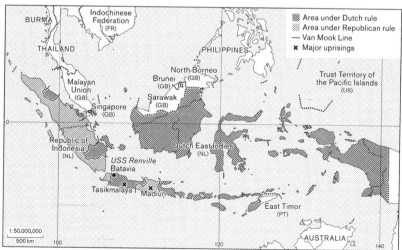

relinquishing would return of their own accord. What's more, it could always ask the UN to allow the Committee to stay longer. The score at half-time: 2–1.

But in the second half, the Indonesians were shut out completely. The long-term political proposals were all to the advantage of the Netherlands: the Republic was to become part of a federal Indonesia and this 'United States of Indonesia' part of a Union with the Netherlands, embodied by the Dutch monarch. This encapsulation of Indonesia within the Kingdom of the Netherlands was a long-standing Dutch goal. Final score: 3-1.

Renville was clearly a victory for the Dutch position, but how impartial had the ref been? When the American negotiator Graham told the Republicans during secret negotiations, 'You are what you are and that is what you will remain,' the Netherlands kicked up a fuss that was justified but also clumsy, given the sacrifices being demanded of the Republic.[55] In general, though, Graham was absolutely on the side of the Dutch. He put the Indonesian delegation under intense pressure to accept the agreement: a chance like this would never come again, the Security Council would not produce a more favourable deal, the UN would take a rejection badly, the Netherlands could launch a new offensive and so on.[56] 'It was a thoroughly unacceptable, unpalatable and unfair proposal,' Sukarno stated later. 'There was no choice.'[57] Especially as his military commanders had just briefed him that their ammunition and supplies were as good as exhausted. On 17 January 1948, with great reluctance, the Republic signed the Renville Agreement on board the American warship. Much later Graham looked back on the lopsided compromise he himself had forced on the Indonesians. Those federal states, he realised, had only been Dutch puppets. 'It would be like forming the United States of America under the Tories [who remained loyal to the British crown]. Just lock George Washington up, and some of the others, and then put the Tories in charge of the several states and call it the United States of America.'[58]

No wonder Renville wasn't well received in the Republic. Withdrawing the troops? Was that why the army had led a guerrilla war? Becoming part of an artificial construction that was still welded to

the European aggressor? Was that what hundreds of thousands of
young people had fought for? The Republic wanted to become an
independent sovereign state, but Renville made it a province. Back
in Yogyakarta, socialist Prime Minister Amir Sjarifuddin was
jeered from all sides, with the exception of his own socialist and
communist supporters, united in a left-wing federation. The Islamists and nationalists, however, thought he had betrayed indigenous
nationalism. Like Sjahrir six months earlier, Amir felt compelled to
resign. Giving in to Dutch demands was bad for your political career. The new prime minister was Vice-President Mohammad
Hatta.

Hatta assembled a new government and immediately set to work
implementing the Renville Agreement. He called the troops back
from the occupied territories. The Siliwangi Division, which had
gone underground in West Java, crossed the border to Central Java
with at least 22,000 men. Goderd van Heek saw them leaving. 'They
were looking pretty scruffy! The Siliwangi was a reasonably well-
organised division, but guerrilla fighting takes a toll.'[59] It was the first
time he'd seen the enemy close up. The soldiers were also withdrawing from East Java. 'I took my cadets back to Solo [Surakarta],' Second
Lieutenant Sukotjo told me. 'After the ceasefire, Malang stayed in
Dutch hands.' He had risked his life for nothing and became an
instructor at an NCO training school.[60]

Van Mook was as slow to execute the political agreement as Hatta
was fast to fulfil the military agreement. The proposed referendums
never got off the ground. The economic blockade was not suspended.
The Dutch army maintained its presence in the demilitarised
zone. Before discussing the future, the Republic must first dissolve its
army. And so it went on. What was even more excessive was that Van
Mook, in complete contravention of Renville, tirelessly continued to
establish new 'states', even in former Republican territory. It was no
longer a question of several large areas; by May 1948 he had thirteen.[61] The local populations had almost no say. He circumvented
revolts by gambling on ever smaller territories, where he entrusted
power to remnants of the old native aristocracy, often with little
legitimacy. They were puppet states, entities that did not in any way

reflect political reality. This was not decolonisation by deliberation but Dutch neo-imperialism.

3–1 to the Netherlands? Definitely, and as a result of the biased referee the Indonesian team also broke up into three factions. America thought it had everything covered by fully supporting the Netherlands but didn't realise that it was also splitting the Republic. The moderate centrist forces – the very people America needed – were exhausted and the political extremes strengthened, both left and right. Sukarno's entire political project consisted of uniting communists, nationalists and Islamists, but 1948 was the year this alliance finally crumbled. Renville drove a deep wedge into Indonesian society, and its effects are felt to this day. The communists are still seen as unpatriotic, the Islamists are still struggling to Islamise the state.

The era in which Indonesia's great ideological movements had eaten together in Tjokroaminoto's boarding house in Surabaya seemed an eternity ago. Young communists like Muso and Semaun, the Islamist Kartosuwirjo and even a very young Sukarno had sat side by side there. Now, after Renville, they were diametrically opposed to each other.

To measure Renville's deep impact on Indonesian history, I travelled by train through the endless Javanese countryside in the dry season of 2016. Among other places, this trip took me to Tasikmalaya in West Java, once the capital of the Islamist resistance. In the mosque I spoke to religious leaders; in a community centre I met descendants of Muslim separatists. 'The people here were not happy with Renville,' Aang Yusuf Syamsuddin explained. 'It was as if Sukarno had sold our independence to the Dutch! That set off the war.'[62] After the Siliwangi Division's forced withdrawal from West Java, only a few irregular units were left, chiefly Islamic youth militias like Barisan Hizbullah that had been formed in the Japanese period. They numbered several thousand and were led by Kartosuwirjo, one of Tjokroaminoto's guests. He had a past in Sarekat Islam, in the Masyumi Movement during the Japanese occupation and in the Masyumi Party after the Proklamasi.[63] Kartosuwirjo had been offered the post of Deputy Minister for Defence under Sjahrir, but now took up arms.[64] That was another effect of Renville. The devout Islamic scholar turned into a fearsome rebel leader. He called his army the Tentara Islam Indonesia (TII, Indonesian Islamic Army) and his territory Darul Islam (DI, House of Islam) and dreamt of jihad, sharia and purity.

Under a wooden lean-to alongside a magnificent paddy field a few hours' drive from Tasikmalaya, I spoke to the very elderly Adjen Muttakin one balmy evening. Year of birth: 1920-something. He didn't speak Indonesian or Javanese, but only Sundanese, the language of West Java. 'There was no TNI here any more! The army had gone back to Yogyakarta! Then we continued the struggle against the Dutch! DI made sure of it! I was a member! In Hizbullah I didn't have a weapon, only a spear, but in the DI the commander gave me a gun. We had a bazooka too! Our leader was Kartosuwirjo. He was very intelligent and a very good speaker! He was our rajah, our king!' This was the crux of it. Although Kartosuwirjo initially fought for the Republic, he assumed more and more political privilege. During the drafting of the Indonesian Constitution in the summer of 1945, political Islam had suffered a major setback: Indonesia would become a nation of believers, but not exclusively Islamic. The Pancasila philosophy was deliberately pluralistic, despite 95% of the country being Muslim. That still stung. Had the hour of rectification struck? Increasingly Kartosuwirjo saw himself as the sole legitimate representative of the Indonesian people. He demanded the total mobilisation and militarisation of the population. In 1949 he went so far as to proclaim the birth of the Indonesian Muslim state, Negara Islam Indonesia – with himself as head of state, supreme commander and imam. The project caught on, not only in large parts of West Java, but also in South Sulawesi, South Borneo and the far north of Sumatra (the ever-rebellious Aceh).[65] Darul Islam formed a real threat to the Republic. Sukarno's territory was already reduced and besieged. Now it was also being menaced by a native Indonesian movement.[66]

The elderly Adjen Muttakin continued: 'After the Dutch we fought the TNI, yes! There were many dead and wounded! The Koran said this and the Pancasila said that. For seventeen years, I fought in the mountains! All that time I stayed single! I didn't get married until 1964, when I was already over thirty!' The struggle between the Republic and Darul Islam would drag on for years, until long after independence, and in 1957 even led to a failed attempt to assassinate Sukarno (three hand grenades, eleven dead, a hundred wounded children). It didn't end until 1962, when a sick and emaciated Kartosuwirjo was captured in a hut in the mountains of West Java and executed. The conflict had cost the lives of 40,000 people. 'The struggle against the TNI was much more difficult than against the Dutch,' said Adjen while we looked out over his small field. And to prove it he showed me his scars: a graze on his left shoulder, a bullet in the right knee, an old wound on his left thumb.[67] America had pushed through Renville and Renville had split the Republic. But the heaviest attack on Yogyakarta was yet to come.

While travelling around Java, I ended up in Surakarta one evening in the living room of a man called Soemardi. Outside, an epic thunderstorm was flooding the streets and turning motorbikes into jet-skis. 'I wasn't happy,' he said, not referring to the heat earlier that day. He too was talking about 1948. 'I wanted to fight but it wasn't allowed any more. I had to surrender my gun. That was because of the rationalisation of the army.' After Renville, what was left of the Republic – only a third of Java – was flooded with troops from East and West Java. There were also countless popular militias – altogether 460,000 men. What was Hatta to do with all those soldiers, especially in times of scarcity?[68] His answer was 'RERA', the *reorganisasi* and *rasionalisasi* of the army. The armed forces were reduced to a professional army of 160,000 men.[69] The demobilised had to serve the country elsewhere. 'I had to go and work in coffee and tea,' Soemardi related. 'Still in uniform. I didn't have anything else. I was given an office job on a plantation that had been in Dutch private ownership, but was now nationalised. We had a lot, a real lot of tea. Five hundred hectares! I did the employee records.'[70] Admittedly, filling in tables of how many people washed, cut and packed tea was a good bit less heroic than fighting for the motherland.

The slimming-down of the army caused a great deal of frustration

among the young, especially in Surakarta, where the newly arrived
Siliwangi Division sometimes seemed rather arrogant to the less
competent local units. But the troops were not the only ones who
were testy. The general populace too had reason to complain. Thanks
to the Dutch naval blockade, the price of a kilogram of rice increased
by a factor of ten in less than a year, from 1.7 to 17.5 rupiah.[71] Everything became more expensive. In the cotton plantations and factories
of Delanggu it led to a very large strike: 20,000 labourers stopped
work for more than a month. Angry soldiers, angry workers and, on
top of all that, angry politicians too. After Renville, the progressive
parties joined forces in a mammoth alliance of the left: the Sajap Kiri
(Left Wing), led by the recently resigned prime minister, Amir Sjarifuddin. They had had enough of America's meddling and put their
faith in other countries. As prime minister, Amir had already begun
talks with Russia and these consultations had proceeded so favourably that in May 1948 the Soviet Union offered to formalise relations
and open consulates in Moscow and Yogyakarta. Prime Minister
Hatta realised, however, that this was the last thing the Americans
wanted and forcefully blocked the offer. In response a familiar figure
returned to Indonesia from Russia: Muso, someone else who had
been a frequent guest at Tjokroaminoto's. When Sukarno saw him
again after all those years, he gave him a very friendly welcome.[72] But
the warmth would soon pass.

Muso was a living legend. A very early member of Sarekat Islam
and the PKI, he had travelled to Moscow in 1926 to discuss plans for
an uprising (the failed communist revolt). In 1935 he had returned to
set up a new, underground PKI, and in 1947 he had taken part in the
discussions with the Kremlin. In Moscow he had married a Russian
and become a confirmed Stalinist. He had never been arrested or
banished. Now he had come back to his embattled motherland and
been welcomed as the saviour of the left. The Left Wing changed its
name to the Popular Democratic Front, and the parliamentary work
became extra-parliamentary opposition. The days of negotiations
were over. Muso was a man of revolutionary action, and the socialist
Amir Sjarifuddin, who admitted to having been a communist for
some time, joined him.

'Brothers,' Muso declared at a mass meeting in September 1948, 'our revolution has now been going on for three years, and yet the workmen, peasants, pemudas and women have not benefited by these results. On the contrary they have suffered badly.' The reason was simple. 'The proclamation of freedom has taken the wrong turning, and now the leadership of the revolution is in the hands of the bourgeoisie and the landed gentry, the proletariat being excluded altogether.' This was straight from the communist handbook. 'It is said that I am an agent from Moscow and that I have received instructions. These are lies.' Instead he was inspired by recent developments in the region: the rapid rise of communism in China, Burma and Indochina. Thailand, Malaya and the Philippines were also in a state of ferment. 'This is the age of the working classes,' he concluded. 'The Soviet Union is the leader of the world revolution, of which our revolution forms a part; consequently we are led by the Soviet Union. If we choose the side of the Soviet Union, we are right.'[73]

The gathering storm cannot have escaped Washington's attention. Was Muso really on his way to becoming the Mao Tse-tung or Ho Chi Minh of Indonesia? It is irrefutable that he managed to acquire an enormous following in a brief space of time: his clear, stirring rhetoric lit up an independence struggle that had grown overcast and gloomy. The people were hungry, the pemuda were angry and the soldiers were weighing tea. It was all taking too long. The young Sumarsono, at least, was enthused. In September '45 he'd played a key role in the flag incident at the Oranje Hotel, after the Battle of Surabaya he had fled to Madiun, a Republican city in East Java that was then free of the British and Dutch. But now the Revolusi seemed to be stalled. 'I still don't understand it. Amir said that he was pressured by the US to accept Renville.' Sumarsono was a member of his socialist party: 'Renville had to succeed, it couldn't become another Linggajati. As prime minister he was called to the American embassy in Jakarta. The US is a mighty country and Amir didn't have much to say. He had to bow to their will. So instead of negotiating with the Netherlands, Renville was all about obeying America. It was pointless.' It still made him shake his head. 'Colonialism was dead everywhere, but not here! Here neo-colonialism was in charge.'

Amir should never have chosen Australia for the Committee of Good Offices, Sumarsono told me. 'We and the party blamed him for that. Why hadn't he chosen the Soviet Union?' It is impossible to know whether that would have brought an agreement any closer, but Muso's arrival definitely stoked the flames. 'Now our goal was to combat the neo-colonialism of Renville!'

Of all the witnesses I met, Sumarsono was the only one to have driven major historical events. In Surabaya he had helped shape the uprising and in Madiun he was appointed military governor to steer important land reform in the right direction. Land had always been in the hands of the feudal aristocracy and the colonial enterprises; now it would be distributed to the landless peasants.[74] Sukarno invited him to dinner at the palace in Yogyakarta. They had met before at the start of the Revolusi. 'You're my younger brother!' the president had laughed at the time. Now there was some reserve. 'During the conversation, he asked me, "Are you a member?" In English of all things! Of course I knew that he was referring to the communist PKI and asked why he asked, when it was a question even my own wife didn't dare put to me! He said he was very fond of the PKI and had gone to high school with Muso. After I heard that, I spoke frankly.'

Sukarno wasn't just asking because of childhood memories. Madiun was the Republic's third city and located in the middle of an extensive agricultural area. The city had undergone its own specific political development. Whereas Yogyakarta was distinctly national-istic and Surakarta was torn between nationalism and communism, Madiun could become the city where the communists triumphed. In Surakarta the conflict between nationalists and communists had led to kidnappings and massacres. Sumarsono was worried the violence could carry over to Madiun. 'I was the leader of the party there and commander of the troops. In Surakarta, on 3 July, Sutarto, head of the Surakarta Division, was assassinated in front of his mother's house.' Sutarto was a colonel of left-wing persuasion.[75] 'The next tar-get was me, Sumarsono. Hatta wanted to murder me and sent someone after me, Dr Moestopo, but he revealed that he'd been sent by Hatta. He was a friend from Surabaya and didn't want to fight against me at all. Later it turned out he was in the PKI too!'

And that was why Sumarsono swung into action. 'I had no desire to be murdered.' On 18 September 1948 at three o'clock in the morning he and 1,500 troops overwhelmed the TNI military police stationed at Madiun. Without any great difficulties, he was able to disarm and confine them. By eight in the morning he had control of the city. At ten he announced on local radio: 'Victory begins in Madiun!'[76] The red-and-white flag was torn up and an emblem with a hammer and sickle was raised in its place. For a long time people thought that Sumarsono had gone rogue and presented the leadership of the Popular Democratic Front with a *fait accompli*, but there had been prior consultation with Muso, Amir and other leading figures about a possible military intervention.[77] Was it a *kudeta* – the Indonesian word for coup d'état? Sumarsono shook his head. 'No, a coup is about seizing central power. In Madiun I only disarmed the local troops because they had been ordered to murder me.' And the accusations that he was aiming to found a Soviet state in Madiun? 'No, that was what the government made of it. It wasn't that at all. I turned Madiun into a place for the opposition to Renville, because the agreement didn't respect our independence. The worst thing was that we had to withdraw our troops from Dutch territory!'

After his intervention, the left-wing leaders – Muso, Amir and other prominent figures – hurried to Madiun to join the rebellion. This could be the decisive spurt. 'And then the fun and games began!' sighed Piet van Staveren, the man who had gone over to the other side. He was the only Dutchman to witness events in Madiun with his own eyes. And not just that, he even lived in the same house as Sumarsono. He was still making publicity programmes for youth radio and spoke to Muso every day. He was very clear about it. 'The Madiun "rebellion" was not actually a rebellion, but a flagrant provocation. There was no plan behind it, it was a reaction to orders from Yogyakarta that the military police round us up. That was why the whole military police force was disarmed and imprisoned one night. Somebody shot a few tiles off the roof, somebody shot someone who had climbed into a tree, and the result was a kind of free state. For a few days, the left-wing front held power. I told Muso, "We've got a couple of big sugar refineries. Hand out the sugar!" The people were dissatisfied, there wasn't any food left. But I don't know if he did that.' Even a few friends of Pratomo's, Indonesians who had been in the Dutch resistance during World War II, participated in the short-lived free state – sometimes compared to the Paris Commune. They had long since stopped expecting any gratitude from the Dutch. 'The Netherlands kept a low profile,' Piet van Staveren said. 'The thinking there was, let them fight it out!'[78] And that's exactly what happened.

In Yogyakarta, Sukarno's reaction to events in Madiun was extraordinarily vehement. 'Brothers,' he said on the radio, 'our Fatherland is facing a great ordeal. While we are involved in a conflict with the Dutch which requires the absolute solidarity of our people behind the Government, while unity is of the utmost importance for our country's sake, this people's unity is broken by a group of rebels. [. . .] Yesterday morning the Communist Party of Muso staged a coup in Madiun and formed a Soviet Government there.'[79] The Republic, he said, was experiencing an 'extremely critical moment' and the population had to choose between Sukarno–Hatta and Muso. One and a half hours later Muso replied from Madiun with a radio speech that was just as fierce, if not fiercer. He called Sukarno and Hatta 'ex-romusha-dealers, the sworn Quislings' who 'have executed a capitulation policy to the Dutch and the British, and at this very moment they are going to sell out Indonesia and her people to the American Imperialists. Can people of this kind claim that they have the just right to govern our Republic?'[80]

Sumarsono still finds it difficult to believe. 'Muso was surprised that Bung Karno turned his back on him like that. There were rumours that Muso wanted to become president with Amir as prime minister, but they were just rumours. Before that speech of Sukarno's, there was no killing in Madiun. The war only started after he gave it.'

Renville was supposed to calm things, but in practice it split the Republic with an unprecedented intensity. Old ideological fault lines became unbridgeable chasms. Within a few months, American diplomacy changed Indonesia's political landscape. It was bad enough that earnest administrators like Kartosuwirjo and Amir Sjarifuddin were abandoning politics to join the armed struggle. But Sukarno's reacting by sending the Siliwangi Division to Madiun was even more extreme: the Indonesian army's elite corps was now fighting against its own people. Sriyono wasn't troubled. 'Darul Islam was far right and Madiun far left,' he explained. 'Muso and his PKI wanted to replace the Pancasila with communism. We went there with fifty battalions.'[81] The TNI advanced on the city with 5,000 troops, where-upon Muso's rebels withdrew into the mountains. En route they committed atrocities against the local population and several conser-vative Muslim leaders; their pursuers in the government army showed a similar lack of restraint. 'I never gave orders to murder Muslims,' said Sumarsono. 'Our ideology was to accept Muslims and include them. We wanted to unite the country.' Rather than splitting up into guerrilla units to continue the struggle, the rebels followed the example of Mao's Long March through China. Piet van Staveren stayed with them. 'We went up into the mountains. In the meantime they'd made me head of the radio service. I loaded three radio trans-mitters onto ox carts. They had water-cooled valves that were a full metre long! Up the mountain, higher and higher. In the end we just chucked it all into a ravine. We left the trucks behind too and con-tinued on foot. We followed the railway, the forest had been burnt down on both sides.'[82] After some time he had trouble with his legs and had to stay behind with wounded soldiers. There he was taken prisoner by members of the Republican army. Others walked 500 kilometres in two months. Sumarsono: 'There were many of us on the Long March. Men and women from the PKI sought protection from our troops so that they wouldn't be captured by the TNI. We wanted to get to Semarang to join the struggle there.' But Semarang was in Dutch territory, wasn't it? 'I preferred to fight against the Netherlands than the Republic! Because that was family. But our plan didn't succeed because we got lost in the swamps south of Demak. The Siliwangi soldiers were pursuing us and we didn't have a compass. That was why we were defeated. Both the TNI and the Dutch were firing on us, and our troops scattered. There were just nine of us left. For three days we didn't have anything to eat.'[83] Sumarsono managed to escape in one piece, but was arrested in Dutch territory shortly afterwards.

The leaders of the People's Democratic Front came off worse. Muso was hunted for weeks before being shot dead in a firefight in the mountain village of Ponorogo. Former prime minister Amir Sjarifuddin was arrested in his pyjamas in late November and executed with ten others on 19 December 1948, the day the Dutch launched their 'Second Police Action'. They sang not only the 'Internationale' but also the Indonesian national anthem just before their deaths; this shows how much they still cherished Indonesian nationalism.[84] But the American approach had driven the two groups woefully far apart.

An ex-prime minister killed by right-wing compatriots as a result of American interference – it seems to foreshadow the murder of Patrice Lumumba, the first prime minister of the Congo, many years later. The US and the Netherlands were not well disposed towards the Madiun experiment. Secretary of State Marshall had revealed himself to be deeply concerned about the 'Communist threat to present moderate Repub regime', and his top negotiator, Merle Cochran, the new head of the Committee of Good Offices, had explicitly told Hatta that this Madiun crisis 'gives the Republican Government opportunity to show its determination to suppress Communism'.[85] The Dutch were also very worried. Former prime minister Beel had just succeeded Van Mook as head of the administration in Indonesia, a country he scarcely knew, but he immediately resorted to hyperbole. 'Never has there been a graver situation than the current one,' he wrote, 'never has an intervention been more justified and internationally defensible than now. It is now or never.' In the 1930s Sukarno and Hatta were reproached for flirting with communism. In 1945 they were labelled fascist collaborators. But in 1948 they were again seen as potential communists. The pendulum of Dutch perception clearly swung from left to right and back again. If Sukarno and Hatta proved to be 'in league with these Muscovites', the Netherlands needed to attack immediately. More than that, 'not taking advantage of this unique God-given opportunity would be fatal'.[86]

But Marshall and Beel could rest at ease: Sukarno and Hatta resolved the problem faster and more thoroughly than they could ever have imagined, crushing communism in 1948 as energetically as the Dutch had in 1926 or the military would in 1965: implacably and on a massive scale. There have been three versions of a communist revolt in Indonesia and all three met with ruthless repression. Ever since, fierce anti-communism, verging on McCarthyism, has been a constant in Indonesian society. During my travels in Java, I visited Madiun and the surrounding area. Particularly graphic monuments recall the atrocities committed by the communists. The stories circulate to this day. 'My father was in the TNI and pursued Muso,' Ryamid told me on the city's main square. 'Muso was dangerous. He had murdered a religious leader and appealed to the young. My father was there when he was shot dead. He liked to talk about it when we had visitors in the evening!'[87] Soekarti was the widow of a TNI commander. 'My husband was against the Dutch and against Muso! We lived here near the sugar refinery. There was no war then. I only heard the executions. I heard the shots at the sugar refinery. Some soldiers let communists live in exchange for their motorbikes, but my husband was very disciplined. He had a pistol and didn't talk about the executions. It happened once a month, several people each time.'[88]

No, Sukarno and Hatta didn't waste any time. The struggle for Java cost thousands of lives; no fewer than 35,000 people were arrested. Dizzying numbers. One evening in Jakarta I was talking to Suradi Surokusumo. He had studied law and been appointed to the military court. The Ministry of Defence sent him to the Madiun region just after events. 'I had to go to the villages to question the population. "Do you know what our country's flag is?" "Red!" they shouted. "No," I said, "red and white!" "You're wrong," they would reply, "that's our enemy's flag!" They were illiterate people who were easy to indoctrinate.' He was sent to the nearby Magetan Regency. 'So many people were sentenced to death there. I believe unjustly. A prison sentence of a few months would have been enough. They had no idea what they had done. They got the death sentence for having cut a telephone cable! Even for a few communist slogans!' He shook his head. Gruesome photos of the executions in Magetan have been preserved. Suspects were tied together with ropes around their necks. They were forced to march through the villages to a pit. There they were shot. Suradi saw worse things. 'A big pit had been dug.

Twenty-seven people were lying blindfolded along the side. The executioner went by with a knife and lifted their heads up one by one. And then . . . I knew him. He was called Tabrani. He was sleeping in the outbuilding where I was staying. After killing ten, he called out, "Bring me water!" It was thirsty work.'[89]

And Sumarsono, the man whose reckless action in Madiun had unintentionally unleashed the Cold War in Indonesia? During the four-hour conversation an Indonesian historian and I had with him, I gained the impression that he would much rather talk about Surabaya than Madiun. One was a source of pride, the other of, well, what actually? He was the only key figure of the People's Democratic Front who was able to escape.[90] Muso was murdered, Amir was murdered, thousands upon thousands were murdered. All those dead for nothing. Simply because America had chosen the side of the Netherlands and rammed an unpalatable deal down the Republic's throat. Sumarsono had been in five different prisons, he lived in banishment in Sumatra for fourteen years, the PKI banned him from political activities. But he was still alive. Ninety-five at the time of the interview. He died a few months later in Sydney.

Sukarno and Hatta's thorough approach reaped a great deal of praise from the Americans. Robert Lovett, the US undersecretary of state, observed that the Indonesian Republic was 'the only govt in Far East to have met and crushed an all-out Communist offensive'.[91] The fear that the Republic would orient itself towards the Soviet Union had proven completely unjust.[92] On the contrary, the State Department 'has come to believe that the Sukarno–Hatta government might well constitute the last bridge between the West and the Indonesian nationalists'.[93] The US could not have hoped for a better ally in the struggle against the communist advance in Asia, where great changes were underway. After Ho Chi Minh established a communist regime in Indochina, North Korea became communist under Kim Il-sung in September 1948. Most worrying to US foreign policymakers were the decisive advances of Mao's communist forces in mainland China in the last months of the year. In 1947 the US feared the possibility of the Netherlands turning red, but by the end of 1948 it saw a dark red

blotch spreading over large parts of Asia, including the most populous country on earth. This put the Netherlands' actions in an
unflattering new light. For months, the former colonial power had
been resisting new proposals, founding statelets and obstructing referendums, while high-handedly rejecting elections and holding up
talks. To make matters worse, the new high representative of the
crown, Beel, showed himself less shrewd than Van Mook. To his
mind, a resolute attitude was sufficient. The Catholics had just won
the election, now they would win back the Indies too. The new minister of overseas territories, Sassen, a Catholic, and the minister of
foreign affairs, Stikker, a liberal, even made a special trip to Indonesia. Meanwhile, however, the American negotiators had serious
doubts about the Netherlands' 'dangerous misconception' concerning sentiments in the Republic; the Dutch position even seemed 'in
part the result of auto-intoxication'.[94] How much longer could the
US afford to fritter away the forces of moderation? They were
stretched very thin. In three years Indonesia had seen five governments. Some had only lasted a couple of months; all had fallen because
they had to defend the indefensible, yet another concession to the
Netherlands. Wasn't it time to change course? When Stikker landed
back at Schiphol after his discussions on 7 December 1948, a memorandum from the American Secretary of State was thrust into his
hands. It said in so many words that any military action by the Netherlands could have consequences for the Marshall aid to the
Netherlands and its colony. An earlier version had even explicitly
stated 'that further allocations would be subject to most critical
examination'.[95] It is not often that allies have to resort to such men-
acing terms. The Netherlands protested vehemently, but America
had no intention of forcing the Republic to make further concessions. The US had changed sides.

Chapter 14

'A Big Hole that Smells of Earth'
The UN year, December 1948–December 1949

The smell of burnt kerosene. The quivering air above the exhaust from the engines. The long slow taxi to the start of the runway. The column of fighters suddenly motionless. And then . . . in the light of early morning . . . while the world is still blue from the night . . . the awe-inspiring, thundering roar of the first plane as it shoots off, screams past the hangar where you're standing with your duffel bag, your mates and your fear, and climbs steeply into the big blue void.[1]

It was the early morning of 19 December 1948. Several hours earlier, at 10 p.m., High Representative of the Crown Louis Beel had ordered military action. In the previous days the government in The Hague had decided to take up arms, but after Hatta had shown himself willing to accommodate virtually all of the Dutch demands, he had been given one last chance – to Beel's displeasure. Encouraged by the army and navy command, the high representative did all he could to prevent a last-minute political solution. Hatta was sick in bed in the mountains thirty kilometres from his government in Yogyakarta. It was pouring with rain, the roads were bad and Beel deliberately gave him too little time to clarify the Republican position. A couple of hours before midnight on Saturday 18 December, he cancelled the Renville Agreement and green-lighted the new offensive.[2]

Joop Hueting was there that Sunday morning. Ministers and padres had just blessed the men. With 2,000 others he was at the airfield at Semarang, where more than twenty fighters took off. These were the first squadrons to fly south to Yogyakarta, 'the bastards' rallying point', as Hueting remembered it being described.[3] There, they bombed the control towers, the anti-aircraft guns and other vital targets. Planes had taken off elsewhere, too, to disable airfields. The bombs were immediately followed by men: sixteen troop carriers flew in formation to Yogyakarta airport to drop 250 paratroopers. The first large-scale airborne landing operation in Dutch military history proceeded smoothly: the paras were able to quickly seize the strategic positions and clear the runway of mines. Circling high in the sky, above the fighters and the paratroopers, was the B-25 of commander-in-chief Spoor, who watched the course of battle through his binoculars like a modern-day Napoleon. Then it was the turn of the troop carriers with the ground forces. For almost all of them, it was the first time they had flown. 'I got on the plane in Semarang and was taken from there to Yogyakarta,' said Hueting. 'I was transported in a DC-3, the Volkswagen of the air force, you could say.' It was a very short flight, less than twenty minutes, but politically a Rubicon had been crossed: from Dutch to Republican territory, right across the demarcation line stipulated by the Renville Agreement. 'We were so weighed down with ammunition my knees buckled when I jumped down out of the plane,' Hueting said. No fewer than 150 planes took part in that morning's surprise attack, thirty of them in Sumatra.[4] 'Jeeps were flown in too,' he added. 'Everything went according to plan. We assumed positions on the edge of the airport.'[5]

This second Dutch offensive, called Operation Crow but better known in the Netherlands as the Second Police Action, consisted not only of a spectacular air offensive, but also a large-scale ground invasion. Just as in the first offensive, motorised columns followed the main roads to push deep into hostile territory and quickly take the most important cities and junctions. In East Java there was even an amphibious landing. This time the Republican troops managed to carry out more sabotage than in July 1947. Goderd van Heek, the officer who had trained in England and considered the first offensive more fun than war, now saw his first real action. 'We took the road from Semarang to Solo,' he said. A distance of sixty kilometres that took him two days. 'The connecting roads were blocked. They'd blown up bridges. They'd placed mines. Kampong residents had been forced to dig under roads and let them be washed away.'[6]

Map 26: Second Dutch offensive in Java (19 December 1948–5 January 1949)

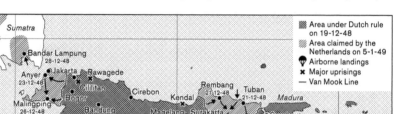

Again the advance went smoothly. Dutch casualties were limited (about a hundred dead between 19 December and 3 January); Republican losses, substantially higher.[7] The numbers can no longer be established, but Soerachman, the young man with the homemade samurai sword and his own little army, was in Yogyakarta at the time. 'The bodies were brought to Yogyakarta by train. From Purwokerto, from Magelang, from Surakarta, from Ambarawa. Sometimes they took three days to get there. The stench . . . The fluid leaking out of the bodies . . . Their clothes were all gone, they were just wrapped in banana leaves. You could tell from the wounds whether they'd been shot or died from bombs: some had a hole in their body, others welts and tears. There were girls among them too: they'd taken care of the nursing or food, some of them had fought alongside the men. Machine-gunned from a plane. I carried the bodies from the train to a truck. One of the guys I'd trained with was among them. At first I didn't recognise him.'[8]

All of Java was overrun. The contrast with Linggajati could not have been greater: according to that two-year-old agreement, the Netherlands would withdraw from its small, urban enclaves and leave Java in its entirety to the Republic – but the former coloniser now had the whole island. The Netherlands had not left Sumatra either, but claimed that island again too. Paratroopers occupied the oil fields of Jambi, Rengat and Airmolek. From Medan, Padang and

Palembang, the soldiers established strategic corridors connecting the east and west coasts. These were more than just new markings on the map. The brutal history of the twentieth century suddenly intruded on the lives of the people of Sumatra's forested interior. 'I had never seen any Dutch or Japanese people before,' related Nursani Tumanggor, a Batak who was fifteen at the time. 'We didn't even have a school or a teacher in our region. We only knew tigers and orangutans. But suddenly the Dutch attacked us and everyone had to hide. We heard shots, we were scared. I didn't see it, but people were killed. Then they came to our market. They asked the pretty girls to cook for them! That included me. There were four of us. I had to cook rice

Map 27: Second Dutch offensive in Sumatra (19 December 1948–5 January 1949)

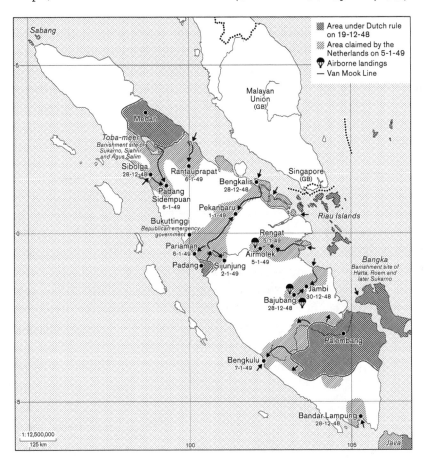

for them. We fetched water from the river and boiled it on a wood fire in the market square. They only stayed here one day, they didn't spend the night, they were just travelling through. I was so nervous. And there were so many of them.'⁹

This second military campaign was not primarily aimed at reconquering production areas to enrich the Dutch treasury, as the first had been. Rather than economic, the main goal was political: the defeat of the Republic. What exactly this meant was, however, far from clear. Eliminating the entire political structure? Recognising it, but replacing the current leaders with straw men? Or simply putting the leaders under pressure with an eye to future negotiations? This was quite a range of options. Incredibly, it is not possible to extract an unambiguous answer to this question from the minutes of the Dutch cabinet or the countless meetings in The Hague.¹⁰ The Netherlands started a war without knowing exactly what it wanted. There was only a broad consensus that Yogyakarta needed to be seized, as Spoor, Van Mook and Wilhelmina had wanted during the first offensive.

Shortly after the airborne landing, special forces advanced on Yogyakarta, followed by infantry. Joop Hueting was among them: 'I was right in the middle of the siege of Yogyakarta. We were the shock troops. We drove from the airport to the city in three-tonners with twenty soldiers in the back. "Hold on tight!" '¹¹ There was some fire when the first Dutch troops drove into the city. They saw slogans and swastikas on the walls: 'Don't do to us what the Germans did to you!' '*Maharadjah* Wilhelmina *lonteh*', Queen Wilhelmina is a whore – her 7 December speech had turned out to be an empty promise.¹² The TNI put up resistance, especially around the presidential palace in the centre of the city, where Sukarno was. The old, classical building with white columns that had once housed the head of the Dutch administration was right next to the kraton, the sultan's extensive palace. Now it was in the line of fire.

Sukotjo Tjokroatmodjo, the man who had fought so bravely during the first Dutch offensive, experienced that crucial day from the other side – and in a special role. He'd had to leave East Java after Renville and had been asked to take on the role of platoon commander in the presidential guard in Yogyakarta. That appealed to him more than being an instructor at a local training centre for sergeants. The anonymous NCO had been promoted to the elite of the Republican armed forces. He moved to the capital and was there on the afternoon of 19 December 1948 when the first Dutch troops arrived, several hours after the landing at the airport. 'The Special Troops Corps were at the door in their green berets. I was in the presidential palace across from Fort Vredeburg with just eighty or ninety soldiers. I suggested to my commander, "Give me thirty lads, you stay here, keep the Hollanders busy, then I can get the president out of here." But my commander kept dithering. Then I went to Major Gandi, who couldn't decide either. In the end I went to President Sukarno himself. He was sitting, I was standing. I said, "You can still escape before the Hollanders take over!" He said, "Red-and-white does not surrender!" He waved his right hand. "But we'll give them this building." ' After news of the attack became known, there were hours of intensive discussion in the presidential palace. Should Sukarno and Hatta flee? Should they opt for exile, like the Dutch queen in World War II? They had planned to go to India to continue the struggle from there with Nehru's support – just as Wilhelmina had done from London with Churchill's support – but it was too late for that now: they had lost the airport. Escaping to Sumatra was not possible any more either. The Republican leaders took a number of very surprising, but in hindsight strategically sound decisions: rather than resisting, Sukarno, Hatta and the Republic's entire political leadership would submit to being arrested. They transferred power to the minister of economic affairs, Sjafruddin Prawiranegara, who, from Bukittinggi in West Sumatra, would guarantee continuity. Finally, Sudirman, the severely ill but irreplaceable head of the armed forces, would slip away from Yogyakarta unseen to continue the struggle from the bush. To keep him from being arrested, his men carried him on a bamboo litter through the forests and over the mountains of Central Java for months, while his commanders, Simatupang and Nasution, took charge of the underground resistance. This safeguarded both military and political continuity and gave the Republic tremendous diplomatic leverage. The imprisonment of its political leaders would not go unnoticed abroad. It's impossible to say now how much they had thought this through tactically, but their gamble astounded our eyewitness. Platoon commander Sukotjo again: 'I had tears in my eyes! We had just smuggled in new weapons from Singapore. Brand-new Lee-Enfield rifles! I broke out in tears! I didn't know anything about Indonesia, but everything about weapons. That was my task as a second lieutenant. I was so angry, I threw down my weapons. I just wanted to keep fighting. They wanted to send me forward with the white flag, but I cried, "That's not my job!" Then they sent someone else. The Dutch accepted him and we threw down our pistols and klewangs.'

The Dutch soldiers entered the presidential palace and ordered everyone to surrender their weapons. But outside it still wasn't over. Sukotjo, who as a child had gone swimming with a nice Japanese grocer and had run around with red-and-white flags after the Proklamasi, would now experience the dramatic nadir of his Republican career. 'We all had to sit in the palace garden with our hands on our heads. There were about sixty of us. As platoon commander, I was the only one wearing insignia. Someone poked me with a machine gun. The Dutch grabbed me and used me as a human shield.' He had to leave the palace garden, go out into the street, onto Malioboro, the city's famous main road, and turn right in front of the kraton, where the last Indonesian troops were. All that time, two soldiers kept their machine guns pointed at him. 'They said, "Tell them to surrender. If we hear one shot, we'll shoot you." It was the day after my twenty-first birthday.' Cautiously he walked down the wide, empty street from the Dutch to the Republican position, right through the no-man's land bordered on both sides by men his age peering tensely through their sights and holding their fingers on their triggers. He could almost feel the gaze of the Dutch machine-gunners stabbing into his back. 'I had no time to be scared. I walked up to our troops and spoke to their commander, a first lieutenant with glasses. You didn't see that often in those days. No shots were fired. Shortly afterwards Sukarno was arrested.'[13]

Yogyakarta had fallen.

Two weeks later. The stylish official residence in Jakarta smelled of *oliebollen*. It was New Year's Eve and, after a hot fish platter, Mrs

Spoor-Dijkema was serving traditional Dutch midwinter dough-nut balls, prepared by her Javanese cook. At midnight her husband, army commander Simon Spoor, raised his glass to everyone's health, especially that of the young, recently inaugurated Queen Juliana in the distant Netherlands and her representative here, Dr Beel, the former prime minister, who was present as a guest. It was a small but elated company. After all, that same day, the military action in Java had been completed – for the first time since the Japanese invasion in March 1942 the whole island was Dutch again – and the war in Sumatra would be concluded within a few days as well. In reply, Beel gave an enthusiastic speech congratulating Spoor on his excellent work. A fortnight earlier it had seemed as if The Hague would once again hesitate, but thanks to their shared determination and extreme pressure – Spoor had even threatened to resign – the politicians had finally given the go-ahead for a short but vigorous campaign. Even before the end of the year, the Republic had been rolled up and its political leaders placed under lock and key. Now a federal Indonesia based on the Dutch template could finally be completed. The party at the Spoors' went on until two-thirty. 'It was a happy evening,' Spoor's wife noted afterwards. Leaving, a friend of hers called it 'the most delightful evening I've had in years'.[14]

But things were not that simple. Yes, Sukarno and the others had been captured, but the Netherlands didn't really know what to do with them. The meticulous planning of the military offensive had not extended to the implausibly messy political reality: when the fighters took off to conquer Yogya and arrest the leaders, nobody knew exactly what to do with them afterwards.[15] For months the Dutch had held meetings and sent telegraphs to and fro, sitting through endless sessions where doubts and calls for action contended, but the hawks – Beel, Spoor, Minister Sassen and the parliamentary leader in the house of representatives, Carl Romme – didn't have a clue what came next. Incomprehensible. The Catholic party had taken charge of the colonial question (Sassen at the ministry of overseas territories; Beel, governor in Jakarta; Romme, parliamentary leader), but a coherent policy plan was nowhere to be seen. After several days' arrest, the Netherlands finally dispatched the seven most important Republican leaders to Sumatra by plane.

'One day I received a telegram in code,' related volunteer Jan Langenberg. He had trained as a radio mechanic and was now a telegraph operator in picturesque Berastagi, a town in the mountains south of Medan. 'Those messages were made up of five-letter codes you had to place a key under. The key was changed weekly. I decoded the message. "Three distinguished guests are coming to visit. Please prepare the *pasanggrahan*."' The pasanggrahan was the official guesthouse. Jan passed the message on to his superiors, but had no idea who would be coming. 'Then an armoured car from Medan pulled up. Sukarno, Sjahrir and Agus Salim got out!' No one less than the Republic's president, former prime minister and minister of foreign affairs. In the meantime Sjahrir had been given a vague position as a presidential advisor. Haji Agus Salim was considered the prudent, non-partisan grand old man of the Hatta government. 'Our commander welcomed them,' Jan Langenberg said. 'Officially they were prisoners, but we pampered them. If they felt like chicken or English cigarettes, they could have them. If Agus Salim needed injections for his health, they were provided. I found that only proper.' During their stay, Langenberg saw that they were nowhere near the demons they had been made out to be. 'Sukarno and Sjahrir presented their credentials to our commander, polite letters in correct Dutch. I thought, they're gentlemen after all. Sjahrir was a fine fellow. Sukarno was the only one with charisma. They should have recognised him right away in 1945, then there wouldn't have been a war. A solution to the advantage of both sides would have been possible.' But Langenberg noticed something else as well. 'Sukarno and Sjahrir didn't get on at all.' That was putting it mildly. Communication had been poor between them for years, but now Sjahrir was furious at Sukarno for letting slip on the radio that they would go into exile in India – his indiscretion contributing to the momentous Dutch decision to move ahead with the second offensive. 'They had surrendered,' Langenberg explained. 'Apparently that had good propaganda value for them. They were held where we were for ten days, then transferred to Parapat on Lake Toba, until they had to go to Bangka

Island.'[16] Confined there, on that swampy, thinly-populated island east of Sumatra, were the other leading Republican figures, among them Prime Minister and Vice-President Hatta and Mohamad Roem, chair of the Indonesian delegation to the Committee of Good Offices. It was like a new Boven Digul! Even if they got English cigarettes and Dutch newspapers, even if Sjahrir was allowed to return to Jakarta to negotiate, the question remained: What was actually the long-term purpose of this? What was the goal behind this nonsensical plan? Did the Netherlands really want to found a new place of banishment for subversive elements? In 1949? The conventional wisdom of 'look before you leap' was seemingly wasted on the trio of Catholic diehards Beel, Sassen and Romme.

And there was something else that should have made the doughballs stick in their throats. The Dutch had reasoned that delaying the launch of their second offensive until 19 December would mean that the UN Security Council would already be recessed for Christmas. A reaction could not be expected until the second half of January at the earliest, by which time the United States of Indonesia would be a fact. But that was failing to account for the great international indignation. Just like last time, Australia raised the alarm at once, but nobody expected the US to immediately join in: together they called an emergency meeting of the Security Council, which led to a resolution on 24 December calling for both parties to immediately suspend hostilities and release the political prisoners.[17] Four days later, two brief resolutions followed, but that New Year's Eve Spoor and Beel weren't particularly troubled. The United Nations response to recent conflicts in Indochina, Palestine and Czechoslovakia had not been that firm either, so it wouldn't amount to very much. If the Soviets could get away with shamelessly supporting a coup in Prague, then the Netherlands could surely liberate Yogyakarta? It was its own overseas territory, after all. First restore law and order and only then talk about a new constitution – that was and remained their motto. Minister of Overseas Territories Sassen had estimated the chance of sanctions as no higher than five per cent.[18] What's more, in the eyes of Spoor, Beel and Sassen, the Indonesian Republic no longer existed. Did the UN still have authority? Hadn't their entire Committee of

Good Offices become irrelevant? How could you negotiate between two parties if one had surrendered? The proponents of military action did not have a very high opinion of the Security Council. Spoor had long seen the Indonesian question as 'a kind of "iron lung" that was needed to keep the institution alive'.[19]

And while the Spoors' guests sipped their champagne and wished each other a prosperous 1949, an hour away by air, the six heads of the Indonesian Republic were being held in dire conditions on Bangka Island. In a tin company's weekend house, they were locked in a single room of six metres by six metres with six beds. Besides that, they had access to a living area of four metres by ten metres, separated from the rest of the room by barbed wire. One of them, Mohamad Roem, had negotiated and signed the Linggajati Agreement alongside Sjahrir. According to that agreement, a free and sovereign Indonesia – the much vaunted United States of Indonesia – would be established on 1 January 1949, the very day that the last barbed wire was nailed in place around their accommodation. Roem noted scornfully: 'Dr Hatta spoke with a smile. He saw wry humour in the fact that fate and history had destined us to be imprisoned and without personal freedom on the day on which the Dutch by the Linggajati Agreement had promised to set free our country.'[20]

There were annoyances – India, Pakistan, Burma and Ceylon, the four newly independent British colonies, banning Dutch planes from their airspace; Saudi Arabia joining them; the boycott resuming in Australia's ports; President Nehru calling an international conference on Indonesia in New Delhi; Burma offering to send an expeditionary force; and even the Americans cancelling the Dutch colony's remaining Marshall aid – but nothing insurmountable.[21] Some international resistance was to be expected. Indonesia-bound Dutch aircraft would just have to refuel somewhere else. There wasn't that much Marshall aid left for Indonesia anyway. And as yet there were no Burmese soldiers in sight. But the US Ambassador to the United Nations, Philip Jessup, delivering a scathing speech to the Security Council on 11 January 1949 – that stung. He didn't hold back. 'My Government in considering the Netherlands–Indonesian dispute cannot but recall a history of non-cooperation on the part of the Netherlands in the work of the Committee of Good Offices in Indonesia. [. . .] Even prior to the resumption of military action against the Republic, the Netherlands pursued a policy which had the effect of weakening the Republic; working unnecessary hardship on the population; isolating the Republican Government economically and politically; and presenting it with a prefabricated interim administration. [. . .] From a purely pragmatic point of view it should be pointed out that the quick military successes of the Netherlands forces will not effect a solution of the Indonesian problem. [. . .] It may well be that the only victory will be that of the forces of anarchy.'[22]

Rarely had the Americans rebuked an ally so harshly, let alone before the eyes of the whole world. The Dutch hard-liners had hoped that the dissolution of the Republic would free their hands again, but their abrupt military offensive had not convinced the United Nations to relinquish control. The resolutions of late December had been mild, but in the course of January the pressure increased. After the British year of 1945–6, the Dutch year of 1947 and the American year of 1948, 1949 would become the momentous year of the United Nations. The Security Council became more actively engaged with the Indonesian question than ever. There were new resolutions, a new commission and new efforts to reach a satisfactory conclusion. From 1 January, the council's five permanent members were joined by Argentina, Canada, Cuba, Egypt, Norway and Ukraine. The consensus they achieved had many fathers. The US was driven by fervent anti-communism, Ukraine and the Soviet Union by fervent anti-imperialism, Norway and Canada had their own motives and so on. America's role remained decisive, but without the international framework of the United Nations, US diplomacy would not have been able to achieve the results it did.

The most important diplomat on the Dutch side was Herman van Roijen, a skilled and invariably polite negotiator whose position was closer to Schermerhorn's than Beel's. Even though Van Roijen had argued against the second Dutch offensive, he now took to the international stage to pick up the pieces.[23] He informed the Security Council that the Netherlands was considering the release of the

imprisoned political leaders, and on 6 January he convinced Queen
Juliana to state publicly once again that the Netherlands' aim was the
decolonisation of Indonesia. On 7 January he announced that
the captive leaders had been granted freedom of movement all over
the island of Bangka. Despite the thanklessness of his task, he applied
himself diligently. But a week later it turned out he'd been deceived.
The Republican leaders on Bangka didn't have any freedom at all;
they were still locked up in their one and a half rooms surrounded by
barbed wire. Van Roijen had no choice but to apologise to the Security Council. He was forgiven his faux pas, but the credibility of the
Netherlands had suffered another heavy blow. Antics like this showed
they were not taking the crisis seriously. The country he was trying
to serve to the best of his abilities had failed the test of history.[24]

On the initiative of the US, feverish work on a new, more forceful
resolution began.[25] On 28 January 1949 it was ready: Resolution 67,
submitted by the US, China, Cuba and Norway, was passed without
any dissenting votes – only France abstained. It was the third-longest
resolution in UN history to that date: four detailed pages instead of
a few measured sentences. What's more, the formulation deviated
from an appeal to both parties or other diplomatic niceties. This time
the Netherlands and the Netherlands alone was declared at fault. The
preamble could not have been clearer: 'continued occupation of
the territory of the Republic of Indonesia by the armed forces of the
Netherlands is incompatible with the restoration of good relations
between the parties.' The resolution is also exceptional in that it not
only 'considers', 'recommends' and 'calls upon' – the usual jargon –
but also stipulates, robustly and point by point, how the future
should unfold: by 15 March 1949 (within six weeks) there had to be an
interim federal government, elections for an Indonesian constituent
assembly had to be completed by 1 October 1949, and a transfer of
sovereignty had to take place no later than 1 July 1950. The Security
Council had had enough and was seizing control. To keep to that
tight schedule, the Netherlands had to immediately and unconditionally release the political leaders, reinstate the Republican government
and relinquish Yogyakarta and its immediate surroundings. Initially
the Americans had even demanded the relinquishment of all territory

seized in the second offensive. After this, new negotiations had to commence under UN supervision. The days of 'good offices' and other non-coercive mediation attempts were over: the Committee of Good Offices was transformed into a much more powerful agency, the UNCI, the United Nations Commission for Indonesia. Never before had a Security Council commission been given so much power. It was charged with supervising the planned elections, mediating during negotiations and formulating recommendations for the transfer of power.[26] It would still be made up of the same three countries (America, Australia and Belgium), but the requirement of unanimity was to be dropped: a simple majority would now suffice. In practice this meant that Belgium's pro-Dutch vote would be much less significant. With Resolution 67, the UN claimed the right to intervene extensively in the Indonesian question. The Dutch had effectively been placed under international supervision in Indonesia.

Diplomatically the Netherlands had its back to the wall, but the Catholic triumvirate of Beel, Sassen and Romme, inspired by Spoor, continued to push their hard line: the Republic was gone; Indonesia was once again an internal question; it was none of the UN's business. As a result, all of the UN instructions were ignored, the imprisoned leaders were not released and Yogya was definitely not relinquished. Instead the Netherlands turned freshly conquered Central Java into a new state and even organised elections there. In February Beel went a step further. Without informing the UNCI, he launched an alternative proposal that astonished friend and foe: the Netherlands was prepared to transfer power to the United States of Indonesia on 1 April 1949, fifteen months before the UN deadline. No transitional period, no interim government, but independence a few weeks after the completion of a round-table conference. Beel called his 'spectacular deed' an attempt to 'prevent international custodianship' and 'emerge from the breakers with our heads held high'. The reasoning was simple: in his opinion, 'no self-respecting sovereign state could swallow' Resolution 67.[27] In New York, Van Roijen severely questioned the plan's chances of success. It was transparently clear that Beel was trying to evade the UN by forcing through his own solution. But wouldn't everyone see that this accelerated 'transfer of sovereignty' remained highly conditional? The Republic would not be re-established and the prisoners would not return. Beel persisted anyway, counting on his excellent local connections: the support of the federal states.

And then something no one had predicted happened, sealing the fate of the Netherlands' late-colonial ambitions. The leaders of the friendly states, the Netherlands' most loyal allies in the archipelago, took the side of the Republic. People like Anak Agung, prime minister of East Indonesia, and Sultan Hamid, head of the government of West Borneo, spoke out against the Dutch approach and refused to participate in the proposed round-table conference while the Republican leaders were still imprisoned. It was either *with* Sukarno, or *without* them. They also demanded that the UN, in the form of the UNCI, be present at the talks as well. 'This was an extremely important and decisive decision,' Anak Agung remembered; the states had made 'the Republic's prior conditions their own'. For Beel, this unexpected *démarche* came as 'a knife in the back'.[28] Until then the 'federalists' had always been Jakarta's puppets, docile fellow travellers who never made common cause with the 'Republicans' in Yogyakarta. But that snug relationship now came to an end: the federalists closed ranks with the Republicans and left Beel out in the cold.

Not having any friends left in New York didn't matter that much, but the loss of the Netherlands' closest friends in the former colony was disastrous. Internationally the Netherlands had been very weak for some time (only Belgium and France still supported it), but from March 1949 it was completely isolated. The brief military success of the second offensive had led to a fiasco. It had been a diplomatic blunder and a psychological stupidity. Beel thought he could play the game harder than his predecessor Van Mook, but he didn't know the terrain well enough and, perhaps more importantly, didn't understand the people. As a governor, that put him on a line with pre-war governors like Fock and De Jonge, who had also made the mistake of believing that only violence can achieve lasting results – a classic fallacy – when a lighter touch that left room for understanding and consultation could have led to a stronger and more permanent outcome. By wanting it all, Beel ended up with nothing. In the

Netherlands, the Indonesian question is often presented as a debate between left and right in Dutch society, and in the parliament it often took that form, but actually it was much more a question of who suffered from psychological myopia and who did not.

Of course, in retrospect it's always easy to judge, but let's not forget that there were also very sharp contemporary critics. People like Jacques de Kadt, a social democratic parliamentarian who in these months went against his own party by writing the remarkable essay *The Indonesian Tragedy*. In the current Dutch administration he discerned 'a staggering lack of national and international responsibility' that had led to a catastrophic outcome. 'We are revealed to the world as tyrants and cheats.' De Kadt didn't mince words: 'Only with policies that allow the quick emergence of a sovereign Indonesian state – without quibbling, and without the constant meddling of Beel, Spoor and Co. – can we rehabilitate ourselves in the eyes of the world.' But there could be no doubt as to the fate of the overseas territory. 'The Netherlands has lost Indonesia. And by "lost" I mean "completely lost".'[29] The words blazed out of his pen. 'That which could have been repaired in 1945 and could have led to the cooperation of two independent states [. . .], this great prospect, which could have raised us up out of provincialism, has been destroyed by the provincial politicians of all the Dutch parties. What is left to us is this: realising what we missed and botched. What is left to us is shame at all our narrow-mindedness, incompetence and conceit. The fools who believe that we are right and the whole world is misled, and the even greater fools who believe that we are a shining example to the world, need to be seen for what they are, people who have proved utterly inadequate and wreaked incalculable damage on our country and nation.'[30]

A short hard jab to force the Republic to its knees? Just as the first Dutch offensive ended up lasting six months instead of a fortnight, the expansionary offensive of December 1948 led to fighting that dragged on for eight months, until mid-August 1949. It became the most intense phase of the whole decolonisation war, with the most dead. For the Dutch troops, these were also the most exhausting months. Many of them had been stationed in the country for more than two and a half years, with no prospect of speedy relief. For the Republican military, it was a question of life and death.

On paper the Netherlands occupied all of Java and a quarter of Sumatra, but in practice it held only the roads and cities. Just as after the first offensive, the interior remained in Republican hands. What's more, the TNI returned to the territories it had been obliged to leave after Renville. That was only logical: if the Netherlands crossed the Van Mook Lines, of course the Republicans would do the same in the opposite direction. These infiltrations had actually been going on for some time. Now Republican troops poured into all of Java. The Siliwangi Division's return to West Java from Central Java became legendary. Thousands and thousands of soldiers walked back home, often accompanied by women and children, a journey of several months through jungle and sawah that many carried out barefoot, occasionally strafed by Dutch planes. 'Then a frenzied panic would break out and the mothers would scream for their children,' Poncke Princen, who was there, related. Like Piet van Staveren he had crossed over to the Republic as a protest against Dutch actions and seen the suffering his fatherland was causing. 'Once a whole family was hit by a bomb about fifty metres away from us. It was like a slaughterhouse: the father and two children were dead, but three women, a little boy and a baby were in a terrible state. Half-severed limbs and big patches of skin burnt off. [. . .] What in the name of God had they done to deserve this: having to run for cover in their own country so as not to be hit by foreign bullets!'[31] Descriptions like this contrasted sharply with commander-in-chief Spoor's rousing words at the start of the offensive, reminding his troops that they were not warriors, 'but bringers of justice and security' to a population that had already 'suffered for too long under terror and oppression'.[32]

The consequence of the expansion was that the Netherlands had to deploy its troops over a much greater area – and therefore disperse them. And this provided the other side with new opportunities. Throughout Java and Sumatra the troops switched back to guerrilla tactics, but much more systematically and fanatically than before. 'We stalked them from the north, south, east and west!' said Johannes

Soewondo.³³ On the Dutch side, Joop Hueting could only confirm it. 'The worst violence started after the Second Police Action. The real combat started after the UN Resolution.'³⁴ The guerrilla warfare was more than the local convulsions of the splintered remnants of an army. It was a conscious, centrally controlled choice. While the ailing commander-in-chief Sudirman was being carried away on his bamboo litter, Siliwangi commander Nasution decided to put Java under military rule. 'That way I was able to arrange within three months that all of Java, down to the smallest hamlets, was one big guerrilla area. That was a struggle the Dutch could never win.' He added: 'Guerrilla warfare is based on the people. You have to harass the enemy everywhere, never let them rest. In turn, their actions get harsher. It keeps getting worse. [. . .] It all comes down to the attitude of the people. If the people support you, you will always win. That is my "science of war". The crux is mobilising the people.'³⁵ If necessary, by resorting to violence. On 5 January 1949 Nasution issued instructions for 'totalitarian' struggle. 'All citizens of Indonesia who collaborate with the enemy will be considered traitors in time of war and tried as such.'³⁶ Anyone who had been paying attention knew what that meant: a bullet in the brain.

But how popular was the Republic now, after Renville, after the Darul Islam uprising, after the Madiun rebellion, after Sukarno's arrest? Its reputation turned out to be largely intact. In Poncke Princen's experience, the villagers 'took it for granted' that they would feed the soldiers and their families and put them up for the night. They were also very willing to share intelligence. How many Dutch soldiers were in the area? How often did they patrol? What was the best route to take to avoid them? Questions like that were quickly answered. 'In the area we covered we had the support of, I would say, eighty to ninety per cent of the population.'³⁷ Others saw it the same way. 'Everywhere we went in West Java, the population had set up communal kitchens and gave us food to take with us, wrapped in banana leaves,' remembered battalion commander Kemal Idris. 'The population was one hundred per cent on our side.'³⁸ The same thing was seen elsewhere too. 'We had the support of the population,' related Piet van Staveren about the mountainous country outside of

Yogyakarta.[39] Outside the areas where Islamists and communists had taken up arms against the nationalists, the population remained largely loyal to the Republican project. Some details were telling. 'The villagers did more than just give us food,' said Johannes Soewondo. 'At the start of their village they would put a *wan* out in the road, one of those baskets for separating the chaff from the rice. That was their way of showing whether the coast was clear.' He summed it up nicely: 'We were like fish, the population was the water.[40]

In other places, too, the fire was still burning brightly. On Bali, Goos Blok was patrolling a village one evening. 'There was a wayang show on. They were projecting the shadows on a sheet. We watched from a distance. It was a play about the Balinese resistance, with Dutch soldiers and Balinese resistance fighters.' The ancient shadow theatre had adapted wonderfully well to the needs of the day. The Wayang Museum in Jakarta preserves a magnificent set of *wayang revolusi* puppets representing Dutch and Indonesian characters. Shows like this helped maintain enthusiasm for the Republic, especially in places where there wasn't any radio. Goos Blok: 'A Balinese resistance fighter put his foot on a Dutchman's neck and shouted "Merdeka!".[41]

And while the shadow play entertained the villagers, young pemuda slipped out into a different kind of shadow world. Farmer's son Ahmad Muhadi went out every night. He lived south of Yogyakarta and saw his area occupied for the first time. 'The Dutch were everywhere. They left women and children alone, but killed ordinary farmers for no reason. They provided for their families!' Aggression like that could not go unanswered. 'We mostly fought at night. Pak Komaruddin was our leader, he was a second lieutenant. In the evening he called us together for the struggle. We ate together. We prayed together. We practised magic so we wouldn't get wounded. Then we set out. The Dutch had much better weapons than us, accurate rifles and lots of planes, but they were scared of the dark. They had Indonesian spies too. As soon as we knew who they were, we killed them. A lot of my friends were killed, others got scared and went away, not everyone was equally brave. After a night's fighting we went back home to sleep. We slept in the daytime. My father didn't ask any questions.[42] Soerachman, too, knew that not everyone supported the Revolusi. 'There were a lot of spies. You saw it from the way they held themselves. They looked around, they acted strange. I was in the security forces and had to identify spies. Then we killed them. We had a lot of places to do that.'[43]

The guerrilla fighters had a mishmash of weapons: rusty carbines from the Dutch era, worn-out pistols and mortars from Japanese arms depots, bombs and aeroplane machine guns that had been left behind, grenades of dubious quality . . . 'Not every soldier had a fire-arm,' said Johannes Soewondo. 'We had one gun for several soldiers and took turns. None of us were familiar with guns, so we missed a lot, even with accurate rifles, whereas the Dutch killed a lot of people.'[44] The Republican forces were short on ammunition too and the supply lines often broke down. Sometimes you had to be lucky, Sukotjo discovered. After serving as a human shield at the fall of Yogya, he escaped to the countryside with sixteen of his men. 'I didn't have a weapon at first, but after two weeks of patrolling we found a house full of grenades. I used four of them in an attack on a Dutch post. We couldn't capture it. I lost a sergeant – his whole belly was torn open – and then I lay in a paddy field for seven hours with a pistol ready until they were gone. Seven hours!'[45]

The Republican soldiers had to make do with what they had. They used old grenades and shells to make incendiary devices. Aeroplane machine guns were often the only automatic weapons they had. They used 100–200-kg aerial bombs to blow up countless bridges. Although, unlike Poncke Princen, Piet van Staveren didn't take up arms himself after deserting, he saw how his comrades set to work. 'There wasn't any real combat, but not a single Dutch transport came through unscathed. On the mountainside, they laid mines you could trigger with a string. When a truck came past they blew it up. And on winding mountain roads they would often build a bank of branches so it looked like the road went straight ahead, whereas it actually curved away. In the twilight, that worked well and the transport would drive into the ravine.'[46] While the Dutch convoys were made up of trucks, jeeps, tanks, armoured cars, weapon carriers and Bren carriers, the TNI had virtually no vehicles. That was why Johannes Soewondo participated in an armed raid on a truck. ' "Get out!" I screamed. "Keys! Line up! Turn around! March!" I shouted the orders in Japanese!' That was the language he'd been trained in. The Dutch soldiers seemed to get the message. 'They walked away and we took the truck.'[47]

It was all make-do, but sometimes those separate initiatives could be combined into collective action. On 1 March 1949 the Republican army delivered the greatest blow of the whole decolonisation war: it recaptured Yogyakarta. They had been working on it for months. Soerachman delivered intelligence from the occupied city to guerrilla units in the country. 'I took a barrow and smuggled documents with me. If they asked me at a checkpoint where I was going, I cried in Dutch, "Fetching rice from the farmers!" Because if they even suspected you were with the guerrillas, they took you away in a jeep and tortured you with electricity. They threw you up against the wall even if you were innocent.' Several thousand soldiers prepared. Soerachman, the man with the improvised samurai sword, began talking faster. 'The night before, our friends came to the city from the forest. On foot! They were tired. I gave them *nasi gudeg*, rice with jackfruit, and arranged places for them to sleep. For myself, I didn't get much sleep that night. At six o'clock in the morning the siren sounded and it was, Wham! They took up arms and pushed through to Fort Vredeburg in the centre of town. Quite a lot of Dutch tanks were destroyed.' It was a spectacular surprise attack led, among others, by Suharto, the later president of Indonesia, but they couldn't hold the city for long. Soerachman related: 'A few hours later the planes came from Semarang and Suharto shouted, "Back! Back!" Afterwards we saw the dead lying everywhere on the streets.' It was a Pyrrhic victory, but of enormous symbolic value. For the outside world, too, it made a lot of difference. 'Palar, our man at the United Nations, had something to show: we still exist.'[48] Exactly.

As far as the real situation was concerned, the United Nations was completely in the dark. The UNCI was in Jakarta and its military observers – several dozen officers from various countries – were not allowed inland. The Dutch authorities did all they could to stop them: the planes were full, they claimed, some areas were too dangerous, others turned out to be temporarily sealed off, et cetera.[49] The UN observers themselves only had eighteen jeeps at their disposal and were dependent on Dutch facilities and cooperation.[50] Anyone who reads the correspondence between the UNCI and the Dutch authorities in Jakarta will find nothing but stonewalling. In early January one of the UNCI's leading negotiators became extremely agitated when, three weeks after the start of the offensive, 'not one military observer is yet in process of returning to the field'.[51] Six months after their second offensive, the Dutch were clearly hiding their activities from the international community. Was it just because the Netherlands still didn't recognise the legitimacy of the Security Council? Or was there more to it?

'In general we didn't like people like that looking over our shoulders,' remarked Lieutenant Van Heek.[52] 'Apart from France and Belgium, the whole world was against us.' After the smooth capture of Surakarta he saw that the spoils were still far from secured. 'It all seemed to be going so well for the Dutch. The Second Police Action was a success. Only after that did things get worse. We were stationed near the racecourse. Soon they began harassing us while we slept.' And that was just the beginning. In the months that followed, he was deployed in various places in Central Java, far from all international observers. Whatever Beel and his friends claimed, the Republic was nowhere near defeated. Van Heek led a platoon of thirty-seven soldiers, but, as he wrote in his memoirs, 'wandering around Yogya were thousands of guerrillas, who were very difficult to get a grip on, as they hid among the population and made use of an excellent warning system'.[53] His worst experiences were in the area between Yogyakarta and Surakarta. The old sultanates were densely populated and 'the region was literally crawling with enemies'. His memoirs leave no room for doubt: 'The Dutch detachments could be compared to islands in a large, hostile sea of *pelopors* [pemuda] and extremists.'[54]

When I interviewed Goderd van Heek at home in Velp, he spoke appreciatively of his adversaries. 'Those guerrillas were no pushover. They wanted to demonstrate that they were in charge. That was why it was so very necessary to keep patrolling. "Unremitting pursuit" was our motto. They wanted to get us out in the open, so we had to keep moving so they didn't know where we were. If they couldn't see us, they'd had it. We often set out on patrol at two in the morning. Around six we'd arrive at a chosen kampong and have an overview of the situation. If the dogs started barking, they'd know we were coming. We'd cut the telephone lines. On a lot of patrols nothing happened and we'd turn back without having accomplished any-thing, but on the way back we'd often set up an ambush. I'd double back in a big circle and outflank them so that *we* could attack *them*. In military terms, I "screwed them good and proper". They suffered losses. Yes, they did. The very first time it's tough. It's you or him, you know that, but later you don't think about it as much. Not that we killed that many anyway.'

After the interview we went through a whole pile of documents he'd laid out in preparation. Photographs, sketches, topographic maps, notes, decorations. Among them was a table from immediately after the war in which he had detailed the results of engagements involving troops under his direct command. Between December 1948 and August 1949 his platoon of a few dozen soldiers killed 104, wounded six and took seven prisoner. They captured some thirty rifles, revolvers and mortars, as well as mortar shells, bombs, bullets, pointed weapons, two typewriters, a pair of binoculars and a bicycle. On his side there were only four wounded. As surprising as these figures may be, killing an armed foe is classified as legitimate – that was decided around 1900 by the Geneva and Hague Conventions. Since then, civilians and unarmed soldiers (for instance those who have been defeated, wounded or captured) have been considered illegitimate military targets. But in a guerrilla war, the boundary between hostile soldiers and innocent civilians is often very vague, especially when the soldiers don't wear uniforms and the civilians are forced to work with them. 'The term "civilian victim" is relative in a guerrilla war,' said Van Heek, 'because civilians helped by keeping watch. They may have done that because they, too, loved freedom, but the soldiers also forced them. Even children and women were forced to keep a lookout.' According to Van Heek, the hazy dividing line was a deliberate tactic on the part of the TNI command. As a result, the Dutch would inflict casualties on the innocent, causing the population 'to hate us even more', until a 'national hatred' of the Dutch existed. He was frank. 'Because of the ruthless guerrilla warfare a lot of innocent blood flowed. Mostly there were more casualties among the population than among the geurrilas.'[55]

Van Heek's testimony is interesting because it identifies the narrow border between the legitimate and illegitimate use of force. He was worshipped by his men – 'one of our best officers', 'someone I will never forget', 'all honour to this lieutenant', wrote one of them – and after the war Queen Juliana decorated him with the Bronze Lion for 'especially courageous and skilful deeds' that demonstrated not only his 'dauntlessness' but also his 'exceptional leadership qualities'.[56] As a disciplined former officer, he explicitly opposed excessive force. 'Houses were set on fire out of spite, but who does that harm? And summary executions? They didn't happen often. Perhaps once. We took prisoners.' He acknowledged that there were abuses, definitely, and added that 'things that were highly disputable were also done on the Republican side. It's easy to point the finger.' What's more, the circumstances were tremendously difficult. 'For a couple of weeks we had to guard the big Gondangwinangoen sugar refinery. Someone shot at a sergeant from a nearby kampong. He was foolish enough to show himself. Then I ordered the men to shell the kampong. A few mortar shells. Then you don't know how many civilian casualties you've caused. I noted the incident in my patrol report.'[57] Military decisions often have to be made in a fraction of a second: it's night, an NCO has just drawn fire, the platoon is under-strength, the enemy is out there somewhere and if you don't react they might advance . . . Firing from a distance with tanks, ships, aircraft or artillery is considered a war crime when the military necessity is uncertain or when the toll on civilians is irresponsibly high. Van Heek acknowledged that his list of victims did not cover this kind of violence at all, but admitted that there were often more civilian than military victims. 'Hekking's squad', he wrote about an action that killed twelve, 'opened fire on a number of fugitives and caused casualties, probably including several guerrilla fighters.'[58]

★

When considering war crimes, it is useful to make a distinction between three forms of unlawful violence: *incidental*, *structural* and *systematic* mass violence.[59] Incidental war crimes occur when several soldiers flout the rules of war and, for revenge or out of rage or sadism, mow down unarmed civilians, burn villages or carry out other actions without any military necessity. Dutch war crimes in Indonesia are often described as 'excesses', regrettable but isolated intemperance that happens in every war but is not an intrinsic part of it. These individual perpetrators can, in principle, be prosecuted – even if that's an extremely rare occurrence. The frequency is low and responsibility does not extend very far up the chain of command.

Structural mass violence goes a step further: here, rather than haphazard events caused by a number of derailed individuals, the war crimes are frequent and the result of a combination of factors such as poor training, insufficient education, bad officers and NCOs, troop shortages, fatigue, boredom, frustration, poor food, a lack of rest and relaxation and so on. In similar circumstances, more soldiers would react similarly. While incidental violence is a failing of individuals, structural violence is a failing of the institutions in which those individuals are embedded. The frequency is higher, and responsibility lies with the senior officers, army command and even the political leadership.

More serious still are systematic war crimes. If incidental and structural war crimes are theoretically avoidable side effects of warfare, systematic violence is intrinsic to it. It is part of the military strategy. The public show trials carried out by Westerling and his troops in South Sulawesi are the best example of this, but the systematic torture of adversaries by Dutch forces to obtain information also falls into this category.[60] These were not interrogations that got out of hand, but standard intelligence-gathering methods that were an inalienable part of the system. Such crimes are not random/haphazard, but deliberate. Accordingly, they occur with the greatest frequency. If the decisions are made or tolerated by the perpetrators' superiors, the guilt lies with the highest levels of military and political authority.

★

In the mid-1970s a man was lying on the street in Brussels. He'd just been hit by a car and felt terribly groggy. He didn't feel any pain. He no longer knew he was a professor of clinical psychology at the Free University of Brussels. Hazy images, impressions, sounds crowded in on him. He was lying in the sun again, lying on the ground. Past and present merged into each other like in a liquid light show. The soil, the mud, the sweat, the heat. 'I was back in the Indonesian sawah again,' Joop Hueting said.

He had spoken about his military service on television and given countless interviews about it. His archives were bursting with news-paper clippings and notes, the issue had occupied him for his entire adult life, but he had hardly published anything about it besides the-oretical considerations. Details and names weren't mentioned; as a clinical psychologist, it was the patterns and structures that interested him. I spoke to him repeatedly in Amsterdam and those conversa-tions were especially informative. If Goderd van Heek testified about legitimate force with incidental peaks of mass violence, Joop Hueting was, without a doubt, the most important voice broaching the issue of structural war crimes.

'We moved from village to village and caught a boy of about eighteen in a black outfit. No weapons, but highly suspicious. Come with us. Questioned. Afterwards Van Diepen, our officer candidate, said to his aide, "Just shoot that boy dead." But he refused. Three times! "Do it yourself!" he said. "Disobeying orders in time of war! You're going to be court-martialled!" The Indonesian boy walked off and we laughed.'

'In another village, near Yogyakarta, a colonel told us that we had to go off the road and into a couple of kampongs and shoot every-thing that moved. We went to that village, he stayed behind. We gave a friendly smile to the women, who were scared to death. We fired a few rounds into the air. When we got back the colonel said, "Brilliant. Well done, lads!" That was in the last few weeks, when it was already a lost cause.'

But how had it started?

'Our group came from secondary school and formed during train-ing. Freek Halbertsma, Wim Brocks, Piet Ouwehand, Jack M., Flip

Cappetti. I was a private, right at the bottom of the ladder. We didn't know anything about politics. On the boat we were briefed, but very poorly. There was a film on board too, *Cavalier of the West*.'

The pamphlet *Onze taak overzee*, 'Our Task Overseas', was distributed on board and explained that the plan wasn't to restore the old colonialism, but to establish 'law and order' together with the country's 'benevolent forces', so that 'new political structures' could develop, within which the people could truly discover 'the blessings of freedom'.[61]

And then the Second Police Action began.

'We noticed that the paras and commandos were opening fire at the drop of a hat. There were holes everywhere. They shot through ceilings, china cabinets, buffaloes and sometimes even people. They were rough characters.

'The town of Kotagede [known for its silverwork] was plundered bare. Wim Brocks got some stuff out of the trailer of a jeep, filled to the rim with silver. The whole place had been shot up. Our platoon filled our pockets with silver coins, traditional daggers, jewels and all kinds of silver objects. I took a lot of stuff too. Bayonets, knives, an Indonesian girl's diary, a Koran in Javanese. Nicked out of some imam's house.

'Those night patrols . . . Weighed down with gear . . . You were forced to support each other, especially if you came under fire. I remember I was lying in the sawah and a snake came slithering past . . .

'In the paddy fields you always felt naked. They were at the edge of the field, in the vegetation. Close by. We both fired. He was lying there. I took his pistol. I got his documents out of his breast pocket. A TNI lieutenant. That strange, crumpled body.'

And then there were your own wounded. 'The pain of others, threatening to demoralise you. You wanted that gone too; at least I did. In some cases you're nothing but flesh with nothing but pain. The lightly wounded would sometimes completely give in to panic. You'd see it slowly taking over. In the heavily wounded who were still conscious you'd sometimes see euphoria too: humming songs, making jokes nobody laughed at. And then the ones who were in tremendous pain. The wounded became a different breed. I didn't like it, but you kept getting stuck with them.'

I asked him if there had been fatalities in his unit too. He nodded with difficulty and gulped for breath. 'Cappetti had been shot and was confused. "Cappetti's going to heaven," he kept saying. He didn't make it. His brother didn't either, by the way. He fell with the shock troops. Later I went to see their parents.'

Moral standards became deeply blurred. 'When we were on patrol, a peasant with a buffalo was walking towards us. The lad in front of me, Henk K., shot him dead for no reason. Blood spurted out of his left shoulder. I screamed, "Stop it!!" but kept walking. Jack M. went trigger-happy too. More and more. He became dangerous to us and was put in hospital. Later he went to Australia or New Zealand and turned Catholic. Or that driver, that boneheaded kid from Brabant, who wanted to test his Owen gun on a few of the badly wounded. All dead. And Sergeant Z. started shooting up a place of worship with his Sten gun. A woman came crawling up to me. Begging on her knees. It was pitch-black. The squad walked on. All the others said to the sergeant was, "Goddammit, be a bit careful, will you? Don't shoot us. Bullets go right through those bamboo walls." '

At that last recollection, tears welled up in his eyes. The image of that woman on her knees had stayed branded on his memory until the last year of his life.

'We had machine guns. "We'll show them who's the most power-ful here." From a distance of 100 or 200 metres, we riddled kampongs with bullets. Court-martial? What are you talking about! I wasn't stupid. Of course I didn't dare report it. That would have been treason.'

According to Joop Hueting, the problems were structural. 'We were badly trained. Too much drilling, too much cleaning, not real-istic enough. And we were badly led. Young commanders. Often dumb and uninterested. Chaotic situations. Poor fire discipline. No pacification plan. Over and over again, platoons and companies needed to be regrouped. Shortages of troops, arms and support. A lot of the men had breakdowns. No leave. Poor-quality food. Having to pay extra for eggs, things from the Chinese shop and so on.'

That food. Hueting's and other accounts talk about sausage and sauerkraut – in the tropics . . . Tinned stew – with coconuts.[62] And the boredom of endless volleyball matches – always that same awful game – and the platitudes in the letters home. 'Everything still fine here', 'how lovely that Nell has had her baby', because why worry them with stories that they, with their crocheted doilies and floral wallpaper and milk bottles on the doorstep, wouldn't understand anyway, stories about mud and blood on a sweltering dirt road and blackened brains crawling with flies, stories about bamboo huts burning so fiercely that the roar of the flames drowns out the screams of the people who lived there, stories about naked fifteen-year-olds writhing on the concrete with electric wires attached to their bodies. No, you couldn't bother them with the friendship and filthy jokes of your mates here, who can't even drink out of a teacup any more, they're so used to canteens, taps and mugs. Why bother the home front with stories like these? What did they know about your body's never-ending dark longing for another body, even if only for a single night, if only for a quarter of an hour, just a moment, to momentarily be allowed to hide your tanned, leathery, grim face in one of those thick heads of dark anonymous hair.[63]

Joop Hueting again: 'The exhaustion, the monotony of the long patrols, the rain, the rivers, the sawah, the drying sweat. Human emotions of fear of dying, terror, sexual intercourse, love, hate . . .'

Silence.

'Years later, when the fireworks went off at Scheveningen, I threw myself on the floor of my room . . .'

Silence.

'Halbertsma got a job at a bank. Piet Ouwehand became an accountant. Wim Brocks worked at a chicken factory in Oss. He was my only friend.'

Deep sigh. Then, haltingly: ' "Blom's cracked," they whispered. They'd crawled around to the rear of the barracks to take cover. Henk was sitting at the front staring at the ground. A big, strapping fellow, over six feet, someone you could count on, but he couldn't take it any more. When he came back from patrol the tea had just been made and was still too hot to drink. He smashed his torch on a mate's shoulder and shot up his own barracks with his Sten gun. Fortunately not at his mates but straight through the roof. Everyone whispered, "Henk Blom's gone mad . . ." Everyone was too scared to move. He was sitting in the shadows with his gun ten metres away and staring at his legs. I went up to him with my knees shaking. I sat down next to him. I put my hand on his knee and said, "Tough, isn't it, Henk?" That was the longest ten minutes of my life.'[64]

On television he was calm, unemotional and analytical. It was 17 January 1969 when Joop Hueting, who had just obtained his doctorate in psychophysiology, broke the great silence about the mass violence in Indonesia in a now-famous television interview aired by the social democratic VARA broadcasting company. It had been scheduled for a month earlier, on 19 December 1968, exactly twenty years after the launch of the Second Police Action, but with Christmas just around the corner, the broadcaster decided to wait so that large numbers of respectable family men would not suddenly be seen as war criminals by their wives and children on that silent night, holy night. A month later it came anyway.

'I hadn't expected it, but it exploded like a bomb.'

That was the least you could say. For weeks the Dutch media, politicians and army steamrollered each other with intense reactions for or against. The VARA received no fewer than 885 letters from veterans confirming or denying Hueting's account on the basis of their own experiences.[65] At home, his telephone didn't stop ringing. He received 200 calls and more than a hundred letters. The international press, too, wanted to hear what he had to say. Some correspondents spoke of their 'admiration' and 'inexhaustible joy' at the way the wall of silence around the theme had been broken open, others called him 'a coward', 'a dirty yellowbelly' and 'a filthy swine'. Psychiatrist H. J. van der Wiel of Gouda called him a 'slimy traitor' trying to suppress his own subconscious by 'disgustingly projecting it into others'. Serious death threats were made. 'That was mostly veterans,' Joop Hueting recalled. 'Those cowards would call to say, "We're across from your house with machine guns."' His archives still contain the proof. Former NCO J. Muller of The Hague asked if he realised that

he had 'signed his own death warrant' with that broadcast. Johan de
Pree, a friend of his late father's, wrote, 'You'll get your just deserts,
hopefully soon!' A group that called itself 'the Spijkerkwartier', after
an area in Arnhem, reported: 'Rubbing you out shouldn't be done
too quickly. We have our own methods. You've had your day, ours is
dawning!!' Another letter writer was disgusted by his 'small head',
considered him 'a suitably psychopathic type and obviously a poof-
ter' and warned: 'The group of five has decided today, tomorrow, in
a month or longer, to give you a punishment you won't forget. [. . .]
But like real war criminals we will show you how it's done. We will
mark your very closest relatives for you; that's why we'll leave you
alive, so you'll be a witness to their marking. [. . .] Your wife and
child will go through life mutilated.' He received telephone calls
with threats to pour sulphuric acid over his two young daughters.
The family was put under police protection and moved to the hotel
De Mallejan in the Veluwe, where Joop and his wife had gone as a
young couple. The newspaper *De Telegraaf*, in the media landscape of
the day the VARA's great adversary, successfully tracked down his
location and gave Joop an ultimatum. 'They said, "Either you give us
an interview or we'll put where you're staying in the paper." They
even wanted to take a photo with the hotel in the background!' Even
more threatening letters. 'Bastard fucking bastard you think fleeing
to the Veluwe makes you safe, no, you bloody *plopper* we're going to
get you, you'll pay for what you've done, we're going to throttle you
you bastard Red traitor we'll throttle you.' Plopper was a term of
abuse for Indonesian freedom fighters, a corruption of *pelopor*, meaning vanguard.

Verbal harassment: it existed in the days before social media too.
Besides threatening and abusive letters, Joop Hueting's archives also
contain many testimonies that have never seen the light of day. It is
bewildering that shortly before his death, the NIOD, the Dutch
Institute for War, Holocaust and Genocide Studies, showed no interest in acquiring his extensive documentation. As a result, the legacy
of the post-war Netherlands' most important whistle-blower is lan-
guishing in the attic of a private house in Amsterdam.

A selection from the letters he received. Ben Verschuuren of

Moergestel, North Brabant, wrote: 'I went into a hut in a kampong. In the gloom I saw two men lying on the ground in a big puddle of blood. Next to them, rifle in hand, a soldier from Den Bosch. I say "They TNI?" "I don't know, but we have to shoot all the men dead."'

J. G. Kroeze of Amsterdam was given a similar task. 'A day later we were told to carry out a punitive expedition. In an area of more or less ten kilometres long and a couple of hundred metres wide all the houses had to be set on fire and all males over fourteen shot dead.' This was pure structural violence ordered from above.

Deliberate cruelty seemed to occur too. Ben Verschuuren saw 'a youth who had been shot exactly in the anus, with the bullet exiting from his lower abdomen'. He was written off for dead and left behind. It wasn't just young men. He also saw 'a woman who had been shot in the lower belly so that the external genitalia were one bloody mess'.

Verschuuren also observed gratuitous violence against innocent Indonesians. 'South of Yogya, a corporal guns a passing peasant down just like that with his Sten. A few of the lads object, but the corporal just grins stupidly, he doesn't give any explanation. It was simply like someone else absent-mindedly picking a leaf off a tree . . .'

Other letters spoke of extreme violence during interrogations. Typist Wim Brocks saw the following: 'A man tied to a post, head back, looking into the sun . . . Walking over rows of prisoners lying on the ground . . . Kicking and hitting every day . . . Making women undress . . . Field telephone on penis and ear . . . Urine flows, make them lick it up . . .'

J. A. M. Landzaat of the 3rd Battalion, Grenadier Pioneer Regiment, of the 7 December Division saw the conditions in a prison. 'At the moment there are three in a cell. They are treated terribly. They are questioned three times a day and everything is beaten out of them. If you don't beat them, you don't find out anything. They've already betrayed a few others. When they run out of things to say, they're shot dead.'

And P. Keulen of the 2nd Company of the Princess Irene Regiment led by Major Sipkes experienced the following. 'On a patrol, when we were dying of thirst, we chased two young farmers up into a coconut tree to throw coconuts down to us. One guy said, "Oh, they don't need to climb down on my account. I'll help them." And shot them out of the tree.'

What didn't help either was the poor moral and spiritual support. At outposts, soldiers only got to see a priest or a minister once a year.[66] It wasn't always very edifying. Some Catholic padres posed for photos bare-chested while holding a gun and ridiculing the enemy.[67] Protestant chaplains, too, could sometimes make peculiar statements. Minister Jacobs of Alphen, for instance, gave a meditation on the concept of trust and told the men: 'A plopper's not to be trusted until he's two foot under the ground.'[68]

The chaplains were much more preoccupied with sexual morality than with the Commandment 'Thou shalt not kill'. That may seem surprising, but only if we forget that in The Hague the most religious politicians, both Catholic and Protestant, were the greatest advocates of the war against Indonesia. War wasn't as bad as illicit sexual contact. Murder on patrol seemed more forgivable than masturbation under a mosquito net. Not that it helped much, all that fulminating against extramarital goings-on in the kampongs. After their return to the Netherlands, it emerged that more than half of the 800 men in one infantry battalion from Catholic Limburg had had sex with an indigenous woman, paid or otherwise.[69] It's impossible to determine how many children or cases of sexually transmitted disease this led to, but given that condoms were also a target of disapproval, presumably thousands.[70] 'Each hospital had a "Ward 9",' said Stef Horvath, 'where only male nurses worked, no females. That was where they sent anyone with the clap or syphilis. They got a nine-day course of treatment and had to make up the time afterwards.'[71] Jaap Tuinder recalled that 'they treated some VDs by scraping the penis'.[72]

As already mentioned, the world press sought out Hueting after his revelations. Several months later, the Dutch government reacted with the *Excessennota*, the List of Excesses, a first, very cautious inventory of war crimes that was intended to form the prelude to a broad official investigation. That investigation, however, never came. On the contrary, the Limitation Law of 1971 guaranteed that war crimes committed in Indonesia could no longer be prosecuted. Only in 2016, after losing several prominent court cases brought by victims of war crimes and their descendants, did the Dutch government make funds available for extensive research. Joop Hueting didn't live to see the results. His archives also include notes for a novel that was to be called *Go Piss in the Kali*. That was what prisoners often heard after their last interrogation. 'Go piss in the river.' Then they'd shoot them in the back and could write in the report that they'd been killed during an 'escape attempt'. I hadn't known that Hueting, who had spent his life searching for a 'theory of undisciplined warfare', sometimes got tired of 'cognition and activation models' and psychophysiological diagrams.[73] They were only beginnings, those literary notes of his, but sometimes fragments evoke the madness better than a polished text: 'War is exhausting, terrifying, it hurts terribly, humiliates everyone and yourself; war is a big hole that gets filled up afterwards by the "home front" with sentimental stories and later by the soldiers themselves with memories of the solidarity, the primitiveness, the total irresponsibility, life at its most primary level. But battle is a big hole that smells of earth, in which you sweat terribly and pant, and time no longer exists.'[74]

Joop Hueting died on 11 November 2018.

Hueting's archives indicated not only structural, but also systematic mass violence. The boundary was often vague. How many kampongs did a company need to wipe out before it became part of the strategy? How many prisoners had to piss in the kali before executions were part of the penitentiary policy? Systematic mass violence doesn't mean that every soldier committed war crimes every day, or that every soldier had committed at least one, but that illegitimate violence was a fundamental part of the methods used.

One of the reasons the reactions to Joop Hueting's revelations were so intense was that the majority of veterans did not commit, witness or hear about acts of extreme violence during their national service. They hadn't been prepared for Hueting's disclosures at all. 'That Mr Hueting on TV with his war crimes!' raged Jan Langenberg, when I first visited him in 2016. 'It was grist to the mill of the Red rats! I never experienced that kind of thing! Was I supposed to feel guilty?' Langenberg, whose father had been in the resistance, had sailed as a highly motivated volunteer. 'And then they go and compare you to the SS! When we had good intentions! I never heard about it, those incidents.' But because of his poor eyesight he'd ended up in the telegraph service and, like the bulk of the troops, never made it to the front. 'I carried a gun, but I never saw any action.'[75]

According to estimates only one in four soldiers was engaged in the fighting.[76] Of the 220,000 troops to serve during the decolonisation war – volunteers, conscripts and professional soldiers – at most 65,000 bore arms in the field.[77] At the start of the second Dutch offensive, commander-in-chief Spoor had 102,000 troops at his disposal in Java, of whom only sixty-five per cent were operational; in Sumatra he had just 22,000 soldiers, of whom eighty-two per cent were available, altogether not even 85,000 men.[78] Many of them were non-combatants. If you realise that in 1949 no fewer than 40,000 troops were active in logistics, it's clear that many were far removed from any war crimes.[79] They were occupied with clothing, equipment, arms, ammunition, tools, tents, food, vehicles, fuel, radio, transport, nursing. And that's not even taking into account the signals units, staff administration, education, welfare, the court-martial and all the other support services based mainly in cities, barracks and compounds.

In brief, there was a curtain drawn through the Dutch army, invisible but sound-proof, separating units that did their jobs and knew nothing from units that knew everything but kept quiet. In one of his notes for his novel, Joop Hueting remarked that the R&R bases in the big cities were marked by mutual tensions between the 'elite troops who did the dirty work and the rest'. The press could not report it at the time either: domestic and foreign journalists were barred from operational areas and military photographers were heavily censored.[80] And the UN, as mentioned above, couldn't send any observers. As a result, the dirt remained hidden for a long time. But three-quarters of a century later, Jan Langenberg had to reconsider his anger after reading *De brandende kampongs van Generaal Spoor* (General Spoor's Burning Kampongs), Rémy Limpach's monumental 2016 study. 'I never knew that so many foul things happened. Was I in the same army? I've had to revise my opinion and I now feel that I've been held personally responsible.'[81]

During my five years of research, it was much easier to find Dutch veterans who categorically denied systematic war crimes than someone who could or was willing to testify about them. But in Bronbeek, the Dutch retirement home for war veterans at Arnhem, I met Bol Kerrebijn. He was the man who had hunted wild pigs with his pack of dogs as a boy in the Indies and had felt so threatened during the Revolusi that he had taken his revenge by joining the KNIL. 'I was a ruffian,' he admitted, 'revenge was my salvation.' His life was atypical – after the death of his European father he had ended up at a boarding school where total obedience to authority was drummed into him. His testimony too was atypical – his intense frankness was dizzying. But everything he told me ultimately said more about the system than it did about Kerrebijn himself.

About the extreme impunity that prevailed, for instance. 'A woman had been raped and I had to console her and question her in Malay, but I only knew dirty words. "I'll help you," she said.' A raped woman having the patience to teach the soldier who was questioning her the right words . . . 'There was a lot of sexual violence between women and Dutch soldiers at the time,' said Kerrebijn. That was no exaggeration. Although sexual violence wasn't ordered from above, there are plenty of known cases. Private Huisman raped a woman in Sumatra under threat of his gun. Lieutenant Schier maltreated and raped an Indonesian woman called Siti Fatima in a shed; he stubbed out burning cigarettes on her nipples and the soles of her feet.[82] On 19 February 1949, for example, the eighteen-year-old Tremini was raped at home in the East Javanese village of Peniwen by five soldiers, while her nine-year-old niece looked on.[83] In Kacen, twenty soldiers, including several senior officers, took turns to rape a girl of twelve. A Protestant chaplain was caught with a girl of nine.[84]

The case Bol Kerrebijn had to investigate involved an adult woman. 'Soldiers had searched a house. In the process her husband, an officer, was shot. She was still alive and was raped. But was it a rape? Or had she offered herself? I was a greenhorn. Policing your own soldiers, that's the hardest thing there is. And writing up every incident? The same bullshit a hundred times. I can't remember that I often . . . I'm not going to throw that lad in the clink, am I? Look, to me, the soldier's never guilty, that's one of my bad sides. I'm a bad policeman.' But the Dutch government also had its bad sides: making the prosecution of serious crimes such a low priority and leaving the investigation of sexual misconduct to subordinates who were more loyal than well-trained. Result: Kerrebijn's case of sexual violence was cast aside, like so many others. In four years of war, only thirteen soldiers were convicted of rape. They were given prison sentences ranging from a few months to one and a half years.[85]

Systematic violence begins with impunity. Henri Schrijver, a KNIL sergeant-major, carried out a reign of terror in and around Cililitan in West Java and had dozens, if not hundreds of people killed. Rather than being punished, he was decorated with the Cross of Merit.[86] At the start of January 1949, Lieutenant Rudy de Mey ordered the Special Troops Corps to clean up the South Sumatran town of Rengat: hundreds, perhaps more than a thousand people died, among them the father of the poet Chairil Anwar. Countless bodies, women and children among them, were thrown off the bridge and into the river, which ran red with blood. It was possibly the largest single war crime of the whole decolonisation war, but the official investigation swept it under the carpet.[87] Nobody was punished, but Lieutenant De Mey earned the praise and appreciation of Captain Westerling. The series of unpunished war crimes is endless, but very few cases went to court: fewer than 150 trials in four years of war with 200,000 soldiers. Mostly ending in acquittal or very light punishments.[88]

Police work? Prosecuting your mates? No, Kerrebijn preferred to go out on patrol with them. He would hang up his white helmet and gear and pull on the khaki combat uniform of the KNIL infantry. In Bali he went out checking kampongs. Each platoon was equipped with a Bren light machine gun and he served as the Bren gunner. He lugged the ten-kilo machine gun between the huts while his assistant carried the ammunition. 'Those clean-up operations were far too polite for me,' he said. 'Sweeping kampongs, collecting guns and krises, taking eggs and chickens with us, all those dogs and pigs. No, no hue and no cry.' After that he was shipped to Java. 'In Probolinggo a train with Dutch soldiers had come under fire. I had to tell them how to act. They still weren't used to fireflies! We responded by sweeping the kampong. Far too polite again! We should have torn it apart!'

All the same, systematic violence was a constant in interrogations. 'We questioned spies at the post. I heard about electric shocks. I was up for it, but I didn't know anything about electricity. We didn't even have electricity. But threatening, intimidating, yes, we did that. He had to blab, I had to make sure he did!' In Hueting's archives I had seen that there are no limits to the human imagination when it comes to interrogation techniques. Tying prisoners to a post and making sure their bare feet are standing on the open rims of tin cans . . . Getting someone to talk by stubbing out cigarettes in their nostrils . . . Tying people's hands and feet together behind their back and then hoisting them up as a 'bird's nest' – or repeatedly throwing someone out of a moving car . . .[89]

And there was another type of systematic violence: disposing of prisoners. Some soldiers noticed that more and more people were being taken prisoner, but the prisons never seemed overcrowded. Bol Kerrebijn knew why. He was stationed at Glenmore, a town in East Java where there had once been an English plantation. 'Shooting prisoners didn't bother me. If there were people who needed to be executed after an investigation or whatever, the commandant said, "I'm looking for a volunteer." Others said, "I'm not doing it," but I said, "Okay, if it has to be done." That's how I was brought up at that boarding school in Sukabumi: intensely loyal. I didn't want my own people burdened. That's the kind of guy I am: so hard it didn't get to me. They arrived from Banyuwangi, that was where the hearings were. A whole column with people who had been sentenced. We had a goods carriage parked in the yard as a prison. It always happened at night. And then I'm not going to ask if he's been sentenced, that doesn't interest me. It's no longer a topic of discussion. I never had any problem with the ones who . . . They left me cold. Evidently they judged me correctly. Somehow he knew he wasn't going to be able to avoid it. Other prisoners had already dug the hole. What am I supposed to say to a bloke like that? I see him as a criminal. He's standing in the hole. I ask him, "Do you need to pray? Are you very religious?" Okay. "And your clothes? Because in a minute, when you're dead, the clothes you're wearing will go to the spy." That's how I talk to him. If a spy reports someone, it's for his own benefit. "Shame to shoot up those clothes," I tell the fellow. He understands. Shirt off. "Take it, have it." I used an Owen, nine millimetre, fully automatic. No, I don't put him out of his misery with a bullet in the back of the head, just a spray in the ribs. We didn't talk about it afterwards. It didn't go in the report, just a summary briefing. A bit spineless, I think sometimes, but I was carrying things out at the lowest level, where you don't have any say.'[90]

Incidental, structural or systematic mass violence – the outside world was in the dark about all of it. Non-combatant troops might have heard stories in the mess, the home front was generally left uninformed, and the United Nations didn't know a thing. But in the entire conflict, the first half of 1949 was without a doubt the phase with the most deaths. In this period, Dutch troops killed an estimated 47,000 adversaries, took 40,000 POWs, and destroyed 11,000 firearms and more than 500 tons of ammunition.[91] The Netherlands lost 1,200 troops, almost half of the Dutch soldiers killed in action during the whole war. This means that from mid-December 1948 to mid-August 1949, the Republic lost an average of 196 people a day, and the Netherlands five.

If you add up all of the phases, the entire war cost the lives of 4,600 to 5,300 Dutch troops, of whom approximately half died by violence (the rest died of disease or in accidents).[92] According to Dutch military reports, 97,000 people died on the Indonesian side, but it could have been many more.[93] Victims of shelling, for instance, could not always be counted precisely and the Republic itself did not keep accurate records. With 19,000 and 59,000 deaths respectively, the years 1947 and 1949 had the highest numbers, not coincidentally in the wake of the two 'police' actions. Definitive figures will probably never be available, but it is quite likely that the majority were civilians and that more people were killed by war crimes than in regular combat. The number of deaths caused by Republican troops among the non-Dutch population (Chinese, Ambonese, 'spies') is unknown.

Putting the numbers into perspective, we see that there were fewer deaths in the decolonisation war than during the Japanese occupation. Even if we take the highest estimate, 200,000 victims for the whole conflict, the monthly average was only 3,846 dead. The figure of four million dead in the Japanese period works out to 95,238 deaths a month – most of them from starvation. Even if the famine of 1944 had cost half as many lives, the period under Japanese rule would still have been more than ten times as lethal as the struggle with the Netherlands.

Unlawful violence was anything but a marginal phenomenon during the decolonisation war. On the Dutch side, it was not limited to a few excesses at the bottom of the military ladder, but ordered and caused by officers in charge of platoons, companies and battalions. In Jakarta the high command tolerated and tacitly allowed it, the highest levels of the civil administration were aware of it, and the supreme judicial authorities did not prosecute it. Responsible figures included Lieutenant Governor-General Van Mook, High Representative of the Crown Beel, military commander-in-chief Spoor and Attorney General Felderhof. But it didn't end there. It would be improper to concentrate on military and administrative culpability in Indonesia without considering who was answerable politically in the Netherlands, as ultimate responsibility lay with the government and parliament in The Hague. From the moment the unilateral tampering with the Linggajati Agreement began at the end of 1946, the quality of political decision-making in the Netherlands slumped with, as disastrous lows, the launching of the first and second Dutch offensives, orders that came from Beel and Drees's Catholic–socialist coalitions (with the liberals joining the latter of those governments). Twice Beel played a crucial role: first in 1947 as prime minister pressing for action, then in 1948 as high representative of the crown blocking a political solution at the last moment. The fact that the Dutch had to deal with large-scale violent resistance in their colony earlier than the Americans, British, French, Belgians and Portuguese can be taken as a mitigating circumstance. The playbook still had to be written. And the Dutch East Indies was certainly many times more important to the Netherlands' self-image and national psyche than the Philippines for the US, Indochina for France or even India for the UK. The Netherlands was entwined with the East, dependent economically, but possibly even more so emotionally. This made letting go even more difficult and, for many, inconceivable. But by the time the order to launch the devastating second offensive was given, the Philippines, India, Ceylon, Pakistan and Burma had all become independent. Although it wasn't a direct order to commit war crimes, that dramatic decision created the conditions that allowed widespread, protracted and, above all, highly predictable mass violence against people who, from the Dutch perspective, were the country's own subjects overseas.

What was the next step? The war was taking place in the heat, rain and mud, but the greatest progress was achieved indoors. Six meetings were decisive, six different interiors too. It began in an office in Washington, DC. April 1949, the American State Department, two men in suits: Dean Acheson, the US Secretary of State, and his Dutch counterpart Dirk Stikker. Acheson was serving under the Democratic President Truman. Stikker, a liberal and former chairman of the board of Heineken, was definitely not a hard-liner when it came to colonial issues. He had travelled to the US to work on the foundation of NATO and it was his second private meeting with Acheson in seven days. More than a week before, the Security Council had voted in favour of a new directive to get the Indonesian question back on track: Beel's stubborn plan for a round-table conference of all the Indonesian states had been accepted and inserted into the Security Council resolution. That meant talks, but first the political leaders needed to be released and Republican rule reinstated. A preparatory conference would remove these major obstacles, under UN leadership of course.

Although high-level discussions seem to be a distinct form of conversation with their own etiquette, they bear a distinct resemblance to negotiations with a used-car salesman. Acheson had informed

Stikker that a Dutch failure to reach agreement with the United Nations could lead to the suspension of US NATO-related military aid. Stikker knew that a great deal of money was at stake: four and a half billion guilders over the coming decade.[94] He also realised that as long as the Netherlands was fighting in Indonesia, it couldn't build up its own national army at home – not ideal during the Cold War. Even so, he risked a countermove: if the US didn't let the Netherlands have its way, his government might no longer see the point of joining NATO. It was bluff poker at the highest possible level. The North Atlantic Treaty was due to be signed just a couple of days later. Acheson didn't flinch. Was that small defenceless country on the North Sea trying to blackmail the mighty victor of World War II? Did it realise that Congress was not at all keen on giving the Netherlands military aid?[95] Stikker knew not to overplay his hand, but he did make it clear that the Dutch government could not possibly release Sukarno and the others without a ceasefire and participation in a round-table conference in return. Acheson nodded. Two days later, Stikker signed the treaty establishing NATO.[96] That was the tipping point. The Netherlands relented not because of Marshall aid, but because of NATO funds.

Just as Indonesia had to accept Renville in 1948, the Netherlands had to accept the loss of Indonesia in 1949. The United States was still the key player, except that it had now changed sides, not because of an anti-colonial impulse, but because of its increasingly virulent anti-communism.[97] The UN was the vehicle for its geopolitical self-interest.

The second interior was a conference room in the stylish Hotel des Indes in Jakarta. It was 7 May 1949, one month after the discussions in Washington. This was the day on which the great change of direction was announced to the world. After Acheson's meeting with Stikker, the Dutch and Republican delegations had carried out intensive consultations under the leadership of the UNCI, the United Nations Commission for Indonesia. The leading American diplomat Merle Cochran, driving force behind the UNCI, found a pragmatic counterpart in the Netherlands' chief negotiator Van Roijen. On the Republican side, he gained the trust of former interior minister

Mohamad Roem, who had also been present at Linggajati and on the *Renville*. The meeting began. Roem stood up to read a three-point declaration on behalf of Sukarno and Hatta: they were willing to stop the guerrilla warfare, restore law and order, and participate in a round-table conference in The Hague. Van Roijen then spoke to present the Dutch government's position: the Republican government would be allowed to return to Yogyakarta, the Netherlands was prepared to suspend hostilities and would not found any new states, and furthermore, consultations in The Hague could commence as soon as possible. It was the biggest breakthrough in years. Following on from Linggajati and Renville, the Roem–Van Roijen Agreement, as it came to be known, was the third major diplomatic agreement of the decolonisation war. If Linggajati had ended in a draw and Renville as 3–1 for the Netherlands, Roem–Van Roijen was a clear victory for the Republic: the political leaders were released, the Republic regained territory and the Netherlands pledged not to found any new states. The price? A ceasefire and a trip to The Hague for talks. 3–2: most of them could live with that.

Beel, on the other hand, was furious. As high representative of the crown he had advocated an unremittingly hard line, averse to the UN, averse to the Republic; unwilling and unable to identify with this new policy, he promptly resigned. The man who had succeeded Van Mook as the head of the Dutch administration in Indonesia had stuck it out for six months, all told, and now went the way of his fellow party member Sassen, who had resigned as minister of overseas territories. Just four months after that convivial New Year's Eve at the Spoors' – where they had been so triumphant in their celebration of the success of the second Dutch offensive – the ranks of that heroic company were severely depleted. Spoor himself was, of course, also far from happy about the Roem–Van Roijen Agreement – the political undoing of his military success – but he resolved to remain at his post, if only to offset the new tendency. He was forty-seven and would see what difference he could still make. Three weeks later, however, at the start of yet another long working day, his heart failed and he collapsed. 'Get a doctor,' he told his secretary. Several days later he died. He had literally worked himself to death.

Two months later again, another room. This time we are in the istana of Yogyakarta, the presidential palace. It was 6 July 1949. Nobody had believed it possible, but here he was again, none other than Sukarno, back from Bangka. The Dutch had just released him and his colleagues. The planned return of the Republic had caused great unrest among certain groups, not least the Chinese, who had been the target of nationalist hatred so often. Now, too, they feared reprisals, for instance for having supplied the Dutch troops. Hameng-kubuwono IX, the pro-Republican sultan of Yogya, had called for calm, but no fewer than 40,000 Chinese left the city, followed by 30,000 Dutch soldiers withdrawing from their zone of operations. The massacres they had dreaded did not take place. The question was, what would the army do? Would the TNI consent to the cease-fire? Why let others decide things in The Hague now that the guerrilla tactics seemed to be working so well? Sukarno sat at his desk in the istana. Four days later there was an uproar in the city: crowds, cheering, a kind of procession. The army had come back from the bush! Commander-in-chief Sudirman was carried to the centre of town on a rickety bamboo litter, emaciated from TB and looking like an ascetic. At the palace, Sukarno embraced him warmly. He still had the support of the TNI, which accepted the Roem–Van Roijen Agreement. Once the emergency government arrived from Sumatra several days later, the Republicans had closed ranks again.

Sukarno and his team then accepted the invitation of Anak Agung, Prime Minister of East Indonesia, to an 'Inter-Indonesian Conference' with the participation of all states. The idea was simple: if we all have to go to The Hague, we're better off putting our heads together here first. The Netherlands had spent long enough trying to divide the federal states and the Republic; now the time for collective consultation had come. This led to surprising and far-reaching results: they soon agreed on a provisional constitution, a name, a language, a flag and a national anthem. Their constitution provided for a federal parliamentary state. The new country would be called the Republik Indonesia Serikat (the Republic of the United States of Indonesia), a convenient combination of terms. The official language would be Indonesian, the official flag red and white, the national anthem would remain 'Indonesia Raya' – all kinds of symbols of the originally Javanese-Sumatran Republic would apply to the whole archipelago. And the most important agreement of all: there would be one military only and it would be the TNI.

The fourth interior was the cabin of an aeroplane. On 12 July 1949, thirteen leading American journalists were on board the KLM plane the *Franeker*, somewhere over the Indian subcontinent on their way back from a luxurious press trip to Indonesia, paid for and organised by the Netherlands. The propaganda goal was evident: to give the American public a more positive impression of Dutch intentions in order to strengthen The Hague's position in the upcoming negotiations. Now that the Netherlands could no longer count on the loyalty of the Indonesian states, it could use all the support from Washington it could get. They were no lightweights on that plane: America's best-known radio voice and Pulitzer Prize-winner, Hubert Knickerbocker, S. Burton Heath of the Newspaper Enterprise Association, another Pulitzer Prize-winner, together with prominent journalists from *The New York Times*, *The Washington Daily News*, *Time Magazine*, *Business Week* and other publications. The timing was perfect: in China, Mao's advance had become unstoppable and in the US, the fear of the Red Menace was greater than ever. The scheme seemed to be working. In their articles most of these leading journalists depicted Sukarno as unreliable and criticised America's treatment of the Netherlands as far too harsh. 'Having lost China, we have now given Moscow the opportunity, for which she has been waiting and working, to move into Indonesia,' wrote the influential Burton Heath from Jakarta. 'Directly and through the United Nations, we have forced the Dutch to free Indonesia so quickly and suddenly that, for the next five years, during which World War III may be made either unavoidable or improbable, there will be no stable government here.' His conclusion: Americans had to realise that 'we have thrown our wholehearted support to the least democratic, least western-minded political group in the islands'.[98] The journalists were flying home to disseminate their new insights. Just before landing in Bombay the monsoon rain was so heavy that the pilots lost visibility in the thick clouds and crashed into a hilltop. Everyone on board was killed.

The Americans who were going to spread a different perspective on the Indonesian question in the coming, decisive months now lay lifeless in the thick wet vegetation, among the burning debris from the *Franeker*.[99]

The fifth interior was once again a conference room in Hotel des Indes. On 1 August this was the location of the final session of the preparatory conference. Dutch and Indonesian negotiators spent hours bending over maps, again under pressure from American UN diplomacy, which would not yield an inch. On that day, the terms of the truce were drawn up, undoubtedly the most difficult step in any negotiation. Who is where? Who has what? Whose troops occupy which territory? Again the discussions went smoothly. Two days later the order to cease fire was given. In Java it was to go into effect on 11 August, in Sumatra on 15 August, almost eight months after the UN had requested it. But announcing a truce is also the best way of making the violence flare up: the conflicting parties quickly make a final attempt to expand their zones. After Linggajati and Renville, the TNI didn't know if the Dutch could be trusted to keep an agreement. Who could guarantee that they would respect Roem–Van Roijen?

Several days before the truce took effect, the always cheerful Lieutenant Van Heek was leading yet another patrol through a kampong. 'Our enthusiasm had gradually waned,' he said. 'After the Roem–Van Roijen Agreement we didn't even know what we were fighting for.' The meaning and purpose of military action were now completely unclear. 'That was why in the end we craved this ceasefire.'[100] The village seemed innocent until he found a few pieces of gear in a small back yard. 'I called the others, but was shot at close range. A lung shot, straight through the thorax. The bullet entered on the left side and exited just in front of the backbone. I was almost paralysed. I took a couple of steps towards our medic, but my lung wasn't working any more.' The orderly gave him blood plasma and morphine. 'He'd never done it before, he was a glassblower from Leerdam.'[101] His men went berserk and started shooting in all directions. Van Heek himself was carried on a bamboo stretcher ten kilometres to the post and then driven to Surakarta for an operation. 'Don't worry,' he wrote to his parents that night, 'I am now being spoilt rotten in the

military hospital in Solo. My only problem is being rather short of
breath, but I hope to be back to my old self in a month or so.'[102] Once
a stoic, always a stoic.

And while Van Heek was laid up in hospital, the Indonesian delegations went to The Hague. The sixth room was perhaps the most
important. On 23 August the long-awaited Round Table Conference, which would last until 2 November, began in the Knights' Hall
at the Binnenhof, home of the Dutch parliament. Late summer in
Holland, golden light in the streets of The Hague, leaves blanketing
the cobbles, shortening days, puddles reflecting the lights of stately
automobiles. In those two long months all the major issues were
raised. Officially there were three parties: the Kingdom of the Netherlands (led by J. H. van Maarseveen, the last Minister of Overseas
Territories), the Republic of Indonesia (led by Hatta) and the Federal
Consultative Assembly (the alliance of federal states, led by Sultan
Hamid of West Kalimantan), but in practice the last two formed a
common front. The United Nations, led by Merle Cochran, was
again present and played a role similar to Lord Killearn's at the Linggajati negotiations: facilitating discussion where possible, intervening
where necessary. In his view, the UNCI should not dominate the
talks, but was prepared to offer its experience and assistance to all
parties.[103] His discreet and informal approach allowed Cochran and
his team to score successes in many areas. Politically, Indonesia
achieved almost all its goals: the federal state would be sovereign, the
'Union' with the Netherlands would be flimsy (the relevant ministers
meeting twice annually), and the new country's army would be
formed by the TNI, not the KNIL. This was Linggajati light. The
fighting had been going on for three years, not over the new state
that would come in the end, but over the transitional period that
would last less than two years. Three years of war for two years of
transition, and the final result was worse for the Netherlands than
what it had started with.

Politically, the Netherlands surrendered Indonesia almost entirely,
but economically it took a very hard line.[104] All of the licenses and
concessions enjoyed by Dutch companies remained fully applicable
so that they could help to fill The Hague's empty coffers. In addition,

Map 28: Round Table Conference (2 November 1949)

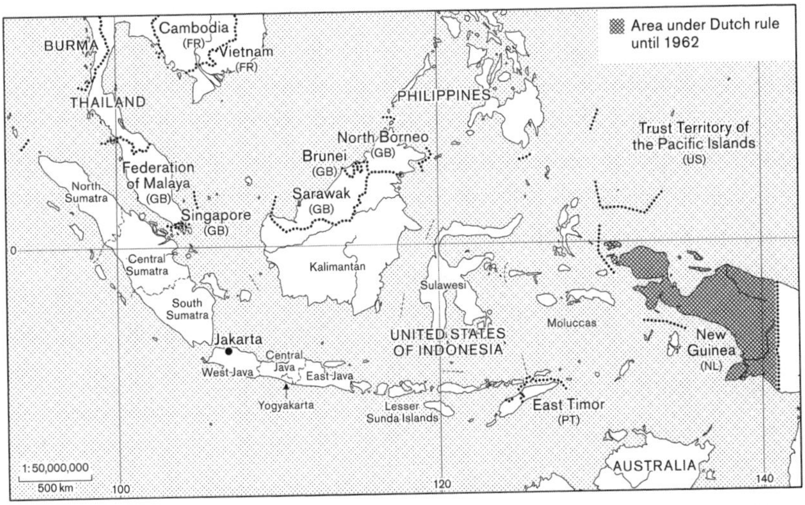

Indonesia had to accept all of the Dutch East Indies' debts. 'They have products that can generate dollars; we don't,' said Prime Minister Drees.[105] That was true, but he seemed to have forgotten that the Netherlands had been profiting from those products for three and a half centuries. He was so preoccupied with expanding the post-war welfare state in the Netherlands that, in his search for funding, he ignored the extremely large contribution Indonesia had already made. The result was bitter. Just as nineteenth-century slaves had to pay their masters for their emancipation, Indonesia now had to purchase its own freedom. For how much? For 6.3 billion guilders – at the time an astronomical amount. That total even included the costs of the recent decolonisation war: could the ex-colony please pay the bill for the Police Actions? The Republic refused to pay for the war that had killed or mutilated so many of its people. Here, too, the US played, through the UN, a significant role: Cochran proposed that the military expenses be scrapped and the total be rounded off at 4.3 billion guilders, still a gigantic sum.[106] Otherwise Indonesia consented to all of the Dutch demands.

For years the Dutch had reasoned that the loss of the Indies would be a catastrophe, but it gradually became clear that clinging to Indonesia would be prohibitively expensive: not only would the

Netherlands lose NATO support and further Marshall aid, it would also have to shoulder the burden of the reconstruction of the Netherlands and Indonesia alone. As always, Finance Minister Lieftinck took a businesslike approach. By relinquishing the colony, the Netherlands received the American funds after all, plus the Indonesian repayments, plus the tax revenue from former colonial enterprises, plus the money saved on Indonesian reconstruction. Altogether that could be seen as a credit of 23 billion guilders, almost eight per cent of the net domestic product for the period 1949–60. Recent calculations suggest that the profit for the Netherlands was much greater: converted to current monetary value, no less than 103 billion euros. In any case, newly independent Indonesia contributed much more to the reconstruction of the Netherlands than the much more visible Marshall Plan.[107] This was how the economic recovery of the Netherlands in the 1950s was financed.[108] The overseas adventure ended with the same argument it began with three and a half centuries earlier: then it had been more profitable for the Dutch to fetch the spices themselves, now it was more profitable for them to go back home.

Still, there was one issue that defeated the Round Table Conference: New Guinea. The agreement would only be accepted by the Dutch parliament if some remnant of the overseas project remained – the right-wing parties in particular insisted on it. The Indonesian delegations wanted that territory included no matter what, but the Netherlands refused to relinquish it – if only because large numbers of Indos could be resettled there after independence. And also because interesting resources had been discovered there. The question of New Guinea developed into the last great stumbling block on the way to independence and for a time it seemed as if all the effort was going to be in vain. Did peace really depend on that one territory? Neither party had ever displayed much interest in it. But it was of great symbolic value. Indonesian politicians wanted to take over the whole colony; the Dutch, on the other hand, did not want to disappear entirely from the East. At the eleventh hour, Cochran suggested leaving New Guinea out of the general agreement and reconsidering it a year later. This compromise froze the issue and saved the Round Table Conference.

On the last day of the conference the Charter of the Transfer of

Sovereignty was ready. Article 1 stated: 'The Kingdom of the Nether-lands unconditionally and irrevocably transfers complete sovereignty over Indonesia to the Republic of the United States of Indonesia and thereby recognises said Republic of the United States of Indonesia as an independent and sovereign State.'[109]

It was 28 December 1949 and a twenty-one-year-old Dutch naval officer was sailing the Java Sea on a minesweeper. He was a midship-man and an acting sub-lieutenant. 'It was terrifically enjoyable. Glorious weather, fabulous sailing . . .' Since 1946 the navy had been working to clear the mines laid by Japan and the Netherlands. 'We were the last to finish.' He had been at it for months. Putting out to sea, towing the sweep, blowing up a mine now and then. He spent whole days using his sextant and updating the sea charts. Both his father and his grandfather had had colonial careers, but he wasn't bothered that the colony was coming to an end. 'If Indonesia wants to become independent, so be it,' he thought.

The transfer of sovereignty had been signed the day before in the Palace on the Dam in Amsterdam in the presence of Queen Juliana and Vice-President Hatta. Afterwards the bells had played the Indonesian national anthem: the cheerful tones of 'Indonesia Raya', the song that had been forbidden for so long, chiming over the roofs and canals of Amsterdam for the first time.[110] In Indonesia people could listen to the ceremony on the radio in a direct broadcast. Immediately afterwards, the transfer of administrative authority took place in Jakarta. The highlight was a brief ceremony on the Koningsplein, henceforth Medan Merdeka, in which the Dutch tricolour was lowered and the Indonesian flag was raised officially for the first time. 'I cried,' said Soeparti Soetedjo, 'really loud sobs. It was so impressive.'[111] In Yogya-karta Sukarno was installed that day as president of all of Indonesia, displaying the flag he had raised on 15 August 1945 in the process.

The following day our midshipman had to conduct the morning colours. 'As the crew commander, the senior non-commissioned offi-cer on deck duty, I had to give the command "raise the flag". We were standing on the deck and had to raise the red-and-white flag on the starboard yardarm for the first time. That's where you fly the flag of the country you're sailing in. My commander was absent from the roll call that day. He'd always ordered his men to shoot at that flag! He was so anti-Republican. Sailors who'd just arrived from the Netherlands had to do the job.'

But the war was over and the young officer couldn't help but notice how worn out both countries were, the Netherlands too. 'I remember someone's shirt hanging open on board: he didn't have any buttons left to do it up!' Indonesia was drained. On shore leave in Surabaya he'd seen that there wasn't much left to buy. 'You used to find jenever glasses there, champagne glasses, sherry glasses, vermouth glasses – now only water glasses.' The country was in shards. The deliberate destruction by the Netherlands in 1942, the invasion and occupation by Japan from 1942 to 1945, the Allied bombing in 1944 and 1945, the Revolusi, the plundering and the British operations of late 1945 and 1946, the Dutch military offensives of 1947 and 1948, the Republican scorched-earth tactics in 1948, the guerrilla warfare that reached its peak in 1949 . . . Thousands of houses had been destroyed, hundreds of plantations, warehouses, workshops, factories and offices. One-third of the rubber businesses had been irreparably ruined, a fifth had suffered heavy damage.[112] Bridges, roads, train stations, schools, hospitals, harbours and airports were in ruins.

Shortly after the transfer of sovereignty, our midshipman saw a small boat being rowed towards the ship. 'We threw down a ladder. An Indonesian captain came on board with a rifle. "What are you doing here?" he asked.' A brief conversation between the officers followed; all very polite. And then his commander, the man who for years had ordered his men to shoot at that flag, spoke the unforgettable words: 'May I offer you a glass of lemonade?'[113]

And that was how they drank to independence: with lemon squash in a simple water glass, somewhere on an endless sea.

Chapter 15

Into the Light of Morning
The Indonesian Revolution and the world after 1950

'A new beginning' was the term Queen Juliana used to describe the transfer of sovereignty. This 'advancing together in freedom' was based, according to her, on 'the deep sympathy of both peoples for each other' and their 'ingrained solidarity'.[1] And it must be said, at first the collaboration between the two countries went well. Indonesia paid the agreed debts faithfully, the Netherlands immediately withdrew its troops and when the first diplomatic representative of the Netherlands presented his letters of credence to President Sukarno in January 1950, he was assigned the number plate CD 1.[2] That said enough.

By the end of 1950 the Dutch government had shipped more than 120,000 troops to Euope.[3] Many of the conscripts were glad to finally be allowed to return home after two or three years, but a volunteer like Goderd van Heek – his perforated lung had healed in the meantime – was not entirely convinced. On board the steamship *Waterman* he wrote a long poem on the last day of 1949 with these opening lines:

> Have they turned out to be in vain,
> Those years we spent out on patrol?
> Was it an error that we made,
> And something we could not control?
>
> We did our best for a righteous cause,
> Establishing order and peace. [. . .]
> But they, too, fought for a righteous cause,
> Giving their lives to be free.[4]

Jan Langenberg said it without poetry. 'The transfer of sovereignty made me feel like I'd been taken for a ride! We'd won the war and then it was all lost because of politics! What use had it all been? Five to six thousand of us "stayed there". When we arrived in Rotterdam, General Kruls came on board. "Ten-shun!" Well, nobody stood up. We'd had it with saluting. He cut his drivel soon enough.' Jan was given an envelope with a couple of hundred guilders, a letter of thanks, and a free driver's licence that was valid for one week. He went to his father's in Bloemendaal. 'You had a fun time of it, I bet. Beautiful weather, nice and sunny.' And when he delivered his kit to the depot he had to pay for a pair of lost socks. The fatherland felt so cold. 'If you tried to talk about it, people started off about coffee being rationed. I just went boozing with mates who were miserable too.' He was twenty-four and decided to rent a room in The Hague. 'I felt unhappy for a very long time. Even now. Sometimes I feel damn lonely.'[5]

The many Indos who had served in the KNIL felt similarly bereft. Once that army had been disbanded in July 1950, there was no clear place for them in Indonesian society. Dick van Steenbergen had always been considered Dutch, but when he arrived in Europe for the first time, people looked askance at him. ' "Where did you learn Dutch? Do you always wear shoes?" I couldn't help but notice how ignorant the Dutch were. They thought we still lived in trees.' In reality he had seen more of the world than they had. He had spent days in the nuclear fallout at Nagasaki, the Americans had taken him to Manila, he'd been trained in Australia and had fought in Borneo and Java. 'The Netherlands made money off us, plenty, but the people were kept ignorant. We knew more about the Netherlands than the other way round.'

Hans Dornseiffer had survived the copper mines of Japan and now had to build a new life in a country he didn't know. 'I wasn't familiar with thick mattresses with blankets on them. I lived very frugally here. I ate once every two days: half a bottle of yoghurt and in the evening some noodle soup.'[6] The evenings were grey for all young men in the fifties, but for nobody were they quite as sombre as for the newly arrived young Indo men. No wonder they responded by adding verve to the parochial life of the Low Countries: they brought a festive variety of hospitality to Europe and became pioneers of popular music. The first real Dutch rock 'n' roll single, 'Rock Little Baby of Mine', was recorded in 1958 by the Tielman Brothers, four brothers from an Indo family in Breda.[7]

The most peculiar trip back was Piet van Staveren's. The man who had made radio programmes for the Indonesians was arrested after the ceasefire. 'For three weeks I was on board in a cell without windows. Soldiers brought me my food.' On arrival in the Netherlands he was immediately put in prison. When his case was brought before the court-martial and the Supreme Military Court, the charge was desertion in time of war and proceeding to territory which was not under Dutch control. 'Who were we at war with?' he asked. Hadn't they just been police actions? Of the twenty-six deserters he received the most severe punishment: eight years, reduced to seven on appeal. He ended up serving five of them. 'After being convicted, I was put in the special prison at Leeuwarden with all those Nazis. The leaders of the NSB and the Dutch SS were there. I considered that an insult.'[8] Years in prison for refusing to take up arms against Indonesian freedom fighters. And meanwhile thousands and thousands of war crimes were hushed up.

The Indonesian government itself was not worrying about the mass violence: the struggle had been won, the country was liberated, the rest was a side issue. The Republican troops hadn't always behaved admirably either, far from it. No, they had to look to the future. For Indonesia it was the dawn of a period of optimism, modernisation and new opportunities. In the cities in particular, it was a time of briefcases and filter cigarettes, cinemas and elegant hairdos, for the upper class at least. For the rest of the country, life gradually grew more expensive and freedom lost its shine.

The good relations with the Netherlands suffered several significant setbacks in the first year of freedom. On 23 January 1950, less than a month after the transfer of sovereignty, Captain Westerling suddenly resurfaced. With a force of 300 men, mainly Ambonese veterans, he seized the Siliwangi Division's Bandung headquarters with the goal of using it as a launching pad to carry out a coup in Jakarta to reverse independence! But besides a hundred dead and some international media attention, his idiotic action achieved little. The Dutch High Commissioner, as the representative of the Dutch-Indonesian Union, helped Indonesia to quickly put down the rebellion. But the subsequent role of senior Dutch military officers in helping Westerling to escape, and the fact that Prime Minister Drees had even given permission for them to do so, obviously stirred up ill feeling in the Republican government.[9] Sukarno decided not to make too much of it.

Soon after it was the Netherlands' turn to be disgruntled. Within just a few months it became clear that federalism was losing momentum and unitarianism was on the rise. A federally structured state had been the keystone of Dutch decolonisation policy and its rapid disintegration felt like a betrayal. From a purely administrative perspective there was much to be said for decentralised rule in such a far-flung archipelago – the Dutch were right about that. But what business did they have to carry on meddling in the internal organisation of an independent country? If the Indonesians wanted to arrange things differently, they had every right to do so. The first few months of 1950 saw widespread mass demonstrations against the system of separate states. Most of the population associated federalism with colonialism and they'd had more than enough of that. On 17 August 1950, the fifth anniversary of the Proklamasi, Sukarno announced that the 'United States of Indonesia' was over and that from then on there would only be '*one* Republic of Indonesia, with *one* territory, with *one* Constitution, with *one* Government'.[10] Many Dutch citizens gnashed their teeth.

One Indonesian island thought differently. On Ambon, where the colonial incursion had begun centuries before, a part of the Christian population had no desire to be subsumed within the 'Javanese' Republic. On 24 April 1950, with the help of local troops, they declared the 'Republic of South Maluku' (Republik Maluku Selatan, RMS). In the Netherlands there was a lot of sympathy for the secession: Ambon was the island where the KNIL had always recruited its best soldiers and where the population had remained loyal to the

Dutch crown; Sukarno wouldn't be able to impose his will on them, they told themselves. So starting in September, when Sukarno did impose his will on Ambon by suppressing the uprising, many in the Netherlands were incensed. The South Moluccan Republic exists to this day. It continues in exile in the Netherlands and has its own flag and president (currently John Wattilete). Despite having lost their representation at the UN, 3,000 Moluccans gather for a memorial in Apeldoorn every year.[11]

In December 1950 things went completely wrong. This was the deadline for the resolution of the question of West New Guinea, but the Netherlands had made very little effort in that direction. On the contrary. In the course of the year it had appointed a governor, drawn up a three-year budget and even minted a new coin (with Juliana on it).[12] The Netherlands was clearly planning on sticking it out there for quite some time. It was an issue that would inflame passions for years. Sukarno changed the name from New Guinea to Irian, as his tone grew curter and his anger grew. He travelled widely, giving speeches in towns and in the countryside in which he whipped up the impoverished population. This allowed him to distract attention from their poverty and unite the country around a common enemy, the Netherlands. In some places he even made things a little clearer for the simple peasants by having local boys painted black and decorated with a few white stripes. Naked, except for penis gourds and some leaves in their hair, it was their task to represent their Papuan brothers.[13] The people neither the Republic nor the Netherlands had ever cared about were now being shamelessly deployed by both sides as a humanitarian fig leaf in a geopolitical altercation.

Westerling, federalism, Ambon, New Guinea: these four dossiers ensured that post-colonial relations soured within a year. From 1951 Indonesian politicians asked themselves if there was any point to this much-vaunted 'Union' with the Netherlands. In 1956 they unilaterally ended it, after a maximum of two meetings. What had once been intended as the embodiment of Dutch–Indonesian cooperation had been revealed as an empty shell. Enthusiasm for the cultural aspect was also waning. Dutch disappeared from the streetscape. Dutch radio shows were cancelled, schoolbooks rewritten. There were still several Dutch professors active in higher education, but primary and secondary schooling soon switched to Indonesian. Even films and newsreel footage of the Dutch royal family were banned.[14]

These acrimonious developments caused a new exodus to the Netherlands. The Ambonese question made the fate of Moluccan KNIL veterans extremely precarious. They had been given the choice of joining the Indonesian army or resigning, but after events around the Republic of South Maluku they no longer felt safe in Indonesia.[15] At the start of 1951 the Dutch government decided to bring 4,000 of them, with their families if married, to the Netherlands, some 12,000 people in total.[16] They were housed in army barracks and even in former concentration camps such as Vught and Westerbork. 'Sukarno was happy to see the back of us, he was glad to be rid of us,' Julius Nunumete explained. 'The Netherlands was right to take us, otherwise we would have kept on fighting. In 1951 I was moved into the barracks of Geesbrug, near Hoogeveen. We got our food from a soup kitchen. Later I moved to Nijverdal and became a welder at an engineering works.'[17] For many, their lives had taken an abrupt turn for the worse. In colonial society they had been the favourites of the Dutch, but in the post-colonial Netherlands they formed the first generation of migrants of colour. Donisius Unawekla had never expected to end up in the Netherlands when he gave up his job as a pearl diver. Day and night he'd sailed between the small, remote island paradises of the eastern Moluccas. Azure waters, white beaches, endless coral reefs . . . On deck he got the pearls out of the shells, but the KNIL paid better. 'I didn't have anything to do with the RMS! I was in Java when it happened. All "Ambonese" soldiers were suddenly suspect, even the ones from other islands! We couldn't go back home.' He too had to go into exile in the Netherlands. 'I left on 29 February 1951 together with my wife. The boat trip took two months.' The contrast was enormous. 'When we arrived, there was deep snow in the Netherlands. We ended up in the Catholic south, in Cuijk, south of Nijmegen. We lived in barracks and were given three guilders a week. The food from the soup kitchen wasn't enough. That's why we started filching potatoes and beetroots from local farms!' From pearls to potatoes: his life. 'My first child was born in a

Dutch army barracks.' It was not until the sixties that he got a home of his own. In the seventies Moluccan militants of the second generation, the children of Ambonese veterans, carried out a series of terrorist acts in the Netherlands. Donisius would spend sixty-one years of his life in the Netherlands, but in his old age he returned to the Moluccas. When I interviewed him he was receiving a modest pension from the Dutch state.[18]

The Moluccans were not the only ones to leave Indonesia. With increased tension around New Guinea, more and more citizens of the Netherlands, both Dutch and Eurasian, packed their bags. At the start of 1950 there were an estimated 226,000 of them living in Indonesia. In the two years that followed 85,000 left for the Netherlands and by the end of 1957 there were only 50,000 Dutch citizens in the whole archipelago. 'The Dutch all lost their jobs,' related Nanny Kooymans, a Eurasian. Her father had been a civil servant, her husband worked in the car industry. The Indonesianisation of the business world had begun and the Indos were mistrusted. 'Sukarno said, a dog can't turn into a cat. We left at once. There was still food in the cupboard, the laundry was still in the room. We couldn't let the Indonesians know we were going. We could only take one small suitcase.' In a period of twelve years, 286,000 people moved from Indonesia to the Netherlands. Nanny was one of them. She had never lived there. During her first winter she wondered why they left all the dead trees standing. Like so many others she found herself in a boarding house that had won a contract to provide lodgings, generally plain accommodation with strict house rules. Hers was in Zandvoort, on the cold, grey North Sea. 'We were allowed to shower once a week – but in Indonesia we washed twice a day! In the bathroom I saw taps with blue and red caps. I turned one on and a flame shot into the water heater! Ahhh! I wrapped myself in a towel and ran out: fire! Fire!' The alienation was caused not just by bare trees and strange taps. It was also what people said to them. 'Chink! Darky! Go back to Sukarno! You have no business here! You shouldn't have surrendered the country!' The Indos: always standing out, never at home anywhere. A month after her arrival in the Netherlands, her mother died. She thought back to her oldest memory: she was three years old, lying in a hammock between two avocado trees and listening to her Indonesian nanny. 'It took me a long time to feel at ease here,' she said at the end of the interview. 'I've been here more than sixty years now and I still get homesick.'

The souring of relations between Indonesia and the Netherlands was written in the stars. More remarkable was that Indonesia also fell out with the US, the country that had helped it gain independence, but that needn't have come as a surprise either. In 1950 Indonesia supplied a third of America's tin and rubber, raw materials whose price had risen substantially because of the Korean War.[19] In exchange for its generous orders, the US expected goodwill and loyalty, but these weren't forthcoming. Yes, Sukarno was grateful for American recognition of Indonesia's right to self-rule, but surely that didn't mean he had to commit himself to America for all eternity. He'd only just liberated the country from the Netherlands! Something that definitely stung in Washington was that the PKI had gained thirteen of the 233 seats in the provisional parliament of 1950. Not many, but hadn't that party been wiped out in 1948 after the Madiun Affair? Apparently not. The government had crushed the rebellion, but not the party. More to the point, by renouncing Stalinism and blending communism and nationalism, the new chairman, Aidit, set the party on a path of enormous growth. With America still reeling from Mao's victory in 1949, concerned about Indochina (Vietnam) and at war with the communists in Korea (1950–53), was Indonesia allowing communism to flare up again too? That wasn't in the plan.

In January 1953 President Eisenhower gained power with a distinctly anti-communist agenda. As former commander-in-chief of the Allied troops in Europe and the first supreme commander of NATO, he was convinced that the Red Menace had to be contained everywhere. His Secretary of State, John Foster Dulles, a strict Christian who divided the world rigorously into good and evil, began negotiations for what would become SEATO, the Southeast Asia Treaty Organization. Just as NATO was intended to counter the Russian threat in Europe, SEATO was designed to form a southern barrier to the People's Republic of China. In September 1954 it was ready. Six months later the Middle East Treaty Organization (METO) joined the others. The plan was to create – with US bases and support – a buffer against the Sino–Soviet bloc. But unlike Turkey, Iraq, Iran, Pakistan, Thailand, Indochina, the Philippines, Australia and New Zealand, Indonesia joined India in refusing to participate. That meant a gigantic breach in the planned geopolitical dam. Indonesia could be inundated! And the PKI was already on its way to becoming the third largest communist party in the world, after the Chinese and Russian parties. To avoid the communists taking over the archipelago, Eisenhower even considered sending troops. During a meeting of the National Security Council in December 1954, he exclaimed, 'Why the hell did we ever urge the Dutch to get out of Indonesia?'[20]

While relations with the Netherlands and the US grew murky, the links to India were strengthened. Nehru, Hatta and Sjahrir had known each other for years. Indonesia had helped India when famine threatened; India had constantly raised the Indonesian question in the Security Council and had even convened an international congress after the second Dutch offensive. It was hardly surprising that President Sukarno's first state visit after independence was to India and the first state visitor Indonesia received, Nehru.[21] Sukarno and Nehru were very different personalities – bon vivant and moral paragon, you might say – but neither believed in the hard-line SEATO policy of the US versus China. Was there no other, worthier form of diplomacy? A window instead of a dam? 'The future of Asia depends upon the relationship of India with China,' Nehru said.[22] He had followed the Indonesian struggle from the beginning and was familiar with Sukarno's Pancasila doctrine, the five political principles of Indonesian society. If they worked for all those far-flung islands, might they not work between the two new superpowers too? In 1954 the historic Panchsheel Agreement with China was signed, the first diplomatic treaty between the world's two largest countries.[23] The Indonesian inspiration was clear.[24] This laid the basis for years of economic, scientific and cultural exchange.[25] 'Live and let live,' said Nehru.[26] The five principles were: mutual respect for each other's territory, mutual non-aggression, mutual non-interference in each other's internal affairs, equality and cooperation for mutual benefit and peaceful co-existence. In 1957 they were unanimously adopted by the UN General Assembly. More than just a new player on the international chessboard, Indonesia was now taking a leading role. Before long, it would leave its mark on the decolonisation of the rest of the world and the geopolitics of the Cold War. It was only to be expected. It had been the first country to declare its independence after World War II. For four years it had fought against the return of colonial rule: one year against the British, three years against the Dutch. It had gained the support of the US and the UN, and established a paradigm of what decolonisation could mean, something that covered the entire territory and all authority, not half-hearted variants like dominion, alliance and commonwealth status. It had done away with all of the old ties, even the linguistic ones, and provided a demonstration of nation-building. It was all very impressive. But the single event that did the most to spread the ideals of the Indonesian revolution around the world was, without a doubt, the Bandung Conference of April 1955.

'Yes, I was there!' It was Sriyono speaking, the man who had taken up arms in 1945 as a fourteen-year-old. 'Hundreds and hundreds of people came to Bandung. Our country hosted all those other countries. All those heads of state and government leaders: Nehru from India, U Nu from Burma, Nasser from Egypt. I saw them all!' In the meantime he had been given the promotion of his life and become one of Sukarno's ten bodyguards. 'We had all been chosen from the military police. We were at our president's command day and night, we were used to that, but now we didn't sleep at all. We had to check everything constantly: access to the building, the chairs, the locations where he was going to give his speeches, everything. We went through all the standard procedures and searched the staff who were present. I even had to taste his food and water to make sure it wasn't poisoned.'[27]

The Bandung Conference, officially known as the Asian–African Conference, was much more than a prestigious international gathering. It was a milestone in world history, *the* moment when non-Western countries collectively combined forces for the first time without the West.[28] The ambitious plan was Sukarno's – Nehru considered it unfeasible at first, Prime Minister Ali Sastroamidjojo envisaged it on a smaller scale – but Sukarno managed to convince India, Ceylon, Burma and Pakistan. Bandung would be the global megaphone for him to trumpet Indonesia's independence.

Western countries were mistrustful. Who was going to be invited? The organisers didn't want to limit themselves to official members of the United Nations. The British government was astonished to see that the Gold Coast (Ghana) had been invited: the country wasn't even independent yet.[29] There was a fear that the popular Dr Kwame Nkrumah would attend, a prominent Pan-African who had already gained a degree of power as part of a transitional agreement. His appearance there could inflame resistance in other British colonies such as Nigeria, Tanzania and Kenya and cause what diplomats in London tactfully described as 'considerable international embarrassment'.[30] They were relieved when the final delegation turned out to be limited to harmless lightweights. Perhaps it really would be no more than the 'political jamboree' a British newspaper had described it as.[31]

France, too, was annoyed that Morocco, Tunisia and Algeria had been invited and would be sending observers. It had already lost its Asian colonies, but now the three Maghreb countries were also rising up. It had been at war with Algeria – not a colony, but an integral part of France – for a year already. No one was coming from its other African colonies (France was in possession of all of West Africa and a large part of central Africa), or from the Belgian or Portuguese territories, as none of these countries were pushing for independence in the near future, but Paris was still fearful of the possible consequences. No one could have suspected that it would lose all of its colonies in the next five years.

America, in turn, was highly disgruntled about the organisers having invited the People's Republic of China. Why communist China and not nationalist China? Only the latter was recognised by the UN, even if its territory had shrunk to the island of Taiwan. Secretary of State Dulles was 'seriously concerned [about] eventual implications' and believed that 'the voice of the free world should be able to blanket the voice of communism at the Afro-Asian meeting'.[32] He hoped to limit the damage at the conference through the US allies Pakistan, Turkey, Iraq and the Philippines.[33] And as a precautionary measure to avoid commotion at home, the State Department confiscated the passport of W. E. B. Du Bois, the father of Pan-Africanism and the first African-American to earn a doctorate, to prevent his departure for Indonesia.[34]

The Netherlands, too, looked on the conference with the utmost suspicion. Was Sukarno really going to stir up the rest of the world with his demagoguery and his harping on about New Guinea? Wouldn't he do better to sort out his own country first? The Dutch press was decidedly scornful. The *Algemeen Handelsblad* anticipated 'a lot of anti-colonial bickering'.[35] According to *de Volkskrant* 'hopeless chaos' was likely to arise, 'a tangle of political disagreements on the road to never-never land' and 'a tumbledown facade of Afro-Asian platitudes'.[36] *De Telegraaf* expected the conference to go off like 'the proverbial damp squib'.[37] The *NRC* thought that the twenty-nine participating countries' only common ground was 'aversion to the colonial regime'. This was 'virtually the only theme all of the conference attendees could discuss sincerely', and beyond that, 'an ideological battlefield' loomed.[38] *Het Parool* concluded: 'That is why nothing fruitful can be expected.'[39]

Doubts in the US were different. For Europe this was an old North–South conflict (retention of the colonies), for America a new East–West conflict (containment of communism). Put differently: Europe was interested in 'coffee plantations', the US in military bases. A week before Bandung, President Eisenhower found it 'very alarming . . . how the communists had managed to identify themselves and their purposes with this emergent nationalism. The US, on the other hand, had failed to utilise this new spirit of nationalism in its own interest . . . The communists seemed to be more successful in this area than we did.[40] On the opening day, he didn't send a congratulatory telegram to the Bandung Conference. His Russian counterpart, Khrushchev, did.

In short, there was tension in the air, a lot of tension. The plane with the official Chinese delegation even crashed on its way to Bandung, with only three survivors. China immediately accused the US of sabotage, which the US denied. Further investigation showed that it had been a bomb, but that Taiwan had planted it. The target had been the Chinese premier, Zhou Enlai, but he had taken another plane for security reasons. The Cold War travelled with him to Bandung. Meanwhile in Indonesia the struggle with Darul Islam was still raging. There were rebels in the mountains a few dozen kilometres from the congress centre. Two thousand police officers patrolled the streets of Bandung. Packages were no longer allowed to be delivered to hotels for fear of bombings.[41] Sriyono's having to taste President Sukarno's food and water was no gimmick.

Walking around Bandung today you can still breathe in the atmosphere of that time. The main road through the centre of town is still called Jalan Asia-Afrika. Across from a stately colonial era department store – 'Warenhuis de Vries' is written on decorative faience tiles, 'Landbouwbenoodigdheden – Kunst – Boek – Papierhandel', agricultural requirements, art supplies, books, stationery – you can visit the building where the conference was held, now home to an excellent museum dedicated to that one week when the provincial city of Bandung was, as Nehru put it, 'the capital of Asia and Africa'.[42] A little further down the street you can still spend the night at the magnificent hotel where the heads of state and government leaders stayed: the Savoy Homann, a modernist masterpiece from 1938 that delights to this day. Just before the conference, the managers installed running hot water and telephone lines.

It was the morning of 18 April 1955. Boy Scouts raised the flags of the participating countries. Thousands of ordinary Javanese thronged together to catch a glimpse of the delegations. A couple of Thai and Cambodian princes in their finery were followed by Saudis in headdresses and long white robes. Several young African leaders approached in suits with bowties and Borsalinos on their heads. A participant from Laos walked up in a plain linen robe, alongside the Emir of Yemen with his highly ornamented dagger. A Liberian politician was in African costume, and a Turkish minister wore the true trademark of a Turkish minister: a cultivated moustache. The observers included the Grand Mufti of Jerusalem, the Archbishop of Cyprus and the African-American author Richard Wright.[43] It was a colourful procession beyond anything any of them had seen before. And it became even more exciting. Here was the new, hastily formed Chinese delegation with Zhou Enlai, Premier of the People's Republic since 1949 and Mao's right-hand man. Here was Colonel Nasser, who had just liberated Egypt from the British, the first independent Egyptian head of state since the pharaohs.[44] He was one of the few in military uniform. The people shouted to catch sight of his handsome, distinctive face. And here was Nehru, walking up to the conference building with his retinue. He was Indonesia's friend, the man who had been at the head of the world's largest democracy since 1947. The crowd whooped. He had his radiant daughter with him, Indira Gandhi, who would later become prime minister. And at last, here came the large Indonesian delegation. A beaming Sukarno and the invariably serious Hatta led the way, the men who had proclaimed independence ten years earlier. Bandung celebrated, Bandung laughed, Bandung exploded with joy.

It was 18 April 1955. While in Europe the last ethnographic exhibitions were still being held with anonymous, dark bodies in reconstructed huts, here a new self-aware generation of political leaders was stepping into the light of morning. It was a 'meeting of the rejected', Richard Wright wrote; these had been 'the despised, the insulted, the hurt, the dispossessed'.[45] Now they were uniting in common cause. Most of the participants were in their forties – the youngest was Nasser at thirty-seven, while sixty-six-year-old Nehru was seen as the grand old man. Some were descendants of aristocrats, others came from the people. Some led feudal kingdoms, others modern democracies. Although countries like China, Nepal and Ethiopia were ancient, most had only just been founded. Or not yet. A country like Sudan didn't even have a flag, a shortcoming that was soon remedied by stitching the name of the country onto a white cloth. Of the participating countries, seventeen were Asian, eight Arabic and four sub-Saharan African. Ten other countries sent observers. It was '*un Evénement universel, planétaire*', as an enthusiastic French observer noted, comparable with 'the French Revolution, the Russian Revolution or the Independence of the United States'.[46]

Monday, 18 April 1955. Two thousand guests, 400 journalists, 200 taxis, fourteen hotels. With demographic giants like China and India, the delegations represented almost one and a half billion people, more than half of the population of the world at the time. They demanded a voice of their own.

'I was very proud of our country,' related Herawati Diah in her quiet living room in Jakarta. The woman who had asked Gandhi if her country would ever be free could not believe her eyes. The building that had once been the exclusive domain of the Dutch Sociëteit Concordia, whose members came there to waltz or play billiards, was now abuzz with a new era. Yes, it was still a man's world – she was one of only two female participants – but in the ballroom where high heels had clicked on the floor and ivory had struck ivory, she still heard the hum of the new. 'It was tremendous to meet so many important people,' she said with a smile. She was there as a journalist. Especially for the conference, she had set up the *Indonesian Observer*, Indonesia's first English-language newspaper. At thirty-eight she had extensive media experience. Her husband and her mother had founded newspapers, now it was her turn. 'I wanted to express the Indonesian nation's struggle and ideals for the rest of the world and wrote articles during the conference. There were so many of us journalists then.'[47]

Sukarno went up onto the podium. Arrayed behind him were the flags of the participating countries. In the press gallery the camera crews were almost knocking each other over. 'Your Excellencies, ladies and gentlemen, sisters and brothers,' he began. 'It is my great honour and privilege on this historic day to bid you welcome to Indonesia.' In the press room you heard the rattle of Remington typewriters. 'This is the first intercontinental conference of coloured peoples in the history of mankind!' Many felt themselves choking up. 'It is a new departure in the history of the world that leaders of Asian and African peoples can meet together in their own countries.' He referred to the historic conference of the League Against Imperialism and Colonialism in Brussels in 1927, in which Hatta, Nehru, Einstein and so many others had taken part. 'But that was a meeting place thousands of miles away, amidst foreign people, in a foreign country, on a foreign continent.' Much had changed since. It was almost too symbolic that, on that same day in a hospital room in Princeton, Albert Einstein was breathing his last – the participants had not yet heard the news. Sukarno spoke: 'Sisters and brothers, how terrifically dynamic is our time! [. . .] The passive peoples have gone.' And in this development they had found each other. 'We are united, for instance, by a common detestation of colonialism in whatever form it appears. We are united by a common detestation of racialism. And we are united by a common determination to preserve and stabilise peace in the world.' And rightly so. 'The states of the world today depend one upon the other and no nation can be an island unto itself. Splendid isolation may once have been possible; it is so no longer.' He thanked his 'good neighbour India' for the international conference in support of Indonesia in New Delhi. The world could learn from the Indonesian experience. 'Sisters and brothers, Indonesia is Asia-Africa in small.' He referred to the country's enormous ethnic and religious diversity. 'But thank God, we have our will to unity. We have our Pancasila. We practise the "Live and let live" principle, we are tolerant to each other. *Bhinneka Tunggal Ika* – Unity in Diversity – is the motto of the Indonesian State. We are one nation. So, let this Asian–African Conference be a great success! Make the "Live and let live" principle and the "Unity in Diversity" motto the unifying force which brings us all together.'[48]

There are conferences that redraw the map of the world and there are conferences that emphasise that the world is more than just a map. The conferences of Vienna (1815), Berlin (1885), Versailles (1919), Yalta and Potsdam (1945) fell into the first category. Bandung was different: here no borders were drawn or territories negotiated, instead new dynamics that transcended national borders were unleashed.

For one week, meetings were held in parallel sessions dealing with political, economic and cultural collaboration. Every day journalists sent some 200,000 words out into the world. It would be an exaggeration to say that all people became brothers in Bandung. There were irreconcilable differences. Regarding the North–South conflict everyone agreed: colonialism was 'an evil thing, and one which must be eradicated from the earth'.[49] But when it came to the new East–West conflict opinions were divided.[50] Former Iraqi prime minister Fadhel Jamali considered communism 'a new form of colonialism, much deadlier than the old one'. John Kotelawala, prime minister of Ceylon, wondered if it should not 'be our duty to declare our opposition to Soviet colonialism?'[51] China's small southern neighbours, countries such as Laos, Cambodia and Thailand, were afraid of becoming satellite states like Latvia and Lithuania. After the Iron Curtain, would a 'bamboo curtain' be raised in Southeast Asia? Premier Zhou Enlai listened attentively, took notes and now and then asked to speak. In affable tones he explained that China sought peaceful coexistence in the region. 'China has no intention whatsoever to subvert the governments of its neighbouring countries. [. . .] We have no bamboo curtain, but some people are spreading a smokescreen between us.'[52] With this reasonable attitude, he made a great impression on the other participating countries, many of which were deeply religious. 'We Communists are atheists,' Zhou said, 'but we respect all those who have religious belief. We hope that those with religious belief will also respect those without.'[53] Whatever else, this didn't sound like a new Stalin. After it was over, many of the delegates agreed with the conference's Indonesian secretary-general: 'We must not think that China is the Asian Russia.'[54]

In short, at Bandung everyone was opposed to colonialism, but not everyone was opposed to communism. This was reflected in the final communiqué: France and the Netherlands were condemned for holding on to Algeria and New Guinea; China and Russia were not for their actions in Tibet and Eastern Europe. But the most important conclusion was that a young country did not have to choose between the superpowers in the new East–West conflict. They could also opt for what Nehru called 'positive neutrality'. This created room between the 'First World' with its economic liberalism (US and Western Europe) and the 'Second World' of the planned state economies (China and the Soviet Union) for a 'Third World'. This

expression would later be associated with starving children and civil
wars, but at the time it was a term that evoked liberation: a new
country didn't need to immediately subject itself to a new master.
Bandung laid the seeds for the establishment of the association of
countries that did not commit themselves to either power bloc, the
Non-Aligned Movement, which in terms of number of members
would grow to become one of the largest organisations in the world.[55]

US Secretary of State Dulles considered the principle of neutrality
'immoral'[56] — anyone who was not against communism was
for it — but reactions elsewhere were cautiously positive, even in the
Netherlands. The demand to surrender New Guinea piqued, of
course, but *Het Parool* found that the final declarations 'looked better

Map 29: Bandung Conference (18–24 April 1955)

than many in the West had expected'.[57] The participants pleaded for world peace, nuclear disarmament, extension of the UN, anti-apartheid and so on. *Het Vrije Volk* called it 'an extraordinary event' and according to *Trouw* the conference was 'no flash in the pan'. 'It is now playing a positive role in the great politics of our times.'[58]

The spirit of Bandung spread around the world. Although the conference did not lead to an international institution with its own budget and a permanent secretariat, its importance can hardly be overstated.[59] At the end of 1955 sixteen new countries were admitted to the UN, among them Cambodia, Ceylon, Jordan, Laos, Libya and Nepal, all present at Bandung. In the years that followed, the 'southernising' of the General Assembly continued unabated.[60] In 1961 more than half of the member countries came from Asia and Africa; in 1945 it had been less than a quarter.[61] Indonesia was at the centre of the world map and Sukarno had become a world leader overnight. Even John Foster Dulles travelled to Jakarta to visit him. To avoid losing him to the communists, he invited him on a state visit to the US. When the Russians heard, they immediately extended an invitation to Moscow as well. Neutrality had its advantages.

In 1956 Sukarno travelled around the world. In the US he met President Eisenhower, Vice-President Nixon and, of course, Dulles. In New York a tickertape parade was held in his honour, in Hollywood he had a private dinner with Marilyn Monroe – and possibly more, according to their biographers.[62] He gave a speech to Congress that was interrupted for applause no fewer than twenty-eight times. 'A sensation,' said a member of Congress afterwards. He called Sukarno's speech the best a visiting head of state had ever given, with the possible exception of Churchill.[63] With his infectious good humour and passionate talk of freedom, Sukarno had no trouble winning over the American public. From there he travelled on to Canada, Italy, the Vatican, West Germany, Austria and Switzerland, and later that year he visited Russia, Yugoslavia, Czechoslovakia, China and Mongolia as well. He consulted with Adenauer, Khrushchev, Mao and the Pope. He visited opera houses, factories, Red Square and the Great Wall of China. En route he collected honorary doctorates and diplomatic gifts: limousines, a Soviet aeroplane and even a horse.

He didn't go to the Netherlands. The Hague didn't invite him once. It is almost impossible to believe, but Sukarno would never visit the country that had been such a fundamental influence on his life. Despite the snub, his status as a global leader and international star gave him the confidence and courage to pay even less attention to the Netherlands.[64] In 1956 he put a definitive end to the Union, annulled the agreements from the Round Table Conference and refused to pay off the remaining debts: eighty per cent had already been paid back.[65] In 1957 he seized the ships of the KPM and cancelled KLM's right to land aircraft. In 1958 he confiscated companies that were still in Dutch hands: political independence without economic independence was meaningless. Finally, in 1960, he broke off diplomatic relations with the Netherlands, again because of West New Guinea. In 1962 the territory was placed under UN control; six months later it was the Republic's.

But it was about more than just Indonesia. Bandung touched every continent. The Arab world, for instance, would never be the same. When Nasser returned to Cairo after the conference, banners in Arabic had been hung across the road: 'Welcome hero of Bandung, champion of peace and liberty! Welcome champion of Africa and Asia!'[66] Although he initially hadn't wanted to go, he said afterwards that it was 'one of the two most important events of modern history' – the other being the discovery of atomic energy.[67] More than anyone else, he used national radio to spread the spirit of Bandung. The whole Arab world already tuned in to his station, Voice of the Arabs, for Umm Kulthum's wistful songs; now he used it for speeches opposing colonialism and neo-colonialism. He called on the populations of Jordan and Iraq to break with their pro-American governments and offered Algerian freedom fighters shelter and broadcasting time.[68] And if his radio waves reached Algiers and Baghdad, they could just as easily go south. Bandung had made him realise that Egypt was the gateway to Africa.[69] He no longer turned his back on the sub-Saharan world, but had programmes produced in Swahili,

Map 30: The United Nations before and after the Bandung Conference

with more percussion and less Islam. They found enthusiastic audiences in Uganda, Kenya, Tanganyika and Zanzibar. 'Africans, Indians and Arabs are brothers, as shown by the Bandung Conference,' was the tenor. 'Brothers, my African national compatriots, I appeal to you to work together with the Arabs and Indians, to fight those white pigs side by side until freedom is attained.'[70]

Nasser had done more in Bandung than just picking up a few ideas for the radio. He had also discreetly discussed weapons with Zhou Enlai; his young country needed them, especially since Israel had established itself in the region by force of arms in 1948. Washington was willing to supply them, but only if Egypt joined the METO, the Middle East Treaty Organization, against Nasser's objections.[71] Zhou listened and nodded. He contacted Russia and Russia contacted Czechoslovakia, known for its arms industry.[72] When Dulles heard after Bandung that Czechoslovakian arms were on their way to Cairo, he was beside himself. It was exactly what he had feared, a breach in his buffer! Now the Cold War would spread to the Arab world! He promptly scrapped all loans for the Aswan Dam. The British did the same.

This colossal dam in the Nile was intended to give a massive boost to the Egyptian economy. The US and the UK had pledged to advance half of the total cost of $400 million, with the World Bank providing the rest. Now Nasser had to find his money elsewhere, by taking advantage of the Suez Canal for instance, operated by an Anglo-French concessionary company. If he nationalised that company, he could draw on the enormous revenue from tolls and be solvent again. To show the seriousness of his resolve, he had a few ships sunk at the entrances. This act stirred up so much ill feeling that the Western press labelled him a 'Pan-Arabic Hitler' and a 'couscous Mussolini'.[73] France and Britain were already nettled by his inflammatory radio broadcasts in Algeria and the British colonies, but closing the Suez Canal made that look like child's play. He had his hands on the throat of international trade. The West would run dry of oil. In top-secret talks, France, Britain and Israel agreed on military action: Israel would bomb the Egyptian positions and destroy the arsenals of Czechoslovakian weapons; the French and British would then intervene to separate the combatants and reconquer the Suez Canal. It was an insane scenario and the most insane thing about it was that the US was kept entirely in the dark. But that was how it happened. On 29 October 1956 Israel attacked. Two days later the French and the British bombed Egyptian positions, including the hated state radio. The military objectives were quickly achieved, but the world was appalled by this imperial aggression and Eisenhower was furious. Of course he was displeased by Nasser's flirtation with China and Russia, but didn't the Europeans realise that this kind of late-colonial display of power would drive more countries into the communists' arms? And how could they possibly launch a campaign like this just when Soviet troops were entering Budapest? The front pages should have been full of horrific news about the Hungarian uprising; now they were focused on Western aggression in Egypt.[74] This outrageous offensive had to be stopped immediately. Eisenhower telephoned London, London telephoned Paris. It's unlikely the conversations were very convivial.

For the French and British, the Suez Crisis was a total debacle. Their days of imperial glory were gone forever. Prime Minister Anthony Eden resigned in the UK and in France the Fourth Republic collapsed. But Gamal Nasser was triumphant, reaping admiration and applause in the souks from Marrakesh to Baghdad. His performance on the international stage was like divinely sweet mint tea pouring from a raised silver teapot into countless glasses across the Arab world. Morocco, Algeria and Tunisia switched up a gear in their struggle against France. Inspired by his example, a military officer called Gaddafi seized power in Libya, Saddam Hussein did the same in Iraq, and in Palestine Yasser Arafat gained in popularity. Arab nationalism – secular, militant, anti-Western – reigned supreme. Even the colonial borders were rejected: Egypt, Libya and Syria became one country and Iraq and Jordan merged, even if these Pan-Arabic constructions didn't last long. Only the United Arab Emirates and the union of North and South Yemen proved more durable.

In 1992, after an archaeological excavation, I drove through the Egyptian desert in a clapped-out four-wheel-drive, a Lada Niva with a Russian dashboard. How did a car with Cyrillic lettering end up in an Arab country? Again, the answer was Bandung. The enormous Aswan Dam ended up being built after all, thanks to the Russians. It was completed in the seventies. Decades later you still occasionally saw a worn-out four-wheel-drive scooting around the desert, as long as the driver could still make sense of the petrol gauge.

Europe too would never be the same after Bandung. On 6 November 1956, West Germany's Chancellor Konrad Adenauer was in the office of French Prime Minister Guy Mollet in Paris when British Prime Minister Eden called him. This was the awkward conversation in which Eden had to tell Mollet that he had just complied with US demands regarding Suez. Mollet knew that France could not carry on by itself. Adenauer interrupted the long silence that followed to tell him that they now needed to unite to make Europe. 'We have no time to waste: Europe will be your revenge.'[75]

The story of European unification is often presented as a series of neat steps: the European Coal and Steel Community in 1951, the European Economic Community in 1957, the European Community in 1967 and so on. In practice, however, there was no logical stairway to heaven. By the time the Bandung Conference was held, the European project was at an impasse; after the fiasco with the European Defence Community (finished off by France in 1954), enthusiasm was low. It was revived not by moral awareness, but by geostrategic realpolitik after the Suez Crisis.

A noble, internal peace mission? Not really. The European Union arose as a reaction to what was happening in Asia and Africa. Committed Europeans wondered if a new power bloc was forming, 'the heavy parallelogram Moscow, Peking, Bandung, Cairo'?[76] What would the consequences be for Africa, historically Europe's backyard? Look what had happened in September 1955. During the first General Meeting of the United Nations after Bandung, France was unable to keep the question of Algeria off the agenda. Algeria was not a colony, Paris insisted, but an integral part of the Republic of France, just as Northern Ireland was part of the United Kingdom. But the Bandung countries disagreed and insisted on discussing the issue. When France lost the vote, its furious diplomats walked out of the meeting. Shortly afterwards the question of West New Guinea was also put on the agenda. This all strengthened the longing to combine Europe's forces to operate separately from both the UN and the US.

Negotiation of the Treaty of Rome – the European Community's founding document – ran from 1955 to 1957. Ten days after the end of the Suez Crisis, the colonial question was raised for the first time. Of the six member states, only one had never had any colonies: the Grand Duchy of Luxemburg. Germany and Italy had lost theirs after World Wars I and II, but the Netherlands, Belgium and France still had them. The idea that Europe began where colonialism ended is not correct. French diplomats, for instance, were still sensitive to arguments such as: 'If the Six do not associate the overseas territories to their exchanges and investments, the Afro-Asian bloc "spearhead of communism" will implant itself on these territories. Already, the Afro-Asians and the communists begin to exercise their harmful activities in Britain's old African colonies. [. . .] If the Europe of the Six, through a truly efficient financial and investment policy, succeeds in making the black populations feel that the Eurafrican Association is capable of producing practical results, the French-Belgian territories [. . .] will not just reject the attempt of the Bandung group and the communists but [. . .] also constitute a symbol of prosperity to its neighbouring colonies.'[77]

During negotiation of the Treaty of Rome, a great deal of attention was given to the colonies and how to involve them in a unified European market. Belgium submitted a request to add its colonies Congo, Rwanda and Burundi to the proposed Eurafrican construction; Italy pleaded the case for Somalia (although it was no longer a colony); the Netherlands wanted to include West New Guinea; and France was thinking of Mauritania, Senegal, Mali, Burkina Faso, Niger, Guinea, Ivory Coast, Benin, Gabon, the Republic of the Congo, Central African Republic, Chad, Togo, Cameroon, French Somaliland and Madagascar. Algeria was still part of France, and Morocco and Tunisia could be invited, as could Libya, a former Italian colony. Altogether this involved more than a quarter of the population of Africa.[78] In return for a contribution to a development fund, the six European member states would gain access to the markets and raw materials of these overseas territories.

The benefit for Germany was unclear – was it really worth pumping money into all those French territories? – but after the Suez Crisis, Adenauer was convinced, stating plainly, 'the free Europe must be prepared to confront this risk, in order not to be crushed, in the foreseeable future, between the peoples of Asia and Africa'.[79] During a night of endless negotiations in Brussels, he even snapped at one of his experts: 'Do you want to make Europe or not? Well then, stop boring us with your bananas, coffee and cacao.'[80]

Without Bandung, no Suez; without Suez, no Europe. European unification was meant as a vigorous riposte to the anti-imperialism of the South. The Belgian former prime minister, Paul-Henri Spaak, driving force behind the Treaty of Rome, had no desire to be 'surrounded by vast masses of humanity indifferent towards or even hostile towards us', because then 'the fate of our civilisation will rapidly be sealed'.[81] Dutch Minister of Foreign Affairs Joseph Luns believed that the Treaty of Rome would not only safeguard Europe's prosperity, but also permit 'the continuation of her grand and global civilising mission'.[82] The mindset underlying Europe was late colonial, rather than post-colonial.

Africa, too, was changed forever by Bandung. On New Year's Eve 1957 a plane from Cairo landed in Accra, capital of newly independent Ghana. On board: a twenty-six-year-old beauty from Egypt, Fathia Halim Ritzk. That same day she married the brand-new head of state, Kwame Nkrumah. The marriage caused a panic in the West. Was this the creation of a political union between Egypt and Ghana, Africa's two most rebellious countries?[83] Was Pan-Arabism merging with Pan-Africanism? After Nkrumah's wedding, Nasser presented him with the Grand Cross of the Order of the Nile, and when a son was born, Nkrumah named him Gamal, after Nasser.

A direct line could be traced from Bandung through Cairo to Accra. In March 1957 Ghana had become the first country to gain its independence in the wave of post-war African decolonisation, and although Nkrumah had not been able to go to Bandung himself, he spread the message with verve. Nkrumah was for Africa what Nasser was for the Arab world, the man everyone looked up to when it came to political emancipation. 'To millions of people living both inside and outside the continent of Africa, Kwame Nkrumah is Africa and Africa is Kwame Nkrumah,' according to an official portrait.[84] His opinion of the Treaty of Rome? It reminded him of the Berlin Conference of 1885. 'The latter treaty established the undisputed sway of colonialism in Africa, the former marks the advent of neo-colonialism in Africa.'[85]

Accordingly it had to be opposed with conferences: prestigious, international gatherings like Bandung. In April 1958, just after the start of the European Economic Community, Nkrumah organised the First Conference of Independent African States, a meeting of eight countries that affirmed 'unswerving loyalty to and support of the Charter of the United Nations and respect for decisions of the United Nations' and 'adherence to the principles enunciated at the Bandung Conference'.[86] In December that same year he convened the All African People's Conference for countries that were not yet independent and now at risk of being swallowed up by a new European imperialism. The participants were trade unionists, student leaders, anti-apartheid activists and artists, including numerous future heads of state and government leaders: Kenneth Kaunda, later president of Zambia, Ahmed Sékou Touré, later president of Guinea, Joshua Nkomo, later vice-president of Zimbabwe, and so on. One of them was an eloquent young man from Congo who had until very recently taken a highly cooperative stance towards his country's coloniser, speaking of 'our beloved King' in Belgium, the colonialists' 'magnificent and humanitarian work' and 'the new, Eurafrican society' that was more important to him at the time than 'the words Independence and Autonomy'.[87] During the conference, however, he would find support for a radical anti-colonial course that would be of great consequence for the political fate not just of his country, but far beyond its borders. His name: Patrice Lumumba.

On 28 December 1958, immediately after arriving home from Accra, Lumumba addressed an audience of no fewer than 10,000 people, the first political mass meeting in Belgian Congo. 'The conference demands the immediate independence of all of Africa and declares that after 1960 no African country may remain under foreign rule.'[88] A week later, large-scale riots broke out in the capital, Léopoldville (Kinshasa). A week after that, King Baudouin promised independence. Without Accra it would never have gone so fast.

1960 became the year of Africa, with no fewer than eighteen countries gaining independence, most of them French colonies. In Paris, Bandung had inspired the *Premier Congrès international des écrivains et artistes noirs*, the first international congress of black writers and artists.[89] Speakers included Léopold Senghor, later president of Senegal, Aimé Césaire, Martinican poet and political leader, Frantz Fanon, psychiatrist and political philosopher in Algeria, Hampâté Bâ, novelist and ethnologist from Mali, Cheikh Anta Diop, essayist and

historian from Senegal, and many others. The congress was held at
the Sorbonne and the poster was designed by Picasso. James Baldwin
and Richard Wright, two African-American authors who lived in
Paris, also participated. Wright had been at Bandung, too, and his
book about it had come out in French. According to Senghor, '*l'esprit
de Bandung*' was nothing less than the beginning of '*notre Renaissance*'.
In 1960 the colonies fell like dominoes, with the British territories
soon to follow. Ten years after Bandung, there were thirty-four new
African countries.

Nkrumah wanted to unite Africa and free it from Europe. He
pleaded for a common African market, African economic policy, an
African currency, an African central bank and even an African constitution.[90] Tanzania's President Nyerere also called for regional
cooperation. Just as in the Arab world, there were attempts to erase
colonial borders: from 1958 Ghana and Guinea formed a single country, joined by Mali in 1960, but this union too proved short-lived. A
real 'United States of Africa' never emerged, but 1963 saw the foundation of the Organisation of African Unity, which became the
African Union forty years later.

South Africa seemed immune to the winds of change; more than
ever the country was in the grip of the apartheid regime. But in the
early sixties, the African National Congress decided that abroad it
would emphatically commit to 'positive neutrality' and the principles of peaceful coexistence adopted at the Bandung Conference.[91]
The anti-apartheid fighters were drawing on the fire of the Revolusi.
From his cell on Robben Island, Nelson Mandela described how
South Africa's case had been pleaded 'in Bombay in 1947, in Bandung
in 1955, at the meetings of the Commonwealth and the Non-Aligned
Movement'.[92] More than once after his release, Mandela praised 'the
visionaries of Bandung', men 'of the calibre of Pandit Nehru, Abdul
Nasser, Kwame Nkrumah, Sukarno, Albert Luthuli, Allende and
others', who had struggled for 'political freedom and socio-economic
development' by initiating and striving 'to build on the spirit of
Bandung'.[93]

Even America would never be the same. Although the great Pan-
Africanist W. E. B. Du Bois had been prevented from attending, he

had followed the conference closely from the US. African-American activists like Paul Robeson expressed their affinity for 'brothers from Africa, India, China, Indonesia and all the people represented at Bandung'. The young Malcolm X saw the Asian–African Conference as 'spelling doom for the "white devils"' and called on black Americans to organise 'a Bandung Conference in Harlem'.[94] The even younger Martin Luther King inspired an audience in Saint Louis, Missouri, in his inimitable way: 'One billion six hundred million of the people of the world are colored. (Yes) [. . .] These people for years have lived under the bondage of colonialism and imperialism. (Yes sir) One day they got tired. (Go ahead) One day these people got tired of being trampled over by the iron feet of oppression. (Yes, Go ahead) [. . .] More than one billion three hundred million of the colored peoples of the world have broken aloose from colonialism and imperialism. (Yes sir) [. . .] They assembled in Bandung some months ago, and that was the word that echoed from Bandung (Yes): "Racism and colonialism must go." (That's right) [applause]'[95]

Eight months after Sukarno's global summit, the Montgomery bus boycott began, a milestone in black history.[96] When Rosa Parks refused to surrender her seat on the bus in December 1955, there was an organisation ready and waiting with twenty-six-year-old Martin Luther King as its spokesman. The court victory and successful campaign that followed became the first great victory for the American civil rights movement and the start of King's national renown. There was a longstanding belief that the US civil rights movement gained momentum purely because of domestic events, but it is now becoming increasingly clear that international developments like Bandung accelerated the process.[97] Richard Wright's *Color Curtain* opened many eyes. His account of the conference ended with the words that this was 'the first attempt in history on the part of man as man to organise himself'.[98] Wright was the son of an illiterate tenant farmer, born on a plantation in Mississippi; all four of his grandparents had been slaves. When it came to oppression, he was an authority. In the forties his autobiographical novels had sold in the hundreds of thousands. His work had been adapted for the theatre and directed by Orson Welles. Wright went to live in Paris and travelled the world:

Zurich, Madrid, Accra, Jakarta ... He knew Sartre, de Beauvoir, Camus, Gertrude Stein and Fanon, but also Nkrumah, Senghor and Sjahrir. As a cosmopolitan intellectual, he informed black America about what was happening in the outside world: the emancipation of Asia and Africa was 'this massive reality, which has, like a volcanic eruption, shot up from the ocean's floor'.[99]

The dominant feeling was that America was miles behind. 'We American Negroes', said Paul Robeson, 'can no longer lead the colored peoples of the world because they far better than we understand what is happening in the world today. But we can try to catch up with them.' That was why civil rights activists needed to 'learn about China and India and the vast realm of Indonesia rescued from Holland'.[100] Others were drawn to independent Ghana: Martin Luther King, Malcolm X, George Padmore, Maya Angelou and Muhammad Ali admired Nkrumah deeply and all went to visit him. Some 300 black Americans even settled permanently in Ghana, among them the very elderly W. E. B. Du Bois. He died there at the age of ninety-five.[101]

The realisation of lagging behind did not pass quickly. Even in April 1963 in his famous *Letter from Birmingham Jail*, Martin Luther King wrote that the 'nations of Asia and Africa are moving with jet-like speed toward gaining political independence, but we still creep at horse and buggy pace toward gaining a cup of coffee at a lunch counter'.[102] Eight years after Bandung, Malcolm X too believed that black America could still learn a lot from events in Indonesia. At a reading in Detroit he said: 'And once you study what happened at the Bandung conference, and the results of the Bandung conference, it actually serves as a model for the same procedure you and I can use to get our problems solved. [. . .] They had a common enemy. And when you and I here in Detroit and in Michigan and in America who have been awakened today look around us, we too realize here in America we all have a common enemy.'[103]

Reverend King differed in style and strategy, but in late 1964, early 1965, he and Malcolm X secretly combined forces when they went to the United Nations to try to get America's race problem on the agenda of the General Assembly. Nothing similar had been done before and it had the potential to be highly embarrassing for the US authorities.

For the first time, the General Assembly was to be chaired by a black diplomat, Alex Quaison-Sackey of – the country you would expect – Ghana. What's more, for the first time, the secretary-general was an Asian, the Burmese U Thant. During his travels in Africa, Malcolm X had already met many ambassadors and ministers and raised the issue with them. The new African countries had to help black Americans 'to take the United States before the United Nations'.[104] In New York he and King also met Che Guevara, with whom they, according to an insider, 'conferred on the Bandung Strategy'.[105] Given the dominance of the Afro-Asian bloc and developments in Latin America, the world would have almost certainly turned against the US with regard to human rights violations. Malcolm X believed that they had 'a strong, airtight case'.[106] But the plans came to nothing. A month later, in late February 1965, Malcolm X was assassinated, Che Guevara was killed in October 1967, Martin Luther King in April 1968. It has been established that the CIA was behind Guevara's murder; with the other two it remains unclear who ordered the assassinations. But Malcolm X's legacy was passed on to the Black Panthers, who for years continued to use Bandung as a benchmark.[107]

'The atmosphere was fantastic! So much international solidarity!' Towards the end of my research I found myself in a modern flat in West Amsterdam. After all those Indonesian islands, Nepali villages and Japanese metropolises, I was almost home. Batik cushions were arranged on the armchairs. Cisca Pattipilohy was ninety-two and still inspired. How many over-nineties had I spoken to in the last few years? And how much life had they brought to a past that once seemed so ossified? It was like lifting blocks of tuff and seeing the smouldering lava of an almost forgotten eruption.

Three days earlier, Pratomo had died, just one week before his 104th birthday. At his funeral in the flat expanse of the 'Head' of North Holland, a few dozen of us sat around his small, white coffin with white flowers. The winter sun shone through the windows and outside on the half-frozen lake, ducks were standing around a hole in the ice. Today the urn with his ashes, together with Stennie's, stands in a niche at the small cemetery of Callantsoog. Burnets grow there, sand blows over the graves, seagulls screech in the sky. So many witnesses have died in the meantime. While writing over the past few years I have constantly received news that someone or other has died. Soerachman, Sukotjo, Iskandar Hadisaputra, Herawati Diah, Purbo S. Suwondo, Sumaun Utomo, Sumarsono, Go Gien Tjwan, Ton Berlee, Felix Jans, Piet van Staveren, Joop Hueting, Lydia Chagoll, Seiji Natsui, Ryuichi Shiono, Nobuyoshi Fukatsu, Bhagta Sing Pun . . . The Gurkha veterans in their inaccessible mountain villages have presumably all died as well. At ninety-seven Goderd van Heek found it 'lonely at the top'. When I phoned him in April 2020 with a question about a detail, he said, 'Yes, we hobble on,' despite coronavirus and other 'unpleasantness'.[108] Joty ter Kulve continued to regularly send me moving emails while I was writing. Johannes Soewondo in Pare and Stef Horvath in Amsterdam read the passages in which they appeared. And with undiminished pugnaciousness and perceptiveness, Cisca Pattipilohy spoke to me on the phone about the latest publications on Indonesia and the Cold War.

As a young woman in the early sixties, Ibu Cisca had had the time of her life working as an interpreter at the Afro-Asian Journalists' Conference in Jakarta, Afro-Asian Writers' Conference in Bali and Afro-Asian Islamic Conference in Bandung. She was one of the few Indonesians able to simultaneously translate into English. And then there were all the Afro-Asian gatherings for youth, workers, women, students, lawyers, paediatricians and so on. In Jakarta you could attend the Afro-Asian Film Festival and even the GANEFO, the Games of the New Emerging Forces, an alternative to the Western-dominated Olympic Games.[109] Cisca's work took her to Hong Kong, Beijing, Budapest and Stockholm, but her most extraordinary travel experience was the tour of nine African countries in 1964. Spending the night on a boat on the Nile, eating French baguettes in Mali, meeting the deputy prime minister of Ghana, seeing a hippo walking around in Tanzania, having the opportunity to translate President Nyerere of Tanzania, trembling before Haile Selassie's lions . . . Two months travelling with an Indonesian, a Chinese and a Japanese journalist to get to know African colleagues – how many young women experience something like that?

'The atmosphere at those meetings was really tremendous. There was this will! This sense of "We don't need the West. We can take charge of our own development." It was like we'd already known each other forever. It really felt like that! We all came from different nations, but we had so much admiration for each other. There was no question of class differences.' The colonial steamship no longer existed. 'No matter how well you spoke Dutch, how educated you were, how hard you tried, you were always a native. In court a native always had to sit on the ground. That was a way of drumming that humiliation into you.' She remembered the African journalists thinking Sukarno was magnificent and wanting to know everything about Indonesia. And then, completely unexpectedly, she added, 'But it all came to nothing of course.'

What did she mean?

'By 1965 the pioneers of the Afro-Asian movement had all been cleared out of the way. Sukarno in Indonesia, Nkrumah in Ghana, Lumumba in Congo, all deposed or even murdered. We were so angry.' She was right: the spirit of Bandung was deliberately smothered and, sadly, Indonesia was once again the forerunner. As early as the elections of 1955 the Eisenhower government gave money to anti-communist conservative parties there in an attempt to prevent the PKI from becoming the world's third largest communist party. In 1958 a rebel movement in Sumatra received generous military and financial support from the CIA, led at that time by Alan Dulles, brother of the Secretary of State.[110] With $10 million it was the then largest covert action in the history of the CIA; that showed how nervous Washington was about Southeast Asia.[111] The operation, however, failed miserably. In the years that followed, Indonesian officers received training in the US and were encouraged to combat and destroy communism. In October 1965 the path was clear for them to brutally suppress a leftist coup attempt, depose Sukarno and install a more right-wing regime. It was one of the Cold War's first large, US-sponsored regime changes. The American agencies were aware that it was immediately followed by a crazed explosion of violence that cost the lives of between 500,000 and one million Indonesians – progressives, communists, Chinese – but this made no difference.[112]

Everything on the left had to go: more than a million journalists, teachers and students were rounded up. General Suharto established a military dictatorship that would last for thirty-two years.[113]

Cisca experienced it first-hand. 'America saw Indonesia moving too far left and then you had all those arrests. My husband disappeared into prison, just for writing for a left-wing newspaper. I was picked up too, but managed to get released again. Not my husband, he died in prison.' As a single mother of four she moved to the Netherlands where she became a librarian. A portrait of her husband hung on the wall. On a necklace, she had worn the same piece of jewellery for half a century, a pendant he had carved for her in his cell from coconut wood.

The 'Jakarta method' was repeated everywhere. A month after Suharto's coup, Mobutu ascended the throne in Congo: another soldier, another friend of the CIA, Mobutu too remained in power for thirty-two years. In the space of a few years, military coups took place in Brazil, Bolivia, Ghana, the Central African Republic, Nigeria and Iraq, mostly with CIA support. In 1965 America sent its first ground troops to Vietnam – the war would cost more than three million lives. And in 1971 one million people died in a genocide in Bangladesh with Nixon and Kissinger's knowledge.[114]

The US had forced European countries to accelerate the relinquishment of their colonies and was now behaving as an imperialist power itself. The dream of Bandung had turned into a nightmare and that nightmare was called Jakarta. Even now Indonesian history remains the point of reference. 'Jakarta' became the code word for regime change and mass slaughter with CIA support. The name the Brazilian dictatorship used for an extermination plan in 1971? *Operação Jacarta*. The code name for the military coup against Allende in Chile in 1973? *Plan Djakarta*. What was daubed on the walls of the streets before Pinochet's coup? *Yakarta viene*, Jakarta is coming.[115]

Cisca picked some fluff off her black jumper. 'Algeria was going to organise the second large Asian–African conference in 1965, but that was cancelled after a coup. So around 1966, the spirit of Bandung was well and truly gone,' she said. And its vestiges grew ever more radical.[116] In that year the Conferencia Tricontinental was held in Havana, with eighty-two countries from the South gathering there.[117] Fidel Castro referred to the 'solidarity movement that began in Africa and Asia' and was spreading to Latin America, 'the third continent that is oppressed and exploited by imperialism'.[118] But the days of positive neutrality were over. The *imperialismo yanqui* had to be opposed with force. A year before his death, in his contribution to the conference, Che Guevara dreamed of 'two, three, many Vietnams' to force America to its knees, revolutionary troops who were filled with 'a relentless hatred of the enemy', a hatred that transforms man 'into an effective, violent, selective and cold killing machine'.[119] This was far removed from the ideal of world peace that had been promoted in 1955. From brotherhood to brutality, that was the tragedy of Bandung.

But American imperialism pushed on. In 1965 there was even a new colony, the last one in the world. In the middle of the Indian Ocean, halfway between Asia and Africa, the tiny islands of the Chagos Archipelago were rechristened as the British Indian Ocean Territory (BIOT), where the US was allowed to build one of the world's most important military bases.[120] After Bandung and Suez they were afraid this part of the world would turn into a strategic vacuum for them. In the Chagos Archipelago, however, the atoll of Diego Garcia turned out to be suitable as a harbour and just large enough to build a runway. The original inhabitants, some 1,000 descendants of African slaves, were forced to move. They are still fighting court battles against that decision to this day.[121]

Cisca Pattipilohy sighed. We had been talking for hours. Outside the twenty-first century raced by. Her expression was downcast. 'You know,' she said to break the silence, 'we never actually became independent. We thought we could make things fairer, but we were three centuries behind. That makes it a difficult struggle. The other side was stronger, the capitalist system has established itself everywhere. But as long as this system carries on, the whole world will be wrecked and the environment devastated. The forests of Sumatra, of Kalimantan, of all of Africa, they're all being destroyed . . .'[122]

She fell silent. It was quiet in the house. Her gaze slid away from the portrait of her husband to the window and the cold Amsterdam rain outside.

Epilogue

The prahu pushed off from the wooden posts in the twilight. I had talked for far too long with a few residents of Pulau Papan, an idyllic fishing village on stilts in Central Sulawesi whose only connection to the island is a long wooden walkway. The interviews had given way to friendly conversation. Sitting cross-legged on the wooden floor of one of the huts, we talked calmly over the turquoise water while the light withdrew from the world. The owner of the prahu wasn't bothered about the long trip back across the sea in the dark. There were stars, after all. The boat was a six-metre-long dugout with a light outboard at the back: fourth millennium BCE meets third millennium CE. He started the motor, I waved to the people and wondered if I would ever return to this magical place again.

My gear was a few kilometres away in a bamboo hut on the beach of the bay. We were staying there with Dr Ating and his wife. Ating was a Chinese-Indonesian doctor from West Java who had abandoned all comforts in favour of an austere life in the service of nature. He grew his own maize, cassava and papayas, but this year the monsoon had failed, and with it all his crops. These were hard times for the island. Malenge was an extraordinary place where you could still find tarsiers, hornbills, babirusas and an extremely rare species of macaque, but Dr Ating had seen biodiversity disappearing before his eyes, despite his efforts to preserve nature. Fishermen here didn't work with lines or nets, but with dynamite, destroying all of the coral reefs in the area. Tropical fish were dazed with cyanide, then sold to aquariums in Hong Kong. And even this remote spot had fallen prey to deforestation – not by large multinationals, but by private citizens who claimed a piece of land they hoped to later sell at a large profit. Giants of the forest were felled, hardwood was worth a fortune, every year more forest was burnt off. Dr Ating was very pessimistic about it. 'They say they need money to feed their

children, but half of the family budget goes on cigarettes. In the last
twenty years it's got much worse. All of the men smoke, sometimes
even toddlers of two. Cardiovascular disease has shot up, but the
richest people in Indonesia are almost all tobacco manufacturers and
the government doesn't do a thing because it's happy with the duties.'
Sometimes he feels despondent about it, but as a Catholic Buddhist
he's found a way to keep going: no expectations, act because you
must. 'If I started waiting for results, I'd go mad,' he said.

Together with those of Brazil and Congo, Indonesia's ecosystems
are among the world's richest. In 1900, eighty-four per cent of the
country was forested, in 2010, only fifty-two per cent. Since then,
many hundreds of thousands of hectares have been cleared, despite new
legislation, the land given over to palm oil plantations and the production of wood pulp. Java and Sulawesi have been largely razed; it's now
the turn of Sumatra and Kalimantan. The planned relocation of the
capital Jakarta to a new administrative centre on Borneo does not bode
well for the surrounding nature. Mass deforestation, illegal logging
and the systematic burning of peatlands has made Indonesia the world's
sixth largest emitter of greenhouse gases. It is also the planet's second
largest plastic polluter, after China. An estimated 93 million straws are
used and discarded every day. Plastic bags? Some ten billion annually –
95 per cent end up in the environment. A full fifteen per cent of the
plastic floating in the world's seas comes from Indonesia.

Deforestation, erosion and overfishing are devastating one of the
most beautiful countries in the world. Mountains of refuse, air pollution and traffic chaos plague the cities, but the population is scarcely
informed about global warming and environmental degradation.
Many people are responsible for that and they are everywhere: in local
education, the national government and multinational corporations.

The prahu slid over the smooth water and the motion cooled us
after yet another sweltering day just below the equator. On our left
was the dark, forested island coast; on our right the open, silver water.
The murmuring water set me to musing: even if we one day come to
terms with the colonialism of the past, we still won't have done anything about the dramatic way we are colonising the future. Mankind
is taking the coming century with the ruthlessness that was once used

to seize control of continents. Colonialism is no longer territorial, but temporal; instead of in the past, the worst might lie before us. We are behaving like the colonists of future generations, depriving them of their freedom, their health, maybe even their lives. We are saddling them with ourselves. The 2020s are ruling over the 2080s with mind-boggling indifference and brutality. And that's not all, because it's not just about people. Even if we could process all of the violence of the past, even if we could stop all of today's violence – verbal, physical and symbolic – even if we could spare the coming generations, the greatest violence would remain: humanity's destruction of the planet. An estimated one million species could become extinct in one or a few generations, an unimaginable massacre.

The sound of a babirusa in the undergrowth. A school of tens of thousands of fish swimming under us. Dolphins swimming alongside a ferry. Monkeys in a tree with a mango. A volcano looming up in the mist. I've seen so much beauty on my trip, so much consolation. And then: the skipper pointing overboard with his torch. Flying fish were trailing us. They shot up, floated elegantly through the air, then disappeared back into the water, emerging over and over again, as if competing with each other. He switched off the torch and laughed. After all these years he still found it a magnificent sight. There was no moon that night, the starry sky was deep and endless. Ten minutes later he turned off the motor. The old, wooden prahu glided silently through the water as old, wooden prahus had glided silently through the water here for thousands of years. '*Lihat*,' said the skipper, 'look.' The sea was dark and smooth and revealed the most beautiful thing I had ever seen. Sparkling in the water were thousands upon thousands of green dots of phosphorescent plankton, a slow, floating carnival of light, without a goal, without a destination, drifting in weightlessness. And suddenly I saw something else glittering in that bright green swarm, minuscule spots of white light. Very delicate, very weak, but glimmering. It was the reflection of the stars above. The plankton and the Milky Way, splashing together, swaying in the night, wandering through the aeons, with or without humanity.

Then he restarted the motor.

Acknowledgements

Revolusi is a book of many voices, sometimes speaking clearly in the foreground and sometimes whispering in the background. I am deeply indebted to all the witnesses I have had the privilege of speaking to over the past five and a half years, for their time, their trust and their stories. My heartfelt thanks to the many hundreds of relatives, acquaintances, colleagues and friends who put me in touch with eye-witnesses, including those whose interviews didn't make it into the final draft of this book.

To thank everyone who has contributed would be impossible, but I would like to mention a number of people by name, because their valuable tips brought my attention to writings, places or individuals that I might never have discovered otherwise. In alphabetical order they are, among others, Udi Baboe, Alfred Birney, Fred Boot, Thijs Broer, Ton Broers, Geert Buelens, Ian Buruma, Bambi Ceuppens, Syahrita Chairaty, Koos van Dam, Soedarmadji Jean Henry Damais, Sylvia Dornseiffer, Douwe Draaisma, David Fontijn, Kenichi Goto, Caroline de Gruyter, Bregje Hofstede, Brad Horton, Waltraud Hüsmert, Luc Huyse, Bert Immerzeel, Elli Izeboud, Karin Jans, Hilde Janssen, Freek de Jonge, Klaas de Jonge, Joty ter Kulve, Wouter Lemm, Michel Maas, Kaori Maekawa, Geert Mak, Nazar Malik, Wim Manuhutu, Valérie Marin La Meslée, Gwen Martèl, Pankaj Mishra, Vincent Monnikendam, Hetty Naaijkens-Retel Helmrich, Karel Ottens, Tino Pattipilohy, Josien Pieterse, Suryantoro Purbo, Anja van Rijs, Shigeru Sato, Mark Schaevers, Willem Schinkel, Christopher Spencer, Lies van Staveren, Klaas Stutje, Ng Sauw Tjhoi, Gerdi Verbeet and Maarten Verberk.

Fred Lanzing fuelled my research with a generous supply of insights, recommended reading and publications. I have good memories of my conversations with him. Jeffry Pondaag tirelessly sent me news items about attitudes towards the colonial past in the present and brought me in contact with a few witnesses in southern Sulawesi. And Marjati Pratomo was exceptionally helpful, scanning documents for me, lending me books and guiding me through the family archives. I also learned a great deal from conversations with fellow writers, including Goenawan Mohamad, Ayu Utami, Seno Gumira Ajidarma, Laksmi Pamuntjak, Sitok Srengenge and Bernice Chauly. I am grateful for my discussions with Chris Keulemans and Willem-ijn Lamp, and it was always very inspiring to converse with Anne-Lot Hoek, who has done noteworthy oral-history research of her own in Sumatra and above all in Bali, exploring the borderlands between academic writing and journalism. I became acquainted with Herman Keppy and Esther Wils of *Indies tijdschrift*, well-read and inspired experts on Indonesian history who energise public debate with their scholarship, flair and nuance. Many thanks to them all!

I would like to express my special gratitude to the fantastic teachers at the Alam Bahasa language school in Yogyakarta and to Didik Agus Prastowo, who continued my Indonesian lessons in Brussels. For the support and hospitality in Jakarta, my thanks to the Belgian ambassador Patrick Herman and his team, especially Heikki Vandermander. It was very important to my research and very enjoyable for me to meet Bonnie Triyana, the editor-in-chief of *Historia*, an outstanding historical monthly in Indonesia. Bonnie combined wide-ranging knowledge of Indonesian history with an incredible network and a delightful sense of humour. He made me feel at home in Jakarta. I was assisted by the journalist Rukardi Achmadi in Semarang, the poet Arif Gumantia in Madiun, the sociologist Anton Novenanto in Malang and Pare, Ruth Ningsih Hastuti in Yogyakarta and the historian Muhajir Salam in Tasikmalaya; my deepest thanks to all of them for the wonderful days we spent together. To the south of Yogyakarta, I stayed with the poet Sitok Srenenge, who shared his knowledge with me very generously. Outside Java, I was fortunate to receive the assistance of other remarkable people: Ika Fuji Rahaya in Tidore and Ternate, Yulia Sahupala and Muhlis Eso in Morotai, Nyoman Sutoyo in Bali, Dr Ating Solihin in North Sulawesi, John Massolo in Tana Toraja, Muhammad Ridwan Alimuddin in West Sulawesi, Horst Liebner and Ilham Mattalatta in Makassar, Dirk

A. Buiskool in Medan in Sumatra and Paulien Joel-Perera in the Moluccas.

Many thanks to all who acted as interpreters for me. Through Couchsurfing, I met Muhammad Fahmi Masdah, a young political science student who spoke good English and proved to have a keen interest in history. It was a pleasure to set off with him again each day. Jeanne Lefèvre, the French freelance journalist who had made her home in Jakarta, was an ideal interpreter, researcher and travelling companion. Without her detective work in the retirement homes of Jakarta, I could never have preserved so many testimonies for posterity. And with Saidah Boonstra, a Dutch-Indonesian historian and curator in Jakarta, I enjoyed marvellous discussions, journeys and museum visits.

In Tokyo, I received a warm welcome from Ambassador Aart Jacobi and political and cultural attaché Ton van Zeeland. I was also assisted there by Yoshiko Tamura, Taeko Sasamoto, Brad Horton and Kjeld Duits. It was again through Couchsurfing that I came into contact with Yukiko Mitsuoka; she became my interpreter, research assistant and translator, all in one, with a combination of precision, modesty and friendliness that was remarkably pleasant. I would also like to thank Nobuteru Iwabuchi of the Pacific War History Museum in Iwate Prefecture. In Nepal, I received assistance from several military officers: Lieutenant Deo Nara, Lieutenant Purna B. Gurung, Major Lalit, Major Sovit, Major Hitman and Lieutenant Colonel John P. Cross. From England, Bishnu Pun helped me to establish contact with his father.

In transcribing and translating the interviews, I was assisted with the Indonesian by Syahrita Chairaty and Elisabeth Ida Mulanyi and with the Japanese by Geert van Bremen. Tomoko Kaji and Luk Van Haute did additional research into Japanese sources.

A special word of thanks to everyone who granted me access to private archives. In particular, I am thinking of Ella Hueting and Hanna Wahab Hueting in Amsterdam, Joop Hueting's daughters; of Marjati Pratomo in Callantsoog, the daughter of Djajeng and Stennie Pratomo-Gret; of the George H. and Charlotte Völker-Müller family in Overveen, the son-in-law and daughter of Martin Müller; and of Goderd van Heek in Velp. I am grateful to Marc Cappon for permission to use the interview he conducted at the age of fourteen (!) with his neighbour, the U-boat survivor Martin Müller. A few Indonesian witnesses gave me access to personal historical documents. I would particularly like to thank Purbo S. Suwondo in Jakarta and Johannes Soewondo in Pare. John P. Cross in Pokhara, Nepal, allowed me especially generous access to his research archives on the subject of Nepalese Gurkhas. My profuse thanks for that too. And lastly, the historian Sytze van der Zee sent me a copy of the famous letter about the plans for a coup d'état in the Netherlands in 1947, a munificent gesture for which I am deeply obliged to him.

During my fieldwork and while writing this book, I was shadowed for more than a month in total by Djoeke Veeninga and Marlou van den Berge, two Dutch documentarians I had worked with earlier. The interest, discretion and integrity they brought to their work made the long days of shooting well worth the trouble. It was also thanks to them that I tracked down certain witnesses, such as the Sultan of Tidore.

During the five and a half years that I worked on this book, I spent one year in Berlin as a guest of the Berliner Künstlerprogramm of the DAAD (Deutsche Akademische Austauschdienst). My thanks to Katharina Narbutovič of the DAAD for the generous reception and for a wonderful stay. Although Germany does not have such a strong historical link to Indonesia as the Netherlands does, I know of no other country in the world that has so impressively demonstrated how, in our own day, you can approach the dark chapters in your history in a calm, mature manner. Humility can have such greatness in it. I should add that the DAAD stipend is the only grant I received while working on this book. To ensure that I could remain independent, I did not apply for any form of public or private financial support in the Netherlands or Belgium.

While writing, I found many people willing to answer my questions, whether about contacts between China and the Roman empire in the ancient world or rainfall in Java in 1944. I wish to thank the employees of the libraries, archival institutions, museums and antiquarian bookshops where I searched for information. My gratitude also extends to the following people, again in alphabetical order: Rosanne D'Arrigo, Manon van den Brekel, Sophie De Schaepdrijver, Frank Dhont, Jonathan Holslag, Hilde Janssen, Gert Oostindie, Marjolein van Pagee, Harry Poeze, Johan Poukens, Bambang Purwanto, Remco Raben, Mikke Susanto, Arjen Taselaar, Gerard Termorshuizen, Valerie Trouet, Marc Waelkens, Abdul Wahid, Kaat Wils, Liesbeth Zegveld and Herwig Zahorka, as well as all the others I thank personally above.

My approach to the structure of this book came to me in Zurich's Kunsthaus museum as I gazed at Nicolas de Staël's painting *Composition en noir* from 1946. The rhythm and the colour scheme were offered to me by *Perahu dan matahari* (Boat and Sun), Affandi's matchless work from 1971. I can't explain exactly how it all worked, but I owe those two works of art my sincerest thanks.

I asked several people to read chapters of the book. I am deeply grateful to Henk Schulte Nordholt, Fred Lanzing, Sadiah Boonstra, Anne-Lot Hoek, Herman Keppy and Esther Wils for the time and trouble they took to supply me with feedback on what I had written. I couldn't have hoped for better first readers. It deserves special note that one of the most elderly witnesses in the book, ninety-five-year-old Francisca Pattipilohy, also took on the task of reading one chapter.

De Bezige Bij publishing house in Amsterdam had faith in me, offered me the time to work undisturbed and gave me the gift of friendship. What a pleasure to work with people like Francien Schuursma, Haye Koningsveld, Marijke Nagtegaal and Liesje Bruin. Wil Hansen turned out to be the finest editor a person could wish for: eagle-eyed, inquisitive, unflagging, strict yet also so very witty. It's often said that an author can never become friends with his editor, but then again, people say all sorts of things. Rob van Rossum, René de Graaff, Michel Wassenaar and Nina van den Broek gave their best as the proofreader, copyeditor, typesetter and indexer, respectively. Once again, Tim Bisschop astounded me with his exceptional talent for graphic design.

Every book is also a hand-knotted carpet of friendships. Bonnie Triyana, Laksmi Pamuntjak, Sadiah Boonstra, Jeanne Lefèvre and Bernice Chauly helped me not only understand but also love Southeast Asia better. In Amsterdam, I enjoyed my inexhaustible conversations with Maaike Pereboom and Julia Akkermans. In Brussels and beyond, I was blessed with friends like Natalie Ariën, Elise Caluwaerts, Yves Dejaeghere, Mohamed El Bachiri, Jan Goossens, Hadja Lahbib, Grazyna Plebanek, Kim Van den Brempt, Stephan Vanfleteren and Francesca Vanthielen. Peter Vermeersch and Emmy Deschuttere, my best friends, went on supporting me unconditionally for the many years that I worked on this book. Their friendship made me sparkle. My mother Bernadette De Bouvere and my brother Tomas Van Reybrouck and his family offered me their warmth, compassion and humour, as always. And while I wrote, Eva Rovers was the greatest pillar of support I was privileged to have, at my side with keen intelligence, encouragement and high spirits. She brought light to my days.

Brussels, October 2020

Bibliographical Essay

Not only is there a great deal of writing about Indonesia, but it is also exceptionally good. It is a true pleasure to immerse yourself in the subject. I would like to share the works that inspired me most and point curious readers towards further information.

For those in search of a compact, accessible introduction, I warmly recommend Elisabeth Pisani's *Indonesia, Etc.: Exploring the Improbable Nation* (London, 2014). Mochtar Lubis wrote the often surprising *Indonesia: Land Under the Rainbow* (Singapore & New York, 1991). Other overviews include Tim Hannigan, *A Brief History of Indonesia: Sultans, Spices, and Tsunamis* (Tokyo & Singapore, 2015), Fritz Schulze, *Kleine Geschichte Indonesiens* (Munich, 2015) and Elsa Clavé-Çelik, *Dictionnaire insolite de l'Indonésie* (Paris, 2012).

One excellent and accurate Dutch-language synthesis is *De garoeda en de ooievaar. Indonesië van kolonie tot nationale staat* by Herman Burgers (Leiden, 2010), a book that has not received the attention it deserved, but that served as a constant guide to me as I wrote. Burgers was building on Loe de Jong's still-astounding achievement: the six volumes that make up Parts 11 and 12 of De Jong's authoritative history of the Netherlands in World War II, *Het Koninkrijk der Nederlanden in de Tweede Wereldoorlog* (The Hague, published between 1984 and 1988). Gerard Termorshuizen's *Journalisten en heethoofden* and *Realisten en reactionairen* is not simply a two-part history of the Dutch East Indies press from 1744 to 1942; it draws on colonial public opinion to offer a marvellous panorama of the Dutch East Indies (Amsterdam & Leiden, 2001 and 2011).

Publications by Indonesian authors include Abdullah Taufik's survey *Indonesia: Towards Democracy* (Singapore, 2009), which sheds light on the continuity between the struggle for emancipation in the colonial period, the fight for independence and the post-colonial Republic. Sartono Kartodirdjo published the two-part survey *Pengantar Sejarah*

Indonesia Baru (New Introduction to Indonesian History), which begins around 1500 (Jakarta, 1987 and 1993). The great novelist Pramoedya Ananta Toer, often seen as a likely winner of the Nobel Prize, worked with Koesalah Soebagyo Toer and Ediati Kamil towards the end of his life on the publication of the five-volume *Kronik Revolusi Indonesia* (Chronicle of the Indonesian Revolution, Jakarta, 1999–2014).

From the English-speaking world, let me mention the survey *A History of Modern Indonesia since c. 1200* (Stanford, 2001) by M. C. Ricklefs. Books specifically about the Revolusi include George McTurnan Kahin, *Nationalism and Revolution in Indonesia* (Ithaca, NY & London, 1952), Benedict Anderson, *Java in a Time of Revolution: Occupation and Resistance, 1944–1946* (Jakarta & Singapore, 2006, originally 1972) and Anthony Reid, *The Indonesian National Revolution 1945–1950* (Hawthorn, 1974).

To those interested in the wider regional context, Henk Schulte Nordholt's crystal-clear, wide-ranging work *Een geschiedenis van Zuidoost-Azië* (Amsterdam, 2016) deserves the very highest recommendation. The *Historical Dictionary of Indonesia*, edited by Robert Cribb and Audrey Kahin (Lanham, MD, 2004), was indispensable to me as I wrote. Anyone who wishes to explore in greater depth will derive great benefit from the *Digital Atlas of Indonesian History*, a DVD compiled with great care by the Australian historian Robert Cribb (Copenhagen, 2010).

On the subject of atlases, Christian Grataloup's *Atlas historique mondial* (Paris, 2019) is the very best historical atlas of which I am aware, although I also made frequent use of Ludwig Könemann's *Historical Atlas of the World* (Bath, 2013).

Prologue

The opening scene is based on what we know about the sinking of the *Van der Wijck* in 1936. My attention was drawn to this disaster by an article on the *Java Post* website ('Een vuurtoren als monument', 28 April 2014). The Dutch captain and legal expert E. A. Bik, president of the Maritime Disciplinary Tribunal of the Netherlands, devoted a brief study to the topic: *Het vergaan van de S.S. 'Van der Wijck'* (n.p., 2006). My description is based on accounts by several survivors, which I was able to track down thanks to Delpher, the superlative online database of the Dutch press. In Indonesia, the disaster has become a subject of interest once again thanks to *Tenggelamnya Kapal Van der Wijck* (2013), a *Titanic*-like film based on Hamka's novel of the same name from 1938.

Chapter 1

The YouGov survey of present-day attitudes towards the colonial past was published on the YouGov website under the title of 'How unique are British attitudes to empire' (www.yougov.co.uk, 11 March 2020). The author was Matthew Smith. Tina van der Vlies was awarded a doctoral degree in November 2019 for her thesis on secondary school history textbooks, *Echoing Events: The Perpetuation of National Narratives in English and Dutch History Textbooks, 1920–2010* (Rotterdam, 2019).

With regard to the population of Southeast Asia, I found the best recent analysis in *Nature*: 'Genomic analyses inform on migration events during the peopling of Eurasia', by L. Pagani, D. J. Lawson, E. Jagoda et al. (*Nature*, 21 September 2016). This type of genetic research provides powerful confirmation of what archaeologists had concluded earlier from excavations. On the origins and spread of agriculture, see the relevant chapters of Peter Bellwood's impressive study *First Farmers: The Origins of Agricultural Societies* (Oxford, 2005) and James C. Scott's *Against the Grain: A Deep History of the Earliest States* (New Haven, 2013). I found a detailed account of the emergence of complex societies in the Paul Michel Munoz's book *Early Kingdoms of the Indonesian Archipelago and the Malay Peninsula* (Singapore, 2006). Henk Schulte Nordholt also offers a very lucid treatment of this subject in his aforementioned *Geschiedenis van Zuidoost-Azië*.

To gain an impression of the importance of sailing and navigation to Austronesian peoples, I read, and took great pleasure in, Bronislaw Malinowski's great classic *Argonauts of the Western Pacific* (London,

1922), the first ethnographic work based on long-term fieldwork, and the study which launched the field of cultural anthropology. Although it is a century old, that is actually one of its strengths; Malinowski witnessed a world that had persisted for thousands of years but changed radically soon afterwards. On the early contacts between East and West, I consulted Peter Frankopan's engaging synthesis *The Silk Roads: A New History of the World* (New York, 2015). Raoul McLaughlin's books address the Roman period specifically: *The Roman Empire and the Silk Routes* (Barnsley, 2016) and *The Roman Empire and the Indian Ocean* (Barnsley, 2018). One especially interesting study of the spice trade with medieval Europe is Paul Freedman, *Out of the East: Spices and the Medieval Imagination* (New Haven & London, 2008). The first direct contacts between Dutch travellers and Javanese and Malay merchants are described by the French scholar Romain Bertrand in his magnificent work *L'Histoire à parts égales. Récits d'une rencontre Orient-Occident (XVIe–XVIIe siècle)* (Paris, 2011), which I call magnificent because the author brings together a wealth of sources in a wide range of languages to break away from the European perspective completely. Rather than primitivism, he offers close attention to the complex and sophisticated nature of local societies. The turbulent history of the two best-known spice islands is described by Willard A. Hanna and Des Alwi in *Turbulent Times Past in Ternate and Tidore* (Banda Neira, 1990).

B. Alkema and T. J. Bezemer, *Volkenkunde van Nederlandsch-Indië* (Haarlem, 1927), a classic anthropological survey of the diverse religions of the archipelago and their history, is still well worth reading. Regarding the unusual ways in which various religious traditions have met – both the frictions and the fusions – Clifford Geertz, perhaps the greatest anthropologist of the second half of the twentieth century, wrote *The Religion of Java* (Chicago & London, 1960).

Chapter 2

The Dutch East India Company (VOC) has inspired a vast body of writing. I consulted a variety of standard reference works, as well as

Ewald Vanvugt, *Roofstaat. Wat iedere Nederlander moet weten* (Amsterdam, 2016) and Piet Hagen, *Koloniale oorlogen in Indonesië. Vijf eeuwen verzet tegen vreemde overheersing* (Amsterdam, 2018). On the origins of Batavia, see Susan Abeyasekere, *Jakarta: A History* (Oxford & New York, 1989).

In connection with the slave trade and slavery, I made use of two excellent studies: Reggie Baay, *Daar werd wat gruwelijks verricht. Slavernij in Nederlands-Indië* (Amsterdam, 2015) and P. C. Emmer, *Geschiedenis van de Nederlandse slavenhandel* (Amsterdam, 2019). P. H. van der Brug wrote a brilliant analysis of malaria as a cause of death in the VOC's second century: 'Malaria in Batavia in the 18th century' (*Tropical Medicine and International Health*, 1997).

Joël Eymeret penned an illuminating study of the often-forgotten French period in Java, 'Les archives françaises au service des études indonésiennes: Java sous Daendels (1808–1811)' (in *Archipel*, 1972). The British interlude in the early nineteenth century is described in Tim Hannigan, *Raffles and the British Invasion of Java* (Singapore, 2012). On the takeover by the Dutch state after 1816 and the development of classical colonialism, I turned to Henk Wesseling, *Europa's koloniale eeuw. De koloniale rijken in de negentiende eeuw, 1815–1919* (Amsterdam, 2003). Gert Oostindie, *De parels en de kroon. Het koningshuis en de koloniën* (Amsterdam, 2006) relates specifically to the role of the monarchy.

I drew on two older, richly illustrated studies of the KNIL's military conquests, which were not entirely free of patriotic sentiment: *Het Koninklijk Nederlands-Indisch Leger 1830–1950* (The Hague, 1977) by H. L. Zwitzer and C. A. Heshusius and *Klamboes, klewangs, klapperbomen. Indië gewonnen en verloren* (Houten, 1977) by Pierre Heijboer. Two more balanced sources are Ben van Kaam, *Ambon door de eeuwen* (Baarn, 1977), about recruitment in the Moluccas, and Fred Lanzing, *Soldaten van smaragd. Mannen, vrouwen en kinderen van het KNIL 1890–1914* (Amsterdam & Antwerp, 2005). For more information about the final decades of 'pacification', see the collection edited by J. van Goor, *Imperialisme in de marge. De afronding van Nederlands-Indië* (Utrecht, 1985). On the Aceh War, Anton Stolwijk wrote *Atjeh. Het verhaal van de bloedigste strijd uit de Nederlandse koloniale geschiedenis* (Amsterdam,

2016), a fascinating read, and Philip Dröge wrote an equally wonderful book about the leading adviser to the Dutch authorities on that war, *Pelgrim. Leven en reizen van Christiaan Snouck Hurgronje* (Houten & Antwerp, 2017).

On the origins of colonial taxation, see Abdul Wahid's thought-provoking doctoral thesis *From Revenue Farming to State Monopoly: The Political Economy of Taxation in Colonial Indonesia, Java c. 1816–1942* (Utrecht, 2013). The uprising against the colonial regime and the tax system is described in great detail in Sartono Kartodirdjo's doctoral thesis, *The Peasants' Revolt of Banten in 1888: Its Conditions, Course and Sequel: A Case Study of Social Movements in Indonesia* (The Hague, 1966). The abominable conditions on the Deli plantations are trenchantly analysed by Jan Breman in a study that has become a classic, *Koelies, planters en koloniale politiek. Het arbeidsregime op de grootlandbouwondernemingen aan Sumatra's oostkust in het begin van de twintigste eeuw* (Dordrecht & Providence, 1987). On small-scale rubber production outside the plantations, see Bambang Purwanto, *From Dusun to the Market: Native Rubber Cultivation in Southern Sumatra, 1890–1940* (London, 1992). On opium addiction, see Abdul Wahid's recent article 'Madat makan orang; opium eats people: opium addiction as a public health issue in late colonial Java, 1900–1940' (in the *Journal of Southeast Asian Studies*, 2020, 51, 1–2, 25–48).

The earliest moving images are not only described in Janneke van Dijk, Jaap de Jonge and Nico de Klerk's beautiful book *J. C. Lamster, een vroege filmer in Nederlands-Indië* (Amsterdam, 2010) but also included on an accompanying DVD.

Chapter 3

The best introduction to the colonial hierarchy in the Dutch East Indies may be the extraordinary documentary *Moeder Dao, de Schildpadgelijkende* by Vincent Monnikendam (1995). This film is made up entirely of historical footage, with music and poetry woven through it as the sole form of commentary. A masterpiece.

When I began my archival research into the *Van der Wijck*, I was so struck by the extensive parallels between the design of steamships and the social stratification of colonial society that I could no longer *stop* seeing them. I found I was not the first to have had this insight; back in 1996, Joop van den Berg had made the same point in an article in the literary magazine *Bzzlletin*, 'Van de brug uit keken ze op ons neer. Rassendiscriminatie in Nederlands-Indië'. Historical research into the role of shipping in the design and conception of colonial society seems to have been on the rise in recent years. Kris Alexanderson published the groundbreaking *Subversive Seas: Anticolonial Networks across the Twentieth-Century Dutch Empire* (Cambridge, 2019) and Coen van 't Veer wrote the very worthwhile doctoral thesis *De kolonie op drift. De representatie en constructie van koloniale identiteit in fictie over de zeereis tussen Nederland en Nederlands-Indië* (Hilversum, 2020).

For a sociological analysis of the colony, I consulted W. F. Wertheim's classic *Indonesian Society in Transition: A Study of Social Change* (The Hague, 1969). A collection edited by Robert Cribb was also very useful: *The Late Colonial State in Indonesia: Political and Economic Foundations of the Netherlands Indies 1880–1942* (Leiden, 1994), especially Cees Fasseur's article 'Cornerstone and stumbling block: racial classification and the late colonial state in Indonesia'. On the European elite, see e.g. Arjen Taselaar, *De Nederlandse koloniale lobby. Ondernemers en de Indische politiek, 1914–1940* (Leiden, 1998). There is an exceptionally large volume of writing about the Eurasian community in the Dutch East Indies. Books I enjoyed included Rob Nieuwenhuys, *Tussen twee vaderlanden* (Amsterdam, 1988) and Marion Bloem, *Indo* (Amsterdam, 2020). Ulbe Bosma, Remco Raben and Wim Willems jointly wrote the more scholarly work *De geschiedenis van Indische Nederlanders* (Amsterdam, 2006). Reggie Baay published the outstanding, taboo-busting *De njai. Het concubinaat in Nederlands-Indië* (Amsterdam, 2008). And Hetty Naaijkens-Retel Helmrich made three eye-opening documentaries: *Buitenkampers* (2013) sheds light on the lives of the Indos during the Japanese occupation, *Contractpensions. Djangan Loepah!* (2008) describes their poor reception in the Netherlands after 1949, and *Klanken van Oorsprong. Poekoel Teroes!* (2018) explores their contributions to pop music. On the Chinese ethnic group, especially the elite, see e.g. Abidin Kusno, *Visual Cultures of the Ethnic Chinese in Indonesia* (London & New York, 2016) and Peter Post and May Ling Thio, *The Kwee Family of Ciledug: Family, Status and Modernity in Colonial Java* (Volendam, 2019). On the lower class, see the study mentioned above by Jan Breman, *Koelies, planters en koloniale politiek* (Dordrecht & Providence, 1987).

I found useful facts about the social system scattered here and there. The census of 1930, the only one ever taken in colonial Indonesia, remains an inexhaustible source of information. The colony's Departement van Economische Zaken (Department of Economic Affairs) published a convenient summary: *Volkstelling 1930. Deel VIII, Overzicht voor Nederlands-Indië* (Batavia, 1936). On what may be the most important aspect of the social hierarchy, access to education, I consulted the very enlightening introduction written by Harry Poeze to the first volume of his collection of primary sources *Politiek-politioneele overzichten van Nederlandsch-Indië* (The Hague, 1982) and the detailed doctoral thesis by Kees Groeneboer, *Weg tot het Westen. Het Nederlands voor Indië 1600–1950* (Leiden, 1993). Figures on income, taxation and labour participation are taken primarily from Anne Booth, 'Living standards and the distribution of income in colonial Indonesia: a review of the evidence' (*Journal of Southeast Asian Studies*, 19, 2, 310–34.) Specifically on the role of the military, I read B. Bouman, *Van driekleur tot rood-wit. De Indonesische officieren van het KNIL, 1900–1950* (The Hague, 1995).

On the role of education in igniting a national consciousness, I recommend Benedict Anderson, *Imagined Communities: Reflections on the Origin and Spread of Nationalism* (London & New York, 1983), one of the most influential studies in the social sciences in the past twenty-five years. Because Anderson was a leading expert on Indonesia, he took many of his examples from the Javanese educational system. The role of maps in the schools was also discussed by Herman Burgers in his book *De garoeda en de ooievaar* (Leiden, 2010). Herman Keppy wrote a novel based on thorough historical research and set partly at STOVIA: *Tussen Ambon en Amsterdam* (Rotterdam, 2004). Harry Poeze and Henk Schulte Nordholt edited an excellent collection of twentieth-century primary source materials about the desire for an independent Indonesia: *De roep om merdeka.*

Indonesische vrijheidslievende teksten uit de twintigste eeuw (Amsterdam & The Hague, 1985).

Chapter 4

There are several outstanding accounts of the origins of political consciousness in Indonesia, starting with J. Th. Petrus Blumberger's classic study *De nationalistische beweging in Nederlandsch-Indië* (Haarlem, 1931), published in facsimile by the Royal Netherlands Institute of Southeast Asian and Caribbean Studies (KITLV) in 1987. R. C. Kwantes edited a superb four-volume collection of the colonial administration's official reports on the phenomenon between 1917 and 1933: *De ontwikkeling van de nationalistische beweging in Nederlandsch-Indië* (Groningen, 1975–1982).

On the early days of Sarekat Islam, the work of A. P. E. Korver is indispensable: *Sarekat Islam 1912–1916. Opkomst, bloei en structuur van Indonesiës eerste massabeweging* (Amsterdam, 1982). See also Takashi Shiraishi's study *An Age in Motion: Popular Radicalism in Java, 1912–1926* (Ithaca, NY, 1990). On the PKI, I refer readers to Petrus Blumberger, *Le communisme aux Indes néerlandaises* (Paris, 1929) and Ruth McVey, *The Rise of Indonesian Communism* (Ithaca, NY, 1965). Exceptionally rich documentation of those early years is provided by the first volume of Harry Poeze's biography of one of the most influential communist leaders: *Tan Malaka: Levensloop van 1897–1945* (The Hague, 1976). On Henk Sneevliet, see the biography by Max Perthus: *Henk Sneevliet. Revolutionair-socialist in Europa en Azië* (Nijmegen, 1976). Joop Morriën's *Indonesië los van Holland. De CPN en PKI in hun strijd tegen het Nederlands kolonialisme* (Amsterdam, 1982) is fascinating because of his access to Russian source materials.

I gained insight into the economic situation in the 1920s thanks to G. Gonggrijp's *Schets eener economische geschiedenis van Nederlandsch-Indië* (Haarlem, 1928) and J. Thomas Lindblad's article 'The late colonial state and economic expansion, 1900–1930' in H. Dick, V. J. H. Houben and T. Kian Wie (eds.), *The Emergence of a National Economy: An Economic History of Indonesia* (Leiden, 2002). I learned a great deal about the systematic absence of a native middle class and the flawed industrialisation of the Dutch East Indies from two above-mentioned works: the biography of Tan Malaka by Harry Poeze and the classic sociological study by W. F. Wertheim. On the major social uprisings, John Ingleson wrote *In Search of Justice: Workers and Unions in Colonial Java, 1908–1926* (Oxford & Singapore, 1986) and *Workers, Unions and Politics: Indonesia in the 1920s and 1930s* (Leiden, 2014).

Alongside macro history, there were also micro processes. Gerard Termorshuizen has put forward the extremely compelling hypothesis that racial segregation was reinforced by the changing structure of the colonial household and especially by greater Europeanisation as a result of the growing number of European women in the Dutch East Indies, in his book *Realisten en reactionairen. Een geschiedenis van de Indisch-Nederlandse pers 1905–1942* (Amsterdam & Leiden, 2011). It reminded me of the changes I had observed in colonial society in the Belgian Congo after World War II; there too, the arrival of European domestic partners led to a more isolated atmosphere in colonial households.

The 'communist' uprising of 1926 and 1927 has been described in various places, including the above-cited studies by Petrus Blumberger, McVey and Ingleson. A few of the most significant sources were collected by Harry Benda and Ruth McVey in *The Communist Uprisings of 1926–1927 in Indonesia: Key Documents* (Jakarta & Kuala Lumpur, 2010 [1960]). As for Boven Digul internment camp, I. F. M. Salim's eyewitness account remains a unique document: *Vijftien jaar Boven-Digoel. Concentratiekamp in Nieuw-Guinea, bakermat van de Indonesische onafhankelijkheid* (Hengelo, 1980). The camp physician also recorded his impressions after a few years of service there. The result was a condescending piece of propaganda: L. J. A. Schoonheyt, *Boven-Digoel* (Batavia, 1936). Rudy Kousbroek wrote beautifully about both men in *Het Oostindisch kampsyndroom* (Amsterdam, 1992).

I learned a great deal about the third movement, nationalism, thanks to John Ingleson, *Road to Exile: The Indonesian Nationalist Movement, 1927–1934* (Kuala Lumpur & Hong Kong, 1979). On the role of non-colonial education as a driving force of the independence struggle, see Abdullah Taufik's recently reprinted study from 1971,

School and Politics: The Kaum Muda Movement in West Sumatra (1927–1933) (Jakarta & Kuala Lumpur, 2009). For documentation of the students in the Netherlands, I relied on Harry Poeze, *In het land van de overheerser, 1. Indonesiërs in Nederland 1600–1950* (Dordrecht, 1986) and Anne van Leeuwen's unpublished doctoral thesis *De Perhimpoenan Indonesia 1929–1941* (Utrecht, 1985). The topic has also been studied by John Ingleson in *Perhimpunan Indonesia and the Indonesian National Movement, 1923–1928* (Melbourne, 1975). Finally, Klaas Stutje wrote the fascinating doctoral thesis *Behind the Banner of Unity: Nationalism and Anticolonialism among Indonesian Students in Europe, 1917–1931* (Amsterdam, 2016), which devotes a great deal of attention to the PI's international contacts. Of course, I also made extensive use of the available biographies of the leading political actors: Lambert Giebels's *Soekarno. Nederlandsch onderdaan* (Amsterdam, 1999), published in abridged form in English as *Sukarno: A Biography* (Amsterdam, 2015); Mavis Rose's *Indonesia Free: A Political Biography of Mohammed Hatta* (Jakarta & Kuala Lumpur, 2010; originally from 1987) and Rudolf Mrázek's *Sjahrir: Politics and Exile in Indonesia* (Ithaca, NY, 1994). The letters written by Sutan Sjahrir from his various places of confinement to his wife Maria Duchâteau are among the greatest works of decolonisation literature: *Indonesische overpeinzingen* (Amsterdam, 1987). Charles Wolf's English-language book *Out of Exile* (Westport, CT, 1969) is based on these letters.

Facts and figures about the economic impact of the stock market crash of 1929 are taken from the doctoral thesis by R. M. Soemitro Djojohadikoesoemo, *Het volkscredietwezen in de depressie* (Haarlem, 1943), J. S. Furnivall's *Netherlands India: A Study of Plural Economy* (Cambridge & New York, 1944), Howard Dick's contribution to the collection *The Emergence of a National Economy* ('Formation of the nation-state, 1930s–1966', Leiden, 2002) and Alexander Claver's article 'Crisis, response and survival: Internatio in the 1930s' (*Economics and Finance in Indonesia*, 55, 2007). I learned how the macroeconomic crisis affected microeconomic developments in rural areas from the doctoral thesis by Erwan Agus Purwanto, *Ups and Downs in Rural Javanese Industry: The Dynamics of Work and Life of Small-Scale Garment Manufacturers and Their Families* (Amsterdam,

2004). Elsbeth Lochter-Scholten focused on the dimension of gender in *Women and the Colonial State: Essays on Gender and Modernity in the Netherlands Indies 1900–1942* (Amsterdam, 2000). The extent of the Dutch business community's influence over colonial politics has been documented in careful detail by Arjen Taselaar in his doctoral thesis *De Nederlandse koloniale lobby. Ondernemers en de Indische politiek, 1914–1940* (Leiden, 1998). The dramatic events of 1933 form the subject of J. C. H. Blom's meticulous doctoral thesis *De muiterij op de Zeven Provinciën* (Bussum, 1975), summarised in his English-language article 'The mutiny on board *De Zeven Provinciën*: reactions and repercussions in the Netherlands' (in *Acta Historiae Neerlandicae X*, 1978), but Herman Keppy had the opportunity to interview one of the Moluccan soldiers involved and shed new light on the motivation for the uprising and on its repression in his collection of essays *Pendek. Korte verhalen over Indische levens* (Amsterdam, 2013).

Chapter 5

I reconstructed the final years of Dutch colonialism on the basis of the authoritative works mentioned above. I also learned a great deal from Tom van den Berge's splendid and beautifully designed biography of the colonial senior official, minister and lieutenant governor-general Hubertus van Mook, *H. J. van Mook. 1894–1965. Een vrij en gelukkig Indonesië* (Bussum, 2014). On Soetardjo's petition and its failure, eighty-year-old N. G. B. Gouka wrote the nuanced doctoral thesis *De petitie-Soetardjo. Een Hollandse misser in Indië? (1936–1938)* (Utrecht, 2001). The peculiar attempt by Indonesian nationalists to enter into dialogue with United States diplomats, with the aim of finding a 'Philippine solution' to the colonial question in the Dutch East Indies, is discussed in various sources, including N. A. Bootsma, *Buren in de koloniale tijd. De Philippijnen onder Amerikaans bewind en de Nederlandse, Indische en Indonesische reacties daarop 1898–1942* (Dordrecht & Riverton, WY, 1986). The rise of the reactionary right was carefully analysed by P. J. Drooglever in his doctoral thesis *De Vaderlandse Club 1929–1942. Totoks en de Indische politiek* (Franeker, 1980).

On the lives of the Indonesians in the Netherlands after the German invasion, see Harry Poeze, *In het land van de overheerser, 1. Indonesiërs in Nederland 1600–1950* (Dordrecht, 1986). Jacob Zwaan gathered together a wealth of documents about the years when the Dutch government had lost the Netherlands but still controlled the Dutch East Indies in *Nederlands-Indië 1940–1946, deel 1: Gouvernementeel intermezzo 1940–1942* (The Hague, 1980). The rise of Japan from the mid-nineteenth century onward and the country's profound humiliation at the peace talks in Versailles are brilliantly described by Margaret MacMillan in her book *Peacemakers: The Paris Conference of 1919 and Its Attempt to End War* (London, 2001). John Toland has written a gripping account of the impact of this event on Japanese fascism and imperialism, *The Rising Sun: The Decline and Fall of the Japanese Empire, 1936–1945* (New York, 2003). As regards the military preparations for the possibility of a Japanese attack by the Dutch East Indies navy, I turned to sources including Jaap Anten, *Navalisme nekt onderzeeboot. De invloed van buitenlandse zeestrategieën op de Nederlandse zeestrategie voor de defensie van Nederlands-Indië, 1912–1942* (Amsterdam, 2011).

Chapter 6

The following titles helped me to make sense of the Japanese period. On the political and military aspects, John Toland, *The Rising Sun: The Decline and Fall of the Japanese Empire, 1936–1945* (New York, 2003). On the racial aspects, John W. Dower, *War without Mercy: Race & Power in the Pacific War* (New York, 1986). The Japanese occupation of Indonesia is the subject of the voluminous and essential reference work *The Encyclopedia of Indonesia in the Pacific War*, edited by Peter Post, William H. Frederick, Iris Heidebrink and Shigeru Sato (Leiden & Boston, 2010). This builds on the earlier *Japan, Indonesia and the War: Myths and Realities*, by the same Peter Post and Elly Touwen-Bouwsma (Leiden, 1997), which also contains a number of very valuable studies. Considerable attention has of course been devoted to the densely populated island of Java. Ethan Mark recently published the noteworthy *Japan's Occupation of Java in the Second World War: A Transnational History* (London, 2018), which concentrates mainly on the years 1942 and 1943. In that respect, it forms the perfect complement to Benedict Anderson's earlier classic *Java in a Time of Revolution: Occupation and Resistance, 1944–1946* (Jakarta & Singapore, 2006).

Books about Pearl Harbor and the start of the Pacific War could fill a library, but the definitive study of Indochina's central role in the events leading up to that conflict was only recently published: Franck Michelin's *La guerre du Pacifique a commencé en Indochine 1940–1941* (Paris, 2019), a magnificent work of diplomatic history that convincingly shows the extent to which the military occupation of northern Indochina and then that of the south were crucial stages in the escalation of the conflict – and therefore in the history of Indonesia. I found essential facts about oil interests and the available oil reserves in Southeast Asia in Jack Boer's exhaustive but well-documented book *Koninklijke olie in Indië. De prijs voor het vloeibare goud 1939–1953* (Bergen, 1997). For military details of the Japanese invasion of Southeast Asia, I made grateful use of the astonishingly detailed *The Invasion of the Dutch East Indies* (Leiden, 2015). This study was published in Tokyo in 1967 and compiled by the War History Office of the National Defense College of Japan. Willem Remmelink translated and annotated this exceptionally detailed collection of primary source materials and reconstruction. The book was my guide during my fieldwork in Japan, and I referred to it several times in interviews with eyewitnesses. That resulted in new stories every time.

The Dutch historians Anne Doedens and Liek Mulder wrote *Slag in de Javazee. Oorlog tussen Nederland en Japan 1941–1942* (Zutphen, 2017), a first-rate, crystal-clear synthesis of the invasion that ranges well beyond the Battle of the Java Sea. As early as 1960, the remarkably interesting collection of primary sources *Nederlandsch-Indië onder Japanse bezetting. Gegevens en documenten over de jaren 1942–1945* (Franeker, 1960) was published by a team headed by I. J. Brugmans. What this book lacks in cohesion, it more than makes up for in vitality; it resembles an exhibition of historical source materials. Fred Lanzing, a survivor of the Japanese internment camps, may be the only Dutch author who has attempted to comprehend the mindset of the Japanese soldier through historical research. His concise study *Toean nippon. De Japanse soldaat in de Pacificoorlog en in Nederlands-Indië, 1942–1947* (Hilversum, 2014) is not clouded by post-traumatic bitterness but offers an honest and impressive attempt to see the human being behind the detested figure of the camp guard.

Chapter 7

I reconstructed Djajeng Pratomo's story from a large number of unpublished documents, but for greater insight into the context, I looked to Harry Poeze's *In het land van de overheerser* (Dordrecht, 1986), mentioned above, and Herman Keppy's *Zijn jullie kerels of lafaards? De Indische en Indonesische strijd tegen de nazi's 1940–1945* (The Hague, 2019). That latter book finally devotes attention to the disproportionately large role played by Indonesians, Eurasians and Dutch people from the colony during the German occupation of the Netherlands. The book reads like a monument to forgotten and, yes, even suppressed heroes.

In connection with the wave of new measures, I made grateful use of the above-cited collection of source materials compiled by Brugmans et al., *Nederlandsch-Indië onder Japanse bezetting* (Franeker, 1960). I found interesting historical photographs and materials for a history of perception in Remco Raben (ed.), *Beelden van de Japanse bezetting van de Indonesië. Persoonlijke getuigenissen en publieke beeldvorming in Indonesië, Japan en Nederland* (Zwolle-Amsterdam, 1999). Harry Benda's *The Crescent and the Rising Sun: Indonesian Islam under the Japanese Occupation, 1942–1945* (The Hague & Bandung, 1958) remains a worthwhile account of how Japan drove a wedge between the nationalists and organised Islam.

The subject of forced prostitution for the military has received particular attention in recent years. For a general overview, I read George Hicks, *The Comfort Women: Japan's Brutal Regime of*

Enforced Prostitution in the Second World War (New York & London, 1997) and Brigitte Ars's outstanding Dutch-language study *Troostmeisjes. Verkrachting in naam van de keizer* (Amsterdam & Antwerp, 2000). Specifically for the Indonesian situation, I read the impressive testimonies collected by Hilde Janssen (with portraits by Jan Banning) in *Schaamte en onschuld. Het verdrongen oorlogsverleden van troostmeisjes in Indonesië* (Amsterdam, 2010) and by Marguerite Hamer-Monod de Froideville in *Geknakte bloem. Acht vrouwen vertellen hun verhaal over Japanse militaire dwangprostitutie* (Delft, 2013).

An overabundance of first-hand accounts of the civilian internment camps, referred to as *jappenkampen* ('Jap camps'), have been preserved and published in the Netherlands. The NIOD collected the most significant ones in the series *De Japanse bezetting in dagboeken* (2001 onwards). The foremost scholarly study of this topic is still Dora van Velden's doctoral thesis *De Japanse interneringskampen voor burgers gedurende de Tweede Wereldoorlog* (Franeker, 1977). I also drew on the personal accounts of Lydia Chagoll, Bep Vuyk, Rudy Kousbroek, Fred Lanzing and Bep Groen (published by Elise Lengkeek), which are included in the bibliography.

Many memoirs of forced labour by prisoners of war have also been published. I read those of the British medical doctor Robert Hardie, the Dutch reserve officer Jan Schneider, the Dutch Jewish conscript Loet Velmans and the well-known Dutch cabaret performer Wim Kan, all relating to the Burma Railway, as well as that of the Dutch conscript Ton Verstraaten, who was sent to Japan. I found *The Burma–Thailand Railway* by the Australian researchers Gavan McCormack and Hank Nelson (St Leonards, 1993) still to be very much worth reading. The British POWs who had to work on the Pekanbaru line in Sumatra form the subject of Lizzie Oliver's recent book *Prisoners of the Sumatra Railway* (London, 2019). Because of the sources available, historical writing on this topic has been heavily skewed towards the Western experience, even though the Asian romusha were much more numerous and had much higher death rates. In recent decades, some attention has finally been devoted to those anonymous, illiterate masses. Paul Kratoska edited the important collection *Asian Labor in the Wartime Japanese Empire*

(Singapore, 2006), and Winnie Rinzema-Admiraal took on the subject of the enormous numbers of Javanese forced labourers spread throughout Southeast Asia in *Romusha van Java. Het laatste front 1942–1945* (Bedum, 2009).

Chapter 8

In 1942 and 1943, Sukarno became a key figure in the Japanese occupation. On his impact on the visual arts from his presidency of Putera onwards, see Mikke Susanto's hefty study *Sukarno's Favourite Painters* (Jakarta, 2018). On Affandi, see Ade Tanesia, *The Stories of Affandi* (Yogyakarta, 2012) and Valentino Suhardjono and Jeremy Allan, *Witnessing Affandi* (Jakarta, 2019). The idea of 'anti-colonial fascism' has been developed and analysed by Ethan Mark in various places, including the conclusion to his aforementioned book *Japan's Occupation of Java in the Second World War* (London, 2018).

I based my account of the radical militarisation of the Javanese youth on the authoritative works listed under Chapter 5 above. For all other aspects of the history of the internment camps, forced prostitution and forced labour, I direct readers to the sources cited in the notes to Chapter 6.

The famine of 1944 is addressed in an illuminating study by Pierre van der Eng, *Food Supply in Java during War and Decolonisation, 1940–1950*, originally published in book form in 1994 by the Centre for South-East Asian Studies at the University of Hull. In 2008, it was reprinted by the Munich Personal RePEc Archive as *MPRA Paper* 8852. Shigeru Sato published *War, Nationalism and Peasants: Java under Japanese Occupation, 1942–1945* (New York, 1994) and shared his findings in a number of scholarly papers.

One publication that is difficult to track down, but from which I learned a great deal, was Anton Lucas's study and collection of primary sources from 1986, *Local Opposition and Underground Resistance to the Japanese in Java, 1942–1945* (Melbourne). This book, with its very plain design, is of crucial importance because it includes the full text and English translation of Sintha Melati's manuscript 'In the service of the underground: the struggle against the Japanese in Java', which she entrusted to him in the early 1980s.

Chapter 9

The Allied advance through Asia has been studied copiously. I used the Toland and De Jong overviews cited above. The encyclopedia by Peter Post et al. was also of great use. For those interested in a heartfelt, intelligent account from a Japanese perspective, the three-part graphic novel *Showa: A History of Japan* by the Japanese master Shigeru Mizuki can't be recommended highly enough (Montreal, 2013–14). One of the founders of Japanese manga, graphic artist Mizuki, lost an arm as a malaria-stricken soldier during a bombing raid off Papua New Guinea. His work is an eye-witness account, history lesson and political satire in one, in which he switches effortlessly between a dramatic, realistic drawing style based on black-and-white photos and an ironic cartoonish version of himself. Anyone who still thinks that graphic novels are a second-rate art form after reading these books has missed something. Anyone who still resorts to the stereotype of 'the Jap' needs to reread them. Another classic in Japan's struggle to come to grips with the war is the disconcerting documentary *Yuki yukite shingun* (*The Emperor's Naked Army Marches On*, 1987) by Hara Kazuo. The film follows veteran Okazaki in his search for the truth about the famine in New Guinea.

There are still gaps in our military knowledge. For instance, it is only in the last few years that there has been significant academic interest in the Gruppe Monsun. In 2017 Lawrence Paterson published *Hitler's Grey Wolves: U-Boats in the Indian Ocean* (New York), while Christian Keimer graduated in 2019 with the research paper *Gruppe Monsun: The U-Boat Operations in the Indian and Pacific Oceans during World War II* (Charles Town, W V).

In his now classic 1972 work, *Java in a Time of Revolution: Occupation and Resistance, 1944–1946* (Jakarta & Singapore, 2006), Benedict Anderson provided a meticulous analysis of the emergence of the young as a significant political category in Java. Anderson built on the work of his teacher George McTurnan Kahin, whose *Nationalism and Revolution in Indonesia* (Ithaca, NY & London, 1952) was not only the first major study dedicated to Indonesian independence, but also opened up the international field of 'Southeast Asian studies'. Anderson's findings from his own interviews with Rear Admiral Maeda gave us a greater understanding of the role of the senior Japanese officers who turned a blind eye to the declaration of independence. In his last work, the autobiographical *A Life Beyond Boundaries* (Selangor, 2016), Anderson wrote beautifully about his conversations with Maeda.

Chapter 10

Much has been written about the turbulent final months of 1945. The classic studies are the above-cited *Nationalism and Revolution in Indonesia* by Kahin and *Java in a Time of Revolution* by Benedict Anderson. The Australian historian Anthony Reid emphasised the national character of the revolution in *The Indonesian National Revolution 1945–1950* (Hawthorn, 1974) and *To Nation by Revolution: Indonesia in the 20th Century* (Singapore, 2011). The Revolusi mobilised extremely diverse segments of the population: rural youth (Anton E. Lucas, *One Soul, One Struggle: Region and Revolution in Indonesia*, Sydney, 1991), petty criminals and juvenile gangs in the cities (Robert Cribb, *Gangsters and Revolutionaries: The Jakarta People's Militia and the Indonesian Revolution 1945–1949*, Singapore, 2009) and devout Muslims (Kevin W. Fogg, *Indonesia's Islamic Revolution*, Cambridge, 2019). The Chinese-Indonesian historian Ong Hok Ham argued that Japan did not bring about the end of the Dutch East Indies, but was merely the catalyst for the centrifugal forces of late colonial society: *Runtuhnya Hindia Belanda* (Jakarta, 1987). Regarding the search for a new constitution, Miriam Budiardjo wrote the article 'The constitutional system of the Republic of Indonesia 1945–1950 with special emphasis on executive-legislative relations' in the collection *De leeuw en de banteng* (The Hague, 1997).

Highly readable works from a Dutch perspective include *De waaier van het fortuin. De Nederlanders in Azië en de Indonesische archipel*

1595–1950 by Joop de Jong (The Hague, 1998), *Afscheid van Indië. De val van het Nederlandse imperium in Azië* by H. W. van den Doel (Amsterdam, 2000) and *Afscheid van de koloniën. Het Nederlandse dekolonisatiebeleid* by John Jansen van Galen (Amsterdam & Antwerp, 2013). The fact that the conflict was more than just a military one, but always had a highly important diplomatic dimension, is shown convincingly in J. J. P. de Jong's voluminous studies: *Diplomatie of strijd. Het Nederlandse beleid tegenover de Indonesische revolutie 1945–1947* (Amsterdam, 1988), *Avondschot. Hoe Nederland zich terugtrok uit zijn Aziatisch imperium* (Amsterdam, 2011) and *De terugtocht. Nederland en de dekolonisatie van Indonesië* (Amsterdam, 2015), even if his perspective remains primarily Dutch. This is often noticeable in the historiography: many Dutch publications are about the Dutch contribution, which is seen favourably or unfavourably, whereas Indonesian, American and Australian studies are more likely to illuminate the Republican side. But perhaps what matters is to study as many approaches as possible, like a night-watchman trying to keep his eye on all the camera images of the terrain he is guarding.

It is only in recent years that attention for the British role has grown. Richard McMillan's *The British Occupation of Indonesia 1945–1946: Britain, the Netherlands and the Indonesian Revolution* (London & New York, 2005) provides, at long last, an authoritative study of the impossible situation in which the British troops found themselves in Indonesia after the end of World War II. For the wider regional context, see Nicholas Tarling, *Britain, Southeast Asia and the Onset of the Cold War, 1945–1950* (Cambridge, 1998) and Peter Lowe, *Contending with Nationalism and Communism: British Policy towards Southeast Asia, 1945–1965* (Basingstoke, 2009).

These months are known in the Netherlands as the 'Bersiap' period, the most chaotic and violent phase of the Indonesian revolution. H. Th. Bussemaker dedicated his substantial study *Bersiap! Opstand in het paradijs. De Bersiap-periode op Java en Sumatra 1945–1946* (Zutphen, 2005) to his wife and sister-in-law, who were both killed in the disturbances. Mary C. van Delden considered a little-known aspect of that period, the civilian internment camps for Eurasians, and argued that they were ordered by Sukarno to avoid bloodshed:

De republikeinse kampen in Nederlands-Indië, oktober 1945–mei 1947. Orde in de chaos? (Kockengen, 2007).

A fascinating report from 'inside' the revolution is provided by the recently published translation of Suhario Padmodiwiryo's *Revolution in the City of Heroes: A Memoir of the Battle that Sparked Indonesia's National Revolution* (Singapore, 2016). Suhario, nicknamed Hario Kecik, was one of the leaders of the popular protest in Surabaya and wrote in detail about the turmoil of late 1945. On the same subject William H. Frederick wrote *Visions and Heat: The Making of the Indonesian Revolution* (Athens, OH, 1988). The most detailed study of events in Surabaya is Willy Meelhuijsen's *Revolutie in Soerabaja, 17 augustus–1 december 1945* (Zutphen, 2000), which often provides a number of differing versions of the facts.

Chapter 11

To better understand the role of the Nepali Gurkhas during the British year, I consulted *Valour: A History of the Gurkhas* by E. D. Smith (Chalford, Stroud, 1997) and *The Gurkhas: Special Force* by Chris Bellamy (London, 2011). One of the few books in which the voices of the Gurkhas themselves are heard is *Gurkhas at War: Eyewitness Accounts from World War II to Iraq* (London, 2007) by John P. Cross and Buddhiman Gurung. Although it does not include any testimonies by Indonesia veterans, the authors did speak to three of them during their fieldwork in Nepal and were kind enough to grant me access to the typescripts of those interviews.

Regarding the make-up of the Dutch military force, I drew on *De geschiedenis van 1 Divisie '7 December', 1946–1996* by Martin Elands, Richard van Gils and Ben Schoenmaker (The Hague, 1996), which is remarkably self-critical. Concerning the laborious recruitment of conscripts, Antoine Weijzen wrote the fascinating *De Indië-weigeraars: Vergeten slachtoffers van een koloniale oorlog* (Utrecht, 2015). I was also grateful to be able to draw on older works such as *Al weer iets groots verricht. Hoe Nederland zijn Indië-deserteurs tot de laatste man berechtte* by Jan Maarten Fiedeldij Dop ar d Yvonne Simons (Amsterdam, 1983),

De Indonesië-weigeraars by Kees Bals and Martin Gerritsen (Amsterdam, 1989) and *Er waren er die niet gingen. Vijftien eeuwen straf voor Indonesië-weigeraars* by Henny Zwart (Amsterdam, 1995).

Regarding the commencement of negotiations, see Idrus Nasir Djajadiningrat's 1956 study, *The Beginnings of the Indonesian–Dutch Negotiations and the Hoge Veluwe Talks* (Jakarta & Kuala Lumpur, 2009). Regarding the process of reaching the Linggajati Agreement, see for instance C. Smit's *Het akkoord van Linggadjati. Uit het dagboek van prof. dr. ir. W. Schermerhorn* (Amsterdam & Brussels, 1959) and especially his complete edition of this exceptional source: C. Smit, *Het dagboek van Schermerhorn. Geheim verslag van prof. dr. ir. W. Schermerhorn als voorzitter der commissie-generaal voor Nederlands-Indië, 20 september 1946–7 oktober 1947* (Utrecht, 1970). The painstaking biography of Willem Schermerhorn by Herman Langeveld is (together with Tom van den Berge's and Rudolf Mrázek's above-mentioned biographies of Van Mook and Sjahrir respectively) essential reading: *De man die in de put sprong. Willem Schermerhorn 1894–1977* (Amsterdam, 2014). Henk Ngantoeng's sketches, *Impressies dari Linggadjati dan sekitarnja pada boelan Nopember 1946* (Jakarta, 1947), were instrumental in letting me soak up the atmosphere of the meetings.

Chapter 12

For the Dutch 'year' of the decolonisation war, I primarily made use of various biographies: those of the prime ministers Gerbrandy (Fasseur 2014), Schermerhorn (Langeveld 2014), Beel (Giebels 1995) and Drees (Daalder 2004), as well as those of Queen Wilhelmina (Fasseur 2001) and her mysterious security advisor François van 't Sant (Van der Zee 2016). The author of that last biography, Sytze van der Zee, very generously gave me access to the letter about the planned coup he had obtained from Van 't Sant's estate.

Regarding the ponderous negotiations following Linggajati, W. H. Helsdingen collected relevant documentation in *Op weg naar een Nederlandsch-Indonesische Unie. Stemmen van hier en ginds* (The Hague, 1947). Essential for studying the Dutch perspective is the unsurpassed, twenty-volume collection of primary sources edited by S. L. van der Wal, P. J. Drooglever and M. J .B. Schouten, *Officiële bescheiden betreffende de Nederlands-Indonesische betrekkingen, 1945–1950* (The Hague, 1971–96), now fully accessible online. Concerning the turbulent events from late May to late July 1947, Ad van Liempt wrote the meticulous *Nederland valt aan. Op weg naar oorlog met Indonesië* (Amsterdam, 2012).

Regarding the so-called 'South Celebes Affair', I consulted, in addition to the recent authoritative work by Rémy Limpach, the biographical study of Westerling by military historian J. A. de Moor, *Westerling's oorlog. Indonesië 1945–1950* (Amsterdam, 1999). I also read the recent, critical popular books by Maarten Hidskes, *Thuis gelooft niemand mij: Zuid-Celebes 1946–1947* (Amsterdam & Antwerp, 2016) and Manon van den Brekel, *Massaexecuties op Sulawesi. Hoe Nederland wegkwam met moord in Indonesië* (Zutphen, 2017). The latter book has the advantage of oral testimonies she was able to gather on location, making it one of the few books that considers the Indonesian perspective and local commemorative culture. Bauke Geersing is critical of the critics and tries to put Westerling's actions in historical perspective in *Kapitein Raymond Westerling en de Zuid-Celebes-affaire (1946–1947). Mythe en werkelijkheid* (Soesterberg, 2019).

Chapter 13

Petra Groen provides an exceptional study of the military aspects of the police actions in *Marsroutes en dwaalsporen. Het Nederlands militair-strategisch beleid in Indonesië 1945–1950* (The Hague, 1991). For the experience of the Dutch troops in West Java, I again recommend the work of Martin Elands, Richard van Gils and Ben Schoenmaker, *De geschiedenis van 1 Divisie '7 December', 1946–1996* (The Hague, 1996). For the logistical side of Operation Product, read B. C. Cats and H. N. J. van den Berg's *Logistiek onder de tropenzon. De verzorgende diensten van KNIL en KL in Nederlands-Indië 1946–1950* (Amsterdam, 2003). Regarding the logistics on the Indonesian side, B. Bouman gathered a great deal of interesting material in *Ieder voor zich en de Republiek voor ons allen. De logistiek achter de Indonesische Revolutie 1945–1950* (Amsterdam, 2006). Concerning the prisoner transport from Bondowoso, Ad van Liempt wrote *De lijkentrein. Waarom 46 gevangenen de reis naar Surabaya niet overleefden* (The Hague, 1997).

This chapter focuses on the extraordinarily important role of American diplomacy in the second half of 1947 and in 1948. The classic study here is Robert J. McMahon's *Colonialism and Cold War: The United States and the Struggle for Indonesian Independence, 1945–1949* (Ithaca, NY & London, 1981). Gerlof D. Homan wrote an exceptional article in the *Journal of Contemporary History*, 'The Netherlands, the United States and the Indonesian Question, 1948' (1990, 25, 123–41) and Robert E. Patterson's *United States–Indonesian Relations, 1945–1949: Negative Consequences of Early American Cold War Policy* (University of Richmond, 1998) also far exceeded the level of the usual master's thesis. Two more recent studies are based on research in American archives: Frances Gouda and Thijs Brocades Zaalberg published *American Visions of the Netherlands East Indies/Indonesia. US Foreign Policy and Indonesian Nationalism, 1920–1949* (Amsterdam, 2002) and Andrew Roadnight wrote *United States Policy towards Indonesia in the Truman and Eisenhower Years* (Basingstoke & New York, 2002). Again and again, American diplomacy is shown to have been fuelled more by anti-communism than by anti-colonialism. Specifically concerning the role of Marshall aid, Pierre van der Eng wrote another extremely thorough contribution, full of figures: 'Marshall aid as a catalyst in the decolonization of Indonesia, 1947–49' (*Journal of Southeast Asian Studies*, 1988, 19, 335–52). As long ago as 1957, Ruth McVey considered the Russian perspective on development in *The Soviet View of the Indonesian Revolution: A Study in the Russian Attitude towards Asian Nationalism* (Jakarta & Kuala Lumpur, 2009). The negotiation of the Renville Agreement was the subject of Ide Anak Agung Gde Agung's publication *'Renville' als keerpunt in de Nederlands-Indonesische onderhandelingen* (Alphen, 1980). The author was interior and later prime minister of the State of East Indonesia, before fulfilling the posts of interior and foreign minister in various Indonesian governments. He also wrote the standard work on the early years of Indonesian diplomacy, *Twenty Years Indonesian Foreign Policy 1945–1965* (Yogyakarta, 1990).

I was able to reconstruct the way the US-sponsored Renville Agreement led to resistance from the left and right from several extremely interesting monographs. With regard to the Darul Islam movement in West Java and beyond, I gratefully consulted C. van Dijk, *Rebellion under the Banner of Islam: The Darul Islam in Indonesia* (The Hague, 1981), Holk H. Dengel, *Kartosuwirjos Kampf um einen islamischen Staat Indonesien* (Stuttgart, 1986), and Chiara Formichi, *Islam and the Making of the Nation: Kartosuwiryo and Political Islam in Twentieth-Century Indonesia* (Leiden & Boston, 2012). Regarding Madiun, I consulted Ann Swift, *The Road to Madiun: The Indonesian Communist Uprising of 1948* (Jakarta & Kuala Lumpur, 2010) and especially volume II of Harry Poeze's monumental biography of Tan Malaka, which covers the period of the decolonisation war, *Verguisd en vergeten. Tan Malaka, de linkse beweging en de Indonesische Revolutie, 1945–1949* (Leiden, 2007). More than a biography, the book is an impressive panorama of the progressive forces during the Revolusi, precise in its details, yet broad in scope.

Chapter 14

The decisive role of the United Nations in the Indonesian question is given relatively little attention nowadays. I made use of several older, but very good studies. J. Foster Collins wrote an exceptional and very early analysis in his long article 'The United Nations and Indonesia' (*International Conciliation*, 1950, 28, 115–202). Moises Montero de Guzman's MA thesis, *The Indonesian Question before the Security Council 1946–1949* (Montana State University, 1952), would make an excellent PhD thesis even today. Rosalyn Higgins edited the indispensable *United Nations Peacekeeping 1946–1967. Documents and Commentary: II. Asia* (London, 1970). And Alastair M. Taylor wrote the brilliant *Indonesian Independence and the United Nations* (London, 1960), without a doubt the best analysis, but evidently now seldom read by Dutch diplomats: the second-hand copy I found turned out to have originated from the library of the Dutch ministry of foreign affairs! That's right, the most important study of the Netherlands' greatest clash with the

UN can no longer be found at the foreign ministry in The Hague. P. J. Drooglever and M. J. B. Schouten brought the most important documents on the Dutch side together in *Het einde in zicht. Stemmen uit het laatste jaar van Nederlands-Indië* (The Hague, 1999). Regarding the important role of the Indonesian states, with their ambivalent position between Dutch and Republican authority, and therefore their power as a 'kingmaker' in settling the Indonesian question, Roel Frakking wrote the PhD thesis '*Collaboration is a very delicate concept': Alliance-Formation and the Colonial Defence of Indonesia and Malaysia, 1945–1957* (Florence, 2017).

The theme of war crimes has received a great deal of attention in recent decades, at least in as much as they were committed by Dutch troops. Besides the abovementioned publications about Westerling and the wide-ranging books of Ewald Vanvugt (*Roofstaat*) and Piet Hagen (*Koloniale oorlogen in Indonesië*), I must first and above all mention Stef Scagliola's doctoral thesis, *Last van de oorlog. De Nederlandse oorlogsmisdaden en hun verwerking* (Amsterdam, 2002), a study which combines archival research and oral history. The year 2012 saw the republication of *Ontsporing van geweld* by J. A. A. van Doorn and W. J. Hendrix (Rotterdam, 1970), a first, large sociological study by two former conscripts. In 2015 Gert Oostindie published *Soldaat in Indonesië 1945–1950. Getuigenissen van een oorlog aan de verkeerde kant van de geschiedenis* (Amsterdam, 2015), the result of research in which he and his team at the KITLV pored through hundreds of letters and diaries written by Dutch soldiers. It includes a very useful typology of war crimes. A year later, Rémy Limpach's weighty PhD thesis came out, *De brandende kampongs van generaal Spoor* (Amsterdam, 2016), a monumental study of the forms, punishment, concealment, control, prevention, registration and causes of extreme violence on the Dutch side and of the responsibility for it. In that same year Alfred Birney published *The Interpreter from Java*, an autobiographical novel that dovetails so closely with his father's memoirs that it can be read as historically relevant. Important work has also been undertaken by independent researchers and freelance journalists such as Anne-Lot Hoek, Manon van den Brekel, Marjolein van Pagee and Maurice Swirc writing in *De Groene Amsterdammer*, *Vrij Nederland* and *NRC*.

Extreme violence on the Republican side, by contrast, has scarcely been investigated.

To gain insight into the court cases decided in the Netherlands since 2007, I used the report that Eefje de Volder and Anne-Marie de Brouwer wrote for the Nuhanovic Foundation, a centre for war reparations: *The Impacts of Litigation in Relation to Systematic and Large-Scale Atrocities Committed by the Dutch Military Forces in the 'Dutch East Indies' between 1945–1949* (Amsterdam, 2019). The suits were brought by the foundation Komite Utang Kehormatan Belanda (Comité Nederlandse Ereschulden) after the Dutch authorities rebuffed founder Jeffry Pondaag and lawyer Liesbeth Zegveld's attempts to reach an amicable settlement of several complaints. *De Memorie van antwoord tevens houdende incidenteel appel Monji c.s. en Yaseman* (Amsterdam, 2019) by the counsels Zegveld and Brechtje Vossenberg, both of the Amsterdam law firm Prakken d'Oliveira, includes an excellent overview of suits brought and historical facts.

Unfortunately the role of army chaplains has not been well researched, perhaps because we, in a secular era, are less interested in religious issues – though they were an important factor at the time. Regarding sexual morals, Annegriet Wietsma and Stef Scagliola wrote the especially original *Liefde in tijden van oorlog. Onze jongens en hun verzwegen kinderen in de Oost* (Amsterdam, 2013). Their innovative approach – a website on which witnesses could reach out to them anonymously – allowed them to break a taboo.

Chapter 15

Hans Meijer's *Den Haag–Djakarta. De Nederlands–Indonesische betrekkingen 1950–1962* (Utrecht, 1994) is the definitive study of the relationship between the former colony and coloniser during the first years after the transfer of sovereignty and strikes a wonderful balance between the big picture and the details. Much became clear to me about the repatriation of the Dutch soldiers thanks to Aart de Ruijter's well-executed master's thesis, *Naar Indonesië en weer terug. Transport van een expeditieleger (1945–1951)* (Leiden, 2017). Griselda Molemans wrote the highly readable *Opgevangen in andijvielucht. De opvang van ontheemden uit Indonesië in kampen en contractpensions en de financiële claims op basis van uitgebleven rechtsherstel* (n.p., 2014) about the experiences of many other repatriates. Andrew Roadnight provides a clear description of the derailment of American–Indonesian relations in *United States Policy towards Indonesia in the Truman and Eisenhower Years* (Basingstoke & New York, 2002). Audrey and George Kahin write about America's secret but totally failed CIA operations in 1957 and 1958 in the too-little-known *Subversion as Foreign Policy: The Secret Eisenhower and Dulles Debacle in Indonesia* (New York, 1995). For US involvement in the genocide of 1965 I refer to Geoffrey B. Robinson's recently published standard work *The Killing Season: A History of the Indonesian Massacres, 1965–66* (Princeton & Oxford, 2018). For the long effect of American support for Suharto's dictatorship see Andre Vltchek, *Indonesia: Archipelago of Fear* (London, 2012).

Interest in the Bandung Conference has grown unmistakably in recent years, but the definitive study of its impact on world politics is yet to be written. David Kimche's PhD thesis *The Afro-Asian Movement: Ideology and Foreign Policy of the Third World* (Jerusalem, 1973) came closest, but is half a century old. Even older is *Bandoung, tournant de l'Histoire* by the French politician and diplomat Arthur Conte (Paris, 1965). One recent publication is *Bandung, Global History, and International Law: Critical Pasts and Pending Futures* by Luis Eslava, Michael Fakhri and Vasuki Nesiah (Cambridge, 2017). Jamie Mackie wrote the accessible and very readable *Bandung 1955: Non-Alignment and Afro-Asian Solidarity* (Singapore, 2005). The renewed academic interest has resulted in several conference volumes of variable quality: *Bandung Revisited: The Legacy of the 1955 Asian–African Conference for International Order* by See Seng Tan and Amitav Acharya (Singapore, 2008); *Making a World After Empire: The Bandung Moment and its Political Afterlives* by Christopher J. Lee (Athens, OH, 2010); *Bandung 1955: Little Histories* by Antonia Finnane and Derek McDougall (Caulfield, Vic., 2010) and *Beyond Bandung: The 1955 Asian–African Conference and its Legacies for International Order*, a special thematic issue of the *Australian Journal of International Affairs* (2016, 70, 4).

The travel account by the American author and civil rights activist

Richard Wright, *The Color Curtain* (New York, 1956), remains well worth reading. The same can be said of the analyses and observations of the great Southeast Asia expert George Kahin, *The Asian–African Conference: Bandung, Indonesia, April 1955* (Ithaca, NY, 1956). Regarding Wright's participation in the conference, there is also the fascinating *Indonesian Notebook: A Sourcebook on Richard Wright and the Bandung Conference* (Durham, NC, 2016), edited by Brian Russell Roberts and Keith Foulcher.

I have puzzled Bandung's impact on the rest of the world together from a chaos of sources. Besides the standard works on the Cold War (Hobsbawm, Judt, Vanden Berghe), I consulted Pankaj Mishra's *From the Ruins of Empire: The Revolt Against the West and the Remaking of Asia* (London, 2013) with much pleasure. I gained insight into the growth of Arab nationalism and Nasser's central role from Eugene Rogan's *De Arabieren* (Amsterdam, 2010) and Chams Zaougui's *Dictators* (Kalmthout, 2016). These books were not only outstandingly well researched but also beautifully written.

I only realised the degree to which the European Union 'owes' its emergence to Bandung and the Suez Crisis after reading Peo Hansen & Stefan Jonsson's *Eurafrica: The Untold History of European Integration and Colonialism* (London, 2014), a milestone of recent historical research. In his recent *De geboorte van Europa: een geschiedenis zonder einde* (Kalmthout, 2017), Rolf Falter also draws a direct line from Suez to the Treaty of Rome.

Kwame Nkrumah's role in stirring the flames of decolonisation has been well documented and described in several places, including by Martin Meredith in *The State of Africa: A History of Fifty Years of Independence* (London, 2005). For the overtures between the American civil rights movement and the new African states, see Kevin Kelly Gaines, *American Africans in Ghana: Black Expatriates and the Civil Rights Era* (Chapel Hill, NC, 2006). Geert Buelens's impressive panorama of culture and politics in the 1960s also pays the theme ample attention: *De jaren zestig. Een cultuurgeschiedenis* (Amsterdam, 2018). Regarding the international sources of black activism in America, see M. L. Dudziak, *Cold War Civil Rights: Race and the Image of American Democracy* (Princeton, NJ, 2011) and, above all, Peniel E. Joseph,

Waiting 'Til the Midnight Hour: A Narrative History of Black Power in America (New York, 2006). Anne G. Mahler wrote the first major study of the radicalisation of the Bandung movement, the rise of tricontinentalism and 'black internationalism': *From the Tricontinental to the Global South: Race, Radicalism, and Transnational Solidarity* (Durham, NC, 2018). A very beautiful overview of the emergence of the Third World and the role of Bandung is provided by Vijay Prashad's *The Darker Nations: A People's History of the Third World* (New York & London, 2007). Jürgen Dinkel dedicated his very solid PhD thesis, *Die Bewegung Bündnisfreier Staaten. Genese, Organisation und Politik (1927–1992)* (Berlin, 2015), to the history of the Non-Aligned Movement. And lastly, on the Chagos Archipelago, see David Vine, *Island of Shame: The Secret History of the US Military Base on Diego Garcia* (Princeton, NJ, 2009) and Peter H. Sand, *United States and Britain in Diego Garcia: The Future of a Controversial Base* (New York, 2009).

Bibliography

Abdulgani, R. 1963: *The Bandung Spirit and the Asian-African Press*. n.p.

Abeyasekere, S. 1989: *Jakarta: A History*. Oxford & New York.

Acri, A. 2015: 'Revisiting the cult of "Śiva-Buddha" in Java and Bali.' In D. Christian Lammerts (ed.), *Buddhist Dynamics in Premodern and Early Modern Southeast Asia*. Singapore, 261–82.

Adams, C. 1965: *Sukarno. An Autobiography*. Indianapolis.

Aghazarian, A. 2012: *'We the Peoples of Asia and Africa': The Bandung Conference and the Southernisation of the United Nations, 1955–1970*. Sydney.

Alexanderson, K. 2019: *Subversive Seas: Anticolonial Networks across the Twentieth-Century Dutch Empire*. Cambridge.

Alkema B. & T. J. Bezemer 1927: *Beknopt handboek der volkenkunde van Nederlandsch-Indië*. Haarlem.

Ampiah, K. 2007: *The Political and Moral Imperatives of the Bandung Conference of 1955: The Reactions of the US, UK and Japan*. Folkestone.

Anak Agung Gde Agung, I. 1980: *'Renville' als keerpunt in de Nederlands-Indonesische onderhandelingen*. Alphen.

Anak Agung Gde Agung, I. 1990: *Twenty Years Indonesian Foreign Policy 1945–1965*. Yogyakarta.

Anderson, B. 1991 (1983): *Imagined Communities: Reflections on the Origin and Spread of Nationalism*. London & New York.

Anderson, B. 2006 (1972): *Java in a Time of Revolution: Occupation and Resistance, 1944–1946*. Jakarta & Singapore.

Anderson, B. 2016: *A Life Beyond Boundaries*. Selangor.

Anon. (E. Brumsteede) 1945: *Jappenspiegel*. Amsterdam.

Anten, J. 2011: *Navalisme nekt onderzeeboot. De invloed van buitenlandse zeestrategieën op de Nederlandse zeestrategie voor de defensie van Nederlands-Indië, 1912–1942*. Amsterdam.

Anwar, R. 1997: 'De revolutie en de openbare mening in Indonesië.' In P. J. Drooglever & M. J. B. Schouten (eds.), *De leeuw en de banteng. Bijdragen aan het congres over de Nederlands-Indonesische betrekkingen 1945–1950*. The Hague, 284–96.

Arpi, C. 2004: *Born in Sin: The Panchsheel Agreement – The Sacrifice of Tibet*. New Delhi.

Arpi, C. 2009: *Tibet: The Lost Frontier*. n.p.

Arpi, C. 2015: 'When Nehru left the Tibetans to their fate.' *The Pioneer*, 5 November.

Ars, B. 2000: *Troostmeisjes. Verkrachting in naam van de keizer*. Amsterdam & Antwerp.

Arta, K. S. & I. K. Margi 2014: *Sejarah Indonesia dari Proklamasi sampai Orde Reformasi*. Yogyakarta.

Asante, M. F. & A. S. Abarry 1996: *African Intellectual Heritage: A Book of Sources*. Philadelphia, PA.

Baay, R. 2008: *De njai. Het concubinaat in Nederlands-Indië*. Amsterdam.

Baay, R. 2015: *Daar werd wat gruwelijks verricht. Slavernij in Nederlands-Indië*. Amsterdam.

Balai Poestaka 1948: *De Indonesische vrouw 1898–1948*. Batavia.

Bals, K. & M. Gerritsen 1989: *De Indonesië-weigeraars*. Amsterdam.

Bank, J. 1983: *Katholieken en de Indonesische Revolutie*. Baarn.

Barcia, M. 2009: ' "Locking horns with the Northern Empire": anti-American imperialism at the Tricontinental Conference of 1966 in Havana.' *Journal of Transatlantic Studies*, 7, 3, 208–17.

Bass, G. J. 2013: *The Blood Telegram: Nixon, Kissinger and a Forgotten Genocide*. New York.

Baudet, H. & I. J. Brugmans (eds.) 1984: *Balans van beleid. Terugblik op de laatste halve eeuw van Nederlands-Indië*. Assen.

Bee, O. J. 1982: *The Petroleum Resources of Indonesia*. Oxford & Kuala Lumpur.

Beets, N. 1981: *De verre oorlog. Lot en levensloop van krijgsgevangenen onder de Japanner*. Meppel.

Bellamy, C. 2011: *The Gurkhas: Special Force*. London.

Bellwood, P. 2005: *First Farmers: The Origins of Agricultural Societies*. Oxford.

Benda, H. J. 1956: 'The beginnings of the Japanese occupation of Java.' *The Far Eastern Quarterly* 15, 541–60.

Benda, H. J. 1958: *The Crescent and the Rising Sun: Indonesian Islam under the Japanese Occupation 1942–1945*. The Hague & Bandung.

Benda, H. J. & R. T. McVey 2009 (1960): *The Communist Uprisings of 1926–1927 in Indonesia: Key Documents*. Jakarta & Kuala Lumpur.

Berg, H., A. Candotti & V. Touw 2014: 'Selamat Sjabbat. De onbekende geschiedenis van Joden in Nederlands-Indië.' *Misjpoge* 27, 4–19.

Berg, J. van den 1984: *Indië-Indonesië in honderd gedichten*. The Hague.

Berg, J. van den 1995–6: 'Van de brug uit keken ze op ons neer. Rassendiscriminatie in Nederlands-Indië.' *Bzzlletin* 25, 43–52.

Berge, T. van den 2014: *H. J. van Mook 1894–1965. Een vrij en gelukkig Indonesië*. Bussum.

Bertrand, R. 2011: *Histoire à parts égales. Récits d'une rencontre Orient-Occident (XVIe–XVIIe siècle)*. Paris.

Beurden, A. I. P. J. van 1985: 'De Indische "goldrush", goudmijnbouw en Nederlands beleid in Noord-Celebes, 1880–1910.' In J. van Goor (ed.), *Imperialisme in de marge. De afronding van het Nederlands-Indië*. Utrecht, 179–226.

Bevins, V. 2020: *The Jakarta Method: Washington's Anticommunist Crusade and the Mass Murder Program that Shaped our World*. New York.

Bijlmer, P. 1986: 'Developments in household incomes and expenditures on Java: a comparative and critical review of budget studies.' In P. J. M. Nas (ed.), *The Indonesian City: Studies in Urban Development and Planning*. Dordrecht, 148–75.

Bik, E. A. 2006: *Het vergaan van het S.S. 'Van der Wijck'*. n.p.

Birney, A. 2016: *De tolk van Java*. Amsterdam. English edition: *The Interpreter of Java* (trans. David Doherty, 2020). London.

Bloem, M. 2020: *Indo: Een persoonlijke geschiedenis over identiteit*. Amsterdam.

Blom, J. C. H. 1975: *De muiterij op de Zeven Provinciën*. Bussum.

Bloom, J. & W. E. Martin Jr. 2016: *Black Against Empire: The History and Politics of the Black Panther Party*. Oakland, CA.

Boateng, C. A. 2003: *The Political Legacy of Kwame Nkrumah of Ghana*. New York.

Boer, J. 1997: *Koninklijke olie in Indië. De prijs voor het vloeibaar goud 1939–1953*. Bergen.

Boer, P. C. 2006: *Het verlies van Java. Een kwestie van Air Power*. Amsterdam.

Boomgaard, P. 2003: 'Human capital, slavery and the low rates of economic and population growth in Indonesia, 1600–1910.' *Slavery and Abolition* 24: 83–96.

Booth, A. 1988: 'Living standards and the distribution of income in colonial Indonesia: a review of the evidence.' *Journal of Southeast Asian Studies*, 19, 2, 310–34.

Bootsma, N. A. 1986: *Buren in de koloniale tijd. De Philippijnen onder Amerikaans bewind en de Nederlandse, Indische en Indonesische reacties daarop, 1898–1942*. Dordrecht & Riverton, WY.

Borch, F. L. 2017: *Military Trials of War Criminals in the Netherlands East Indies 1946–1949*. Oxford.

Bosatlas 2011: *Bosatlas van de Geschiedenis van Nederland*. Groningen.

Bosma, U., R. Raben & W. Willems 2006: *De geschiedenis van Indische Nederlanders*. Amsterdam.

Bosman, E. 2005: 'Stipt neutraal. Jan Greshoff en *Het Hollandsche Weekblad*.' *ZL* 5, 46–64.

Boudiguet, B. 2012: *Une anthologie, discours politiques africains et antillais: 1933–2012*. n.p.

Bouman, B. 1995: *Van driekleur tot rood-wit. De Indonesische officieren uit het KNIL, 1900–1950*. The Hague.

Bouman, B. 2006: *Ieder voor zich en de Republiek voor ons allen. De logistiek achter de Indonesische Revolutie 1945–1950*. Amsterdam.

Boyd, D. 1975: 'Development of Egypt's Radio: "Voice of the Arabs" under Nasser.' *Journalism & Mass Communication Quarterly* 52, 4, 645–53.

Brekel, M. van den 2017: *Massaexecuties op Sulawesi. Hoe Nederland wegkwam met moord in Indonesië*. Zutphen.

Breman, J. 1987: *Koelies, planters en koloniale politiek. Het arbeidsregime op de grootland-bouwondernemingen aan Sumatra's Oostkust in het begin van de twintigste eeuw.* Dordrecht.

Brennan, J. R. 2010: 'Radio Cairo and the decolonization of East Africa, 1953–64.' In C. J. Lee (ed.), *Making a World After Empire: The Bandung Moment and its Political Afterlives.* Athens, OH: 173–95.

Bronkhorst, D. & E. Wils 1996: *Tropenecht. Indische en Europese kleding in Nederlands-Indië.* The Hague.

Brug, P. H. van der 1997: 'Malaria in Batavia in the 18th century.' *Tropical Medicine and International Health* 2, 9, 892–902.

Brugmans, I. J., H. J. de Graaf, A. H. Joustra & A. G. Vromans 1960: *Nederlandsch-Indië onder Japanse bezetting. Gegevens en documenten over de jaren 1942–1945.* Franeker.

Budiardjo, M. 1997: 'The constitutional system of the Republic of Indonesia 1945–1950 with special emphasis on executive–legislative relations.' In P. J. Drooglever & M. J. B. Schouten (eds.), *De leeuw en de banteng. Bijdragen aan het congres over de Nederlands-Indonesische betrekkingen 1945–1950.* The Hague, 148–67.

Buelens, G. 2018: *De jaren zestig. Een cultuurgeschiedenis.* Amsterdam.

Buiting, W. 2006: *Dagboek van Wim Buiting, pionier van 5–5 R.I.* Vriezenveen.

Burgers, H. 2010: *De garoeda en de ooievaar. Indonesië van kolonie tot nationale staat.* Leiden.

Buruma, I. 2013: *1945. Biografie van een jaar.* Amsterdam.

Bussemaker, H. T. 2005: *Bersiap! Opstand in het paradijs. De Bersiap-periode op Java en Sumatra 1945–1946.* Zutphen.

Campen, J. P. 2002: *De golfglorie van tempo doeloe. Golf in Nederlands Indië.* n.p.

Campo, J. à 1985: 'Een maritiem BB. De rol van de Koninklijke Paketvaart Maatschappij in de integratie van de koloniale staat.' In J. van Goor (ed.), *Imperialisme in de marge. De afronding van het Nederlands-Indië.* Utrecht, 123–77.

Campo, J. à 1994: 'Steam navigation and state formation.' In R. Cribb (ed.), *The Late Colonial State in Indonesia: Political and Economic Foundations of the Netherlands Indies 1880–1942.* Leiden.

Castro, F. 1966: *Clausura de la Primera Conferencia de Solidaridad de los Pueblos e Asia, Africa y America Latina (Tricontinental).* Departamento de versiones taquigraficas del gobierno revolucionario, www.cuba.cu/gobierno/discursos/1966/eso/f150166e.html.

Cats, B. C. & H. N. J. van den Berg 2003: *Logistiek onder de tropenzon. De verzorgende diensten van KNIL en KL in Nederlands-Indië 1946–1950.* Amsterdam.

Centre for the Study of Asian–African and Developing Countries 1983: *Collected Documents of the Asian–African Conference, April 18–24, 1955.* (Jakarta.)

Chagoll, L. 1986: *Buigen in jappenkampen.* Leuven & Purmerend.

Chagoll, L. 1988: *Hirohito, keizer van Japan. Een vergeten oorlogsmisdadiger?* Antwerp & Baarn.

Chairil Anwar 1993: *The Voice of the Night: Complete Poetry and Prose* (trans. and ed. Burton Raffel). Athens, OH.

Claudio, L. E. 2015: 'The anti-communist Third World: Carlos Romulo and the other Bandung.' *Southeast Asian Studies* 4, 1, 125–56.

Clavé-Çelik, E. 2012: *Dictionnaire insolite de l'Indonésie.* Paris.

Claver, A. 2007: 'Crisis, response and survival: Internatio in the 1930s.' *Economics and Finance in Indonesia,* 55, 3, 305–26.

Claver, A. 2015: 'A money paradox in the Netherlands Indies: coins, commerce and consumers in late colonial life (1800–1942).' In A. Schrikker & J. Touwen (eds.), *Promises and Predicaments: Trade and Entrepreneurship in Colonial and Independent Indonesia in the 19th and 20th centuries.* Singapore, 80–97.

Cochran, H. M. 1949: 'Rede van de voorzitter der UNCI.' In *Redevoeringen gehouden ter gelegenheid van de plechtige opening der Ronde Tafel Conferentie, 's Gravenhage, 23 augustus 1949.* The Hague.

Colijn, H. 1980 (1928): 'De inlandse beweging.' In C. Fasseur (ed.), *Geld en geweten. Een bundel opstellen over anderhalve eeuw Nederlands bestuur in de Indonesische archipel, deel II: Het tijdvak tussen 1900 en 1942.* The Hague, 96–101.

Commando exécutif pour le dixième anniversaire de la première Conférence Afro-Asiatique (1965): *La flamme révolutionnaire de Bandung.* Jakarta.

Commission on the Struggle in South Africa and its Programme n.d.: *Appendix.* African National Congress Digital Archives/ANC Collections/Documents/ Oliver Tambo Papers/029/0248/11, ancarchive.org.

Conte, A. 1965: *Bandoung, tournant de l'Histoire (18 avril 1955).* Paris.

Coolhaas, W. P. 1985: *Controleur B.B. Herinneringen van een jong bestuursambtenaar in Nederlands-Indië.* Utrecht.

Cribb, R. (ed.) 1994: *The Late Colonial State in Indonesia: Political and Economic Foundations of the Netherlands Indies 1880–1942.* Leiden.

Cribb, R. 2009: *Gangsters and Revolutionaries: The Jakarta People's Militia and the Indonesian Revolution 1945–1949.* Singapore.

Cribb, R. 2010a: *Digital Atlas of Indonesian History.* Copenhagen.

Cribb, R. 2010b: 'Institutions.' In P. Post, W. H. Frederick, I. Heidebrink & S. Sato (eds.), *The Encyclopedia of Indonesia in the Pacific War.* Leiden & Boston, 102–13.

Cribb, R. & A. Kahin 2004: *Historical Dictionary of Indonesia.* Lanham, MD.

Cross, J. P. 2016a: *It Happens with Gurkhas: Tales from an English Nepali, 1944–2015.* Brimscombe Port.

Cross, J. P. 2016b: *A Gurkha Remembers: A Lifetime in Asia* (CD). London & Pokhara.

Cross, J. P. & B. Gurung 2007: *Gurkhas at War: Eyewitness Accounts from World War II to Iraq.* London.

Curaming, R. 2003: 'Towards reinventing Indonesian nationalist historiography.' *Kyoto Review of Southeast Asia 3*, https://kyotoreview.org/issue-3-nations-and-stories/an-introduction-to-indonesian-historiography/.

Curaming, R. 2005: 'Behind, between and beyond politics: the "political" history in the writing of textbook in Indonesia and the Philippines.' *Asia–Pacific Forum* 28, 1–20.

Daalder, H. 2004: *Vier jaar nachtmerrie. Willem Drees 1886–1988. De Indonesische kwestie 1945–1949.* Amsterdam.

Dahm, B. 1964: *Soekarno en de strijd om Indonesië's onafhankelijkheid.* Meppel.

D'Arrigo, R., R. Wilson, J. Palmer, P. Krusic, A. Curtis, J. Sakulich, S. Bijaksana, S. Zulaikah & L. O. Ngkoimani 2006: 'Monsoon drought over Java, Indonesia, during the past two centuries.' *Geophysical Research Letters* 33, 4.

Daum, P. A. 1894: *Aboe Bakar.* The Hague.

Davidson, B. 1973 (2007): *Black Star: A View of the Life and Times of Kwame Nkrumah.* Oxford.

Decraene, P. 1961: *Le panafricanisme.* Paris.

Delden, M. C. van 2007: *De republikeinse kampen in Nederlands-Indië, oktober 1945–mei 1947. Orde in de chaos?* n.p.

Dengel, H. H. 1986: *Kartosuwirjos Kampf um einen islamischen Staat Indonesien.* Stuttgart.

Denham, T. 2010: 'The roots of agriculture and arboriculture in New Guinea: looking beyond Austronesian expansion, Neolithic packages and indigenous origins.' *World Archaeology* 36, 610–20.

Departement van Economische Zaken (Ministry of Economic Affairs) 1936: *Volkstelling 1930. Deel VIII: Overzicht voor Nederlands-Indië.* Batavia.

Derksen, J. B. D. & J. Tinbergen 1980 (1945): 'Berekeningen over de economische betekenis van Nederlandsch-Indië voor Nederland.' In C. Fasseur (ed.), *Geld en geweten. Een bundel opstellen over anderhalve eeuw Nederlands bestuur in de Indonesische archipel, deel II: Het tijdvak tussen 1900 en 1942.* The Hague, 225–40.

Diah, H. 2005: *An Endless Journey: Reflections of an Indonesian Journalist.* Jakarta.

Dick, H. 2002: 'Formation of the nation-state, 1930s–1966.' In H. Dick, V. J. H. Houben, J. T. Lindblad & T. Kian Wie (eds.) 2002, *The Emergence of a National Economy: An Economic History of Indonesia.* Leiden, 153–93.

Dick, H., V. J. H. Houben, J. T. Lindblad & T. Kian Wie (eds.), *The Emergence of a National Economy: An Economic History of Indonesia.* Leiden.

Dijk, C. van 1981: *Rebellion under the Banner of Islam: The Darul Islam in Indonesia.* The Hague.

Dijk, J. van, J. de Jonge & N. de Klerk 2010: *J. C. Lamster, een vroege filmer in Nederlands-Indië.* Amsterdam.

Dinkel, J. 2015: *Die Bewegung Bündnisfreier Staaten. Genese, Organisation und Politik (1927–1992)*. Berlin.

Diong, N. J. N. 2015: 'Sawt Al-Arab or Sawt Al-Nasser? The case of mass media under Gamal Abdel Nasser and the convoluted rise of pan-Arabism.' *Journal of Georgetown University-Qatar*, 5.

Djajadiningrat, I. N. 2009 (1956): *The Beginnings of the Indonesian–Dutch Negotiations and the Hoge Veluwe Talks*. Jakarta & Kuala Lumpur.

Doedens, A. & L. Mulder 2017: *Slag in de Javazee. Oorlog tussen Nederland en Japan 1941–1942*. Zutphen.

Doel, H. W. van den 1996: *Het Rijk van Insulinde. Opkomst en ondergang van een Nederlandse kolonie*. Amsterdam.

Doel, H. W. 2000: *Afscheid van Indië. De val van het Nederlandse imperium in Azië*. Amsterdam.

Doorn, J. A. A. van 1995: *De laatste eeuw van Indië. Ontwikkeling en ondergang van een koloniaal project*. Amsterdam.

Doorn, J. A. A. van & W. J. Hendrix 1970: *Ontsporing van geweld*. Rotterdam.

Dower, J. W. 1986: *War without Mercy: Race and Power in the Pacific War*. New York.

Dröge, P. 2015: *De schaduw van Tambora. De grootste natuurramp sinds mensenheugenis*. Houten.

Dröge, P. 2017: *Pelgrim. Leven en reizen van Christiaan Snouck Hurgronje*. Houten & Antwerp.

Drooglever, P. J. 1980: *De Vaderlandse Club 1929–1942. Totoks en de Indische politiek*. Franeker.

Drooglever, P. J. & M. J. B. Schouten 1999: *Het einde in zicht. Stemmen uit het laatste jaar van Nederlands-Indië*. The Hague.

Du Bois, W. E. B. 1993 (1954): 'Africa and the American Negro intelligentsia.' In G. Early (ed.), *Speech and Power: The African-American Essay and its Cultural Content, from Polemics to Pulpit*, 2. Hopewell, NJ: 413–26.

Dudziak, M. L. 2011: *Cold War Civil Rights: Race and the Image of American Democracy*. Princeton, NJ.

Duijs, J. E. W. 1928: *De vervolging tegen de Indonesische studenten*. Amsterdam.

Edis, R. 2004: *Peak of Limuria: The Story of Diego Garcia and the Chagos Archipelago*. London.

Elands, M., R. van Gils & B. Schoenmaker 1996: *De geschiedenis van 1 Divisie '7 December', 1946–1996*. The Hague.

Elias, W. H. J. [1988]: *De Japanse bezetting van Nederlands-Indië*. Zutphen.

Elout, C. K. 1936: *Indisch Dagboek*. The Hague.

Elson, R. E. 2008: *The Idea of Indonesia: A History*. Cambridge.

Emmer, P. C. 2019: *Geschiedenis van de Nederlandse slavenhandel*. Amsterdam.

Eng, P. van der 1988: 'Marshall aid as a catalyst in the decolonization of Indonesia, 1947–49.' *Journal of Southeast Asian Studies*, 19, 335–52.

Eng, P. van der 2008 (1994): 'Food supply in Java during war and decolonisation, 1940–1950.' *MPRA Paper* 8852, https://mpra.ub.uni-muenchen.de/8852/.

Eslava, L., M. Fakhri & V. Nesiah 2017: *Bandung, Global History, and International Law: Critical Pasts and Pending Futures.* Cambridge.

Esterik, C. van & K. van Twist 1980: '*Daar werd iets grootsch verricht' of hoe het Koninkrijk der Nederlanden zijn grootste kolonie verloor.* Weesp.

Eymeret, J. 1972: 'Les archives françaises au service des études indonésiennes: Java sous Daendels (1808–1811).' *Archipel* 4, 151–68.

Falter, R. 2017: *De geboorte van Europa: een geschiedenis zonder einde.* Kalmthout.

Farid, H. 2016: 'Rethinking the legacies of Bandung.' *Inter-Asia Cultural Studies*, 1, 12–18.

Fasseur, C. 1980a: 'De geest van het gouvernement.' In C. Fasseur (ed.), *Geld en geweten. Een bundel opstellen over anderhalve eeuw Nederlands bestuur in de Indonesische archipel, deel I: 19e eeuw.* The Hague, 32–58.

Fasseur, C. 1980b: 'Het cultuurstelsel opnieuw in discussie.' In C. Fasseur (ed.), *Geld en geweten. Een bundel opstellen over anderhalve eeuw Nederlands bestuur in de Indonesische archipel, deel I: 19e eeuw.* The Hague, 131–51.

Fasseur, C. 1994: 'Cornerstone and stumbling block: racial classification and the colonial state in Indonesia.' In Robert Cribb (ed.), *The Late Colonial State in Indonesia: Political and Economic Foundations of the Netherlands Indies 1880–1942.* Leiden, 31–56.

Fasseur, C. 2001: *Wilhelmina. Krijgshaftig in een vormeloze jas.* Amsterdam.

Fasseur, C. 2014: *Eigen meester, niemands knecht. Het leven van Pieter Sjoerds Gerbrandy, minister-president van Nederland in de Tweede Wereldoorlog.* Amsterdam.

Ferro, M. 1982: *Suez: naissance d'un tiers monde.* Brussels.

Fiedeldij Dop, J. M. & Y. Simons 1983: *Al weer iets groots verricht. Hoe Nederland zijn Indië-deserteurs tot de laatste man berechtte.* Amsterdam.

Finnane, A. & D. McDougall (eds.) 2010: *Bandung 1955: Little Histories.* Caulfield, Vic.

Fogg, K. W. 2019: *Indonesia's Islamic Revolution.* Cambridge.

Fontaine, A. 2007: *Het rode gevaar. De geschiedenis van de Koude Oorlog.* Amsterdam.

Formichi, C. 2012: *Islam and the Making of the Nation: Kartosuwiryo and Political Islam in Twentieth-Century Indonesia.* Leiden & Boston.

Frakking, R. 2017: '*Collaboration is a very delicate concept': Alliance-Formation and the Colonial Defence of Indonesia and Malaysia, 1945–1957.* Florence.

Franken, B. 2007: *Daar sta je dan . . . Indië-dagboek van een Betuwse dienstplichtige.* Kesteren.

Frankopan, P. 2015: *The Silk Roads: A New History of the World.* New York.

Frederick, W. H. 1988: *Visions and Heat: The Making of the Indonesian Revolution.* Athens, OH.

Frederick, W. 2010: 'The aftermath.' In P. Post, W. H. Frederick, I. Heidebrink & S. Sato (eds.), *The Encyclopedia of Indonesia in the Pacific War.* Leiden & Boston, 46–60.

Freedman, P. 2008: *Out of the East: Spices and the Medieval Imagination.* New Haven, CT.

Frost, M. R. & Y.-M. Balasingamchow 2016: *Singapore: A Biography.* Singapore.

Foster Collins, J. 1950: 'The United Nations and Indonesia.' *International Conciliation* 28, 115–202.

Fuller, D. Q. & L. Qin 2009: 'Water management and labour in the origins and dispersal of Asian rice.' *World Archaeology* 41, 88–111.

Furnivall, J. S. 1944: *Netherlands India: A Study of Plural Economy.* Cambridge & New York.

Gaines, K. K. 2006: *American Africans in Ghana. Black Expatriates and the Civil Rights Era.* Chapel Hill, NC.

Galen, J. J. van 2013: *Afscheid van de koloniën. Het Nederlandse dekolonisatiebeleid 1942–2012.* Amsterdam & Antwerp.

Geerken, H. 2015: *Hitlers Griff nach Asien. Der Anfang vom Ende der Kolonialzeit. Deutsche Hilfe für Soekarnos Freiheitskämpfer und Indiens Subhas Chandra Bose. Eine Dokumentation.* n.p.

Geersing, B. 2019: *Kapitein Raymond Westerling en de Zuid-Celebes-affaire. Mythe en werkelijkheid. Een markante episode uit de geschiedenis van Nederlands-Indië.* Soesterberg.

Geertz, C. 1960: *The Religion of Java.* Chicago & London.

Ghosh, A. 2017: 'Before 1962: the case for 1950s China–India history.' *Journal of Asian Studies* 76, 3, 697–727.

Giebels, L. 1995: *Beel. Van vazal tot onderkoning. Biografie 1902–1977.* The Hague & Nijmegen.

Giebels, L. 1999: *Soekarno. Nederlandsch onderdaan. Biografie 1901–1950.* Amsterdam.

Giebels, L. 2001: *Soekarno. President. Biografie 1950–1970.* Amsterdam.

Goedhart, F. J. 1953: *Een revolutie op drift.* Amsterdam.

Gonggrijp, G. 1928: *Schets eener economische geschiedenis van Nederlandsch-Indië.* Haarlem.

Goor, J. van 1985 (ed.): *Imperialisme in de marge. De afronding van het Nederlands-Indië.* Utrecht.

Goor, J. van 2000: *Indische avonturen. Opmerkelijke ontmoetingen met een andere wereld.* The Hague.

Gouda, F. & T. Brocades Zaalberg 2002: *American Visions of the Netherlands East Indies/Indonesia. US Foreign Policy and Indonesian Nationalism, 1920–1949.* Amsterdam.

Gouka, N. G. B. 2001: *De petitie-Soetardjo. Een Hollandse misser in Indië? (1936–1938).* Utrecht.

Graaf, H. J. de 1958: *De regering van Sultan Agung, vorst van Mataram, 1613–1645, en die van zijn voorganger Panembahan Séda-Ing-Krapjak, 1601–1613* (Verhandelingen van het KITLV 23). The Hague.

Graaff, B. de 1997: *'Kalm temidden van woedende golven'. Het ministerie van Koloniën en zijn taakomgeving 1912–1940*. The Hague.

Grataloup, C. 2019: *Atlas historique mondial*. Paris.

Groen, P. 1991: *Marsroutes en dwaalsporen. Het Nederlands militair-strategisch beleid in Indonesië 1945–1950*. The Hague.

Groeneboer, K. 1993: *Weg tot het westen. Het Nederlands voor Indië 1600–1950. Een taalpolitieke geschiedenis*. Leiden.

Guevara, E. C. 2017: *Textes, discours, interviews*. Marseilles.

Hagen, P. 2018: *Koloniale oorlogen in Indonesië. Vijf eeuwen verzet tegen vreemde overheersing*. Amsterdam.

Haley, A. 2015 (1964): *The Autobiography of Malcolm X*. New York.

Hamer-Monod de Froideville, M. 2013: *Geknakte bloem. Acht vrouwen vertellen hun verhaal over Japanse militaire dwangprostitutie*. Delft.

Hanna, W. A. & D. Alwi 1990: *Turbulent Times Past in Ternate and Tidore: Early East–West Encounters in the Clove Islands*. Banda Neira.

Hannigan, T. 2014. *Raffles and the British Invasion of Java*. Singapore.

Hannigan, T. 2015: *A Brief History of Indonesia: Sultans, Spices, and Tsunamis: The Incredible History of Southeast Asia's Largest Nation*. Tokyo.

Hansen, P. & S. Jonsson 2014: *Eurafrica: The Untold History of European Integration and Colonialism*. London.

Hara, K. 1987: *Yuki yukite shingun* (The Emperor's Naked Army Marches On). Documentary.

Hardie, R. 1983: *The Burma–Siam Railway: The Secret Diary of Dr Robert Hardie 1942–45*. London.

Harinck, C., N. van Horn & B. Luttikhuis 2017: 'Wie telt de Indonesische doden?' *De Groene Amsterdammer*, 26 July 2017.

Harinck, C. H. C. & J. Verwey 2015: *Wie kwamen, wie zagen, wie schreven?* www.kitlv.nl.

Hatta, M. 1980 (1928): 'Kielstra-Colijn als profeten van het Nederlandse koloniale imperialisme.' In C. Fasseur (ed.), *Geld en geweten. Een bundel opstellen over anderhalve eeuw Nederlands bestuur in de Indonesische archipel, deel II: Het tijdvak tussen 1900 en 1942*. The Hague, 102–11.

Hazelhoff Roelfzema, E. 2003: *In Pursuit of Life*. Stroud.

Hazeu, W. 2018: *Lucebert. Biografie*. Amsterdam.

Heath, B. 1949: 'Key to the Pacific.' In *Last Testimony: An American Document*. New York.

Heek, G. van 1952: *Front op Java. Mijn diensttijd in Indonesië 1947–1950*. Hengelo.

Heidebrink, I. 2010: 'Prisoners of war.' In P. Post, W. H. Frederick, I. Heidebrink & S. Sato (eds.), *The Encyclopedia of Indonesia in the Pacific War*. Leiden & Boston, 174–9.

Heijboer, P. 1977: *Klamboes, klewangs, klapperbomen. Indië gewonnen en verloren*. Houten.

Heijden, C. van der 2001: *Grijs verleden. Nederland en de Tweede Wereldoorlog.* Amsterdam.

Heilbron, M. 2019: 'Het geschiedenisonderwijs is eurocentrisch.' *De Correspondent*, 25 May 2019.

Hendraparya, T. A. 2011: *Onderafdeeling Bagansiapapi: Negeri Penghasil Ikan Terbesar di Dunia.* Pekanbaru.

Hengel, M. van 2018: *Een knipperend ogenblik. Portret van Remco Campert.* Amsterdam.

Hellwig, T. & E. Tagliacozzo (eds.) 2009: *The Indonesia Reader: History, Culture, Politics.* Durham, NC.

Helsdingen, W. H. van 1946: *De plaats van Nederlandsch-Indië in het Koninkrijk. Stemmen van overzee.* Leiden (2 vols).

Helsdingen, W. H. 1947: *Op weg naar een Nederlandsch-Indonesische Unie. Stemmen van hier en ginds.* The Hague.

Hesselink, L. 2011: *Healers on the Colonial Market: Native Doctors and Midwives in the Dutch East Indies.* Leiden.

Hicks, G. 1997: *The Comfort Women: Japan's Brutal Regime of Enforced Prostitution in the Second World War.* New York & London.

Hidskes, M. 2016: *Thuis gelooft niemand mij. Zuid-Celebes 1946–1947.* Amsterdam & Antwerp.

Higgins, R. 1970: *United Nations Peacekeeping 1946–1967. Documents and Commentary: II. Asia.* London.

Hobsbawm, E. 1995: *The Age of Extremes: The Short Twentieth Century, 1914–1991.* London.

Hoek, A.-L. 2016a: 'Ook op Sumatra richtte Nederland een bloedbad aan.' *NRC Handelsblad*, 13 February.

Hoek, A.-L. 2016b: 'Rengat, 1949.' *Inside Indonesia*, insideindoneisa.org/rengat 1949-part-1.

Hoek, A.-L. & E. van der Kleij 2020: 'De prijs van de onafhankelijkheid. Hoe Nederland profiteerde van "Indië".' *De Groene Amsterdammer* 34, 19 August.

Hoëvell, W. R. van 1980 (1860): 'De inlandsche hoofden en de bevolking op Java (Max Havelaar, of de koffij-veilingen der Nederlandsche Handel-Maatschappij, door Multatuli).' In C. Fasseur (ed.), *Geld en geweten. Een bundel opstellen over anderhalve eeuw Nederlands bestuur in de Indonesische archipel, deel I: 19e eeuw.* The Hague, 173–83.

Homan, G. D. 1990: 'The Netherlands, the United States and the Indonesian Question, 1948.' *Journal of Contemporary History* 25, 123–41.

Hoornik, E. 1972: *Verzamelde gedichten.* Amsterdam.

Horst, L. van der. 2007: *Het Verzetsmuseum Amsterdam.* Amsterdam.

Hovinga, H. 2006: 'End of a forgotten drama: the reception and repatriation of rōmusha after the Japanese capitulation.' In P. H. Kratoska (ed.), *Asian Labor in the Wartime Japanese Empire.* Singapore, 213–34.

Hueting, J. H. 1973: 'Oorlogsmisdaad of exces? – of hoe je onbegrijpelijk gedrag begrijpelijk kunt maken.' *Transaktie* 2, 5, 11–15.

Huyse, L. 2006: *Alles gaat voorbij, behalve het verleden.* Amsterdam & Leuven.

Ibnoe Hadjar, M. 1941: *Korte handleiding voor de Bahasa Indonesia. Ook voor zelfstudie.* Leiden.

Immerzeel, B. R. & R. van Esch (eds.) 1993: *Verzet in Nederlands-Indië tegen de Japanse bezetting 1942–1945.* The Hague.

Ingleson, J. 1975: *Perhimpunan Indonesia and the Indonesian National Movement 1923–1928.* Melbourne.

Ingleson, J. 1979: *Road to Exile: The Indonesian Nationalist Movement 1927–1934.* Kuala Lumpur & Hong Kong.

Ingleson, J. 1986: *In Search of Justice: Workers and Unions in Colonial Java, 1908–1926.* Oxford & Singapore.

Ingleson, J. 2014: *Workers, Unions and Politics. Indonesia in the 1920s and 1930s.* Leiden.

Jacobs, A. 1913: *Reisbrieven uit Afrika en Azië.* Almelo.

Jacobs, E. M. 1991: *Varen om peper en thee. Korte geschiedenis van de Verenigde Oostindische Compagnie.* Amsterdam.

James, J. 2011: *Rimbaud in Java: The Lost Voyage.* Singapore.

Jansen, L. F. 1988: *In deze halve gevangenis. Dagboek van mr dr L. F. Jansen, Batavia/Djakarta 1942–1945.* Franeker.

Janssen, H. 2010: *Schaamte en onschuld. Het verdrongen oorlogsverleden van troostmeisjes in Indonesië.* Amsterdam.

Jaquet, F. G. P. 1987: *Kartini. Brieven aan mevrouw R. M. Abendanon-Mandri en haar echtgenoot met andere documenten.* Dordrecht.

Jaquet, L. G. M. 1982: *Minister Stikker en de souvereiniteitsoverdracht aan Indonesië.* The Hague.

Jo, H. 2017: 'Si Pitung dari Ciamis.' *Historia*, https://historia.id/politik/articles/si-pitung-dari-ciamis-PKNbe.

Jong, J. J. P. de 1988: *Diplomatie of strijd. Het Nederlands beleid tegenover de Indonesische revolutie 1945–1947.* Meppel & Amsterdam.

Jong, J. J. P. de 1998: *De waaier van het fortuin. Van handelscompagnie tot koloniaal imperium. De Nederlanders in Azië en de Indonesische archipel 1595–1950.* The Hague.

Jong, J. J. P. de 2011: *Avondschot. Hoe Nederland zich terugtrok uit zijn Aziatisch imperium.* Amsterdam.

Jong, J. J. P. de 2015: *De terugtocht. Nederland en de dekolonisatie van Indonesië.* Amsterdam.

Jong, L. de 1979: *Het Koninkrijk der Nederlanden in de Tweede Wereldoorlog. 9. Londen.* The Hague.

Jong, L. de 1984: *Het Koninkrijk der Nederlanden in de Tweede Wereldoorlog. 11a. Nederlands-Indië I* (2 vols). The Hague.

Jong, L. de 1985: *Het Koninkrijk der Nederlanden in de Tweede Wereldoorlog. 11b. Nederlands-Indië II* (2 vols). The Hague.

Jong, L. de 1986: *Het Koninkrijk der Nederlanden in de Tweede Wereldoorlog. 11c. Nederlands-Indië III*. The Hague.

Jong, L. de 1988: *Het Koninkrijk der Nederlanden in de Tweede Wereldoorlog. 12. Epiloog.* The Hague.

Joseph, P. E. 2006: *Waiting 'Til the Midnight Hour: A Narrative History of Black Power in America.* New York.

Joseph, P. E. 2009: 'The Black Power movement: a state of the field.' *Journal of American History* 96, 3, 751–77.

Joustra, A. 2009: *Instructions for American Servicemen in Dutch Indonesia during World War II.* Amsterdam.

Judt, T. 2007: *Postwar: A History of Europe Since 1945.* London.

Kaam, B. van 1977: *Ambon door de eeuwen.* Baarn.

Kadt, J. de 1949: *De Indonesische tragedie. Het treurspel der gemiste kansen.* Amsterdam.

Kahin, A. (ed.) 1985: *Regional Dynamics of the Indonesian Revolution: Unity from Diversity.* Honolulu.

Kahin, G. 1956: *The Asian–African Conference: Bandung, Indonesia, April 1955.* Ithaca, NY.

Kahin, G. 1970 (1952): *Nationalism and Revolution in Indonesia.* Ithaca, NY & London.

Kahin, A. R. & G. Kahin 1995: *Subversion as Foreign Policy: The Secret Eisenhower and Dulles Debacle in Indonesia.* New York.

Kan, W. 1986: *Burmadagboek 1942–1945.* Amsterdam.

Kawilarang, A. E. 1993: *Officier in dienst van de Republiek Indonesië.* Breda.

Keimer, C. 2019: *Gruppe Monsun: The U-Boat Operations in the Indian and Pacific Oceans during World War II.* Charles Town, WV.

Kemperman, J. 2002: *De Japanse bezetting in dagboeken. Buiten de kampen.* Amsterdam.

Kemperman, J. 2010: 'Internment of civilians.' In P. Post, W. H. Frederick, I. Heidebrink & S. Sato (eds.), *The Encyclopedia of Indonesia in the Pacific War.* Leiden & Boston, 163–73.

Keppy, H. 2004: *Tussen Ambon en Amsterdam.* Rotterdam.

Keppy, H. 2013: *Pendek. Korte verhalen over Indische levens.* Amsterdam.

Keppy, H. 2019: *Zijn jullie kerels of lafaards? De Indische en Indonesische strijd tegen de nazi's 1940–'45.* The Hague.

Keppy, H. 2020: 'Een president op zoek naar de dialoog.' *Indies Tijdschrift* 1, 6–7.

Keppy, P. 2006: *Sporen van vernieling. Oorlogsschade, roof en rechtsherstel in Indonesië 1940–1957.* Amsterdam.

Keyser, A. 2016: *Teaching and Tuition of Neurology and Neurosurgery in Indonesia during one Century (1850–1950).* Nijmegen.

Kimche, D. 1973: *The Afro-Asian Movement: Ideology and Foreign Policy of the Third World*. Jerusalem.

King, M. L. 1957: 'A realistic look at the question of progress in the area of race relations.' Address delivered at St Louis Freedom Rally, https://kinginstitute.stanford.edu/king-papers.

King, M. L. 1963: *Letter from Birmingham Jail*, https://kinginstitute.stanford.edu/king-papers.

Kobong, T. 2008: *Injil dan Tongkonan: inkarnasi, kontekstualisasi, transformasi*. Jakarta.

Koch, J. 2013: *Koning Willem I, 1772–1843*. Amsterdam.

Koch, J. 2018: *Oranje in revolutie en oorlog. Een Europese geschiedenis 1772–1890*. Amsterdam.

Könemann, L. 2012: *Historica. Grote atlas van de wereldgeschiedenis*. Bath.

Koetsier-Korvinus, H. & T. 1995: *Vijftig jaar 'Merdeka'. In gesprek met Indonesiers en Nederlanders*. Kampen.

Kok, R., E. Somers & L. Zweers 2009: *Koloniale oorlog 1945–1949. Van Indië naar Indonesië*. Amsterdam.

Korver, A. P. E. 1982: *Sarekat Islam 1912–1916. Opkomst, bloei en structuur van Indonesië's eerste massabeweging*. Amsterdam.

Kossmann, E. H. 2001: *De Lage Landen 1780–1980. Twee eeuwen Nederland en België. Deel 1. 1780–1914*. Amsterdam.

Kossmann, E. H. 2002: *De Lage Landen 1780–1980. Twee eeuwen Nederland en België. Deel 2. 1914–1980*. Amsterdam.

Kousbroek, R. 1995: *Terug naar Negri Pan Erkoms*. Amsterdam.

Kousbroek, R. 2005 (1992): *Het Oostindisch kampsyndroom*. Amsterdam.

KPM 1935: *Romance Calling: Java Bali Sumatra Nias Siam Indo-China*. n.p.

KPM 1941: *Een halve eeuw paketvaart 1891–1941*. Amsterdam.

Kratoska, P. H. (ed.) 2006: *Asian Labor in the Wartime Japanese Empire*. Singapore.

Kropman, M., C. van Boxtel & J. van Drie 2015: 'Small country, great ambitions: prospective teachers' narratives and knowledge about Dutch history.' In A. Chapman & A. Wilschut (eds.), *Joined-Up History: New Directions in History Education Research*. Charlotte, NC, 57–84.

Kubitschek, H. D. & I. Wessel 1981: *Geschichte Indonesiens. Vom Altertum bis zur Gegenwart*. Berlin.

Kuijper, J., B. Peperkamp, M. Salverda & G. A. M. Willem 1990: *Het Vroman-effect*. Amsterdam.

Kusno, A. 2016: *Visual Cultures of the Ethnic Chinese in Indonesia*. London & New York, 2016.

Kurasawa, A. 1987: 'Propaganda media on Java under the Japanese 1942–1945.' *Indonesia*, 44, 59–116.

Kurasawa-Inomata, A. 1997: 'Rice shortage and transportation.' In P. Post & E. Touwen-Bouwsma (eds.), *Japan, Indonesia and the War. Myths and Realities*. Leiden, 111–33.

Kurasawa, A. 2010: 'The education of *pribumi*.' In P. Post, W. H. Frederick, I. Heidebrink & S. Sato (eds.), *The Encyclopedia of Indonesia in the Pacific War*. Leiden & Boston, 320–27.

Kwantes R. C. 1975–1982: *De ontwikkeling van de nationalistische beweging in Nederlandsch-Indië. Bronnenpublikatie*. Groningen, 4 vols.

Ladwig III, W. C., A. S. Erickson & J. D. Mikolay 2014: 'Diego Garcia and American security in the Indian Ocean.' In C. Lord & A. S. Erickson (eds.), *Rebalancing US Forces: Basing and Forward Presence in the Asia-Pacific*. Annapolis, MD, 131–79.

Langeveld, H. 2014: *De man die in de put sprong. Willem Schermerhorn, 1894–1977*. Amsterdam.

Lanzing, F. 2005: *Soldaten van smaragd. Mannen, vrouwen en kinderen van het KNIL 1890–1914*. Amsterdam & Antwerp.

Lanzing, F. 2007: *'Voor Fredje is het kamp een paradijs'. Een jeugd in Nederlands-Indië 1933–1946*. Amsterdam & Antwerp.

Lanzing, F. 2014: *Toean nippon. De Japanse soldaat in de Pacificoorlog en in Nederlands-Indië, 1942–1947*. Amsterdam.

Leakey, R. A. & J. Slikkerveer 1993: *Man-Ape, Ape-Man: The Quest for Humans' Place in Nature and Dubois' Missing Link*. Amsterdam.

Lee, C. J. 2009: 'At the rendezvous of decolonization: the final communiqué of the Asian–African Conference, Bandung, Indonesia, 18–24 April 1955.' *Interventions: International Journal of Postcolonial Studies* 11, 1, 81–93.

Lee, C. J. 2010: *Making a World After Empire: The Bandung Moment and its Political Afterlives*. Athens, OH.

Leeuwen, A. van 1985: *De Perhimpoenan Indonesia 1929–1941*. Unpublished doctoral thesis, Utrecht.

Legum, C. 1965: *Pan-Africanism: A Short Political Guide*. New York.

Lengkeek, E. G. 2010: *De hel van Tjideng. Een persoonlijk verslag van een jappenkamp*. Amsterdam.

Levy, W. J. 1982: *Oil Strategy and Politics, 1941–1981*. Boulder, CO.

Liempt, A. van 1997: *De lijkentrein. Waarom 46 gevangenen de reis naar Surabaya niet overleefden*. The Hague.

Liempt, A. van 2012: *Nederland valt aan. Op weg naar oorlog met Indonesië*. Amsterdam.

Limpach, R. 2016: *De brandende kampongs van Generaal Spoor*. Amsterdam.

Lindblad, J. T. 1985: 'Economische aspecten van de Nederlandse expansie in de Indonesische archipel ten tijde van het moderne imperialisme (1870–1914).' In J. van Goor (ed.), *Imperialisme in de marge. De afronding van het Nederlands-Indië*. Utrecht, 227–65 (also published as 'Economic aspects of the Dutch expansion in Indonesia, 1870–1914', *Modern Asian Studies* 23, 1989, 1–23).

Lindblad, J. T. 1989: 'The petroleum industry in Indonesia before the Second World War.' *Bulletin of Indonesian Economic Studies* 25, 53–77.

Lindblad, J. T. 2002: 'The late colonial state and economic expansion, 1900–1930.' In H. Dick, V. J. H. Houben, J. T. Lindblad & T. Kian Wie (eds.), *The Emergence of a National Economy: An Economic History of Indonesia*. Leiden, 111–52.

Lindblad, J. T. 2006: 'Macroeconomic consequences of decolonization in Indonesia.' Paper presented at the XIVth conference of the International Economic History Association, Helsinki, 21–25 August.

Locher-Scholten, E. 2000: *Women and the Colonial State: Essays on Gender and Modernity in the Netherlands Indies 1900–1942*. Amsterdam.

Lowe, P. 2009: *Contending with Nationalism and Communism: British Policy towards Southeast Asia, 1945–1965*. Basingstoke.

Lubis, M. 1990: *Indonesia: Land Under the Rainbow*. Singapore & New York, 1990.

Lucas, A. (ed.) 1986: *Local Opposition and Underground Resistance to the Japanese in Java, 1942–1945*. Melbourne.

Lucas, A. E. 1991: *One Soul, One Struggle: Region and Revolution in Indonesia*. Sydney.

Lumumba, P. 1961: *Le Congo, terre d'avenir, est-il menacé?* Brussels.

Maar, R. van der & H. Meijer 2013: *Herman van Roijen (1905–1991). Een diplomaat van klasse*. Amsterdam.

Mackie, J. 2005: *Bandung 1955: Non-Alignment and Afro-Asian Solidarity*. Singapore.

MacMillan, M. 2001: *Peacemakers: The Paris Conference of 1919 and its Attempt to End War*. London.

Maekawa, K. 2006: 'The Heiho during the Japanese occupation of Indonesia.' In P. H. Kratoska (ed.), *Asian Labor in the Wartime Japanese Empire*. Singapore, 179–96.

Mahin, M. 2006: *Hausmann Baboe: Tokoh Pergerakan Rakyat Dayak Yang Terlupakan*. Jakarta.

Mahler, A. G. 2018: *From the Tricontinental to the Global South: Race, Radicalism, and Transnational Solidarity*. Durham, NC.

Malinowski, B. 1978 (1922): *Argonauts of the Western Pacific: An Account of Native Enterprise and Adventure in the Archipelagoes of Melanesian New Guinea*. London.

Mandela, N. 1995: *Rajiv Gandhi Foundation Lecture*. Nelson Mandela Foundation Archive/ZA COM MR-S-224, https://nelsonmandela.org/.

Mandela, N. 1998: *Address by the President of the Republic of South Africa, Nelson Mandela, at the inaugural Session of the 12th Conference of Heads of State or Government of the Movement of Non-Aligned Countries*. Nelson Mandela Foundation Archive/ ZA COM MR-S-621, https://nelsonmandela.org/.

Marable, M. 2011: *Malcolm X: A Life of Reinvention*. London.

Margolin, J.-L. & C. Markovits 2015: *Les Indes et l'Europe: Histoires connectées XVe–XXIe siècle*. Paris.

Mark, E. 2011: 'Indonesian nationalism and wartime Asianism: essays from the "Culture" column of Greater Asia, 1942.' In S. Saaler & C. W. A. Szpilman (eds.), *Pan-Asianism: A Documentary History*. Lanham, MD, 233–42.

Mark, E. 2018: *Japan's Occupation of Java in the Second World War: A Transnational History*. London.

Mattalatta, A. 2002: *Meniti Siri' dan Harga Diri. Catatan dan Kenangan*. Makassar.

McAlexander, R. J. 2010: 'Couscous Mussolini: US perceptions of Gamal Abdel Nasser, the 1958 intervention in Lebanon and the origins of the US–Israeli special relationship.' *Cold War History* 11, 363–85.

McCormack, G. & H. Nelson 1993 (eds.): *The Burma–Thailand Railway: memory and history*. St Leonards.

McLaughlin, R. 2016: *The Roman Empire and the Silk Routes: The Ancient World Economy and the Empires of Parthia, Central Asia and Han China*. Barnsley.

McLaughlin, R. 2018: *The Roman Empire and the Indian Ocean: The Ancient World Economy and the Kingdoms of Africa, Arabia and India*. Barnsley.

McMahon, R. J. 1981: *Colonialism and Cold War: The United States and the Struggle for Indonesian Independence, 1945–1949*. Ithaca, NY & London.

McMillan, R. 2005: *The British Occupation of Indonesia 1945–1946: Britain, the Netherlands and the Indonesian Revolution*. London & New York.

McMillan, R. 2009: 'British military intelligence in Java and Sumatra, 1945–46.' *Indonesia and the Malay World* 37, 107, 65–81.

McVey, R. 1965: *The Rise of Indonesian Communism*. Ithaca, NY.

McVey, R. 2009 (1957): *The Soviet View of the Indonesian Revolution: A Study in the Russian Attitude towards Asian Nationalism*. Jakarta & Kuala Lumpur.

Meelhuijsen, W. 2000: *Revolutie in Soerabaja, 17 augustus–1 december 1945*. Zutphen.

Meijer, H. 1994: *Den Haag-Djakarta. De Nederlands-Indonesische betrekkingen 1950–1962*. Utrecht.

Meijer, H. 1997: 'Pieter Lieftinck en de Indonesische dekolonisatie 1945–1949. Financier of politicus?' In P. J. Drooglever & M. J. B. Schouten (eds.), *De leeuw en de banteng. Bijdragen aan het congres over de Nederlands-Indonesische betrekkingen 1945–1950*. The Hague, 61–72.

Meredith, M. 2005: *The State of Africa: A History of Fifty Years of Independence*. London.

Mets, J. & F. van der Herberg 2014: 'Een onstuitbaar streven. Raden Mas Djajeng Pratomo, 22 February 1914.' http://www.dachau.nl/wp-content/uploads/2018/04/Biografie-Djajeng-Pratomo-opmaak-DEF.pdf.

Michel Munoz, P. 2006: *Early Kingdoms: Indonesian Archipelago & the Malay Peninsula*. Singapore.

Michelin, F. 2019: *La guerre du Pacifique a commencé en Indochine 1940–1941*. Paris.

Mishra, P. 2013: *From the Ruins of Empire: The Revolt Against the West and the Remaking of Asia*. London.

Mizuki, S. 2013–14: *Showa: A History of Japan* (3 vols). Montreal.

Molemans, G. 2014: *Opgevangen in andijvielucht. De opvang van ontheemden uit Indonesië in kampen en contractpensions en de financiële claims op basis van uitgebleven rechtsherstel.* Amsterdam.

Molen, S. van der 1939: *Populair Maleis.* Deventer.

Molen, S. van der 1945: *Populair Maleis. Uitgebreid met Maleis voor militairen.* Deventer.

Monnikendam, V. 1995: *Moeder Dao, de Schildpadgelijkende.* Documentary.

Montero de Guzman, M. 1952: *The Indonesian Question before the Security Council 1946–1949.* Montana State University, https://scholarworks.umt.edu/cgi/viewcontent.cgi?article=9680&context=etd.

Moor, J. A. de 1999: *Westerling's oorlog: Indonesië 1945–1950.* Amsterdam.

Moor, J. A. de 2011: *Generaal Spoor. Triomf en tragiek van een legercommandant.* Amsterdam.

Morriën, J. 1982: *Indonesië los van Holland. De CPN en PKI in hun strijd tegen het Nederlands kolonialisme.* Amsterdam.

Mrázek, R. 1994: *Sjahrir. Politics and Exile in Indonesia.* Ithaca, NY.

Mrázek, R. 2010: *A Certain Age: Colonial Jakarta through the Memories of its Intellectuals.* Durham, NC & London.

Multatuli 1955 (1860): *Max Havelaar of de koffieveilingen der Nederlandsche Handel-Maatschappij.* Amsterdam. English edition: *Max Havelaar: Or, the Coffee Auctions of the Dutch Trading Company* (trans. Ina Rilke & David McKay 2019). New York.

Naaijkens-Retel Helmrich, H. 2008: *Contractpensions. Djangan Loepah!* Documentary.

Naaijkens-Retel Helmrich, H. 2008: *Buitenkampers.* Documentary.

Naaijkens-Retel Helmrich, H. 2018: *Klanken van Oorsprong. Poekoel Teroes!* Documentary.

Nehru, J. 1970 (1958): *Jawaharlal Nehru's Speeches. Vol. 3 (March 1953–August 1957).* New Delhi.

Ngantoeng, H. 1947: *Impressies dari Linggadjati dan sekitarnja pada boelan Nopember 1946* (Impressions of Linggajati and surroundings in November 1946). Jakarta.

Nieuwenhuys, R. 1978: *Oost-Indische spiegel. Wat Nederlandse schrijvers en dichters over Indonesië hebben geschreven, vanaf de eerste jaren der Compagnie tot op heden.* Amsterdam.

Nieuwenhuys, R. 1988 (1959): *Tussen twee vaderlanden.* Amsterdam.

NIOD Institute for War, Holocaust and Genocide Studies et al. 2022: *Over de grens: Nederlands extreem geweld in de Indonesische onafhankelijkheidsoorlog, 1945–1949.* Amsterdam. English edition: *Beyond the Pale: Dutch Extreme Violence in the Indonesian War of Independence, 1945–1949.* Online summary: https://ind45-50.nl/sites/default/files/2022-02/Samenvatting%20onderzoeksresultaten%20ODGOI%20EN.pdf.

Ohler, N. 2015: *Der totale Rausch. Droge im Dritten Reich.* Cologne.

Oliver, L. 2019: *Prisoners of the Sumatra Railway: Narratives of History and Memory.* London.

Ong Hok Ham 1987: *Runtuhnya Hindia Belanda* (The Fall of the Netherlands East Indies). Jakarta.

Ooi, K. G. 2010: 'Calculated strategy or senseless murder? Mass killings in Japanese-occupied South and West Kalimantan.' In P. Post, W. H. Frederick, I. Heidebrink & S. Sato (eds.), *The Encyclopedia of Indonesia in the Pacific War.* Leiden & Boston, 212–17.

Ooms, A. 2010: 'Prisoners of war put to work on the Thailand–Burma railway.' In P. Post, W. H. Frederick, I. Heidebrink & S. Sato (eds.), *The Encyclopedia of Indonesia in the Pacific War.* Leiden & Boston, 179–84.

Oostindie, G. 2006: *De parels en de kroon. Het koningshuis en de koloniën.* Amsterdam.

Oostindie, G. 2015: *Soldaat in Indonesië 1945–1950. Getuigenissen van een oorlog aan de verkeerde kant van de geschiedenis.* Amsterdam.

Padmodiwiryo, S. 2016: *Revolution in the City of Heroes: A Memoir of the Battle that Sparked Indonesia's National Revolution.* Singapore.

Pagani, L., D. J. Lawson, E. Jagoda et al. 2016: 'Genomic analyses inform on migration events during the peopling of Eurasia.' *Nature,* 21 September 2016.

Paranjpe, V. V. 2004: 'Panchsheel: the untold story.' *Hindustan Times,* 26 June 2004.

Parker, J. 2006: 'Cold War II: the Eisenhower administration, the Bandung Conference, and the reperiodization of the postwar era.' *Diplomatic History* 30, 5, 867–92.

Paterson, L. 2017: *Hitler's Grey Wolves: U-Boats in the Indian Ocean.* New York.

Patterson, R. E. 1998: *United States–Indonesian Relations, 1945–1949: Negative Consequences of Early American Cold War Policy.* Richmond, VA.

Perhimpoenan Indonesia 1933: *25 jaren Perhimpoenan Indonesia.* n.p.

Perhimpunan Indonesia 1945: Duitsland is verslagen! Leve de vrijheid! *Indonesia* (unnumbered issue), May 1945.

Perron, E. du 1943: *Scheepsjournaal van Arthur Ducroo.* Amsterdam.

Perthus, M. 1976: *Henk Sneevliet. Revolutionair-socialist in Europa en Azië.* Nijmegen.

Petrus Blumberger, J. T. 1929: *Le communisme aux Indes néerlandaises.* Paris.

Petrus Blumberger, J. T. 1931: *De nationalistische beweging in Nederlandsch-Indië.* Haarlem.

Philips, A. 2016: 'Beyond Bandung: the 1955 Asian–African Conference and its legacies for international order.' *Australian Journal of International Affairs* 70, 4.

Pisani, E. 2014: *Indonesia Etc.: Exploring the Improbable Nation.* London.

Pitman, T. & A. Stafford 2009: 'Transatlanticism and tricontinentalism.' *Journal of Transatlantic Studies* 7, 3, 197–207.

Poelgeest, L. van 1999: *Japanse besognes. Nederland en Japan 1945–1975.* The Hague.

Poeze, H. 1976: *Tan Malaka. Strijder voor Indonesië's vrijheid. Levensloop van 1897 tot 1945.* The Hague.

Poeze, H. A. 1982: *Politiek-politioneele overzichten van Nederlandsch-Indië. Bronnenpublikatie. Deel 1: 1927–1928.* The Hague.

Poeze, H. A. 1986: *In het land van de overheerser. 1. Indonesiërs in Nederland 1600–1950.* Dordrecht.

Poeze, H. A. 2006: 'The road to hell: the construction of a railway line in West Java during the Japanese occupation.' In P. H. Kratoska (ed.), *Asian Labor in the Wartime Japanese Empire.* Singapore, 152–78.

Poeze, H. A. 2007: *Verguisd en vergeten. Tan Malaka, de linkse beweging en de Indonesische Revolutie, 1945–1949.* Leiden.

Poeze, H. & H. Schulte Nordholt (eds.) 1995: *De roep om Merdeka: Indonesische vrijheidlievende teksten uit de twintigste eeuw.* Amsterdam & The Hague.

Poll, W. van de 1947: *Kerels van de daad. Onze oorlogsvrijwilligers in Malakka en Indië.* The Hague.

Post, P. & E. Touwen-Bouwsma (eds.) 1997: *Japan, Indonesia and the War: Myths and Realities.* Leiden.

Post, P., W. H. Frederick, I. Heidebrink & S. Sato (eds.) 2010: *The Encyclopedia of Indonesia in the Pacific War.* Leiden & Boston.

Post, P. & M. L. Thio 2019: *The Kwee Family of Ciledug: Family, Status and Modernity in Colonial Java.* Volendam.

Poukens, J. 2018: 'Cultivateurs et commerçants'. *Huishoudelijke productie, consumptie en de industrious revolution in het hertogdom Brabant (1680–1800).* Antwerp.

POW Research Network n.d.: *Sunken Japanese Ships with the Allied POWs in Transit.* www.powresearch.jp/en/archive/ship/index.html, consulted on 8 January 2020.

Pramoedya Ananta Toer 1988: *De pionier.* Amsterdam.

Pramoedya Ananta Toer, Koesalah Soebagyo Toer & Ediati Kamil 1999–2014: *Kronik Revolusi Indonesia* (5 vols). Jakarta.

Prashad, V. 2007: *The Darker Nations: A People's History of the Third World.* New York & London.

Pratomo, D. 1940: 'Economische belangen der verschillende mogendheden in Indonesia.' *Soeara Roepi* v, 5.

Pratomo, D. (1996): 'Einde van een nachtmerrie.' In M. Verseput, N. Planjer, M. J. de Loos & R. Schutrup (eds.), *Nationaal Dachau Monument.* n.p., 16–17.

Présence Africaine 1956: *Actes du Premièr congrès international des écrivains et artistes noirs.* Paris-Sorbonne, 19–22 September.

Princen, P. 1995: *Een kwestie van kiezen.* The Hague.

Purwanto, B. 1992: *From Dusun to the Market: Native Rubber Cultivation in southern Sumatra, 1890–1940.* London.

Purwanto, E. A. 2004: *Ups and Downs in Rural Javanese Industry: The Dynamics of Work and Life of Small-Scale Garment Manufacturers and their Families.* Amsterdam.

Queuille, P. 1965: *Histoire de l'Afro-Asiatisme jusqu'à Bandung.* Paris.

Raben, R. (ed.) 1999: *Beelden van de Japanse bezetting van Indonesië. Persoonlijke getuigenissen en publieke beeldvorming in Indonesië, Japan en Nederland.* Zwolle & Amsterdam.

Raben, R. 2006: 'Indonesian *rōmusha* and coolies under naval administration: the Eastern archipelago, 1942–45.' In P. H. Kratoska (ed.), *Asian Labor in the Wartime Japanese Empire.* Singapore, 197–212.

Ray, C. 2006: 'The marriage that sent the West into a panic.' *New African,* 448.

Rebling, E. 1989: *Die Tanzkunst Indonesiens.* Wilhelmshaven.

Reid, A. 1974: 'Marxist attitudes to social revolution, 1946–1948.' *Review of Indonesian and Malaysian Affairs,* 8, 1, 45–56.

Reid, A. 1974: *The Indonesian National Revolution 1945–1950.* Hawthorn.

Reid, A. 2011: *To Nation by Revolution: Indonesia in the 20th Century.* Singapore.

Reinsma, R. 1980: 'De cultuurprocenten in de praktijk en in de ogen der tijdgenoten.' In C. Fasseur (ed.), *Geld en geweten. Een bundel opstellen over anderhalve eeuw Nederlands bestuur in de Indonesische archipel, deel I: 19e eeuw.* The Hague, 59–90.

Renders, H. 2004: *Gevaarlijk drukwerk. Een vrije uitgeverij in oorlogstijd.* Amsterdam.

Rey, M. 2014: ' "Fighting colonialism" versus "non-alignment": two Arab points of view on the Bandung conference.' In N. Mišković, H. Fischer & N. Boškovska (eds.), *The Non-Aligned Movement and the Cold War: Delhi–Bandung–Belgrade.* London & New York, 163–83.

Ricklefs, M. C. 2001: *A History of Modern Indonesia since c. 1200.* Stanford, CA.

Ricklefs, M. C. 2012: *Islamisation and its Opponents in Java: A Political, Social, Cultural and Religious History, c. 1930 to the Present.* Singapore.

Rinkes, D. A., N. van Zalinge & J. W. de Roever 1925: *Het Indische Boek der Zee.* Weltevreden.

Rinzema-Admiraal, W. 2009: *Romusha van Java. Het laatste front 1942–1945.* Bedum.

Roadnight, A. 2002a: 'Sleeping with the enemy: Britain, Japanese troops and the Netherlands East Indies, 1945–1946.' *History. The Journal of the Historical Association,* 87, 286, 245–68.

Roadnight, A. 2002b: *United States Policy towards Indonesia in the Truman and Eisenhower Years.* Basingstoke & New York.

Roberts, B. R. & K. Foulcher (eds.) 2016: *Indonesian Notebook: A Sourcebook on Richard Wright and the Bandung Conference.* Durham, NC.

Robinson, C. 1983: *Black Marxism: The Making of Black Radical Tradition.* London.

Robinson, G. B. 2018: *The Killing Season: A History of the Indonesian Massacres, 1965–66.* Princeton, NJ.

Rodriguez, B. 2006: ' "Long live Third World unity! Long live internationalism": Huey P. Newton's revolutionary intercommunalism.' *Souls,* 8, 3, 119–41.

Rogan, E. 2010: *De Arabieren. Een geschiedenis.* Amsterdam.

Romein, J. 1956: *De eeuw van Azië. Opkomst, ontwikkeling en overwinning van het modern-Aziatisch nationalisme.* Leiden.

Rooy, P. de 2014: *Ons stipje op de waereldkaart. De politieke cultuur van modern Nederland.* Amsterdam.

Rose, M. 2010 (1987): *Indonesia Free: A Political Biography of Mohammed Hatta.* Jakarta & Kuala Lumpur.

Ruijter, A. 2017: *Naar Indonesië en weer terug. Transport van een expeditieleger (1945–1951).* Leiden.

Rutgers, S. J. & A. Huber. 1937: *Indonesië.* Amsterdam.

Salim, I. F. M. 1980: *Vijftien jaar Boven-Digoel. Concentratiekamp in Nieuw-Guinea, bakermat van de Indonesische onafhankelijkheid.* Hengelo.

Sand, D. 2009: *United States and Britain in Diego Garcia: The Future of a Controversial Base.* New York.

Sartono Kartodirdjo 1966: *The Peasants' Revolt of Banten in 1888: Its Conditions, Course and Sequel: A Case Study of Social Movements in Indonesia.* The Hague.

Sartono Kartodirdjo 1987: *Pengantar Sejarah Indonesia Baru. Jilid 1. 1500–1900. Dari Emporium sampai Imperium.* Jakarta.

Sartono Kartodirdjo 1993: *Pengantar Sejarah Indonesia Baru: Jilid 2. Dari kolonialisme sampai nasionalisme.* Jakarta.

Sato, S. 1994: *War, Nationalism and Peasants: Java under the Japanese Occupation 1942–1945.* New York.

Sato, S. 1997: 'The pangreh praja in Java under Japanese military rule.' In P. Post & E. Touwen-Bouwsma (eds.), *Japan, Indonesia and the War: Myths and Realities.* Leiden, 64–86.

Sato, S. 2006: ' "Economic soldiers" in Java: Indonesian laborers mobilized for agricultural projects.' In P. H. Kratoska (ed.), *Asian Labor in the Wartime Japanese Empire.* Singapore, 129–51.

Sato, S. 2010a: 'Administrative changes in Java.' In P. Post, W. H. Frederick, I. Heidebrink & S. Sato (eds.), *The Encyclopedia of Indonesia in the Pacific War.* Leiden & Boston, 92–102.

Sato, S. 2010b: 'The PETA.' In P. Post, W. H. Frederick, I. Heidebrink & S. Sato (eds.), *The Encyclopedia of Indonesia in the Pacific War.* Leiden & Boston, 132–46.

Scagliola, S. I. 2002: *Last van de oorlog. De Nederlandse oorlogsmisdaden en hun verwerking.* Amsterdam.

Schmidt-Colinet, A., A. Staufer & K. Al-As'ad 2000: *Die Textilien aus Palmyra: neue und alte Funde.* Mainz am Rhein.

Schneider, J. 2019: *In de hel van Birma. Ooggetuigenverslag uit de kampen langs de Birma-Siam Spoorlijn 1942–1945.* Amsterdam.

Schneider, J. & G. van de Westelaken 2018: *De bus uit Dachau. Achttien Nederlanders en hun weg terug uit Nacht und Nebel.* Amsterdam.

Schöttli, J. 2012: *Vision and Strategy in Indian Politics: Jawaharlal Nehru's Policy Choices and the Designing of Political Institutions*. London & New York.

Schoonheyt, L. J. A. 1936: *Boven-Digoel*. Batavia.

Schulte Nordholt, H. 2016: *Een geschiedenis van Zuidoost-Azië*. Amsterdam.

Schulze, F. 2015: *Kleine Geschichte Indonesiens*. München.

Scott, J. C. 2013: *Against the Grain: A Deep History of the Earliest States*. New Haven, CT.

Sena Utama, W. 2016: 'From Brussels to Bogor: contacts, networks and the history of the Bandung Conference 1955.' *Journal of Indonesian Social Sciences and Humanities* 6, 1, 11–24.

Shibata, Y. 1997: 'The monetary policy in the Netherlands East Indies under the Japanese administration.' In P. Post & E. Touwen-Bouwsma (eds.), *Japan, Indonesia and the War. Myths and Realities*. Leiden, 177–202.

Shiraishi, T. 1986: *Islam and Communism: An Illumination of the People's Movement in Java, 1912–1926*. Ithaca, NY.

Shiraishi, T. 1990: *An Age in Motion: Popular Radicalism in Java, 1912–1926*. Ithaca, NY.

Sjahrir, S. 1946: *Onze strijd*. Amsterdam.

Sjahrir, S. 1987 (1945): *Indonesische overpeinzingen*. Amsterdam.

Slauerhoff, J. J. 1930: *Schuim en asch*. Bussum.

Smilde, H. P. 2017: *Helden van toen. The Tielman Brothers en de Nederlandse rock-'n-roll 1957–1967*. Amsterdam.

Smit, C. 1959: *Het akkoord van Linggadjati. Uit het dagboek van prof. dr. ir. W. Schermerhorn*. Amsterdam & Brussels.

Smit, C. 1970: *Het dagboek van Schermerhorn. Geheim verslag van prof. dr. ir. W. Schermerhorn als voorzitter der commissie-generaal voor Nederlands-Indië, 20 september 1946–7 oktober 1947*. Utrecht.

Smith, E. D. 2007: *Valour: A History of the Gurkhas*. Chalford, Stroud.

Smith, M. 2020: 'How unique are British attitudes to empire?' YouGov, 22 March 2020, http://yougov.co.uk.

Snodgrass, K. 1928: *Copra and Coconut Oil*. Stanford, CA.

Soebardi, S. 1983: 'Kartosuwiryo and the Darul Islam rebellion in Indonesia.' *Journal of Southeast Asian Studies* 14, 109–33.

Soekarno 1950: *From Sabang to Merauke! President Soekarno's speech on the occasion of the Fifth Anniversary of Indonesia's Independence, 17th August 1950*. Jakarta.

Soemitro Djojohadikoesoemo 1943: *Het volkscredietwezen in de depressie*. Haarlem.

Soper, T. 1965: 'The EEC and aid to Africa.' *International Affairs* 41, 3, 463–77.

Speerstra, H. 2015: *Op klompen door de dessa. Indiëgangers vertellen*. Amsterdam & Antwerp.

Spoor-Dijkema, M. 2004: *Achteraf kakelen de kippen. Herinneringen aan Generaal KNIL S. H. Spoor*. Amsterdam.

Stalin, Joseph. 2017. *Leninism: Volume One.* London.

Stevens, H. 2015: *Gepeperd verleden. Indonesië en Nederland sinds 1600.* Amsterdam & Nijmegen.

Stevens, H. & E. Wils 2020: 'Revolusi: het Rijksmuseum maakt een wending.' *Indies Tijdschrift* 1, 18–20.

Stolwijk, A. 2016: *Atjeh. Het verhaal van de bloedigste strijd uit de Nederlandse koloniale geschiedenis.* Amsterdam.

Stutje, J. W. 2008: 'Ferdinand Domela Nieuwenhuis (1846–1919), Revolte en melancholie: romantiek in Domela's kritiek op de moderniteit.' *Tijdschrift voor Sociale en Economische Geschiedenis* 5, 3–28.

Stutje, K. 2013: 'Indonesian identities abroad: international engagement of colonial students in the Netherlands, 1908–1931.' *BMGN – Low Countries Historical Review*, 128, 151–72.

Stutje, K. 2015a: 'The complex world of the Chung Hwa Hui: international engagements of Chinese Indonesian *peranakan* students in the Netherlands, 1918–1931.' *Bijdragen tot de Taal-, Land- en Volkenkunde* 171, 516–42.

Stutje, K. 2015b: 'To maintain an independent course: interwar Indonesian nationalism and international communism on a Dutch–European stage.' *Dutch Crossing: Journal of Low Countries Studies* 39, 204–20.

Stutje, K. 2016: *Behind the Banner of Unity: Nationalism and Anticolonialism among Indonesian Students in Europe, 1917–1931.* Amsterdam.

Suhardjono, V. & J. Allan 2019: *Witnessing Affandi.* Jakarta.

Suherdjoko 2014: 'Sarekat Islam building gets restoration.' *The Jakarta Post*, 4 October 2014.

Sukarno, D. 2010: *Devi sukaruno kaisōki* (Memoirs of Ratna Sari Dewi Sukarno). Tokyo.

Susanto, M. 2014: *Bung Karno: Kolektor & Patron Seni Rupa Indonesia.* Yogyakarta.

Susanto, M. 2018: *Sukarno's Favourite Painters.* Jakarta.

Suwondo, P. S. & A. Nurdin 2016: *The PETA Army and the Struggle for Indonesia's Independence.* Bogor.

Swift, A. 2010: *The Road to Madiun: The Indonesian Communist Uprising of 1948.* Jakarta & Kuala Lumpur.

Swirc, M. 2019: ' "Gelijke monniken, gelijke kepie gaat niet op". De Verjaringswet als doofpot.' *De Groene Amsterdammer*, 25 September 2019.

Tambo, O. 1983: *Speech to the Non-Aligned Summit of Heads of State and Government,* New Delhi, India, 7–11 March 1983. ANC Digital Archives/Oliver Tambo Papers/Documents/Processed/Box0017/FLR0137/ITEM007, https://ancarchive.org.

Tan, S .S. & A. Acharya (eds.) 2008: *Bandung Revisited: The Legacy of the 1955 Asian–African Conference for International Order.* Singapore.

Tanesia, A. 2012: *The Stories of Affandi.* Yogyakarta.

Tarling, N. 1992: ' "Ah-Ah": Britain and the Bandung Conference of 1955.' *Journal of Southeast Asian Studies* 23, 1, 74–111.

Tarling, N. 1998: *Britain, Southeast Asia and the Onset of the Cold War, 1945–1950.* Cambridge.

Tas, S. 1973: *De onderontwikkelde vrijheid. Indonesia toen en nu.* Baarn.

Taselaar, A. 1998: *De Nederlandse koloniale lobby. Ondernemers en de Indische politiek, 1914–1940.* Leiden.

Taufik, A. 2009 (1971): *Schools and Politics: The Kaum Muda Movement in West-Sumatra (1927–1933).* Jakarta & Kuala Lumpur.

Taufik, A. 2009: *Indonesia: Towards Democracy.* Singapore.

Taylor, A. M. 1960: *Indonesian Independence and the United Nations.* London.

Taylor Atkins, E. 2017: *A History of Popular Culture in Japan: From the Seventeenth Century to the Present.* London & Oxford.

Termorshuizen, G. 2001: *Journalisten en heethoofden. Een geschiedenis van de Indisch-Nederlandse pers 1744–1905.* Amsterdam & Leiden.

Termorshuizen, G. 2011: *Realisten en reactionairen. Een geschiedenis van de Indisch-Nederlandse pers 1905–1942.* Amsterdam & Leiden.

Toland, J. 2003 (1970): *The Rising Sun: The Decline and Fall of the Japanese Empire, 1936–1945.* New York.

Utami, N. A. 2016: 'Revisiting the Bandung Conference: berbeda sejak dalam pikiran.' *Inter-Asia Cultural Studies*, 17, 1, 140–47.

Utrecht, E. 1991: *Twee zijden van een waterscheiding. Herinnering aan Indonesië voor en na de onafhankelijkheid.* Amsterdam.

Vaillant, R. E. F. 1987: 'Van "Banzai" tot "Bersiap": Indische Nederlanders in ontreddering, 1942–1946.' *Basis* 18, 7/8, 23–7.

Valk, G. 2017: *Vechten voor vijand en vaderland. SS'ers in Nederlands-Indië en Korea.* Amsterdam.

Van Lierde, J. 1963: *La pensée politique de Patrice Lumumba.* Brussels.

Vanden Berghe, Y. 2008: *De Koude Oorlog. Een nieuwe geschiedenis (1917–1991).* Leuven.

Vanvugt, E. 2016: *Roofstaat. Wat iedere Nederlander moet weten.* Amsterdam.

Veer, C. van 't 2020: *De kolonie op drift. De representatie en constructie van koloniale identiteit in fictie over de zeereis tussen Nederland en Nederlands-Indië.* Hilversum.

Velden, D. van 1977: *De Japanse interneringskampen voor burgers gedurende de Tweede Wereldoorlog.* Franeker.

Velmans, L. 2003: *Terug naar de River Kwai. Herinneringen aan de Tweede Wereldoorlog.* Zutphen.

Verstraaten, T. 2008: *Ooggetuige. Krijgsgevangen in Indië en Japan 1942–1945.* Zutphen.

Veur, P. W. van der 1984: 'De Indo-Europeaan: probleem en uitdaging.' In H. Baudet & I. J. Brugmans (eds.), *Balans van beleid. Terugblik op de laatste halve eeuw van Nederlands-Indië.* Assen, 81–101.

Vine, D. 2009: *Island of Shame: The Secret History of the US Military Base on Diego Garcia*. Princeton, NJ.

Vlekke, B. H. M. 1947: *Geschiedenis van den Indischen archipel. Van het begin der beschaving tot het doorbreken der nationale revolutie*. Roermond & Maaseik.

Vlies, T. van der 2019: *Echoing Events: The Perpetuation of National Narratives in English and Dutch History Textbooks, 1920–2010*. Rotterdam.

Vltchek, A. 2012: *Indonesia: Archipelago of Fear*. London.

Voerman, J. 1950: *Gedenkboek van de Utrechtsche Indologen Vereeniging 1925–1950*. n.p.

Volder, E. de & A. de Brouwer 2019: *The Impact of Litigation in relation to Systematic and Large-Scale Atrocities Committed by the Dutch Military Forces in the 'Dutch East Indies' between 1945–1949*. Amsterdam.

Vosse, L. B. 2001: *Dai Nippon: Catalogue of the Postage Stamps of The Netherlands East Indies under Japanese Occupation 1942–1945*. n.p.

Vuyk, B. 1941: *Het laatste huis van de wereld*. Utrecht.

Vuyk, B. 1989: *Kampdagboeken*. Utrecht & Antwerp.

Wahid, A. 2013: *From Revenue Farming to State Monopoly: The Political Economy of Taxation in Colonial Indonesia, Java c. 1816–1942*. Utrecht.

Wahid, A. 2020: ' "*Madat makan orang*"; opium eats people: opium addiction as a public health issue in late colonial Java, 1900–1940.' *Journal of Southeast Asian Studies*, 51, 1–2, 25–48.

Wal, S. L. van der 1968: *Herinneringen van Jhr. Mr. B. C. de Jonge*. Groningen.

Wal, S. L. van der 1979: *Officiële bescheiden betreffende de Nederlands-Indonesische betrekkingen, 1945–1950. Deel 8: 21 maart–20 mei 1947*. The Hague.

War History Office of the National Defense College of Japan 2015 (1967): *The Invasion of the Dutch East Indies* (ed. and trans. Willem Remmelink). Leiden.

Ward, O. G. 1988: *De militaire luchtvaart van het KNIL 1945–1950*. Houten.

Weijzen, A. 2015: *De Indië-weigeraars. Vergeten slachtoffers van een koloniale oorlog*. Utrecht.

Wertheim, W. F. 1969: *Indonesian Society in Transition: A Study of Social Change*. The Hague.

Wertheim, W. & H. Wertheim-Gijse Weenink 1991: *Vier wendingen in ons bestaan. Indië verloren, Indonesië geboren*. Breda.

Wesseling, H. L. 2003: *Europa's koloniale eeuw. De koloniale rijken in de negentiende eeuw, 1815–1919*. Amsterdam.

Westerling, R. P. P. 1982: *De eenling*. Amsterdam.

Wietsma, A. & S. Scagliola 2013: *Liefde in tijden van oorlog. Onze jongens en hun verzwegen kinderen in de Oost*. Amsterdam.

Witte, R. 1998: *De Indische radio-omroep. Overheidsbeleid en ontwikkeling 1923–1942*. Hilversum.

Woodard, K. 2019: 'Citizen Malcolm X blueprint for black liberation: coming of age with Rod Bush on race, class and citizenship in the Bandung era.' *Human Architecture: Journal of the Sociology of Self-Knowledge* 12, 1, 171–83.

Wright, R. 2008 (1956): *The Color Curtain*. In R. Wright, *Black Power: Three Books from Exile*. New York.

Wright-Nooth, G. 1995: *Prisoner of the Turnip Heads: Horror, Hunger and Heroics, Hong Kong, 1941–1945*. Barnsley.

X, M. 1963: 'Message to the grass roots.' Northern Negro Grass Roots Leadership Conference, King Solomon Baptist Church, Detroit, 10 November 1963. https://www.rev.com/blog/transcripts/message-to-the-grassroots-speech-transcript-malcolm-x

Young, R. J. C. 2005: 'Postcolonialism: from Bandung to the Tricontinental.' *Historein*, 5.

Zahorka, H. 2010: 'Die Geschichte des deutschen Soldatenfriedhofs Arca Domas in Indonesien', https://nanopdf.com/download/deutsche-botschaft-jakarta-seitebildergaleriecikopo_pdf.

Zaougui, C. E. 2016: *Dictators. Een Arabische geschiedenis*. Kalmthout.

Zed, M. 2001: 'Menggugat Tirani Sejarah Nasional' (Addressing the Tyranny of National History). 7th National History Conference, Jakarta, 28–31 October.

Zee, S. van der 2016: *Harer majesteits loyaalste onderdaan. François van 't Sant 1883–1966*. Amsterdam.

Zegveld, L. & A. Vossenberg 2019: *Memorie van antwoord tevens houdende incidenteel appel Monji c.s. en Yaseman*. Amsterdam.

Zinn, H. 2007: *Geschiedenis van het Amerikaanse volk*. Antwerp.

Zolov, E. 2016: 'La Tricontinental y el mensaje del Che Guevara: encrucijadas de una nueva izquierda.' *Palimpsesto* 9, 6, 1–13.

Zwaan, J. 1980: *Nederlands-Indië 1940–1946. I. Gouvernementeel intermezzo 1940–1942*. The Hague.

Zwart, H. 1995: *Er waren er die niet gingen. Vijftien eeuwen straf voor Indonesië-weigeraars*. Amsterdam.

Zweers, L. 1995: *Agressi II: Operatie Kraai. De vergeten beelden van de tweede politionele actie*. The Hague.

Zweers, L. 2002: *De crash van de Franeker. Een Amerikaanse persreis naar Nederlands-Indië in 1949*. Amsterdam.

Zweers, L. 2013: *De gecensureerde oorlog. Militairen versus media in Nederlands-Indië 1945–1949*. Zutphen.

Zwierstra, R. P. 2009: 'Van vaccinateur tot academisch opgeleide arts. Over de geschiedenis van het medisch onderwijs in Nederlands-Indië.' *Tijdschrift voor Medisch Onderwijs* 28, 81–9.

Zwitzer, H. L. & C. A. Heshusius 1977: *Het Koninklijk Nederlands-Indisch Leger 1830–1950*. The Hague.

Zwitzer, H. L. 1982: 'Verwikkelingen rondom de capitulatie van het Koninklijk Nederlandsch-Indisch Leger in maart 1942.' In G. Teitler (ed.), *De val van Nederlands-Indië*. Dieren, 92–112.

Notes

Chapter 1: The VOC Mentality

1. Wright 2008 (1956): 598.
2. Conte 1965.
3. *De Standaard*, 11 August 2017.
4. Arta & Margi 2014.
5. Curaming 2003 and 2005; Zed 2001.
6. Van Doorn 1995; Van den Doel 2000; Jansen van Galen 2013; De Jong 2015; Scagliola 2002; Oostindie 2015; Vanvugt 2016; Hagen 2018; Limpach 2016.
7. Smith 2020.
8. Leakey & Slikkerveer 1993.
9. Pagani et al. 2016.
10. Denham 2010.
11. Bellwood 2005: 128–45; Fuller & Qin 2009.
12. Grataloup 2019: 35.
13. Rinkes et al. 1925: 15–18.
14. Michel Munoz 2006: 39–43; Schulze 2015: 16.
15. Hellwig & Tagliacozzo 2009: 19.
16. Michel Munoz 2006: 123; Hannigan 2015: 26.
17. Acri 2015.
18. Schulte Nordholt 2017: 79.
19. Geertz 1960.
20. Mets & Van der Herberg 2014; Poeze 1986: 307–9.
21. Interview Djajeng Pratomo, Callantsoog, 11 August 2016 and 27 January 2017.
22. Freedman 2008: 26.
23. McLaughlin 2018.
24. McLaughlin 2016.
25. Schmidt-Colinet et al. 2000.
26. Frankopan 2015: 17; Schulte Nordholt 2017: 36.
27. Freedman 2008: 216–19.
28. Freedman 2008: 127.
29. Freedman 2008: 115.
30. Schulte Nordholt 2017: 90.
31. Freedman 2008: 208–10.
32. Vanvugt 2016: 84.
33. Jacobs 1991: 38, 47, 63.
34. Van Goor 2000: 61.
35. Bertrand 2011: 180–88.
36. Bertrand 2011: 185.

Chapter 2: Assembling the Jigsaw Puzzle

1. Lubis 1990: 193.
2. Hanna & Alwi 1990: 145.
3. Interview Sultan Husain Syah, Tidore, 6 July 2016 (translation Syahrita Chairaty).
4. Abeyasekere 1989: 7–12.
5. Baay 2015.
6. Rutgers & Huber 1937: 47.
7. Hagen 2018: 485.
8. Emmer 2019: 291.
9. Abeyasekere 1989: 19–20.
10. Baay 2015: 54.
11. Hagen 2018: 117.
12. Vanvugt 2016: 136.
13. Freedman 2008: 219.
14. Poukens 2018: 261–314.
15. Van der Brug 1997.
16. Burgers 2010: 57.
17. Margolin & Markovits 2015: 376–86.
18. Vanvugt 2016: 386.
19. Vlekke 1947: 288.
20. Eymeret 1972: 160.
21. Eymeret 1972: 166.
22. Hannigan 2015.
23. Oostindie 2006: 23.
24. Stolwijk 2016; Hagen 2018: 310–38.
25. Hellwig & Tagliacozzo 2009: 123.
26. Interview Djajeng Pratomo, Callantsoog, 11 August 2016 and 27 January 2017.
27. Private archives Marjati Pratomo, Callantsoog, 'De eeuw van Raden Mas Djajeng Pratomo', 22 February 2014.
28. Kossmann 2001, I: 140.
29. Reinsma 1980: 61.
30. Burgers 2010: 86; De Rooy 2014: 68.
31. Fasseur 1980a: 40.
32. Fasseur 1980b: 127.
33. Fasseur 1980a: 32.
34. Zwierstra 2009.
35. Departement van Economische Zaken 1936: 11.
36. Multatuli 1955 (1860).
37. Termorshuizen 2001: 74–5.
38. Van Hoëvell 1980 (1860): 175.
39. Nieuwenhuis 1978: 136–54.
40. Stutje 2008: 8.
41. Boomgaard 2003.
42. Lindblad 1985: 242.
43. Wahid 2013.
44. Hagen 2018: 292–5.
45. Zwitzer & Heshusius 1977.
46. Van Goor 1985; Wesseling 2003.
47. Lanzing 2005: 120.
48. James 2011.
49. Interview Nanny Kooymans, Ede, 29 May 2016.
50. Interview Dutch veteran, [n.p.], 29 May 2016.
51. Vanvugt 2016: 495–6.
52. Hagen 2018: 374–6.
53. Interview Tjokorda Gde Agung Samara Wicaksana,

Klungkung, 2 December 2017
(interpreter Nyoman Sutoyo).

54. Burgers 2010: 121.

55. Burgers 2010: 100.

56. Claver 2015.

57. Sartono Kartodirdjo
1966.

58. De Jong 1984: 197.

59. De Jong 1984: 198.

60. Interview Harjo Utomo,
Prambanan Klaten, Central
Java, 19 June 2016 (interpreter
Ruth Hastuti Ningsih).

61. Breman 1987: 43–5.

62. Van den Doel 1996: 121.

63. Breman 1987: 45.

64. Lindblad 1989.

65. Bee 1982: 1–7.

66. Campo 1985.

67. Dröge 2015.

68. Poeze 1982: xxiii.

69. Schulte Nordholt
2017: 202.

70. Van Dijk et al. 2010.

71. Bronkhorst & Wils 1996:
50–67.

Chapter 3: The Colonial Steamship

1. *De Indische Courant*, 26
October 1936.

2. Daum 1894: 59, 61.

3. Van den Berg 1995–1996: 43.

4. Jacobs 1913: 398.

5. *Het Nieuws van den Dag voor
Nederlandsch-Indië*, 20 October
1936.

6. *Bataviaasch Nieuwsblad*,
22 October 1936.

7. Groeneboer 1993: 476.

8. Bloem 2020: 6.

9. Nieuwenhuys 1988 (1959): 29.

10. Van der Veur 1984: 91.

11. *Het Nieuws van den Dag voor
Nederlandsch-Indië*, 23 & 24
October 1936.

12. Keppy 2019; Bloem 2020.

13. Nieuwenhuys 1978: 385.

14. Van der Veur 1984: 93.

15. Departement van
Economische Zaken 1936: 15.

16. *Indische Courant*, 2 December
1936.

17. *Bataviaasch Nieuwsblad*, 24 July
1937; Bik 2006.

18. *Algemeen Brabants Dagblad*,
21 October 1936.

19. *Het Nieuws van den Dag voor
Nederlandsch-Indië*, 24 October
1936.

20. *Bataviaasch Nieuwsblad*,
22 October 1936.

21. KPM 1941: 209.

22. Fasseur 1994.

23. *Bataviaasch Nieuwsblad*, 30
March 1937.

24. Van den Berg 1995–1996:
48–9.

25. Post & Thio 2019: 159.

26. *De Sumatra Post*, 22 April 1933.

27. *De Sumatra Post*, 28 November
    1929.

28. *Het Nieuws van den Dag voor
    Nederlandsch-Indië*, 7 March
    1934.

29. *Soerabaiasch Handelsblad*,
    20 June 1935.

30. *De Sumatra Post*, 22 April 1933;
    *Het Nieuws van den Dag voor
    Nederlandsch-Indië*, 7 March
    1934.

31. Du Perron 1943: 362–9.

32. De Jong 1984: 184.

33. Vaillant 1987: 23–7.

34. Burgers 2010: 134.

35. Kahin 1952: 35.

36. Lindblad 2002: 141–2.

37. Booth 1988: 334.

38. Kahin 1952: 36.

39. Groeneboer 1993: 470.

40. Departement van Economische
    Zaken 1936: 122–5.

41. Houben 1996: 110–19.

42. G. W. Overdijkink 1946: *Het
    Indonesische probleem. De feiten.*
    The Hague.

43. Slauerhoff 1930: 128–9.

44. Van den Berg 1995–1996: 49.

45. *Nieuws van den Dag voor
    Nederlandsch-Indië*, 11
    November 1931.

46. *Soerabaiasch Handelsblad*,
    31 May 1929.

47. Groeneboer 1993: 237.

48. Poeze 1982: xxiii; De Jong
    1998: 527.

49. Interview Hamad Puag Abi,
    Lekopadis, 17 and
    19 February 2016 (interpreter
    Muhammad 'Iwan' Ridwan
    Alamuddin).

50. Departement van
    Economische Zaken 1936: 30.

51. Poeze 1982: xvii.

52. Interview Chisma
    Widjajasoekma, Jakarta,
    20 January 2016.

53. Interview Sri Lestari,
    Yogyakarta, 25 August 2015
    (interpreter Eny Guntari).

54. Interview Soeparti 'Oma
    [Grandma] Ted' Soetedjo,
    Jakarta, 20 January 2016.

55. Interview Sukotjo
    Tjokroatmodjo, Jakarta,
    22 January 2016.

56. Interview Benny Bastian,
    Jakarta, 21 January 2016
    (interpreter Rizky Wahyu
    Perdana).

57. Interview Dorothea 'Dora'
    Tatiwibowo, Jakarta,
    20 January 2016.

58. Poeze 1982: xxiv.

59. Interview Anna Christina
    Gunawan Bosschieter,
    Jakarta, 29 February 2016.

60. Interview Constance Amy
    'Ca' Pattiradjawane, Jakarta,
    22 January 2016.

61. Interview Hans Dornseiffer,
    The Hague, 16 November 2015.

62. Interview Nanny Kooymans, Ede, 29 May 2016.
63. Interview Leonard 'Nora' van Dorp, Jakarta, 21 January 2016.
64. Interview Joty ter Kulve, Wassenaar, 15 July 2015.
65. Interview Johannes Soewondo, Sambirejo, Pare, 25 June 2016 (interpreter Anton Novenanto); cf. Utrecht 1991: 21.
66. Departement van Economische Zaken 1936: 20–22, 98–9.
67. Interview Purbo S. Suwondo, Jakarta, 1 July 2016.
68. Interview Francisca 'Cisca' Pattipilohy, Amsterdam, 8 October 2017.
69. Van den Berg 1984: 92; Van den Berg 1995–1996.
70. Poeze 1986: 14.
71. Jaquet 1987: 61.
72. Poeze 1986: 66.
73. Poeze 1982: xxvi.
74. Hesselink 2011; Keyser 2016.
75. Keyser 2016: 35; Balai Poestaka 1948: 21.
76. Private archives Marjati Pratomo, Callantsoog, File Dr Pratomo.
77. Hendraparya 2011: 74.
78. Interview Djajeng Pratomo, Callantsoog, 11 August 2016 and 27 January 2017.
79. Burgers 2010: 154–5, Anderson 1991: 116–23.
80. Morriën 1982: 24.
81. Keppy 2004: 93.
82. Poeze & Schulte Nordholt 1995: 26; Pramoedya Ananta Toer 1988: 112.
83. Poeze & Schulte Nordholt 1995: 34–8.

Chapter 4: 'Flies Spoiling the Chemist's Ointment'

1. Adams 1965: 38, 40.
2. Shiraishi 1986.
3. Interview Harjo Utomo, Prambanan Klaten, 19 June 2016 (interpreter Ruth Hastuti Ningsih).
4. Korver 1982: 53.
5. Ricklefs 2001: 212–16.
6. Korver 1982: 194.
7. Korver 1982: 197.
8. Korver 1982: 194, 207.
9. Cribb & Kahin 2004: 433.
10. Korver 1982: 35.
11. Korver 1982: 84.
12. Ricklefs 2001: 211.
13. Termorshuizen 2011: 146.
14. *Nieuws van den Dag*, 3 July 1915.
15. De Jong 1984: 227.
16. *Java-Bode*, 19 August 1913; cf. *De Expres*, 20 January 1914.
17. Korver 1982: 24.

18. De Jong 1984: 231.
19. Kwantes 1975: 104.
20. Suherdjoko 2014.
21. Ingleson 1986: 74–87.
22. Perthus 1976: 137–8.
23. Interview Rukardi Achmadi, Semarang, 18 June 2016.
24. Interview Sumaun Utomo, Semarang, 21 June 2016 (interpreter Muhammad Fahmi Masdah).
25. Hagen 2018: 530.
26. Tas 1973: 111; Vlekke 1947: 436.
27. Coolhaas 1985: 27.
28. Poeze 1976: 281, 332–4.
29. Gonggrijp 1928: 214–30.
30. De Graaff 1997: 214.
31. Wertheim 1969: 99–105.
32. Hagen 2018: 566–74.
33. Ingleson 1986: 239.
34. Poeze 1976: 281–2.
35. Morriën 1982: 9–20.
36. Kwantes 1978: 484, 489.
37. Poeze 1976.
38. Departement van Economische Zaken 1936: 8.
39. Termorshuizen 2011: 201–72.
40. Salim 1980: 30–1.
41. Kwantes 1978: 201.
42. Morriën 1982.
43. Hagen 2018: 577.
44. Morriën 1982: 62; Poeze & Schulte Nordholt 1995: 50.
45. De Graaff 1997: 216.
46. Salim 1980: 107.
47. Salim 1980: 108.
48. Morriën 1982: 63.
49. Schoonheyt 1936: 263.
50. Petrus Blumberger 1929: 132–3.
51. Schoonheyt 1936: 185.
52. Interview Dharyanto Tito Wardani, Tasikmalaya, West Java, 27 June 2016; cf. Jo 2017.
53. Salim 1980: 26.
54. Salim 1980: 151.
55. Schoonheyt 1936: 103.
56. Salim 1980: 296–305.
57. Sjahrir 1987: 119–21.
58. Salim 1980: 302–03.
59. Salim 1980: 289.
60. Rose 2010: 47–8.
61. Elson 2008: 1–4.
62. Poeze 1986: 176.
63. Poeze 1986: 176.
64. Petrus Blumberger 1987 (1931): 189.
65. Petrus Blumberger 1987 (1931): 188.
66. Interview Djajeng Pratomo, Callantsoog, 11 August 2016 and 27 January 2017.
67. Stutje 2013, 2015b.
68. Van Leeuwen 1985: 7.
69. Interview Ananda B. Kusuma, Jakarta, 14 June 2016 (interpreter Sadiah Boonstra).
70. Sena Utama 2016.
71. Stutje 2016.
72. Tas 1973: 121.

73. Duijs 1928: 41–2.
74. Colijn 1980 (1928): 98, 100.
75. Hatta 1980 (1928): 102, 107, 108.
76. Mahin 2006.
77. Poeze 1982: xxii.
78. De Graaff 1997: 231.
79. Interview Jefferson Dau, Jakarta, 15 June 2016.
80. Interview Eli Kansil, Rijswijk, 2 March 2019.
81. Interview Djadju Wiratakoeroman, Tasikmalaya, West Java, 27 June 2016 (interpreter Muhammad Fahmi Masdah).
82. Interview Francisca 'Cisca' Pattipilohy, Amsterdam, 8 October 2017 and 18 February 2018.
83. Anderson 1991.
84. Kwantes 1981: 177.
85. Interview Ananda B. Kusuma, Jakarta, 14 June 2016 (interpreter Sadiah Boonstra).
86. Interview Herawati Diah, Jakarta, 14 July 2016.
87. Diah 2005: 12.
88. Ingleson 1979: 62, 88, 98.
89. Mrázek 1994: 72.
90. Drooglever 1980: 31.
91. Snodgrass 1928: 7–9.
92. Snodgrass 1928: 51.
93. Soemitro 1943: 24.
94. Soemitro 1943: 74–5.
95. Soemitro 1943: 10.
96. Interview Badora, Malenge, 2 and 3 February 2016 (interpreters Jeanne Lefèvre and Ating Solihin).
97. Vlekke 1947: 442.
98. Taselaar 1998: 367.
99. Schulte Nordholt 2017: 235–6.
100. Dick 2002: 155–6.
101. Purwanto 2004: 95.
102. De Jong 1998: 513.
103. Locher-Scholten 2000.
104. Furnivall 1944: 430–33.
105. Ingleson 1979: 159–62.
106. Ingleson 1979: 171.
107. Burgers 2010: 221.
108. Van Helsdingen 1946: 173.
109. Blom 1975: 265.
110. Blom 1975: 55.
111. Blom 1975: 44–64.
112. Termorshuizen 2011: 347.
113. Termorshuizen 2011: 388.
114. Termorshuizen 2011: 259–60.
115. Termorshuizen 2011: 388.
116. Blom 1975: 63.
117. Keppy 2013: 47.
118. Termorshuizen 2011: 258.
119. Taselaar 1998: 508–12.
120. *Deli Courant*, 4 April 1936; cf. Van der Wal 1968: 351.
121. Ingleson 1979: 76.

Chapter 5: Silence

1. *De Indische Courant*, 13 September 1937.

2. Bijlmer 1986: 159.

3. *Java Post*, 28 April 2014.

4. Campen 2002: 35–6, 41.

5. Schulte Nordholt 2016: 237.

6. Departement van Economische Zaken 1936: 20–22.

7. Departement van Economische Zaken 1936: 2–30.

8. Interview Brigitte Melissande Sparwer-Abrams and Marianne Constance Pulle, The Hague, 8 April 2018.

9. Baudet & Brugmans 1984: 358.

10. Van der Molen 1939.

11. Wertheim & Wertheim-Gijse Weenink 1991: 80–81.

12. Vuyk 1941: 55.

13. Interview Mulyono Darsono, Yogyakarta, Kotagede, 24 August 2015 (interpreter Jeanne Lefèvre).

14. Sjahrir 1987: 101–02.

15. Sjahrir 1987: 123.

16. De Jong 1984: 367.

17. Blom 1975: 246.

18. Zwaan 1980: 39.

19. Sjahrir 1987 (1945): 123.

20. De Jong 1984: 370.

21. De Graaff 1997: 226.

22. Sjahrir 1987: 175.

23. Sjahrir 1987: 115.

24. Sjahrir 1987: 127.

25. Sjahrir 1987: 179.

26. Gouka 2001.

27. Interview Francisca 'Cisca' Pattipilohy, Amsterdam, 8 October 2017.

28. Interview Iskandar Hadisaputra, Jakarta, 1 July 2016 (interpreter Muhammad Fahmi Masdah).

29. Interview Sukotjo Tjokroatmodjo, Jakarta, 22 January 2016.

30. Sjahrir 1987: 103, 163, 171.

31. MacMillan 2001: 315–30.

32. Ars 2000: 29.

33. Sjahrir 1987: 84–5.

34. Sjahrir 1987: 105–06.

35. Sjahrir 1987: 117.

36. Sjahrir 1987: 183.

37. De Jong 1984: 432–5.

38. De Jong 1984: 435.

39. Bootsma 1986: 109–11.

40. Interview Sumaun Utomo, Semarang, 21 June 2016 (interpreter Muhammad Fahmi Masdah).

41. Morriën 1982: 94–5.

42. Private archives Marjati Pratomo, Callantsoog, correspondence Stijntje Gret–Djajeng Pratomo.

43. Mets & Van der Herberg 2014.

44. Interview Djajeng Pratomo, Callantsoog, 11 August 2016 and 27 January 2017.

45. *Indonesia* (jubilee issue) 1938: 170, 189, 197.

46. Kossmann 2002: 141–5.
47. Fasseur 2014: 283.
48. Van den Berge 2014: 172–5.
49. Poeze 1986: 297–302.
50. *Soeara Roepi*, October 1940, V, 6.
51. Ibnoe Hadjar 1941.
52. De Graaff 1997: 243.
53. Pratomo 1940.
54. Interview Soerachman Koesoemorachmanto, Jakarta, 15 January 2016.
55. Burgers 2010: 249–52.
56. De Jong 1984: 571–6.
57. Boer 1997: 69.
58. Van den Berge 2014: 153–9.
59. Interview Fred Lanzing, Amsterdam, 28 July 2015 and 2 March 2019.
60. Van der Horst 2007: 128.
61. Keppy 2019: 32–9.
62. De Jong 1984: 642.
63. De Jong 1984: 611–15; Quispel 1945: 17–27.
64. Zwaan 1980: 55–65.
65. Interview Hans Dornseiffer, The Hague, 16 November 2015.
66. Interview Dick Buchel van Steenbergen, Waalre, 17 May 2017.
67. Interview Felix Jans, The Hague, 4 June 2017.
68. Interview Sukotjo Tjokroatmodjo, Jakarta, 22 January 2016.

69. Van Kaam 1977: 38–60.
70. Interview Julius Nunumete, Hative Besar, Ambon, 4 July 2016 (interpreter Paulien Joel-Perera).
71. De Jong 1984: 631, 612–13.
72. Interview Sumaun Utomo, Semarang, 18 June 2016 (interpreter Rukardi Achmadi).
73. Interview Sumarsono, Jakarta, 11 July 2016 (interpreter Bonnie Triyana, translation Syahrita Chairaty and Elisabeth Ida Mulyani).
74. Interview Purbo S. Suwondo, Jakarta, 1 July 2016.
75. Dower 1986.
76. De Jong 1984: 614.
77. Interview Nippon Sembiring, Medan, 29 November 2017 (interpreter Adam Damrin Nainggolan).

Chapter 6: The Pincer and the Oil Fields

1. Levy 1982: 25.
2. Levy 1982: 32–3, 40.
3. Michelin 2019: 211, 227.
4. Michelin 2019: 217.
5. Levy 1982: 33.
6. Michelin 2019: 225–33; Toland 2003: 85–6.
7. Fasseur 2014: 274.

8. Fasseur 2014: 275.

9. De Jong 1984: 739.

10. De Jong 1984: 733.

11. Zahorka 2010.

12. War History Office 2015: 183.

13. Zwaan 1980: 147.

14. Interview Hendrik Pauned Muntuuntu, Manado, 25 January 2016.

15. Interview Ventje Memah by Jeanne Lefèvre, Manado, 25 January 2016.

16. Interview Indonesian veteran, Manado, 25 January 2016 (interpreter Frans B. Maramis).

17. Boer 1997: 118.

18. Boer 1997: 119.

19. Wesseling 2003: 340.

20. Brugmans et al. 1960: 98.

21. Boer 1997: 128.

22. Boer 1997: 112.

23. Boer 1997: 55, 134–6.

24. War History Office 2015: 329.

25. Interview Ton Berlee, Leiden, 7 April 2018.

26. Boer 1997: 112.

27. www.youtube.com, 14 November 2019.

28. Doedens & Mulder 2017: 83.

29. Anten 2011.

30. Interview Julius Nunumete, Hative Besar, Ambon, 4 July 2016 (interpreter Paulien Joel-Perera).

31. Doedens & Mulder 2017: 131.

32. Elias 1988: 19.

33. Interview Bhagta Sing Pun, Pokhara, Nepal, 13 April 2017 (interpreters Karna Bahadur Thapa and Narbahadur Pun).

34. Doedens & Mulder 2017: 152.

35. Toland 2003: 282.

36. Boer 2006: 181.

37. Doedens & Mulder 2017: 150, 153.

38. Doedens & Mulder 2017: 160.

39. Interview Felix Jans, The Hague, 4 June 2017.

40. War History Office 2015: 567.

41. Boer 2006: 201, 211.

42. Interview Seiji Natsui, Niigata, 28 March 2017 (interpreter Yukiko Mitsuoka).

43. Interview Ton Berlee, Leiden, 7 April 2018.

44. Beets 1981: 194.

45. Interview Hans Dornseiffer, The Hague, 16 November 2015.

46. Interview Sumarsono, Jakarta, 11 July 2016 (interpreter Bonnie Triyana, translation Syahrita Chairaty and Elisabeth Ida Mulyani).

47. Interview Iskandar Hadisaputra, Jakarta, 21 January 2016 (interpreter Rizky Wahyu Perdana).

48. Beets 1981: 203–04.
49. Frost & Balasingamchow 2016: 242.
50. Interview Dick Buchel van Steenbergen, Waalre, 17 May 2017.
51. Brugmans et al. 1960: 115.
52. De Jong 1984: 1002.
53. De Jong 1984: 1046–8.
54. Lanzing 2014, p. 23; Taylor Atkins 2017: 171.
55. McCormack & Nelson 1993: 71.
56. Lanzing 2014: 23.
57. Brugmans et al. 1960: 233–4.
58. Doedens & Mulder 2017: 180.
59. De Jong 1984: 970.
60. Mark 2018: 137.
61. Brugmans et al. 1960: 124.
62. Interview Purbo S. Suwondo, Jakarta, 1 July 2016.
63. Interview Iskandar Hadisaputra, Jakarta, 21 January 2016 (interpreter Rizky Wahyu Perdana) and 1 July 2016 (interpreter Muhammad Fahmi Masdah).
64. Interview Sukotjo Tjokroatmodjo, Jakarta, 22 January 2016.
65. War History Office 2015: 531–3.
66. Zwitzer 1982: 109.
67. Witte 1998: 153.
68. War History Office 2015: 7.
69. War History Office 2015: 588.
70. War History Office 2015: 568.
71. War History Office 2015: 569.
72. Doedens & Mulder 2017: 190.
73. De Jong 1984: 1084; Immerzeel & Van Esch 1993: 223–6.
74. Interview Sumarsono, Jakarta, 11 July 2016 (interpreter Bonnie Triyana, translation Syahrita Chairaty and Elisabeth Ida Mulyani).
75. Interview Ton Berlee, Leiden, 7 April 2018.
76. Interview Felix Jans, The Hague, 4 June 2017.
77. Interview Hans Dornseiffer, The Hague, 16 November 2015.
78. Interview Dick Buchel van Steenbergen, Waalre, 17 May 2017.

Chapter 7: The Land of the Rising Pressure

1. Mark 2011: 240–1.
2. Kwantes 1982: 637.
3. Kwantes 1982: 645.
4. Kwantes 1982: 639.
5. Interview Djajeng Pratomo, Callantsoog, 11 August 2016, 27 January 2017.
6. Poeze 1986: 297–330.

7. Keppy 2019.

8. *De Bevrijding*, 26 May 1945, 7.

9. *De Bevrijding*, 2 June 1945, 22.

10. *De Bevrijding*, 26 May 1945, 8.

11. *De Bevrijding*, 2 June 1945, 21.

12. De Jong 1986: 440; Keppy 2019: 191.

13. Van der Heijden 2001: 280–81.

14. Keppy 2019: 182–7, 210–11.

15. Poeze 1986: 302.

16. Keppy 2019: 101–02; 120–39.

17. Hazelhoff 2003: 8–9.

18. Private archives Pratomo, Callantsoog: File Resistance Indonesians, 'Indonesiërs in bezet Nederland ook in ondergronds verzet', unpublished typescript, Djajeng Pratomo 1985.

19. Keppy 2019: 10.

20. Private archives Pratomo, Callantsoog: File Resistance Indonesians.

21. Private archives Pratomo, Callantsoog: hand-written memo Djajeng Pratomo.

22. Private archives Pratomo, Callantsoog: File Resistance Indonesians, 'Verzetsrapport', unpublished typescript Gondho Pratomo.

23. Private archives Pratomo, Callantsoog: File Resistance Indonesians, letter Gondho Pratomo to Stichting 1940–1945, 5 May 1974.

24. Private archives Pratomo, Callantsoog: File Resistance Indonesians, 'Verzetsrapport', unpublished typescript Gondho Pratomo.

25. Rebling 1989.

26. Poeze 1986: 308.

27. Brugmans et al. 1960: 138.

28. Kemperman 2002: 618.

29. Kurasawa 1987.

30. Kurasawa 1987.

31. Mark 2018: 58.

32. Vosse 2001: 9–20.

33. Shibata 1997: 178–81.

34. Interview Chisma Widjajasoekma, Jakarta, 20 January 2016.

35. Sato 2010a: 95–7.

36. Interview Go Gien Tjwan, Amstelveen, 9 October 2017.

37. Interview Benny Bastian, Jakarta, 21 January 2016 (interpreter Rizky Wahyu Perdana).

38. Interview Yusuf Surya, née Tjong King Poek, Medan, 29 November 2017 (interpreter Adam Damrin Nainggolan).

39. Interview Leonard 'Noortje' van Dorp, Jakarta, 21 January 2016.

40. Interview W. F. G. L. 'Bol' Kerrebijn, Arnhem, 9 October 2017.

41. Interview Nanny Kooymans, Ede, 29 May 2016.

42. Mark 2018: 89.
43. Mark 2018: 94.
44. De Jong 1985: 1022.
45. Brugmans et al. 1960: 169–70.
46. Benda 1956; 1958: 110–19, 135.
47. Kurasawa 2010: 324.
48. Interview Toenggoel Siagian, Jakarta, 19 January 2016.
49. Kurasawa 2010: 322.
50. Interview Soerachman Koesoemorachmanto, Jakarta, 15 January 2016.
51. Interview Liza Yusuf, Jakarta, 20 January 2016.
52. Interview Francisca 'Cisca' Pattipilohy, Amsterdam, 8 October 2017.
53. Interview Indonesian veteran, Manado, 25 January 2016 (interpreter Frans B. Maramis).
54. Interview Chisma Widjajasoekma, Jakarta, 20 January 2016.
55. Interview Anna Christina Gunawan, Jakarta, 29 February 2016.
56. Interview Madjodin, Benteng, Pulau Togean, 31 January 2016 (interpreter Lani Jaelani).
57. Interview Leonard 'Noortje' van Dorp, Jakarta, 21 January 2016.
58. Interview Soeparti 'Oma [Grandma] Ted' Soetedjo, Jakarta, 20 January 2016.
59. Hamer-Monod de Froideville 2013: 62.
60. Hamer-Monod de Froideville 2013: 59–81.
61. Ars 2000: 27.
62. *Kyodo News*, 6 December 2019.
63. Ars 2000: 145.
64. Hicks 1997: 143–4.
65. Borch 2017: 149.
66. Hicks 1997: 143–4.
67. Ars 2000: 145.
68. Janssen 2010: 51, 81–2.
69. Janssen 2010: 14.
70. Ars 2000: 148.
71. Hamer-Monod de Froideville 2013: 34.
72. Adams 1965: 164.
73. Ars 2000: 107.
74. Lanzing 2007: 41.
75. Brugmans et al. 1960: 131.
76. Kemperman 2010: 165.
77. Interview Kartika Affandi, Yogyakarta, Pakem, 16 June 2016.
78. Interview Joty ter Kulve, Wassenaar, 15 July 2015 and 27 January 2017.
79. Berg, Candotti & Touw 2014: 4.
80. Chagoll 1986; 1988.
81. Bosman 2005.
82. Interview Lydia Chagoll, Overijse, 27 January 2018.
83. Van Velden 1977: 252–3.

84. Interview Soerachman
    Koesoemorachmanto,
    Jakarta, 15 January 2016.
85. Velmans 2003: 87–8.
86. Ooms 2010: 180.
87. McCormack & Nelson 1993:
    75; Hovinga 2006: 214.
88. McCormack & Nelson
    1993: 27.
89. McCormack & Nelson 1993:
    19.
90. Veltmans 2003: 82.
91. Beets 1981: 241–54.
92. Ooms 2010: 180.
93. Hovinga 2006: 214.
94. Interview Brigitte Melissande
    Sparwer-Abrams, The
    Hague, 8 April 2018.
95. Hicks 1997: 133.
96. Interview Ton Berlee, Leiden,
    7 April 2018.
97. POW Research Network n.d.
98. Interview Felix Jans, The
    Hague, 4 June 2017.
99. Interview Kazuko Kawai,
    Tsuga, Chiba, 30 March 2017
    (interpreter Yukiko
    Mitsuoka).
100. Poeze 2006: 165.
101. Oliver 2019: 26, 30.
102. Hovinga 2006: 214.
103. Heidebrink 2010.
104. Interview Nanny Kooymans,
    Ede, 29 May 2016.
105. Post et al. 2010: 21–4.
106. Heidebrink 2010: 178.

107. Interview Dick Buchel van
    Steenbergen, Waalre, 17 May
    2017.
108. Kuijper et al. 1990: 60.
109. Verstraaten 2008: 157–99.
110. Interview Hans Dornseiffer,
    The Hague, 16 November
    2015.

Chapter 8: 'Colonialism is Colonialism'

1. Giebels 1999: 287.
2. Mark 2018, p. 203; Adams
   1965, p. 210.
3. Jansen 1988: 85.
4. Jansen 1988: 87, 85.
5. Mark 2018: 242.
6. Burgers 2010: 304.
7. Kemperman 2002: 255.
8. Dahm 1964: 206, 219.
9. Giebels 1999: 291.
10. Susanto 2014: 2018.
11. Interview Kartika Affandi,
    Yogyakarta, Pakem, 16 June
    2016.
12. Tanesia 2012: 25, 79.
13. Anwar 1993: 163.
14. Anwar 1993: 88–9.
15. Anwar 1993: 6–7.
16. Mark 2018: 209.
17. Interview Soemardi Mau
    Sudarmo, Surakarta, 22 July
    2016 (interpreter Muhammad
    Fahmi Masdah).

18. Post et al. 2010: 505; Maekawa 2006: 189–91.
19. Interview Johannes Soewondo, Sambirejo, Pare, 25 June 2016 (interpreter Anton Novenanto).
20. Interview Soenaryo Goenwiradi, Yogyakarta, 24 August 2015 (interpreter Eny Guntari).
21. Interview Soejono Sastrodiwirjo, Malang, 26 June 2016 (interpreter Muhammad Fahmi Masdah).
22. Interview Sumaun Utomo, Semarang, 21 June 2016 (interpreter Muhammad Fahmi Masdah).
23. Sato 2010b: 134–5.
24. Anderson 1991; Cribb 2010b: 108.
25. Interview Purbo S. Suwondo, Jakarta, 1 July 2016.
26. Adams 1965: 181.
27. Benda 1958: 150, 155–7.
28. Mark 2018: 250.
29. Mark 2018: 235.
30. Interview Johannes Soewondo, Sambirejo, Pare, 25 June 2016 (interpreter Anton Novenanto).
31. Kemperman 2002: 313.
32. Jansen 1988: 257, 259, 262, 268; Van der Eng 2008: 14.
33. Kemperman 2002: 324.
34. Kemperman 2002: 351, 371.
35. D'Arrigo et al. 2006.
36. Sato 1997: 65.
37. Van der Eng 2008: 24.
38. Kurasawa-Inomata 1997: 114.
39. Kurasawa-Inomata 1997: 113.
40. De Jong 1985: 537, 550.
41. Van der Eng 2008: 26, 37, 78–9.
42. Van Velden 1977: 519–44.
43. Van Velden 1977: 347–8.
44. Interview Joty ter Kulve, Wassenaar, 15 July 2015 and 27 January 2017.
45. Interview Tineke & Berthe Korvinus, Heemstede, 11 August 2016.
46. Interview Marianne Constance Pulle, The Hague, 8 April 2018.
47. Interview Lydia Chagoll, Overijse, 27 January 2018; Chagoll 1986: 130.
48. Interview Brigitte Melissande Sparwer-Abrams, The Hague, 8 April 2018.
49. Ars 2000: 102.
50. Hamer-Monod de Froideville 2013: 167.
51. Borch 2017: 139.
52. Interview Tineke & Berthe Korvinus, Heemstede, 11 August 2016.
53. Interview Joty ter Kulve, Wassenaar, 15 July 2015 and 27 January 2017.
54. Kousbroek 2005: 515–22.

55. Lanzing 2007.

56. Lanzing 2007: 53, 47–8.

57. Interview Fred Lanzing, Amsterdam, 28 July 2015 and 2 March 2019.

58. Borch 2017: 81–6; Lengkeek 2010: 123–37.

59. Interview Lydia Chagoll, Overijse, 27 January 2018; Chagoll 1986: 130.

60. Interview Brigitte Melissande Sparwer-Abrams, The Hague, 8 April 2018.

61. Vuyk 1989: 104.

62. De Jong 1985: 537–52.

63. Kemperman 2002: 324.

64. Interview Antonius Sumartono, Jakarta, 20 January 2016.

65. Interview Dorothea 'Dora' Tatiwibowo, Jakarta, 20 January 2016.

66. Interview Soenaryo Goenwiradi, Yogyakarta, 24 August 2015 (interpreter Eny Guntari).

67. Interview Benny Bastian, Jakarta, 21 January 2016 (interpreter Rizky Wahyu Perdana).

68. Interview Eman Sulaiman, Cengkareng, 21 January 2016 (interpreter Rizky Wahyu Perdana).

69. Interview Soenaryo Goenwiradi, Yogyakarta, 24 August 2015 (interpreter Eny Guntari).

70. Interview Soerachman Koesoemorachmanto, Jakarta, 15 January 2016.

71. Interview Madjodin, Benteng, Pulau Togean, 31 January 2016 (interpreter Lani Jaelani).

72. Interview Yomi Rauf, Daruba, Morotai, 8 July 2016 (interpreter Yulia Sahupala).

73. Interview W. F. G. L. 'Bol' Kerrebijn, Arnhem, 9 October 2017.

74. Interview Eman Sulaiman, Cengkareng, 21 January 2016 (interpreter Rizky Wahyu Perdana).

75. Interview Ca Pattiradjawane by Jeanne Lefèvre, Jakarta, 30 October 2015.

76. Interview Anna Christina Gunawan, Jakarta, 29 February 2016.

77. Interview Benny Bastian, Jakarta, 21 January 2016 (interpreter Rizky Wahyu Perdana).

78. Interview Lan Chong Fin by Jeanne Lefèvre, Jakarta, 30 October 2015.

79. Interview Suhut by Jeanne Lefèvre, Jakarta, 5 November 2015.

80. Interview Iskandar Hadisaputra, Jakarta, 1 July

2016 (interpreter Muhammad Fahmi Masdah).

81. Kemperman 2002: 321.
82. Jansen 1988: 296.
83. Kemperman 2002: 354.
84. Diah 2005: 55.
85. Interview Soerachman Koesoemorachmanto, Jakarta, 15 January 2016.
86. Interview Soenaryo Goenwiradi, Yogyakarta, 24 August 2015 (interpreter Eny Guntari).
87. Interview Mulyono Darsono, Yogyakarta, 24 August 2015 (interpreter Jeanne Lefèvre).
88. Interview Suhut by Jeanne Lefèvre, Jakarta, 5 November 2015.
89. Interview Madjodin, Benteng, Pulau Togean, 31 January 2016 (interpreter Lani Jaelani).
90. Interview Badora, Malenge, 2 and 3 February 2016 (interpreters Jeanne Lefèvre and Ating Solihin).
91. Interview Iskandar Hadisaputra, Jakarta, 1 July 2016 (interpreter Muhammad Fahmi Masdah).
92. Sintha Melati in Lucas 1986: 200.
93. Interview Eman Sulaiman, Cengkareng, 21 January 2016 (interpreter Rizky Wahyu Perdana).
94. Sintha Melati in Lucas 1986: 204.
95. Interview Soenaryo Goenwiradi, Yogyakarta, 24 August 2015 (interpreter Eny Guntari).
96. Interview Eman Sulaiman, Cengkareng, 21 January 2016 (interpreter Rizky Wahyu Perdana).
97. Interview Mendila Pongpadati, Rantepao, 8 February 2016 (interpreter John Massolo).
98. Interview Iskandar Hadisaputra, Jakarta, 1 July 2016 (interpreter Muhammad Fahmi Masdah).
99. Interview Iskandar Hadisaputra, Jakarta, 21 January 2016 (interpreter Rizky Wahyu Perdana).
100. Interview Nanny Kooymans, Ede, 29 May 2016.
101. Lucas 1986: 200.
102. Kemperman 2002: 316.
103. Interview Soenaryo Goenwiradi, Yogyakarta, 24 August 2015 (interpreter Eny Guntari).
104. Kemperman 2002: 354.
105. Kemperman 2002: 375.
106. Lucas 1986: 200.
107. Interview Bu Law Ennie by Jeanne Lefèvre, Jakarta, 2 November 2015.

108. Interview Toenggoel Siagian, Jakarta, 19 January 2016.

109. De Jong 1985: 557.

110. De Jong 1985: 559; Dower 1986: 296.

111. Kossmann 2002: 205.

112. Van der Eng 2008.

113. Sato 2006.

114. McCormack & Nelson 1993: 67; Hovinga 2006: 214; Rinzema-Admiraal 2009: 22, 114.

115. Raben 2006: 209.

116. Interview Eman Sulaiman, Cengkareng, 21 January 2016 (interpreter Rizky Wahyu Perdana).

117. Interview Julius Nunumete, Hative Besar, Ambon, 4 July 2016 (interpreter Paulien Joel-Perera).

118. Interview Madjodin, Benteng, Pulau Togean, 31 January 2016 (interpreter Lani Jaelani).

119. Interview Indonesian veteran, Manado, 25 January 2016 (interpreter Frans B. Maramis).

120. Interview Zulfikar by Jeanne Lefèvre, Jakarta, 4 November 2015.

121. Koetsier-Korvinus 1995: 83.

122. Interview Corrie by Jeanne Lefèvre, Jakarta, 29 October 2015.

123. Rinzema-Admiraal 2009: 62.

124. Raben 2006: 214.

125. Hovinga 2006: 214–15.

126. Adams 1967: 221.

127. Giebels 2001: 183.

128. Giebels 2001: 360; Sukarno 2010.

129. Interview Dewi Soekarno, Tokyo, 6 April 2017.

130. Tanesia 2012: 81.

131. Interview Kartika Affandi, Yogyakarta, Pakem, 16 June 2016.

132. Interview Madjodin, Benteng, Pulau Togean, 31 January 2016 (interpreter Lani Jaelani).

133. Post et al. 2010: 590–91.

134. Post et al. 2010: 516.

135. Post et al. 2010: 419–21.

136. Interview Donisius Unawekla, Ambon, 4 July 2016 (interpreter Paulien Joel-Perera).

137. Koetsier-Korvinus 1995: 51.

138. Lucas 1986: 144, 148, 155.

139. Lucas 1986: 163.

140. Lucas 1986: 181.

141. Adams 1965: 191.

142. Dahm 1964: 261–4, 270–75.

143. Lucas 1986: 198.

144. Ooi 2010: 212–17.

145. Interview Jefferson Dau, Jakarta, 15 June 2016.

146. Mahin 2006: 77–81.

147. Lucas 1986: 213–16.

Chapter 9: 'Our Blood is Forever Warm'

1. Burgers 2010: 321–3.
2. Toland 2003: 483.
3. Interview Nobuteru Iwabuchi, Ichinoseki, Iwate, 5 April 2017 (interpreter Yukiko Mitsuoka).
4. De Jong 1986: 353.
5. De Jong 1986: 293–4.
6. De Jong 1986: 294.
7. Interview Nobuteru Iwabuchi, Ichinoseki, Iwate, 5 April 2017 (interpreter Yukiko Mitsuoka).
8. Wright-Nooth 1995: 238.
9. Van Poelgeest 1999: 88, 102–03; Borch 2017.
10. Interview Nobuyoshi Fukatsu, Tokyo, 2 and 4 April 2017 (interpreter Yukiko Mitsuoka, translation Geert van Bremen).
11. Interview Hatijah 'Yaya' Rauf and Yomi Rauf, Daruba, Morotai, 8 July 2016 (interpreter Yulia Sahupala).
12. Interview Naji Baronga, Dehegila, Morotai, 8 July 2016 (interpreter Yulia Sahupala).
13. Interview Hatijah Kira, Morotai, 8 July 2016 (interpreter Yulia Sahupala).
14. Interview Ryuichi Shiono, Tokyo, 4 April 2017 (interpreter Yukiko Mitsuoka, translation Geert van Bremen).
15. https://www.bbc.co.uk/history/ww2peopleswar/stories/27/a4138427.shtml
16. Geerken 2015; Paterson 2017.
17. Ohler 2015: 185–91.
18. Keimer 2019.
19. Interview Martin Müller by Marc Cappon, Overveen, 11–12 May 2014; Private archives Völker-Müller family, Overveen.
20. Hoornik 1972: 184, 173.
21. Pratomo 1996: 16.
22. Private archives Marjati Pratomo, Callantsoog.
23. Pratomo 1996: 17.
24. Private archives Marjati Pratomo, Callantsoog.
25. Interview Djajeng Pratomo, Callantsoog, 11 August 2016, 27 January 2017.
26. Anon. 1945.
27. *De Bevrijding*, 28 April 1945.
28. Perhimpunan Indonesia 1945.
29. Private archives Völker-Müller family, Overveen, email correspondence with Herwig Zahorka, 2001.
30. Interview Martin Müller by Marc Cappon, Overveen, 11–12 May 2014.

31. Kahin 1970: 114–15.
32. Schneider & Van de Westelaken 2018.
33. De Jong 1986: 441.
34. Van der Molen 1945: 70–71.
35. Interview Jan Langenberg, Zierikzee, 16 May 2016.
36. Interview Goderd van Heek, Velp, 28 May 2016.
37. Valk 2017: 20–24.
38. De Moor 2011: 152.
39. De Jong 1986: 167–276.
40. Lucas 1986: 183–4.
41. Post et al. 2010: 582.
42. Anderson 2006: 50–53.
43. De Jong 1985: 949; Hagen 2018: 642.
44. Chairil Anwar 1993: 75.
45. Interview Hans Dornseiffer, The Hague, 16 November 2015.
46. Interview Dick Buchel van Steenbergen, Waalre, 17 May 2017.
47. Dahm 1964: 277.
48. Interview Ryuichi Shiono, Tokyo, 4 April 2017 (interpreters Yukiko Mitsuoka and Geert van Bremen).
49. Interview Hans Dornseiffer, The Hague, 16 November 2015.
50. Interview Dick Buchel van Steenbergen, Waalre, 17 May 2017.
51. Private archives Marjati Pratomo, Callantsoog, correspondence Djajeng Pratomo-Stennie Gret, May–August 1945.
52. Mrázek 1994: 258–60.
53. Anderson 2006: 66–7.
54. Adams 1965: 209.
55. Interview Piet van Staveren, Assen, 7 October 2017.
56. Mrázek 1994: 265–6.
57. Anderson 2016: 83.
58. Anderson 2006: 80.

Chapter 10: 'Free! Of! Everything!'

1. Dower 1986: 296.
2. Figures calculated based on Wikipedia article 'World War II casualties'.
3. Suwondo & Nurdin 2016.
4. Interview Toernowo Hadiwidjojo, Semarang, 21 June 2016 (interpreter Muhammad Fahmi Masdah).
5. Interview Goderd van Heek, Velp, 28 May 2016.
6. Joustra 2009: 47.
7. De Jong 1986: 462.
8. Van den Berge 2014: 205.
9. Hovinga 2006: 216.
10. Interview Herawati Diah, Jakarta, 14 July 2016.
11. Diah 2005: 67–8.

12. Frederick 2010: 54.
13. De Jong 2015: 23.
14. Derksen & Tinbergen 1980: 234, 238.
15. Interview Djajeng Pratomo, Callantsoog, 11 August 2016, 27 January 2017.
16. Burgers 2010: 395.
17. Van der Eng 2008: 47.
18. Anderson 2006: 133.
19. Frederick 2010: 48–9.
20. De Jong 1986: 548, 555.
21. De Jong 1986: 556.
22. McMillan 2009: 67.
23. Burgers 2010: 393.
24. Kok, Somers & Zweers 2009: 22–3.
25. Tanesia 2012: 25, 83.
26. Interview Bu Law Ennie by Jeanne Lefèvre, Jakarta, 2 November 2015.
27. Interview Sumarsono with Bonnie Triyana, Jakarta, 11 July 2016 (translation Syahrita Chairaty and Elisabeth Ida Mulyani).
28. Interview Sumaun Utomo, Semarang, 21 June 2016 (interpreter Muhammad Fahmi Masdah).
29. Meelhuijsen 2000: 74 ff.
30. Padmodiwiryo 2016: 42.
31. De Jong 1986: 625.
32. Van den Berge 2014: 205.
33. Van Delden 2007: 127.
34. Interview Joty ter Kulve, Wassenaar, 15 July 2015 and 27 January 2017.
35. Interview Tineke & Berthe Korvinus, Heemstede, 11 August 2016.
36. Interview Ton Berlee, Leiden, 7 April 2018.
37. Interview Toenggoel Siagian, Jakarta, 19 January 2016.
38. Reid 1974: 2011.
39. Interview Nanny Kooymans, Ede, 29 May 2016.
40. Interview W. F. G. L. 'Bol' Kerrebijn, Arnhem, 9 October 2017.
41. NIOD 2022: xxx.
42. Interview Toenggoel Siagian, Jakarta, 19 January 2016.
43. Bussemaker 2005: 343.
44. Kemperman 2002: 251.
45. Interview Soerachman Koesoemorachmanto, Jakarta, 15 January 2016.
46. Interview Ahmad Muhadi, Plered, Segoroyoso, 22 August 2015 (interpreter Jeanne Lefèvre).
47. Interview Johannes Soewondo, Sambirejo, Pare, 25 June 2016 (interpreter Anton Novenanto).
48. Interview W. Sriyono, Jakarta, 15 June 2016 (translation Jeanne Lefèvre).

49. Interview Toto, Cikatomas, 28 June 2016 (translation Muhajir Salam).

50. Interview Soemardi Mau Sudarmo, Surakarta, 22 July 2016 (interpreter Muhammad Fahmi Masdah).

51. Interview Suradi Surokusumo, Jakarta, 18 January 2016.

52. Interview Toernowo Hadiwidjojo, Semarang, 21 June 2016 (interpreter Muhammad Fahmi Masdah).

53. Interview Sumaun Utomo, Semarang, 21 June 2016 (interpreter Muhammad Fahmi Masdah).

54. Interview Iskandar Hadisaputra, Jakarta, 21 January 2016 (interpreter Rizky Wahyu Perdana).

55. Interview Benny Bastian, Jakarta, 21 January 2016 (interpreter Rizky Wahyu Perdana).

56. Interview Go Gien Tjwan, Amstelveen, 9 October 2017.

57. Van Delden 2007: 79–81.

58. Frederick 2010: 54.

59. Interview Soemardi Mau Sudarmo, Surakarta, 22 July 2016 (interpreter Muhammad Fahmi Masdah).

60. Interview Soenaryo Goenwiradi, Yogyakarta, 24 August 2015 (interpreter Eny Guntari).

61. Interview W. Sriyono, Jakarta, 15 June 2016 (translation Jeanne Lefèvre).

62. Interview Ahmad Muhadi, Plered, Segoroyoso, 22 August 2015 (interpreter Jeanne Lefèvre).

63. Interview Johannes Soewondo, Sambirejo, Pare, 25 June 2016 (interpreter Anton Novenanto).

64. Interview Iskandar Hadisaputra, Jakarta, 1 July 2016 (interpreter Muhammad Fahmi Masdah).

65. Mark 2018: 277.

66. Padmodiwiryo 2016: 68.

67. Bussemaker 2005: 208.

68. Padmodiwiryo 2016: 64.

69. Padmodiwiryo 2016: 74.

70. Interview Sukotjo Tjokroatmodjo, Jakarta, 22 January 2016.

71. Interview Soemardi Mau Sudarmo, Surakarta, 22 July 2016 (interpreter Muhammad Fahmi Masdah).

72. Interview W. Sriyono, Jakarta, 15 June 2016 (translation Jeanne Lefèvre).

73. Van Delden 2007.

74. Interview Iskandar Hadisaputra, Jakarta, 1 July

2016 (interpreter Muhammad Fahmi Masdah).

75. Interview Huri Prasetyo, Semarang, 21 June 2016 (interpreter Muhammad Fahmi Masdah, translation Elisabeth Ida Mulyani).

76. Interview Toernowo Hadiwidjojo, Semarang, 21 June 2016 (interpreter Muhammad Fahmi Masdah).

77. Roadnight 2002a; Post et al. 2010: 587.

78. Interview Kazuko Kawai, Tsuga, Chiba, 30 March 2017 (interpreter Yukiko Mitsuoka).

79. Roadnight 2002a: 267.

80. Interview Yoshida Tomio, Agano, Niigata, 28 March 2017 (interpreter Yukiko Mitsuoka).

81. Buruma 2013: 128.

82. McMillan 2005: 35.

83. McMillan 2005: 36.

84. Padmodiwiryo 2016: 127.

85. McMillan 2005: 44.

86. Interview Sumaun Utomo, Semarang, 21 June 2016 (interpreter Muhammad Fahmi Masdah).

87. Bouman 2006: 379–80.

88. Interview Goderd van Heek, Velp, 28 May 2016.

Chapter 11: 'An Errand of Mercy'

1. Interview Kartika Affandi, Yogyakarta, Pakem, 16 June 2016.

2. Mrázek 1994: 301.

3. Rose 2010: 213.

4. Interview Toernowo Hadiwidjojo, Semarang, 21 June 2016 (interpreter Muhammad Fahmi Masdah).

5. Diah 2005: 82.

6. Budiardjo 1997.

7. Sjahrir 1946: 23.

8. Sjahrir 1946: 13–15.

9. Sjahrir 1946: 19.

10. Foster Collins 1950: 117–19.

11. Montero de Guzman 1952: 31.

12. Van Delden 2007: 124.

13. Smith 1997: 18.

14. Cross & Gurung 2007.

15. Bellamy 2011: xxv.

16. Cross 2007: 23.

17. Cross 2016a: 43–6.

18. Cross 2016b.

19. Cross 2016b.

20. Interview John P. Cross, Pokhara, 13 April 2017.

21. Interview Bhagta Sing Pun, Pokhara, 13 April 2017 (interpreters Karna Bahadur Thapa and Narbahadur Pun).

22. Interview Lal Bahadur Khatri, Pakawadi, Rogdi,

17 April 2017 (interpreter Krishna Hari Subedi).

23. Interview Purna Bahadur Gurung, Pokhara, 19 April 2017.

24. Interview Khamba Sing Bura, Gumchal, 24 April 2017 (interpreter Suresh Acharya).

25. Interview Hari Bahadur Chhetri, Ghokreswanra, Bhoteodar, 15 April 2017 (interpreter Ramchandra Subedi).

26. Van den Berge 2014: 203–04.

27. Interview Sop Bahadur Rana, Nayar, Narayanmatales, 22 April 2017 (interpreter Suresh Acharya).

28. Interview Tul Bahadur Thapa, Palung Chaurtole, Palung Mainadi, 22 April 2017 (interpreter Suresh Acharya).

29. Interview Hari Bahadur Chhetri, Ghokreswanra, Bhoteodar, 15 April 2017 (interpreter Ramchandra Subedi).

30. Interview Lal Bahadur Khatri, Pakawadi, Rogdi, 17 April 2017 (interpreter Krishna Hari Subedi).

31. Interview Purna Bahadur Chhetri, Butwal, 22 April 2017 (interpreter Suresh Acharya).

32. Van Velden 1977: 469.

33. Interview Khamba Sing Bura, Gumchal, 24 April 2017 (interpreter Suresh Acharya).

34. Bussemaker 2005: 339.

35. Interview Lal Bahadur Khatri, Pakawadi, Rogdi, 17 April 2017 (interpreter Krishna Hari Subedi).

36. Bussemaker 2005: 171.

37. Interview Indra Bahadur Thapa, Syangja, Humdi Bhanjhang, 18 April 2017 (interpreter Krishna Hari Subedi).

38. Interview Purna Bahadur Gurung, Pokhara, 19 April 2017.

39. Interview Hari Bahadur Chhetri, Ghokreswanra, Bhoteodar, 15 April 2017 (interpreter Ramchandra Subedi).

40. Interview Champa Singh Thapa, Khangrang, Rangmang, 18 April 2017 (translation Krishna Hari Subedi).

41. Interview Lal Bahadur Khatri, Pakawadi, Rogdi, 17 April 2017 (interpreter Krishna Hari Subedi).

42. Interview Champa Singh Thapa, Khangrang, Rangmang, 18 April 2017

(translation Krishna Hari Subedi).

43. Interview Champa Singh Thapa, Khangrang, Rangmang, 18 April 2017 (translation Krishna Hari Subedi).

44. Interview Hari Bahadur Chhetri, Ghokreswanra, Bhoteodar, 15 April 2017 (interpreter Ramchandra Subedi).

45. Interview Purna Bahadur Chhetri, Butwal, 22 April 2017 (interpreter Suresh Acharya).

46. Interview Hari Bahadur Chhetri, Ghokreswanra, Bhoteodar, 15 April 2017 (interpreter Ramchandra Subedi).

47. Interview Hari Bahadur Chhetri, Ghokreswanra, Bhoteodar, 15 April 2017 (interpreter Ramchandra Subedi).

48. Interview Buddhiraj Limbu by Buddhiman Gurung, 1999–2000, Private archives John P. Cross, Pokhara.

49. Interview Buddhiraj Limbu by Buddhiman Gurung, 1999–2000, Private archives John P. Cross, Pokhara.

50. Interview Birbahadur Pun by Buddhiman Gurung, 1999–2000, Private archives John P. Cross, Pokhara.

51. Interview Purna Bahadur Gurung, Pokhara, 19 April 2017.

52. Limpach 2016: 225–43.

53. Interview Buddhiraj Limbu by Buddhiman Gurung, 1999–2000, Private archives John P. Cross, Pokhara.

54. Interview Lal Bahadur Khatri, Pakawadi, Rogdi, 17 April 2017 (interpreter Krishna Hari Subedi).

55. Interview Champa Singh Thapa, Khangrang, Rangmang, 18 April 2017 (translation Krishna Hari Subedi).

56. Interview Khamba Sing Bura, Gumchal, 24 April 2017 (interpreter Suresh Acharya).

57. Van Delden 2007: 124; Roadnight 2002: 267; Limpach 2016: 236.

58. De Moor 2011: 196.

59. Weijzen 2015: 35–6, 39.

60. Zwart 1995: 11–13; Elands et al. 1996: 22–4.

61. Weijzen 2015: 59.

62. Princen 1995: 49.

63. Weijzen 2015: 71.

64. Zwart 1995: 16.

65. Interview Piet van Staveren, Assen, 22 July 2015.

66. Elands et al. 1996: 34.

67. Private archives Pratomo,
    Callantsoog, Centrale
    Veiligheidsdienst, Overzicht
    No. 9, 12 October 1946.
68. Weijzen 2015: 162–3.
69. Bals and Gerritsen 1989: 12.
70. Van de Poll 1947; Weijzen
    2015: 69.
71. Email correspondence
    Raymond van het
    Groenewoud, April–May
    2020.
72. Princen 1995: 50.
73. Weijzen 2015: 34–5.
74. Interview Remco Campert,
    23 December 2015.
75. Van Hengel 2018: 79; Hazeu
    2018: 135.
76. Fiedeldij Dop & Simons 1983:
    31–2.
77. Weijzen 2015: 149.
78. Zwart 1995.
79. Langeveld 2014: 377–8.
80. Djajadiningrat 1956.
81. Smit 1970: 1.
82. Smit 1970: 18, 19, 26, 23.
83. Smit 1970: 41, 43, 39.
84. Smit 1970: 34.
85. Smit 1970: 53, 62, 63, 64.
86. Smit 1970: 97, 67.
87. Smit 1970: 93.
88. Interview Joty ter Kulve,
    Wassenaar, 15 July 2015 and
    27 January 2017.
89. Smit 1970: 110.
90. Smit 1970: 73.

91. Smit 1970: 111, 119, 116.
92. Smit 1959: 52–63.
93. Smit 1970: 127.
94. Smit 1970: 129.
95. Smit 1970: 130.

Chapter 12: The Trap

1. Lowe 2009: 37.
2. McMahon 1981: 138.
3. Interview Piet van Staveren,
   Assen, 22 July 2015.
4. Princen 1995: 56.
5. Smit 1970: 132, 140.
6. Smit 1970: 131.
7. De Jong 1988: 784, 786.
8. Smit 1970: 145.
9. Smit 1970: 139.
10. Smit 1970: 150.
11. Smit 1970: 151.
12. De Jong 1988: 782.
13. Smit 1970: 157.
14. Smit 1970: 158, 157.
15. Smit 1970: 159.
16. Smit 1970: 164.
17. Smit 1970: 185.
18. Van Helsdingen 1947: 410,
    414, 421, 427, 429.
19. Smit 1970: 167.
20. Van Helsdingen 1947:
    396–429.
21. Smit 1970: 182, 355.
22. Smit 1970: 200.
23. Smit 1970: 202.
24. Giebels 1999: 431.

25. Interview Johannes Soewondo, Sambirejo, Pare, 25 June 2016 (interpreter Anton Novenanto).

26. Interview W. Sriyono, Jakarta, 15 June 2016 (translation Jeanne Lefèvre).

27. Interview W. F. G. L. 'Bol' Kerrebijn, Arnhem, 9 October 2017.

28. Cats & Van den Berg 2003: 103.

29. Interview Murtini Pendit, Jakarta, 21 January 2016.

30. Interview Siti Aishah, Jakarta, 13 January 2016 (interpreter Sri Ramadhani Asda and Jeanne Lefèvre).

31. Interview Donisius Unawekla, Ambon, 4 July 2016 (interpreter Paulien Joel-Perera).

32. Bee 1982: 8.

33. Interview Julius Nunumete, Hative Besar, Ambon, 4 July 2016 (interpreter Paulien Joel-Perera).

34. Interview Puling Daeng Rannu, Makassar, 20 February 2016 (interpreter Muhammad Fahmi Masdah).

35. Mattalatta 2002: 293.

36. Interview Ilhamsyah 'Ilham' Mattalatta, Makassar, 15 February 2016.

37. Interview H. Bachtiar, Makassar, 21 February 2016 (interpreter Muhammad Fahmi Masdah).

38. Testimony Piet Scheele, http://www.pietscheele.nl/members.chello.nl/pscheele/kapiteinwesterling.html

39. Van Galen 2013: 316.

40. Geersing 2019.

41. Westerling 1982: 221–6.

42. Westerling 1982: 233.

43. Limpach 2016: 284.

44. Limpach 2016: 295.

45. Interview Puling Daeng Rannu, Makassar, 20 February 2016 (interpreter Muhammad Fahmi Masdah).

46. Interview Sitti Saerah by Muhammad Fahmi Masdah, Makassar, 22 February 2016.

47. Interview Bachtiar, Makassar, 20 February 2016 (interpreter Muhammad Fahmi Masdah).

48. Interview Hajah Puang Kuneng, Makassar, 20 February 2016 (interpreter Muhammad Fahmi Masdah).

49. https://historibersama.com/grandson-refuses-damages-from-the-netherlands-cnn-indonesia/

50. Interview H. Bachtiar, Makassar, 21 February 2016 (interpreter Muhammad Fahmi Masdah).

51. Limpach 2016: 322.

52. Interview Arifin, Sudiang, 13 February 2016 (interpreter Risky Amaliah).
53. Limpach 2016: 308, 321.
54. Interview Muhammad 'Iwan' Ridwan Alimuddin, Pambusuang, 16 February 2016.
55. Van den Brekel 2017: 94–6.
56. Interview Yusuf Rambe, Galung Lombok, 16 February 2016 (translation Muhammad Ridwan Alamuddin).
57. Interview Isa, Galung Lombok, 16 February 2016 (translation Muhammad Ridwan Alamuddin).
58. Limpach 2016: 279.
59. Interview Hafsah, Baruga, 16 February 2016 (translation Muhammad Ridwan Alamuddin).
60. Interview Abdul Samad Bonang, Lawarang, 16 February 2016 (translation Muhammad Ridwan Alamuddin).
61. Interview Maemunah, Galung Lombok, 19 February 2016 (translation Muhammad Ridwan Alamuddin).
62. Interview Umi, Lekopadis, 17 February 2016 (translation Muhammad Ridwan Alamuddin).
63. Interview Harun Masa, Lemosusu, 17 February 2016

(translation Muhammad Ridwan Alamuddin).
64. Interview Hamad Puag Abi, Lekopadis, 17 February 2016 (translation Muhammad Ridwan Alamuddin).
65. Kahin 1952: 201.
66. Limpach 2016: 293–4.
67. Smit 1970: 335.
68. Smit 1970: 360, 399, 490.
69. De Jong 1988: 797.
70. Smit 1970: 355.
71. Van der Zee 2016: 295–307.
72. Hazelhoff 2003: 209.
73. Fasseur 2001: 525.
74. Fasseur 2001: 529.
75. Van der Zee 2016: 306.
76. Van der Wal 1979: 313–20.
77. Giebels 1995: 209.
78. Van der Wal 1979: 353–65.
79. De Jong 1988: 778.
80. Smit 1970: 509.
81. Burgers 2010: 543.
82. Van der Wal 1979: 191.
83. Interview Siti Rabyah Parvati 'Upik' Sjahrir, Jakarta, 2 July 2016.

Chapter 13: 'Unacceptable, Unpalatable and Unfair'

1. Interview Goderd van Heek, Velp, 28 May 2016 and 26 February 2017.

2. Interview Dick Buchel van Steenbergen, Waalre, 17 May 2017.

3. Interview W. F. G. L. 'Bol' Kerrebijn, Arnhem, 9 October 2017.

4. De Moor 2011: 266.

5. Groen 1991: 79; De Moor 2011: 224, 272–3.

6. Groen 1991: 79; Bouman 2006: 130, 159.

7. Interview Goderd van Heek, Velp, 28 May 2016 and 26 February 2017.

8. Spoor-Dijkema 2004: 205.

9. Cats & Van den Berg 2003: 78–81.

10. Cats & Van den Berg 2003: 113.

11. Meijer 1997: 67.

12. Bank 1983: 305–06.

13. Homan 1990: 135; De Moor 2011: 276.

14. Interview Sukotjo Tjokroatmodjo, Jakarta, 22 January 2016.

15. Groen 1991: 106.

16. Langeveld 2014: 470.

17. Fasseur 2001: 529–30.

18. Interview Piet van Staveren, Assen, 22 July 2015 and 7 October 2017.

19. Vanden Berghe 2008: 101–03.

20. Fontaine 2007: 96.

21. Fontaine 2007: 103.

22. McMahon 1981: 172; Gouda & Zaalberg 2002: 214.

23. Foster Collins 1950: 127–8; McMahon 1981: 185–6.

24. Taylor 1960: 50.

25. Fasseur 2001: 529.

26. Spoor-Dijkema 2004: 222.

27. Higgins 1970: 63.

28. Kawilarang 1993: 86.

29. Higgins 1970: 63.

30. Interview Iskandar Hadisaputra, Jakarta, 21 January 2016 (interpreter Rizky Wahyu Perdana).

31. Interview Goderd van Heek, Velp, 28 May 2016 and 26 February 2017.

32. Interview Sukotjo Tjokroatmodjo, Jakarta, 22 January 2016.

33. Langeveld 2014: 475.

34. Interview Soerachman Koesoemorachmanto, Jakarta, 15 January 2016.

35. Interview Johannes Soewondo, Pare, 25 June 2016 (interpreter Anton Novenanto).

36. Interview Jan Langenberg, Zierikzee, 16 May 2016 and 26 January 2017.

37. Interview Ton Berlee, Leiden, 7 April 2018.

38. Interview Goos Blok, Heemskerk, 29 May 2016.

39. Interview S. A. T. Horvath, Amsterdam, 1 October 2015.
40. Interview Joop Hueting, Amsterdam, 30 April 2016 and 25 February 2017.
41. Oostindie 2015: 152.
42. Oostindie 2015: 162–4, 313.
43. Interview Sukotjo Tjokroatmodjo, Jakarta, 22 January 2016.
44. Van Liempt 1997: 32.
45. Van Liempt 1997: 35, 46.
46. Interview S. A. T. Horvath, Amsterdam, 1 October 2015.
47. Limpach 2016: 325–6.
48. De Volder & De Brouwer 2019: 19–22.
49. Van Liempt 1997: 83.
50. Limpach 2016: 330.
51. McMahon 1981: 191–2.
52. Patterson 1998: 69.
53. Diah 2005: 91.
54. Anak Agung Gde Agung 1980: 63–4.
55. McMahon 1981: 204.
56. Kahin 1952: 227–8.
57. Adams 1965: 215–17.
58. McMahon 1981: 200.
59. Interview Goderd van Heek, telephone, 28 April 2020.
60. Interview Sukotjo Tjokroatmodjo, Jakarta, 22 January 2016.
61. Burgers 2010: 583.
62. Interview Aang Yusuf Syamsuddin, Tasikmalaya, 27 June 2016.
63. Dengel 1986.
64. Soebardi 1983: 115–17.
65. Van Dijk 1981.
66. Romein 1956: 338.
67. Interview Adjen Muttakin, Cikatomas, 28 June 2016.
68. Bouman 2006: 128–9, 158–9, 247–64.
69. Bouman 2006: 210.
70. Interview Soemardi Mau Sudarmo, Surakarta, 22 July 2016 (interpreter Muhammad Fahmi Masdah).
71. Kahin 1952: 252.
72. Poeze 2007: 1091.
73. Poeze 2007: 1190–95.
74. Reid 1974.
75. Poeze 2007: 1151–7.
76. Poeze 2007: 1206.
77. Poeze 2007: 1201, 1389.
78. Interview Piet van Staveren, Assen, 22 July 2015 and 7 October 2017.
79. Swift 2010: 155–6.
80. Swift 2010: 160.
81. Interview W. Sriyono, Jakarta, 15 June 2016 (interpreter Jeanne Lefèvre).
82. Interview Piet van Staveren, Assen, 22 July 2015 and 7 October 2017.
83. Interview Sumarsono with Bonnie Triyana, Jakarta,

11 July 2016 (translation
Syahrita Chairaty and
Elisabeth Ida Mulyani).

84. Poeze 2007: 1324.
85. Poeze 2007: 1212; McMahon
    1981: 243.
86. Poeze 2007: 1214.
87. Interview Ryamid, Madiun,
    23 June 2016 (interpreter
    Muhammad Fahmi Masdah).
88. Interview Soekarti, Madiun,
    24 June 2016 (interpreter
    Muhammad Fahmi Masdah
    and Arif Gumantia).
89. Interview Suradi
    Surokusumo, Jakarta,
    18 January 2016.
90. Poeze 2007: 1299.
91. McMahon 1981: 44.
92. Patterson 1998:
    70–71.
93. Patterson 1998: 83.
94. Homan 1990: 127.
95. Homan 1990: 133.

Chapter 14: 'A Big Hole that Smells of Earth'

1. Buiting 2006: 175–6.
2. De Jong 1988:
   961–4.
3. Interview Joop Hueting,
   Amsterdam, 30 April 2016
   and 25 February 2017.
4. Ward 1988: 308–14.

5. Private archives Joop
   Hueting, Amsterdam, 'Van
   dag tot dag' (Day to Day).
6. Interview Goderd van Heek,
   Velp, 28 May 2016 and
   26 February 2017.
7. Taylor 1960: 176; De Moor
   2011: 341.
8. Interview Soerachman
   Koesoemorachmanto,
   Jakarta, 15 January 2016.
9. Interview Nursani
   Tumanggor, Medan,
   29 November 2017 (interpreter
   Adam Damrin Nainggolan).
10. Burgers 2010: 629.
11. Interview Joop Hueting,
    Amsterdam, 30 April 2016
    and 25 February 2017.
12. Private archives Joop
    Hueting, Amsterdam, report
    Ben Verschuuren.
13. Interview Sukotjo
    Tjokroatmodjo, Jakarta,
    22 January 2016.
14. Spoor-Dijkema
    2004: 263.
15. Burgers 2010: 629.
16. Interview Jan Langenberg,
    Zierikzee, 16 May 2016 and
    26 January 2017.
17. Foster Collins 1950: 196.
18. Van der Maar and Meijer
    2013: 190.
19. Spoor-Dijkema
    2004: 236.

20. UN Archives, Security Council, CGO, 16 January 1949.

21. Montero de Guzman 1952: 183.

22. Higgins 1970: 50.

23. Van der Maar and Meijer 2013: 189.

24. Van der Maar and Meijer 2013: 207.

25. Van der Maar and Meijer 2013: 198–203.

26. Taylor 1960: 408.

27. Anak Agung 1980: 249.

28. Anak Agung 1980: 269–70.

29. De Kadt 1949: 11, 197, 199.

30. De Kadt 1949: 203.

31. Princen 1995: 94.

32. De Moor 2011: 335.

33. Interview Johannes Soewondo.

34. Interview Joop Hueting, Amsterdam, 30 April 2016 and 25 February 2017.

35. Koetsier-Korvinus 1995: 27.

36. Bouman 2006: 294.

37. Princen 1995: 95, 104–05.

38. Bouman 2006: 304.

39. Interview Piet van Staveren, Assen, 22 July 2015 and 7 October 2017.

40. Interview Johannes Soewondo, Pare, 25 June 2016 (interpreter Anton Novenanto).

41. Interview Goos Blok, Heemskerk, 29 May 2016.

42. Interview Ahmad Muhadi, Plered, Segoroyoso, 22 August 2015 (interpreter Jeanne Lefèvre).

43. Interview Soerachman Koesoemorachmanto, Jakarta, 15 January 2016.

44. Interview Johannes Soewondo, Pare, 25 June 2016 (interpreter Anton Novenanto).

45. Interview Sukotjo Tjokroatmodjo, Jakarta, 22 January 2016.

46. Interview Piet van Staveren, Assen, 22 July 2015 and 7 October 2017.

47. Interview Johannes Soewondo, Pare, 25 June 2016 (interpreter Anton Novenanto).

48. Interview Soerachman Koesoemorachmanto, Jakarta, 15 January 2016.

49. Higgins 1970: 51–2.

50. Higgins 1970: 36, 55.

51. Higgins 1970: 55–7.

52. Van Heek 1952: 40.

53. Van Heek 1952: 96.

54. Van Heek 1952: 107.

55. Van Heek 1952: 123–4.

56. Franken 2007: 96, 121; private archives Goderd van Heek, Velp.

57. Interview Goderd van Heek, Velp, 28 May 2016 and 26 February 2017.
58. Private archives Goderd van Heek, Velp, typescript, 6 March 1950.
59. Oostindie 2015: 176–8; Limpach 2016: 737–9.
60. Limpach 2016: 450–55.
61. Ruijter 2017: 34.
62. Van Heek 1952.
63. Private archives Hueting, Amsterdam, n.d. typescript.
64. Interview Joop Hueting, Amsterdam, 30 April 2016 and 25 February 2017.
65. Scagliola 2002: 295–321; Limpach 2016: 39.
66. Franken 2007: 122.
67. Bank 1983: 256.
68. Franken 2007: 122.
69. Bank 1983: 254–9.
70. Wietsma & Scagliola 2013; Oostindie 2015: 257–67.
71. Interview S. A. T. Horvath, Amsterdam, 1 October 2015.
72. Interview Jaap Tuinder, Groningen, 7 October 2017.
73. Hueting 1973.
74. Private archives Hueting, Amsterdam, n.d. typescript.
75. Interview Jan Langenberg, Zierikzee, 16 May 2016 and 26 January 2017.
76. Oostindie 2015: 153.
77. Harinck & Verwey 2015.
78. De Moor 2011: 337–8.
79. Cats & Van den Berg 2003: 166.
80. Zweers 1995; 2013: 83–100.
81. Interview Jan Langenberg, Zierikzee, 16 May 2016 and 26 January 2017.
82. Limpach 2016: 463.
83. De Volder & De Brouwer 2019: 29–30; Zegveld & Vossenberg 2019: 26–7.
84. Oostindie 2015: 185.
85. Limpach 2016: 464.
86. Limpach 2016: 344.
87. Hoek, 2016 a & b.
88. Limpach 2016: 498.
89. Private archives Joop Hueting, Amsterdam, letter Jacob Singer; cf. Limpach 2016: 453, 24.
90. Interview W. F. G. L. 'Bol' Kerrebijn, Arnhem, 9 October 2017.
91. Groen 1991: 256–65.
92. Limpach 2016: 57.
93. Harinck, Van Horn & Luttikhuis 2017.
94. Van der Eng 1988: 352.
95. McMahon 1981: 293.
96. Jaquet 1982: 256–68.
97. Roadnight 2002b: 55–77.
98. Heath 1949: 3.
99. Zweers 2002.
100. Van Heek 1952: 115, 118, 147.
101. Interview Goderd van Heek, Velp, 28 May 2016 and 26 February 2017.

102. Private archives Goderd van Heek, Velp, telegram 7 August 1949.
103. Cochran 1949: 82.
104. Meijer 1997.
105. Daalder 2004: 383.
106. Anak Agung 1980: 327–8, Jaquet 1982: 316.
107. Hoek & Van der Kleij 2020.
108. Van der Eng 1988.
109. Burgers 2010: 666.
110. Anwar 1997.
111. Interview Soeparti 'Oma [Grandma] Ted' Soetedjo, Jakarta, 20 January 2016.
112. Keppy 2006: 77, 232.
113. Interview Dutch veteran, n.l., 29 May 2016.

Chapter 15: Into the Light of Morning

1. Daalder 2004: 394–5.
2. Meijer 1994: 13.
3. Ruijter 2017: 55–8.
4. Private archives Goderd van Heek, Velp.
5. Interview Jan Langenberg, Zierikzee, 16 May 2016 and 26 January 2017.
6. Interview Hans Dornseiffer, The Hague, 16 November 2015.
7. Smilde 2017.
8. Van Esterik & Van Twist 1980: 87.
9. Meijer 1994: 111–19.
10. Soekarno 1950: 11.
11. Keppy 2020.
12. Burgers 2010: 706.
13. Goedhart 1953: 30.
14. Meijer 1994: 279–83.
15. Meijer 1994: 239.
16. Ruijter 2017: 57–8.
17. Interview Julius Nunumete, Hative Besar, Ambon, 4 July 2016 (interpreter Paulien Joel-Perera).
18. Interview Donisius Unawekla, Ambon, 4 July 2016 (interpreter Paulien Joel-Perera).
19. Roadnight 2002: 90.
20. Roadnight 2002: 123.
21. Giebels 2001: 42.
22. Arpi 2015.
23. Arpi 2004; Schöttli 2012: 138.
24. Paranjpe 2004.
25. Ghosh 2017.
26. Arpi 2009.
27. Interview W. Sriyono, Jakarta, 15 June 2016 (interpreter Jeanne Lefèvre).
28. Queuille 1965; Sena Utama 2016.
29. Tarling 1992.
30. Ampiah 2007: 129.
31. Wright 2008 (1956): 493.
32. Parker 2006: 873–4.
33. Parker 2006.
34. Rodriguez 2006.

35. *Algemeen Handelsblad*, 16 April 1955.
36. *De Volkskrant*, 18 April 1955.
37. *De Telegraaf*, 16 April 1955.
38. *NRC*, 20 April 1955.
39. *Het Parool*, 18 April 1955.
40. Parker 2006: 877.
41. Wright 2008 (1956): 536.
42. Nehru 1970 (1958): 287.
43. Kahin 1956; Wright 2008 (1956).
44. Rogan 2010: 388.
45. Wright 2008 (1956): 438.
46. Conte 1965: 11.
47. Interview Herawati Diah, Jakarta, 14 July 2016.
48. Centre for the Study of Asian-African and Developing Countries 1983: 3–12.
49. Centre for the Study of Asian-African and Developing Countries 1983: 141.
50. Rey 2014; Claudio 2015.
51. Kahin 1956: 12–21.
52. Centre for the Study of Asian-African and Developing Countries 1983: 46–7.
53. Centre for the Study of Asian-African and Developing Countries 1983: 45.
54. Abdulgani 1963: 12.
55. Lee 2009; Dinkel 2015.
56. Mackie 2005.
57. *Het Parool*, 26 April 1955.
58. *Het Vrije Volk*, 14 April 1955; *Trouw*, 26 and 28 April 1955.
59. Prashad 2007; Tan & Acharya 2008.
60. Aghazarian 2012.
61. Kimche 1973: 91.
62. Giebels 2001: 126.
63. Roadnight 2002: 137.
64. Utami 2016.
65. Lindblad 2006.
66. Kimche 1973: 82.
67. Kimche 1973: 82.
68. Boyd 1975; Diong 2015; Rey 2014.
69. Legum 1965: 39.
70. Brennan 2010: 181–2.
71. Rogan 2010: 391–4.
72. Rogan 2010: 401–03.
73. McAlexander 2010.
74. Ferro 1982; Judt 2007: 294–9.
75. Falter 2017: 525, Hansen & Jonsson 2014: 163.
76. Hansen & Jonsson 2014: 165.
77. Hansen & Jonsson 2014: 190.
78. Soper 1965.
79. Hansen & Jonsson 2014: 234–5.
80. Falter 2017: 528.
81. Hansen & Jonsson 2014: 212.
82. Hansen & Jonsson 2014: 238.
83. Ray 2006; Davidson 1973.
84. Meredith 2005: 179.
85. Hansen & Jonsson 2014: 270.

86. Asante & Abarry 1996; Lee 2009: 533.

87. Lumumba 1961: 21, 150, 173, 201.

88. Van Lierde 1963: 13.

89. Présence Africaine 1956.

90. Boudiguet 2012.

91. Commission on the Struggle n.d.

92. Tambo 1983.

93. Mandela 1995; 1998.

94. Rodriguez 2006: 120; Marable 2011.

95. King 1957.

96. Zinn 2007: 550.

97. Joseph 2006; 2009; Dudziak 2011.

98. Wright 2008 (1956): 597.

99. Wright 2008 (1956): 599.

100. Rodriguez 2006: 126.

101. Gaines 2006.

102. King 1963.

103. X 1963.

104. Haley 2015 (1964): 357, 368.

105. Woodard 2019: 179.

106. Haley 2015 (1964): 368.

107. Robinson 1983; Rodriguez 2006; Bloom & Martin 2016: 312.

108. Telephone conversation Goderd van Heek, 28 April 2020.

109. Commando exécutif pour le dixième anniversaire de la première Conférence Afro-Asiatique (1965).

110. Kahin & Kahin 1995.

111. Roadnight 2002: 162.

112. Robinson 2018: 115–17.

113. Robinson 2018.

114. Bass 2013.

115. Bevins 2020.

116. Farid 2016.

117. Young 2015; Pitman & Stafford 2009; Mahler 2018.

118. Castro 1966.

119. Guevara 2017 (1966): 22, 23; Zolov 2016.

120. Edis 2004; Ladwig et al. 2014.

121. Vine 2009.

122. Interview Francisca 'Cisca' Pattipilohy, Amsterdam, 8 October 2017 and 18 February 2018.

Index

Great Britain 7, 49, 56, 59, 118, 133, 135,
  157, 158, 213, 255, 291, 292, 294,
  297, 301, 325, 333, 382, 392, 399,
  433, 525
Great East 354, 362, 366
Grote Postweg 41–4
Gubeng convoy 324
guerrilla warfare 45, 176, 187, 291, 325,
  341, 367, 368, 405, 406–7, 409,
  413, 415, 417–18, 427, 448–9,
  451, 452, 453–5, 474, 475, 482
Gunawan Bosschieter, Anna Christina
  80
Gurkha 307, 308, 311, 321, 327, 328,
  331–40, 343, 369, 514
Gurung, Purna Bahadur 339, 340

Hadisaputra, Iskandar 130–31, 176, 184,
  315–18, 321, 404, 40
Hadiwidjojo, Toernowo 289, 315, 321,
  327
Hafsah 377
Haga, Dr 253
Haile Selassie 514
Hakkenberg, Seaman 169
Halbertsma, Freek 457, 460
Hamad Puag Abi 76–7, 379–80
Hamid, Sultan 446, 478
Hampel, Hertha Anna 237
Hartman, Mrs 66
Hatta, Mohammed 108–11, 115, 116,
  118–19, 136, 144, 159, 194, 202,
  225, 226, 234–6, 272, 278, 283,
  285–8, 297, 300, 303, 306, 322,
  323, 328, 349, 353, 355, 359, 360,
  389, 398, 418, 421, 422, 424, 426,
  428–430, 432, 437, 440–2, 474,
  478, 481, 491, 496, 498
  arrest and exile 121, 144, 159, 194
  and Nehru 109–10
  in the Netherlands 108, 109

and Perhimpunan Indonesia 108
return to Indonesia 118
and Sjahrir 118–19, 136, 144, 159,
  202, 225, 272, 285, 328, 349, 359,
  360, 389, 398, 491
and Sukarno 119, 136, 144, 225, 234,
  235, 278, 283, 285–8, 297, 300,
  303, 306, 322, 323, 328, 349, 353,
  355, 359, 389, 398, 426, 428–30,
  437, 474, 496
youth and education 108
Hazelhoff Roelfzema, Erik 194, 382, 383
Heath, Burton 476
Heek, Goderd van 274, 291, 294, 298,
  325, 391, 392, 405, 406, 418, 433,
  453–455, 457, 477, 478, 483, 514
Heiho 231–233, 279, 286, 295, 298, 318
Helfrich, Conrad 159, 160, 166–7, 169,
  177, 308, 360, 382, 383
Heutsz, Jo van 373
Hinduism 19–20, 22, 26, 57, 277, 338,
  367, 414
Hirohito, Emperor 154, 203, 205, 235,
  283, 285
Hitler, Adolf 120, 129, 134, 135, 265,
  504
Ho Chi Minh 300, 423
Hoge Veluwe Talks 348, 349
Homo erectus 14–16
Homo sapiens 15, 16
Hoornik, Ed. 267
Horvath, Stef 410, 412, 413, 464, 514
Houtman, Cornelis de 27–8
Hovinga, Henk 294
Hudson, E.C. 66
Hueting, Joop 410, 411, 432, 433, 436,
  449, 457, 459–62, 464–6, 469,
  514
Hughes, Billy 132
Huisman, Private 467
Hussein, Saddam 505

About the Author

David Van Reybrouck is the author of *Congo: The Epic History of a People*, which won twenty prizes, sold over half a million copies and has been translated into a dozen languages. His book *Against Elections* has been translated into more than twenty languages and has led to trials of participatory democracy throughout the Netherlands, Belgium, Spain and elsewhere. His plays *Mission* and *Para* have been performed across Europe, and his novel *Zinc* won the European Book Prize 2017. *Revolusi* was first published in the Netherlands, where it was a major bestseller. David Van Reybrouck has been described as 'one of the leading intellectuals in Europe' (*Der Tagesspiegel*) and 'one of the most brilliant European intellectuals of the moment' (*Le Soir*). He is Belgian, writes in Dutch and is based in Brussels.

About the Translators

David Colmer is an Australian writer, translator and editor based in Amsterdam. He translates Dutch-language literature in a range of genres and has won numerous awards, most notably the IMPAC Dublin Literary Award and the Independent Foreign Fiction Prize (both with novelist Gerbrand Bakker) and the NSW Premier's Translation Prize for his body of work.

David McKay's translations from the Dutch have been awarded the Vondel Prize and nominated for various international prizes. They include *Max Havelaar*, the scathing nineteenth-century critique of Dutch colonial misdeeds in the East Indies (co-translated with Ina Rilke), and the classic anti-colonial manifesto *We Slaves of Suriname* by Afro-Surinamese activist Anton de Kom.